"This is a sensitive, patient, sophisticated evangelical response to evangelical questions concerning the religions. Tiessen takes the biblical witness with utter seriousness—a seriousness lacking in most books on this and related subjects. Those from the Reformed tradition will be especially pleased with the nuanced attention given to problems of salvation and revelation in the religions."

GERALD R. McDERMOTT, ROANOKE COLLEGE

"Professor Tiessen has produced a major work on a cluster of issues that are as complex as they are controversial. One need not agree with all of his conclusions to benefit from this carefully crafted theological and missiological study."

HAROLD NETLAND, TRINITY EVANGELICAL DIVINITY SCHOOL

"The product of many years of reading, thinking and discussion, this is one of the most satisfactorily comprehensive treatments of salvation ever attempted by an evangelical in the Reformed tradition. Even those—like me—who do not share in that tradition, will discover in Tiessen an immensely well-informed, trustworthy and fair-minded guide through the labyrinthine maze of questions issuing from Christian understanding of and response to the Bible's teaching on salvation. Unless I am greatly mistaken, this book will serve as the benchmark reference on the subject for evangelical teachers, pastors, missionaries and students for years to come."

JONATHAN J. BONK, OVERSEAS MINISTRIES STUDY CENTER

"While not endorsing all of the author's conclusions, I recommend this book as an excellent introduction to the contemporary discussion on the boundaries of Christian faith.

"The strength of this theology is that it is both exclusive and inclusive. It is exclusive because it upholds Jesus Christ as the only way to salvation. It is inclusive because it sees God's grace at work in all religions and among all peoples."

DONALD G. BLOESCH, UNIVERSITY OF DUBUQUE THEOLOGICAL SEMINARY

"*Who Can be Saved?* is a bold and significant contribution to evangelical theological and missiological thinking on a very controversial issue. Its theological depth and its missiological grounding sets it apart from many other books."

"Terrance Tiessen reshapes the paradigm for Christian thinking about religions, taking us beyond the inadequate language of exclusivism, inclusivism and pluralism, and offering fresh analyses and stimulating insights. He offers what many of us have longed for—a fully worked-out, carefully biblical and Reformed case for the conviction that the sovereignty of God's saving grace in all human history, while it is exclusively grounded in the person and work of Jesus Christ, is not exclusively limited to the church's evangelistic obedience (or lack of), and presented in a way that does not thereby diminish the evangelistic mandate or motive. . . . Few books I have read have been so doctrinally thorough, closely and cautiously argued, and thought-provoking on the twin subjects of the destiny of the unevangelized and the status and role of religions in the purposes of God."

"This book does two things impressively well: It skillfully clarifies many issues that too often are blurred in the discussion of world religions, and it argues the author's own views with gracefulness, maturity and cogency. Professor Tiessen thus takes his proper place in the forefront of evangelical theology of religions with a book that will become a reference point for all further work in the field."

Who Can Be Saved?

REASSESSING SALVATION IN CHRIST

AND WORLD RELIGIONS

Terrance L. Tiessen

InterVarsity Press
Downers Grove, Illinois
Leicester, England

InterVarsity Press
P.O. Box 1400, Downers Grove, IL 60515-1426
World Wide Web: www.ivpress.com
E-mail: mail@ivpress.com

Inter-Varsity Press, England
38 De Montfort Street, Leicester LE1 7GP, England
World Wide Web: www.ivpbooks.com
E-mail: ivp@uccf.org.uk

InterVarsity Press® is the book-publishing division of InterVarsity Christian Fellowship/USA®, a student
movement active on campus at hundreds of universities, colleges and schools of nursing in the United States of
America, and a member movement of the International Fellowship of Evangelical Students. For information about
local and regional activities, write Public Relations Dept., InterVarsity Christian Fellowship/USA, 6400 Schroeder
Rd., P.O. Box 7895, Madison, WI 53707-7895, or visit the IVCF website at <www.ivcf.org>.

Inter-Varsity Press, England, is the book-publishing division of the Universities and Colleges Christian Fellowship
(formerly the Inter-Varsity Fellowship), a student movement linking Christian Unions in universities and colleges
throughout the United Kingdom and the Republic of Ireland, and a member movement of the International
Fellowship of Evangelical Students. For information about local and national activities write to UCCF, 38 De
Montfort Street, Leicester LE1 7GP.

All Scripture quotations, unless otherwise indicated, are taken from the Holy Bible, New International
Version®. NIV®. *Copyright © 1973, 1978, 1984 by International Bible Society. Used by permission of Zondervan*
Publishing House. *Distributed in the U.K. by permission of Hodder and Stoughton Ltd. All rights reserved. "NIV"*
is a registered trademark of International Bible Society. UK trademark number 1448790.

Design: Kathleen Lay Burrows

Images: Roberta Polfus

USA ISBN 0-8308-2747-1
UK ISBN 1-84474-031-5

Printed in the United States of America ∞

Library of Congress Cataloging-in-Publication Data

Tiessen, Terrance L., 1944-
  Who can be saved? : reassessing salvation in Christ and World
religions/by Terrance L. Tiessen.
     p. cm.
Includes bibliographical references and indexes.
  ISBN 0-8308-2747-1 (pbk.: alk. paper)
  1. Salvation. 2. Salvation outside the church. I. Title.
  BT751.3.T54 2004
  234—dc22

                                                                              2003023199

British Library Cataloguing in Publication Data
A catalogue record for this book is available from the British Library

---

P	19	18	17	16	15	14	13	12	11	10	9	8	7	6	5	4	3	2	1
Y	20	19	18	17	16	15	14	13	12	11	10		09		08	07	06		05	04

To Gail,

my wife and partner in ministry,

who will not need to read this book

because we have talked about

these ideas for many years

Contents

Acknowledgments

I AM GRATEFUL TO THE ADMINISTRATION OF Providence Theological Seminary for granting me a half-year sabbatical, during which much of this book came together, and for giving me some course teaching relief to finish the project. I am also thankful to Jonathan Bonk and the staff at the Overseas Ministry Studies Center, in New Haven, Connecticut, for the invitation to be a Senior Mission Scholar in residence. The seminar I taught at OMSC on the theology of religions was the context out of which the idea for this book emerged. It was delightful to have a keen group of missionaries and scholars, international both in their origin and in their missionary experience, to think through these ideas with me. I am also grateful to the faculty of Yale University Divinity School for granting me a research fellowship during my time in New Haven, which gave me access to their splendid library, whose staff was very helpful.

My editor, Daniel Reid, has once again been helpful in numerous ways. I am thankful to him for his wise counsel throughout the process of my writing and for his vast knowledge of the Bible, gained through personal study and the reading of numerous books and dictionary articles during many fruitful years as an editor. His cheerful encouragement has been a blessing. Harold Netland brought a different expertise to the reading of my manuscript and gave me significant help. One other reader obtained by IVP remained anonymous but gave me further invaluable help and I hope that she or he will read this note of thanks. Sections of an earlier version of my manuscript were read by one of my seminary classes. Their feedback was helpful, and I owe particular thanks to Theodore Van Raalte, a Reformed Church pastor, whose comments from within our shared theological perspective were particularly beneficial to me. This is a better book than it would have been without the help of these astute critics. My thanks are also due to Jennifer Conrad Seidel, who made good suggestions for

clearer wording of my thoughts, and to William Eichhorst (formerly president and chancellor of our Seminary), for similar help when he read an
early draft of this work with care. As always, of course, I must take responsibility for any weaknesses that remain in this manuscript.

In the process of writing about the grace of God in saving sinners, I have
often been deeply stirred by a spirit of thankfulness to God for the great
grace with which he has blessed me and for the many evidences of that
grace in the lives of other people. It is an inexpressible joy to know myself
a child of God, saved by his grace and appointed to inherit all the family
privileges that God has stored up for his children in and through Christ. It
is my prayer that God will use this book to the praise of his name and as
an instrument of his grace in the lives of all who truly seek him.

Where Are We Going?

THE HORROR OF WHAT HAPPENED IN New York and Washington, D.C., on September 11, 2001, has aroused new interest in the ways that people's actions are affected by their religious faith. Responses to this event have been complex and varied. Some people have concluded that religions are dangerous and should be avoided because they inevitably cause conflict. Other people suggest that only some religions are harmful in this way but that other religions are beneficial, including, of course, the one to which they belong. Then again, we hear frequent calls for mutual tolerance among the members of different religions. Some of these pleas include statements that because all religions are valid, no one should attempt to convert a person from one religion to another. Others, however, argue that peaceful coexistence between religions is possible even if they make conflicting truth claims and even if their members attempt to persuade other people that a change in religious commitment would be good for them.

In countries that foster genuine religious freedom, the religious diversity of the population is visible. Increasingly, city dwellers have neighbors of a different religion. As religious diversity has grown through immigration in many Western nations, Christian churches have reexamined their attitudes toward other religions, and they have not all agreed on what the proper attitude should be. For decades, evangelicals have discussed the state of those who do not hear the gospel—whether the unevangelized can be saved. But we have not been as engaged in the discussion of the religions themselves and in the assessment of the role they play within God's purposes in the world. As Gerald McDermott notes,

When evangelicals have considered the world religions, for the most part they have focused on the questions of truth (do all the religions teach the same essential truths? Is truth propositional or ineffable?) and salvation (can non-Christians be saved?), not revelation (is there divine revelation in the other religions?). Evangelicals' concern for revelation has extended only to the point at which it affects the question of salvation.[1]

I will address both the issue of salvation and the issue of the world's religions in the two parts of this book, and I invite you to ponder with me these two important questions: how does God save people, and how do the religions fit into God's purposes in the world? Once again, I want to examine what Scripture tells us about the state of those people who do not hear the gospel. I also want to discover what God thinks about the religions of the world, what he may be doing in the context of those religions and what our attitude as Christians should be toward other religions and their members. Moving beyond the issue of salvation, I will raise the broader question of divine providence, probing how God's general purposes for humankind are being fulfilled in a world full of religions.

THE QUESTIONS WE NEED TO ADDRESS

In the pages that follow, I hope to address a number of key questions which we face when we ask the two large questions that I have posed above. It may help if we identify those questions before we get into the more detailed analysis. I begin with questions related to the general theme of how God saves people.

What is the natural state of humankind? When and how do people become sinners? This issue is not often addressed directly in discussions of the salvation of the unevangelized, but it is a critical starting point. We need to ascertain who *needs* to be saved before we can say how such people *can* be saved. In particular, we face a disagreement between those who believe that we are all guilty "in Adam" ("original guilt") as well as corrupt and those who only believe in "original corruption." The implications of this difference are significant, particularly when we consider the situation of children who die as infants or the situation of those who are mentally disabled. If such people never come under God's condemnation as sinners, then we need not worry about whether or how they might be saved. But if

---

[1]Gerald R. McDermott, *Can Evangelicals Learn from World Religions? Jesus, Revelation and Religious Traditions* (Downers Grove, Ill.: InterVarsity Press, 2000), p. 39.

all human beings are sinners needing salvation, their situations become a matter of urgent theological inquiry.

Who are the "unevangelized"? Evangelical discussions of the possibility of salvation for the unevangelized frequently speak only to the situation of rationally competent adults who do not hear the gospel. I am convinced that whatever doctrine of salvation one confesses, it needs to account for all categories of the unevangelized. Thus, when we ask whether the unevangelized can be saved, we must put forward a doctrine of salvation that includes at least the following five groups:

- people whose lives come to an end (naturally or by force) before they are born

- infants who die before reaching an age at which they could understand this good news

- the mentally handicapped who never attain such an ability

- everyone who lived before the incarnation of the Son of God, who gave his life for sinners

- those living after Jesus' resurrection who are never told this good news in a comprehensible manner that places before them the choice of faith or disbelief in Jesus, including those who hear the proclamation of Jesus as Savior but are unable to recognize it as good news because of their memory of atrocities committed by people whom they identify (or who identified themselves) as Christians

Obviously, we are speaking of a very large number of people, which makes this a highly significant issue. When this question is raised, people often think only of those people in the fifth category, but such an understanding is inadequate to deal with the total situation. Our answer to the question of the prospects of the unevangelized must be broad enough to address all of the above categories, and our cultural context may determine which categories appear most important. Thus, Americans may struggle particularly with the issue of infants and the unborn, whereas Christians in Asia are more likely to wonder about their ancestors who died before the gospel reached their country.[2]

The importance of keeping all these categories in mind as we formulate a biblical response was evident at the Evangelical Affirmations conference

---

[2]I am grateful to Harold Netland for this observation.

held at Trinity Evangelical Divinity School in May 1989. John Sanders has described what happened there:

> J. I. Packer was chosen to speak on the unevangelized. He warned against speculating about the salvation of the unevangelized, yet he was careful not to shut the door so firmly as to rule out all hope. As the participants voted on the statements being produced, Robertson McQuilken [sic] objected that the wording of the affirmations did not specifically rule out the possibility of salvation for the unevangelized. He proposed a stricter formulation to the effect that explicit knowledge of Jesus is necessary for salvation and without it no one can be saved. This was a tremendously important modification for, if accepted, it would establish in a somewhat official way *the* evangelical position. A brief debate ensued but came to an abrupt halt when theologian Roger Nicole (himself not an advocate for the wider hope) pointed out that McQuilken's proposal would consign all infants who die to hell. The tide turned abruptly after that. Apparently evangelicals are simply not willing to consign all such infants to eternal damnation. The final draft affirmed that all are saved only through Christ and that God reaches out to save all who believe in him, but that was as close as the conference came to answering the key question.[3]

Whom did God intend to save by means of the death and resurrection of Jesus? The key difference here is between those who believe in universal atonement (that Christ died with the intention of saving everyone) and those who believe in particular redemption or "limited atonement" (that Christ died with the intention of saving those whom God had chosen to salvation, or "the elect").

How does God save sinners? A number of questions arise in this area. What is the essential instrument in the appropriation of God's saving work in Christ? Is it faith alone, faith plus good works or good works accepted in lieu of faith? If salvation is by faith, what must one know in order to have saving faith? That is, what is the content or object of saving faith? Furthermore, what ability do sinful people have to believe, even when they receive God's self-revelation? Assuming that the Fall of humankind into sin has disabled all of us spiritually so that faith in God is impossible without God's gracious enablement, *whom* does he enable to believe and *when* and *how* does he do this enabling work?

By what means does God make himself known to sinners in order that they

---

might be saved? Here a question is often raised about the value of general revelation: can people be saved through God's revelation in nature and conscience? Or, alternately, must people know that Jesus died and rose again from the dead in order to be saved? Is there special revelation apart from Christian Scripture that can lead people to a saving knowledge of God?

What about your unevangelized ancestors? Were they irrevocably lost because of their ignorance? This is obviously a particularly critical question in those cultures where ancestors are highly valued, which is true in much of the world, the exception perhaps being individualistic Western countries. It was raised, for instance, by Hawaiians who were converted in the nineteenth century when the gospel was carried from Boston to the mid-Pacific Sandwich Islands by Congregational missionaries.[4]

What are the grounds of God's final judgment, and does ignorance of Christ constitute an "excuse"? If not, how can God be considered just and loving? The idea that the unevangelized cannot be saved is common in the evangelical tradition, particularly with regard to the adults in the fifth group identified above, but this has been a serious stumbling block to many who cannot understand how God can justly condemn to hell those who never hear of Jesus. So we must examine Scripture's teaching concerning the criteria by which God judges people and demonstrate God's justice in condemning all those whom he does not acquit.

As we try to discern the role of the world's religions in God's overall program in the world, a number of further questions arise.

What meaning does the plurality of religions in the world have in God's own intentions for humankind? In spite of vigorous missionary work by Christian groups, particularly in the last few centuries, other religions persist and, in some cases, seem virtually impervious to Christian missionary efforts. This has led some Christians to conclude that it is a mistake to try to convert people from other religions. In a spirit of relativism, some have even concluded that the persistence of the religions is indication that they are alternate ways in which God does his work among the various peoples of the world. Evangelicals have written books to combat such relativism, and I will not repeat their arguments, but my own proposal is clearly not in the vein of that relativistic pluralism. Nevertheless, even evangelicals

---

[4]Gabriel Fackre, "Divine Perseverance," in *What About Those Who Have Never Heard? Three Views on the Destiny of the Unevangelized*, ed. John Sanders (Downers Grove, Ill.: InterVarsity Press, 1995), p. 71.

who deny that God has raised up the religions as vehicles of salvation
need to ask whether the religions have any place in the providential work
and purposes of God in the world.

How do the religions fit into God's plan of salvation for humankind, if at all?
Are the religions completely idolatrous, sinful or demonic? Or, on the contrary, might they be God's primary way of salvation for people in the areas
of the world where they are dominant? Then again, is it possible that the
truth falls somewhere in the middle of these alternatives and that God
saves people who practice the rituals of other religions because of God's
gracious work in their hearts in spite of the errors of the traditions within
which they live?

*Is there divine revelation in the other religions? If so, does that make them di-
vinely ordained means of salvation?* Other religions have flourished, even in
the presence of intensive Christian missionary activity. Their views of God
often conflict with the teachings of the Christian religion, but occasionally
they agree. How should we explain both the differences and the similarities? By what means has God made himself known to people? In particular, what forms of divine revelation may have contributed to the specific
religious construct that we encounter as we speak with non-Christians? If
we were to grant that God may have revealed himself in a direct and personal way to individuals outside the people with whom he established a
special covenantal relationship, what status would that give to the religions that developed from the religious activity of those individuals? Furthermore, how should we regard the things written by key figures in other
religions, those whose writings are viewed with the same sort of respect
that Christians give to the Bible?

*Are other religions preparatory to Christianity, as Judaism is assumed to be in
most of the Christian tradition?* Some Christian writers have proposed, for
instance, that Islam or traditional African religions or Native American religions were developed through the work of God as means of preparing
them for the gospel of Christ. In this regard, Judaism would then not be
unique. This would also give those religions an efficacy in the saving program of God, in their own right, prior to the arrival of the gospel. And, the
writings produced within these religious movements might then be
viewed as parallel to the Old Testament, so that the Qur'an, for instance,
would be the "Old Testament" for Arab peoples. Unlike the relativistic
pluralists who give all the religions continued validity, this position is
sometimes referred to as the *fulfillment theory.* It gives Christianity a superior role as the goal to which the other religions are moving, but it sees

those religions as divinely intended and as valid in a preliminary way for those who do not have the gospel. I will not reach that conclusion myself, but I think that we must address the question and put forward a clear biblical alternative.

If religions are ambiguous in their value (containing both truth and error), how should Christians assess what is good and what is bad? Two groups of theologians need not face this question: Those who are convinced that the non-Christian religions are demonic and completely wrong do not need to distinguish between the truth and error within the teaching and practice of the religions of the world. But neither need those who believe that all the religions are equally valid. If we conclude that the religions are ambiguous, as I will propose, then we have to decide by what means we will assess them and how our conclusions in this regard affect our relationships with the adherents of those religions.

Should Christians seek dialogue with or cooperate with members of other religions? And, if so, what should be the goal of such dialogue or the limits of such cooperation? Much has been said about interreligious dialogue in recent years, and serious efforts to conduct such dialogue have been undertaken. Whether we should seek to dialogue and, if so, why and how we should do so will be determined by the answers we reach to the questions posed above. Once having answered those questions, I will suggest some implications of the convictions put forward in these practical areas.

THE PERSPECTIVE FROM WHICH I WILL APPROACH THESE QUESTIONS

Evangelicalism. I approach this study as a Christian theologian and, more specifically, as an evangelical. I affirm the unique authority of Scripture as the means by which we know truth about God, ourselves and the world. I also believe that salvation comes about only through a work of God's grace in the life of sinners, which causes them to believe in God and to entrust themselves to his gracious mercy. The moment at which people move from darkness into God's light is frequently hidden from us, but without such a transition, salvation does not occur. Consequently, God has placed an obligation on all of us who know him to be witnesses of what we know. By means of this Christian witness, evangelism and mission, God is daily reconciling people to himself.

Monergism. A major theological watershed in Christian theology has to do with understandings of the extent of God's control in the world and with the respective roles of God and his creatures. What we conclude on this basic issue has widespread effects throughout our theology and in the ways we live out our faith in the world. There are finely nuanced differences between theological traditions on this issue, but all of the various positions can be categorized as either *monergistic* or *synergistic* understandings. Between these two there is no middle ground.

Monergists believe that everything comes about because God has determined that it will occur. Synergists, as the name implies, believe that events occur through a cooperation of God and his creatures, such that God does not always have his way. Indeed, God has chosen to give creatures a significant say in how things turn out in the world so that human beings determine a great deal of human history, often against God's wishes and efforts. Among evangelicals, these two fundamentally different approaches are frequently identified as Calvinism and Arminianism because of a dispute on the matter that arose within the Reformed churches in the seventeenth century. The argument had occurred many times before, but that particular discussion has left a strong imprint on the theological formation of evangelicals. Like the much earlier dispute between Augustine and Pelagius, the seventeenth-century argument was focused on sin and grace. It applied the different perspectives of monergism and synergism particularly to the issue of salvation, which is our focus in this book. The "orthodox" Calvinists of the day were monergists. They believed that helpless sinners are saved because God chose particular individuals to salvation; he sent the Son to die for those whom he had chosen, and he blesses these people with grace, which effectively draws them to saving faith. The followers of Arminius, on the other hand, believed that God wanted everyone to be saved, that he sent the Son to accomplish this, and that he graciously enables everyone to respond. But, being "genuinely" free, people are free to reject God's grace, and so God's will to save everyone is thwarted by some human wills. In this discussion of salvation, then, we meet the essential difference between monergism and synergism.

These two different understandings of God's control of the world have entailed competing understandings of the nature of creaturely freedom, often identified as *compatibilist* and *libertarian* notions of freedom. Monergists affirm what philosophers call *compatibilistic* freedom, a term derived from the proposal that God is comprehensively in control of all that occurs in the world but that this is *compatible* with free agency on the part of moral creatures in that world. Thus, it is asserted that humans have genuine agency in the world and the sort of freedom that is necessary to be morally responsible, but that this freedom is compatible with God's always achieving the will of his eternal purpose.[5]

Libertarians frequently assert that authentic freedom entails "the power of contrary choice." A person must have been able to act otherwise than she has acted, all things being equal, or she was not "free." Compatibilists, on the other hand, argue that people are free in the sense that grounds moral responsibility, provided they act as they wished (i.e., voluntarily). Unlike compatibilists, who assert that the will of God's eternal purpose is always accomplished, libertarians allow for a measure of divine self-limitation. Hence, the synergism, or cooperation, identified above.

For two reasons, I will generally refer to monergism and synergism rather than to Calvinism and Arminianism, despite the common use of the latter terms in evangelical discussion. First, self-professed Calvinist philosophers sometimes affirm this libertarian notion of freedom, making it difficult to say categorically that Reformed or Calvinist thought is monergistic these days. Second, this more basic terminology will keep us from the anachronism of calling the early fathers of the church or a Reformer such as Menno Simons "Arminians" because they were synergists.

My own understanding of God's relationship with the world is clearly monergistic.[6] Unfortunately, the term *monergism* gives the impression that creatures do not have genuine agency within the world—that God is the *only* one with causative power, the only one "working."[7] On the contrary, monergists in the Calvinist tradition affirm that creatures (both human and angelic) have genuine agency. People have wills and they act according to them, which is what gives their actions moral quality. It is because people (and angels) *choose* to do what they do that they are morally respon-

---

[5]This classic Calvinistic understanding of God's providence is expounded in chapter 11 of Terrance Tiessen, *Providence and Prayer: How Does God Work in the World?* (Downers Grove, Ill.: InterVarsity Press, 2000.)

[6]The outworking of this theological framework in a doctrine of divine providence and its correlative theology of petitionary prayer is spelled out in ibid., chapters 13 and 14.

[7]To avoid the misunderstanding that the term *monergism* may easily create, Donald Bloesch dubs his position "a monergy that embraces synergy," which he describes thus: "God's grace brings about the desired effect—faith and obedience, but it does this by animating and motivating the human subject to believe and obey. Synergism as such means that we contribute to our salvation through our own power, that God does some and we do some. We need to avoid both monergism and synergism by maintaining that God does all—but in and through human action. We believe and overcome through the power of grace, not through our own power—even in part." Donald G. Bloesch, *The Church: Sacraments, Worship, Ministry and Mission*, Christian Foundations (Downers Grove, Ill.: InterVarsity Press, 2002), p. 62. This is precisely what I mean by *monergism*.

sible for their actions. Monergists believe, however, that God *always* achieves the will of his eternal purpose (traditionally identified in the Reformed tradition as God's "decree"), even though his moral creatures act voluntarily or spontaneously to bring about the history that God has purposed. God works in the minds and hearts of human beings in a way that ensures the outcome but that does not destroy the human act of volition. Contemporary Calvinists or monergists therefore describe their position as a "soft" determinism, to differentiate it from the hard determinism that is mechanistic and that allows for no morally responsible human freedom. This is the framework within which I will examine the questions I have identified above.

Critical realism. In this book, I aim to further the Christian pursuit of truth by putting forward my own understanding of Scripture's answers to the questions I have raised. Speaking of truth is controversial these days, so I should indicate that I approach this study as a "critical realist." I believe that truth exists and that it can be known, but I also recognize that no one seeks this truth, even in the study of Scripture, without presuppositions that significantly shape what we hear there. This does not lead me to complete subjectivism, but it fosters a sober humility about the extent to which I (or others) have grasped the truth. Truth is not merely a social construction, but I am a knower who is embedded in a social context that affects my view of truth. Consequently, we are called to a self-conscious and self-critical knowing, and we must listen to others whose different contexts (even different religious contexts) may have enabled them to hear or see truth that we have not heard or seen as clearly.

I believe that "a statement (proposition, belief . . .) is true if and only if what the statement says to be the case actually is the case."[8] This notion is often called the *correspondence theory of truth,* which holds that "for a statement to be true, there must be some appropriate *correspondence* between true statements and actual features of the world."[9] Thus, as I reassess salvation in Christ and seek to understand the role of the religions within God's purposes in the world, I will be forthright about what I presently understand to be the correct answers to the questions under consideration.

---

[8]William Alston, *A Realist Conception of Truth* (Ithaca: Cornell University Press, 1996), p. 5, quoted in Harold Netland, *Encountering Religious Pluralism: The Challenge to Faith and Mission* (Downers Grove, Ill.: InterVarsity Press, 2001), p. 198.

[9]Paul K. Moser, Dwayne H. Mulder and J. D. Trout, *The Theory of Knowledge: A Thematic Introduction* (New York: Oxford University Press, 1998), p. 65, quoted in Netland, *Encountering,* p. 198.

On the other hand, my own mind has changed through the years, so I now offer this proposal in the spirit of a seeker after truth. I am sure to be wrong at some points, but I hope that I can stimulate a conversation that will lead me and others closer to the truth, which only God knows completely.

The globalization of Christianity. Both the success and failure of Christian mission has contributed to the rethinking that is going on within the Christian church relative to the saving program of God within the world and the proper attitude toward other religions (or even to our own). Because of the success of Christian mission, Christianity is now established in many parts of the world where it was not some centuries ago. This has required Christian churches to live and witness in communities where other religions are also actively present. Particularly in Asia, the Christian church has become conscious of the significance of the other great religious traditions that are dominant there.

Experiences of "failure" in Christian mission have also prompted Christian theologians to reexamine their assumptions about God's saving work in the world. Some Christian missionary efforts assumed that once the gospel was clearly proclaimed and properly lived out in an area, its superiority to other religious options would be obvious and conversion would result. If this did not occur, the assumption may have been that it was because of the inherent depravity and hardness of heart of the devotees of those religions. But Christianity has now been active in the context of other religions for centuries and, in many parts of the world, conversion rates from those other religions have been very slow. Furthermore, as dialogue between Christians and the devotees of other religions has gone on through the years, Christians have met people whose lives they came to admire and have discovered aspects of the teaching and practice of those religions that they respected. This has sometimes raised questions about the initial assumptions that Christianity alone is good and other religions are bad. It is within this context that I will seek a biblical understanding of God's saving and providential program in the world.

MY GOAL IN THIS BOOK

Even within evangelicalism there is not a clear consensus on the questions that I have raised above.[10] A host of books have been written on the sub-

---

[10]See Harold Netland, *Dissonant Voices: Religious Pluralism and the Question of Truth* (Grand Rapids, Mich.: Eerdmans, 1991), p. 264; "The WEF Manila Declaration," in *The Unique Christ in Our Pluralist World*, ed. Bruce J. Nicholls (Grand Rapids, Mich.: Baker, 1994), p. 15.

jects I am addressing, from a wide range of perspectives. Many of these books have laid out the alternative answers proposed by various other theologians or have offered careful critiques of the positions taken by those with whom the author disagrees. My own purpose is constructive rather than critical: I will try to define the issues clearly and will occasionally refer to some of the different ways in which the questions of our study have been answered by other people, but I will do this only when it clarifies the presentation of my own understanding of the biblical teaching. It is my hope and prayer that readers will listen to my proposal carefully, especially when it differs from the position to which they have been inclined, and that the result will be progress in the common pursuit of truth regarding these important matters.

MY PROPOSAL

At the beginning of each chapter of the constructive proposal, I offer the thesis statement (or statements) developed in that chapter. To give you a quick road map for the theological journey on which I will be taking you, I present here those thirty theses.

Thesis 1: Accessibilism can be traced in Christian thought back to the second century. It is now strongly affirmed in official Roman Catholic documents, but it can also be found among noted Protestant and evangelical theologians. It is the logical position for synergistic theologies but can also be well grounded in monergistic frameworks.

Thesis 2: By God's appointment, the entire human race was represented in Adam in his moral probation in the Garden of Eden. When he sinned, we all sinned, and so we all die. The consequence of that original sin was that everyone is born a sinner, alienated from God, guilty of enmity toward God and certain to commit acts of personal disobedience as soon as we are capable of making moral judgments. Thus, there are no "innocent" people, whether they be unborn, infant, disabled or competent and adult. Every human being, therefore, needs to be saved from the guilt of sin and its terrible consequences.

Thesis 3: There is only one means by which salvation of sinners can be accomplished. Jesus Christ is the world's only Savior. All who have ever been, are now or ever will be saved are reconciled to God because Jesus Christ lived, died and rose again for them. Salvation is a work of the triune God whom Christians worship. Before creating the world, God the Father chose whom he would save and God the Son then became a man and laid down his sinless life to accomplish salvation for those people. Just as the whole race became sinners in their natural head, Adam, so too the new race that God establishes in union with Christ (the second Adam) is made alive and righteous (i.e., "saved") in Christ. The Spirit of God then works in the lives of these people so that they respond willingly to God in the way necessary for the appropriation of Christ's saving work. Thus, God saves everyone whom he chose to save in the will of his eternal purpose (or his "decree"). On the other hand, God's gracious work extends beyond salvation so that everyone benefits from Christ's death in numerous ways.

Thesis 4: People experience the salvation that God has accomplished in Christ only when they respond to God in a way that satisfies him, which the Bible calls "faith." Therefore, God makes himself known to all people, but not everyone receives an equally full revelation. God reveals his being and work and something of his moral nature to everyone (i.e., "generally"). He does this by his works of creation and providence and through the moral consciousness and intrinsic religiousness of human beings. Thus, no one lacks the revelation necessary to elicit a response to God. But a much fuller revelation of God's nature, purposes and work has been made to particular individuals whom God uses to establish a covenant people (both old and new). This community and its members then serve as instruments of God's special revelation in the world, so that the effects of salvation can be extended to all areas of an individual's life and for the well-being of human society. God also reveals himself to particular individuals in a manner that is neither related to the formation of his covenant people nor universally normative. As with every form of God's special revelation, individuals' response to that revelation is part of their fundamental orientation of faith or unbelief in God.

Thesis 5: Whatever information, religious or moral, a person accepts as ultimately authoritative truth (whether this is understood to be from a personal God or not) must be believed and obeyed. It makes a claim upon that person. Just as one is obligated to obey one's moral conscience, so one is required to believe one's religious consciousness.

Thesis 6: Since faith is essential for reconciliation with God, unbelief and its attendant disobedience leave people under God's just condemnation. But people are held accountable by God only for their response to the revelation that they have received. People are guilty, even when they act ignorantly if they can be charged with having brought about their own state of ignorance. On the other hand, there is a form of ignorance for which individuals are inculpable, or not held accountable. God does not sentence people to judgment for acts they did that were morally wrong if, first, they were morally ignorant through no act of their own doing and, second, they acted with a clear conscience, not knowing their actions to be contrary to the truth. Consequently, it is possible that God may graciously save some who do not believe in Jesus as Savior if they are ignorant of him through no fault of their own.

Thesis 7: Salvation has always been by grace through faith, but the faith that God expects (and gives) is appropriate to the revelation of himself that he has given to a particular individual. God requires people who receive general revelation to honor him as the Creator and Provider, to be thankful to him, to obey their consciences and to cast themselves on his mercy when they are aware of their failure to do what is right. If the Spirit of God were graciously to elicit this response in anyone's heart, they would be saved. But there are eight reasons why we might doubt that there are people who receive only general revelation in the course of their lives. Even so, however, we can expect that God saves some people who have very incomplete knowledge of his person and work.

Thesis 8: God's knowledge of what people would do if they heard the gospel does not make salvation more accessible, but it enables him to bring about the salvation of the elect without coercion.

Thesis 9: Old Testament believers were saved by faith in God and in God's sure fulfillment of his promises to them, although the manner in which those promises would be fulfilled became clear only gradually. Their faith in God was frequently demonstrated in their obedience to his instructions or in deeds that expressed their confidence in God. We are not told much about the revelation to which Old Testament believers outside the covenant people (e.g., Job, Melchizedek and Jethro) were responding. It may have been general revelation or traditional remnants of much earlier special revelation, but I think it most likely that God revealed himself to them personally, as he did to the covenant people. From the experience of Old Testament believers, we can assert that God may save people today who do not hear the gospel. He could graciously save them by similar means of revelation and by the same kinds of faith, trust in God and acceptance of the truthfulness of his promise.

Thesis 10: From observing the experiences of people who met Jesus during his earthly ministry, we notice that God led them through a process that sometimes happened quickly and sometimes went more slowly. The point at which people were saved is impossible for us to discern, but it was frequently earlier than the moment at which they became Christians, that is, when they acknowledged Jesus to be the Messiah, the Son of God, and worshiped him. This paradigm still operates today, so that some people are saved who have not yet become Christians. Some of these are ignorant of Jesus; others have heard about him but have not yet been convinced of his identity by the Holy Spirit. We are reasonably able to discern when a person becomes a Christian, but only God knows the moment at which a person is saved.

Thesis 11: The implications of the principles derived from both the Old Testament situation and from the lifetime of Jesus are particularly important for our perspective on Jewish people today. We can assert that the faith of Abraham still saves, and we can acknowledge that some Jews may be believers (with an old covenant faith) and hence be saved, although they are not Christians. This is only true, however, of Jews who do not know the real identity of Jesus and who have not knowingly rejected the Messiah. Evangelism among Jewish people is as necessary today as it was in the time of the apostles. Not only does God want people to be saved, but he wants them to experience all the blessings of the new covenant in the fellowship of the new covenant community, the church of Jesus Christ.

Thesis 12: The possibility and the process of salvation are no different for infants and the mentally incompetent than for competent adults. Those whom God elects to salvation are saved by grace through faith. Scripture is silent about how many of the infants who die in infancy are included among the elect, but we place our hope for their salvation in God's great mercy. The capabilities of infants and the mentally challenged to relate to God cannot be measured by their ability to communicate with us; we must not assume that the capabilities of their bodies and brains are indicative of the abilities of their souls and minds. Infant faith, like adult faith, would be a trusting response to God and his self-revelation by the means God chooses.

Thesis 13: All people meet Jesus Christ personally at the moment of death, and they respond to him in a manner consistent with the response they had been giving to God and his revelation during their lifetime. At that moment, those who had received forms of revelation less complete than the gospel but who had responded in faith, by a work of the Holy Spirit, will joyfully find in Christ the fulfillment of all their hopes and longings. Consequently, there is a sense in which we can say that only those who believe in Jesus will be (finally) saved, even though we affirm that some can be (initially) saved without knowing about Jesus.

Thesis 14: God's saving grace is universally sufficient so that, on at least one occasion in each person's life, one is enabled to respond to God's self-revelation with a faith response that is acceptable to God as a means of justification. Only those whom God effectively persuades (i.e., recipients of efficacious grace) will believe. Nevertheless, the universally sufficient grace vindicates God's judgment of unbelievers, and it removes from the doctrine of original sin a burden that it could not otherwise sustain, given the biblical witness concerning the grounds of final judgment.

Thesis 15: Accessibilism is not detrimental to the church's missionary motivation. The point of accessibilism is not to undermine the uniqueness of the gospel or to diminish the necessity of its proclamation; it is to vindicate God's justice toward people who have not heard the gospel. God's ordinary means for saving people, since Pentecost, is through the proclamation of the gospel by the church, empowered by the Spirit. We engage zealously in evangelism out of obedience to the example and request of our Lord and out of our love for Christ and for our neighbor. Above all, we do Christian mission for the glory of God whose name will be magnified by those who come to know him as Father. Although God may be saving people beyond the reach of the church's gospel proclamation, he desires for them a fullness of life, here and now, that is impossible apart from full knowledge of Christ's blessings and life in a community of followers of Jesus.

Thesis 16: Scripture is silent about the final numbers of the saved relative to the unsaved, but we have reason to be very hopeful concerning the proportion of the human race that will enjoy life with God in the glorious new earth that he plans to bring about when his redemptive program is complete.

Thesis 17: Religions develop as inherently religious people respond to God's revelation in the forms that are accessible to them. Consequently, religions are ambiguous constructions, incorporating both the appropriation of divine truth and its suppression, due to human fallenness and demonic deception. The value of religions is therefore measured both by the completeness of the revelation to which they have responded and by the extent to which they have believed and obeyed, rather than suppressed, the truth that God has revealed.

Thesis 18: Among the religions of the world, Christianity has the great advantage of being constructed in response to God's revelation in Jesus Christ and the Scriptures of the New and Old Testaments. But even so, there is no particular communion or congregation of the Christian church that is a pure appropriation of God's revealed truth. As we construct the Christianity that we teach and practice, we must beware of syncretism. Nevertheless, the Christian religion we formulate should be at home in its cultural context to the fullest extent possible while faithfully living out God's revealed truth.

Thesis 19: The biblical writers consistently bear witness to the uniqueness of the God who created all that exists and who established a covenant relationship with the people of Israel, which was later extended to the Gentiles, in the church. The gods worshiped by the other nations are not real and are unable to save; in fact, the worship of these gods might be stirred up by demonic forces as a means to hold people in spiritual bondage. To his covenant people, God gave special revelation of himself and prescribed the way in which he was to be worshiped. Sadly, despite this great privilege, idolatry was always a grave threat among the covenant people. The people of Israel were called to bear witness to the true God primarily by the purity of their own lives and worship, but God also acted on their behalf and in the lives of neighboring nations to exalt his own name. As is true in the areas of theological and moral truth, the practice of religion for which God holds people accountable is assessed by the revelation of God's will that they have received.

Thesis 20: God appropriated divine names and religious forms from contemporary culture without endorsing the religion of Israel's neighbors. Thus, God modeled accommodation and assimilation without syncretism, and this should be our own goal as we establish Christian communities in the contexts of the religions of our own day.

Thesis 21: Formalized religions are ambiguous responses to divine revelation, and so are the religious commitments of individual members of those religions. Both the institutional religions and the persons within them are responding to general revelation, but they may also be responding to universally normative special revelation that they have encountered or to remnants of such revelation that may exist in the traditions that have been passed down. Additionally, there may have been instances of particular, but not universally normative, revelation that contributed to the formation of an established religion or to the personal religious commitment of an individual within one of those religions.

Thesis 22: The scriptures of other religions are not themselves instances of divine revelation. Because these scriptures lack the Holy Spirit's inspiration, they are a mixture of truth and error, depending on the relative extent to which they have appropriated and suppressed revealed truth, whether through human rebellion or error, or through demonic deception.

Thesis 23: After the supreme self-revelation of God in Jesus, the incarnate Word, there have been no divinely appointed prophets on the order of those in the old covenant, such as Moses and Isaiah. In the church, the Spirit of God gifts individuals for prophecy, and this may include the reception of messages from God that are beneficial to the building up of the congregation in their lives of faith. Such new covenant prophecies are fallible reports of messages believed by the reporter to have been received from God, and these must be judged within the congregation by others who have spiritual discernment. God may reveal to individuals outside the church messages containing truth that would further God's purposes in the world if it were appropriated. Only in a very limited sense could the communication of such messages be dubbed "prophecy," and the communicators could not be called "prophets" of God by any but the most restricted definition. They lack the charism of the Spirit that operates in the Christian church. Obviously, the human communication of such messages from God is fallible and liable to an admixture of error that greatly exceeds the communication of messages from God by individuals who are indwelt by the Spirit of God. Such messages, particularly when regarded by members of the religious community as having come from God, will contribute significantly to the formation and development of the religion.

Thesis 24: In God's gracious providence, he may have caused or allowed ideas to emerge within a religious context that provide a bridge or stepping stone toward the gospel, thereby facilitating communication of the gospel to those people and becoming an instrument of the Spirit of God in eliciting faith in Christ.

Thesis 25: No religion saves people—only God does. But, because religions are ambiguous responses to divine revelation and because they pass along to their devotees aspects of God's truth that have been appropriated by the religious tradition, God may graciously give faith to individuals while they live in the context of a non-Christian religion. In such instances, God may use the revealed truth that people encounter as a part of their religious tradition to elicit that saving faith. The religions that have not arisen primarily from God's universally normative special revelation cannot be viewed as having been raised up by God with the intent that they should serve as vehicles of special (saving) grace.

Thesis 26: We can observe signs of the work of God's common grace in the world through religions, and we should give thanks to God for this when we discern it in religions we encounter. Religions, like governments, may be used (and perhaps even intended) by God to restrain sin and evil and to create an environment where good may flourish. In religions, as in cultures, God may work graciously for the well-being of his creatures. Christians can engage in worthwhile ministry activities that serve only the purposes of God's common grace, but our greatest desire is to be useful to God in his purposes of special, saving grace. On the other hand, the line between God's works of common and special grace is not something that we are well able to discern.

Thesis 27: We can discern the work of God's grace in the teaching and life of other religions and in the lives of individuals who adhere to other religions by using three criteria. Most important for our process of discernment is the extent to which the truth revealed in Scripture is attested and practiced, that is, the degree to which the religion or the individual is orthodox. A second criterion is the morality taught and practiced by religions and their members (i.e., *orthopraxy*). By the fruit, we know the nature of the tree. God's grace is evident where human well-being is fostered—where personal morality and social justice are valued, encouraged and practiced. Although human theory is often better than its practice, the grace of God may be discernible particularly in situations where we are led to commend good behavior that seems unlikely to have been derived from the erroneous religious theory being propounded. The third criterion is most important from God's perspective but is most difficult for us to use, namely, the orientation of an individual's heart or even a community's heart. Only God knows the motives from which people do good, but his moral assessment is largely determined by that attitude of heart. Religions can teach ideas and foster forms of behavior, but only God can turn hearts toward himself.

Thesis 28: Dialogue with members of other religions is valuable. It is not a substitute for evangelism, but it is also not simply a means of evangelism. Nevertheless, Christians engaged in dialogue will be hopeful that God might use their conversations to lead dialogue partners to faith in Christ or to further other good purposes that God may have for the lives of those with whom we are in dialogue. Christians can also benefit personally from dialogue in various ways, learning as well as teaching.

Thesis 29: Some concerns are common to various religions, such as the dangers of secularism, the protection of innocent human life, the protection of the ecosystem and the quest for social justice. Peace through justice in the world is the desire of all people of goodwill but, regrettably, religious differences frequently contribute to both injustice and violence. In the face of these issues of global importance, whatever the members of different religions can do together for the common good, for the shalom of God's world, without compromising their distinctive faith allegiances, is to be pursued. Religious communities need to work together against common threats in ways that do not compromise or syncretize their different belief systems.

Thesis 30: It is impossible for Christians to join in worship with members of other religions. To do so would be to deny the uniqueness of the triune God whom Christians worship through Christ by the impulse of God's Spirit.

Words and acts of worship to God, even when offered in the name of Jesus, are not acceptable to him when the heart of the worshiper is not right. On the other hand, we do not know to what extent God may receive the prayers and worship of people whose theology is inadequate but whose hearts are rightly oriented toward God. Nevertheless, we are not authorized to worship together, as though the differences in our understanding of the God whom we worship were not significant. In civic events where there is a common desire to acknowledge our human finitude and to seek the help and blessing of the Supreme Being, Christians may pray, as long as they are free to do so in the name of Jesus their Lord, as participants in a series of prayers offered by members of different religions. This is not an act of common worship, provided each participant prays according to his or her own faith and so long as no effort is made to formulate a generic prayer to be prayed by all participants, regardless of religious differences.

2

What Are the Options?

IT WOULD TAKE AN ENCYCLOPEDIA TO BRING TOGETHER the diverse answers Christians have given to the questions I raised in the first chapter. As is usually true, however, these many answers can be grouped together in broad categories of shared understanding. One common way in which this has been done is the threefold typology of pluralism, inclusivism and exclusivism.[1] Although years of use have made the terms fairly comprehensible, the usefulness of the classification is now frequently questioned. Tim Perry, for instance, suggests "that this typology tends to misrepresent non-pluralist approaches as theologically deficient and/or ethically insensitive."[2] Similarly, Harold Netland posits that *exclusivism* has been used as "a pejorative term with unflattering connotations: exclusivists are typically branded as dogmatic, narrow-minded, intolerant, ignorant, arrogant and so on."[3] In fact, Perry contends, an analysis of actual exclusivist and pluralist proposals demonstrates "that exclusivist accounts have more nuance while pluralist ones are more problematic than the typology indicates."[4]

Now that the threefold typology has been so widely criticized, numerous authors have proposed alternatives, but none of these has been widely

---

[1]The typology is often traced back to Alan Race, *Christians and Religious Pluralism* (London: SCM Press, 1983).

[2]Tim S. Perry, *Radical Difference: A Defence of Hendrik Kraemer's Theology of Religions*, Editions SR, ed. H. Martin Rumscheidt and Theodore S. de Bruyn (Waterloo, Ontario: Wilfrid Laurier University Press, 2001), 27:11. See his excellent discussion in chapter 2, "Typological Issues," 27:9-28.

[3]Harold Netland, *Encountering Religious Pluralism: The Challenge to Faith and Mission* (Downers Grove, Ill.: InterVarsity Press, 2001), p. 46.

[4]Perry, *Radical Difference*, 27:11.

adopted. Consequently, I have deemed it best to construct my own categories, using terms that encapsulate for me the ideas being represented.
Some of these terms have been used by others, but not in this combination.
This will force readers to attend to my own definition of these terms, and
it should avoid the difficulty that occurs when a widely used term like *inclusivism* is used differently from one book to another. I see the major answers as falling into five positions, which I will identify as *ecclesiocentrism,
agnosticism, accessibilism, religious instrumentalism* and *relativism.* Amos
Yong has observed that "exclusivism is first and foremost a soteriological
category," which might be helpful regarding the question concerning the
unevangelized but "is not well equipped for engaging the task of theology
of religions broadly considered."[5] I have been aware of this difficulty in se-
lecting the categories and terminology for my own work, which addresses
both the question of the unevangelized and the issue of the religions. My
first three categories arise from analysis of the fate of the unevangelized,
and the last two are more focused on the role of religions. I suggest, however, that one's answers to the first question determine to some extent the
options available on the second issue. Along the way, I will indicate where
I see some overlap in application of the categories. At this point, I will give
a brief definition of each of these understandings, and then I will outline
the rationale that leads theologians to adopt them. I begin with the most
conservative option, which is probably also the majority position among
evangelical clergy today, particularly among monergists.

DEFINING THE OPTIONS

Ecclesiocentrism. Ecclesiocentrism is characterized particularly by the
conviction that ever since Christ ascended and sent the Holy Spirit, only
those who hear the gospel can be saved. This means that the possibility of
salvation is coextensive with the presence of the church, which makes the
church and its gospel proclamation essential to God's work of salvation.
Thus, the reason for designating this position *ecclesiocentrism* should be obvious. Ecclesiocentrists believe that salvation is accomplished only
through Jesus Christ, but that conviction is shared by the first four of my
five categories, so this does not constitute a distinctive of the position. Ecclesiocentrism also contends that the non-Christian religions, as such, do
not have saving instrumentality. But again, since this conviction is shared

---

[5]Amos Yong, *Beyond the Impasse: Toward a Pneumatological Theology of Religions* (Grand Rapids,
Mich.: Baker, 2003), pp. 26-27.

by agnostics and accessibilists, it cannot be the primary identifying characteristic. Very negative assessments of other religions and their value are frequently found in the writings of ecclesiocentrists, but this is not consistently the case, particularly in recent years. The distinctive of this position, therefore, is the contention that salvation is only accessible to those who hear the gospel, at least in the case of competent adults.

Agnosticism. The theologians whose position I identify as *agnosticism* do not know for sure that God has means by which to save people who do not hear about Christ. But they do not think that Scripture clearly indicates that none of the unevangelized are ever saved. They acknowledge that the New Testament bears strong witness to the normative importance of explicit faith in Jesus for salvation, but they doubt that the God revealed to us in Scripture would condemn eternally so many people who die in ignorance of Christ. At most, they find the Bible silent about the fate of the unevangelized. As to the means by which such people might be saved, if any are, the agnostics I have encountered are no less certain than the ecclesiocentrists that the sacrifice of Christ is the only ground of salvation. This would be true whether or not these people are fully aware of what Christ has done for them. Evangelicals who take this standpoint in regard to the possible salvation of the unevangelized also tend to be more affirming of relative good in the context of other religions, while insisting that the religions are not themselves God's instruments of salvation.

Accessibilism. Accessibilism[6] asserts that Jesus Christ is exclusively God's means of salvation and that the covenantal relationships God established with Israel and the church, in working out his saving program, are unique and unparalleled. Accessibilists believe, however, that there is biblical reason to be *hopeful* (not simply agnostic) about the possibility of salvation for those who do not hear the gospel. So they do not restrict God's saving work to the boundaries of the church as ecclesiocentrists do. On the contrary, they posit that God makes salvation *accessible* to people who do not receive the gospel. Although they grant that non-Christians can be saved, they do not regard the religions as God's instrument in their salvation.

Religious instrumentalism. What I am calling *religious instrumentalism* goes beyond the accessibilist belief that God saves some people who do

---

[6]I have appropriated this term from William Lane Craig, "Politically Incorrect Salvation," in *Christian Apologetics in the Postmodern World,* ed. Timothy P. Phillips and Dennis L. Okholm (Downers Grove, Ill.: InterVarsity Press, 1995), p. 84.

not hear about Christ's saving work and argues that "God's salvation is available *through* non-Christian religions. Jesus is still held to be, in some sense, unique, normative and definitive; but God is said to be revealing himself and providing salvation *through* other religious traditions as well"[7] (emphasis mine). What I have just quoted is Netland's definition of *inclusivism*. Unfortunately, many other evangelicals use the term *inclusivism* to identify the position that I am calling *accessibilism*. It is to avoid this confusion that I am not using *inclusivism* for either of the two positions in my classification scheme. Gavin D'Costa also defines as "inclusivist" theologies which claim that "the one revelation or religion is the only true and definitive one, *but* truth and therefore salvation can be found in various, incomplete forms within other religions and their structures."[8] It should be obvious why I have, instead, chosen the term *religious instrumentalism* to describe the position that has been defined in these citations from Netland and D'Costa.[9] I hope that the distinction between this position and accessibilism is now clear: accessibilists believe that God may save people who are members of other religions, but religious instrumentalists believe that God has raised up those religions as his instruments in salvation.

   Relativism. To the question posed in part one of this book (how does God save people?), relativism's basic answer is that salvation is universally accessible *through* the various religions that are part of the divine program. Thus, their answer to the question of part two (how do the religions fit into God's purposes in the world?) is a straightforward answer to the previous question as well. D'Costa's definition of *pluralism* represents well what I mean by *relativism:* "All the major religions have true revelations in part, while no single revelation or religion can claim final and definitive truth."[10] All of them are, therefore, more or less equally true and valid as paths to salvation. The value of this perspective is presumed to be the respect and autonomy it grants to different religions.

---

[7]Harold Netland, *Dissonant Voices: Religious Pluralism and the Question of Truth* (Grand Rapids, Mich.: Eerdmans, 1991), p. 10; see also Netland, *Encountering,* pp. 51-52.

[8]Gavin D'Costa, *The Meeting of Religions and the Trinity,* Faith Meets Faith (Maryknoll, N.Y.: Orbis, 2000), p. 21.

[9]Similar definitions of *inclusivism,* which fit my category of *religious instrumentalism,* can be found in D. A. Carson, *The Gagging of God: Christianity Confronts Pluralism* (Grand Rapids, Mich.: Zondervan, 1996), p. 27; Harvie M. Conn, "Do Other Religions Save?" in *Through No Fault of Their Own? The Fate of Those Who Have Never Heard,* ed. William V. Crockett and James G. Sigountos (Grand Rapids, Mich.: Baker, 1991), p. 199; and Calvin E. Shenk, *Who Do You Say that I Am? Christians Encounter Other Religions* (Scottdale, Penn.: Herald, 1997), p. 43.

[10]D'Costa, *Meeting of Religions,* p. 21.

Not every expression of a religion is approved, however, and a distinction is often made between small minor cults and major religions.

One of the major problems with using the term *pluralism* to define the position that I am calling *relativism* is that *pluralism* is widely used to describe contexts in which diverse viewpoints are permitted. In that sense, societies that grant religious freedom to their members are pluralist. But most people in all four of the other categories are committed to this sort of plurality, or pluralism. I think that *relativism* identifies the distinctive in the theology of religions that has regularly been called *pluralist* in the three-fold schematic.

The following chart will help to identify the differences between these five proposals.

Chart of the Theological Spectrum

	Ecclesiocentrism	Agnosticism	Accessibilism	Religious Instrumentalism	Relativism
Is Christ the only Savior in the world?	Yes	Yes	Yes	Yes	No
Can unevangelized adults be saved?	No	Don't know	Yes	Yes	Yes
Does God raise up various religions as instruments of salvation?	No	No	No	Yes	Yes
Are religious books other than the Bible normative divine revelation?	No	No	No	Possibly yes	Yes
Should Christians evangelize devout members of other religions?	Yes	Yes	Yes	Generally, yes	No

An Outline of the Rationale for Each of These Approaches

In putting forward my own understanding of the answers to the questions raised in this book, I will occasionally interact with writers who reach a different conclusion than I do. At this point, however, I will trace briefly the major reasons cited by proponents of the five approaches I have identified.[11]

Ecclesiocentrism. Ecclesiocentrists have a strong sense of support within Christian tradition, going back at least to the statement by Cyprian (ca. 200-258), bishop of Carthage, that "outside the church there is no salvation." Cyprian used this phrase to refer to heretics and schismatics, people who had been part of the church and had departed from it. A couple of centuries later, however, Fulgentius of Ruspe (468-533) applied the axiom to pagans and Jews, and this extended application of the statement was formalized in the conclusions of the Council of Florence (1431-1438).[12]

In a letter from Pope Innocent III to the archbishop of Tarragona (dated December 12, 1208), the following profession of faith was demanded of Durandus de Osca on his return to the Roman Catholic Church from the Waldensians: "We heartily believe and orally confess the one Church, not of heretics, but the Holy, Roman, Catholic, apostolic [Church], outside which we believe no one can be saved." Soon afterward, the Fourth Lateran Council (1215), which was directed against spiritualist and antiecclesial movements, declared, "There is indeed one universal Church of the faithful outside which no one at all is saved, and in which the priest himself, Jesus Christ, is also the sacrifice *(idem ipse sacerdos est sacrificium Jesus Christus)*."[13] Strong statements of ecclesiocentrism are obviously not difficult to find in the tradition of the church.

For evangelical heirs of the Reformation's *sola Scriptura*, even more significant than these statements from the church in the middle ages is the teaching of Scripture. Ecclesiocentrists recognize that the severity of God's judgment is according to the degree of revelation that people receive (Rom 2:12-13), but they still assert that the absolute line between salvation and

---

[11]For readers who want a more extensive review of the various proposals for a Christian theology of religions, see Veli-Matti Kärkkäinen, *An Introduction to the Theology of Religions* (Downers Grove, Ill.: InterVarsity Press, 2003).

[12]See Fulgentius *De fide ad Petrum* 37-38, quoted in Jacques Dupuis, *Toward a Christian Theology of Religious Pluralism* (Maryknoll, N.Y.: Orbis, 1997), p. 92.

[13]Dupuis, *Toward a Christian Theology,* p. 94.

condemnation is found in explicit faith in Christ. They frequently insist that even those who were saved before the incarnation had to have an anticipatory faith regarding the coming Messiah or Savior.

In Acts 4:12, Peter stated that "there is no other name under heaven given among mortals by which we must be saved." Ecclesiocentrists take this to "imply that the requirement of salvation by belief in Jesus' name is universal."[14] They consider it "difficult to argue that Peter allows that salvation of which he speaks in Acts 4:12 did not require knowledge of the person of Jesus."[15] This is deemed to be borne out by Peter's use of the term *name*.[16] Furthermore, "Peter does not appear to be referring to Jesus merely as the ontological ground of salvation—that is, as the sole *source* of atonement. Rather, he is indicating what must be acknowledged about Jesus before one can be saved."[17]

From John 14:6, Douglas Geivett and Gary Phillips "infer that anyone who wants to come to the Father must find that way that uniquely leads to the Father, namely, Jesus himself." And they note that, in his intercessory ministry, Jesus prays for "those who will believe in me *through their word*" (Jn 17:20, emphasis mine), which "implies a direct link between the future salvation of those who are not of his immediate Jewish fold (10:16) and the explicit proclamation of the apostolic word."[18] Although the Bible tells us of individuals who received some special revelation, they were still required to believe further redemptive truth in order to be saved. Examples of this are the Samaritans (Jn 4:9, 24), devout Jews from every nation (Acts 2:5, 38), zealous Jews (Rom 10:1-3) and God-fearing Gentiles (Acts 9:2; 10:33, 43). Much of what these people believed was true, but it was not enough for salvation.[19]

Few texts have been memorized more often by evangelicals than John 3:16, and it seems clear to restrictivists not only that Jesus is God's ordained means of salvation, but also that one must, therefore, know and believe in him to be saved. Commenting on Romans 10:9-10, Geivett and Phillips argue that

> it is difficult to account for the evangelistic mandate, and for the sufferings God's witnesses are called upon to endure, on the supposition that the un-

---

[14]Douglas R. Geivett and Gary W. Phillips, "A Particularist View: An Evidentialist Approach," in *More Than One Way? Four Views on Salvation in a Pluralistic World*, ed. Dennis L. Okholm and Timothy R. Phillips (Grand Rapids, Mich.: Zondervan, 1995), p. 230.
[15]Ibid., p. 231.
[16]Ibid., p. 232.
[17]Ibid., pp. 232-33.
[18]Ibid., p. 237.
[19]Ibid., p. 238.

evangelized do not need to hear in order to be saved. To be saved, a specific confession has to be made, and a specific set of truths must be believed.[20]

Missionary work is critical, therefore, because "apart from the faithful labor of the human evangelist, the unbeliever will have no opportunity to hear that which must be believed in order to be saved."[21]

Ecclesiocentrism has, therefore, been used as a powerful motivation to Christian missions, a point clearly heard by Carl Braaten, a Lutheran theologian:

> They now teach as dogmatic truth and as a criterion of being faithful to the gospel of Jesus Christ that all who die or who have died without conscious faith in Jesus Christ are damned to eternal hell. If people have never heard the gospel and have never had a chance to believe, they are lost anyway. The logic of this position is that children who die in infancy are lost. The mentally retarded are lost. All those who have never heard of Christ are lost. Nevertheless, evangelicals cling to this view as the heart of the gospel and the incentive to mission.[22]

It is interesting to notice, however, how widely evangelicals reject this logic regarding infants and the mentally incapable. The validity of this distinction between those who *do* not hear and those who *cannot* hear the gospel will be examined later in our study.

Agnosticism. The agnostic standpoint is stated succinctly by John Stott:

> I believe the most Christian stance is to remain agnostic on this question. . . . The fact is that God, alongside the most solemn warnings about our responsibility to respond to the gospel, has not revealed how he will deal with those who have never heard it. We have to leave them in the hands of the God of infinite mercy and justice, who manifested these qualities most fully in the cross. Abraham's question, "will not the Judge of all the earth do right?" (Genesis 18:25) is our confidence too.[23]

In these few words, Stott captures the features that I find recurring in the statements of other evangelical "agnostics" on this issue, namely, the silence of Scripture on the fate of the unevangelized, the mercy and grace of God, and the justice of God.

---

[20]Ibid., p. 235.

[21]Ibid., p. 236.

[22]Carl E. Braaten, "The Uniqueness and Universality of Jesus Christ," in *Faith Meets Faith*, Mission Trends, ed. Gerald H. Anderson and Thomas F. Stransky (Grand Rapids, Mich.: Eerdmans, 1981), 5:73.

[23]David L. Edwards and John Stott, *Evangelical Essentials: A Liberal-Evangelical Dialogue* (Downers Grove, Ill.: InterVarsity Press, 1988), p. 327.

While sharing Stott's agnosticism about whether any people who do not know the gospel will actually be saved, J. I. Packer has spelled out why or how it might be that God could save some who are ignorant of Christ:

> We may safely say *(i)* if any good pagan reached the point of throwing himself on his Maker's mercy for pardon, it was grace that brought him there; *(ii)* God will surely save anyone he brings thus far (cf. Acts 10:34f; Rom. 10:12f); *(iii)* anyone thus saved would learn in the next world that he was saved through Christ. But what we cannot safely say is that God ever does save anyone in this way. We simply do not know.[24]

Similarly, church-growth specialist Donald McGavran was explicit about the means by which God might save any who are ignorant of Jesus and his work: "All we can say, humbly yet boldly, is that if anyone *is* saved it will not be through any religion or human attainment, but solely through the objective, atoning death and resurrection of Jesus Christ, whether consciously appropriated or not."[25]

Although D. A. Carson generally speaks in ecclesiocentric terms, he does not deny the possibility that God might save some of the unevangelized, although he is pessimistic about their numbers. Commenting on Romans 2:14-16, Carson writes, "One might imagine some pagan, afflicted by conscience, crying to his Maker for mercy." Although that is "not what the text *says* . . . it does not absolutely shut the door to the possibility."[26] He suggests that "the text does not rule out the possibility for which Packer allows, but it does not explicitly sanction it either."[27] Regarding Acts 17:24-30, he observes, "God's creative power, his creation of the human race from one man and his providential rule over them were all done, we are told, 'so that men would seek him and perhaps reach out for him and find him' (17:27)."[28] Again, Carson is cautious and says that "strictly speaking, the text does not say that some would find God by this means; it says, rather, that at least one of God's purposes in his providential rule is to lead people to know him. Clearly, that was the

---

[24]J. I. Packer, *God's Words: Studies of Key Bible Themes* (Downers Grove, Ill.: InterVarsity Press, 1981), p. 210; see also J. I. Packer, "What Happens to People Who Die Without Hearing the Gospel?" *Decision,* January 2002, p. 11.

[25]Donald McGavran, "Contemporary Evangelical Theology of Mission," in *Contemporary Theologies of Mission,* ed. A. F. Glasser and Donald McGavran (Grand Rapids, Mich.: Baker, 1983), p. 103.

[26]Carson, *Gagging of God,* p. 311.

[27]Ibid., p. 312.

[28]Ibid., p. 308.

'hope.'"[29] Carson observes that although the Athenians had *not* found
God by this means,

> it *may* be the case that God has in some cases opened the eyes of some people
> to recognize the existence and graciousness of their Maker and turn to him
> in repentance and faith, imploring him for mercy. But the text does not say
> that this has taken place. . . . The least that must be said is that the passage
> offers no comfort for the view that there are millions and millions of pagan
> anonymous Christians out there.[30]

Accessibilism. My own response to the questions raised in this book
falls into the category of accessibilism, and so I will not present the rationale for this approach now. The rest of the book will serve that purpose.
At this point, however, it may be helpful for me to relate something of
my pilgrimage toward this position, since I was for many years a convinced ecclesiocentrist. In the early 1980s, while taking a course on the
doctrine of divine revelation, I became aware of the way in which Roman
Catholic theologians were appealing to second-century theologians in
support of positive views of God's saving work outside the church. With
that in mind, I did a study of the doctrine of revelation in the writings of
Clement of Alexandria, Justin Martyr and Irenaeus. I concluded that
there was some ground for citing Clement of Alexandria and Justin as
forerunners of a positive view of God's self-revelation and grace beyond
the covenant community.

I was more skeptical that Irenaeus should be included with Clement
and Justin on this issue. But I was intrigued by his own situation as a missionary to the Gauls, and I had gained an appreciation for his passionate
apologetic for Christian faith against the Gnostics. So I then narrowed and
intensified my study in a dissertation on the theology of divine revelation
in the work of Irenaeus, with particular attention to his understanding of
the state of the unevangelized. At the time of that study, I was an ecclesiocentrist myself. And although I wanted to hear and represent Irenaeus as
fairly as I could, I fully expected him to be an ecclesiocentrist too. I certainly found statements that sounded ecclesiocentrist, but I quickly real-

---

[29]Ibid., p. 309.

[30]Ibid. Others who have made similar agnostic statements about the salvation of the unevangelized include Harold Netland (*Encountering*, p. 323); veteran missionary and church
leader in India Lesslie Newbigin (*The Open Secret: An Introduction to the Theology of Mission*,
rev. ed. [Grand Rapids, Mich.: Eerdmans, 1995], p. 173); Mennonite missiologist Calvin
Shenk (*Who Do You Say*, p. 242); and Vinoth Ramachandra (*The Recovery of Mission: Beyond
the Pluralist Paradigm* [Carlisle, U.K.: Paternoster, 1996], p. 274).

ized that Irenaeus believed the world to have been evangelized in his time through the travels of the apostles throughout the world. Consequently, in the worldview of Irenaeus, there were no people out of contact with the church. Thus, I was bringing to his work a question that he had not personally contemplated. Given my own ecclesiocentrism at the time, I cannot be accused of having imported accessibilist presuppositions into the thought of Irenaeus. But as my study proceeded, I came to the conclusion that features in his theological position would have led him to accessibilism if he had known of the existence of the unevangelized. I recognize that people sometimes change their theological position when they discover that it has unwanted implications, so I could only say where Irenaeus was headed, not what he would actually have taught. Some years later, I revised the work for publication, but in the revision process I found no reason to change my interpretation of Irenaeus.[31]

For the next twelve years or more, I continued to hear ecclesiocentrism in the Bible's language concerning salvation. I preached it in missionary conferences, and I taught it in my classes. One summer in the early 1990s, I wrote a review of three books dealing with the subject of the salvation of the unevangelized from an evangelical perspective.[32] One of the books was a collection of essays from differing viewpoints, one was a survey of the various understandings in the history of Christian thought, and the third made a case for an accessibilist (or "wider hope") position.[33] I had read all three books and was still a convinced ecclesiocentrist when I started to write the review article. But then something happened—what has been called a "paradigm shift," I guess. I found myself reexamining biblical texts and hearing them differently than I used to. I concluded that I had been reading Scripture through ecclesiocentrist lenses, which I had inherited and gotten used to. But when I stood back and examined the lenses themselves, I decided that they had been keeping me from seeing some things that now jumped out at me from the biblical pages. From that time forward, I have been refining my position, but I have not yet found reason to reject

---

[31]Terrance Tiessen, *Irenaeus on the Salvation of the Unevangelized*, ATLA Monograph 31 (Metuchen, N.J.: Scarecrow, 1993).

[32]Terrance Tiessen, "Can the Unevangelized Be Saved? A Review Article," *Didaskalia* 4 (fall 1993): 77-91.

[33]The books I reviewed were William V. Crockett and James G. Sigountos, eds., *Through No Fault of Their Own? The Fate of Those Who Have Never Heard* (Grand Rapids, Mich.: Baker 1991); John Sanders, *No Other Name: An Investigation into the Destiny of the Unevangelized* (Grand Rapids, Mich.: Eerdmans, 1992); and Clark H. Pinnock, *A Wideness in God's Mercy: The Finality of Jesus Christ in a World of Religions* (Grand Rapids, Mich.: Zondervan, 1992), respectively.

my new set of accessibilist lenses. Having changed my understanding once, I am not averse to doing so again, but this book lays out the way in which I now hear the biblical message. This journey has not always been comfortable, given the significant anxiety that accessibilism arouses among evangelical theologians, who frequently identify it as "inclusivism" and who see it as a threat to the church's motivation in evangelistic mission.

Given these significant evangelical fears, I have devoted a chapter to the reasons why we should be energetically involved in global evangelism, even if God has chosen to save some people to whom we have not yet "delivered" the gospel. At this point, however, I want to acquaint you with my involvement in the global mission of the church. I grew up in a missionary home in India, and my life has been greatly influenced by the evangelistic fervor of my parents. My father had a brother who also served as a missionary in India and a sister who was a missionary in the West Indies. One of my mother's brothers was a missionary among First Nations peoples in Canada. So I certainly learned early that Christian mission is an excellent way to spend one's life.

I have vivid and fond memories of the citywide evangelistic tent meetings that my father used to organize each year, during the time that I was at home from boarding school for the long winter vacation. I recall very early childhood dreams of becoming a missionary doctor in Africa, stirred by books in the "jungle doctor" series. When I was fifteen years of age, I experienced a particular moving of the Spirit of God in my life as I read a series of missionary biographies loaned to me by a boarding school master, including two dense but fascinating volumes on the life and work of Hudson Taylor. Meanwhile, God was at work in the life of a girl in Toronto who developed a similar desire for missionary service. We met at a Bible college (where she was a missions major), got married and eventually spent sixteen years as missionaries in the Philippines. We now have a son and daughter-in-law who live dangerously in Central Asia in order to further the great task of getting God's Word into the languages of people to whom God wants to speak about his great salvation.

Although I was no longer a full-time missionary at the time I became an accessibilist, I have not found that this change in perspective has in any way diminished my sense of the urgency and privilege of proclaiming the good news concerning Jesus, which God uses powerfully to work salvation in people's lives. I would be distressed if my theological proposal discouraged anyone from enthusiastic involvement in the "great commission" that Christ gave to the church, but I consider that an unlikely result. I believe that we have great motivation to give our lives for the furthering of God's redemptive program in the world and for the magnification of God's name among the nations.

Religious instrumentalism. Religious instrumentalism has found particular favor in the thought of major Roman Catholic theologians. It finds its rationale less in the explicit teaching of Scripture or tradition than in a desire to view other religions in a more positive light than Christians have often done. Thus, these theologians posit that some elements in other religions are actually willed by Christ and that "non-Christian religions have a positive saving potential similar to Judaism in the Old Testament. . . . They can be the means by which God's salvation reaches those who have not yet heard the gospel."[34] In this paradigm, however, rival religious truth claims are judged by the criteria arising from the one true revelation or religion. Thus, Christianity may be seen as the fulfillment of other religions in a manner analogous to its relationship to Judaism. Indeed, the statement by Jesus that he had "come not to abolish but to fulfill" (Mt 5:17) became paradigmatic for religious instrumentalists.[35]

Religious instrumentalists insist that Jesus Christ is the only Savior of the world and that no one has ever been or ever will be saved apart from the redemptive work of Christ; his righteous life and death are the only grounds of salvation. They also assert, however, that God has a universal salvific will and that he is graciously at work in and through all the great religions of the world. I would put Karl Rahner's "anonymous Christian" proposal in this category.[36] In Rahner's perception, non-Christian religions before Christ "in principle were positively willed by God as legitimate ways of salvation," though they were overtaken and rendered obsolete by the coming of Christ and his death and resurrection.[37] Rahner proposes,

---

[34]Shenk, *Who Do You Say*, p. 43.

[35]Kenneth Cracknell's fine study of the perspectives of theologians and missionaries concerning world religions in the period from 1846 to 1914 suggests that F. D. Maurice's use of Matthew 5:17 as a definition of "fulfilment" was "a chief source for the use of 'fulfilment' as the basic category for the relationship of the Eastern religious traditions to Christianity" (*Justice, Courtesy and Love: Theologians and Missionaries Encountering World Religions, 1846-1914* [London: Epworth, 1995], pp. 58-59). Cracknell describes the views of four other theologians (B. F. Westcott, A. M. Fairbairn, A. V. G. Allen and C. C. Hall) and eight missionaries (T. E. Slater, T. Richard, R. A. Hume, J. P. Jones, A. Lloyd, B. Lucas, J. N. Farquhar and C. F. Andrews) whose positions generally fall under my category of "religious instrumentalism." He also demonstrates the extent to which this approach predominated at the 1910 World Missionary Conference in Edinburgh.

[36]See my exposition of Rahner's position in *Irenaeus*, 31:11-28.

[37]Karl Rahner, "Church, Churches and Religions," in *Theological Investigations* (New York: Herder & Herder, 1973), 10:46.

however, that we cannot define the precise moment at which that obsolescence takes place in the experience of any particular people and their religion.[38] It happens only when "Christianity in its explicit and ecclesiastical form becomes an effective reality,"[39] which is to say, when the church asserts "its claims in history in the relevant cultural sphere to which the non-Christian religion concerned belonged."[40] Rahner proposes, therefore, that

> until the moment when the gospel really enters into the historical situation of an individual, a non-Christian religion (even outside the Mosaic religion) does not merely contain elements of a natural knowledge of God, elements, moreover, mixed up with human depravity which is the result of original sin and later aberrations. It contains also supernatural elements arising out of the grace which is given to men as a gratuitous gift on account of Christ. For this reason, a non-Christian religion can be recognized as a *lawful* religion (although only in different degrees) without thereby denying the error and depravity contained in it.[41]

Religious instrumentalism has been stated with particular clarity by Hans Küng. He proposes that there is an "ordinary" way of salvation within the world religions but an "extraordinary" way within the Christian church. The ordinary way is valid only in the interim until a person is confronted with the claims of the Christian religion:

> Since God seriously and effectively wills that *all* men should be saved and that none should be lost unless by his own fault, every man is intended to find his salvation within his own historical condition . . . within the religion imposed upon him by society. . . . But since God seriously and effectively wills the universal salvation history of the whole of humankind, whilst he does not, indeed, legitimize every element (some being erroneous and depraved) in these religions (even the old covenant was not perfect!), yet he *does* sanction the *religions as such*—as social structures. These, though in different senses and degrees, are "legitimate religions." A man is to be saved within the religion that is made available to him in his historical situation. Hence it is his right and duty to seek God within that religion in which the hidden God has already found him. All this until such time as he is confronted in an existential way with the revelation of Jesus Christ. The religions with their forms of belief and cult, their categories and values, their

---

[38]Ibid., p. 48.

[39]Ibid., p. 47.

[40]Ibid.

[41]Karl Rahner, "Christianity and the Non-Christian Religions," in *Theological Investigations* (New York: Herder & Herder, 1966), 5:121.

symbols and ordinances, their religious and ethical experience, thus have a "relative validity," a "relative providential right to existence." They are the *way of salvation* in universal salvation history; the general way of salvation, we can even say, for the people of the world religions: the more common, the *"ordinary"* way of salvation, as against which the way of salvation in the Church appears as something very special and extraordinary.[42]

Recently, S. Mark Heim has put forward a new paradigm that strikes me as fitting well into the category of religious instrumentalism.[43] Whereas relativists have spoken of the many religions as all being ways to the same ultimate end (which Christians call salvation), Heim posits that there is a plurality of religious ends. Salvation is the distinctive end to which Christian believers are led, but the practice of other religions can be effective in bringing the faithful to the particular ends that those religions define as the goal of human life. Heim therefore "affirms the legitimacy of Christian confession of Christ as the one decisive savior of the world."[44] But he also asserts "that other religious traditions truthfully hold out religious ends which their adherents might realize as alternatives to communion with God in Christ. These are not salvation, the end Christians long for. But they are real."[45] This approach thus attributes real value to other religions without completely relativizing them all and "distinguishes between transitional eschatology and final eschatology"[46] through a fascinating appropriation of aspects of Dante's vision of the next world in *The Divine Comedy*.

Relativism. Well-known proponents of a relativist perspective include John Hick, Paul Knitter, Raimundo Panikkar and Stanley Samartha. They seem to be influenced particularly by their sense that exclusivism has serious problems. The heart of what these relativists identify as "exclusivism" (the conviction that Christ is the world's only Savior) is affirmed by all four of the groups we have already considered, but their objections appear to be aimed most strongly at what I have called ecclesiocentrism. Relativists see Christians as a minority in the world and assert that their number,

---

[42]Hans Küng, "The World Religions in God's Plan of Salvation," in *Christian Revelation and World Religions*, ed. Josef Neuner (London: Burns & Oates, 1965), pp. 51-53. A more recent statement of religious instrumentalism has been presented by Dupuis in *Toward a Christian Theology* (see esp. pp. 305-26).

[43]S. Mark Heim, *Salvations: Truth and Difference in Religion* (Maryknoll, N.Y.: Orbis Books, 1995), and *The Depth of the Riches: A Trinitarian Theology of Religious Ends* (Grand Rapids, Mich.: Eerdmans, 2001). Heim calls himself "a convinced inclusivist" (*Depth of the Riches*, p. 8).

[44]Heim, *Depth of the Riches*, p. 7.

[45]Ibid.

[46]Ibid., p. 10.

relative to the other religions, is declining. Hence, if only Christians can be saved, this "casts a massive shadow over any assumption that it is God's will that all mankind shall be converted to Christianity."[47] People's religious commitment is deemed to be almost always a consequence of where they are born, but this is hard to coordinate with the Christian teaching of a loving God who desires all persons to be saved.[48] Christianity has not been very successful in converting people from the major religions; most converts come from animism and polytheism.[49]

The quality of the life of people in other religions in which saints, prophets, martyrs and mystics are encountered demonstrates that they are "intensely aware of the divine presence" and have genuine devotion.[50] In light of this, exclusivism is deemed to have resulted from ignorance of other religions.[51] Using the criterion of "the universally recognized sense of goodness," Hick sees a broad similarity among religions, and he notes that the fruit of the Spirit is no more evident in Christian than in non-Christian lives.[52] He contends that "one cannot establish the unique moral superiority of any one of the great world religions"[53] because "from a religious point of view basically the same thing is going on in all" of the religions.[54] Conceptions of the higher power show great resemblance—a common sense of transcendence that deserves our reverence.[55]

Knitter argues for a "unitive pluralism" because religion should be a tool in building a common world, although it has characteristically brought about division and conflict.[56] The exclusivism that is found in New Testament texts (e.g., Jn 1:14; 14:6; Acts 4:12; 1 Cor 15:21-22; 1 Tim 2:5; Heb 9:12) is to be understood as "more a requirement of the medium" than as the core message of the New Testament. In the historical context of the early church, Christians needed a message with a universal or absolute

---

[47]John Hick, *God Has Many Names* (Philadelphia: Westminster John Knox, 1986), p. 61.

[48]John Hick, *God and the Universe of Faiths: Essays in the Philosophy of Religion* (New York: St. Martin's, 1973), pp. 100, 132.

[49]Paul Knitter, *No Other Name? A Critical Survey of Christian Attitudes Toward the World Religions* (Maryknoll, N.Y.: Orbis, 1985), p. 4.

[50]Hick, *God and the Universe*, p. 130.

[51]Hick, *God Has Many Names*, p. 30.

[52]John Hick, "A Pluralist View," in *More Than One Way? Four Views on Salvation in a Pluralistic World*, ed. Dennis L. Okholm and Timothy R. Phillips (Grand Rapids, Mich.: Zondervan, 1995), p. 41.

[53]Ibid., p. 42.

[54]Ibid., p. 38, and Hick, *God Has Many Names*, pp. 62-63.

[55]Hick, *God Has Many Names*, pp. 40-41.

[56]Knitter, *No Other Name*, p. 31.

quality. They worked in a culture that thought of truth as unitary, unchanging, certain and normative, and so they had to express their message in absolutist fashion in order to have any impact. They had also inherited a philosophy of history from Judaism that led them to expect a new and definitive stage of history, and they were a minority movement that had to ensure their own survival.[57] So we should understand the absolutist language of the early church as confession and testimony, but we should not hear in it a scientific or literal intention.

Hick proposes that if religion is defined

> as an actual human change, a gradual transformation from natural self-centeredness (with all the human evils that flow from this) to a radically new orientation centered in God and manifested in the "fruit of the Spirit," then it seems clear that salvation is taking place within all of the world religions— and taking place, so far as we can tell, to more or less the same extent.[58]

Consequently, Hick posits "a plurality of religious traditions constituting different, but apparently more or less equally salvific, human responses to the Ultimate."[59] In short, according to relativism, anyone can be saved, and they can be saved *through* the religions in which they are born and raised.

SUMMING UP

The answers that Christian theologians give to the questions I have raised can usually be placed within one of five overall approaches. I will call these *ecclesiocentrism* (only those who hear the gospel through the church's witness can be saved), *agnosticism* (we don't know whether the unevangelized can be saved or not), *accessibilism* (God does save some of the unevangelized, but he has not raised up the world's religions as instruments for achieving this), *religious instrumentalism* (the various religions of the world are instruments of God's saving work through Christ among the various peoples of the world) and *relativism* (any of the religions have salvific potential in and of themselves, apart from the specific saving work God does through Christ within the Christian church). Before proceeding to lay out my own accessibilist proposal, let us take a brief look at some others who have had this understanding in earlier times.

---

[57]Millard J. Erickson, *The Word Became Flesh: A Contemporary Incarnational Christology* (Grand Rapids, Mich.: Baker, 1994), p. 300 (presenting Knitter's view).
[58]Hick, "Pluralist View," p. 43.
[59]Ibid., p. 47.

3

Is Accessibilism a New Idea?

Thesis 1: Accessibilism can be traced in Christian thought back to the second century. It is now strongly affirmed in official Roman Catholic documents, but it can also be found among noted Protestant and evangelical theologians. It is the logical position for synergistic theologies but can also be well grounded in monergistic frameworks.

ECCLESIOCENTRISM HAS BEEN SO WIDELY ASSUMED at certain times and in particular segments of the Christian church that accessibilism may sound like a new idea to some readers. So we will take a quick look at a few theologians in previous centuries who have had a more hopeful vision of God's gracious work in the world. This is, obviously, very far from a complete historical review, and the names of others who have conceived of salvation within this general framework will arise as you read the book. But this should suffice to give an indication that accessibilism has had significant representation through the history of Christian thought.

PATRISTIC THEOLOGY

In the second century, Justin Martyr posited that when the philosophers, such as Plato, wrote about "immortality of the soul, or punishments after death, or contemplation of things heavenly," they had "received such suggestions from the prophets." This led Justin to the conclusion that "there seem to be seeds of truth among all men," even though these are not accurately understood.[1] Justin did not assume that knowledge of God and his

---

[1]Justin Martyr, *1 Apology* 44, in *The Apostolic Fathers with Justin Martyr and Irenaeus*, vol. 1 of *The Ante-Nicene Fathers*, ed. Alexander Roberts and James Donaldson (reprint, Grand Rapids, Mich.: Eerdmans, 1989).

truth could have come to people who lived before Christ only through contact with the Jewish people and the special revelation they had received. Nevertheless, Justin was concerned that some of his critics might "cry out against us as though all men who were born before [Christ] were irresponsible."[2] To "anticipate and solve that difficulty," Justin observes that

> [Christ is the] Word of whom every race of men were partakers; and those who lived reasonably are Christians, even though they have been thought atheists; as among the Greeks, Socrates and Heraclitus, and men like them; and among the barbarians, Abraham, and Ananias, and Azarias, and Misael, and Elias, and many others whose actions and name we now decline to recount, because we know it would be tedious.[3]

These people were, therefore, "Christians" before the time of Christ. Consequently, none of Justin's readers should be surprised that the Word of God incarnate as Jesus was crucified, since "even they who lived before Christ, and lived without reason, were wicked and hostile to Christ, and slew those who lived reasonably."[4]

Clement of Alexandria believed that some elementary knowledge of God was attainable through human reason (logos) in a natural way. "For there was always a natural manifestation of the one Almighty God, among all right-thinking men."[5] But there was also an operation of the divine Logos in the thinking of the philosophers that constituted a divine economy which paralleled, to some extent, the Jewish economy of the law. God intended both of these to lead people to Christ. Thus Clement proposed that God had given the law to the Jews and philosophy to the Greeks and, by this means, he "shut up unbelief to the Advent" so that "everyone who believes not is without excuse. For by a different process of advancement, both Greek and Barbarian, He leads to the perfection which is by faith."[6] Similarly, Clement said,

> To the Jews belonged the Law and to the Greeks Philosophy, until the Advent; and after that came the universal calling to be a particular people of righteousness, through the teaching which flows from faith, brought to-

---

[2] *1 Apology* 46.
[3] Ibid.
[4] Ibid.
[5] Clement of Alexandria *Stromata* 5.13, in *Fathers of the Second Century*, vol. 2 of *The Ante-Nicene Fathers*, ed. Alexander Roberts and James Donaldson (Grand Rapids, Mich.: Eerdmans, 1962).
[6] Clement of Alexandria *Stromata* 7.2.

gether by one Lord, the only God of both Greeks and barbarians, or rather of the whole race of men.[7]

Both the Law and Prophets, which were "given to the barbarians," and philosophy, which was given to the Greeks, were intended "to fit their ears for the Gospel."[8] Thus, philosophy had a preliminary and pedagogical function among the Greeks, yet "those among the Greeks who have philosophized accurately, see God."[9]

One of the difficulties we face in trying to determine what early Christian theologians thought about the possibility of salvation for the unevangelized is that they generally assumed the gospel had been taken throughout the world by the apostles. Thus, no one was effectively out of contact with the church and its preaching. We find this assumption in Irenaeus, late in the second century. Regarding the Gnostics, who had separated themselves from the true church and deprived themselves of the life of grace, Irenaeus also insisted that guilty separation from the church excludes one from salvation, for "Where the Church is, there is the Spirit of God, and where the Spirit of God is, there is the Church."[10] Irenaeus could say this because he believed that the world had been evangelized.[11] Nevertheless, in my work on Irenaeus, I have set out my reasons for believing that Irenaeus would have been optimistic about the salvation of the unevangelized if he had known of their existence.[12] I will simply sum up those reasons here:

(1) God wills the salvation of humankind, who are condemned only in consequence of their voluntary unbelief and disobedience.

(2) The revelation by the Word in creation and providence is life-giving and necessitates a response of faith on the part of humans, which is made possible by an illumination by the Word.

(3) The Word's immanence in creation, symbolized by a cosmic cross, has a cohesive and reconciliatory effect on all of creation, which is not only physical, but also moral and supernatural.

---

[7]Ibid., 6.17.

[8]Ibid., 6.6.

[9]Ibid., 1.19.

[10]Irenaeus *Against Heresies* 3.24. (Quotations are translated from the volumes in *Sources Chrétiennes* [Paris: Editions de Cerf, 1965-82].)

[11]Terrance Tiessen, *Irenaeus on the Salvation of the Unevangelized*, ATLA Monograph (Metuchen, N.J.: Scarecrow, 1993), 31:64-81.

[12]Ibid. These points sum up the detailed analysis found in chaps. 4-8.

(4) In Christ's incarnation, obedient life, death and resurrection, a recapitulation of the history of fallen humanity was made, which objectively accomplished the salvation of humankind.

(5) Within the economy of salvation, the same reward (knowledge of the Son of God, or immortality) is eventually given to all whom God calls, regardless of the particular stage of the economy in which they lived and in which they are called.

(6) God's just judgment of sinful people assumes their voluntary rejection of divine saving revelation to *all* people.

(7) Those who believe and follow God are given a greater illumination of the mind.

(8) People will be judged according to the privilege of revelation that they have received.

(9) During the millennium, those who have not known the incarnate Word but who have had some form of "anticipation" of him will become accustomed to living with him and will be prepared for the vision of the Father.

It is easy to see in Irenaeus's theology the sort of synergism that characterizes evangelical Arminianism today. He places a strong emphasis on the first and the sixth items above, and he clearly has a libertarian understanding of human freedom. That synergism naturally inclines Arminians toward hopefulness concerning the salvation of the unevangelized, as I will observe later in this chapter. For this reason and the others I have mentioned, I concluded that Irenaeus was headed in the direction of accessibilism.

Early assertions that there was no salvation possible outside the church must be put in the context of concern about Christians who had once been a part of the household of faith but who had left that ark of salvation in order to join a heretical or schismatic sect:

> Many of the early church leaders who could affirm with certainty God's saving activities among all peoples from the beginning of time, when confronted by threats to the unity of the church could just as unequivocally warn those separated from the body of Christ, either by their own actions or those taken by church authorities, that they had absolutely no hope of salvation.[13]

After Christianity became the official religion, the phrase was applied to

---

[13]Don A. Pittman, Ruben L. F. Habito and Terry C. Muck, eds., *Ministry and Theology in Global Perspective: Contemporary Challenges for the Church* (Grand Rapids, Mich.: Eerdmans, 1996), p. 46.

Jews and pagans who failed to become Christians but, once again, it was assumed that the gospel had been proclaimed everywhere and all had the opportunity to accept it.[14]

Some of the early fathers made statements suggesting that everyone will eventually be saved, and some theologians at later points in history have held forms of "universalism."[15] This might be deemed a highly optimistic form of accessibilism, but I consider the two positions to be radically different. The accessibilism put forward in this book, and anticipated in others whom I cite in this chapter, acknowledges that some people will be eternally lost, but it denies that this will ever be because of their ignorance of the gospel. We should note that there is an incoherence in the position of most universalists, who have generally also been synergists. If one affirms libertarian freedom, it is impossible to insist that everyone will libertarianly freely respond to God's overtures with repentance and faith.

POSTCOLONIAL AND CONTEMPORARY ROMAN CATHOLIC THEOLOGY

However unacceptable the Roman Catholic concept of an infallible magisterium may be to Protestants, we must admit that it has served to protect classical orthodoxy to an extent not true in Protestant contexts. Yet, it is widely granted in official statements of the Roman Catholic Church today that the unevangelized can be saved, although there is still significant controversy among Catholic theologians about the role that non-Christian religions may play in that salvation.[16] This may seem surprising, given the strongly ecclesiocentric statements made at the Council of Florence (1442). But Roman Catholic theologians now argue that Florence was addressing the situation of heretics and schismatics, not speaking about the unevangelized.[17] Cardinal Juan De Lugo (1583-1660) later posited that

---

[14]Ibid., p. 47.

[15]See the helpful discussions by Trevor Hart, "Universalism: Two Distinct Types," and Frederick W. Norris, "Universal Salvation in Origen and Maximus," in *Universalism and the Doctrine of Hell: Papers Presented at the Fourth Edinburgh Conference in Christian Dogmatics, 1991,* ed. Nigel M. de S. Cameron (Grand Rapids, Mich.: Baker, 1993). For a very interesting but ultimately unconvincing biblical case for universal salvation, from a Reformed theological perspective, see Jan Bonda, *The One Purpose of God: An Answer to the Doctrine of Eternal Punishment* (Grand Rapids, Mich.: Eerdmans, 1998).

[16]Gavin D'Costa, *The Meeting of Religions and the Trinity,* Faith Meets Faith (Maryknoll, N.Y.: Orbis, 2000), p. 99.

[17]Francis Sullivan, *Salvation Outside the Church? Tracing the History of the Catholic Response* (New York: Paulist, 1992), p. 66.

people who had never had a chance to hear the message of the gospel . . . would receive the grace with which they could observe the natural law; and if they keep this, they would be enlightened so that they could arrive at faith in God, and with this they could have the implicit desire for Christian faith, baptism and membership in the church that would suffice for their salvation.[18]

Pope Pius IX's *Singulari Quadem,* in 1854, was reportedly the first document to speak of some who are invincibly ignorant of the true religion revealed in the Roman Catholic Church. In this allocution, these people are not deemed guilty by God:

It must, of course, be held as of faith that no one can be saved outside the Apostolic Roman Church, that the Church is the only ark of salvation, and that whoever does not enter it will perish in the flood. Yet, on the other hand, it must likewise be held as certain that those who are in ignorance of the true religion, if this ignorance is invincible, are not subject to any guilt in this matter before the eyes of the Lord. Now, who could presume for oneself the ability to set the boundaries of such ignorance, taking into consideration the natural differences of peoples, lands, talents and so many other factors? Only when we have been released from the bonds of this body and "shall see God as he is" [1 Jn 3:2] shall we understand how closely and wonderfully the divine mercy and justice are linked.[19]

The same doctrine of "invincible ignorance" was reiterated by Pius IX in *Quanto Conficiamur Moerore* (1863), but it was applied not only to non-Catholic Christians, but also to people of other religions, as follows:

There are, of course, those who are struggling with invincible ignorance about our most holy religion. Sincerely observing the natural law and its precepts inscribed by God on all hearts and ready to obey God, they live honest lives and are able to attain eternal life by the efficacious virtue of divine light and grace. Because God knows, searches and clearly understands the minds, hearts, thoughts, and natures of all, his supreme kindness and clemency do not permit anyone at all who is not guilty of deliberate sin to suffer eternal punishments.[20]

A particularly significant incident in the development of the Roman Catholic Church's official aversion to ecclesiocentrism occurred in a letter from Pope Pius XII to the Bishop of Boston in 1949. He condemned Father

---

[18]Ibid., p. 31.

[19]Jacques Dupuis, *Toward a Christian Theology of Religious Pluralism* (Maryknoll, N.Y.: Orbis, 1997), p. 124, quoting Denzinger 1647.

[20]The encyclical can be found at <www.papalencyclicals.net/Pius09/p9quanto.htm>.

Leonard Feeney for applying the axiom "there is no salvation outside the church" too rigorously. Pius then reiterated the concept of implicit faith or of the baptism by desire:

> No one who knows that the Church has been divinely established by Christ and, nevertheless, refuses to be a subject of the Church or refuses to obey the Roman Pontiff, the vicar of Christ on earth, will be saved. . . . As regards the helps to salvation which are ordered to the last end only by divine decree, not by intrinsic necessity, God, in his infinite mercy, willed that their effects which are necessary to salvation can, in some circumstances, be obtained when the helps are used only in desire and longing. We see this clearly stated in the Council of Trent about the sacrament of regeneration and about the sacrament of penance.[21]

Thus, "when one is invincibly ignorant," God also accepts an implicit desire, a desire that is "informed with perfect charity" and that is effective because the "person has supernatural faith."[22]

Roman Catholic theologians disagree about the church's position on the instrumentality of the religions in salvation. Vatican II affirmed that elements of "truth and grace can be found among the nations, as a sort of presence of God," but it made this statement in the context of a strong call to missionary activity.[23] For the purpose of this mission in the world, church members are called to be active participants in the communities where they live, to be "familiar with their national and religious traditions, gladly and reverently laying bare the seeds of the Word which lie hidden in them."[24] It is "by the seeds of the Word and by the preaching of the gospel" that the Holy Spirit "stirs up in [people's] hearts the obedience of faith."[25] The Catholic Church "rejects nothing of what is holy and true in these [non-Christian] religions," which "often reflect a ray of that truth which enlightens all men."[26] But, whether the Catholic Church teaches that the religions have a *salvific* function is still a matter of controversy.[27]

---

[21]Dupuis, *Toward a Christian Theology*, p. 128, quoting Denzinger 3870.

[22]Dupuis, *Toward a Christian Theology*, p. 129.

[23]*Ad Gentes* ("Decree on the Missionary Activity of the Church") 9, in *The Documents of Vatican II*, ed. Walter M. Abbott, S.J. (New York: Guild, 1966).

[24]Ibid., 11.

[25]Ibid., 15.

[26]*Nostra Aetate* 2, in *The Documents of Vatican II*, ed. Walter M. Abbott, S.J. (New York: Guild, 1966).

[27]See discussion by Dupuis, *Toward a Christian Theology*, pp. 165-69.

Vatican II was clear, however, that salvation is accessible to everyone, so that ecclesiocentrism is excluded:

> Those also can attain to everlasting salvation who through no fault of their own do not know the gospel of Christ or His Church, yet sincerely seek God and, moved by grace, strive by their deeds to do His will as it is known to them through the dictates of their conscience. Nor does divine Providence deny the help necessary for salvation to those who, without blame on their part, have not yet arrived at an explicit knowledge of God, but who strive to live a good life, thanks to His grace.

Once again, this is not seen as diminishing at all the church's painstaking missionary work.[28]

The Congregation for the Doctrine of the Faith issued a declaration "on the unicity and salvific universality of Jesus Christ and the Church" on August 6, 2000, referred to as *Dominus Iesus*.[29] It offers strong reasons for "supporting the evangelizing mission of the Church, above all in connection with the religious traditions of the world."[30] Against relativistic pluralism, it also reaffirms that all people "who are saved share, though differently, in the same mystery of salvation in Jesus Christ through his Spirit,"[31] but that full revelation of divine truth is given only in Jesus Christ,[32] and "the universal salvific will of the One and Triune God is offered and accomplished once for all in the mystery of the incarnation, death, and resurrection of the Son of God."[33] Consequently, it identifies interreligious dialogue as "part of the Church's evangelizing mission."[34] Nevertheless, "the salvific action of Jesus Christ, with and through his Spirit, extends beyond the visible boundaries of the Church to all humanity," and "the Holy Spirit offers to all the possibility of being made partners, in a way known to God, in the paschal mystery."[35]

Dominus Iesus admits that there are elements in the sacred writings of other religions "which may be *de facto* instruments by which countless people throughout the centuries have been and still are able today to nour-

---

[28]*Lumen Gentium* 16.
[29]*Dominus Iesus* can be found at <www.vatican.va/roman_curia/congregations/cfaith/documents/rc_con_cfaith_doc_20000806_dominus-iesus_en.html>
[30]*Dominus Iesus* 2.
[31]Ibid.
[32]Ibid., 5.
[33]Ibid., 13.
[34]Ibid., 2.
[35]Ibid., 12.

ish and maintain their life-relationship with God," but it "reserves the designation of *inspired texts* to the canonical books of the Old and New Testaments."[36] God "desires to call all peoples to himself in Christ," and he
makes himself present "to entire peoples through their spiritual riches, of
which their religions are the main and essential expression even when
they contain 'gaps, insufficiencies and errors.'"[37] The church is the "universal sacrament of salvation" but,

> for those who are not formally and visibly members of the Church, "salva
> tion in Christ is accessible by virtue of a grace which, while having a myste
> rious relationship to the Church, does not make them formally part of the
> Church, but enlightens them in a way which is accommodated to their spir
> itual and material situation. This grace comes from Christ; it is the result of
> his sacrifice and is communicated by the Holy Spirit."[38]

Only God knows how this grace, which has a mysterious relationship to the
church, comes to individual non-Christians.[39] It is at least clear that the
church is not simply one way of salvation "alongside those constituted by
other religions."[40] Knowing that God saves people who have no knowledge
of Christ through the church's proclamation does not diminish the importance of evangelism but, rather, increases the duty and urgency of the proclamation of salvation and of conversion to the Lord Jesus Christ.[41]

It is clear, then, that the options for contemporary Roman Catholics now
begin with accessibilism as the most conservative option. Some theologians are attracted to a religious instrumentalism, but relativism is clearly
condemned by the magisterium.

EARLY PROTESTANT THEOLOGIANS

Martin Luther rarely spoke of the unevangelized, but John Sanders cites a
couple of instances in which Luther speaks of them with a measure of
hopefulness. In his commentary on Romans (1515), Luther wrote,

> Original sin God could forgive [the unevangelized] (even though they may
> not have recognized it and confessed it) on account of some act of humility
> towards God as the highest being that they know. Nor were they bound to

[36]Ibid., 8.
[37]Ibid.
[38]Ibid., 20.
[39]Ibid., 21, making reference to *Ad Gentes* 7.
[40]*Dominus Iesus* 21.
[41]Ibid., 22.

the Gospel and to Christ as specifically recognized, as the Jews were not either. Or one can say that all people of this type have been given so much light and grace by an act of prevenient mercy of God as is sufficient for their salvation in their situation, as in the case of Job, Naaman, Jethro and others.[42]

In a letter written about 1522, Luther addresses the issue of the salvation of a person who dies without faith, and he stops short of ecclesiocentrism. He insists that no one can be saved apart from faith, but he says that "it would be quite a different question whether God can impart faith to some in the hour of death or after death so that these people could be saved through faith. Who would doubt God's ability to do that? No one, however, can prove that he does do this."[43] Luther may not have been a convinced accessibilist, but he appears to have been at least agnostic concerning the salvation of the unevangelized.

John Calvin was definitely an ecclesiocentrist, and his influence within the Reformed theological tradition is obvious. Ulrich Zwingli, on the other hand, was an early representative of accessibilism within the Reformed tradition. In his *Exposition of the Faith,* Zwingli addressed King Francis, assuring him that when the faithful die, they "fly away to God" where they "may expect to see the communion and fellowship of all the saints and sages and believers and the steadfast and the brave and the good who have ever lived since the world began." Zwingli told the king,

> You will see the two Adams, the redeemed and the Redeemer, Abel, Enoch, Noah, Abraham, Isaac, Jacob, Judah, Moses, Joshua, Gideon, Samuel, Phinehas, Elijah, Elisha, Isaiah and the Virgin Mother of God of whom he prophesied, David, Hezekiah, Josiah, the Baptist, Peter, Paul; Hercules too and Theseus, Socrates, Aristides, Antigonus, Numa, Camillus, the Catos and Scipios; Louis the Pious and your predecessors the Louis, Philips, Pepins and all your ancestors who have departed this life in faith. In short, there has not been a single good man, there has not been a single pious heart or believing soul from the beginning of the world to the end, which you will not see there in the presence of God. Can we conceive of any spectacle more joyful or agreeable or indeed sublime?[44]

---

[42]*Luther's Works,* ed. Jaroslav Pelikan (St. Louis: Concordia, 1972), 25:181, quoted in John Sanders, *No Other Name: An Investigation into the Destiny of the Unevangelized* (Grand Rapids, Mich.: Eerdmans, 1992), p. 141.

[43]*Luther's Works,* ed. Helmut Lehmann (Philadelphia: Fortress, 1968), 45:51-55, quoted in Sanders, *No Other Name,* p. 141.

[44]Ulrich Zwingli, "An Exposition of the Faith," in *Zwingli and Bullinger,* ed. Geoffrey Bromiley (Philadelphia: Westminster Press, 1953), pp. 275-76.

For Zwingli, salvation is the result of divine election, which is an election to good works, so that election and reprobation are seen in outward signs; faith and good works assure both the individuals themselves and others of their election. An evil life gives evidence of reprobation, but people who live such lives may be predestined to salvation and not yet manifest as elect.[45] It is important to note that people are not saved on account of their faith and works; salvation is without regard to ethical or religious qualities in people, but God, in divine freedom, may elect children or even heathen. On the other hand, the death of infants is not a sign of their election. Luther and his friends contended that this nullified the work of Christ, but Zwingli denied it. Christ is the only way to the Father, and people are elected in Christ, but this does not mean that all elect people have to hear of Christ in their lifetime. The elect who hear of Christ respond in faith, and the elect who do not hear of Christ respond with a virtuous life, because the law is written on their hearts.

In support of his accessibilism, Zwingli did not appeal to universal revelation in nature, nor to the meritorious deeds of the unevangelized, but to the gratuitous election by God, from which faith follows even though "some of those elected outside the visible sphere of Christendom might never come to faith in this life."[46] This perspective on the unevangelized angered Luther, who saw it as presumption on the grace of God and a capitulation to rationalistic humanism such as he had opposed in Erasmus.[47] It was also different from Calvin's perspective, since he considered lack of opportunity to hear the gospel to be one of the likely marks of reprobation.[48]

REFORMED CONFESSIONS

The Second Helvetic Confession (1566) asserted that there is no salvation outside the church, but its concern was schismatics who "separate themselves from the true Church of Christ."[49] The Confession goes on to acknowledge that "God had some friends in the world that were not of the

---

[45]Justo L. González, *From the Protestant Reformation to the Twentieth Century,* vol. 3 of *A History of Christian Thought* (New York: Abingdon, 1975), p. 69, quoting G. W. Locher, "Die Praëdestinations-lehre Huldrych Zwinglis," *Theologische Zeitschrift* 12 (1956): 526-48.

[46]Timothy George, *Theology of the Reformers* (Nashville: Broadman, 1988), p. 125.

[47]Ibid., pp. 124-25.

[48]John Calvin *Institutes of the Christian Religion* 3.24.12, ed. J. T. McNeill, trans. F. L. Battles, Library of Christian Classics, vols. 20-21 (Philadelphia: Westminster Press, 1961).

[49]Second Helvetic Confession, chapter 17, in *Creeds of the Churches: A Reader in Christian Doctrine from the Bible to the Present,* rev. ed., ed. John H. Leith (Richmond: John Knox Press, 1973), p. 147.

commonwealth of Israel."[50] In the first chapter, the confession affirms the necessity of illumination by the Spirit for the Word of God to be fruitful in people's lives. An important observation is then made that God's "usual way of instructing men" is by the preaching of the Word but that "God can illuminate whom and when he will, even without the external ministry, which is a thing appertaining to his power."[51]

The Westminster Confession (1647) asserts that "elect infants, dying in infancy, are regenerated and saved by Christ through the Spirit, who worketh when, and where, and how he pleaseth."[52] Here is one of our groups of the unevangelized for whom salvation is obviously possible. But the confession adds, "So also are all other elect persons, who are incapable of being outwardly called by the ministry of the word."[53] W. G. T. Shedd points out that "this is commonly understood to refer not merely, or mainly, to idiots and insane persons, but to such of the pagan world as God pleases to regenerate without the use of the written revelation."[54]

With an explicitly accessibilist tone, the Church of Scotland's Declaratory Act (1879) stated that "while none are saved except through the mediation of Christ . . . it is not required to be held that . . . God may not extend his grace to any who are without the pale of ordinary means, as it may seem good in his sight."[55]

PURITANS, REFORMED THEOLOGIANS AND EVANGELICALS

Puritan preacher Richard Baxter (1615-1691) had "argued that if all nations of the world have some kind of religion, then all may hope to obtain mercy for their sins. 'Those that know not Christ nor his redemption, are yet his Redeemed.'"[56] Baxter did not deny that Christ's atoning work is necessary for anyone to be saved, but he posited that "the efficacy of Christ's work

---

[50]Second Helvetic Confession, chapter 17.
[51]Ibid., chapter 1.
[52]Westminster Confession 10.3, in *Evangelical Protestant Creeds*, vol. 3 of *The Creeds of Christendom*, 6th ed., ed. Philip Schaff (reprint, Grand Rapids, Mich.: Baker, 1993).
[53]Ibid.
[54]William G. T. Shedd, *Dogmatic Theology* (1888; reprint, Grand Rapids, Mich.: Zondervan, 1969), 2:707-8. Such a reading might appear to be excluded by Westminster Confession 10.4, which denies that "people not professing the Christian religion" can "be saved in any other way whatsoever, be they never so diligent to frame their lives according to the light of nature and the law of that religion they do profess." Accessibilists probably take the confession to be excluding salvation by works in this phrase.
[55]Church of Scotland's Declaratory Act 4, quoted in Sanders, *No Other Name*, pp. 143-44.
[56]Cited by B. A. Gerrish, "What Do We Mean by Faith in Jesus Christ?" *Christian Century* 116 (October 6, 1999): 932.

extends to some, at least, who have never heard of him."[57]

Gerald McDermott, who has paid close attention to the thought of Jonathan Edwards regarding these issues, "acknowledges that Edwards never consciously embraced inclusivism, 'at least in his published writings or private notebooks,'" but he concludes that Edwards's thought contained elements that might eventually have led him to it. Indeed, he finds in Edwards's own theology "the groundwork for such an interpretation,"[58] the "theological foundations upon which a more hopeful soteriology could quite naturally have been erected," although Edwards himself never chose to do it.[59] In *Miscellanies* (1338), Edwards states that the heathen world "are not so entirely and absolutely cast off, but that there is a possibility of their being reconciled; and God has so ordered the case, that there is an equal possibility of their receiving the benefit of divine revelation."[60]

Seventeenth-century deists like Lord Herbert of Cherbury depicted the God of Reformed theology as a monster on grounds of ecclesiocentrism. Since "geographers of the day estimated that only one-sixth of the planet had heard the gospel," Calvinistic ecclesiocentrists were left with the conclusion that "at least five-sixths of the world's population was doomed to hell."[61] In defense of Reformed orthodoxy, Edwards used the idea of *prisca theologia* (ancient theology) to argue that there were vestiges of true religion in non-Christian tradition, so that not all of those people without Christian preaching had been deprived of the truths of the gospel. Edwards "developed an elaborate typological system to show that God is constantly communicating Reformed truths wherever the eye can see and the ear can hear—in nature, history, and even the history of religions."[62] Of particular importance, I think, is Edwards's contention that regeneration can take place before explicit conversion to Christ and that it is evident in the "disposition" of a person. Specifically, it would be manifest in "a sense of the dangerousness of sin, and of the dreadfulness of God's anger . . . [such a conviction of] their wickedness, that they trusted to nothing but the mere mercy of God, and then bitterly lamented and mourned for their

---

[57]Ibid., p. 932.

[58]Gerald R. McDermott, *Jonathan Edwards Confronts the Gods: Christian Theology, Enlightenment Religion and Non-Christian Faiths* (New York: Oxford University Press, 2000), p. 137.

[59]Gerald R. McDermott, "Response to Gilbert: 'The Nations Will Worship: Jonathan Edwards and the Salvation of the Heathen,' " *Trinity Journal* 23 (spring 2002): 79.

[60]Edwards, *Miscellanies* (1338), quoted in McDermott, "Response," p. 80.

[61]Gerald R. McDermott, "Holy Pagans," *Christian History* 22 (winter 2003): 38. See also McDermott, *Jonathan Edwards*, chapter 11, "American Indians."

[62]McDermott, "Holy Pagans," p. 38.

sins."[63] McDermott has concluded from Edwards's private correspondence and notebooks that "in his last decade, while in exile, the great theologian might have concluded that he had found [among the Stockbridge Indians] holy pagans who, like Cornelius, were sincerely seeking the gospel."[64]

Shedd contended, in 1888, that "the electing mercy of God reaches to the heathen":

> It is not the doctrine of the Church, that the entire mass of pagans, without exception, have gone down to endless impenitence and death. That some unevangelized men are saved, in the present life, by an extraordinary exercise of redeeming grace in Christ, has been the hope and belief of Christendom. It was the hope and belief of the elder Calvinists, as it is of the later.[65]

Shedd cites a lengthy section from Herman Witsius (1636-1708) to illustrate "the hopeful view which the elder Calvinism took of the possible extent to which God's decree of election reaches."[66] Such a perspective on the Reformed tradition would probably be quite surprising to many Calvinistic evangelicals today, who speak as though ecclesiocentrism has always represented the tradition within which they stand.

Shedd also cites Jerome Zanchius (1516-1590) who had commented on the many nations that never had the privilege of hearing the word: "It is not indeed improbable that some individuals in these unenlightened countries may belong to the secret election of grace, and the habit of faith may be wrought in them."[67] Examples of people who had this "habit of faith" are Cornelius and the Ethiopian eunuch. "These men, under the teaching of the Spirit, were conscious of sin, and were anxiously inquiring if, and how, it could be forgiven."[68] Shedd posits that

> the true reason for hoping that an unevangelized heathen is saved is not that he was virtuous, but that he was *penitent*. A penitent man is necessarily virtuous; but a virtuous man is not necessarily penitent. Sorrow for sin produces morality; but morality does not produce sorrow for sin.[69]

John Wesley accepted the possibility of salvation apart from the gospel because of his conviction regarding universal prevenient grace:

---

[63]Cited in ibid.
[64]Ibid., 39.
[65]Shedd, *Dogmatic Theology*, 2: 706.
[66]Ibid.
[67]Jerome Zanchius, *Treatise on Predestination*, chapter 4, quoted in Shedd, *Dogmatic Theology*, 2: 708.
[68]Ibid.
[69]Ibid., 2: 710.

> The benefit of the death of Christ is . . . extended . . . even unto those who are inevitably excluded from this knowledge. Even these may be partakers of the benefit of His death, though ignorant of the history, if they suffer His grace to take place in their hearts, so as of wicked men to become holy.[70]

In support of this point, "Wesley appealed to the account of Cornelius in Acts 10, whose prayers he judged to be a response to the secret working of prevenient grace."[71] He suggested that those who were saved but were outside the Christian community are *servants*, but not *sons*; "if they continue in their faith, they will become sons."[72] In that Wesleyan tradition, Richard Watson (d. 1833), the first Methodist systematic theologian, similarly argued that "by virtue of universal prevenient grace the heathen are supplied with the means of salvation. He [John Wesley] believed that virtuous heathen in all ages have been saved apart from written revelation or explicit hearing of the Gospel (Rom 2:7, 10)."[73]

Baptist Calvinist theologian Augustus H. Strong claimed that

> the patriarchs, though they had no knowledge of a personal Christ, were saved by believing in God so far as God had revealed himself to them; and whoever among the heathen are saved, must in like manner be saved by casting themselves as helpless sinners upon God's plan of mercy, dimly shadowed forth in nature and providence.[74]

Similarly, Presbyterian A. T. Pierson, who has been described as "the foremost spokesperson for foreign missions in the late nineteenth century,"[75] wrote: "If there be anywhere a soul feeling after God, following the light of nature and conscience, in hope and faith that the Great Unknown will somehow give more light, and lead to life and blessedness, we may safely leave such to His fatherly care."[76]

---

[70]John Wesley, *Letters,* 2:118 (cf. 6:214; 7:168), quoted in Bruce Demarest, *The Cross and Salvation: The Doctrine of Salvation,* Foundations of Evangelical Theology (Wheaton, Ill.: Crossway, 1997), p. 58.

[71]Demarest, *Cross and Salvation,* p. 58.

[72]Calvin E. Shenk, *Who Do You Say that I Am? Christians Encounter Other Religions* (Scottdale, Penn.: Herald, 1997), p. 230.

[73]Richard Watson, *Theological Institutes* (New York: Lane & Scott, 1851), 2:447, quoted in Demarest, *Cross and Salvation,* pp. 58-59.

[74]Augustus H. Strong, *Systematic Theology* (Westwood, N.J.: Revell, 1907), p. 842.

[75]Harold Netland, *Encountering Religious Pluralism: The Challenge to Faith and Mission* (Downers Grove, Ill.: InterVarsity Press, 2001), p. 50.

[76]A. T. Pierson, *The Crisis of Mission: Or, the Voice out of the Cloud* (New York: Carter & Brothers, 1886), p. 297, quoted in Netland, *Encountering,* 51.

A veteran missionary in India, Lesslie Newbigin denied that the church is "the exclusive possessor of salvation"[77] and stated that his position included aspects of all three of the traditional categories:

> The position which I have outlined is exclusivist in the sense that it affirms the unique truth of the revelation in Jesus Christ, but it is not exclusivist in the sense of denying the possibility of the salvation of the non-Christian. It is inclusivist in the sense that it refuses to limit the saving grace of God to the members of the Christian Church, but it rejects the inclusivism which regards the non-Christian religions as vehicles of salvation. It is pluralist in the sense of acknowledging the gracious work of God in the lives of all human beings, but it rejects a pluralism which denies the uniqueness and decisiveness of what God has done in Jesus Christ.[78]

Newbigin reminds us about the surprise of people in the end (Mt 22:1-14), but believes that "God will shock the righteous by his limitless generosity and by his tremendous severity" and he warns us "to judge nothing before the time (1 Cor 4:1-5)."[79]

Another evangelical missionary and theologian, J. N. D. Anderson, put it thus:

> Where the "God of all grace" has been at work by his Spirit in the hearts of individuals from other religious backgrounds, revealing to them something of their sin and need and enabling them (as he alone can) to throw themselves on his mercy, they too may profit from this "specific remedy" for man's spiritual sickness and this "unique historic deed" which still stands as "the turning point of history," but about which they have never had the opportunity to hear.[80]

Anderson strongly affirms the uniqueness of Jesus Christ as the means of salvation, but then he insists that

> these categorical statements about the one and only "specific remedy" for "the human sickness" and the "unique historic deed, which we confess as the true turning point of universal history, "do not of themselves *exclude* any-

[77]Lesslie Newbigin, *The Open Secret: An Introduction to the Theology of Mission*, rev. ed. (Grand Rapids, Mich.: Eerdmans, 1995), p. 203.
[78]Lesslie Newbigin, *The Gospel in a Pluralist Society* (Grand Rapids, Mich.: Eerdmans, 1989), pp. 182-83.
[79]Lesslie Newbigin, *The Open Secret: Sketches for a Missionary Theology* (Grand Rapids, Mich.: Eerdmans, 1978), p. 196, quoted in J. N. D. Anderson, *Christianity and World Religions: The Challenge of Religious Pluralism* (Downers Grove, Ill.: InterVarsity Press, 1984), p. 148.
[80]Anderson, *Christianity and World Religions*, p. 32.

one, except those who with open eyes persist in rejecting them.[81]

The saints of the Old Testament were saved by the death of Christ, despite the fact that they did not know about it,[82] and "so too are those today, from whatever religion, who have never heard the gospel."[83] The Spirit can still speak directly to people in their need, "through dreams, visions, conscience, or an inner voice." And what of those in other religions whom the Spirit convicts of their sin "and enables them to throw themselves on the mercy of the God whom they seek in the twilight, will they not also be saved in Christ—on the basis, that is, of what God himself did in Christ on the cross for the sins of the whole world?"[84]

More recently, but working within a Reformed and somewhat neo-orthodox framework, Neal Punt posits that "all persons are elect in Christ (that is 'will be saved,' 'justified,' 'on the way to heaven,' 'under grace,' 'children of God') except those who the Bible expressly declares will be finally lost."[85] And, Donald Bloesch writes,

> The missionary proclamation must go out to the whole world, but we dare not presume on where or how the Spirit of God may work, nor should we deny that the hidden Christ may be at work in the most unexpected places in preparing people for the new dispensation of grace.[86]

From a contemporary evangelical Anglican perspective, Alister McGrath states,

> We are assured that those who respond in faith to the explicit preaching of the gospel will be saved. We cannot draw the conclusion from this, however, that *only* those who thus respond will be saved. God's revelation is not limited to the explicit human preaching of the good news, but extends beyond it. We must be prepared to be surprised at those whom we will meet in the

---

[81]Ibid., p. 31. Anderson takes the quote "unique historic deed . . . " from Newbigin, *Open Secret*, p. 56.

[82]Anderson, *Christianity and World Religions*, pp. 31-32.

[83]Norman Anderson, "Christianity and the World's Religions," in *Introductory Articles*, vol. 1 of *The Expositor's Bible Commentary*, ed. Frank E. Gaebelein and J. D. Douglas (Grand Rapids, Mich.: Zondervan, 1979), p. 155. It is particularly significant that Anderson was invited to write the article on this very important subject, given the intention of the editors to produce a series from the stance of "a scholarly evangelicalism committed to the divine inspiration, complete trustworthiness, and full authority of the Bible" (p. vii).

[84]Ibid., p. 155.

[85]Neal Punt, *What's Good About the Good News? The Plan of Salvation in a New Light* (Chicago: Northland, 1988), p. 2.

[86]Donald G. Bloesch, *The Church: Sacraments, Worship, Ministry and Mission*, Christian Foundations (Downers Grove, Ill.: InterVarsity Press, 2002), p. 41.

kingdom of God. In his preaching of the good news of the kingdom, Jesus lists some who will be among its beneficiaries—the Ninevites, the queen of Sheba, and those who lived in the cities of Tyre, Sidon, Sodom, and Gomorrah (Matt. 10:15; 11:11; 12:41-42).[87]

McGrath goes on to state that if we affirm ecclesiocentrism, we

> write off the vast majority of those who have ever lived, who are deprived of salvation by matters of geographical and historical contingency. But this is a flawed theology, which limits God's modes of action, disclosure, and saving power. . . . A human failure to evangelize cannot be transposed into God's failure to save. In the end, salvation is not a culturally conditioned or restricted human accomplishment; it is God's boundless sovereign gift to his people. . . . Where the word is not or cannot be preached by human agents, God is not inhibited from bringing people to faith in him, even if that act of hope and trust may lack the fully orbed character of an informed faith. . . . Perhaps we need to be more sensitive to the ways in which God is at work and realize that, important though our preaching may be, in the end God does not depend on it. . . . God's saving work must never be exclusively restricted to human preaching, as if the Holy Spirit was silent or inactive in God's world, or as if the actualization of God's saving purposes depended totally on human agencies.[88]

Synergists such as John Sanders, Clark Pinnock and Amos Yong have written from an accessibilist perspective,[89] but we also find hopefulness in the moderately Calvinist work of Baptist theologian Millard Erickson. He analyzes texts such as Romans 1:19-20; 2:12-16; 10:14-18; and Psalm 19:4 and concludes that "the essential nature of saving faith can be arrived at without the special revelation. . . . Perhaps, in other words, it is possible to receive the benefits of Christ's death without conscious knowledge-belief in the name of Jesus."[90] From a more classically Calvinist perspective, Paul Helm has defended what he calls "opaque exclusivism": "It is possible to think of the Saviour exercising his exclusivism through bringing some men and women to unwittingly confess him as

---

[87]Alister McGrath, "A Particularist View: A Post-Enlightenment Approach," in *More Than One Way? Four Views on Salvation in a Pluralistic World,* ed. Dennis L. Okholm and Timothy R. Phillips (Grand Rapids, Mich.: Zondervan, 1995), p. 178.

[88]Ibid., pp. 178-79.

[89]Sanders, *No Other Name;* Clark H. Pinnock, *A Wideness in God's Mercy: The Finality of Jesus Christ in a World of Religions* (Grand Rapids, Mich.: Zondervan, 1992); Amos Yong, *Beyond the Impasse: Toward a Pneumatological Theology of Religions* (Grand Rapids, Mich.: Baker, 2003).

[90]Millard J. Erickson, "Hope for Those Who Haven't Heard? Yes, But . . ." *Evangelical Missions Quarterly* 11 (April 1975): 124.

Saviour and Lord, by worshipping Christ in ignorance."[91]

REFLECTIONS ON THE CALVINIST-ARMINIAN DISCUSSION IN REGARD TO THIS PARTICULAR STUDY

In recent years, the accessibilist understanding of God's saving work has been most often defended, within evangelicalism, by Arminians. This might give the impression that Calvinism is naturally ecclesiocentrist whereas Wesleyanism is more likely to be accessibilist. Indeed, some would argue that, logically, Arminian theology *must* be so. Pinnock states that "if God really loves the whole world and desires everyone to be saved," as Arminians believe, "it follows logically that every one must have access to salvation."[92] Stuart Hackett argued that

> if every human being in all times and ages has been objectively provided for through the unique redemption in Jesus, and if this provision is in fact intended by God for every such human being, then it must be possible for every human individual to become personally eligible to receive that provision—regardless of his historical, cultural, or personal circumstances and situation, and quite apart from any particular historical information or even historically formulated theological conceptualization—since a universally intended redemptive provision is not genuinely universal unless it is also and for that reason universally accessible.[93]

I find this line of reasoning from Arminian (synergistic) premises to be quite compelling. Nevertheless, D. A. Carson observes that many Arminians (he suggests "most" of them) hold that God desires the salvation of all people but that getting the gospel to them is our task.[94] Of course, it is a basic Arminian tenet that humans, having been given libertarian free will by God, can prevent God from realizing his desires. This is true of the individuals who hear the gospel and are graciously enabled to believe it but refuse to do so, and it is true also of the Christians whom the Spirit prompts to become missionaries but who refuse to go. Nevertheless, it

---

[91]Paul Helm, "Are They Few That Be Saved?" in *Universalism and the Doctrine of Hell: Papers Presented at the Fourth Edinburgh Conference in Christian Dogmatics, 1991*, ed. Nigel M. de S. Cameron (Grand Rapids, Mich.: Baker, 1993), p. 278. See his argument for the position on pp. 279-81.

[92]Pinnock, *Wideness in God's Mercy*, p. 157.

[93]Stuart C. Hackett, *The Reconstruction of the Christian Revelation Claim* (Grand Rapids, Mich.: Baker, 1984), p. 244, quoted in Pinnock, *Wideness in God's Mercy*, p. 159.

[94]D. A. Carson, *The Gagging of God: Christianity Confronts Pluralism* (Grand Rapids, Mich.: Zondervan, 1996), p. 289.

does seem to me that Arminians are theologically compelled toward an accessibilist position in a way that Calvinists are not. If one believes that God wants everyone to be saved, that Christ died for everyone and that the Spirit enables all to respond properly to God's self-revelation, it is difficult, if not impossible, to believe that God does not make himself known to everyone in a potentially saving manner.

Calvinist theologian Loraine Boettner also saw the situation this way. He argues that "the fact that, in the providential working of God, some men are left without the Gospel and the other means of grace virtually involves the principle set forth in the Calvinistic doctrine of Predestination."[95] He observes that

> in all ages the greater portion of mankind has been left destitute even of the external means of grace.... Multitudes were left with no chance to hear the Gospel, and consequently died in their sins. If God had intended to save them undoubtedly he would have sent them the means of salvation. If he had chosen to Christianize India and China a thousand years ago, He most certainly could have accomplished His purpose.

Consequently, Boettner contends that if Arminians were correct, "namely, that Christ died for all men and that the benefits of His death are actually applied to all men," then

> we would expect to find that God had made some provision for the Gospel to be communicated to all men. The problem of the heathens, who live and die without the Gospel, has always been a thorny one for the Arminians who insist that all men have sufficient grace if they will but make use of it.[96]

Implicit in the general framework of a synergistic understanding of God and his work in the world is the assumption that God always does the most that God can do. This has been very clearly stated by Open Theists, but it is not less true of classic Arminians or Molinists, even though they believe that God is able to do more than Open Theists think he can.[97] The principle is

---

[95]Loraine Boettner, *The Reformed Doctrine of Predestination* (Philadelphia: Presbyterian & Reformed, 1969), p. 117.

[96]Ibid., p. 118.

[97]Molinists, like Arminians, are synergists. Their distinctive is a proposal that from God's knowledge of what everyone would do in every circumstance, God has chosen this particular world in which libertarianly free creatures make their choices. I will interact with this Molinist proposal later in the book. A brief exposition of the idea can also be found in Terrance Tiessen, *Providence and Prayer: How Does God Work in the World?* (Downers Grove, Ill.: InterVarsity Press, 2000), chapter 8.

commonly assumed, even if not stated. From the Open Theist perspective, Gregory Boyd has addressed this very explicitly. He discerns that

> the classical understanding of omnipotence holds that God can intervene in the world anytime, anywhere and in any way he wants. . . . Hence, there must always be a divine reason as to why God intervenes when he does and does not intervene when he does not. . . . If one child is miraculously protected while another is allowed to be abducted, it must ultimately be because it fit God's plan to protect the first but not the second.[98]

In reference to our topic of salvation, then, monergists believe that God determines whom he will save. Consequently, we do not assert that God wished to save more people but was unable to do so, due to limits he had placed on himself when he created morally responsible creatures.

Boyd sums up his synergistic perspective:

> God genuinely faces in every particular situation a reality distinct from himself that has some say-so over and against himself. By giving every free agent an irrevocable domain of genuine say-so in the flow of history, God has to that extent limited his own unilateral say-so in the flow of history. God is everywhere and at all times present in his creation maximizing good and minimizing evil. But to the extent that he has given creatures say-so, God has restricted the exercise of his own omnipotence.[99]

There is widespread unease with Open Theism, even among classic Arminian evangelicals, because of its denial that God knows the future comprehensively. But it seems clear that even those more traditional Arminians would affirm Boyd's general contention regarding God's voluntary self-limitation in his granting of libertarian freedom to angels and humans. To deny that "God always does the most God can do" would be to assert that God has chosen not to save people whom he could have saved if he willed.[100] That proposal is inconceivable to the minds of the

---

[98]Gregory A. Boyd, *Satan and the Problem of Evil: Constructing a Trinitarian Warfare Theodicy* (Downers Grove, Ill.: InterVarsity Press, 2001), p. 210.

[99]Ibid., p. 213.

[100]It is interesting to find the same perspective in the thought of a theologian who was once classically Calvinist but who abandoned that position in order to deal with the evil of the death of his baby while maintaining his faith in God. Lewis Smedes proposes that, on September 11, 2001, "God was right there doing what God always does in the presence of evil that is willed by humans—fighting it, resisting it, battling it, *trying God's best* to keep it from happening" but that time evil won ("What's God Up To? A Father Grieves the Loss of a Child," *Christian Century*, May 3, 2003, p. 39 [emphasis mine]). The article is excerpted from his book *My God and I: A Memoir* (Grand Rapids, Mich.: Eerdmans, 2003).

many synergists I have met or whose books I have read. As a monergist of the Calvinist variety, therefore, I find it very difficult to see how anyone who affirms that "God always does the most God can do" can take an ecclesiocentric position. I would find it impossible to assert that God wills to save everyone, that he is doing all that he can do to save everyone (within his self-imposed limitations) and that hearing the gospel is necessary for salvation.

Additionally, I have a practical problem with synergism, which compounds the fact that I hear the biblical account of salvation as monergistic. I find it totally implausible that God could not do more than he has done to get the gospel to the unevangelized. One need only think of the numerous Muslims who come to faith in Jesus as God only after they have had a vision of Christ. Given the frequent efficacy of this means of divine encounter, it is hard to imagine what would prevent God from giving every Muslim in the world such a vision, even within the synergistic assumption that God cannot guarantee a believing response, regardless of his best efforts.

Because accessibilism is the most natural approach for a synergist to take, I have particularly mentioned a number of Calvinistic or monergistic theologians who have not been ecclesiocentrists. More could be cited, but some of their names will arise as I put forward my own Calvinistic, or monergistic, proposal. What my brief review should have demonstrated, at least, is that, even within the Reformed tradition, various approaches taken by Reformed theologians have provided ground for optimism concerning the salvation of the unevangelized.

Summing Up

Two things have become clear from declarations prepared by conferences of evangelicals in recent years. First, there is no consensus among evangelicals on the state of the unevangelized. Second, this is clearly not a hindrance to the energetic pursuit of evangelistic mission. The Evangelical Affirmations conference (convened at Trinity Evangelical Divinity School in May 1989) asserted the uniqueness of Christ's saving work and rejected universalism, but "the conferees could not agree" on the state of the unevangelized.[101] Similarly, the Manila Declaration (1992) clearly affirms the uniqueness of Jesus Christ as Savior and denies that religions have the

---

[101]Sanders, *No Other Name*, p. 145.

power to save.[102] But, regarding the question of the possible salvation of the unevangelized, it concludes, "We did not achieve a consensus on how to answer this question."[103]

As I head into my constructive proposal, I hope to further the pursuit of a biblically informed position on these issues, particularly among evangelical monergists. I hope that my use of terms is now clear. A review of the chart in chapter two should be helpful if you are in doubt. The proposal I am putting forward is clearly accessibilist and, because concern about this position has been expressed by evangelicals who fear that it will undermine the church's missionary passion, I will present my position very carefully. Since I am firmly convinced that this is no threat to the church's missionary task but that it glorifies the God who alone is able to save rebellious sinners, I have no fear that this message will discourage gospel witness. Our first steps are to identify who *needs* to be saved and how God accomplishes that salvation.

---

[102]The Manila Declaration was formulated by eighty-five theologians from twenty-eight countries in June 1992, at the conclusion of the conference on the theme "The Unique Christ in Our Pluralistic World," sponsored by the Theological Commission of the World Evangelical Fellowship (now known as the World Evangelical Alliance).

[103]"The Unique Christ in Our Pluralistic World," in *Biblical Theology in Asia*, ed. Ken Gnanakan (Bangalore: Theological Book Trust, 1995), p. 307.

PART 1

HOW DOES GOD
SAVE PEOPLE?

4

Who Needs to Be Saved?

Thesis 2: By God's appointment, the entire human race was represented in Adam in his moral probation in the Garden of Eden. When he sinned, we all sinned, and so we all die. The consequence of that original sin was that everyone is born a sinner, alienated from God, guilty of enmity toward God and certain to commit acts of personal disobedience as soon as we are capable of making moral judgments. Thus, there are no "innocent" people, whether they be unborn, infant, disabled or competent and adult. Every human being, therefore, needs to be saved from the guilt of sin and its terrible consequences.

WHEN WE TALK ABOUT GOD'S SAVING WORK IN THE WORLD, we must start from an understanding of who needs to be saved. Who is a sinner, and how does one get that way? In particular, we are faced with the question of "original sin," that is, of the consequences of Adam's sin for the rest of humanity. Are all human beings under God's condemnation from the beginning of their lives, or do they only become guilty when they personally disobey God's moral law? We face this important question every time an infant dies or someone is born without the mental capacity to comprehend the gospel, even if they are in a situation where they would hear it.

ORIGINAL SIN

As I understand the condition of the human race, all of humanity is both guilty (under God's condemnation) and corrupt (inclined toward sin) through solidarity with Adam. This sinfulness is "original" not just because it was the first human sin; that distinction would go to Eve's disobedience. But Adam's transgression is critical because it is the origin of *all* the human sin that followed that primal Fall. This doctrine is found most clearly in Paul's letter to the Romans, where he tells us that "sin came into the world through one man, and death came through sin, and so death spread to all" because all sinned (Rom 5:12).[1] All who were "in Adam" sinned when Adam, as appointed head of the human race, made his fatal decision to disobey God, and that is why we all die.

There are many theories about original sin. Since the church condemned Pelagius for stating that we all begin life in the same condition that Adam and Eve had before they fell, it has been almost universally accepted that everyone descended from Adam and Eve is inclined toward sin, that we begin life with a nature that is "corrupt" or "polluted." But not everyone agrees with Augustine and his theological heirs that *guilt*, as well as corruption, is entailed in original sin. The difference is significant for our analysis of who needs to be saved. If not everyone is born guilty, it is possible that some never do become guilty and, therefore, do not need to have their sins forgiven. If the sin for which one is guilty before God is only the sin committed when one is morally conscious of sin, then significant numbers of the human race may be considered not guilty. These would include infants who die before they reach that "age of moral accountability" or people whose mental development prevents them from making moral distinctions. Here are my reasons for concluding from Scripture that everyone is, in fact, guilty in Adam and that *everyone*, therefore, needs to be saved in the sense of being forgiven of sin and declared not guilty in the presence of the righteous and holy God.

First reason for affirming original guilt. Scripture is clear that no one can be saved by keeping the law (Ps 143:2; Rom 3:20; Acts 13:39; Gal 2:16). Part of our problem is that we are unable to keep the law because of an inherited corruption[2] that constitutes a "dire propensity to sin."[3] But, more fundamentally, no one can be saved by keeping the law, because we are already guilty and hence condemned. Rather than becoming guilty because of the sin we do as a result of our being corrupted, we are inclined to sin because we are guilty and hence alienated from God, on whom we depend for our moral righteousness. Even Adam and Eve, in their pristine goodness before the Fall, were dependent on God for their physical life and for

---

[1]The NRSV has "all have sinned," but I believe that "all sinned" better represents the aorist that Paul uses here, and this conviction is shared by the translators of the NIV, the TNIV, the ESV, the NASB and the NLT.

[2]As per C. E. B. Cranfield, *A Critical and Exegetical Commentary on the Epistle to the Romans*, International Critical Commentary (Edinburgh: T & T Clark, 1979), 1:278-79.

[3]Alan F. Johnson and Robert E. Webber, *What Christians Believe: A Biblical and Historical Summary* (Grand Rapids, Mich.: Zondervan, 1989), p. 206.

their continuance in moral goodness. Their sin alienated them from God
and cut them off from fellowship with him, which was the source of their
moral goodness.

According to Romans 5:12, everyone sinned in Adam; they did not just
become prone to sin.[4] That message can be heard also in Romans 3:23,
where Paul tells his readers that "all sinned" (an aorist tense in Greek) and
are falling short (present tense) of the glory of God. N. T. Wright argues,
accordingly, that the aorist in this verse indicates "a single moment, despite the almost universal perfect tense ('all have sinned') in the translations," with the exception of the Jerusalem Bible.[5] Wright notes that "Paul
seems to be thinking of Adam, hiding under the argument as in 1:18-25
and 7:7-12, emerging into daylight only in 5:12-21."[6] Thus, everyone needs
salvation because we all sinned in Adam and because we continue to sin,
thereby falling short of the glory of God or of the image of God in which
we were created. In Jewish literature of the period, losing God's glory is
closely associated with the Fall of Adam, just as the sense of regaining
Adam's glory is a key feature of the expected redemption.[7]

Augustine's concept of universal guilt in Adam is sometimes attributed
to the faulty translation of Romans 5:12 by Ambrosiaster, which influenced
Augustine. That mistranslation led Augustine to render Paul's *eph hō* as
"in whom," but "*epi* would not be the right preposition, and *hō* would be
too far removed from its antecedent" for this to be a proper translation.[8] It
is important to note, however, that the concept of original guilt, which Augustine derived from Romans 5, does not depend on his mistranslation.
The aorist verb ("all sinned") carries the sense of universal guilt in Adam
even when the phrase is properly translated. The phrase *eph hō* is probably
best given a causal sense, "*because* all sinned,"[9] as is evident where *because*

---

[4]This point was made by Francis Turretin, whose argument that it pointed to one act of sinning
rather than to habitual sin has been followed by S. Lewis Johnson, Leon Morris, P. E. Hughes
and many others in the Reformed tradition. See Henri Blocher, *Original Sin: Illuminating the
Riddle*, New Studies in Biblical Theology (Downers Grove, Ill.: InterVarsity Press, 1997), p. 72.

[5]N. T. Wright, "The Letter to the Romans: Introduction, Commentary and Reflections," in *The
New Interpreter's Bible* (Nashville: Abingdon, 2002), 10:470. Earlier, Philip Edgcumbe Hughes
had argued for the same interpretation; see *The True Image: The Origin and Destiny of Man in
Christ* (Grand Rapids, Mich.: Eerdmans, 1989), p. 1.

[6]Wright, "Letter to the Romans," 10:470.

[7]Ibid.

[8]William Sanday and Arthur Headlam, *A Critical and Exegetical Commentary on the Epistle to
the Romans*, 5th ed. (Edinburgh: T & T Clark, 1980), p. 133.

[9]Stanley E. Porter, "The Pauline Concept of Original Sin, In Light of Rabbinical Background,"
Tyndale Bulletin 41 (1990): 22-24. Hence, also, the NRSV and NIV translations.

is used in 2 Corinthians 5:4 and Philippians 3:12. So then, what Paul says in Romans 5:12 is that death spread to the whole human race through one man *"because* all sinned" rather than that we all die because of Adam *"in whom* all sinned." Both readings support the notion that we all sinned when Adam sinned and that this is why we all die. As Wright sums it up, "Paul's meaning must in any case be both that an entail of sinfulness has spread throughout the human race from its first beginnings and that each individual has contributed their own share to it."[10]

In Romans 4:15, Paul had indicated that there is no transgression where there is no law, but then in Romans 5:13 he tells us that "sin was indeed in the world before the law" and that "the trespass multiplied" when the law came in (Rom 5:20). In spite of the fact that Torah, the Law of Moses, had not yet been given, death was experienced by people in the world in the time between Adam and Moses. Here Paul's point is clarified by Wright's proposal that Paul's Adam-Christology is "based on the Jewish view that saw Israel as the last Adam."[11] It was in Israel that sin abounded, finding fresh opportunity when the Law was given at Sinai; but there, too, grace abounded. The existence of sin prior to the giving of the Law also offers ground for the culpability of the Gentiles, as Paul had stated in Romans 2:14.[12] Death is the universal human experience because "sin came into the world through one man, and death came through sin" (Rom 5:12). It is possible that death prior to the giving of the Law is a result of original corruption rather than of guilt.[13] I concur with Leon Morris, however, that it is better to see death as coming to all through a solidarity in Adam's transgression, because of the way Paul links death with condemnation.[14]

Original sin is what determines human nature and what directs our actions; we sin because we are sinners. We are alienated from God, and so we lack the pure moral goodness that is only possible for creatures who live in fellowship with God. Henri Blocher puts it nicely: "Sinfulness has become our quasi-nature while remaining truly our anti-nature."[15]

Second reason for affirming original guilt. My second reason for hearing original guilt in Romans 5 is that Romans 5:12-19 so clearly relates the

[10]Wright, "Letter to the Romans," 10:527.
[11]N. T. Wright, *The Climax of the Covenant: Christ and the Law in Pauline Theology* (Minneapolis: Fortress, 1991), p. 39.
[12]Wright, "Letter to the Romans," 10:527.
[13]Sanday and Headlam, *Critical and Exegetical Commentary,* pp. 134-35.
[14]Leon Morris, *The Epistle to the Romans* (Grand Rapids, Mich.: Eerdmans, 1988), p. 233.
[15]Blocher, *Original Sin,* p. 30.

passage of sin and death to the sin of the "one man." Four times (in verses 15, 16, 17 and 18) Paul writes of "the one man's trespass" or "the one man's sin." This one act of disobedience—not Adam's descendants' many acts of disobedience—is contrasted with the one act of righteousness by Christ. Blocher rightly observes:

> Paul's emphasis in Romans 5:18ff. on the *one* act of disobedience, which constituted all human beings sinners, is so insistent that the idea of Adam simply as the remote cause of sin's introduction fails to match the force of Paul's language. Apart from the disputed clause in verse 12, "because all have sinned," nowhere does the apostle put forward the actual sinful tendencies or behaviour of humankind as the ground for their condemnation. . . . Nor does the scheme that focuses on universal corruption fit with the unique phrase of verse 14, describing Adam as a *type* of the One who was coming. According to the looser reading, Adam's role is very different from Christ's in justification (for Christ does not justify his own by transmitting to them a "good inclination").[16]

Millard Erickson makes an interesting proposal regarding the imputation of sin, but I do not consider it correct, for reasons that will emerge as we go along. Nevertheless, it deserves careful consideration because I find that people are attracted to it. Erickson proposes that

> until the first conscious or responsible moral action or decision by a person, there is no imputation of the Adamic sin, just as there is no imputation of Christ's righteousness until there is a conscious acceptance of that work. In the case of the sin, there is, in effect, actually no awareness of the concept of rightness and wrongness or of responsibility. This is prior to what we term the "age of accountability."[17]

He does not suggest that one is "innocent and free of any guilt until he or she commits a first act of personal sin. . . . It is rather that in the moment one becomes conscious of the reality of right and wrong, that person becomes aware that past actions he or she has performed are indeed sinful."[18] A person then "becomes aware of the inclination toward sin, or the sinful nature, or depravity," and the proper response to this is abhorrence and rejection. "By failing to reject that sinful inclination, one acquiesces in it or accepts it. This constitutes a ratification of the first sin of the

---

[16]Ibid., p. 67.
[17]Millard J. Erickson, *How Shall They Be Saved? The Destiny of Those Who Do Not Hear of Jesus* (Grand Rapids, Mich.: Baker, 1996), p. 250. Compare Deut 1:39; Is 7:15-16; Jon 4:11.
[18]Ibid.

human race, an accepting it as one's own, and therefore guilt comes on the person as well."[19] That moment of acquiescence to Adam's act of sin is thus analogous to the moment of acquiescence to Christ's act that occurs in saving faith.

Erickson's proposal has the merit of preserving the parallelism between the acts of Adam and of Christ. I question, however, that his scheme of voluntarily appropriated depravity completely avoids the key problem of Pelagianism and semi-Pelagianism, since actual guilt does not really occur for all people through Adam. In this scheme, children who die in infancy were never actually guilty. But then why do they die? If sin does not become theirs through Adam, why does death? Paul clearly puts the two together. Indeed, these infants are excellent examples of those who die, although they have not sinned after the manner of Adam (Rom 5:14).

The major problem with the doctrine of the "age of accountability," which suggests that children do not become guilty sinners until they knowingly commit personal acts of sin, is that it portrays a situation in which large numbers of people will eventually enjoy fellowship with God, for all eternity, in the new earth, without ever having needed Christ's atoning work to make it possible. If we are conceived and even born guiltless and in fact only become guilty of sin when we commit an act of intentional violation of our moral conscience, then a great many people never become sinners and never need a savior. To the contrary, however, Scripture clearly teaches that the new earth will be populated by the bride of Christ, "the wife of the Lamb" (Rev 21:9). They are there because God graciously saved them from sin and death through the righteous act of the Son of God, who became a man in order to reverse the curse that began in Adam and to inaugurate a new race redeemed by Christ's righteousness.

David Smith has proposed that "sin is not imputed against innocents. Until there is awareness of guilt (i.e., of breaking the law), the penalty for sin—eternal death—is not imposed. It is evidently covered by the Saviour's atonement."[20] But Blocher rightly observes the serious ambiguity "in the joint affirmations of innocence and of the role of atonement. If the infant is not to be charged with sin, where does the need for atonement come in? Innocence does not need to be 'covered.'"[21] Consequently, we are left with only two coherent alternatives. Either morally unaware infants are not

---

[19]Ibid., p. 251.
[20]David L. Smith, *With Wilful Intent: A Theology of Sin* (Wheaton, Ill.: Victor 1994), p. 298.
[21]Blocher, *Original Sin*, p. 24.

guilty, in which case they do not need to be saved, or they are guilty in Adam and can be saved only if they are justified through union with Christ, the Righteous One. I will discuss the issue of infant salvation later, but now I will simply underline the fact that the occupants of heaven are there because of the atoning work of Christ. Consequently, if there are going to be in heaven any people who died as infants, they must have been sinners redeemed by Christ. Their sinfulness and need of such redemption is most easily understood in terms of the guilt of the whole human race in Adam.

Third reason for affirming original guilt. A third reason for believing that the human race is guilty in Adam is that it is important to avoid the errors of both works-righteousness and universalism, which might otherwise follow from Paul's analogy between Adam and Christ. If the analogy is carried through in the mode of "voluntarily appropriated depravity," then it leads to salvation by actual and voluntary righteousness after Christ's example. If we become sinners only because we personally commit an act of sin, thereby appropriating Adam's choice, then we become righteous because we personally commit an act of righteousness. Presumably, that act would be the faith by which we appropriate Christ's righteousness. But, if we follow this path and make faith the act by which we become righteous, it becomes the one meritorious act necessary for our salvation. Calvinists regularly complain that this is entailed in Arminian views of salvation, but evangelical Arminians have been strenuous in their denial that faith is a human work for which believers deserve credit. If Paul's analogy between Adam and Christ is to be maintained, voluntarily appropriated depravity parallels voluntarily appropriated righteousness, and the graciousness of salvation has been fatally compromised. A better reading of the purpose of the law is provided by Wright's Adam-Israel-Christ schematic: "The Torah possesses, Paul asserts, the divinely intended function of drawing sin on to Israel, magnifying it precisely within the people of God ([Rom] 7:13-20), in order that it might then and thus be drawn on to Israel's representative and so dealt with on the cross ([Rom] 8:3)."[22]

Fourth reason for affirming original guilt. As a fourth point, we should note that Paul is not concerned with giving an explanation of the universality of sin or the manner of its propagation. This has been pointed out by G. C. Berkouwer, Herman Ridderbos and others.[23] What does come through clearly is that all people sinned in Adam and that this is not an

---

[22]Wright, *Climax of the Covenant,* p. 39.

alien sin but a personal or proper one. *How* that is so, Paul does not clearly spell out, but it is clear that all were involved in Adam's sin.

> Alienation from God, the condition of being deprived and depraved, follows immediately upon the first act of sinning—for Adam himself and for his seed after him. It affects his descendants from the very start of their existence because of their relationship to him. It is voluntary inasmuch as it implies a disposition of the will, even in its most embryonic form; it is guilty.[24]

Right from the beginning of fetal life, "the will, though undeveloped, does exist, and its anti-God tendency already constitutes a wilful exercise,"[25] an enmity toward God that carries guilt. Being born sinners is, therefore, "not a penalty, or strictly the result of transference, but simply an existential, spiritual, *fact* for human beings since Adam."[26]

Facing the scandal of original guilt. In our individualistic Western culture, the concept of becoming guilty sinners in Adam frequently stirs strong resistance. I recall vividly the outrage of one of our sons when he was just three years old. I was teaching the boys a children's catechism, and I loved to hear them recite the answers even though the language was often pretty difficult. Then came the day when I read the question and answer concerning original sin. Instead of the repetition that usually followed my stating of a new answer, my son said, "But that's not fair!" This is not an unusual response to what sounds as though we are being held accountable for something someone else did. As strange as the concept of Adam's representative headship or of our solidarity with him seems, however, we need to realize that it is the same structure of headship or union that is the ground of our salvation in Christ. No one who rejoices in being righteous because of union with Christ dare protest at being guilty because of union with Adam.

Paul's point is that all who were "in Adam" sinned and became subject to death but, more importantly, that all those who are represented "in Christ" are made alive. Wright notes, helpfully, that the "question of numerically universal salvation" is not in Paul's mind. "His universalism is of the sort that holds to Christ as the way for all."[27] The main point of the

---

[23]Herman N. Ridderbos, *Paul: An Outline of His Theology* (Grand Rapids, Mich.: Eerdmans, 1975), p. 95.
[24]Ibid.
[25]Ibid., p. 129.
[26]Ibid.
[27]Wright, "Letter to the Romans," 10:529.

contrast between Adam and Christ is in the act of each one and in its outcome. Just as condemnation and death came into the world through the
one act of disobedience of one man, so justification and life came into the
world through the one act of obedience of one man. Jesus was not "in
Adam" in this corporate solidarity that God established between Adam
and the human race. Thus, Jesus was free of original guilt. This is essential,
because there would otherwise have been no means by which his own
guilt in Adam could have been addressed. He was protected from the corruption (or pollution) of sin by the "overshadowing" of the Holy Spirit
who assured that, in his conception, he was born holy (Lk 1:35). The grace
that comes to us in Christ is greater because it is able to counteract the initial trespass and to deal with a multitude of trespasses that followed it. "In
Christ," we die and rise again to new life (Rom 6:3-11). There are thus two
humankinds: each of us exists originally in Adam, but through faith in
Christ, we become incorporated into him, into the new humanity that God
views as righteous in Christ. And that very faith itself was part of the grace
that Christ secured for those whom the Father chose in him.

ACTUAL SIN

In addition to the guilt incurred in Adam, human beings who live long
enough have a long list of their own transgressions of God's law. We all fall
short of the glory of God, that is, of the image of God in which humankind
was created and for which we were intended (Rom 3:23). Universal sinfulness is a tragic fact that includes the painful reality that this sin separates us
from a holy God in whose righteous presence no sinner can live. (See
1 Kings 8:46; Job 9:2-3; 14:4; 15:14; Ps 51:5; Eccles 7:20; Rom 5:12; Eph 2:3.) It
is important, however, to note that in passages like Romans 1:24-32; 3:10-
18; and 2 Timothy 3:2-8, Paul is depicting "human nature in the raw, when
not restrained or prompted by either 'common' or 'special' grace."[28] No one
seeks after God perfectly, and no one seeks him without God's gracious enabling. This does not diminish the significance of the "very numerous references and promises in the Scriptures to those who 'seek God.'"[29]

Given the previous affirmation of original guilt, it is significant to observe that Scripture always relates the ultimate judgment to our own
moral "works," which fall short of God's standards, and not in the first in-

---

[28]J. N. D. Anderson, *Christianity and World Religions: The Challenge of Pluralism* (Downers
Grove, Ill.: InterVarsity Press, 1984), p.152.
[29]Ibid.

stance to our union with Adam (e.g., Mt 7:21-27; 13:41; 25:31-46; Lk 3:9; Rom 2:5-10; Rev 20:11-14.)[30] This is significant in regard to the weight we place on original guilt, but it does not negate the human solidarity in Adam that makes Christ's saving work necessary for the whole human race.

SUMMING UP

Who needs to be saved? Everyone does. No one who matures to the point of moral awareness does only and always what they believe they should do. And even when we obey our consciences, we do not do so for the right reason—to glorify God—unless God graciously transforms us. As Paul told the Romans, "Whatever does not proceed from faith is sin" (Rom 14:23). On the other hand, a very large number of human beings never achieve moral awareness. Many die before birth, and many more die in early infancy. But these people are also sinners. By God's appointment, Adam acted on behalf of the race, in his moral probation in the Garden of Eden, so that when he sinned we all did; this is why we die, even if we do not mature physically to moral awareness. We can all say with David, "I was born guilty, a sinner when my mother conceived me" (Ps 51:5). Unless our sin is dealt with, we cannot be reconciled with God. So next we must ask how sinners can be saved. Paul has taught us that the free gift of God "in the grace of the one man, Jesus Christ," brings justification (Rom 5:15-16). Just as all who are "in Adam" die, so all who are "in Christ" will be made alive (1 Cor 15:22). That leads us to our next question. Who is it that will be "made alive in Christ"? Whom does God save through incorporation "in Christ"?

---

[30]This is noted by Bruce Milne, *Know the Truth: A Handbook of Christian Belief* (Leicester, U.K.: Inter-Varsity Press, 1982), p. 106.

5

Whom Is God Trying to Save?

Thesis 3: There is only one means by which salvation of sinners can be accomplished. Jesus Christ is the world's only Savior. All who have ever been, are now or ever will be saved are reconciled to God because Jesus Christ lived, died and rose again for them. Salvation is a work of the triune God whom Christians worship. Before creating the world, God the Father chose whom he would save and God the Son then became a man and laid down his sinless life to accomplish salvation for those people. Just as the whole race became sinners in their natural head, Adam, so too the new race that God establishes in union with Christ (the second Adam) is made alive and righteous (i.e., "saved") in Christ. The Spirit of God then works in the lives of these people so that they respond willingly to God in the way necessary for the appropriation of Christ's saving work. Thus, God saves everyone whom he chose to save in the will of his eternal purpose (or his "decree"). On the other hand, God's gracious work extends beyond salvation so that everyone benefits from Christ's death in numerous ways.

THE PICTURE OF THE HUMAN CONDITION, which we have considered, is bleak. The story of the tragic Fall of humankind into sin comes very early in the biblical narrative, but the rest of the story is a wonderful account of God's work of grace to restore sinful human beings to fellowship with himself and, ultimately, to renew the whole cosmos. Now we will observe how salvation is accomplished through one of the descendants of Eve, by whom the chief adversary of God in the world is defeated (Gen 3:15). God gradually implements his program of restoration through a series of covenants. With Noah and his descendants God makes a covenant that includes every living creature or "all flesh that is on the earth" (Gen 9:8-17). The focus then narrows, and God establishes a covenant with Abram and his descendants (Gen 12:1-3), the nation of Israel (see Ex 2:24; 19:3-20:17). But a new covenant is finally established through Jesus Christ, through whom all the earlier stages of the covenant promise are fulfilled (Heb 9:11-18). The covenant had always been intended as a means of universal blessing, and its universal scope is realized in Jesus and the sending of the Spirit of the risen Christ, who equips the new covenant people of God for their role as witnesses of Christ to the ends of the world and the end of this age (Mt 28:19-20; Acts 1:8).

JESUS CHRIST IS THE WORLD'S ONLY SAVIOR

Contrary to the proposal of relativists, accessibilists insist that anyone who has ever been, is now or ever will be saved is saved because of the atoning work of Jesus Christ, the prophet greater than Moses, the priest greater than Aaron, the king greater than David. As the Westminster Confession puts it, "Although the work of redemption was not actually wrought by Christ til after his incarnation, yet the virtue, efficacy and benefits thereof were communicated unto the elect in all ages successively from the beginning of the world."[1]

There is strong witness in the New Testament to the exclusive efficacy of the redemptive work of Jesus the Christ. Indeed, this exclusivism is integral to the biblical teaching regarding the incarnation of the Son of God, the Word made flesh, in whom the new covenant is established. Jesus himself insisted that no one can come to the Father except by him, "the way, and the truth, and the life" (Jn 14:6). These and other "I am" sayings by Jesus in John's Gospel "deliberately refer to similar sayings in Isaiah and thus identify Jesus with the God of the Old Testament."[2] In these texts (Jn 8:24, 28, 58), Jesus appropriates to himself a phrase that is reserved for Yahweh, a phrase that identifies him as the Lord, without any rivals.[3] Not only does Jesus identify himself with the one true God of Israel, but he "also claims to fulfil the day when God's salvation would be seen."[4] The phrase "you will die in your sins unless you believe that I am he" (Jn 8:24) suggests that Jesus has an exclusive role in the forgiveness of sins, and it implies that this forgiveness is experienced only by those who believe that he is Yahweh.[5] In regard to the latter point, how-

---

[1]Westminster Confession 8.6.
[2]David M. Ball, " 'I Am . . .': The 'I Am' Sayings of Jesus and Religious Pluralism," in *One God, One Lord: Christianity in a World of Religious Pluralism*, 2nd ed., ed. Andrew D. Clarke and Bruce Winter (Grand Rapids, Mich.: Baker, 1992), p. 65.
[3]Ibid., pp. 76, 79.
[4]Ibid., p. 83.
[5]Ibid., p. 79.

ever, it is important to remind ourselves that Jesus made the statement specifically to people to whom he was revealing his identity. It is critical that we not overextend such statements to the unevangelized, who are, by definition, without such revelation.

The apostle Peter informed the rulers of Israel that "there is salvation in no one else, for there is no other name under heaven given among mortals by which we must be saved" (Acts 4:12). At the time, Peter was speaking about the healing of the crippled beggar at the Beautiful Gate of the Temple.

> He was saying that Jesus of Nazareth is the source of every act of healing and salvation that has ever happened. He knew perfectly well that vast numbers of people had been healed without any knowledge of Jesus, yet he made the astounding claim that Jesus was the hidden author of all healing. He was the totally unique savior because he was totally universal.[6]

As Paul asserts, possibly in quotation of an early Christian hymn or confession, "There is one God; there is also one mediator between God and humankind, Christ Jesus, himself human, who gave himself a ransom for all" (1 Tim 2:5-6).

Just as sin came into the world through the disobedience of one man (Rom 5:12, 15, 17-19), so that all who were "in Adam" sinned and died, so life came into the world through the obedience of one man (Rom 5:18-19), so that all who are "in Christ" are made alive. In order for God to remain just while justifying sinners, the righteous demands of his law had to be met (Rom 3:25-26). God accomplished this in a wonderful way. He took on himself the penalty of our sin, so that God can justly view us as righteous in Christ. The New Testament speaks of this amazing act as "justification," the declaration that we are righteous or without guilt (Rom 3:24; 5:9, 19; 8:1; 10:4; 1 Cor 1:30; 6:11; 2 Cor 5:21; Phil 3:9; cf. Is 53:4-6). Anyone who ever has been, is now or ever will be saved is accepted by God on the grounds of the righteous sacrifice of Christ and our identification or union with him. There is no other ground.

Paul says to Timothy that the grace "given to us in Christ Jesus before the ages began" was revealed historically in his incarnation (2 Tim 1:9-10).[7] To Titus, Paul says that our faith and knowledge rest "in the hope of eter-

---

[6]John V. Taylor, "The Theological Basis of Interfaith Dialogue," in *Faith Meets Faith*, Mission Trends, ed. Gerald H. Anderson and Thomas F. Stransky (Grand Rapids, Mich.: Eerdmans, 1981), 5:100-101.
[7]Daniel Clendenin, *Many Gods, Many Lords* (Grand Rapids, Mich.: Baker, 1995), p. 125.

nal life that God, who never lies, promised before the ages began" and that
he has revealed "through the proclamation" with which Paul was entrusted, "in due time" (Tit 1:2-3). The secret wisdom of the cross has been
hidden, but God decreed it "before the ages for our glory." It was not understood by the "rulers," but is revealed to Paul and the Corinthians, by
the Spirit (1 Cor 2:7-10). Writing to the Ephesians, Paul stated that all people, Jew and Gentile, are naturally dead in their sins and in need of being
raised from the dead "together with Christ" (Eph 2:5).[8] Likewise Peter says
that Christ was "destined before the foundation of the world, but was revealed at the end of the ages" (1 Pet 1:20).

Thus, the good news is declared to be "the gospel of your salvation"
(Eph 1:13), in the objective sense of that which God has accomplished to
bring about human salvation. "The gospel is a declaration of what God *has
done* for us and a call to respond. It is God 'who saved us and called us with
a holy calling, not in virtue of our works but in virtue of his own purpose
and grace which he gave us in Christ Jesus ages ago' (2 Tim 1:9)."[9] Particularly in the later New Testament writings, Jesus is designated as "God"
and "Savior" (e.g., Tit 2:13; 2 Pet 1:1, 11; 2:20; 3:2, 18).[10] The title *savior* is applied, either to God or Christ, fifteen times in the Pastoral Epistles and
2 Peter but only nine times in the rest of the New Testament.[11] F. F. Bruce
suggests that this is "a reaction against the claims being made, especially
in the second half of the first century, to the *Theoi soteres* and in particular
the Roman Emperor."[12]

The biblical claim that Jesus is unique as the world's Savior is a scandal
that we cannot avoid as the messengers of his grace in the world. Perhaps
it helps us, however, to look at it from Colin Gunton's perspective:

> It is only when we appreciate that it is in and through Jesus of Nazareth
> that God meets humanity where it is, in its alienation and fallenness, and
> so liberates it for an imitation of that love, that we shall begin to under-
> stand that the assertion of Jesus' uniqueness, far from being immoral or il-

---

[8]Thorsten Moritz, " 'Summing Up All Things': Religious Pluralism and Universalism in Ephesians," in *One God, One Lord: Christianity in a World of Religious Pluralism,* 2nd ed., ed. Andrew D. Clarke and Bruce Winter (Grand Rapids, Mich.: Baker, 1992), pp. 115-16.
[9]Neal Punt, *What's Good About the Good News? The Plan of Salvation in a New Light* (Chicago:
Northland, 1988), p. 4.
[10]Russell F. Aldwinckle, *Jesus—A Savior or the Savior? Religious Pluralism in Christian Perspective* (Macon, Ga.: Mercer University Press, 1982), p. 40.
[11]Ibid., p. 41.
[12]S. G. F. Brandon, *The Saviour God* (Manchester, U.K.: Manchester University Press, 1963),
p. 52, quoted in Aldwinckle, *Jesus,* p. 41.

logical, is the presupposition for an understanding of the love of God for all of his creation.[13]

Jesus is the stone that human religious builders reject but that God makes the capstone (Acts 4:11). To unbelievers he is a "stumbling stone" (Ps 118:22, as used to conclude the parable of the tenants in all the Synoptic accounts; see Mk 12:1-12; Mt 21:33-46; Lk 20:9-19), but to believers he is precious (1 Pet 2:4-8). Either people stumble over him, or they are established on him.[14] In spite of the persecution, social marginalization and intellectual scorn that we may experience—as the apostles did—we must not be ashamed of the gospel (Rom 1:16; Phil 1:20; 2 Tim 1:8, 12, 16), even in its exclusivity. Carl Braaten sums up this situation well:

> He is the one and only Christ or he is not the Christ at all. He is the one and only Son of God, or he is not God's Son at all. He is the one and only Savior or he is not Savior at all. The exclusive claim is not a footnote to the gospel; it is the gospel itself. Not part of the husk, it is the kernel itself. The answer of the gospel to John the Baptist's question, "Are you the one who is to come?" is "Yes, and we shall not look for another" (Mt. 11:3).[15]

The uniqueness of Jesus lies precisely in "his universal meaning. . . . He is the universal Savior."[16]

WHAT DOES CHRIST ACCOMPLISH FOR THE SINNERS WHOM HE SAVES?

We are asking who can be saved, so it would be wise to describe briefly the salvation that is accomplished by the triune God. God the Father willed to save many sinners, and he achieved this through the atoning work of the Son, which is completely effective for the purpose God intended. Through Christ's death and resurrection, God accomplishes exactly what he intended, and that finished work of Christ is now being applied for the salvation of God's people through the ongoing work of the Holy Spirit. To describe that work, the New Testament uses many metaphors, and we dare

---

[13]Colin Gunton, *Yesterday and Today: A Study of Continuities in Christology* (London: Darton, Longman & Todd, 1983), p. 164, quoted in Vinoth Ramachandra, *The Recovery of Mission: Beyond the Pluralist Paradigm* (Carlisle, U.K.: Paternoster, 1996), p. 238.

[14]Clendenin, *Many Gods*, pp. 148-51.

[15]Carl E. Braaten, "The Uniqueness and Universality of Jesus Christ," in *Faith Meets Faith, Mission Trends*, ed. Gerald H. Anderson and Thomas F. Stransky (Grand Rapids, Mich.: Eerdmans, 1981), p. 75.

[16]Ibid., p. 78.

not reduce the biblical teaching concerning the atonement to any one of them (such as penal substitution). Indeed, it is probably unwise even to venture a suggestion as to which metaphor is primary.[17]

Sinners are covenant breakers who fail to give God the honor and obedience that are his due as Creator. For this, God wreaked destruction on the earth through a great flood, from which he saved Noah and his family. God then established a covenant with all living creatures (Gen 9:1-17). But sin again developed quickly in human society, and God established a special covenant relationship with Abraham, with the aim of blessing the whole world (Gen 12:1-3). In Christ, God established the *new covenant and the new creation*, thereby addressing the effects of the Fall in all of creation. This new covenant was superior to the one established at Sinai because it internalized and personalized the relationship between God and his people and because it was established by a better mediator (Heb 9:15). In this new covenant people, the wall between Jew and Gentile is broken down, and they are made one new covenant community through the cross (Eph 2:12-19). "The old obstacles and hostilities that had made *shalom* (peace or well-being) impossible have been abolished (see Gal 3:26-29; Col 3:9-17). . . . And the new community of salvation is a community of faith and freedom empowered and guided by the Spirit of Christ."[18]

Because of sinners' habitual disobedience, they live under God's condemnation, guilty before the demands of his moral law. Christ's death was a *sacrifice*, which addressed the problem of human guilt. As Isaiah foresaw so beautifully, "the LORD has laid on him the iniquity of us all" (Is 53:6). Thus, he became the "ransom for many" (Mk 10:45), the righteous one who died in place of sinners. Sin produces a terrible alienation from God, which is also manifested in countless forms of human alienation and social disorder. Christ accomplished *reconciliation*, addressing the enmity and alienation that exist between God and sinners and the shame that this entails on the part of sinners. God restores us to his own favor, removing all obstacles to our access to the Father and providing the ground for our justification or acquittal. Reconciliation deals with the shame that sin brings with it, a shame that results in the sinner's exclusion from the community,

[17]In personal conversation at the Regent College Theology Conference, in 2001, Gordon Fee suggested to me, quite plausibly, that the reason why penal substitution is given such a high priority among evangelicals is our tendency to prioritize Paul and to read Paul largely through the eyes of Galatians and Romans.
[18]C. Norman Kraus, *Jesus Christ our Lord: Christology from a Disciple's Perspective*, rev. ed. (Scottdale, Penn.: Herald, 1990), p. 177.

because of either self-loathing or social rejection. Divine forgiveness addresses both the personal and the social aspects of this shame and restores the sinner to harmony within the community and particularly with God.

Sinners live under the judgment of God for their sin, which includes his righteous wrath "against all ungodliness and wickedness of those who by their wickedness suppress the truth" (Rom 1:18). We can only escape this wrath and judgment through the gift of Christ's righteousness. Whether or not Christ's act of deliverance on behalf of his people is to be understood as an appeasement of God's wrath against sin has been much discussed.[19] Two things are clear: first, only the righteousness of Christ can deliver us from the judgment of God; and second, God is, therefore, the one who has provided the means of our *deliverance from his wrath*. Whether Christ's death effects our deliverance by appeasing the wrath of God or by expiating our sin is less clear. It is worth noting, however, that the concepts of penal substitution and of propitiation have both been severely criticized in recent years because of concerns that they may foster abuse.[20] It is essential, therefore, that we see salvation as a thoroughly trinitarian work. The Father does not subject the Son to suffering to satisfy his own demands, however just those were. The Son willingly gives himself for the salvation of those whom the Father has given to him (Jn 6:38-39). No one took his life from him; he willingly laid it down for the sheep, even though he does so in obedience to the Father's command (Jn 10:11, 15, 18). As a new covenant *mercy seat* (Rom 3:25), Christ is "the place of God's atoning presence."[21]

As *redeemer*, Christ leads us in a great new exodus, addressing both the shame or guilt of our sin and the pollution or power of sin to which we were in bondage, as to a foreign master (Rom 7:14). With reference to guilt, this issues in our justification (Rom 3:24; Eph 1:7; Col 1:14; Heb 9:15) and reconciliation. In regard to pollution, it produces the renewal of our nature, or regeneration, which is carried forward in sanctification and glorification. It also brings about deliverance from the enslaving defilement and power of sin (Tit 2:14; 1 Pet 1:18). We are now able not to sin but to

---

[19]J. M. Gundry-Volf provides a helpful review of the arguments for and against interpreting *hilastērion* as "propitiation" in Rom 3:25; Heb 2:17; and 1 Jn 2:2; 4:10 ("Expiation, Propitiation, Mercy Seat," in *Dictionary of Paul and His Letters*, ed. Gerald F. Hawthorne, Ralph P. Martin and Daniel G. Reid [Downers Grove, Ill.: InterVarsity Press, 1993], pp. 279-82).

[20]See the discussion in Joel B. Green and Mark D. Baker, *Recovering the Scandal of the Cross: Atonement in New Testament and Contemporary Contexts* (Downers Grove, Ill.: InterVarsity Press, 2000).

[21]Gundry-Volf, "Expiation," p. 283.

please God, which was impossible before Christ delivered us. There is an interrelationship between redemption and propitiation in Romans 3:24-26, indicating the juridical nature of the redemption.

In a great cosmic *victory,* Christ "abolished death" (2 Tim 1:10) through his fulfillment of the law, which we are powerless to keep and, thereby, he overcomes the power of sin (1 Cor 15:55-57). He overcame the hostile spiritual forces and stripped them of their power (Col 2:15). The resurrected Christ has been given authority over the rulers or powers (Eph 1:19-21). He made a public spectacle of them on the cross (Col 2:15), and he "rescued us from the power of darkness and transferred us into the kingdom of his beloved Son" (Col 1:13). The demonic powers are defeated foes; they continue to work until Christ fully subdues all his enemies (1 Cor 15:24-26), but we need not fear them and, in Christ, we are able to struggle against them.

It is true that Jesus provided a wonderful moral *example* for us, but this should not be considered a complete description of the purpose of Christ's work. We are not saved by following his example; rather those who are saved should and will follow Christ as Christ's life transforms them and as Christ lives in and through them (see Eph 5:1-2; Phil 2:3-8; 2 Cor 5:14; 1 Pet 1:21; cf. 1 Pet 4:1-2; Heb 12:2).

The salvation accomplished by Christ thus addresses every aspect and effect of sin in the lives of those to whom it is applied. Knowing *what* Christ has done, however, leads us to wonder *for whom* he did it. Whom was Christ attempting to deliver from the guilt and power of sin through his sinless life and death and his triumphant resurrection? Who is actually saved because the Word came as a man, lived a perfect human life, died a guiltless life and rose again?

THE INTENT AND EFFECTIVENESS OF CHRIST'S SAVING WORK

Alternative proposals. To the question of God's *intent,* we can identify two main answers. Not surprisingly, these distinguish synergistic from monergistic theologies. Synergistic theologians argue that God wills to save *everyone* and that Christ died in order to make this possible. Monergists, on the other hand, believe that God chose *particular people* whom he would save (that is, the "elect") and that Christ died and rose again for these people, as the head of a new race in him. These two alternatives are described, therefore, as *universal* and *particular atonement.*

Both of these positions can be further divided as to the *effectiveness* of

Christ's atoning work. Concerning the effectiveness of God's intention to save *everyone,* some believe that God succeeds in his purpose and that everyone will ultimately be saved. This is complete *soteric universalism* and should not be confused with Arminians' belief in the *universal atonement.* In the universalist model, the work of Christ is effective. He died to save everyone, and ultimately he will succeed in doing so. Many who hold this position believe that hell is purgatorial and that it will ultimately be emptied because everyone (at least all people, if not all fallen angels) will go to heaven. But others believe that God's universal salvific intent does *not* succeed. This is usually explained on the basis of the free will of God's creatures, which is understood in libertarian terms (i.e., as the power of contrary choice). God wanted to save everyone, and he sent Christ to accomplish that goal, but he can only forgive those who repent and believe. Sadly, some people choose to reject God's gracious overtures toward them.

Those who believe that God has a *particular* intention—to save only certain people—also divide into two groups. On the one hand, we have a minority who posit that God chose everyone in Christ and so everyone is ultimately redeemed by him—in other words, universalism. (These people might argue, legitimately I think, that universalism is only possible if creatures have the sort of freedom that allows God always to achieve his own purposes, that is, "compatibilistic freedom." In other words, synergists can hope for universal salvation, but only the God of monergism can guarantee it.) The majority of monergists believe that God graciously chose only a part of the human race (though possibly a majority of it) and that he justly leaves the rest to suffer the consequences of their own choice to sin.

These alternatives can be diagrammed as follows:

God's *intent*	To save everyone (universal atonement)		To save the elect (particular atonement)	
The *effect* of Christ's work	Salvation of everyone, though the choice is their own	Salvation only of those who freely choose to believe, which some never do	Election and salvation of everyone	Election and salvation of only part of the human race

Defining the issue. This issue is often discussed under the subject of the *extent* of the atonement, but that term is unhelpful because it focuses on the number who are saved rather than on the purpose or design of God's saving acts. Furthermore, it is important to avoid emotive judgments through terminology. Hence, I prefer to use the terms *effective* and *provisional.* The question is whether God *effectively saves* sinners or whether he *provides the possibility* for them to be saved.[22] The point at issue, therefore, is *not* whether the satisfaction made by Christ was sufficient for the salvation of all people. Anyone who understands election to be a choice of individuals for inclusion in God's salvation can agree with Augustine that it was "sufficient for all, efficient for the elect." Where people disagree, however, is on whether God's choosing to save particular individuals was based on his foreknowledge that they would believe ("conditional") or whether God chose people unconditionally, not based on any act by those people. The atonement is infinite in its value and, therefore, in its potentiality; no sinner will be lost because there was insufficient atoning power in the death of Christ!

The issue among evangelicals is usually *not* whether the saving benefits of Christ are actually applied to everyone. Those who affirm a "universal atonement" generally do not believe that everyone will be saved. Most Christians are agreed that salvation is particular in its *results*; the difference is in the explanation of *why* that is so. Is it because only some people libertarianly freely choose to believe in God and Christ in spite of God's best efforts to draw everyone to himself? Or is it because God has only chosen to save some people and that he only draws these people effectively to himself?

The issue is *not* whether a genuine offer of salvation can be made to all who hear the gospel on condition of repentance and faith. *Nor* is it whether the nonelect enjoy any benefits of the death of Christ. Everyone enjoys some benefits of the mediatorial dominion of Christ, which is universal.[23] Common grace has its origin in the atonement of Christ. This includes the common blessings of life, the restraint of evil, an objective provision sufficient for all, the future resurrection of the dead and the objective overthrow of the devil and his hosts. Paul worked hard as an evangelist because he had his "hope set on the living God, who is the Savior of all people, especially of those who believe" (1Tim 4:10). This statement is sometimes cited to indicate a twofold purpose: general benefits for all and saving benefits for elect believers.[24]

The point at issue then is God's *intention*. Did the Father send the Son, and did the Son give himself up to death *in order to* save all people or only the elect? But also at issue is our understanding of the nature of the atone-

---

[22]Robert Letham, *The Work of Christ* (Downers Grove, Ill.: InterVarsity Press, 1993), p. 229.

[23]John Murray, *Redemption Accomplished and Applied* (Grand Rapids, Mich.: Eerdmans, 1955), p. 61.

[24]See Bruce Demarest, *The Cross and Salvation: The Doctrine of Salvation,* Foundations of Evangelical Theology (Wheaton, Ill.: Crossway, 1997), p. 163.

ment. Arminians assert that Christ died to make salvation possible for all people without exception, even though not all will be saved. Salvation is offered on condition of faith, a condition that sinners can meet because of enabling grace that is universal and prevenient. Stanley Grenz, for instance, makes use of a common illustration: a general amnesty for jailed persons is announced, but only those who personally appropriate the offer walk out of jail. "Until we appropriate the new status he offers us, our Savior's death is of no salvific effect."[25]

A case for particular intention. It is not surprising that Arminians or synergists, in general, assert that Christ died for everyone, making salvation possible for all but not actually achieving it for anyone, since it requires a human act (faith) that is not secured by God's act to complete the saving process. It is surprising, however, that many Calvinistic Baptist theologians balk at asserting that Christ died with the intention of saving the elect alone. Since this form of Calvinism is so common, however, I think it wise to describe briefly my nine chief reasons for believing *that God's intention in sending Christ as a ransom for sin and Christ's intention in laying down his life were to save a great number (possibly the majority) of the sinners who would be conceived in the process of human history and that this is effectively accomplished through the work of the Spirit of God.*

First, *the atonement is effective.* Scripture speaks of Christ actually accomplishing salvation by his death, not just making people savable. Christ ransomed us (Rev 5:9), he obtained eternal redemption (Heb 9:12), and he "gave himself for us that he might redeem us from all iniquity and purify for himself a people of his own who are zealous for good deeds" (Tit 2:14). He "who knew no sin" was "made . . . to be sin," "so that in him we might become the righteousness of God" (2 Cor 5:21), and he "gave himself for our sins to set us free from the present evil age" (Gal 1:4). He "redeemed us from the curse of the law by becoming a curse for us" (Gal 3:13).

If Christ *actually bore* the punishment for sins in a substitutionary way— if he paid the penalty for our sins and if the Father accepted that payment— it would be grossly unjust of him to demand it again from an unbeliever. If he bore the punishment vicariously for everyone, we have full-blown universalism. As John Owen said, if Christ died for the sins of all and if unbelief is a sin, then he died for their unbelief too, in which case they cannot be punished for it. Hence, either unbelief is not a sin or Christ did not die for

---

[25]Stanley J. Grenz, *Theology for the Community of God* (Nashville: Broadman & Holman, 1994), p. 455.

it and his death was, therefore, not universal in its intent and effect.[26]

Some Wesleyan theologians now reject the penal substitutionary view of the atonement because they have come to realize that "the logical conclusion of the penal theory is either universalism or a limited atonement."[27] I believe that this assertion is correct. I wish that many other evangelical Arminians who affirm both universal atonement and penal substitution would realize the incoherence of such a position. I also wish, however, that the many Calvinists who assert that Christ died to save everyone would recognize the problem they generate for themselves when they also state that, in his death, Christ bore the penalty of all for whom he died. Robert Letham rightly points out that

effective atonement + universal intent = universalism

Therefore, universal intent requires limited effectiveness.[28] Grenz continues to speak of substitution, of Christ's death "for us," but he clearly makes it provisional rather than effective.[29] This has significant implications for the conceptualization of what Christ actually accomplished by dying for our sins.

I am reminded of a church that printed on its envelopes the statement "Christ died for you. Have you ever thanked him?" From the pulpit of that church, I frequently heard it said that Christ had died as a substitute for sin, bearing the penalty on behalf of those for whom he died. Few people seemed to be aware of the problem these two messages were creating. Obviously, the envelopes were not only sent to believers in Christ; they were used to mail payments for utility bills, purchases of stationery and so on. Yet all who received the envelope were informed that Christ had died "for them." If those same people heard that in dying "for them" Christ had already paid the penalty for their sins, they could logically conclude that they were now acquitted (that is, justified), and this would have to be so whether or not they were thankful for it. The church could have avoided this problem in a number of ways. The envelopes could have said, "Christ died for sinners. Have you ever thanked him?" That would have left open the possibility that there are some sinners for whom Christ did not die. Al-

---

[26]Letham, *Work of Christ*, p. 232.

[27]H. Ray Dunning, *Grace, Faith and Holiness: A Wesleyan Systematic Theology* (Kansas City, Mo.: Beacon Hill, 1988), p. 363.

[28]Letham, *Work of Christ*, p. 230.

[29]Grenz, *Theology for the Community*, p. 460.

ternatively, if they wanted to continue asserting that Christ died for everyone, they could have stopped preaching that Christ had been a penalty-bearing substitute for everyone for whom he died.

As I recall, it was Charles Spurgeon who used to point out that everyone "limits" the atonement; we either limit its intent or its effect. Either the work of Christ is a narrow bridge that serves only the elect but reaches completely across the gap between sinners and God, or it is a broad bridge that includes everyone but goes only part way across the gap. The human acts of repentance and faith are necessary to get people all the way across.

Unquestionably, Scripture makes statements concerning the death of Christ that use the language of universality, so it is understandable that many Christians, including many who are otherwise Calvinistic (or monergistic), have concluded that we must affirm that Christ died "for" everyone. I suggest, however, that we should formulate our position on the basis of biblical teaching regarding the actual effect *achieved* by Christ's death and resurrection. In that regard, within all the metaphors I briefly identified above, I hear frequent and strong statements that Christ *saved* people. God did not simply make sinners savable, he redeemed them, reconciled them to himself, satisfied the demands of justice on their behalf, paid the penalty for their sin and overcame the powers of evil that bound them. It is also clear, however, that not everyone will be saved. Putting together the strong assertion that Christ saved those for whom he died and that not everyone will be saved, I have had to reexamine the texts that sound initially as though they are stating that Christ died with the intention of saving everyone. If you are interested in how I (and many other Calvinists) understand those texts, you can read appendix one, "A 'Particular Atonement' Reading of the Apparently Universal References Concerning Salvation."

Second, *the completeness of Christ's saving work and the graciousness of salvation are undermined if humans must add something to what Christ did in order to be saved.* Many Christians, as synergists, believe that God and humans cooperate in salvation. Christ died *for* everyone, but only those who trust in him are saved *by* his death. This creates a serious problem. If Christ actually atoned for the sins of no one until people believe, then the atoning effectiveness of Christ's work ultimately rests on the human decision.[30] Thus, there are people for whom Christ died who are not saved by his work, which means that salvation comes about only when we add something to Christ's work. As in the illustration of the bridge, salvation is only

---

[30]Letham, *Work of Christ,* p. 230.

accomplished when people add faith to what Christ has done. Furthermore, it is our additional contribution (faith) that is determinative.

Admittedly, Wesleyans believe that faith is only possible for sinners because of God's enabling grace, which goes before, or precedes, the human act. The problem is that because this prevenient grace is universal, it is not the grace of God but the choice of the human believer that differentiates the saved from the unsaved. It becomes very difficult for monergists to grasp why we should not congratulate those who are saved for their decision to believe—something that Paul specifically rules out when he insists that we are saved by grace through faith, which is not our "own doing" or "the result of works, so that no one may boast" (Eph 2:8-9).

Third, *provisional universal atonement seriously undermines the union with Christ that is the heart of biblical soteriology.* Christ died and rose again for us, and we died and rose again with him. If it turns out that some for whom Christ died and rose again are not raised to eternal life, then it is clear that Christ did not represent anyone and was in the place of no one specifically.[31] But Scripture clearly attests that those for whom Christ died have also died with Christ (Rom 6:3-11; 2 Cor 5:14-15; Eph 2:4-7; Col 3:3) and that those who died with Christ rose again with him (Rom 6:5). Therefore, only those who die to sin and live to righteousness are those for whom Christ died and for whom he rose again.[32] Particularly in the soteriology of the apostle Paul, union with Christ is critical. If everyone died with Christ, then everyone will rise with him, and we have universalism. On the other hand, if only those who believe die with Christ, then Christ only died for *them*. Hence, even an evangelical or Wesleyan Arminian ought to assert particular atonement, regardless of the fact that they consider the decision of faith to be exercised by libertarianly free people who had the power not to believe if they so chose. In other words, the issue here is not between those who believe that election is conditioned on faith and those who believe that faith is the consequence of God's elective grace. The issue is this: for whom did Christ die—for everyone or only for believers?

Fourth, *there are limiting statements in the biblical description of Christ's saving work.* Thus, Scripture speaks of the work of Christ as being for his people (Mt 1:21), for his sheep (Jn 10:11, 15) or for the "church of God that he obtained with the blood of his own Son" (Acts 20:28). "Christ loved the church and gave himself up for her, in order to make her holy by cleansing

---

[31]Ibid., pp. 235-36.
[32]Murray, *Redemption Accomplished*, pp. 69-71.

her" and "present the church to himself in splendor" (Eph 5:25-27). He died in covenant union with his people, and his death brings justification and life (Rom 5:12-21) "at least as surely as Adam's sin brought death and condemnation."[33]

It could rightly be pointed out, of course, that the above passages do not have to be taken exclusively. Christ did die for his people, but that does not mean that he died for no one else. On the other hand, if Ephesians 5:25-27 describes Christ's intention for all people (namely, to make them holy so that he can present them "to himself in splendor," "without a spot or wrinkle"), then he failed to realize his intention. This makes it particularly surprising that so many contemporary Calvinist theologians affirm four of the so-called five points of Calvinism but balk at the statement of Christ's particular intent in atoning for sin.[34] Romans 8:32-39 is even more problematic for the perspective of a universal atonement, for Paul gives assurance of God's preserving care for those for whom Christ died. If God "did not withhold his own Son, but gave him up for all of us," asks Paul, "will he not with him also give us everything else?" To those for whom Christ died, Paul confidently promises justification, Christ's intercession, inseparability from Christ and final victory over all afflictions.

Fifth, *particular intent preserves the co-extensiveness of Christ's sacrificial and intercessory work as two sides of his priestly work.* Two of the priests' primary activities were to offer sacrifices for the sins of the people and to intercede on their behalf. The intercession was made on the basis of the sacrifice. As our great High Priest, Christ offers up his own life—being both priest and sacrifice—and he intercedes for us on the basis of that perfect sacrifice. In his intercessory prayer, in John 17, Jesus prays specifically for those whom the Father gave to him (Jn 17:9) and for "those who will believe" in him through the teaching of the original disciples (Jn 17:20). It is to these people that the Father has given the Son authority to give eternal life (Jn 17:2). He prays that the Father will protect them from the evil one and sanctify them in truth (Jn 17:15, 17) and that they might all be one, with the unity that exists between Father and Son. Thus, in Romans 8:33-34, Paul is confident that Christ intercedes for God's elect, whom God justifies and preserves. Earlier in the chapter, Paul assures the Romans that

---

[33]Letham, *Work of Christ*, p. 245.
[34]The "five points" of Calvinism are often remembered by the acronym TULIP, to designate total depravity, unconditional election, limited atonement, irresistible grace and perseverance of the saints. It is the third of these that "four point Calvinists" usually do not affirm.

the Spirit "intercedes for the saints" (Rom 8:26-27), indicating the harmony between the work of Son and Spirit that we always find in the work of the Trinity. Scripture never speaks of either the Son or Spirit as interceding for anyone but God's people. If God wants everyone to be saved and Christ died for them all, in an attempt to save them, it seems extraordinary that intercession for everyone would not also be offered up by Christ and the Spirit.

Sixth, *by his death, Christ obtained the conditions of application of the benefits of his death—namely, faith and repentance—to his people.* Salvation is conditional on human repentance and faith, but these are secured for the elect by Christ's death for them, which is why we cannot boast about having chosen to believe when others choose not to (Eph 2:8-9). For instance, Paul tells us that "Christ redeemed us . . . in order that in Christ Jesus the blessing of Abraham might come to the Gentiles, so that we might receive the promise of the Spirit through faith" (Gal 3:13-14). God "has blessed us in Christ with every spiritual blessing in the heavenly places, just as he chose us in Christ before the foundation of the world to be holy and blameless before him in love" (Eph 1:3-4). Thus, Paul informed the Philippians that God "has graciously granted you the privilege not only of believing in Christ, but of suffering for him as well" (Phil 1:29). The appearance of "the goodness and loving kindness of God our Savior" brings about the whole complex of salvation, including rebirth, renewal by the Holy Spirit, justification by grace and the hope of eternal life (Tit 3:5-6).

Seventh, *particular intent maintains the parallel between our solidarity with Adam and our solidarity with Christ.* As Neal Punt puts it, Romans 5:15-17

[does] not say that one of the differences between Adam's transgression and Christ's obedience is that the transgression resulted in actual death while the obedience merely established a potential or possibility for life. Instead of making such a distinction, Paul, using the *identical* grammatical construction, makes a parallel application of actual death and actual life in verse 18. Calvinists are unmistakably correct in noting that Romans 5:12 through 21 says "acquittal and life" actually come to all those represented by Christ *just as certainly* as it declares that "sin and death" actually came upon all those represented by Adam.[35]

Eighth, *harmony is maintained within the Trinity when God's saving intent*

---

[35]Punt, *What's Good?* p. 11.

is seen as particular. Those whom God elects and to whom the Holy Spirit applies Christ's saving work are those for whom Jesus died. Again, I find four-point Calvinism very difficult to comprehend. Why would the Son die with the intention of saving those whom the Father had not chosen to salvation and whom the Spirit would not effectually call? In the economy of the triune Godhead, the three persons always work in complete harmony. As Letham notes, it is significant that Episcopius, leader of the Remonstrants at Dort, did reject the Trinity.[36]

Ninth, *evangelical Arminians share with Calvinists the belief that even though God, in some sense, wills the salvation of all people, they are not all saved.* They simply differ concerning what it is that God values more highly than the salvation of everyone, which accounts for the fact that some are not saved. This point was made by Jonathan Edwards centuries ago:

> All must own that God sometimes wills not to hinder the breach of his own commands, because he does not in fact hinder it. . . . But you will say, God wills to permit sin, as he wills the creature should be left to his freedom; and if he should hinder it, he would offer violence to the nature of his own creature. I answer, this comes nevertheless to the very same thing that I say. You say, God does not will sin absolutely; but rather than alter the law of nature and the nature of free agents, he wills it. He wills what is contrary to excellency in some particulars, for the sake of a more general excellency and order. So that the scheme of the Arminians does not help the matter.[37]

John Piper puts the point succinctly: "God wills not to save all, even though he is willing to save all, because there is something else that he wills more, which would be lost if he exerted his sovereign power to save all."[38] For Arminians, this higher commitment by God is to "human self-determination and the possible resulting love relationship with God." To Calvinists, it is "the manifestation of the full range of God's glory in wrath and mercy (Rom 9:22-23) and the humbling of man so that he enjoys giving all credit to God for his salvation (1 Cor 1:29)."[39]

---

[36]Letham, *Work of Christ*, p. 237.

[37]Jonathan Edwards, "Concerning the Decrees in General, and Election in Particular," in *The Works of Jonathan Edwards* (Edinburgh: Banner of Truth Trust, 1974), 2:529, quoted in John Piper, "Are There Two Wills in God?" in *Still Sovereign: Contemporary Perspectives on Election, Foreknowledge and Grace,* ed. Thomas R. Schreiner and Bruce A. Ware (Grand Rapids, Mich.: Baker, 2000), p. 123.

[38]Piper, "Are There Two Wills?" p. 123.

[39]Ibid., p. 124.

UNIVERSAL EFFECTS OF THE SAVING WORK OF CHRIST

Up to this point, I have been specifically addressing the question of whom Christ died to save, but it is important to recognize that the eternal salvation of believers is not the only benefit derived from Christ's life, death and resurrection. In fact, there is no one in the world—regardless of one's religious affiliation, one's ignorance or knowledge of Christ, one's submission to or rebellion against Christ—who does not experience benefits of the grace of God that are grounded in Christ's incarnate work.

First, we need to recall that the redemptive work of Christ is *sufficient* for every one. No further sacrifice would be necessary for everyone to be saved. Second, the death of Christ is *to be proclaimed to all* because there is no other means of salvation. The free offer of the gospel by Christian witnesses is sincere because it is true. Whoever trusts in Christ will be saved. Letham proposes that the relationship between the particularity and the universality of the atonement is like the wave and particle theories of light. Both are true though they seem self-contradictory. The intent of Christ's atoning was for the elect, but its worth and scope were sufficient for everyone. God's "sovereign election of some, however, stands side by side with his expressed will that sinners should repent and be saved."[40] Hence, we invite sinners to repent, and we assure them that if they do, they will be saved because Christ died for them.

Third, the atonement has cosmic outworkings, for the *renovation of the entire universe* is grounded on the atonement. Christ's *decisive victory* over Satan and the fallen angels through his resurrection and ascension has implications much wider than salvation; this constitutes a fourth benefit extending beyond the company of the elect. Fifth, and perhaps most obvious, are the *kindnesses of God* that sinners experience though they do not deserve to. Reformed theologians refer to this as "common grace." All the good things that the unregenerate experience are undeserved and are, therefore, possible only because of the grace of God that derives from Christ's mediatorial work. This includes the general order of nature, which provides for human needs (Job 37:13; Ps 65:9; Mt 5:45; Acts 14:17), and God's sustaining the existence of living things (Ps 36:6; Is 42:5; Acts 17:28), including provision of what they need for survival, such as food, water and shelter (Gen 27:28; Ps 65:9; 104:14). These generate a measure of gladness, even in the unsaved (Acts 14:17). God's facilitating of what is

---

[40]Letham, *Work of Christ*, p. 246.

true and good in philosophy, arts, science and technology (Ex 31:2-11; 35:30-35) is a further fruit of this "common" grace of God accomplished for sinners in the righteous satisfaction of Christ.

Sixth, we must mention the *restraint of the power of sin* within human relationships (Gen 6:3; Rom 13:1-4; 2 Thess 2:6-7; cf. 1 Sam 16:14), including the maintenance of the social and political order. Nor can we forget, as a seventh benefit of Christ's work, the *patience of God,* for he does not immediately execute judgment on sinners in spite of their rebellion (Gen 8:21-22; Rom 2:4). This grace of God is intended to lead to repentance (Rom 2:4). All of these benefits have been commonly affirmed in Reformed theological treatments of common grace. To them, I now add two others for your consideration.

As an eighth universal blessing proceeding from Christ's work of atonement, I suggest that it covers all of the *unintentional sins* that are committed both by those who are saved and by those who are not. This proposal follows from a couple of assumptions that I will revisit later: all disobedience against God's moral law incurs *objective* guilt, but God only holds people accountable for their *subjective* guilt, that is, for the things they do in willful rebellion. Some of these acts are objectively wrong and some are not, but they are all sins, by virtue of the agent's intention. (I will expand on this point in chapter seven.) Since the sins for which people are not held accountable are still sins, in an objective sense, they need to be atoned for and forgiven. I postulate that these sins were covered by Christ's death, so that God is able to judge us only for those sins that we do in conscious violation of our conscience, that is, in rebellion against what we believe to be God's moral will in a situation.

On the Day of Atonement, the high priest made atonement for the sanctuary "because of the uncleannesses of the people of Israel, and because of their transgression, all their sins" (Lev 16:16). I assume that this includes both the sins they had done intentionally ("with a high hand") and those of which they were ignorant. All of those transgressions of God's moral will had polluted the holy place in the tabernacle or the temple, which was God's special dwelling place among the people. The writer to the Hebrews saw the earthly tabernacle as patterned after the heavenly one and pictured Christ's perfect sacrifice as purifying the heavenly sanctuary. He seems to have envisioned human sin as polluting the very dwelling place of God, which then needed to be cleansed by Christ's righteous sacrifice. I assume that this included the totality of the sins of God's people, those committed both consciously and unconsciously, but it seems necessary to me that the unconsciously committed sins of unbelievers must also be dealt with by the sacrifice of Christ, since they are not charged against the human agents that commit them. Perhaps there is a progression in John's mind, in 1 John 1:7-9: First, he tells us that "the blood of Jesus [God's] Son cleanses us from all sin," but then he goes on to speak about the sins of which we are aware and which need to be confessed so that they can be forgiven and cleansed.[41] Admittedly, John's first statement is made concerning those who walk in the light, but if it does imply that "all sin" is a larger category than that which is conscious and confessed, then the principle of distinguishing between two aspects of Christ's cleansing is established.

The last benefit coming to all people from Christ's death is what I will refer to as "universal enabling grace." I will develop this concept in chapter eleven, where I will argue that at least once in every person's life, one receives an enabling by the Holy Spirit so that one *could* respond in saving faith to the revelation of God that has been given, if one *would* do so.

SUMMING UP

To recapitulate, everyone needs to be saved, but there is only one Savior for all of humankind, Jesus Christ, the Righteous One. Because Christ is the Lamb who was slain before the foundation of the world, all of God's saving work among the peoples of the world, in all times and places, has been objectively accomplished in and through the one act of obedience of the incarnate Son of God. All sinners who will stand before God in the final judgment and hear God's wonderful declaration that they are found not guilty will be justified because Christ completely obeyed the righteous demands of God in all the ways that they did not. They will be invited to live with God forever in the glorious new earth and heaven because they died to sin and rose again to new life in union with Christ.

We say that someone *was* saved, or *is* now saved, but the fullness of salvation is something that still lies ahead of us. The saved are people who once were lost but now have been found; they were blind but now see; they were dead in sin but now are alive in Christ. All of this was accomplished for us totally by God's grace through a work of the triune God; having been chosen by the Father, God's people were redeemed by the Son who gave his life for those whom the Father chose in him; they were illumined, regenerated and sanctified by the Spirit.

---

[41]I am indebted to my colleague, Edmund Neufeld, for stimulating my reflection in this matter and for suggesting the significance of John's way of speaking in this text.

So then, everyone needs to be saved, and the Word became flesh, lived a perfect life, died a sinless death and was raised from the dead to accomplish salvation for those whom the Father chose in him. Adam, Noah, Job, Abraham and David, who all lived before Christ, were saved because of Christ's sacrifice for them. None of them knew what we now know about the triune nature of God or the means by which God reconciles sinners to himself, but they were saved by Christ's work nevertheless. We are left wondering, however, about the many people who had no contact with any of these figures familiar to us because of the biblical record. When Abraham was called, there were people in North America and Australia who were completely ignorant of God's covenant promises to Abraham. Must we conclude that all of those people were outside God's saving purposes, that none of them were among the elect? What about people who do not hear the good news concerning what Christ has done to save sinners even now? Must we assume that God has not chosen even one of them to salvation? On the other hand, if some of the elect were among those who had no contact with revelation concerning God's covenant with sinners, how was God making himself known to them and what did he ask of (and give to) them by way of an acceptable response that would constitute "saving faith"? Furthermore, how significant are the nonsaving benefits of God's gracious work in Christ to such people? To such questions we now proceed.

6

To Whom Does God Reveal Himself?

Thesis 4: People experience the salvation that God has accomplished in Christ only when they respond to God in a way that satisfies him, which the Bible calls "faith." Therefore, God makes himself known to all people, but not everyone receives an equally full revelation. God reveals his being and work and something of his moral nature to everyone (i.e., "generally"). He does this by his works of creation and providence and through the moral consciousness and intrinsic religiousness of human beings. Thus, no one lacks the revelation necessary to elicit a response to God. But a much fuller revelation of God's nature, purposes and work has been made to particular individuals whom God uses to establish a covenant people (both old and new). This community and its members then serve as instruments of God's special revelation in the world, so that the effects of salvation can be extended to all areas of an individual's life and for the well-being of human society. God also reveals himself to particular individuals in a manner that is neither related to the formation of his covenant people nor universally normative. As with every form of God's special revelation, individuals' response to that revelation is part of their fundamental orientation of faith or unbelief in God.

Thesis 5: Whatever information, religious or moral, a person accepts as ultimately authoritative truth (whether this is understood to be from a personal God or not) must be believed and obeyed. It makes a claim upon that person. Just as one is obligated to obey one's moral conscience, so one is required to believe one's religious consciousness.

WE HAVE SEEN THAT GOD HAS DONE EVERYTHING NECESSARY to objectively accomplish the salvation of needy and helpless sinners through the life, death and resurrection of Christ. But in order for people to experience the benefits of this saving work, they must respond positively to God and his overtures to them. Consequently, God must make himself known to people in order to elicit a response. One of the pressing questions arising out of our general query, Who can be saved? is, therefore, whether everyone receives the revelation they need in order to believe and be saved. Might there be some sinners who never know the information they would need to be saved? Ecclesiocentrists believe that this is so, that the unevangelized (people who are ignorant of the gospel) cannot be saved. In this chapter, therefore, we will examine the ways in which God makes himself known to people. This will lay the groundwork for my later proposal that God gives to every human being a revelation sufficient to elicit saving faith, provided they are enabled by grace. In other words, no one who will be eternally condemned will have lacked the revelation or the enabling to be saved; no one will be lost through no fault of their own.

I recognize that ecclesiocentrists have appealed to the irrevocable lostness of the unevangelized in order to motivate people to be involved in evangelistic mission. They often state their fear that accessibilism will cut the nerve of missionary motivation. I will respond to that important concern in chapter twelve, but first we need to consider the reasons for believing that even the unevangelized can be saved. We start with the matter of divine revelation, without which no one could be saved.

THE NECESSITY OF DIVINE SELF-REVELATION

Knowledge of God has never been possible apart from God's will to be known and his disclosure of himself. As a text like 1 John 1:1-3 indicates, revelation was not the product of human seeking or imagination but a divine gift to creatures who otherwise have only distorted ideas about the divine: we were "dead" in our sins and "darkened in our understanding" of God when God took the initiative to open our eyes and ears to see God's reality and redemptive designs (Eph 2:1; 4:18; cf. Mt 11:25-27; 16:17; 2 Cor 4:6). Apart from revelation, our speculations about the divine are only "foolishness" and in fact contradict true knowledge of God (Rom 1:21-26; 1 Cor 2:14).[1]

UNIVERSAL OR "GENERAL" REVELATION

Graciously, God has left no one without witness of himself, but not everyone has been given an equally full revelation of God. Commonly, we distinguish between general and special revelation to indicate the difference between the knowledge that God gives of himself to all people everywhere

---

[1] Gerald R. McDermott, *Can Evangelicals Learn from World Religions? Jesus, Revelation and Religious Traditions* (Downers Grove, Ill.: InterVarsity Press, 2000), pp. 46-47.

and the knowledge that he gives more particularly on special occasions.[2]

Creation. The first way by which God speaks universally is through his creative work in the physical world (Job 36:24—37:24; 38:1—39:30; Ps 19:1-6; 104; 148; Rom 1:18-21). Psalm 19:4, in particular, says that the voice of God in the cosmos "goes out through all the earth, and [his] words to the end of the world," which "seems to speak of God's revelation going to those who have not heard the Lord of Israel—not just to Israelites, as Barth had suggested."[3] According to Romans 1:19-20, "God communicates to every person individually ('to them') through what can be seen in the world."[4] Just as the invisible God is visibly proclaimed in Jesus (Col 1:15-16), so "the God who cannot be seen is visibly proclaimed by what God created."[5] God's invisible qualities, his everlasting power and deity, can be seen clearly or plainly. "In other words, when creation is contemplated with a receptive will, which looks to discern the significance of creation, then God's unseen nature can be seen distinctly."[6]

To describe this knowledge which God has made available to all people, Paul uses the term *ginōskō*, which "can refer to personal experiential knowledge of theological truths as in knowledge of peace (Rom 3:17), sin (Rom 7:7; 2 Cor 5:21), grace (2 Cor 8:9), God's will (Rom 2:18), or God's wisdom (1 Cor 2:8)" or to "experiential knowledge of a person" (Rom 11:34; 1 Cor 1:21; 2:11; 4:19; 8:3; 2 Cor 5:16; Gal 4:9).[7] "Paul is saying that humans can have an experiential knowledge of God by contemplating God's creation."[8] Paul speaks of this universal revelation to make the point that the Gentiles, who do not have the inspired scriptures, can still be guilty before God because God has made himself known to them. Hence,

---

[2]Admittedly, as Hendrik Kraemer noted, "every kind of revelation is a 'special' revelation" (*Religion and the Christian Faith* [London: Lutterworth, 1956], p. 353, quoted in Tim S. Perry, *Radical Difference: A Defence of Hendrik Kraemer's Theology of Religions*, Editions SR, ed. H. Martin Rumscheidt and Theodore S de Bruyn [Waterloo, Ontario: Wilfrid Laurier University Press, 2001], 27:80). But we need to recognize that God reveals himself to all people in certain ways, while other acts of his revelation are addressed more limitedly to particular individuals or groups. Kraemer preferred to call this "original revelation" or "fundamental revelation" (Perry, *Radical Difference*, 27:80).

[3]McDermott, *Can Evangelicals Learn*, p. 54.

[4]Aída Besançon Spencer, "Romans 1: Finding God in Creation," in *Through No Fault of Their Own? The Fate of Those Who Have Never Heard*, ed. William V. Crockett and James G. Sigountos (Grand Rapids, Mich.: Baker, 1991), p. 126.

[5]Ibid., p. 127.

[6]Ibid.

[7]Ibid., pp. 128-29.

[8]Ibid., p. 129.

they are without excuse when they do not honor God as God but instead worship the things that God has made, or when they do not give him thanks for his provisions, that is, when they do not respond to God's self-revelation in praise and thanksgiving (Rom 1:21).

Particularly significant, from our perspective as Christians, who know the fullness of God's speaking in the last days, in the Son (Heb 1:2), is the fact that creation is a mediatory work of the Son (Gen 1:3; Jn 1:3; cf. 1 Cor 8:6; Col 1:16; Heb 1:3). Telford Work draws out Athanasius's point that

> though the *logos* came to creation in a fundamentally new way in the incarnation, nevertheless "he was not far from it before, for no part of creation had ever been without Him Who, while ever abiding in union with the Father, yet fills all things that are." By virtue of this participation, the works of creation are a "means by which the Maker might be known"—by "pondering the harmony of creation." For Athanasius, what we call general revelation and natural theology are grounded Christologically. Creation's power to signify derives from the creative agency of the *logos*.[9]

Similarly, Donald Macleod observes that Christianity has no difficulty assimilating the fact of "overlap between Christianity and world religions." Christians believe that no one knows the Father except through the Son (Mt 11:27), but we also believe that "the Old Testament is revelatory precisely because the Spirit of Christ spoke in the prophets (1 Pet 1:11); and that creation is revelatory precisely because the aeons were made through the divine Son (Heb 1:2)."[10]

Moral consciousness. The second means by which God reveals himself to all people is through the individual moral conscience (Rom 2:14-15) and the innate consciousness of the existence of God that is the root cause of the intrinsic religiousness of humankind (Acts 17:22-31), created in God's own image (Gen 1:26-27). As to the former, the moral consciousness, Romans 2:14-15 teaches us that although the Gentiles do not have the law of Moses (special revelation), they do "by nature" (NIV) or "instinctively" (NRSV) the things that are contained in the law because the work of the law is written on their hearts. Commonly, this text, along with Romans 1:32, is understood as indicating that humans have an innate knowledge of the law. I am

---

[9]Telford Work, *Living and Active: Scripture in the Economy of Salvation,* Sacra Doctrina (Grand Rapids, Mich.: Eerdmans, 2002), p. 38, quoting Athanasius *On the Incarnation of the Word* 8, 12.

[10]Donald Macleod, *The Person of Christ,* Contours of Christian Theology (Downers Grove, Ill.: InterVarsity Press, 1998), p. 239.

inclined to concur with Mark Mathewson, however, that nothing in either of these texts "insists that the law is an innate part of the human makeup. Paul simply asserts that humans generally have some degree of knowledge that the actions and behaviors of which he speaks in 1:21-31 violate God's moral standard and deserve punishment."[11] Mathewson proposes that "what is part of the human's constitutional makeup is the cognitive ability to grasp or apprehend the law,"[12] that "humans are born with a natural ability of the mind to grasp immediately God's moral demands in an a priori manner."[13] Conscience is an "inner tribunal which determines whether behavior (in the broad sense, including thinking, willing, speaking and acting) agrees with the moral norms and requirements affirmed by the mind and which testifies of this verdict to the subject."[14]

Two difficult questions arise if the moral knowledge is considered to be innate: First, how can we conceptualize any knowledge as innate? And second, what is the content of the law innately known?[15] Consequently, it seems better to view this moral cognitive ability as parallel to the innate ability we have to grasp physical reality in Romans 1. Our knowledge of God's creation is not something innate in humans. Rather, we are "born with the capacities to apprehend immediately and directly and non-inferentially know the created order around us." Similarly, we are born "with the capacity to perceive moral reality (God's moral demands) immediately and directly and come to non-inferentially know it." In neither case, then, is our knowledge of the reality innate to us.[16] This ability is part of our being created in the image of God, and it is negatively affected by the Fall, so our moral knowledge is not trustworthy and will vary from one person to another (1 Cor 8:7-12; 10:25-29). There is no guarantee that we have intuited moral principles or judgments correctly.[17]

As a result of either innate moral knowledge or the natural capacity to apprehend the moral order, we all have some knowledge of God's moral demands, and we are obligated to live according to that knowledge, how-

---

[11]Mark D. Mathewson, "Moral Intuitionism and the Law Inscribed on Our Hearts," *Journal of the Evangelical Theological Society* 42 (December 1999): 631.

[12]Ibid., p. 630.

[13]Ibid., p. 633.

[14]J. M. Gundry-Volf, "Conscience," in *Dictionary of Paul and His Letters*, ed. Gerald F. Hawthorne, Ralph P. Martin and Daniel G. Reid (Downers Grove, Ill.: InterVarsity Press, 1993), p. 153.

[15]Mathewson, "Moral Intuitionism," p. 632.

[16]Ibid., p. 633.

[17]Ibid., p. 641.

ever wrong it may be, following the dictates of our consciences. Paul urges Christians not to repay evil for evil "but [to] take thought for what is noble *in the sight of all*" (Rom 12:17, emphasis mine). I assume that this is witness to the objective fact of the divinely created moral order and to the fact that sin has not completely obliterated some remnant common moral judgment. It is clear, however, that there are also significant differences in what people in different contexts consider to be obviously or naturally immoral or moral. Yet everyone has a conscience, a sense of obligation, a sense of the moral rightness of certain kinds of behavior. Even "evil" parents know how to give good gifts to their children (Mt 7:11), and the universal human practice of marriage is testimony to the preservation of the creational order (Mt 19:1-9; Mk 10:1-9). This helps us to understand some of the similarity of moral teaching that we encounter between different cultures and the religions that predominate within them, but it also accounts for the differences that occur.

Religious consciousness. In addition to the universal occurrence of moral consciousness, everyone also has a sense of deity *(sensus deitatis)*, a religious consciousness. This is the basis of human religion (cf. Acts 17:22-31). Because humans are themselves revelational of God (Gen 1:27), they are able to receive divine revelation. It is possible that John 1:4, 9 offers further testimony to a universal illumination of human intellectual and moral faculties by the Logos. Macleod observes that "many theologians of unobjectionable orthodoxy have taken this to refer to a work of Christ, the eternal *Logos*, in the heart of Everyman,"[18] and he cites John Calvin's statement that

> from this *light* the rays are diffused over all mankind. . . . For we know that men have this particular excellence which raises them above other animals, that they are endued with reason and intelligence, and that they carry the distinction between right and wrong engraven on their conscience. There is no man, therefore, whom some perception of eternal *light* does not reach.[19]

To Macleod's mind, "the presence of this *light* gives a perfectly coherent explanation, from the standpoint of Christian exclusivism, for all that is true and valuable in the religions of the world."[20]

---

[18]Macleod, *Person of Christ*, p. 239.

[19]John Calvin, *Commentary on the Gospel of John* (Edinburgh: Calvin Translation Society, 1847), 1:38, quoted in Macleod, *Person of Christ*, p. 240.

[20]More recently, this reading of John 1:9 has been affirmed by Bruce Demarest and Gordon Lewis (*Integrative Theology* [Grand Rapids, Mich.: Zondervan, 1987], 1:71), and they cite R. V. G. Tasker and William Plummer in support of the idea.

More cautiously, D. A. Carson states that "it might be better and simpler to say that John 1:9 insists that the Word of God, the incarnate Jesus, enlightens everyone without distinction"[21] rather than to speak of him as enlightening every human person. On the other hand, given that creation reveals God through the mediating activity of the Logos, so that the Word does make God known to every person, it would not be surprising if the Word was also active in enlightening the creatures who bear God's image. Though illumination is usually referred to the Spirit within the divine economy, the close relationship that Christ describes between his own work and that of the Spirit, whom he will send from the Father, prevents us from drawing too hard a line between the work of Son and Spirit (Jn 15:26; 16:7-14).

William Temple wrote:

> From the beginning divine light has shone; it has always enlightened every man alive in his reason and his conscience. Every check on animal lust felt by the primitive savage, every stimulation to a nobler life, is God self-revealed within his soul. But God in self-revelation is the Divine Word, for precisely this is what that term means.[22]

For Lesslie Newbigin there is here an affirmation "that the presence and work of Jesus are not confined within the area where he is acknowledged."[23] The idea is also latent in the work of early Greek theologians like Justin Martyr, who spoke of the "Word implanted" *(logos emphytos)* in pagans[24] and stated that "all who have thought and acted rationally and rightly have participated in Christ the universal Logos."[25]

Clement of Alexandria spoke of the Old Testament and Greek philosophy as "two tributaries of one great river."[26]

On the basis of Hebrews (1:1) he asserts that it was to the whole of mankind

---

[21]D. A. Carson, *The Gagging of God: Christianity Confronts Pluralism* (Grand Rapids, Mich.: Zondervan, 1996), p. 303.

[22]William Temple, *Readings in St. John's Gospel,* quoted in R. W. F. Wootton, *Christianity and Other Faiths: An Evangelical Contribution to Our Multi-Faith Society* (Exeter: Paternoster, 1983), p. 20.

[23]Lesslie Newbigin, *The Open Secret: An Introduction to the Theology of Mission,* rev. ed. (Grand Rapids, Mich.: Eerdmans, 1995), p. 174. Clark Pinnock also affirms this; see *A Wideness in God's Mercy: The Finality of Jesus Christ in a World of Religions* (Grand Rapids, Mich.: Zondervan, 1992).

[24]Justin Martyr *1 Apology* 46.

[25]Justin Martyr *2 Apology* 10, 13.

[26]Clement of Alexandria *Stromata* 1.28-29; 4.67, 117.

and not only to Israel that "God spoke in former times in fragmentary and varied fashion." Mankind as a whole is subject to a process of education (a pedagogy: we should remember that, for Paul, the pedagogue was the Law and the pupil in his care was Israel). It is not a case here of a natural or a rational law, for "the *Logos* of God . . . ordered our world, and above all this microcosm man, through the Holy Spirit."[27]

Clement saw the philosophy of the Greeks as "given to the Greeks as their Testament."[28] Pagan and Greek philosophies are "scattered fragments of a single whole which is the *Logos*."[29] Irenaeus asserted that "there is only one God who from beginning to end, through various economies, comes to the help of mankind,"[30] and "Gregory Nazianzus declared that a number of philosophers, like Plato and Aristotle 'caught a glimpse of the Holy Spirit.'"[31]

Providence. The fourth way in which God makes himself known to everyone is through his providential work, which includes his upholding of all that he has created (Col 1:17), his kindness in providential care for all his creatures (Mt 5:45; Acts 14:17) and his ordering of the affairs of nations, which is specifically done in hope that people will reach out for God (Acts 17:26-27; cf. God's working through the Assyrians [Is 10:5-6] and the Chaldeans [Hab 1:5-6]). A continual reminder (both to us and to God) of God's covenant to preserve creation is the rainbow, but this is a sign whose covenantal significance is understood only by believers (Gen 9:16-17). Malachi 1:11 says: "For from the rising of the sun to its setting my name is great among the nations, and in every place incense is offered to my name, and a pure offering; for my name is great among the nations." R. W. F. Wootton notes that "the context requires the present tense, not the future, and any reference to a wide-spread Jewish dispersion—'from furthest east to furthest west'—is inappropriate in the fifth century B.C. when Malachi was writing."[32] John V. Taylor wonders whether it might be

likely that this haunting reference to the rising and going down of the sun was in the mind of Jesus when he pointed to the faith of the Roman centu-

---

[27]Georges Khodr, "The Economy of the Holy Spirit," in *Faith Meets Faith,* Mission Trends, ed. Gerald H. Anderson and Thomas F. Stransky (Grand Rapids, Mich.: Eerdmans, 1981), 5:39; citing Clement of Alexandria *Protreptikos* 1:5.

[28]Clement of Alexandria *Stromata* 5.8.3.

[29]Khodr, "Economy of the Holy Spirit," 5:39.

[30]Irenaeus *Against Heresies* 3.12-13.

[31]Khodr, "Economy of the Holy Spirit," 5:40; citing Gregory of Nazianzus *Oratio in laudem Basilii* 31.5.

[32]Wootton, *Christianity and Other Faiths,* p. 18.

rion, saying: "Many shall come from the East and from the West and shall sit down with Abraham and Isaac and Jacob in the Kingdom of heaven, but the sons of the Kingdom shall be cast out into outer darkness" (Matthew 8:11-12). The Church cannot read those words today without applying them to itself, and, indeed, they strike at the heart of all exclusive religious claims.[33]

It is this general revelation of God to all people that helps us to account for the fact that many of the adherents of religions which are officially nontheistic nevertheless pray as if there were a god. Ajith Fernando notes:

> Mahayana Buddhists [the majority within Buddhism] worship the Buddha and the *Bodhisattvas* and address their prayers to them as they would to gods. Hinayana Buddhism is practiced in countries such as Sri Lanka, Burma, Thailand, and Cambodia. It prides itself in being closer to the teachings of the Buddha and the early Buddhist (Pali) scriptures. Yet Buddhists belonging to this branch have also included the divine factor into the practice of their religion. Many Buddhists of Sri Lanka have literally deified the Buddha, a practice he would have opposed. These Buddhists often talk about the gods who protect them.[34]

J. H. Bavinck notes that "each person, no matter how deeply fallen and how far departed, still is within the reach of God's common grace. God has not left himself without a witness."[35] He then cites Romans 1:19 and observes that God has had a great deal to do with people even before they have any contact with a missionary, prompting them to wonder anxiously if they might be on a false path.

> A missionary who worked for years in the prison of Pretoria among the Bantu natives who were condemned to death, says in one of his writings, "When a person moves every day in a terrain where only the fundamental things remain, wherever he tries to serve as an instrument in God's hands, he discovers with moving surprise that God has already been at work in this soul. No matter how strange this may sound, I have frequently found God in the soul of the South African Bantu. Certainly, it is not the full revelation of the Father. But nevertheless, God himself is the one who lies hidden behind a curtain, as a shadowy figure, but the main outline is visible. A surpris-

---

[33]John V. Taylor, "The Theological Basis of Interfaith Dialogue," in *Faith Meets Faith*, Mission Trends, ed. Gerald H. Anderson and Thomas F. Stransky (Grand Rapids, Mich.: Eerdmans, 1981), 5:99-100.

[34]Ajith Fernando, *The Christian's Attitude Toward World Religions* (Wheaton, Ill.: Tyndale, 1987), pp. 106-7.

[35]J. H. Bavinck, *An Introduction to the Science of Missions*, trans. David Hugh Freeman (Kampen: J. H. Kok, 1954; Philadelphia: Presbyterian & Reformed, 1960), p. 227.

ing and glorious experience! And when I experienced the moment that a soul surrenders, I understood that the Master had been there earlier."[36]

SPECIFIC REVELATION TO PARTICULAR INDIVIDUALS

Biblical instances within the covenant. Even before sin occurred, God made more particular revelation of his person and will by speaking with Adam and Eve (Gen 1:28-30; 2:16-17). This divine speaking continued after Adam and Eve's sin, when it took the form of pronouncing judgment on the first sinners but also of announcing God's gracious plan for overcoming sin (Gen 3:9-19). God then continued to speak quite immediately to specific individuals (Gen 4:9-15; 6:13-7:4), and eventually he established a special covenantal relationship with Abraham and particular descendants whom he chose (Gen 12:1-3; 26:24; 28:13-15; Rom 9:6-13). The purpose of this covenant was not simply the salvation of Abraham and his family but the blessing of the world through God's testimony in the life and preservation of his people and, ultimately, through the Messiah who would come from the line of Abraham and bring salvation to humankind.

When God intervened in history to deliver Israel from bondage in Egypt, he chose Moses to be his representative and began a pattern of speaking to his people, as well as to other nations, through designated prophets (Heb 1:1). To communicate to these prophets, God used a number of different forms of revelation, including speech (audible or inaudible), visions and dreams (Gen 12:1—25:8; Acts 9:3-5; 16:9-10; 27:23-24; Gal 1:11-12, 16; 2:2).[37] Some of these prophets were instructed to write down their prophecies; and, when they did so, the Holy Spirit worked in them (2 Pet 1:19, 21) so that those writings became themselves the permanent, authoritative and normative revelation of God (2 Tim 3:16-17). In the most complete way possible, God the Son ultimately revealed the Godhead by taking human form (Jn 1:14-18; Heb 1:2-3). Eyewitnesses of this revelation and others who knew eyewitnesses were further inspired by the Spirit of God to write additional works that had the same divine authority as those of the pre-Christian scriptures (1 Pet 1:10-12; 2 Pet 3:15-16; 1 Tim 5:18).

Biblical instances outside the covenant. In addition to God's normal means of making himself known through the written and preached scriptures, there are instances of other fascinating forms of communication, in-

---

[36]Ibid.; citing H. Ph. Junod, *Condamnation à mort et message de vie* (Lausanne: Mission Suisse dans l'Afrique du Sud, 1950), pp. 35-36.

[37]J. N. D. Anderson, *Christianity and World Religions: The Challenge of Pluralism* (Downers Grove, Ill.: InterVarsity Press, 1984), p. 150.

cluding some using people outside the covenant community. Abimelech received a message from the one true God rebuking him for taking Abraham's wife Sarah (Gen 20:1-3). Joseph told the Egyptian Pharaoh that God had "revealed to Pharaoh what he [was] about to do" (Gen 41:25, 28). God spoke to Balaam in a way that is not described (Num 22:9); he was a "heathen diviner who accepted a fee to curse the people of God from the altar of Baal," but "that did not prevent the Spirit of God from coming upon him so that in the end he offered a divine blessing" (Num 23:11; 24:2-9).[38] He accurately delivered the word of God more than four times,[39] and yet Balaam himself gives no evidence of God's saving work in his life and was "among those killed when God asked the Israelites to take vengeance on the Midianites (Numbers 31:1-8)."[40]

King Hyram of Tyre told Solomon that he knew it was the God of Israel who made the heaven and the earth (2 Chron 2:11-12).[41] When Pharaoh Neco of Egypt "went up to fight at Carchemish on the Euphrates" (2 Chron 35:20), Josiah, king of Judah, went out against him. Neco told Josiah that this was unnecessary since he was not making war on Judah and told Josiah, "God has commanded me to hurry. Cease opposing God, who is with me, so that he will not destroy you" (2 Chron 35:21). The chronicler then tells us that Josiah "did not listen to the words of Neco from the mouth of God, but joined battle in the plain of Megiddo" (2 Chron 35:22). As C. F. Keil notes, "the God who had commanded Pharaoh to make haste, and whom Josiah was not to go against, is not an Egyptian god . . . but the true God, as is clear from verse 22."[42] This does not mean, however, that God had spoken directly or through a human messenger to Neco, although Neco was anxious to convince Josiah that God did not want him to intervene. In retrospect, after the battle, in which Josiah was in fact killed, the chronicler recognizes Neco's warning as from God. In any event, it is significant to our current analysis that the chronicler did not hesitate to describe words attributed to God (Elohim) by Neco, as "words . . . from the mouth of God."

The Lord "stirred up the spirit" of Cyrus, the king of Persia, to send the

---

[38]Daniel Clendenin, *Many Gods, Many Lords* (Grand Rapids, Mich.: Baker, 1995), p. 133.

[39]Walter C. Kaiser Jr., *Mission in the Old Testament: Israel as a Light to the Nations* (Grand Rapids, Mich.: Baker, 2000), p. 41.

[40]Fernando, *Christian's Attitude*, p. 138.

[41]McDermott, *Can Evangelicals Learn*, p. 79.

[42]C. F. Keil and F. Delitzsch, *Biblical Commentary on the Old Testament: The Books of the Chronicles* (Grand Rapids, Mich.: Eerdmans, 1966), p. 505.

Jews back to their land and to build the temple. Cyrus declares in a written edict that "the LORD [Yahweh], the God of heaven, has given me all the kingdoms of the earth, and he has charged me to build him a house at Jerusalem, which is in Judah" (2 Chron 36:23; cf. Ezra 1:2). Cyrus then refers to this God, however, as "the God of Israel . . . the God who is in Jerusalem" (Ezra 1:3), and Cyrus has other gods in whose house were stored the treasures that had been taken from Jerusalem by Nebuchadnezzar (Ezra 1:7). There is no suggestion here that Cyrus had been led to monotheistic worship of Yahweh, but clearly God worked in his mind and spirit, prompting him to send the Jews back and to support them in reestablishing their house of worship. From the perspective of the Isaiah's prediction, Cyrus was God's "shepherd" who would carry out all God's purposes (Is 44:28); Cyrus was the Lord's "anointed" (Is 45:1).

When Nebuchadnezzer was choosing between his options for conquest—Rabbah of the Ammonites or Judah and Jerusalem—he used his habitual means of divination. He shook arrows, consulted the teraphim (oracular deities) and examined a liver. God purposed to use Nebuchadnezzar as his instrument of judgment against Jerusalem, and so he determined the outcome of Nebuchadnezzar's pagan methods for discerning the right course of action (Ezek 21:18-23). This is obviously not because God approves of such divination or authorizes it as a means by which we might discern his will. But, as Keil says, "all that is proved by this fact is, that even heathenism is subject to the rule and guidance of Almighty God, and is made subservient to the accomplishment of the plans of both His kingdom and His salvation."[43] Unquestionably, it is the teaching of Scripture that God directed Nebuchadnezzar toward Jerusalem but used Nebuchadnezzar's pagan means of seeking direction. Unusual though the means were, this was an instance of divine direction or "revelation," what we might consider providential direction.

God later spoke to Nebuchadnezzar in dreams and gave the interpretation of these to Daniel (Dan 2:1, 29-45), and Nebuchadnezzar made several "startling confessions of faith" (Dan 2:47; 3:28-29; 4:34, 37).[44] God gave a vision to Belshazzar and again gave the interpretation to Daniel (Dan 5:5). Darius acknowledged that Yahweh is the living God and ordered his subjects to "tremble and fear before the God of Daniel" (Dan 6:26-28).

---

[43]C. F. Keil and F. Delitzsch, *Biblical Commentary on the Old Testament: Biblical Commentary on the Prophecies of Ezekiel* (Grand Rapids, Mich.: Eerdmans, 1966), 1:298.
[44]Clendenin, *Many Gods*, p. 134.

I think that Gerald McDermott's assessment of these revelations received by pagan kings, which led them to recognize the sovereignty of the God of Israel, is accurate (although I will discuss his terminology later). He notes that this does not count as knowledge coming from outside the Jewish tradition because it came from encounters with Yahweh and it did not result in their salvation, but "like general revelation, it shows that there is true knowledge of God outside the sphere of special revelation."[45] It was not "general revelation," because it was not available to all; nor was it "special" revelation of the covenantal kind, because it did not point to salvation. "But," says McDermott, "it was true knowledge of the true God given by God directly or through an encounter with God's works."[46]

Moving into the New Testament narrative, we quickly meet the Magi from the East who were led by God to worship young king Jesus through their practice of astrology, which took them to Herod. Herod, through the Jewish priests, put them in touch with the Scriptures that led them to the child in Bethlehem. David Wells comments, "But there is no indication that they were saved by their religion; instead, God brought them to worship Jesus as their king."[47] And D. A. Carson suggests that

> one could as easily infer from the narrative that their coming to see the baby Jesus demonstrates how God may sometimes use even the wrath and follies of human beings to praise him—in this case to provide a pregnant symbol of how his Son will someday meet the aspirations of Gentiles as well as of Jews—as infer that the Magi are true believers while still being pagans.[48]

I wonder, however, how quickly we should deny any significance of their following the "call" that led them to Jesus.

Postbiblical instances. In more recent years, we find numerous testimonies by people to whom God made himself known in a dream or a vision. All of the experiences about which we know are, of course, experiences of people who later had contact with the gospel through human messengers, but can we assume that this is always so? We commonly hear of people who come to believe in Jesus as God as a result of a dream or vision that convinced them of this truth. This seems to be particularly true of Muslims, for instance. We need to take a closer look at this phenomenon

---

[45]McDermott, *Can Evangelicals Learn*, p. 79.
[46]Ibid., p. 80.
[47]David F. Wells, *God the Evangelist: How the Holy Spirit Works to Bring Men and Women to Faith* (Grand Rapids, Mich.: Eerdmans, 1987), p. 23.
[48]Carson, *Gagging of God*, p. 299.

as it occurs within the context of other religions, but I will delay that discussion until the second part of the book, where I address the religions more directly. At this point in our study, however, it may be profitable to cite a few instances of extrabiblical revelation that have been reported as occurring to non-Christians, although within a predominantly Christian context or where gospel proclamation was taking place.

Phillip Wiebe describes many of these experiences in *Visions of Jesus*, indicating that they do not only happen outside the modernized West.[49] In a Canadian incident, about 1962,

> Jim Link was watching a movie on television one evening in his home in Newmarket, Ontario, when the screen suddenly became invisible. The first thought that occurred to him, which he knew to be absurd, was that maybe he had watched so much television that he had become blind! He next realized that he was unable to hear the television set, and he thought, "Have I been watching so much TV that it is affecting my vision and my hearing?" He stood up to look out of the window next to him just to make sure his eyesight was still intact, but he couldn't see the walls. It seemed as though he was enclosed in a curtain, but he couldn't really see a curtain. A human figure then came into view at the end of the room, starting with an outline that became clearer and clearer, until he could see someone wearing long robes and sandals. He wondered, "What's going on here? Who is this? What is this?" The figure turned to face Jim, extended an arm, and beckoned him three times to come to him. Jim immediately thought to himself, "That is Jesus!" and the lines came to him from the New Testament, "Come to me all you who are weak and heavy laden, and I will give you rest." He thought to himself, "It's real, then, it's real. I have to ask for forgiveness and repent and receive him." At that instant everything in the room returned to normal, and he decided to become a Christian.[50]

Prior to this visionary encounter with Jesus that transformed Jim's life, he

> had been wondering about the meaning of life, what his purpose in life was, and whether he was just on earth to work and maintain a home and watch television! He had been attending church with his wife, just to please her, but having this experience, at twenty-seven years of age, changed his outlook on life.[51]

---

[49]Phillip H. Wiebe, *Visions of Jesus: Direct Encounters from the New Testament to Today* (New York: Oxford University Press, 1997).
[50]Ibid., p. 3.
[51]Ibid., p. 4.

Another interesting experience is that of Robin Wheeler, from Abbotsford, British Columbia, in 1984. Robin had little contact with Christians or the church for the first thirty-eight years of his life, though he occasionally attended an Anglican or Catholic church when he was young. Through Christian neighbors, his wife became a Christian and Robin was annoyed, particularly when she prayed openly for him.

One Saturday night several weeks after her conversion he had what he described as a battle with an evil creature as he was trying to sleep. Its face resembled a human face without skin, and it frightened him. He tried to fight off this creature, but he was not successful. Just off to his right stood a man wearing a brown sackcloth robe with a sash around his waist. Robin never did see above the shoulders of this second figure, but he considers it to have been Jesus. Robin tried to tie up the creature with the sash from Jesus, and as he did so Jesus disappeared. Again and again he would struggle with the monster, and each time Jesus would appear long enough for Robin to grab the sash, and then would disappear.... Robin's wife was with him while this struggle was taking place. She told me that he levitated for long periods of time that coincided with the struggles, and seemed to go in and out of consciousness. She says that Robin floated in midair in a horizontal position about a foot above the bed. His body was in a perfectly rigid position, and all the veins in his body were bulging. His head was bent so far back, she says, that she thought it would break. Although she did not see the figures that appeared to him, she could ask him what was happening, and he would describe the events taking place. She estimates that the various struggles occurred over a six-hour period, but he had no sense of the passing of time. When a fight sequence came to an end, his body would drop back onto the bed, and he would relax until a new struggle began. But Robin was not aware of his levitation. During the fights he could see his wife as well as these two other beings, and they seemed as real as ordinary persons.... The struggles finally ended when Robin found that his efforts to tie up the monster did not succeed, and he requested help from Jesus who bound the monster for him. Robin considers this to be symbolic of his own inability to restrain the powers of evil that tried to envelop him. The next day Robin decided to become a Christian.[52]

Rather different was the experience of Hugh Montefiore, an instructor in the New Testament at Cambridge University and later a bishop of the Church of England.

[52]Ibid., pp. 44-45.

He was brought up in the Jewish faith, and as a child never attended Christian worship or read the New Testament. He credits his conversion to Christianity to a vision he experienced at sixteen years of age. The figure that appeared to him said, "Follow me," and "knowing it to be Jesus," . . . [he] decided to embrace the Christian faith, although he says he has not ceased to be a Jew. Only later did he discover that the invitation "Follow me" was in the New Testament.[53]

Wiebe further cites an account from legislative assistant Karen Feaver, who

reports the following incident as a message was preached to a crowd unfamiliar with Christianity: "A vision of Jesus walking among them and then suffering on the cross appeared to all gathered. When the teacher told of Jesus rising from the dead, the vision showed Jesus ascending to heaven gloriously."[54]

Wiebe concludes from his study that

Christic visions are evidently more common than is ordinarily believed, although a lack of documentation currently makes this conclusion unprovable. The numerous accounts of recent experiences in the books by Sparrow and the Huyssens indicate that they may happen quite often, and the fact that so many of the percipients I interviewed were in British Columbia, a province with fewer than four million inhabitants, suggests that they are quite ubiquitous.[55]

Similarly, Richard Peace suggests that we should

build into our evangelistic efforts the awareness that a lot of people have had mystical experiences but most people have not responded to them. In other words, it makes good sense to ask people to recall those moments in their lives in which they were aware of the presence, power, and love of God and then invite them to respond to the God they met in such mystical moments. Our point of contact is with their deepest aspirations, since mystical experiences create a longing for the Divine. For such people Jesus becomes the bridge between an experience of God and a lifestyle rooted in the presence of God.[56]

There is benefit in this suggestion, but we need to remember that not all

---

[53]Ibid., p. 82.

[54]Ibid., pp. 84-85, quoting *Christianity Today*, May 16, 1994.

[55]Wiebe, *Visions*, p. 212.

[56]Richard V. Peace, *Conversion in the New Testament: Paul and the Twelve* (Grand Rapids, Mich.: Eerdmans, 1999), p. 304.

mystical experiences are created by God; there are also other spirits at work in the world.

THE NATURE AND SIGNIFICANCE OF PARTICULAR NONUNIVERSALLY NORMATIVE DIVINE REVELATION

In our review of the biblical accounts of revelation that occurred outside the covenant community, I cited McDermott's conclusion these were not "general revelation" because they were not available to all, but that these were also not "special revelation" of the covenantal kind, because they did not point to salvation. By "special revelation," it is apparent that McDermott means *universally normative covenantal revelation.* This is the way in which that term has generally been used within Reformed theology. Given the instances of God's revelation to particular individuals on the occasions that we identified, McDermott is correct that we need to account for another form of revelation to individuals. It is "special" in its particularity or limited address, but it is not "special" in the sense of being revelation from God intended for everyone, everywhere—that is, it is not universally normative. Thus, we must distinguish between two categories of particular revelation: universally normative covenant revelation and specific revelation given to an individual for a limited time and purpose.

It might help us to clarify the situation if we look first at the experience of particular divine revelation within the covenant community. In recent years, so-called charismatic Christians have given special prominence in their private and public worship to particular, nonuniversally normative revelation, and they call it "prophecy." Noncharismatics have often objected to this designation because they reserve the term *prophecy* for the universally normative revelation that God gave to individuals who were recognized in the covenant community as God's authoritative spokespersons.[57] Many of the "prophecies" given in charismatic worship services are general exhortations or reminders of truth that anyone could have gleaned from the universally normative Bible. Although I am not likely to be identified as a "charismatic," I see no reason to doubt that the Spirit of God can bring truths learned from Scripture to the mind of one of his children at a time when this truth is particularly appropriate and that the individual who receives the insight is able to minister to the congregation by passing it along. It seems probable to me that this was part of what Paul had in

---

[57]A helpful discussion of the differences on this subject is found in Wayne Grudem, ed., *Are Miraculous Gifts for Today? Four Views* (Grand Rapids, Mich.: Zondervan, 1996).

mind when he gave the Christians in Corinth instructions concerning the proper exercise of prophecy (1 Cor 14). The communication of this spiritual insight can be for the congregation's "upbuilding and encouragement and consolation," which is precisely what Paul identified as the purpose of prophecy in the congregational meeting (1 Cor 14:3).

God does not give Christians insight into the application of only biblical truth to their circumstances. The process of divine guidance in a believer's life may include revelation of specific new information, as it did in the early church.[58] Luke tells us that Paul and his missionary team were "forbidden by the Holy Spirit to speak the word in Asia" (Acts 16:6) and then that they attempted to go into Bithynia, "but the Spirit of Jesus did not allow them" (Acts 16:7). Commentators sometimes surmise that this might have been providential guidance, such as circumstances that prevented Paul from going somewhere. Paul and his team recognized these hindrances as God's doing. It could also, however, have been a prophetic message such as the congregation in Antioch received, as "they were worshiping the Lord and fasting" —a specific instruction to set Barnabas and Saul apart for missionary work (Acts 13:2). We cannot rule out the possibility that God will speak to us today in dreams and visions. Though I have not had this experience myself, I have no reason to doubt the veracity and wisdom of others who testify to having had these experiences and acted accordingly. On occasion, in Scripture, God sent angels to give direction, and numerous accounts of such instances have come out of China in recent years, from very credible witnesses, including a personal friend of mine who has traveled there frequently. God continues to speak to his children by way of new covenant guidance, but these messages are not to be added to the covenant scriptures, which are universally normative. God also gives very specific information to individuals to enable them to minister effectively at the time. Charles Spurgeon, a nineteenth-century Calvinist Baptist preacher whom no one would ever have accused of being Pentecostal, testified to a number of such instances.[59]

---

[58]My appreciation of a dynamic ongoing work of the Spirit of God in the lives of Christians has been helped particularly by the work of Reformed theologian Klaus Bockmuehl, who argues persuasively that the Reformers' commitment to Scripture alone unwittingly restrained the Spirit's activity in the life of believers and of the community in the new covenant age. See his *Listening to the God Who Speaks: Reflections on God's Guidance from Scripture and the Lives of God's People* (Colorado Springs, Colo.: Helmers & Howard, 1990).

[59]Charles H. Spurgeon, Susannah Spurgeon, and W. I. Harrald, *Autobiography of Charles H. Spurgeon* (London: Curtis & Jennings, 1899), 2:226-27.

Once we acknowledge that God makes himself known to particular individuals both inside and outside the covenant community, in ways that are not universally normative, we have accepted a truth that is very important for our current inquiry. God's continuing self-revelation is not limited to the universally accessible means that we call "general revelation." Nor is revelation limited to the universally normative covenant revelation that is now confined to Scripture. God makes himself known to individuals in very particular ways, and every one of these divine encounters calls for a response of faith and obedience. This is true, whether it be revelation given to a Christian believer within the church or messages communicated to someone who is completely ignorant of God's universally normative covenant revelation. Every instance of divine revelation requires a response from those who receive it, and only the response of obedient faith will satisfy God. The revelation makes a claim on that person. Just as one is obligated to obey one's moral conscience, so one is required to believe one's religious consciousness.

SUMMING UP

The God who graciously established a means by which his righteous enmity against sinners could be removed—through the sending of the very Son of God in human form—has also been ceaselessly at work making himself known to all people. In some forms, this divine self-revelation is accessible to everyone, but God has also taken special steps to speak more clearly and in greater detail to particular individuals. No one has been left without witness of God, but not everyone has been given equally full or clear knowledge of who God is, what he has done for us and what he asks from us.

What we need to look at next, therefore, is what God requires *from* human beings in order for Christ's saving work to be effective in their individual lives or in and through their religious communities. This will enable us to answer more directly whether salvation is accessible to everyone or not. Although God has made himself known to everyone, might it be that some levels of that revelation are sufficient to justify God's condemnation of them for sinfully rejecting him but not sufficient to make saving faith possible for these people? How useful are behavior and belief that are exercised in "good faith" and with a clear conscience when the information eliciting these acts and commitments is incomplete or untrue? In the next chapter, we will examine the grounds of God's judgment and then, in the three following chapters, we will consider how much knowledge of God a person must have to be saved.

7

By What Standard Are People Judged?

Thesis 6: Since faith is essential for reconciliation with God, unbelief and its attendant disobedience leave people under God's just condemnation. But people are held accountable by God only for their response to the revelation that they have received. People are guilty, even when they act ignorantly, if they can be charged with having brought about their own state of ignorance. On the other hand, there is a form of ignorance for which individuals are inculpable, or not held accountable. God does not sentence people to judgment for acts they did that were morally wrong if, first, they were morally ignorant through no act of their own doing and, second, they acted with a clear conscience, not knowing their actions to be contrary to the truth. Consequently, it is possible that God may graciously save some who do not believe in Jesus as Savior if they are ignorant of him through no fault of their own.

HAVING OBSERVED THE VARIED AND WONDERFUL WAYS in which God reaches out to sinners in order to reestablish with them the relationship that was ruptured by sin, we now examine what response God is seeking from us, the one response that will satisfy him and actually result in restored fellowship with him. We also contemplate what accountability sinners might have for failing to respond to forms of revelation that they have not received.

FAITH: THE ONE ESSENTIAL RESPONSE THAT CONSISTENTLY RESTORES HUMAN FELLOWSHIP WITH GOD

From the coming of sin into the world, God has graciously made it possible for people to be saved through faith. The human experience of God's wonderful gift of salvation in Christ is now, and has always been, solely by grace through faith, and it involves a conversion from darkness to light. This was just as true before Christ's coming as it is after that saving event. As the apostle Paul has taken pains to argue, God's people of the old covenant were justified by faith, not by works of their own, even if those works were in obedience to the law given through Moses (Rom 3:25-30; 4:1—5:1; Gal 2:15-16; 3:6-14; Eph 2:8-9; Phil 3:9). The writer to the Hebrews likewise stresses the fundamental instrumentality of faith in acceptance by God. "Without faith it is impossible to please God, for whoever would approach him must believe that he exists and that he rewards those who seek him" (Heb 11:6). He then proceeds to a lengthy description of people in Old Testament times who were "commended for their faith" (Heb 11:39).

From a study of the New Testament, we come to understand faith as an act of the will toward God that is manifested in various ways. For Abraham, faith was accepting as true what God had said (Gen 15:6), but it was also seen in his obedience to God's command (Jas 2:21-24; Heb 11:8, 17). The same was also true of Noah (Heb 11:7). Faith has been demonstrated by entrusting oneself to God and remaining true to him through adversity (Hab 2:4, 17-19; Heb 10:36-39; 11:30-38), by giving honor to God as God and being thankful for his gifts (Rom 1:21), by turning from sin and entrusting oneself to Jesus as Savior (Jn 3:16-18; Acts 2:38; 3:19; 13:48; 16:31; Rom 3:25, 28, 30; 5:1; Gal 2:16; Phil 3:9) and by serving him and eagerly awaiting his return (1 Thess 1:9-10).

A common theme in regard to human salvation is the concept of turning from an old to a new way, which we refer to as "conversion." Richard Peace identifies three elements of conversion:

- "They need to *see* their true state in relationship to God. Perception is foundational to change."

- "They must *turn*. They must turn *from* the way in which they are walking, which is the way of darkness, the way of Satan. They must turn *to* the way of light, which is the way of God."

- And, "having seen and turned, they will receive forgiveness and sanctification by faith. A new life begins for them."[1]

We can use the term *faith* in an objective sense, as when Christians in Judea heard that Saul, who had been persecuting them, was now "proclaiming *the faith* he once tried to destroy" (Gal 1:23, emphasis mine). Thus,

---

[1]Richard V. Peace, *Conversion in the New Testament: Paul and the Twelve* (Grand Rapids, Mich.: Eerdmans, 1999), p. 25.

we can speak of "the Christian faith." Because of this use, however, it is easy to think that the subjective use of "faith," when exercised by a "believer," is believing the doctrines of the church, which makes it primarily a matter of the mind and emphasizes the knowledge required for faith to occur. Without ignoring the importance of this cognitive dimension of faith, we must keep in mind the deep element of trust that biblical faith entails. Above all, we must view faith as an orientation of the entire person. Likewise, when we speak of an "unbeliever," we should think of unbelief as an act of the total personality that includes practical, theoretical and emotional elements. Ted Peters captures this well when he defines *unbelief* as "the act or state in which a person in the totality of his or her being turns away from God."[2] As I speak of faith and of unbelief, in this study of salvation, I have in mind this sense of the total orientation of a person's life toward or away from God.

GOD HOLDS PEOPLE ACCOUNTABLE ONLY FOR THE REVELATION THAT HAS BEEN MADE AVAILABLE TO THEM

Since God has consistently required faith from us if we are to be saved from our sin and restored to fellowship with God, a critical question arises: how much must we *know* in order to have the kind of faith that pleases God and results in salvation? This is one place at which ecclesiocentrists and accessibilists often part company. Both groups agree that God is just and that he only holds people accountable for the revelation concerning God and his will that he himself has made available to them. People are not condemned for not responding to revelation that they did not receive. Here is where they disagree: accessibilists believe that *everyone receives* potentially saving revelation; ecclesiocentrists believe that *some people do not receive* saving revelation, yet that these people are still justly condemned to hell for rejecting the insufficient revelation that they do receive.

There is widespread discomfort among evangelical church members about the teaching that everyone who does not hear the gospel about Jesus will be damned. Interestingly, Lutheran theologian George Lindbeck suggests that the general failure of Protestant theologians to address the question of the salvation of non-Christians is due to their university orientation. They are unaware of the concerns held by many people in the churches. In this regard, he considers Catholic theology to be more rele-

---

[2]Ted Peters, *Sin: Radical Evil in Soul and Society* (Grand Rapids, Mich.: Eerdmans, 1994), p. 67.

vant pastorally.[3] Back in the 1970s, a questionnaire was distributed to students at InterVarsity's student mission convention in Urbana, Illinois. Of the five thousand who replied, only 37 percent believed that a "person who does not hear the gospel is eternally lost," and 25 percent believed that a "man will be saved or lost on the basis of how well he followed what he did know."[4] These statistics might, conceivably, reflect an insufficient knowledge of Scripture, but I think that there is a basic truth that intuitively leads Christians to reject the idea that God would condemn people for not believing in one of whom they have never heard, when only that faith would save them.

Culpable and inculpable ignorance. When the question arises about the salvation of the unevangelized, whether they be infants who have died or adult pagans, I have often heard evangelicals plead ignorance about the eternal destiny of others and then appeal to the words of Abraham. Considering the prospect that the righteous in Sodom would be destroyed with the wicked, Abraham asked rhetorically, "Shall not the Judge of all the earth do what is just?"(Gen 18:25). We all know that he will.

Furthermore, we recognize that a distinction has to be made between culpable and inculpable ignorance. I was reminded of that by the policeman who pulled me over one night because I had driven out of a parking lot and turned the wrong way down a one-way street. I told him that I did not know it was a one-way street, assuming that this ignorance would absolve me of guilt. He assured me, however, that there was a sign at the point where I had entered the street, so I was responsible to know this fact and was, therefore, culpably ignorant. We all recognize, however, that a fundamental injustice is done when people who are inculpably ignorant of some fact are condemned for not having acted according to a truth they did not know. The critical question, therefore, is whether Scripture depicts anyone as *inculpably* ignorant or whether there is some reason why even people who are ignorant of the gospel may be *justly* held guilty for their failure to trust in Christ.

This leads me to the proposition I stated above: that, being just, God holds people accountable only for the revelation that he has given to them. This does not mean that every person who does not receive the gospel is

---

[3]George Lindbeck, "*Fides ex auditu* and the Salvation of the Non-Christians: Contemporary Catholic and Protestant Positions," in *The Gospel and the Ambiguities of the Church*, ed. Vilmos Vajta (Philadelphia: Fortress, 1974), pp. 108-9.

[4]J. Ronald Blue, "Untold Billions: Are They Really Lost?" *Bibliotheca Sacra* 138 (October-December 1981): 340-41.

not condemned. All of them are sinners needing God's salvation; they are justly condemned for sinful refusal to acknowledge God, to thank him and to believe what he makes known about himself, even if it is only through means of general revelation. The ground of their condemnation, however, can only be the revelation that they have received; it *cannot* be the revelation that they have *not* received. *All* have received divine revelation, and *all* have sinned by failing to obey what they understand to be morally right or to believe and live according to what they know to be true. Paul clearly states this principle of proportionate responsibility in Romans 2:12: "All who have sinned apart from the law will also perish apart from the law, and all who have sinned under the law will be judged by the law." By "the law," he means the law as given by special revelation to Moses. He is not suggesting that anyone is completely without knowledge of God's law. That would render all the unevangelized sinless. On the contrary, he asserts that the Gentiles also have a knowledge of God's moral will through their consciences, the law of God "written on their hearts" (Rom 2:15).

Although the judgment of the conscience is not reliable and must be re-educated on the basis of Scripture, we must treat it formally as God's voice to us. Paul spells this out, specifically with regard to believers, in Romans 14. Those who violate the voice of conscience sin against God, even if they do not break God's moral law. "Those who have doubts are condemned if they eat, because they do not act from faith" (Rom 14:23). The conscience mediates God's demand and verdict to humans. As such an instrument, it is something that God has given to everyone (Rom 2:15). It is that which testifies within the person, both before and after action, either warning or commending, acquitting or condemning (cf. Rom 9:1; 13:5; 1 Cor 4:4; 8:7; 2 Cor 1:12). In the previous chapter, I offered my understanding of the conscience as a faculty of moral discrimination that does not include the content according to which it bears witness. Humans have an innate *ability*, however, to know the moral order, just as they have an innate *ability* to know the physical order; and God holds them responsible for the knowledge that they deduce from these aspects of God's creative work.

The critical point being made by Paul, then, regardless of what one understands by "conscience," is that God has left no one without a moral witness, and we are obligated always to obey this internal voice, though we must also educate it by the normative written Word of God. We are judged, however, according to the knowledge we have, not according to a knowledge that we do not have. Those who do not have Scripture will not be judged according to Scripture (Rom 2:12). On this basis we acknowledge that people who lived before Jesus were saved by grace through faith, though not through faith *in Jesus*. They did not know about Jesus, and so they were not obligated to believe in him. When that knowledge came to them, of course, their obligation changed.

As we saw earlier, John 3 is very explicit about the fate of those who see the light in Jesus and reject it because they prefer darkness. It says nothing, however, about those on whom that light has not shone. The principle that Paul stated concerning the Old Testament Scripture is equally true of the New Testament. In short, judgment will be according to knowledge.

Accepting this principle of just judgment, D. A. Carson cautiously grants that "one might imagine some pagan, afflicted by conscience, crying to his Maker for mercy"; and although that is "not what the text *says* . . . it does not absolutely shut the door to the possibility."[5] At that point, Carson cites the statement of "even so conservative a writer as J. I. Packer":

> We may safely say *(i)* if any good pagan reached the point of throwing himself on his Maker's mercy for pardon, it was grace that brought him there; *(ii)* God will surely save anyone he brings thus far (cf. Acts 10:34f; Rom. 10:12f); *(iii)* anyone thus saved would learn in the next world that he was saved through Christ.[6]

In Carson's opinion, "the text does not rule out the possibility for which Packer allows, but it does not explicitly sanction it either."[7]

In both of Paul's sermons to Gentile audiences (in Acts), he makes intriguing use of this principle that judgment is proportionate to revelation. To the audience of idolaters in Lystra, Paul said that "in past generations he [God] allowed all the nations to follow their own ways; yet he has not left himself without a witness in doing good—giving you rains from heaven and fruitful seasons, and filling you with food and your hearts with joy" (Acts 14:16-17). It is highly implausible that Paul is suggesting that God accepted all the various forms of worship and conduct that the nations chose in their ignorance of God through lack of revelation. His point is twofold: First, God had given them some revelation in the form of his providential care for them. As indicated in Romans 1:21, this left them culpable if they did not respond by honoring God as God and giving him thanks. And sec-

---

[5] D. A. Carson, *The Gagging of God: Christianity Confronts Pluralism* (Grand Rapids, Mich.: Zondervan, 1996), p. 311.

[6] J. I. Packer, *God's Words: Studies of Key Bible Themes* (Downers Grove, Ill.: InterVarsity Press, 1981), p. 210, quoted in Carson, *Gagging of God*, p. 311.

[7] Carson, *Gagging of God*, p. 312.

ond, in Paul's generation, they were receiving a clearer revelation of God's truth and of his will, so their obligation was increasing accordingly.

To the philosophers of Athens, Paul is even more explicit about this principle. He says that "God has overlooked the times of human ignorance" but that "now he commands all people everywhere to repent, because he has fixed a day on which he will have the world judged in righteousness by a man whom he has appointed, and of this he has given assurance to all by raising him from the dead" (Acts 17:30-31). Clearly, there is an ignorance that is not culpable. When the gospel concerning the resurrected Jesus is preached and the Spirit illumines the hearers, the ignorance is dispelled and God's "overlooking" is, therefore, no longer appropriate.

The meaning and import of the Athenians'"ignorance" needs careful attention. Darrell Bock has argued that "ignorance is not an excuse. One is still culpable before God for actions that are outside the truth. Those in ignorance must repent."[8] He observes that the people had "acted willfully when they executed Jesus" (Lk 23) and that the "ignorance" about which Peter speaks (Acts 3:17) is not really knowing what they were doing. Since Peter calls on his hearers to repent, Bock concludes that Peter did not consider the ignorance of Jesus' crucifiers to have constituted an excuse. Similarly, says Bock, Paul had persecuted the church "ignorantly" (1 Tim 1:13), but "he needed God's grace to save him from his sinful past as the 'worst of sinners.' . . . Ignorance was no excuse."[9] In the epistles, states Bock, "the term *ignorance* most often describes the lifestyle of the saved before conversion. Christians are exhorted not to live as they once did" (Eph 4:18; 1 Pet 1:14; 2 Pet 2:12)."Yet, the immoral life, although it reflects ignorance, still remains culpable for its acts before God."[10] It was because Paul's fellow Jews were "ignorant of the righteousness that comes from God, and seeking to establish their own" that they had not "submitted to God's righteousness" (Rom 10:3). So Paul indicates to the Athenians that they "must respond to the returning King who will surely sit in judgment on the last day" (Acts 17:31).[11]

Bock's identification of key New Testament texts that speak of ignorance is helpful, but his conclusion from these texts misses a critical point,

---

[8]Darrell L. Bock, "Athenians Who Have Never Heard," in *Through No Fault of Their Own? The Fate of Those Who Have Never Heard*, ed. William V. Crockett and James G. Sigountos (Grand Rapids, Mich.: Baker, 1991), p. 121.
[9]Ibid.
[10]Ibid., p. 122.
[11]Ibid.

in my view. It is true that Christian preachers are commissioned to call all people to repentance because all are guilty sinners and because none are inculpable before God on account of ignorance. This is because no one is completely ignorant and no one's conscience is completely clear. Concerning many actions, people's consciences may "excuse" them, but every one will have done actions for which their consciences "accuse" them on the day when Christ judges "the secret thoughts of all" (Rom 2:15-16). Observe, however, that given the fact that everyone is guilty, we cannot conclude that they are held accountable for all of their actions outside the truth—both those actions they do willfully against the truth that they know and those actions they do willfully but with a clear conscience, not knowing these actions to be contrary to the truth. These two kinds of actions are treated differently in Scripture. Both kinds make the perpetrator objectively guilty; both are, by definition, sin. But God holds us accountable only for the first class of actions, those that are objectively sinful and that we know to be wrong, that is, those actions that we do contrary to the witness of our own conscience. In fact, so important is the inner witness (conscience) that we sin when we disobey it, even if we do not objectively transgress the law of God. That is Paul's point to the Romans in regard to the eating of meat offered to idols. It was not sin, in and of itself, but it *was* sin if one did it "without faith" or without a clear conscience before God (Rom 14:23).

Romans 2:12 clearly teaches us that we are held accountable for the actions that we do in spite of the fact that we believe them to be wrong, that is, in spite of our knowledge that they are contrary to the moral standard (law) that we understand to be our obligation. Although only sinning subjectively, we are accounted guilty. This is the important distinction between actions that are *objectively* wrong and actions that are *subjectively* wrong. "An act is objectively sinful if it disturbs shalom and makes its agent guilty," but "an act is subjectively sinful if its agent thinks that it is objectively sinful (whether or not it is) and purposely (or in some other accountable way) does it anyhow."[12]

Jesus applies this principle of culpability and inculpability, due to knowledge or ignorance, to the Pharisees who were disturbed about the man who claimed that Jesus had healed his blindness. The man knew that it was Jesus who had healed him but he knew nothing more about Jesus'

---

[12]Cornelius Plantinga Jr., *Not the Way It's Supposed to Be: A Breviary of Sin* (Grand Rapids, Mich.: Eerdmans, 1995), p. 20.

identity. When Jesus later revealed himself to be the Son of Man, the healed man believed that self-testimony and worshiped him (Jn 9:35-38). Jesus made the enigmatic statement that he had come into the world "for judgment so that those who do not see may see, and those who do see may become blind" (Jn 9:39). His coming increases the culpability of those who encounter him but do not believe in him. When some of the Pharisees overheard his remark, they asked, "Surely we are not blind, are we?" And Jesus replied: *"If you were blind, you would not have sin.* But now that you say, 'We see,' your sin remains" (Jn 9:41, emphasis mine).

A significant group of manuscripts of Luke record Jesus on the cross interceding for forgiveness for those who put him there because they did not know what they were doing (Lk 23:34). Obviously, they *did know* that they were crucifying Jesus but they *did not know* that they were crucifying the Son of God. They assumed Jesus to be guilty of blasphemy as charged. On the day of Pentecost, when the Spirit has come on Peter and the other believers in power, Peter informs the bewildered crowd that the Jesus whom they had crucified was none other than the "Lord and Messiah" whom God had raised from the dead and exalted to his right hand and who had now poured out the promised Holy Spirit on his followers (Acts 2:33-36). With the Spirit now at work in the minds of Peter's hearers, they were "cut to the heart," and they asked Peter what they could do now. Peter calls them to repentance so that their sins might be forgiven (Acts 2:38). They were to repent of *all* their sins, including particularly the one of which they had only now become aware, the sin of putting to death their own Messiah.

On a later occasion, while preaching in Solomon's portico, Peter tells the crowd—who were "filled with wonder and amazement" at the healing of the crippled beggar (Acts 3:10)—that he knew that they had "acted in ignorance" when they "killed the Author of life," but then he called on them to repent. Bock is certainly correct that this is always our twin obligation: to make people aware of their sin (even though we increase their guiltiness when we do so) and to call them to repentance. But no one can be expected to repent of wrongdoing of which they are ignorant, except in a very general way, as in the Old Testament sacrifice for "sins of ignorance." The moment that the Spirit of God makes us aware that what we have done was wrong, however, we become accountable for it.

By application to our study of the proclamation of the gospel to those who are ignorant, no one in the world is guiltless of sin, because God has left no one without witness. Furthermore, no one has ever remained faultless in regard to the moral standard according to which his or her own conscience brings conviction. All sinned and are falling short of God's glory, and all are aware of this. What makes the gospel good news is that when we tell the story concerning Jesus, the Word incarnate, crucified as the one righteous man for many unrighteous people, we announce to people how their guilty consciences can be appeased and their sins can be forgiven. In so doing, we give them even greater revelation for which they are now culpable *to the extent that they understand it through the Spirit's illumination*. In short, no one is without guilt, but not everyone is guilty for the same sins; and each person's guilt is proportionate to their knowledge, that is, not what they have been *told* but what they have actually *comprehended*. Spiritual truth is understood only when the Spirit of God gives us understanding.

One is only culpably ignorant if one's ignorance is brought about by one's own action. Thus, the suppression of truth and repeated disobedience to the conscience will ultimately sear it so that it no longer convicts concerning sin about which it was once sensitive (1 Tim 1:19; 4:2; Eph 4:18-19). It is because much of our ignorance is self-incurred that "ignorance" becomes a handy way to describe the state of those who are alienated from God, as Bock notes. Not *all* ignorance excuses us, *but some* of it does—not absolutely, but at least in regard to the particular objective law breaking we have unconsciously committed.

There is, therefore, *culpable* ignorance, and there is *inculpable* ignorance, but *no one* is completely, inculpably ignorant, because of the universal self-revelation of God and the absolute moral obligation placed on humans to do what they believe to be right, whether or not they are correct in that regard (Rom 14:22-23). Consequently, there is no one who does not need to be saved by God's grace in Christ on account of being completely inculpable through ignorance. But those who do not know of Christ are not guilty of rejecting him. The critical question is whether they can benefit from Christ's atoning work without knowing about it, and I will address that matter directly, in the next three chapters.

Coming back to the Athenians, John Piper has said,

> It is a stunning New Testament truth that since the incarnation of the Son of God all saving faith must henceforth fix on him. This was not always true. And those times were called the "times of ignorance" (Acts 17:30). But now it is true, and Christ is made the conscious center of the mission of the church.[13]

---

[13]John Piper, *Let the Nations Be Glad! The Supremacy of God in Missions* (Grand Rapids, Mich.: Baker, 1993), p. 115; cf. p. 131.

Piper assumes that the end of the "times of ignorance" is the point at which Christ's earthly work is done. I am suggesting, rather, that Paul locates it at the point of knowledge of that event. For the Athenians, it did not happen until Paul proclaimed this truth to them. The same would then be true for all people prior to the proclamation of the gospel. But Paul was now informing them of the coming day of judgment and calling them to turn toward the only one who can save them from that judgment, Jesus Christ who rose from the dead in vindication of his role as Judge. I. Howard Marshall also understands the text in this way:

> Until the coming of the revelation of God's true nature in Christianity, men lived in *ignorance* of him. But now the proclamation of the Christian message brings this time to an end *so far as those who hear the gospel are concerned;* they no longer have an excuse for their ignorance. God was prepared to *overlook* their ignorance, but now he will do so no longer.[14]

To the Athenians, then, Paul reiterates the principle that responsibility is proportionate to one's knowledge. It is those who know about Jesus (both through information concerning him and by means of the Spirit's gift of understanding) who are responsible to believe in him. Those who are ignorant of Jesus through no fault of their own are not condemned for not believing in him, but they have done many other sins consciously and willingly, and for these they face the righteous condemnation of God. For these sins they must receive God's forgiveness or pay the just penalty. Paul was not saying that the Athenians were guiltless before God; they were not "saved" simply because they were ignorant. But he is also not saying that it was impossible for them to be saved without knowing about Jesus. Nevertheless, once Paul made known to them the good news concerning Jesus, they were no longer inculpably ignorant of that truth.

Implications of the category of inculpable ignorance. Someone who re-

---

[14]I. Howard Marshall, *The Acts of the Apostles: An Introduction and Commentary,* Tyndale New Testament Commentaries (Grand Rapids, Mich.: Eerdmans, 1980), pp. 289-90, emphasis mine. John E. Goldingay and Christopher J. H. Wright also posit that "the progress of history does change things. Joshua's renewal of the covenant in Joshua 24 implies that, whatever kinds of polytheistic worship may have been part of Israel's ancestry, polytheism was no longer appropriate in the light of Yahweh's great redemptive achievements of exodus and conquest. Fresh choices had to be made 'today.' This seems consistent with Paul's affirmation of God's apparently differential attitude toward human religion at different stages of either history or awareness, in Acts 17:27-31. The knowledge of Christ requires repentance even from things God had previously overlooked" (" 'Yahweh Our God Yahweh One': The Oneness of God in the Old Testament," in *One God, One Lord: Christianity in a World of Religious Pluralism,* 2nd ed., ed. Andrew D. Clarke and Bruce Winter [Grand Rapids, Mich.: Baker, 1992], p. 51).

alizes that people are only responsible for the knowledge of God that he has revealed to them might be tempted to conclude that it is better not to remove people's ignorance by preaching the gospel to them, because preaching increases their culpability. That would be a seriously incorrect conclusion to draw from what I have been arguing. The people to whom we take the gospel were already culpable of sin with regard to the revelation they had received before we got there, and they will be eternally condemned if they remain unrepentant of the sin of which they are aware and fail to respond to God in the manner appropriate to the revelation they already have. (I'll say more on this in the next three chapters.) God has graciously overlooked their ignorance in the past, however culpable their ignorance was, in that he did not punish them instantly.[15] Their ignorance was never so total as to completely vindicate them. It is certainly true that the gospel will increase the guilt of those who reject it, but to those who believe, it is the power of God to salvation. Precisely because we know that God has chosen to call many of the elect to himself through the church's proclamation of the gospel, we can go with the joyful expectation that those who have been "destined for eternal life" will become believers through our proclamation (Acts 13:48).

Scripture is very clear about the fact that people who believe in Jesus are saved and that those who reject Jesus remain condemned, but many of the passages (such as John 3) that speak of these two possible destinies necessarily assume knowledge, a point that has been missed by ecclesiocentrists. Christ came to his own, and they did not receive him. That is the context of the statement that those who do not believe are condemned. They are condemned precisely because they did know Christ and yet rejected him (Jn 3:18, 36). Judgment is on "those who do not know God and on those who do not obey the gospel of our Lord Jesus" (2 Thess 1:8). Jesus is ashamed of those who are ashamed of him (Mk 8:38), and he denies those who deny him (Mt 10:32-33), which assumes that there is knowledge of him. Only people aware of Jesus have no excuse, as Jesus told his disciples: "If I had not come and spoken to them, they would not have sin: but now they have no excuse for their sin" (Jn 15:22).

The implications of this distinction between culpable and inculpable ignorance for places such as Japan, Taiwan and many African contexts are immense. In those cultures, there is very high regard for the ancestors; their memory is perpetuated in family rituals, and it is often be-

---

[15]Carson, *Gagging of God*, p. 310.

lieved that they have a continuing involvement in the family's life. In such contexts, when people hear Christian missionaries teach that salvation only comes through Christ and that those who do not believe in Christ are condemned to eternity in hell, they become very concerned about their ancestors. The desire not to offend them or not to be separated from them by religious difference is often a large stumbling block to the acceptance of the Christian life. Paul Hiebert, Daniel Shaw and Tite Tiénou note this concern and suggest that "rather than [making] a harsh condemnation of the dead, proclaimers of the gospel should take a pastoral approach by encouraging the living to follow Christ, and to commit their ancestors to God knowing that his judgments are totally loving and just."[16] This statement is clearly not representative of an ecclesiocentric position; it may simply be agnostic, but it implies to me a latent doubt that a just God could have eternally condemned all those generations of ancestors who lacked a human preacher of the gospel. Japanese and Taiwanese believers today are right to have grave doubts about the justice and mercy of a God who would condemn to hell all their ancestors without having given them a means of salvation. I believe that we can confidently affirm to them that the just and merciful God has always made himself known to people and that it has always been possible for people to respond to that self-revelation in a saving manner. This still leaves us ignorant of the destiny of our ancestors as individuals, but at least it does not permit (or obligate) us to pronounce all of them certainly damned for their ignorance of Jesus.

I am reminded of Matteo Ricci (1552-1610), Jesuit missionary to China, who was asked whether Confucius (551-479 B.C.) was in hell. He replied: "All those who know God and love Him above all things, and passed out of this life with such knowledge and love, are saved. If Confucius knew God and loved Him above all things, and passed out of this life with such knowledge and love, without doubt he is saved."[17] This response demonstrates the proper caution. Without presuming to make a pronouncement

---

[16]Paul G. R. Hiebert, Daniel Shaw and Tite Tiénou, *Understanding Folk Religion: A Christian Response to Popular Beliefs and Practices* (Grand Rapids, Mich.: Baker, 1999), p. 131. Harold Netland comments that, while serving as a missionary in Japan, he found many Japanese pastors who adopted this approach when questions arose concerning the ancestors.

[17]Ralph R. Covell, *Confucious, the Buddha and Christ: A History of the Gospel in Chinese* (Maryknoll: Orbis, 1986), p. 60, quoted in Don A. Pittman, Ruben L. F. Habito and Terry C. Muck, eds., *Ministry and Theology in Global Perspective: Contemporary Challenges for the Church* (Grand Rapids, Mich.: Eerdmans, 1996), p. 51.

regarding the eternal state of another person, it identifies the criterion according to which the person would have been saved.

The situation of the unborn and of young infants. Consideration of this principle—that judgment is proportionate to the revelation that people have received—underlines how important it is that we define a doctrine of salvation that is comprehensive enough to take account of all the categories of unevangelized people. Piper, for instance, has made the statement that "apart from a knowledge of him [Jesus], *none who has the ability to know will be saved*" (emphasis mine).[18] This sounds very much like the position of accessibility that I am proposing rather than the ecclesiocentric position that Piper himself puts forward. He explains this apparent discrepancy in his footnote: "I state it like this so as to leave open salvation for infants and imbeciles who do not have the physical ability to even apprehend that there is any revelation available at all."[19] I appreciate Piper's sensitivity in this regard, but I suggest that he expand the application of his principle to include those who have other reasons for not being able to know of Christ. The numbers of these people are immense when we consider that in the United States alone, it could be said in 2002 that "since abortion was legalized in 1973, American doctors have terminated 39 million pregnancies."[20] Add to that number the intentional abortions in countries like India and China and the many unintended miscarriages. Then, if one holds that life begins at fertilization, consider the immense number of human beings who are never even implanted. Clearly this group of the unevangelized is so numerous as to boggle the mind, constituting a very significant portion of the entire human race. But why should we restrict our concern to those who are ignorant of Christ through a lack of physical ability when the numbers of those who are ignorant because of the circumstances of their place of birth and life are also so large?

SUMMING UP

God has always had only one subjective means by which the saving work of Christ became effective in people's life, namely, faith. This makes the problem of ignorance extremely important. Can people be held accountable for believing in Jesus as Savior if they have never heard of him? Our study of Scripture in this chapter has led to the conclusion that God holds

---

[18]Piper, *Let the Nations*, p. 135.
[19]Ibid., p. 165 n. 26.
[20]Stan Guthrie, "RU-486 Deaths Prompt Outcry," *Christianity Today*, June 10, 2002, p. 16.

people accountable only for the revelation of himself that he has given to them. It might be argued, however, that even though people who are ignorant of Christ are not condemned for not believing in Christ, they are justly condemned for not having responded to God in faith in ways appropriate to the revelation that God has given them. Many Calvinist theologians, for instance, have argued that general revelation is sufficient to make everyone guilty but that it is not sufficient to lead to salvation. That leaves billions of people, throughout human history, without the revelation necessary for salvation, and yet it leaves them eternally condemned. Given that no one *deserves* grace, this would not be unjust, if it were the real outcome, but is this the case? In the next three chapters, I will argue that God does in fact give *everyone* revelation that is sufficient for salvation if it is responded to properly but that the necessary faith varies with the kind of revelation an individual receives. We will examine what sorts of faith God requires from the various groups of the unevangelized that I previously listed.

8

Can People Be Saved If
They Only Have General Revelation?

Thesis 7: Salvation has always been by grace through faith, but the faith that God expects (and gives) is appropriate to the revelation of himself that he has given to a particular individual. God requires people who receive general revelation to honor him as the Creator and Provider, to be thankful to him, to obey their consciences and to cast themselves on his mercy when they are aware of their failure to do what is right. If the Spirit of God were graciously to elicit this response in anyone's heart, they would be saved. But there are eight reasons why we might doubt that there are people who receive only general revelation in the course of their lives. Even so, however, we can expect that God saves some people who have very incomplete knowledge of his person and work.

Thesis 8: God's knowledge of what people would do if they heard the gospel does not make salvation more accessible, but it enables him to bring about the salvation of the elect without coercion.

IN THE LAST CHAPTER, I MENTIONED THAT MANY CULTURES teach a strong respect for and sense of attachment to their ancestors. Suppose that you are a Christian missionary who brings to these people the good news concerning God's work of salvation and that you invite them to believe in Christ, warning them that to reject him will mean eternal condemnation. They ask you about the state of their ancestors who lived and died in complete ignorance of the gospel that you now relate to them. If you were an ecclesiocentrist, you would have to tell these hearers of the gospel that their ancestors are all condemned to hell, however sorry we may be that such is the case and however prepared we may be to confess that Christians bear some responsibility for failing to take the gospel to them. Without the knowledge of Christ, even those who were completely ignorant would be eternally cut off from God in just punishment for the sins they committed, even though they are not being punished for rejecting a Savior of whom they did not know. By comparison, what answer might be given by a Christian missionary who appropriates the accessibilist proposal that has been made thus far?

We accessibilists must tell our listeners that their ancestors (like ourselves and our hearers) were, indeed, all sinners who fell short of God's moral demands on them and who knew this to be the case. None of the ancestors will have obeyed their own consciences continuously throughout their lives. We can also tell them, however, that God has made himself known to all of the ancestors in various ways and that an appropriate response to each kind of revelation would have been necessary to experience God's grace in forgiveness and salvation. Because of God's most basic revelation in his creative work, he expected the ancestors to acknowledge that there is a Creator and to be thankful to him (Rom 1:21). Every demand of their moral conscience had to be treated as the voice of God and obeyed. Some of those ancestors may even have been given experiences of particular but nonuniversally normative revelation, and that would have placed them under further obligation to respond in trust and obedience. We can assure our hearers that none of their ancestors have been held accountable for any revelation that they did not receive. But that will be very small comfort indeed, if we must also inform them that the ancestors had revelation sufficient to leave them guilty but not to make salvation possible. In this chapter and the following ones, we will examine what else Scripture allows us to say. Do we have reason to believe that any of those ancestors might have responded to the revelation they received in a manner that God would account as faith and have been saved by Christ's atoning sacrifice? I think that we do, although we must plead ignorance as to whether God did work graciously in the life of any of those individuals about whose lives we know nothing. I hope to demonstrate that *while we cannot assure our hearers that any of their ancestors were saved, we need not insist that all of them are certainly lost, and we can be hopeful of the great mercy of God*, a mercy that we are profoundly thankful to have received in our own lives.

SALVATION IS ONLY BY GRACE THROUGH FAITH

The restoration of sinners to God's favor has always been by grace, and it has always been appropriated by faith. It is the grace that produces the faith, not vice versa. As Donald Bloesch says, "Faith is the medium of grace, the sign that grace is already at work, but it is not the condition for receiving grace. When grace falls upon us we will then invariably believe."[1] Of course, he is speaking about the efficacious grace that God gives to those whom he wills to save, since there are obviously distributions of grace that are not saving and that are resistible. While the principle of salvation by grace through faith has been God's way ever since the tragic human disobedience that alienated us from God, the content of the faith that justifies has obviously not always been the same. What we must believe is determined by what God reveals of himself to us. How might that faith look for people who only know God through the general means of his self-revelation?

GOD'S PURPOSE IN GIVING GENERAL REVELATION

The problem of salvation looms largest when we think about those who do not have the special revelation that God gave to Israel. We have asserted that all people are sinners deserving eternal damnation, that the righteousness of Jesus Christ is the only ground on which sins can be forgiven, that salvation is therefore by grace and has always been by faith and that God's just judgment is according to the knowledge that one has been given by God. Clearly, everyone has enough knowledge to be justly condemned. Apart from original guilt in Adam, all who live to moral consciousness violate their own consciences. All fall short of God's glory (Rom 3:23).

The crucial question before us is this: *Is it possible that God may have given some people revelation that was sufficient to constitute them justly condemned but insufficient to permit them to be saved?* Romans 1:18-23 is frequently cited by ecclesiocentrists as evidence that general revelation provides sufficient grounds to condemn people but that it is insufficient to lead them to salvation.[2] This is because people have the law written on their hearts and they break it. They are culpable sinners. But the revelation of God in conscience, creation and providence offers no knowledge that could elicit a faith that would be instrumental in justification. Special revelation is necessary for salvation to occur.

Both Jonathan Edwards and John Calvin taught that "nature points only to God the Creator, not God the Redeemer, and that knowledge of

---

[1]Donald G. Bloesch, *The Church: Sacraments, Worship, Ministry and Mission*, Christian Foundations (Downers Grove, Ill.: InterVarsity Press, 2002), p. 66.

[2]For example, Bruce A. Demarest, *General Revelation* (Grand Rapids, Mich.: Zondervan, 1982), pp. 69-70, 248; Ronald Nash, *Is Jesus the Only Savior?* (Grand Rapids, Mich.: Zondervan, 1994), pp. 20-21, 119.

only the former is insufficient for salvation."[3] But the implications of that position have troubled many Christians. If Scripture teaches it, we must accept it, however disturbing we find it; but should we not examine God's Word carefully to be sure that this is a necessary burden to carry? Are we sure that there are people who have no revelation other than what God gives in creation? Much more importantly, does the Bible categorically assert that *none* of the people who only have creational revelation *ever* honor God as Creator or are thankful to him?

I suggest that many Christians have been inclined to push Paul's statement in Romans 1:18 further than it goes in Paul's own argument. Paul teaches that "the wrath of God is revealed from heaven against all ungodliness and wickedness of *those who* by their wickedness suppress the truth" (emphasis mine), and many have assumed that Paul is indicating that *everyone* ultimately and *finally* does this. That is, for instance, the reading given by John Piper.[4] But Paul does not say this is so. What he clearly states is that those who *do suppress* the truth of creational revelation and who *do not honor* God as God or give him thanks (Rom 1:21) are without excuse and that this sinful response to general revelation, when it persists, leads to increasingly more serious forms of sin. The most negative statement we could make from Romans 1, therefore, is that "there may be those who respond positively, but Paul makes no mention of them."[5] This is different from hearing a positive *assertion* that no one does respond. After all, it is probable that each of you who reads this book is a person who acknowledges that God created the world and that you are earnestly seeking him in confidence that God will let himself be found. But you were not naturally or always such a person. God graciously opened your eyes to see beyond the works of his hands to the One who created the wonders that now elicit your praise and thanksgiving. We, too, once suppressed God's truth in unrighteousness but, thanks to his grace, we no longer do so.[6]

---

[3]Gerald R. McDermott, *Can Evangelicals Learn from World Religions? Jesus, Revelation and Religious Traditions* (Downers Grove, Ill.: InterVarsity Press, 2000), p. 51.
[4]John Piper, *Let the Nations Be Glad! The Supremacy of God in Missions* (Grand Rapids, Mich.: Baker, 1993), 164 n. 23, 166 n. 39.
[5]Millard J. Erickson, *How Shall They Be Saved? The Destiny of Those Who Do Not Hear of Jesus* (Grand Rapids, Mich.: Baker, 1996), p. 149.
[6]Aída Besançon Spencer observes that Paul does not clearly address "the situation of the eternal state of the *devout* human who has not been told by another human that Jesus is Lord and that God raised him from the dead (Rom. 10:9) because Paul is, after all, writing to the *churches* in Rome." Spencer relies "on God's loving and just character to judge such people" ("Romans 1: Finding God in Creation," in *Through No Fault of Their Own? The Fate of Those Who Have Never Heard*, ed. William V. Crockett and James G. Sigountos [Grand Rapids, Mich.: Baker, 1991], 134 n. 32).

David Clark hits the right note with his suggestion that Romans 1:18-23 is "consistent with the claim that natural revelation fails to bring salvation to those who are rebellious and wicked, but potentially leads to salvation for those who respond to it."[7] I think that Clark is correct to observe that those who find in Romans 1:18-23 a demonstration that special revelation is necessary for salvation "do so because they assume on some other ground that only those with special revelation can be saved."[8] We must remember, of course, that a positive response to *any* divine revelation is a fruit of God's gracious working in the heart of sinners, not a response that comes naturally to us in our sinfulness. If this response is a response of faith, it is by grace, as is true of all faith, regardless of the fullness of the revelation to which it responds.

If we portray God's judgment in ways that run counter to everything we expect in proper human jurisprudence, we will have to provide good explanation for doing so. God's ways are often beyond our comprehension, but God's justice is the standard of human justice, and I fail to see why we would attribute to him something that we would never accept from a human judge. Millard Erickson's approach strikes me as much more plausible. He writes concerning Romans 1:20,

> If they are condemnable because they have not trusted God through what they have, it must have been possible somehow to meet his requirements through this means. If not, responsibility and condemnation are meaningless. . . . If individuals, on the basis of the inner law, come to realize their own sinfulness, guilt, and inability to please God, then that law would also have the effect of bringing them to grace.[9]

Since "these persons actually knew God but suppressed the truth, then it must be correct to say that on some level persons responding to the God of general revelation are genuinely responding to the true God."[10]

The work of Christ was effective for Old Testament believers who did

---

[7]David K. Clark, "Is Special Revelation Necessary for Salvation?" in *Through No Fault of Their Own? The Fate of Those Who Have Never Heard*, ed. William V. Crockett and James G. Sigountos (Grand Rapids, Mich.: Baker, 1991), pp. 40-41. Similarly, Paul Jewett says that "since the Christian doctrine of revelation includes God's witness to himself in creation and in history, it is not necessary to deny the saving efficacy of this witness, in every conceivable instance, in order to secure the ultimate truth claims of Christianity" (*God, Creation and Revelation: A Neo-Evangelical Theology* [Grand Rapids, Mich.: Eerdmans, 1991], p. 73).

[8]Clark, "Is Special Revelation Necessary," p. 41.

[9]Erickson, *How Shall They*, p. 194.

[10]Ibid.

not know specifically about Christ but who threw themselves on the mercy of God. In the same way, I assume, people with guilty consciences who are under conviction by the Holy Spirit would be led to stop depending on themselves and would entrust themselves to the mercy of the Creator and Judge whom they encounter in creation and in the voice of their conscience.[11] Accordingly, Erickson proposes that

> the inner moral impulse, the law written within, could serve the same function as the Mosaic or written law. That would, properly speaking, be to bring about repentance. What the law requires is perfect obedience, and, lacking that, repentance. It would, in that sense, bring an awareness of the need of divine grace, and might also cause one to cast oneself upon the mercy of God.[12]

Calvin, commenting on Romans 1, notes that "even during the time in which the Lord confined the favor of his covenant to Israel, He did not withdraw the knowledge of Himself from the Gentiles, without continually inflaming some spark of it among them."[13] Norman Anderson is correct, I believe, to doubt that God continues to inflame some spark of grace among them "*only* that they might all be 'without excuse,' and without any possibility of salvation."[14] He asks, "May it not be compatible, both within Scripture and experience, to suggest that God sometimes so works in men's hearts by his grace that, instead of them 'holding down the truth,' he opens their hearts to it and enables them to embrace such of it as has been revealed to them?"[15] Anderson sees Peter's words to Cornelius about God's acceptance of "anyone in every nation who fears him and does what is right" as indicating that this can be so (Acts 10:35). This is not to say that such a person merits salvation by these right deeds but that this is evidence of the Spirit's work of grace in the life of sinners who throw themselves on the mercy of God.

GOD'S COSMIC COVENANT, AS ANNOUNCED TO NOAH

Another point deserves mention as we ponder God's work of grace on the universal plane. It is significant that the covenant God proclaimed to Noah

---

[11]See John D. Ellenberger, "Is Hell a Proper Motivation for Missions?" in *Through No Fault of Their Own? The Fate of Those Who Have Never Heard*, ed. William V. Crockett and James G. Sigountos (Grand Rapids, Mich.: Baker, 1991), p. 225.
[12]Erickson, *How Shall They*, p. 152.
[13]John Calvin *Romans* 233, quoted in J. N. D. Anderson, *Christianity and World Religions: The Challenge of Pluralism* (Downers Grove, Ill.: InterVarsity Press, 1984), pp. 150-51.
[14]Anderson, *Christianity and World Religions*, p. 151.
[15]Ibid.

was with the whole of humankind and with the cosmos (Gen 9:10), "an 'everlasting' and irrevocable covenant (Gen 9:16) which manifests God's fidelity to his creation, of which the rainbow appears as the sacramental sign (Gen 9:12-15)."[16] Although there are significant differences between the specific promises God made in the covenant with Noah and the one later with Abraham, we should not ignore the significance of God's relationship with the whole of creation. Andreas Köstenberger and Peter O'Brien, for instance, note that Genesis 9:1-7 speaks of God's "keeping" his covenant with Noah's family and a representative group of animals, birds and reptiles, "a statement that apparently refers to the plan which God brought into being at creation (cf. 9:1-7)." They also observe that Noah and his family are commissioned "in terms recalling [Genesis] 1:28," indicating that "despite the ongoing presence of sin, God intends to maintain the covenant with the created order, that is, with man and his world (9:9-13)."[17] And Clark Pinnock suggests that "the promise to Noah prepares the way for the blessing of all nations through Abraham. . . . The call of Abraham implements the promise to Noah. Both covenants are universal in scope."[18]

THE FAITH WHICH GOD DEMANDS FROM THOSE WHO RECEIVE GENERAL REVELATION

If God does leave some people with no more than the general revelation of himself given in nature and conscience and yet chooses to save them by grace through an appropriate faith response, then the apostle Paul has provided a clue to the form that such faith would take. When speaking of God's self-revelation in creation, Paul describes the *unbelieving* response of those who suppress the knowledge of God in unrighteousness. Such people "knew God" but "they did not honor him as God or give thanks to him" (Rom 1:21). The faith response to God's revelation of his eternal power and divine nature through his work of creation would, therefore, include a worship of the Creator God and a spirit of thankfulness for what he has made and provided for us. As to the revelation of God's moral demands, discerned through the human moral consciousness, Paul describes

---

[16]Jacques Dupuis, *Toward a Christian Theology of Religious Pluralism* (Maryknoll, N.Y.: Orbis, 1997), p. 36.

[17]Andreas J. Köstenberger and Peter T. O'Brien, *Salvation to the Ends of the Earth: A Biblical Theology of Mission*, New Studies in Biblical Theology, ed. D. A. Carson (Downers Grove, Ill.: InterVarsity Press, 2001), 11:28.

[18]Clark Pinnock, *A Wideness in God's Mercy: The Finality of Jesus Christ in a World of Religions* (Grand Rapids, Mich.: Zondervan, 1992), p. 21.

obedience to this law, which is possessed by those who do not have Scripture, as the righteousness that pleases God. These people are not justified by their works, but this righteousness gives evidence of the work of God in their lives.

John's Gospel provides an interesting parallel account. It tells us that "all who do evil hate the light and do not come to the light. . . . But those who do what is true come to the light, so that it may be clearly seen that their deeds have been done in God" (Jn 3:20-21). A couple of things stand out here. First, we note the statement of the principle that God draws people toward himself and that they respond to him in ways made possible by the particular revelation with which he has graced them. Christ is the light who came into the world (Jn 3:19), and those who reject him remain in the condemnation that is the natural state of the entire race in the aftermath of the Fall (Jn 3:18). But God draws people toward Christ, the light, and they believe and are saved. The second thing to note, however, is John's indication that God may be at work in people's lives *before* they encounter Christ and that his work is evident in their good deeds (Jn 3:20-21), as Paul had also noted (Rom 2:13-16). There are people whose lives were admirable before they had faith in Christ; when they meet Christ and believe in him, we recognize that their commendable deeds done *prior* to their coming to Christ were "done in God" (Jn 3:21).

EXTRABIBLICAL INSTANCES OF PEOPLE WITH NO EVIDENCE OF SPECIAL REVELATION WHO HAVE SHOWN REMARKABLE FAITH

Don Richardson tells of Yamqui Salcamayugua Pachacuti, the fifteenth-century Incan king who built the renowned structure of Machu Picchu. As Richardson tells the story, Pachacuti was a devout sun worshiper and rebuilt the temple of Inti, the sun god, in Cuzco. But Pachacuti "later began to question his god's credentials" when it dawned on him that the sun was a mere thing. Instead, Pachacuti revived the worship of Viracocha, the god who had created all things. This god was described as

> ancient, remote, supreme, and uncreated. Nor does he need the gross satisfaction of a consort. He manifests himself as a trinity when he wishes, . . . otherwise only heavenly warriors and archangels surround his loneliness. He created all peoples by his "word," . . . as well as all huacas [spirits]. He is man's Fortunus, ordaining his years and nourishing him. He is indeed the very principle of life, for he warms the folk through his created son, Punchao

[the sun disk, which was somehow distinct from Inti]. He is a bringer of peace and an orderer. He is in his own being blessed and has pity on men's wretchedness. He alone judges and absolves them and enables them to combat their evil tendencies.[19]

Here, we seem to have a man whom God moved *back* from worship of the creature to worship of the Creator.

John Ellenberger cites encouraging examples of "individuals in their pre-Christian states who nonetheless sought after God with a clearer vision of the light than their contemporaries had."[20] Among his examples are "the Chinese youth in Jakarta, Indonesia, who refused to dust the household idols 'because they don't care whether they get dusted or not, and probably they don't hear us when we pray to them either'";[21] "the Dayak leader in Kalimantan . . . who realized that his charms and fetishes were creations of his own hands, and resolved to worship instead the deity that created his hands";[22] "a Lobi man from Burkina Faso, West Africa" who "claimed God had told him to put away his fetishes and wait for a messenger who would come to tell him the true way."[23] In Laos, southeast Asia, "a Hmong female shaman prophesied about the coming of a messenger who would tell them of the true God."[24]

In each of these cases, "they identified Jesus as the fulfillment of their searching when they heard the gospel message," though not always immediately. "It took the Chinese youth years of exposure to Christian faith before he fully believed." The Dayak leader more quickly perceived in Jesus the one he looked for when the missionary who visited his village spoke of "the God that made you, who made your hands." The Lobi African was the first to accept the gospel when it came to his village, after ten years of ostracism and persecution. The Hmong shaman was instrumental in bringing about a "people movement" to Christ because of her position.[25]

---

[19]B. C. Brundage, *Empire of the Inca* (Norman: University of Oklahoma Press, 1963), p. 165, quoted in Don Richardson, *Eternity in Their Hearts,* rev. ed. (Ventura, Calif.: Regal, 1984), p. 38.

[20]Ellenberger, "Is Hell," p. 223.

[21]Ibid., from an interview with Eddy Susanto, Jaypura, Indonesia, December 1975.

[22]Ibid., from an interview with Christian Missionary Alliance missionary Ruth Rudes, August 1990.

[23]Robert S. Roseberry, *The Niger Vision* (Harrisburg, Penn.: Christian Publications, 1934), p. 117, quoted in Ellenberger, "Is Hell," p. 223.

[24]G. Linwood Barney, "The Meo: An Incipient Church," in *Readings in Missionary Anthropology,* 2nd ed., ed. William A. Smalley (Pasadena, Calif.: William Carey Library, 1978), p. 469, quoted in Ellenberger, "Is Hell," p. 223.

[25]Ellenberger, "Is Hell," p. 223.

In all of the above incidents, the gospel eventually reached these people in whose hearts the Spirit of God had been at work beforehand, but the critical question is what to make of people like them who are never reached with the good news. Particularly compelling is the story Ellenberger tells of Mugumende, an Irian Jayan "who had been a spiritual seeker but died without hearing of Christ." When Christian missionaries arrived in Mugumende's village years later, Mugumende's stepson received the gospel and led a people movement to follow Christ. But, he said, "If Mugumende had been here when the gospel came to our valley, he would have been the first Christian (instead of me)."[26] However rare such people may be, it seems very unlikely to me that people who clearly *would have believed* had they heard the gospel will be damned because they did not hear. This is not to say that such people are saved on the ground of what they *would* have done but that the attitude observed in Mugumende—which made his stepson assert what Mugumende would have done—demonstrated the quality of the faith that is instrumental in justification.

N. L. Niswander wrote of a missionary who was impressed with the openness and interest shown by a man who was listening to his preaching.

> The subject of Christ as Savior brought him delight and joy. Later, when he talked with the missionary, the man spoke of three crises in his life. The first one was of his becoming aware of the perfection and wonder of the universe. Nature revealed to him the awesome wonder of the Mighty One. The next crisis was a serious condemnation and conviction of sin. His knowledge of the grandeur of nature brought to light his own imperfections. He realized then the close relationship between the physical laws and the moral law and the holiness of God. In the third crisis he became an earnest seeker for God's answer to this confusion in his heart and mind. He testified that when he sought God's forgiveness, he was conscious of a Savior's presence. And now, he continued, "Since I have heard you speak, I recognize in Jesus the Person who has made atonement for my sin."[27]

Ajith Fernando comments, "Here was a modern Cornelius indeed. We note that this person responded as best he could to the light he received until he was finally led to Christ."[28] The principle of response is

[26] Alice Gibbons, *The People Time Forgot* (Chicago: Moody Press, 1981), pp. 212-17, quoted in Ellenberger, "Is Hell," p. 223.
[27] J. Oswald Sanders, *How Lost Are the Heathen?* (Chicago: Moody Press, 1972), pp. 67-70, referring to N. L. Niswander's article in *The Alliance Weekly*, July 2, 1958, quoted in Ajith Fernando, *The Christian's Attitude Toward World Religions* (Wheaton, Ill.: Tyndale House, 1987), p. 134.
[28] Fernando, *Christian's Attitude*, p. 134.

worth noting. This man did not have the advantage that Cornelius had—namely, the old covenant scriptures that were taught in the synagogue—but Niswander depicts a Spirit-illumined response to general revelation in nature and conscience. Here was a man who was not like those of whose condemnation Paul wrote in Romans 1 but who did, indeed, respond properly to those forms of revelation. We can rejoice that he was reached by a Christian missionary, but I see no reason to assume that God was not already doing a saving work in the life of this repentant sinner. Suppose that his first personal encounter with Christ had been at the moment of death rather than through the proclamation of the gospel. I think we can assume that he would then have responded to Jesus in exactly the way he responded to Jesus when he encountered him in the missionary's preaching. The man knew, then, that Jesus was the One for whom he had been looking, but note that he had been blessed with a sense of "a Savior's presence" even earlier, when he had sought forgiveness.

AN ASSESSMENT OF THE POTENTIALLY SALVIFIC VALUE OF GENERAL REVELATION

Daniel Clendenin observes that all people have equal access to natural revelation but not all respond equally positively. "Some people respond in ways that conform to truth, beauty, and goodness—and these the Christian freely acknowledges. Others respond in counterproductive ways, bringing forth evil, falsehood, and ugliness."[29] The same is true of special revelation, so the additional revelation does not guarantee a positive religious response, "nor is the lack of special revelation necessarily an obstacle to experiencing true religion." People will be judged according to what they have done (Rev 20:12-13; cf. Mt 25:31-46). "The ultimate difference," Clendenin proposes, "rests in the human response to God's revelation (natural or special), the synergistic encounter between divine grace and human freedom. Whether that grace proves effective or vain depends upon our response (1 Cor 15:10-11; 2 Cor 6:1; Phil 2:12-13)."[30] Clendenin's synergistic approach fits best within a Catholic, Lutheran or Wesleyan reading, but its basic point is valid, even from the standpoint of a monergist. Monergists do not deny the necessity of human response, but we believe that positive response is the fruit of God's own effective work in a

---

[29]Daniel Clendenin, *Many Gods, Many Lords* (Grand Rapids, Mich.: Baker, 1995), p. 57.
[30]Ibid.

sinner's heart. God accepts people from every nation who fear him and do what is right (Acts 10:34-35), but both the fear of God and obedience to the law are fruits of efficacious grace.

I have identified the sort of faith that Scripture describes as what God expects from those to whom he makes himself known through the media of general revelation, but I find no biblical examples of people who were saved through general revelation alone. Most of the Old Testament people who are outside Israel and yet evidence a proper relationship to God all had special revelation in some form. For this reason, it seems rather inappropriate to classify people such as Abel, Noah, Enoch and Job as "holy pagans."[31] Nor does Cornelius seem a good candidate in the New Testament, because he was certainly blessed with special revelation through his synagogue worship. On the other hand, God's relationships with Job and Melchizedek are striking, but we know nothing of the means by which these relationships came about. They certainly seem to have happened apart from the narrowly focused program through which God developed his relationship with the people of the older covenant. (This will get a closer look in the next chapter.)

On the other hand, the lack of examples in the Bible of people saved through general revelation should not be overemphasized; such arguments from silence have limited value. Consequently, we need to consider more carefully *how* general revelation might function in the salvation of people for whom it is the only means of knowing God. Erickson suggests that there are five elements that constitute "the essential nature of the gospel message" and that are available through general revelation:

> (1) The belief in one good powerful God. (2) The belief that he (man) owes this God perfect obedience to his law. (3) The consciousness that he does not meet this standard, and therefore is guilty and condemned. (4) The realization that nothing he can offer God can compensate him (or atone) for this sin and guilt. (5) The belief that God is merciful, and will forgive and accept those who cast themselves upon his mercy.[32]

Accordingly, Erickson asks, "May it not be that if a man believes and acts on this set of tenets he is redemptively related to God and receives the benefits of Christ's death, whether he consciously knows and understands the details of that provision or not?"[33]

---

[31]This objection is noted by Erickson, *How Shall They,* p. 188.
[32]Millard J. Erickson, "Hope for Those Who Haven't Heard? Yes, But . . ." *Evangelical Missions Quarterly* 11 (April 1975): 125.
[33]Ibid.

In Acts 17:24-30, Paul tells the Athenians that God's creation of the cosmos, his creation of the human race from one ancestor and his providential rule over all of the nations were "so that they would search for God and perhaps grope for him and find him" (Acts 17:27). Even Carson, made cautious by his concerns about relativism, notes that "at least one of God's purposes in his providential rule is to lead people to know him. Clearly, that was the 'hope.'"[34] Carson observes that the Athenians had *not* found God by this means but, he says, "it *may* be the case that God has in come cases opened the eyes of some people to recognize the existence and graciousness of their Maker and turn to him in repentance and faith, imploring him for mercy."[35] Carson is very cautious about the extent to which God's saving grace may be at work outside special covenantal revelation, but it would be hard to deny that Paul laid out before the Athenians a description of God's gracious purposes in his universal self-revelation, which opens the door to accessibilism. God does not make himself known only in order to compound people's guilt; he makes himself known in this universally accessible manner so that people would search for him and "perhaps grope for him and find him" since "he is not far from each one of us" (Acts 17:27).

On the other hand, evangelicals who have spoken optimistically about the salvific potential of general revelation may have underestimated the extent to which special revelation is experienced. I suggest, therefore, that a realistic assessment of the situation of the peoples of the world in regard to divine revelation must take into account the following eight factors:

- the remnants of special revelation that have been passed on (however distortedly) in cultural and religious traditions of the peoples dispersed throughout the world

- the long period of time between the Fall and God's inspiration of written revelation, during which it seems highly implausible that God made no special contact with people in revelations of the nonuniversally normative kind

- the contact of the peoples and of the religions of the world with the in-

---

[34]D. A. Carson, *The Gagging of God: Christianity Confronts Pluralism* (Grand Rapids, Mich.: Zondervan, 1996), p. 309.
[35]Ibid.

spired scriptures of the Old and New Testaments

- the fact that God still encounters people directly (in dreams, visions and theophanies), as he did in the Old Testament, and that a host of angels also serve him as messengers

- the fact that the Word operates throughout the world, just as he did before and during the incarnation, in ways not limited by his embodiment

- the work of the Holy Spirit, who was poured out "upon all flesh" (Acts 2:17), and who operates in a special way in and through those whom he indwells in new covenant blessing, but whose work is not restricted to the church

- God's promise that those who sincerely seek him with all their hearts will find him (Jer 29:13; Jas 4:8)

- the possibility of universal at-death encounters with Christ—not a "second chance" for salvation but the first-time meeting with Christ—that will elicit from all a response consistent with their prior response to God's overtures toward them through less complete modes of revelation (I will expand on this last factor in chapter ten).

A CLOSER EXAMINATION OF SOME OF THE FACTORS THAT MAY MAKE IT UNLIKELY THAT ANYONE LACKS SPECIAL REVELATION

Each of the eight factors I have just identified could be expanded, but I will comment further on just a few of them. I note, first, that we must speak tentatively when we speculate on the source or causes of someone's knowledge of God. The possible sources are numerous, and we are unlikely to be able to separate out which of the strands identified above may have taken someone beyond what he or she could have learned about God simply through general revelation and the Holy Spirit's illumination of his or her mind in connection with that revelation. Thus, in the material that follows, we will frequently see that it is possible for two or more of the above factors to have come together in the situations we meet as we bear witness to Christ throughout the world.

Traces of earlier revelation. We may note, for instance, the remarkable parallels between the biblical account of the creation and the flood and other similar myths among some people long out of contact with biblical covenant people, but we cannot discern conclusively how to account for these similarities.[36] Among those who have showed a special interest in our first factor—the traces of early revelation in the traditions of cultures and religions—is Jonathan Edwards, who called this the *prisca theologia*, or "ancient theology." Few, if any, have given more careful attention to the work of Edwards in regard to our subject than has Gerald McDermott.[37] He observes that Edwards "went to great lengths detailing in his notebooks the religious truths possessed by the heathen."[38] Edwards explained these truths as revelation received directly or indirectly from God by the "fathers of the nations" and "passed down, by tradition, from one generation to the next."[39] Edwards generally viewed these distorted remnants of special revelation as preparatory to the gospel; among the many absurdities in heathen religion and philosophy "there were enough 'scraps of truth' to show the way to salvation."[40] Unfortunately, the revelation was distorted because of human finitude and corruption, so people fell into superstition and idolatry.[41] Nevertheless, McDermott posits that Edwards's "private correspondence and notebooks suggest that in his last decade, while in exile, the great theologian might have concluded that he had found holy pagans who, like Cornelius, were sincerely seeking the gospel."[42]

More recently, striking evidence of the remnants of knowledge of special revelation has been cited by New Tribes missionaries Bob and Cecilia Brown, who work in the village of Simpang, among the Saluan people in remote jungle mountains of Sulawesi, Indonesia. The Browns wondered how they could "teach these people whose social control was so effective that there had not been one theft, divorce, wife-beating or adultery episode in the village as long as [they] had known them. They were proud

---

[36]See for instance, Tokunboh Adeyemo's treatment of African concepts of God that bear similarities to the biblical narrative. He posits that "the principle of cultural diffusion explains in part the elements of truth observable in non-Christian religions" ("Unapproachable God: The High God of African Traditional Religion," in *The Global God: Multicultural Evangelical Views of God*, ed. Aída Besançon Spencer and William David Spencer [Grand Rapids, Mich.: Baker, 1998], p. 144; see esp. pp. 140-44).

[37]Gerald McDermott's seminal work on our subject is *Jonathan Edwards Confronts the Gods: Christian Theology, Enlightenment Religion and Non-Christian Faiths* (New York: Oxford University Press, 2000), but he has made the fruit of this work accessible in various other writings to which I will also allude along the way.

[38]Ibid., p. 94.

[39]Ibid., pp. 94-95.

[40]Ibid., p. 96.

[41]Ibid., p. 95.

[42]Gerald R. McDermott, "Holy Pagans," *Christian History* 22 (Winter 2003): 39.

of their superiority over the corrupt and scandalous lives of the 'civilized,' religious, coastal people."[43] The Browns often prayed about what name they should use for God and sensed that God had answered that prayer when they encountered the traditional Saluan story of "the Snake and the Man."

> The One-Who-Formed-Our-Fingers had made a beautiful place. When he made the man and the woman he told them that they could live in that beautiful place. So, they lived there, and their fire never went out, and their water flasks never went dry. The One-Who-Formed-Our-Fingers said that he was going away and that they must not eat of the fruit of one tree while he was gone. Then he left. While he was gone, the snake came. Now, the man and the snake were brothers. The snake told the man that the fruit was so good and that he should try some. The man did eat the fruit. Then he was afraid of The-One-Who-Formed-Our-Fingers. When The-One-Who-Formed-Our-Fingers returned, he knew right away what had happened. He chased the man away from the beautiful place and said, "From now on the water won't come by itself, and the firewood won't come by itself, and the food won't come by itself. The sweat will drip off your jaw and your fingernails won't get long because you will have to work to get food."[44]

The Browns report that the Saluan "knew nothing else about the The-One-Who-Formed-Our-Fingers except that when he wanted somebody to die, there was no amount of ritual that could stop that death. He was above all and very far away." This story, along with another account telling of a flood that covered the mountains, "provided a starting point for evangelism."[45] As the Browns taught the Saluan people the biblical narrative, it was many months before they got to the story of Jesus, and the Spirit of God brought a conviction of sin and the joy of faith to many of the people in the village.[46] But what is important to the point I am making here is that the people in this remote village had not lived through the centuries with general revelation alone. However distorted, the memory of basic aspects of the divine revelation that God preserved accurately in his inspired Scriptures had remained with those people. God had not left himself without witness, and that witness went beyond the general revelation in God's creative work, although it attested to that

---

[43]Bob and Cecilia Brown, "The Power of the Creation Message," *Impact*, February 1997, p. 1.
[44]Ibid., p. 2.
[45]Ibid.
[46]Ibid., p. 4.

most fundamental form of God's self-disclosure, the self-revelation of The-One-Who-Formed-Our-Fingers.

J. H. Bavinck comments on the main resemblances between "the religious ideas and customs of all races and peoples," such as the similarity between the myths, religious rites and customs of the Indian tribes in America, the Bantu tribes in Africa, and people in widely separated parts of Asia and the islands of the Pacific.[47] In accounting for this similarity, Bavinck appeals first to "the unity of mankind" and suggests, "It is not only possible but even likely that there are still some common traditions which go back to a past that we have no knowledge of."[48]

Winfried Corduan sums up this first point well, under what he calls "original monotheism."

> Once one has acknowledged the reality of a special revelation, one ought not to ignore the possibility of a continuity of such a special revelation through tribal memory. To be more specific, according to special revelation, the history of humanity began with the creation of human beings who had a direct relationship with God, the Creator. After the human beings disobeyed the Creator, their relationship with him was broken, but certainly not their knowledge of him. Two generations into their existence outside of paradise, they began regular worship practices, and that tradition has continued ever since. Since there is good reason to believe in the common descent of all human beings from the original pair, both on revelatory and scientific grounds, it is logical that the monotheistic religions practiced by preliterate tribes do, in fact, derive from the same monotheistic beliefs and practices attributed to the earliest humans in special revelation. . . . The continuity of monotheism is based on an original special revelation and reinforced by general revelation.[49]

Corduan thinks that this makes it unnecessary to posit special revelation outside the covenant community.[50]

The delay between the Fall and the giving of Scripture. Moving on to a different point, consider the second factor I identified above: the long period of time between humankind's Fall into sin and God's inspiration of written revelation. This presents a very significant difficulty to those

---

[47]J. H. Bavinck, *The Church Between Temple and Mosque: A Study of the Relationship Between the Christian Faith and Other Religions* (Grand Rapids, Mich.: Eerdmans, 1966), p. 30.
[48]Ibid., p. 31.
[49]Winfried Corduan, *A Tapestry of Faiths: The Common Threads Between Christianity and World Religions* (Downers Grove, Ill.: InterVarsity Press, 2002), pp. 41-42.
[50]Ibid., 42 n. 25.

who insist that the special revelation given in Scripture is necessary to salvation. John Feinberg defends the view that God created the universe in periods of approximately twenty-four hours.[51] The dispute concerning the timing of God's creative work need not trouble us here, but I am interested in one of the arguments Feinberg uses to bolster his own position on the matter. People died between Adam and Moses because they "were guilty of at least one sin (Adam's), but God apparently revealed no remedy, no word of salvation, to most of them."[52] Feinberg suggests that "it is already hard enough to uphold God as just in condemning such people, who never heard and never read a Bible because there was none,"[53] but he considers the problem reduced if the length of time between Adam and Moses is as short as it could be with a modified twenty-four-hour-creative-day position. He notes that "God revealed himself to people like Noah, Enoch, and Abraham in special ways, but these people seem to have been unusual cases."[54] Of course, the difficulty Feinberg is wrestling with is only experienced in an ecclesiocentrist position. If we begin with the assumption that the Spirit of God works in a saving way with all people, although the means and content of his self-revelation vary, the problem does not exist. The people who lived between Adam and Moses—those who lived without the special forms of revelation experienced by the likes of Noah, Enoch and Abraham—then become a category of people whose counterpart may still exist in parts of the world. If we need not assume that those people before Moses were completely outside God's saving work, then we need not assume the same today of people in an analogous situation.

The Holy Spirit's work outside the church. We can skip on to the sixth of my eight factors: the Holy Spirit's work outside the church. When reading evangelical statements that general revelation is insufficient to elicit saving faith, I am struck by the apparent exclusion of the Holy Spirit's work of illumination and calling in connection with general revelation as well as special revelation. For instance, James Hoffmeier does fine exegetical work on Psalm 19 as he demonstrates how the psalmist draws out the superiority of "the perfect law of Yahweh (vv. 7-11)" over "the Glory of God as revealed in creation (vv. 2-6)." Hoffmeier then con-

---

[51]John Feinberg, *No One Like Him: The Doctrine of God*, Foundations of Evangelical Theology (Wheaton, Ill.: Crossway, 2001), pp. 623-24.
[52]Ibid., p. 623.
[53]Ibid., pp. 623-24.
[54]Ibid., p. 623.

cludes that the intent of Psalm 19 "is to show that from creation one can only obtain an impression of God, whereas through special revelation a clearer picture is obtained."[55]

I cannot imagine that anyone would deny that God's acts of special revelation make his nature known to us in much clearer and fuller ways than do his works of creation and providence. This would be true even if creation had not been "subjected to futility" by the Fall (Rom 8:20) and even if our minds were not darkened by sin. When we know God through his speaking by the prophets and culminatively through the Son, we contemplate God's creative work and are led to glorify God in ways to which creation alone could never lead us. The movement in Psalm 19 from general to special revelation is, therefore, one that we can easily understand. Even as we glorify Elohim, the God who created, we are most grateful that we know him as Yahweh, the one who graciously brought us into covenant relationship with himself. But note what Hoffmeier does with this truth: he asserts that "special revelation is necessary to make general revelation result in salvation because fallen, sinful humans cannot comprehend the inaudible message of natural revelation"[56]—*unless we include in our definition of "special revelation" the inner work of the Holy Spirit* that is necessary even for verbal revelation to be salvific.

I think that Hoffmeier's statement takes us in a different direction than the one he intended. It reminds us that no revelation (general or special) has saving power in itself. It must be accompanied by an illuminating and enabling work by the Spirit of God. Evangelical theologians frequently distinguish between God's work of revelation and his work of illumination, but Hoffmeier's comment (unwittingly) draws our attention to the fuzziness of this distinction. If revelation is the process of God's making himself known to people, then the Spirit's work of illumination is an intrinsic part of God's self-revelatory work. Thus, while a distinction between the divine acts of revelation and of illumination is sometimes helpful, we cannot ignore that illumination is itself part of the full process of God's self-disclosure to us. This is a very helpful contribution to our understanding of the universal accessibility of salvation because it makes it impossible to state, without very careful qualification, that no one can be saved by general revelation alone.

---

[55]James K. Hoffmeier, " 'The Heavens Declare the Glory of God': The Limits of General Revelation," *Trinity Journal*, n.s., 21 (2000): 23.
[56]Ibid.

If we make a hard distinction between revelation and illumination, we may legitimately say that salvation is impossible through general revelation alone. But we would have to say, likewise, that salvation is impossible through *special* revelation alone. That is to say, without the Spirit's illumination, no form of revelation results in a person's salvation. On the other hand, this also opens up for us the distinct possibility that general revelation *plus* illumination may lead to salvation just as is true when special revelation is illuminated. *If illumination is defined as a form of special revelation,* as Hoffmeier intimates, *then we can say that no one can be saved by general revelation alone, and still not be saying that people whose knowledge is restricted to universally accessible modes of revelation cannot be saved.* Thus, I cannot emphasize too strongly the immense importance of the Holy Spirit's role in opening the eyes of the spiritually blind to the truths of God's self-revelation and softening (or "opening") the hearts of the spiritually hardened to reception of the truth revealed.

Putting together a number of the factors that I have identified, Bavinck expressed his own reluctance to overstate the extent to which any of the peoples of the world are left with only general revelation:

> For while there are disturbing depths, and terrible degenerations, there are also unexpected high points, and exalted exceptions. These high points are extremely noteworthy. Do they go back to ancient stories which continue to live among the people, and in which there is still alive in bastard form much of the primeval history of humanity, the primeval revelation of God, the fall into sin, and the lost paradise? Do such histories sometimes suddenly appear and do they then begin to stimulate the spirit of man? Or has Israel, the nation to whom God has particularly revealed himself in a special manner, exercised a greater influence upon the ancient world than we have frequently surmised? May we assume that a certain ray of special revelation has gone forth? Various scholars have assumed with respect to India, China, and Japan that some forms of Hinduism and Buddhism in these lands originated under the influence of Nestorian Christianity, which had established itself in the Far East during the first centuries.[57]

In short, although we may doubt that many people come to God in acceptable faith through general revelation *alone,* we dare not underestimate the extent to which special revelation reaches people throughout the world and the extent to which the Holy Spirit's "special" convicting and enlightening work uses that revelation to draw them to God.

---

[57]J. H. Bavinck, *An Introduction to the Science of Missions,* trans. David Hugh Freeman (Kampen: J. H. Kok, 1954; Philadelphia: Presbyterian & Reformed, 1960), p. 236.

DOES GOD'S KNOWLEDGE OF HOW PEOPLE WOULD RESPOND IF THEY HEARD THE GOSPEL MAKE SALVATION MORE ACCESSIBLE?

I have alluded to the sense of injustice that Christians commonly have when they hear ecclesiocentrists say that the unevangelized cannot be saved. Two responses are common. First, monergistic ecclesiocentrism defends God's justice by arguing that the unevangelized are not condemned for not believing in a Jesus of whom they were ignorant but are condemned only for the sins they committed knowingly. Synergistic ecclesiocentrism may make that same point, but it often adds a second: the attribution of responsibility to Christians who did not carry the gospel to those who die in ignorance. For many objectors, the first response is small comfort since the unevangelized still spend eternity in hell, even though their punishment is less severe than of people who consciously rejected Christ. The second response is, likewise, not very satisfying, because the Christians in heaven have been absolved of their neglect of evangelism but the unevangelized still suffer in hell. A further objection to the second response might also arise, namely, that people's lack of special revelation was often not remediable by those who had the knowledge. Indeed, for centuries, the covenant people of Israel were given no commission by God to take their special revelation to the nations. So what are we to say about the people who lived in North America and Australia after God had made his covenant with Abraham? Abraham's descendants could not have reached these people with the gospel promise even if they had known of their existence.

To address this sense of injustice created by the ecclesiocentric message, another response has been developed through asking another question: What would happen if God knew that some of the unevangelized *would* have believed *if* they had heard the gospel promise (given to Abraham) or the complete good news concerning Jesus? Those who pose such a question are generally synergists, who make use of the "middle knowledge" proposal put forward by Luis de Molina; he proposed that creatures have libertarian freedom, so they do what they choose (indeterministically) in this world, but God sovereignly chose this world history from among all the worlds that might have been.[58] The middle-knowledge position asserts that, in addition to his knowing

---

[58]See chapter 8 of Terrance Tiessen, *Providence and Prayer: How Does God Work in the World?* (Downers Grove, Ill.: InterVarsity Press, 2000), for an exposition of Molinism.

innately all actual truths (natural knowledge) and his knowing those things that are actual because he wills them to be (free knowledge), God knows counterfactuals, that is, things that never happen but that *would* happen if different circumstances existed. In the classic form of this view, it was from his knowledge of all the possible worlds that might have come about if people had chosen differently, that God chose to bring into being this particular world, in which people (libertarianly) freely make their actual choices.

Two Molinist (synergistic) strategies for dealing with the state of the unevangelized. This Molinist proposal has been applied to the salvation of the unevangelized in two different ways. First, it has been proposed by some people that God elects to salvation all those whom he knew *would* believe if they heard the gospel. Donald Lake, for instance, says that "God knows who would, under ideal circumstances, believe the gospel, and on the basis of his foreknowledge, applies that gospel even if the person never hears the gospel during his lifetime."[59] Brethren evangelist George Goodman asks,

> What if an omniscient God, seeing that [the unevangelized] take a true attitude to the light they have, is able to see that had the Greater Light, the True Light, been given to them, they would have rejoiced in the light? Does the fact that the light never reached them prevent the outflow of His grace to them?[60]

This proposal provides a Molinist version of accessibilism. The unevangelized can be saved if they would have believed the gospel had they received it. These Molinists could tell our hypothetical inquirers that their ancestors might have been saved, that their salvation would depend on whether they had hearts that were responsive to God in the ways in which they knew about him.

A second approach is taken by William Lane Craig, probably the leading evangelical proponent of Molinism. Although Craig admits that accessibilism might be true, he is not very hopeful and he does not use God's middle knowledge to support it. He grants that "perhaps some do access salvation by means of general revelation" but opines that "if we take Scrip-

---

[59]Donald M. Lake, "He Died for All: The Universal Dimensions of the Atonement," in *Grace Unlimited,* ed. Clark H. Pinnock (Minneapolis: Bethany Fellowship, 1975), p. 43.

[60]Quoted by J. Oswald Sanders, *How Lost,* p. 62, quoted in John Sanders, *No Other Name: An Investigation into the Destiny of the Unevangelized* (Grand Rapids, Mich.: Eerdmans, 1992), pp. 168-69.

ture seriously we must admit that these are relatively few."[61] Craig proposes, rather, that "God in his providence so arranged the world that those who never in fact hear the gospel are persons who would not respond to it if they did hear it. God brings the gospel to all those who he knows will respond to it if they hear it."[62] In regard to "persons who do not respond to His grace under especially disadvantageous circumstances, God can so order the world that such persons are exclusively people who would *still* not have believed even had they been created under more advantageous circumstances."[63] Consequently, we need not be troubled about any injustice in God's condemnation of the unevangelized or even about those evangelized with great obstacles to their believing the gospel. We know that God will get the gospel to anyone who would respond to it.

To those who have complained that divine judgment is inconsistent with an affirmation that God is all-loving, Craig gives a Molinist response. He asserts that "an all-powerful God can create a world in which everybody hears the gospel."[64] But he believes that

> so long as people are free, there is simply no guarantee that everybody in that world would freely be saved. . . . So long as God desires free creatures, . . . even he cannot guarantee that all will freely embrace his salvation. In fact, there is not even any guarantee that the balance between saved and lost in that totally evangelized world would be any better than it is in the actual world![65]

In fact, Craig grants that there may be "possible worlds in which everyone hears the gospel and is freely saved," but he denies that God's love compels him to prefer one of these worlds to the actual world. It might be that "the only worlds in which everybody hears and believes the gospel are worlds with only a handful of people in them. In any world in which God creates more people, at least one person refuses to receive God's salvation."[66] Craig concludes that "so long as God provides sufficient grace for

---

[61]William Lane Craig, "Politically Incorrect Salvation," in *Christian Apologetics in the Post-Modern World*, ed. Timothy P. Phillips and Dennis L. Okholm (Downers Grove, Ill.: InterVarsity Press, 1995), p. 89. A version of the essay can also be found in *Faith and Philosophy* 6 (April 1989): 172-88.

[62]William Lane Craig, *The Only Wise God: The Compatibility of Divine Foreknowledge and Human Freedom* (Grand Rapids, Mich.: Baker, 1987), pp. 150-51.

[63]Craig, "Politically Incorrect," p. 94.

[64]Ibid., p. 91.

[65]Ibid., pp. 91-92.

[66]Ibid., p. 92.

salvation to every person in any world He creates, He is no less loving for preferring one of the more populous worlds, even though that implies that some people would freely reject Him and be lost."[67] Craig considers it possible that the actual world has the "optimal balance," that "in order to create this many people who are saved, God also had to create this many people who are lost."[68]

A parallel monergist strategy. Craig's appeal to God's knowledge of counterfactuals within a synergistic model is paralleled from within a monergistic framework by Augustine.

> He realized there were some barbarian tribes located in the distant southern reaches of Africa that remained unaware of Jesus Christ and geographically beyond the current ministries of the church. Yet, in order to maintain both his ecclesial perspective on salvation and the justice of God, he asserted that the gospel had not been made known to these people precisely because it was foreknown by God that they would not believe.[69]

This seems a peculiar thing for a monergist to say, however, since God's foreknowing that those tribes would not believe is really a foreknowledge of God's choice not to give them faith. The major scandal of monergism is its doctrine of unconditional election, as some Calvinist scholars have noted. If God did not choose those tribes for salvation, they would not have believed, no matter how many evangelists were sent to them or how many miracles were done among them, because the Spirit of God would not have produced faith. On the other hand, if God did choose to save them he would have gotten the gospel message to them in some way. So God's knowledge of counterfactuals does not significantly reduce the scandal of Augustinian monergism in the eyes of synergists.[70]

An assessment of the Molinist (synergistic) strategies. Both of the applications of Molinist (synergistic) middle knowledge address the concern about possible injustice in the case of the unevangelized. In the first pro-

---

[67]Ibid.

[68]Ibid., p. 93.

[69]Don A. Pittman, Ruben L. F. Habito and Terry C. Muck, eds., *Ministry and Theology in Global Perspective: Contemporary Challenges for the Church* (Grand Rapids, Mich.: Eerdmans, 1996), pp. 48-49.

[70]Frankly, many of us monergists feel that scandal quite keenly, too, but we live with it because we are convinced that Scripture teaches it. Our primary form of reconciliation with the apparent problem is to remind ourselves that no one deserves to be saved. Since all sinners deserve condemnation and since salvation is by grace, we need to focus on the wonderful grace of God that saves so many unworthy sinners rather than acting as though an injustice had been done to those who do not receive this grace.

posal (Lake and Goodman), the concern is allayed by the possibility that
worthy people among the unevangelized can be saved. The second proposal (Craig) addresses the concern by postulating that none of the unevangelized who are lost would have chosen otherwise, even if they had received the gospel.

One problem with the first Molinist approach, the accessibilist approach,
is that it requires no faith at all.[71] I think that a synergist who wishes to appeal to middle knowledge would do better to posit that this group of the
elect would have some form of faith proportional to the revelation they received. At first glance, it might appear that Anderson has used an accessibilist appeal to God's knowledge of counterfactuals similar to the one made
by Lake and Goodman. Anderson asks, "Is it not possible that an omniscient
God will judge such people, if they have never heard the gospel, on the basis
of what he knows would have been their response if they had heard . . . ?"[72]
But before concluding his question, Anderson indicates *how* God knows
what the response of these unevangelized people would have been. He describes it as "a response manifested instead, in their ignorance, by that
search after God and abandonment to his mercy that only the Holy Spirit
could have inspired."[73] This is a very important qualifier, for it indicates that
God has given these people repentance and faith during their lifetime. It is
through *this* faith that such people are saved by Christ's atoning work, not
through a faith that *would* have occurred *if* they had heard the gospel. This
is the response of the elect who are ignorant of the gospel through no fault
of their own. Anderson expects, as I do, that if these people had heard the
gospel later in their lives, they would have accepted it quickly and have said
to the messenger, "Why did you not come and tell me this before? It is what
I have been waiting for all my life." Of those who never do hear the gospel
in this life, Anderson surmises that they "will awaken, as it were, on the
other side of the grave to worship the one in whom, without understanding
it, they found forgiveness."[74] (In chapter ten, I will expand on that concept.)

The *critical problem* for both of the Molinist approaches, however, is
what is frequently called the *grounding objection*.[75] The problem is that

---

[71]This problem has been identified by Pinnock, *Wideness in God's Mercy*, p. 161.

[72]Norman Anderson, "Christianity and the World's Religions," in *Introductory Articles*, vol. 1
   of *The Expositor's Bible Commentary*, ed. Frank E. Gaebelein and J. D. Douglas (Grand Rapids,
   Mich.: Zondervan, 1979), p. 156.

[73]Ibid.

[74]Ibid.

[75]See the discussion in Tiessen, *Providence and Prayer*, p. 317.

knowing future counterfactuals of libertarian human freedom is impossible for *anyone,* including God. There is nothing that would ground God's knowledge of what creatures would do in situations that never occur. Even God cannot know how libertarianly free people who never hear the gospel *would* respond if they did hear it. By definition, to be libertarianly free is to have the power to choose otherwise, so that a free person's decision is unpredictable with certainty, even if one knows everything else about the situation.

A comprehensive foreknowledge of counterfactuals is only possible if creatures have compatibilist freedom, the freedom of spontaneity or volition. Only if some form of determinism is correct can God know what a person *would* do in a situation that never actually occurs, because he not only knows the situational factors completely, but he also knows the person so completely that her action is predictable. We act freely, but we act out of the complex of habits, motives, preferences, inclinations and so on that constitute our nature. It is because God knows us so thoroughly in our inner being, what Scripture calls the "heart," that he can know what a person would do in a given situation. Within the context of God's sovereign and unconditional elective grace, God chooses those to whom he gives faith. So the concept of his simply foreknowing who *would not* believe is not useful to the discussion of the unevangelized; it does not make salvation more accessible.

God's knowledge of counterfactuals *is* useful to God, however, in working out his saving purpose, because he knows what it would take for each person to repent and believe. He is, therefore, able to bring about the salvation of the elect without coercion. Although God's choice of sinners is completely gracious, and hence sovereign, no one is saved unwillingly. This has always been believed by Calvinists, whether or not they affirm divine middle knowledge, despite common Arminian misunderstanding. One can only be saddened by misrepresentation such as we hear in Pinnock's statement that B. B. Warfield's "view holds that the saved are saved by divine coercion."[76]

SUMMING UP

Although salvation has always been by God's grace through faith, the kind of faith God requires varies depending on the revelation with which he has blessed an individual. If God gives a person only general revela-

---

[76]Pinnock, *Wideness in God's Mercy,* p. 42.

tion, then he requires them to believe and obey only according to the knowledge that they have received. In principle, then, it is possible that God might graciously save someone through general revelation by eliciting the appropriate kind of faith in that person's mind and heart. Some of the ancestors might, therefore, have been saved if only by worshiping the Creator and being thankful to him for his provision. On the other hand, I have identified eight factors that, taken together, may make it unlikely that there are actually any people who live "normal" lives in the world and are completely ignorant of any form of special revelation. Thus, it is certainly possible that some of God's elect are people who do not receive the gospel (including some of the ancestors of those who are just now being reached by missionaries), but we need not assume that their salvation comes about only through means of general revelation.

The introduction of God's knowledge of counterfactuals into the discussion of the possibility of salvation for the unevangelized might sound helpful to the accessibilist proposal, but this turns out not to be the case. I have raised two objections: First, it is problematic to propose that some people are saved by potential rather than actual faith. And second, it is impossible for God to know counterfactuals concerning the decisions that people would make if they have the libertarian freedom that synergists assume they have. On the other hand, I do affirm the usefulness of God's knowledge of counterfactuals in regard to people who have compatibilist freedom. This enables God to save people without forcing them to believe.

In the next chapter, we want to look at the situation of the many people whom God saved without their having faith in Jesus, both before and during Jesus' ministry on earth. What might we learn from their salvation that will be helpful in considering the situation of people in our own day who do not know about Jesus?

9

What About the Saved
Who Did Not Believe in Jesus?

Thesis 9: Old Testament believers were saved by faith in God and in God's sure fulfillment of his promises to them, although the manner in which those promises would be fulfilled became clear only gradually. Their faith in God was frequently demonstrated in their obedience to his instructions or in deeds that expressed their confidence in God. We are not told much about the revelation to which Old Testament believers outside the covenant people (e.g., Job, Melchizedek and Jethro) were responding. It may have been general revelation or traditional remnants of much earlier special revelation, but I think it most likely that God revealed himself to them personally, as he did to the covenant people. From the experience of Old Testament believers, we can assert that God may save people today who do not hear the gospel. He could graciously save them by similar means of revelation and by the same kinds of faith, trust in God and acceptance of the truthfulness of his promise.

Thesis 10: From observing the experiences of people who met Jesus during his earthly ministry, we notice that God led them through a process that sometimes happened quickly and sometimes went more slowly. The point at which people were saved is impossible for us to discern, but it was frequently earlier than the moment at which they became Christians, that is, when they acknowledged Jesus to be the Messiah, the Son of God, and worshiped him. This paradigm still operates today, so that some people are saved who have not yet become Christians. Some of these are ignorant of Jesus; others have heard about him but have not yet been convinced of his identity by the Holy Spirit. We are reasonably able to discern when a person becomes a Christian, but only God knows the moment at which a person is saved.

Thesis 11: The implications of the principles derived from both the Old Testament situation and from the lifetime of Jesus are particularly important for our perspective on Jewish people today. We can assert that the faith of Abraham still saves, and we can acknowledge that some Jews may be believers (with an old covenant faith) and hence be saved, although they are not Christians. This is only true, however, of Jews who do not know the real identity of Jesus and who have not knowingly rejected the Messiah. Evangelism among Jewish people is as necessary today as it was in the time of the apostles. Not only does God want people to be saved, but he wants them to experience all the blessings of the new covenant in the fellowship of the new covenant community, the church of Jesus Christ.

WE HAVE EXAMINED THE SORT OF FAITH that God expects from, and that he might give to, people who receive his general revelation. I have also suggested that the number of people who have only general revelation may actually be very small. We now turn our attention to another issue that should contribute to our understanding of salvation, namely, the situation of individuals within the biblical narrative who did not believe in Jesus as their Savior but who were clearly saved. What can we learn from their experience of salvation that may be helpful to us today as we ask whether people who do not know Jesus can be saved by his atoning work? In particular, what is the situation of Jewish people today? Can they be saved without becoming Christians? Should we try to convert them? I'll begin with some general comments about the faith that saved Old Testament believers, then I'll focus specifically on the salvation of people who were outside the covenant community, and finally I'll examine the experience of people who knew Jesus in the time of his public ministry on earth.

THE SAVING FAITH OF OLD TESTAMENT BELIEVERS

"Old Testament believers" within Israel were saved by grace through faith, although they did not know of Jesus' death and did not, therefore, put their trust in him. Millard Erickson neatly summarizes the nature of the "faith" that was always involved in salvation, as described in the Old Testament: "This faith was an utter abandonment of reliance on one's own strength, righteousness, effort, or that of anyone other than God himself. It was also a belief in the gracious, merciful provision of that holy, loving God."[1]

Hebrews 11 has much to say about the faith of old covenant believers, so it is a key passage for our present considerations. The writer identifies the minimum content of saving faith: "Without faith it is impossible to please God, for whoever would approach him must believe that he exists and that he rewards those who seek him" (Heb 11:6). "God commends all who penetrate beyond the veil of things seen to understand that they are made from things that are not seen (Heb 11:3) and that the things that are seen testify that God exists."[2] And he rewards those who seek him, this reward being "his commendation, the verdict of righteousness (cf. Heb 11:7)."[3] This reward is neither something merited by the seekers nor some-

[1] Millard J. Erickson, *How Shall They Be Saved? The Destiny of Those Who Do Not Hear of Jesus* (Grand Rapids, Mich.: Baker, 1996), pp. 191-92.
[2] Thomas R. Schreiner and Ardel B. Caneday, *The Race Set Before Us: A Biblical Theology of Perseverance and Assurance* (Downers Grove, Ill.: InterVarsity Press, 2001), p. 90.
[3] Ibid.

thing additional to salvation; it is a reward that God gives "purely out of his grace."[4]

The particular faith that was exercised by individuals under the older testament is very instructive. "In every case, faith sprang into faithful action,"[5] but the action varies, depending on the way in which God's summons was given. The content of divine revelation varied greatly, but the acts of obedience that were done in response to God's call pleased God as evidence of faith in him. These deeds demonstrated that God was working in the lives of the doers for their salvation. Noah "built an ark . . . and became an heir to the righteousness that is in accordance with faith" (Heb 11:7). Abraham "obeyed . . . and he set out, not knowing where he was going" (Heb 11:8); he "considered him faithful who had promised" (Heb 11:11) and so "offered up Isaac," believing "that God is able even to raise someone from the dead" (Heb 11:17, 19). "Isaac invoked blessings for the future on Jacob and Esau" (Heb 11:20), and Jacob blessed the sons of Joseph (Heb 11:21). Joseph in turn "made mention of the exodus of the Israelites and gave instructions about his burial" (Heb 11:22).

Moses' parents hid him for three months. Moses left Egypt unafraid, "for he persevered as though he saw him who is invisible. By faith he kept the Passover" (Heb 11:27-28). Moses himself "considered abuse suffered for the Christ to be greater wealth than the treasures of Egypt, for he was looking ahead to the reward" (Heb 11:26). Rahab "received the spies in peace" (Heb 11:31), and many others underwent unspeakable forms of persecution for their faith but refused to give up their firm trust in God and the future that he had prepared for them (Heb 11:32-38). The people of Israel demonstrated their faith in God by obedience, by trust in his faithfulness and by an expectation of the fulfillment of his promises. It was not the mere practice of the prescribed rituals of sacrifice that brought them forgiveness of sin, but rather their sincere faith in God demonstrated in acts of obedience and mercy that elicited God's approval. In retrospect, we know that they were saved not by the animal sacrifices but by the perfect sacrifice of Christ who was to come (Heb 9), but Old Testament believers did not have the perspective with which we are blessed in the new covenant.

Commenting on the statement made by the author of Hebrews that Moses unwittingly "considered abuse suffered for the Christ to be greater wealth than the treasures of Egypt" (Heb 11:26), William Abraham sug-

---

[4]Ibid., p. 91.
[5]Ibid., p. 95.

gests, "Surely this implies that it is perfectly consistent to hold both that Jesus is the exclusive path to God and that people may genuinely encounter God outside the Christian church without explicitly knowing about Jesus of Nazareth."[6] Abraham sees here the "high Christology" that the classical tradition represents, in which "the activity of Christ, although crucially related to the events of his life, ministry and death in Palestine, is not confined to that short segment of history. Jesus is the incarnate embodiment of the cosmic Christ who is at work enlightening all people (Jn 1:9)."[7]

The statement regarding Moses points us to Christ's work in Israel, centuries before the incarnation of the Word. It is from this perspective that we can understand Paul's identification of Abraham as the model of the justified believer, though Abraham had never heard the gospel about Jesus. "If one has to know about Jesus of Nazareth to be saved, then Abraham could not have been saved. Abraham did not have such knowledge, yet he was saved; hence it must be possible to be saved without knowing about Jesus."[8] William Abraham rightly notes, of course, that this does not mean that anyone is "saved apart from the activity of God's Son."[9]

D. A. Carson wisely observes that "these believers on the Old Testament side were responding in faith to special revelation, and were not simply exercising some sort of general 'faith' in an undefined 'God.'"[10] I agree—the saving faith of people within the old covenant community was a response to very significant self-disclosures by God through his messengers. The situation of these old covenant believers is relevant to our situation today in a very limited way, namely, when we contemplate the situation of Jewish people to whom the Spirit has not made clear the identity of Jesus but who have the faith that Abraham had. I am not suggesting that we should not declare to Jews the good news that Jesus is their Messiah. The apostles did it and we should do so too. But I am recognizing that Jews who do not have that knowledge are in the same position as were their forebears who lived prior to Messiah's coming. Because they are ignorant concerning Jesus or concerning his true identity, they can hardly be deemed to be "rejecting" him.

---

[6]William J. Abraham, *The Logic of Evangelism* (Grand Rapids, Mich.: Eerdmans, 1989), p. 219.
[7]Ibid.
[8]Ibid., p. 220.
[9]Ibid.
[10]D. A. Carson, *The Gagging of God: Christianity Confronts Pluralism* (Grand Rapids, Mich.: Zondervan, 1996), p. 298.

Hebrews 11 tells us nothing about people who are ignorant even of old covenant special revelation. Nevertheless, one can concur with J. O. Buswell Jr. when he grants that he does not "know what kind of conviction came to Abel, to Enoch, or even to Abraham," but that he does "know that they were convicted by the same Holy Spirit, that they were justified by faith, and thus we know that they are among the elect of God."[11] Buswell admits that he does not know "how much knowledge is necessary for faith," referring "not merely to the Old Testament saints, but to ignorant believers in extremely dark circumstances even in America today." He believes "the essence of a childlike faith" to be "a simple surrender of oneself to the grace of God in Christ." And although he does not "know how simple that surrender may be," he knows "that Abraham 'believed God, and it was reckoned to him for justification.' "[12]

Buswell is careful to state, as I want to do, that he does not mean to say "that every savage in the jungle has anything like the light which Abraham had." But he does believe that

> as God sees the matter, every savage in the jungle is [in] some way or another confronted with the grace of God in the universal convicting work of the Holy Spirit, that he makes a choice for which God is justified, even in our finite minds, according to God's revelation—God is justified in holding him responsible.[13]

OLD TESTAMENT EXAMPLES OF OLD COVENANT BELIEVERS OUTSIDE ISRAEL

The salvation of people outside Israel, in Old Testament times, is significant for our inquiry, but we are told little about it. Nevertheless, J. N. D. Anderson is correct that "the knowledge of God and the experience of his grace were never limited to Israel under the covenant of Sinai. God had called Abram, and subsequently made a covenant with him, hundreds of years before that of Sinai (Gal 3:17)."[14] As Yahweh had told Moses: "I will be gracious to whom I will be gracious, and will show mercy on whom I will show mercy" (Ex 33:19). Those who experienced the mercy of God outside Israel are sometimes referred to by Christian theologians as "pa-

---

[11]J. O. Buswell, *A Systematic Theology of the Christian Religion* (Grand Rapids, Mich.: Zondervan, 1963), p. 160.

[12]Ibid.

[13]Ibid., pp. 160-61.

[14]J. N. D. Anderson, *Christianity and World Religions: The Challenge of Pluralism* (Downers Grove, Ill.: InterVarsity Press, 1984), p. 145.

gan saints" or "holy pagans," but I do not find this terminology helpful, because the term *pagan* gives the impression that people are ignorant about and alienated from God.

The Jews spoke of these people as "God-fearers" (cf. Job 1:8), in contrast with people such as Amalek who "did not fear God" (Deut 25:18). They were people of faith, which R. V. G. Tasker helpfully defines as "a practical response to the divine initiative."[15] But Bryan Widbin finds

> never a hint that Israel saw "the fear of God" among the nations as something less than a redemptive experience. She accepted it on both practical and theological grounds. Israel's exclusive calling was to be a testimony to the nations. What happened apart from that was Yahweh's business.[16]

Among those in the Old Testament who were saved but came from outside the covenant people, I would include the following: Abel, Enoch (Heb 11:5-6; Sirach 44:16), Noah (Ezek 14:14; Sirach 44:17; Mt 24:37-39; Heb 11:7-8; 1 Pet 3:20; 2 Pet 2:5), Job (who was designated as a "just pagan" by Gregory the Great [540-604]),[17] Melchizedek, Lot, Jethro, Naaman, Rahab (Josh 2:11; 6:23; Heb 11:31; Jas 2:25), Ruth (Ruth 1:16-17) Bathsheba (2 Sam 11:3-4) and Ebed-melech (a pagan Ethiopian eunuch in the court of evil King Zedekiah, who rescued Jeremiah from the pit and was saved by Yahweh because he "trusted in" him [Jer 39:15-18]). Possibly, we can include some of the Ninevites who responded well to Jonah's call for repentance. And perhaps some of the foreigners were saved—those whose prayers Solomon asked God to answer when they were offered toward the temple, "so that all the peoples of the earth may know your name and fear you, as do your people Israel" (1 Kings 8:41-43).

Most of these had special revelation about which we know. Either God made himself specially known to them in a personal way (e.g., Abel, Enoch, Noah, Job, Abimelech), or they had contact with Jews (e.g., Lot, Ruth, Naaman), or they at least had knowledge of the Israelites' faith or of God's activity among them (e.g., Rahab, Naaman, the foreigners whom Solomon

---

[15]Quoted by Anderson, *Christianity and World Religions,* p. 145.

[16]R. Bryan Widbin, "Salvation for People Outside Israel's Covenant?" in *Through No Fault of Their Own? The Fate of Those Who Have Never Heard,* ed. William V. Crockett and James G. Sigountos (Grand Rapids, Mich.: Baker, 1991), p. 82.

[17]R. W. F. Wootton, *Christianity and Other Faiths: An Evangelical Contribution to Our Multi-Faith Society* (Exeter: Paternoster, 1983), p. 17. As Daniel Reid commented to me, even if "Job is a literary dialogue, a piece of wisdom literature, with little or no basis in historical figures and events," we can observe "that Scripture (and Israel) is comfortable with the understanding that such revelation could be given to a non-Israelite."

anticipated would come to pray toward the temple). I am left with only Melchizedek and Jethro as individuals whose experience may offer us insight into the work of God's grace outside the covenant community.

Melchizedek (Gen 14:18-20; Ps 110:4; Heb 7) is presented as a priest of El Elyon, "a Canaanite deity whose identity here is curiously merged with Abraham's God" for they both worship God by the same name, El Elyon.[18] We are not told how Melchizedek came to know God, but at least three possibilities have been proposed: general revelation, remnants of original revelation or special revelation.

First, Don Richardson deems Melchizedek "a figurehead or type of God's *general* revelation to mankind," a counterpart to Abraham who represented "God's covenant-based, canon-recorded *special* revelation."[19] The parallelism is neat, but the concept is hard to ground in the biblical text, which does not tell us for certain that Melchizedek obtained his knowledge of God through general revelation alone.

The second option is suggested by Jonathan Edwards, who believed that Melchizedek "could have been saved through the traces of original revelation that still remained among his people," since he lived long before the final apostasy of the Gentile nations, which Edwards thought happened about the time of Moses.[20] Winfried Corduan, likewise, appeals to "original monotheism" as the source of Melchizedek's knowledge of God:

> And the God of original monotheism is none else but the God who revealed himself particularly to the Jews and later in Jesus Christ. Thus, it is possible to say that Melchizedek and others are ultimately saved just as the Jews of the Old Testament are, namely, by implicit faith in Christ, worked out within the context of their explicit faith in God as presently known to them.[21]

I am presently inclined to see the third option as the most plausible, as found, for instance, in Widbin's opinion that Melchizedek and Abram

---

[18]Gerald R. McDermott, *Can Evangelicals Learn from World Religions? Jesus, Revelation and Religious Traditions* (Downers Grove, Ill.: InterVarsity Press, 2000), p. 77.

[19]Don Richardson, *Eternity in Their Hearts,* rev. ed. (Ventura, Calif.: Regal, 1984), p. 31.

[20]Jonathan Edwards, *History of Redemption,* the work of ed. John F. Wilson, in *The Works of Jonathan Edwards,* ed. Harry S. Stout (New Haven, Conn.: Yale University Press, 1989), 9:179, 298, quoted in Greg D. Gilbert, "The Nations Will Worship: Jonathan Edwards and the Salvation of the Heathen," *Trinity Journal,* n.s., 23 (spring 2002): 69.

[21]Winfried Corduan, *A Tapestry of Faiths: The Common Threads Between Christianity and World Religions* (Downers Grove, Ill.: InterVarsity Press, 2002), p. 162.

"came by their knowledge of El Elyon independently, perhaps through their distinct revelations of God."[22]

Sent by God to Abram to receive the tithe to serve for the worship of God (Gen 14:20), Melchizedek blessed Abram by El Elyon and said that El Elyon is "maker of heaven and earth" (Gen 14:19). Then Melchizedek blessed El Elyon and declared that he had delivered Abram's enemies into his hand (Gen 14:20). Abram then tells the king of Sodom that he cannot take any of the spoils because "I have sworn to the LORD [Yahweh], God Most High [El Elyon], maker of heaven and earth, that I would not take a thread or a sandal-thong or anything that is yours, so that you might not say, 'I have made Abram rich'" (Gen 14:21-23). (I will have more to say about the significance of this for other religions in part two of this book.)

Melchizedek is the type of Christ (Heb 7:1-3) who would "assume and bring to perfection all sacrifices in his eternal offering (Heb 9:11)."[23] Hebrews thus gives anticipatory significance to the sacrifices prescribed by God in the old covenant. Might this also be true of other sacrifices offered by devout people outside the Mosaic covenant? I leave the answer to that question open, at this point in the discussion; but if we *were* eventually to grant that God might accept the sacrifices of some non-Christians because the Spirit works faith in their lives, then those sacrifices would also derive their efficacy from Christ's sacrifice.

Widbin notes parallels between Jethro and Melchizedek. Both of them, as priests of foreign nations, "appear at times of Israel's deliverance to give independent testimony to God's gracious activity. Both are contrasted with nations who do not fear God but intend to profit from Israel. Both remain part of their 'heathen' nations after the event."[24] Walter Kaiser, though working with ecclesiocentric assumptions, has no hesitation about declaring Jethro saved. He notes that "this Midianite priest broke out into paeans of praise to Yahweh, the Name of God reserved for those who had a personal relationship to the Lord" (Ex 18:10-11). Kaiser comments: "Once again, we are baffled. When did Jethro come to know such saving grace?"[25]

In the study made by the Evangelical Alliance in Britain, Wootton sums

---

[22]Widbin, "Salvation," p. 81. Similarly, Erickson suggests that "it is at least logically possible that God manifested himself to Melchizedek, just as he did to Abraham, but that we simply have no biblical record of it" (*How Shall They,* p. 137).
[23]Widbin, "Salvation," p. 81.
[24]Ibid., pp. 80-81 n. 15.
[25]Walter C. Kaiser Jr., *Mission in the Old Testament: Israel as a Light to the Nations* (Grand Rapids, Mich.: Baker, 2000), p. 40.

up conclusions from the Old Testament:

> We may conclude therefore that though God chose Israel as his special chan-
> nel of blessing to mankind, acting powerfully on their behalf and giving
> them the law and the prophets, he did not confine to Israel his dealings with
> the children of Adam; he still had his faithful ones in other nations, men and
> women enlightened by his wisdom, conscious of his majesty and offering ac-
> ceptable worship to him, though continuing in the traditions of their own
> people, and others whom he used in various ways, though they lacked a liv-
> ing relationship with him.[26]

On the other hand, it is intriguing to note the lengths to which an exe-
gete with ecclesiocentric presuppositions will go to find his assumptions
supported in the biblical text. Kaiser states his bottom line:

> A belief in one God, admirable as that may be, is still not saving faith. The
> New Testament makes the point in Acts 4:12. . . . Likewise, John 17:3 agrees
> that a belief in God is not enough. Some may want to argue that saving faith
> was different in the Old Testament, but that would go against the plain
> teaching of the text. All, of course, will agree that salvation in the Old Testa-
> ment was by grace and faith alone. Most will also agree that when Abraham
> believed, and as recorded in Genesis 15:6, he was also justified. The differ-
> ence begins to appear when we ask if the object of faith is the same in the Old
> Testament as it is in the New. Must Naaman believe in the coming Man of
> Promise, the "Seed" of the woman and of Abraham and David? And the an-
> swer is "Yes." Even in Genesis 15:6, Abraham did more than merely become
> a monotheist; he believed and put his faith in the promise God had just fin-
> ished giving (Gen. 15:1-5) about the "Seed" that would come through the
> line established by God. Faith terminated and was grounded in the Messiah
> who was to come. Thus, both the method and object of saving faith in both
> Testaments was the same.[27]

With this assumption in mind, Kaiser approaches the narratives regarding "individual believing Gentiles" in the Old Testament. Of Melchizedek,
Kaiser writes,

> Where, when, and how had this king and priest, in the midst of a pagan cul-
> ture, become a true believer in the Man of Promise who was to come? The
> text does not supply even a hint. Yet few can deny that he was indeed a be-
> liever. He is one of many hints in the Old Testament that many Gentile indi-

---

[26]Wootton, *Christianity and Other Faiths*, p. 19.
[27]Kaiser, *Mission*, pp. 46-47.

viduals were coming to know the One who would later be called the Messiah, or Jesus.[28]

Concerning Jethro, who had known "saving grace," Kaiser wonders: "Had Moses shared the Abrahamic promise with him and had he put all his trust in the coming 'Seed' of the woman, the 'Seed' of Shem and Abraham's line? He must have done so, for there is no other way to account for the results the text affirms so clearly."[29] Kaiser affirms that Rahab had saving faith, citing Hebrews 11:31 and James 2:25 and states:

> Thus, her confession that "Yahweh is God" included a confession that she looked forward to the coming Messiah. The God who had promised the land to Israel was the same God who had promised that he would send his Seed, the Messiah. To believe in one part of this promise was to affirm that one believed in all the promise, for how could this one great promise of God be segmented, divided, or bifurcated into that which was only temporally real and that which was eternal? . . . [And] the same case could be made for Ruth, the Moabite woman.[30]

Kaiser goes on to wonder,

> Had General Naaman been told more not only about the prophet in Israel, but also about the promise God had given, a promise that was to all the people of the earth? Had the captured maiden witnessed not only about the miracle-working power of Elisha, but about Yahweh whose plan embraced all the families of the earth? One thing is for sure: Naaman is the first one to mention (2 Kings 5) the name "Yahweh," both before (v. 11), and after (v. 15) his healing. He could just as easily have used the plural noun "Elohim," "God," to refer to the God of Israel. The Old Testament is careful about the times it chooses to refer to Yahweh. That name was reserved for those who had a personal relationship to him, otherwise Elohim was accurate enough.[31]

The process of Kaiser's logic is clear: Melchizedek, Jethro, Rahab, Ruth and Naaman were saved. People cannot be saved without faith in the promised Seed. Therefore, they must have had knowledge of and faith in that Seed. Ironically, with this approach to the salvation of people outside the covenant community, one could take an ecclesiocentrist position, keeping the bar high on what one must know in order to have saving faith, but

---

[28]Ibid., p. 40.
[29]Ibid., p. 41.
[30]Ibid., pp. 41-42.
[31]Ibid., p. 47.

still be optimistic about widespread salvation, since one could claim ignorance of *how* God made Christ known to people while assuming that he
did. This is not likely the direction Kaiser intends to take, but his reading
of these Old Testament incidents offers an intriguing precedent for another
form of accessibilism.

New Testament Examples of Old Covenant Believers Outside Israel

Cornelius. In the Gospels, "the pagan Samaritan or social outcast often enters the kingdom of God before people of the religious establishment,"[32]
but Cornelius is probably the most important individual in the New Testament for the focus of this inquiry. Although he lived at the time of Jesus
and became a Christian after Pentecost, he exemplifies the Gentiles who
lived outside the community of the old covenant people of God but who
worshiped that God. In Luke's narrative, we learn that Cornelius was a
"devout man who feared God" and who "gave alms generously to the
people and prayed constantly to God" (Acts 10:2); his "prayers and alms"
had "ascended as a memorial before God" (Acts 10:4); and when Peter met
Cornelius, Peter realized that "in every nation anyone who fears [God]
and does what is right is acceptable to him" (Acts 10:35).

In its context, the primary meaning of Peter's statement is that "God is
not prejudiced in restricting salvation to a particular nation."[33] As Carson
notes, the Greek term translated "acceptable" *(dektos)* "is never used in reference to whether or not a person is accepted by God in some saving
sense."[34] The million-dollar question, of course, is whether Cornelius
would have gone to be with Christ if he had died *before* his encounter with
Peter. One line of ecclesiocentric interpretation asserts that he would have
gone to hell; it hears a clear statement that Cornelius was not saved in the
angel's instructions, which told him that Peter would give him a message
"by which you and your entire household will be saved" (Acts 11:14). If
one starts with an ecclesiocentric assumption, the salvation spoken about
by the angel is identified as the present experience; people are not saved,
therefore, until they actually encounter Christ. Thus, David Wells, for instance, concludes: "That his salvation occurred during Peter's preaching

---

[32]Daniel Clendenin, *Many Gods, Many Lords* (Grand Rapids, Mich.: Baker, 1995), p. 51.
[33]Bruce A. Demarest, "General and Special Revelation: Epistemological Foundations of Religious Pluralism," in *One God, One Lord: Christianity in a World of Religious Pluralism,* 2nd ed.,
ed. Andrew D. Clarke and Bruce Winter (Grand Rapids, Mich.: Baker, 1992), p. 191.
[34]Carson, *Gagging of God,* p. 307.

is expressly declared by the centurion himself (Acts 11:14),"[35] a sentiment echoed by John Stott, despite his general agnosticism regarding this topic: "It is clear then that, although in some sense 'acceptable' to God, Cornelius before his conversion had neither 'salvation' nor 'life.'"[36]

Some other ecclesiocentrists, however, have proposed that Cornelius was indeed saved before Peter arrived but that his case is exceptional. Noted examples of those who hold this position are John Calvin and Thomas Aquinas, who wrote:

> At the time, Cornelius was not an unbeliever, else his works would not have been acceptable to God, whom none can please without faith. However, he then had implicit faith [in Christ], when the truth of the Gospel had not yet been manifested to him. Hence Peter was sent to him, to give him full instruction in the faith.[37]

But Aquinas saw Cornelius as an exception since explicit faith is necessary after Christ: "After grace had been revealed, all, both the learned and the simple, are bound to have explicit faith in the mysteries of Christ, especially with respect to those mysteries which are publicly and solemnly celebrated in the Church, as those which refer to the mystery of the incarnation."[38] The problem Aquinas creates for ecclesiocentrism, of course, is that one "exception" leaves us wondering whether there might be others.

Similarly, in his commentary on Acts 10:4, Calvin concludes that Cornelius was saved before Peter's instruction since "the fear of God and godliness do plainly prove that he was regenerate by the Spirit."[39] In his *Institutes of the Christian Religion*, Calvin also wrote:

> Indeed, Cornelius must have been already illumined by the Spirit of wisdom, for he was endowed with true wisdom, that is, the fear of God; and he was sanctified by the same Spirit, for he was a keeper of righteousness, which the apostle taught to be the Spirit's surest fruit [Gal 5:5]. All those

---

[35]David F. Wells, *God the Evangelist: How the Holy Spirit Works to Bring Men and Women to Faith* (Grand Rapids, Mich.: Eerdmans, 1987), p. 23.

[36]John R. Stott, "Dialogue, Encounter, Even Confrontation," in *Faith Meets Faith*, Mission Trends, ed. Gerald H. Anderson and Thomas F. Stransky (Grand Rapids, Mich.: Eerdmans, 1981), 5:167.

[37]Thomas Aquinas *Summa Theologica* II-II, q.10, a.4, ad3, quoted in Jacques Dupuis, *Toward a Christian Theology of Religious Pluralism* (Maryknoll, N.Y.: Orbis, 1997), p. 114.

[38]Aquinas *Summa Theologica* II-II, q.2, a.7, quoted in Dupuis, *Toward a Christian Theology*, p. 114.

[39]John Calvin, *Calvin's Commentaries: John-Acts* (Wilmington, Del.: Associated Publishers & Authors, n.d.), p. 1095.

things in him which are said to have pleased God he received from God's grace.[40]

But given Calvin's ecclesiocentric position, he takes the tack we observed earlier in Kaiser's analysis. Asserting "that faith cannot be separated from Christ," Calvin concludes that Cornelius must have "heard somewhat of the promised Mediator." Thus, "Cornelius must be put in the catalogue of the fathers, who hoped for salvation of the Redeemer before he was revealed."[41] Once again, Calvin opens a door, as Aquinas had done. If Cornelius could be saved by old covenant anticipation after Jesus had ascended to heaven, why might not there be others in the same position?

An accessibilist position was intimated by Edwards, who considered Cornelius saved because he "did already in some respect believe in [Christ] even in the manner that the Old Testament saints were wont to do."[42] Likewise, G. Campbell Morgan identified Cornelius as "not to be accounted for, as we first meet him, by Christianity, or by Judaism."[43] Cornelius was an example of John 1:9 ("the true light, which enlightens everyone") and provides a contrast to the Gentiles who suppress the truth in unrighteousness, that is, who "had not obeyed the light they had."[44] He was a man "who had been true to the light that was within him. He had followed it, yielded himself to it, and had become a worshipper of the one true living God," but he had "not passed into the fullness of life or of light. He also needed Christ."[45] Cornelius was saved through his obedience to the light he had, but he needed "the fuller light" so that he could become "all he might be."

When Peter defended his eating with uncircumcised Gentiles, he reported that the angel who appeared to Cornelius had said that Peter would bring him "a message through which you and your entire household will be saved" (Acts 11:14). Scripture speaks of salvation as past (accomplished by Christ), present (now enjoying fellowship with God) and future (the consummation of our salvation in the end). This text may,

---

[40]John Calvin *Institutes of the Christian Religion* 3.17.4, Library of Christian Classics (Philadelphia: Westminster Press, 1960), 20:806.

[41]Calvin, *Calvin's Commentaries*, p. 1096 (commenting on Acts 10:4).

[42]Jonathan Edwards, *Miscellanies* 40, quoted in Gerald R. McDermott, "Response to Gilbert: 'The Nations Will Worship: Jonathan Edwards and the Salvation of the Heathen,' " *Trinity Journal* 23 (spring 2002): 78.

[43]G. Campbell Morgan, *The Acts of the Apostles*, 13th ed. (New York: Revell, c. 1924), p. 266.

[44]Ibid.

[45]Ibid., p. 267.

therefore, be an indication of the eschatological dimension of salvation, the sense in which salvation is still future for all of us. Paul has this in view when he tells the Corinthians that they "are being saved" through the good news that he had proclaimed to them, if they "hold firmly" to the message (1 Cor 15:2). Looked at from this eschatological perspective, the angel's statement to Cornelius was an indication that God wanted him to know of the work of Christ, on the basis of which he and his household would be saved in the last day (Acts 11:14), and to "experience the fullness of salvation that comes from a personal relationship with Christ."[46]

The acknowledgment by the likes of Aquinas, Calvin, Edwards, Morgan and even Ronald Nash (a convinced ecclesiocentrist) that Cornelius was saved after Pentecost, but before he became a Christian, provides hope for others who have an old covenant faith.[47] Thus, R. W. F. Wootton asks rhetorically, "There are those too who, like Cornelius, have a sense of loving dependence upon God and a hope in his mercy without ever having heard that message—can we doubt that God's mercy extends to them?"[48]

The critical question is, therefore, when (if ever) does salvation cease to be possible for Jews with an Old Testament faith and for God-fearing Gentiles who do not know of Jesus? Ronald Nash suggests "that whole first-century community of Believers in Yahweh was a kind of transition generation."[49] But why must the transition be limited to one generation? Why may it not extend throughout this age to all who remain ignorant of Jesus and of his identity and work? Why might not people today who have the faith of an old covenant believer or of a Gentile god-fearer be saved today, just as they were then?

The Athenians. Another group of interest are the Athenians, whom we considered in the last chapter from the perspective of the usefulness of general revelation. Paul describes them as "extremely religious . . . in every way" (Acts 17:22) and states that God had "overlooked" their unbelief in ignorance (Acts 17:30). Orthodox theologian Georges Khodr says,

---

[46]John Sanders, *No Other Name: An Investigation into the Destiny of the Unevangelized* (Grand Rapids, Mich.: Eerdmans, 1992), p. 222.

[47]In his ecclesiocentric proposal (identified in that book as "restrictivism"), Ronald Nash says that "Cornelius was a believer in the same sense as every believing Jew prior to Christ" ("Restrictivism," in *What About Those Who Have Never Heard? Three Views on the Destiny of the Unevangelized,* ed. John Sanders [Downers Grove, Ill.: InterVarsity Press, 1995], p. 122) and that he was "a faithful believer in Yahweh" whose "relationship to Yahweh was similar to that of an Old Testament believer" (p. 138).

[48]Wootton, *Christianity and Other Faiths,* p. 24.

[49]Ronald Nash, *Is Jesus the Only Savior?* (Grand Rapids, Mich.: Zondervan, 1994), p. 138.

The view of the apostle as expressed in his Areopagus speech is that the Athenians worshipped the true God without recognizing Him as the Creator. His face had not been unveiled to them. In other words, they were Christians without knowing it. Paul gave their God a name. The Name, together with its attributes, is the revelation of God. We find here the germ of a positive attitude to paganism which goes hand in hand with its complete negation, inherited from Judaism.[50]

I would definitely not want to speak of them as being "Christians without knowing it." To be Christian is to consciously trust in Jesus the Christ. Furthermore, caution is necessary about the statement that "the Athenians worshipped the true God." F. F. Bruce, for instance, does say that "this God whom they venerated . . . was the God whom he now proposed to make known to them," but Paul "used neuter, not masculine, forms: 'what therefore you worship as unknown, this I proclaim to you' (RSV)," indicating that he was not "unreservedly identifying the 'unknown god' of the inscription with the God whom he proclaimed."[51] A better description might be to use Richardson's category of "redemptive analogies" to indicate the way in which Paul built on the Athenian religious experience and introduced them to the God whom they sought but of whom they were still very ignorant.[52]

Conclusions for our situation today. Like John Hick, many of us have met moral Buddhists, generous almsgiving Muslims and non-Christians who show traits of goodness, faith, love, joy and righteousness;[53] but we cannot assume that these are always the fruit of *saving* grace because we are aware that God is graciously at work in the lives of people and communities in ways that are not saving, which we identify as instances of *common* grace. As we draw conclusions for the situation of people outside the covenant community in our own day, it appears to me that we gain some help from these Old and New Testament examples. Original monotheism (the remnant of special revelation in cultural and religious traditions) persists as a category, though the number of people to whom it might apply is growing smaller. Particular help would be gained, however, if we could assume that God may still encounter people personally when necessary, beyond their memory of original special revelation. As indicated in the last chapter, I do

---

[50]Georges Khodr, "The Economy of the Holy Spirit," in *Faith Meets Faith,* Mission Trends, ed. Gerald H. Anderson and Thomas F. Stransky (Grand Rapids, Mich.: Eerdmans, 1981), 5:38.

[51]F. F. Bruce, *The Book of the Acts* (Grand Rapids, Mich.: Eerdmans, 1988), p. 336.

[52]Richardson, *Eternity in Their Hearts.*

[53]John Hick, *God Has Many Names* (Philadelphia: Westminster John Knox, 1986), pp. 17-18.

not think that we can eliminate this possibility.

J. Dudley Woodberry and Russell Shubin report the findings of their ten-year study of about six hundred Muslim-background believers, and they comment: "For someone who has not had extended exposure to Muslim-background believers in Christ, probably the most striking surprise is the powerful role that dreams and visions have played in drawing people to Jesus."[54] Rick Love, international director of Frontiers, a missions organization, writes, "Just as God used a vision to convert Paul, in like manner He reveals Himself to Muslims through dreams and visions. Just as God prepared Cornelius to hear the Gospel through a vision, so God is preparing a multitude of Muslims to respond to His good news."[55] Woodberry and Shubin contend that "it is difficult to consider engaging in ministry to Muslims without a recognition of and an openness for God to continue drawing people to Himself through what may be viewed as unconventional means."[56]

The biblical instances cited above do demonstrate that one *can* be saved *by* Christ without knowing *about* him, at least not by means of a human messenger, and this provides ground for our hopefulness about God's work of grace outside the church now. Even an ecclesiocentrist like Loraine Boettner, who insists on the impossibility of salvation apart from special revelation, allows that such a "miracle of pure grace" might occur, although it would be an extraordinary hearing of the gospel.[57]

An intriguing account of God's use of the faint memory of earlier revelation and of eager anticipation for more is worth repeating here. In this case, the revelation must have initially come through contact with a Christian messenger. The story, which comes out of the killing fields in Cambodia, in 1979, was told to Pastor Tuy Seng, who carried the gospel to a remote area in Khampong Tom Province, in September 1999.[58] The villagers welcomed Seng eagerly, and most of them committed their lives to Christ in a short time, which prompted him to comment that it seemed as if they had been waiting for him. An old woman replied: "We *have* been waiting

---

[54]J. Dudley Woodberry and Russell G. Shubin, "Why I Chose Jesus," *Mission Frontiers*. This is also available at <http://www.missionfrontiers.org/2001/01/muslim.htm>, p. 5.

[55]Rick Love, *Muslims, Magic and the Kingdom of God* (Pasadena, Calif.: William Carey Library, 2000), p. 156, quoted in Woodberry and Shubin, "Why I Chose Jesus," p. 5.

[56]Woodberry and Shubin, "Why I Chose Jesus," p. 7.

[57]Loraine Boettner, *The Reformed Doctrine of Predestination* (c. 1932; Philadelphia: Presbyterian & Reformed, 1974), p. 119.

[58]The story is told by Dois I. Rosser and Ellen Vaughn in *The God Who Hung on the Cross* (Grand Rapids, Mich.: Zondervan, 2003), pp. 235-37.

for you for twenty years." She then told of the time in 1979 when soldiers of the Khmer Rouge had come to their village. Those who resisted were immediately killed, and the rest were ordered to dig what they knew would be their own mass grave. When the pit was ready, they were ordered to face it, with their backs to the soldiers. Knowing that their end was near, many began to cry out in desperation.

"Some screamed to Buddha, to ancestors, or to demon spirits. A few cried for their mothers." The one woman recalled "the faint echo of a story told her by her mother about the God who hung on the cross. She called out to that God," hoping that the one who had suffered personally might have compassion on those who were going to die. "Suddenly the screams around her became one great wail, as the entire village called out as one, crying for their lives to the God who hung on the cross." The place went silent and when they finally turned around the soldiers were gone. Since that day they had been waiting for someone to come and tell them more about the God who hung on the cross, and Seng fulfilled that longing. I doubt that anyone would deny that the true and living God who did, indeed, hang on a cross, had heard and answered their prayer. But, of course, an answered prayer is no sign of reconciliation to God in salvation through Christ's righteousness. It seems unlikely, however, that everyone who had been there in 1979 had lived for another twenty years, as they waited expectantly for further knowledge. I see no reason why we should conclude that for those who died in that interim, the gospel came too late for their salvation. Indeed, some of those who responded in faith in Christ, when he was proclaimed by Seng, may well have been living in a trust in God that God accounted as righteousness.

A quite comprehensive theory of implicit faith was actually developed by some of the Catholic theologians in the sixteenth and seventeenth centuries. Dominican theologian Domingo Soto, writing in 1549, posited that God would provide the unevangelized with the light necessary for an implicit faith in Christ—and for salvation in him—which Thomas had said was sufficient for those who lived before Christ.[59] Robert Bellarmine, a Jesuit at the Roman College (1576-1592), took a similar view, while Juan de Lugo, at the same school (1621-1643), went further and applied the solution not only to people who never heard the gospel but also to people who knew about Christ but lacked orthodox faith. Not just pagans, therefore, but heretics, Jews and Muslims could be saved through their sincere faith in God.

---

[59]Dupuis, *Toward a Christian Theology*, p. 119.

A Jew or other non-Christian could be saved; for he could have supernatural
faith in the one God and be invincibly ignorant about Christ. But such a person would not be a Christian, because one is called a Christian by reason of
one's knowledge of Christ. . . . The possibility of salvation for such a person
is not ruled out by the nature of the case; moreover, such a person should not
be called a non-Christian, because, even though he has not been visibly
joined to the Church, still, interiorly he has the virtue of habitual and actual
faith in common with the Church, and in the sight of God he will be reckoned with Christians.[60]

From an evangelical standpoint, Vinoth Ramachandra has nicely described the combination of the particularity of Christ's saving work and
the variety of revelation and faith experiences:

The problem of particularity should not be confused with the problem of the
ultimate status of those who are not Christians. The claim that God has revealed his truth in historical events does not entail, at least without further
premises, that those who lack this revelation are excluded from the benefits
of that revelation.[61]

It may be maintained that "even as the Old Testament saints looked forward to God's gracious redemption and trusted in the Christ in whom redemption took shape without clearly understanding how that redemption
would come about, so there are many who are saved by Christ and serve
him without realizing who it is they trust."[62]

Similarly, Gerald McDermott posits that

we can infer that if there were different expectations for Old Testament saints
under a different dispensation with different degrees of revelation, we
should not dismiss other religions as completely lacking revelation merely
because they make different requirements of their adherents. In fact we
might *expect* there to be different requirements where lesser degrees of revelation have been given.[63]

A very similar conclusion was drawn from Cornelius's experience by
Morgan, who wrote:

---

[60]Juan de Lugo, *De virtute fidei divinae*, disp. 12, n. 104 (Lyon, 1646), col. 3, p. 300; (Paris:
L. Vivès, 1868), 1:425, quoted in Dupuis, *Toward a Christian Theology*, p. 119.
[61]Vinoth Ramachandra, *The Recovery of Mission: Beyond the Pluralist Paradigm* (Carlisle, U.K.:
Paternoster, 1996), p. 130.
[62]Ibid.
[63]McDermott, *Can Evangelicals Learn*, pp. 103-4.

No man is to be saved because he understands the doctrine of the Atonement. He is saved, not by understanding it, but because he fears God, and works righteousness. Oh, the glad and glorious surprise of those ultimate days when we find that there will be those who walked in the light they had, and wrought righteousness, and were acceptable to Him; not because of their morality, but by the infinite merit of the Cross, and by the fact that they yielded themselves to the light they possessed. The sin of the Gentile is not that he does not believe the thing of which he never heard. It is that he holds down the truth which he knows, in unrighteousness.[64]

Amos Yong does well to remind us that the work of the Son and of the Spirit cannot be divided and that "pneumatology is the key to overcoming the dualism between christological particularity and the cosmic Christ."[65] The Spirit who is at work outside the church is the Spirit of Jesus, just as he is the Spirit of God. People who have responded to elementary forms of God's self-revelation and who later hear and understand the gospel will welcome and accept it as the Spirit of God illumines their minds concerning this more specific truth. They are the people who, when they hear the gospel, express their sense that this is what they have been waiting for. It is wonderful when we encounter such people in our proclamation of the gospel, people like Cornelius. But we have no way of knowing how many others like them may not hear the gospel in this life.

When Richardson wrote *Eternity in Their Hearts* in 1984, he was cautious about the salvific effect of the special revelations made by God to people who were not in contact with the covenant community, the church.[66] Reflecting on the experience of the Mbaka, for instance, who had once been told by Koro, the Creator, that "He has already sent His Son into the world to accomplish something wonderful for all mankind," Richardson proposes "that these particular facets of Mbaka lore be described as "redemptive" but not as "redeeming.""[67] He defines "redemptive" as "contributing to the redemption of a people, but not culminating it."[68] The proposed distinction between that which is *redemptive* and that which *redeems* is a confusing use of related terms. More important, it draws a line that we are not

---

[64]Morgan, *Acts of the Apostles*, p. 281.

[65]Amos Yong, "Discerning the Spirit(s) in the World of Religions: Toward a Pneumatological Theory of Religions," in *No Other Gods Before Me? Evangelicals and the Challenge of World Religions*, ed. John G. Stackhouse Jr. (Grand Rapids, Mich.: Baker, 2001), p. 49.

[66]More recently, I have heard him make statements more in tune with the tenor of my own proposal in this book, but I have not seen published record of this.

[67]Richardson, *Eternity in Their Hearts*, p. 57.

[68]Ibid., p. 59.

in a position to draw because it requires us to know how God judges the hearts of people; but that judgment is hidden from us until the day on which it is gloriously revealed.

Presbyterian scholar J. Gresham Machen was right to observe that only God knows how much a person must know in order to be saved.[69] Here, we must emphasize our limitations in judging when a person's relationship to God includes a faith that God has worked as means of justification. We need to be careful not to assume that people have rejected Christ when they have rejected our proclamation of Christ or have rejected Christianity as they have experienced it.

> Frederick and Margaret Stock, analyzing a ninety-seven percent Muslim Pakistan, comment, "Too often we assume that theological differences are the primary barriers to winning Muslims. This has been repeatedly disproved. Many are theologically convinced of Christianity, but cannot hurdle the social and cultural obstacles to faith."[70]

Peter McNee, writing of Bangladesh,

> dreads to "think of . . . how many Muslims have been turned away because of their inability to adjust to the Hindu thought forms through which Christianity is expressed in Bangladesh, or consider how many Muslims have reverted because they were never trusted in a Hindu convert church."[71]

"A random sampling taken by Avery Willis in Java of non-Christians generally sympathetic to Christianity reveals that '93.4 percent said lack of acculturation by the churches was a hindrance to their becoming Christians.'"[72] We can grieve these problems of church growth, but we must not confuse them with judgments regarding the salvation of the individuals affected by them.

THE SALVATION OF JEWS WHO MET JESUS

Identifying the time of the salvation of those Jewish people who knew

---

[69]J. Gresham Machen, *The Virgin Birth of Christ* (1930; reprint, Carlisle, Penn.: Banner of Truth, 1991), p. 395.

[70]Harvie M. Conn, "The Muslim Convert and His Culture," in *Faith Meets Faith*, Mission Trends, ed. Gerald H. Anderson and Thomas F. Stransky (Grand Rapids, Mich.: Eerdmans, 1981), 5:215, quoting Frederick and Margaret Stock, *People Movements in the Punjab* (South Pasadena, Calif.: William Carey Library, 1975), p. 202.

[71]Conn, "Muslim Convert," p. 216, quoting Peter McNee, *Crucial Issues in Bangladesh* (Pasadena, Calif.: William Carey Library, 1976), p. 122.

[72]Conn, "Muslim Convert," p. 223, quoting Avery Willis, *Indonesian Revival: Why Two Million Came to Christ* (Pasadena, Calif.: William Carey Library, 1977), p. 195.

Jesus and eventually came to acknowledge him as the Messiah is significant, but it is less obvious than it might, at first, seem to be. Let's look at
some examples.

Saul of Tarsus. Richard Peace notes that the dramatic, sudden experience
of Saul of Tarsus is what many people have in mind when they think about
conversion, and Saul does make an interesting case study.[73] David Wells
says of Paul: "He met the risen Christ on the Damascus road, but his sins
were not formally forgiven and he did not join the disciples until Ananias
led him to call upon the name of Jesus and be baptized (Acts 22:16; 9:17-
18)."[74] *That was when Paul became a Christian, but was it when he became saved?*

Noting the scholarly disagreement regarding the nature of Paul's encounter with Christ, Andreas Köstenberger and Peter O'Brien propose that
"it is best to regard it as *both* a conversion *and* a calling."[75] They find "conversion" appropriate because "it led to a dramatic 'paradigm shift' in Paul's
thinking."[76] He came to a new understanding of the identity of Jesus as Israel, Messiah and Son of God and a new understanding of justification as by
God's grace alone. In his accounts of Paul's Damascus experience, Luke focuses on Paul's call as an apostle to the Gentiles, but this is less central for
Paul's self-perception. In Galatians 1, Paul emphasizes the call because he is
defending his gospel, but he does not mention it in Philippians 3.[77]

Concerning the Ethiopian eunuch, the Ephesian disciples of John the
Baptist and Paul, Wells states, "Whatever contact these people had with
God in their own religious settings was not itself salvific. Their salvation
did not occur until they were explicitly led to an explicit and conscious
faith in Christ through preaching of the gospel."[78] But that seems impossi-
bly definitive of the moment of salvation, given our limited perspective,
particularly regarding the "disciples" in Ephesus (Acts 19:1-7), and it inap-
propriately confuses the moment of being saved and the moment of be-

---

[73]Richard V. Peace, *Conversion in the New Testament: Paul and the Twelve* (Grand Rapids, Mich.:
Eerdmans, 1999), p.17.
[74]Wells, *God the Evangelist*, p. 23.
[75]Andreas J. Köstenberger and Peter T. O'Brien, *Salvation to the Ends of the Earth: A Biblical Theology of Mission*, New Studies in Biblical Theology, ed. D. A. Carson (Downers Grove, Ill.:
InterVarsity Press, 2001), 11:162.
[76]Ibid.
[77]J. M. Everts, "Conversion and Call of Paul," in *Dictionary of Paul and His Letters*, ed. Gerald
F. Hawthorne, Ralph P. Martin and Daniel G. Reid (Downers Grove, Ill.: InterVarsity Press,
1993), p. 161. For Paul's own accounts, see particularly 1 Cor 9:1; 15:8-10; Gal 1:13-17; Phil
3:4-11; but it is probably also in Paul's view in Rom 10:2-4; 1 Cor 9:16-17; 2 Cor 3:4-4:6; 5:16;
Eph 3:1-3; Col 1:23-29; and 1 Tim 1:11-14 (Peace, *Conversion*, pp. 29-30).
[78]Wells, *God the Evangelist*, p. 23.

coming Christian. In both instances, a "conversion" may take place, but we should not confuse conversion to another religion with conversion to God, as in salvation. When Paul urges the Philippians to imitate him, it is in regard to his commitment to "press on toward the goal for the prize of the heavenly call of God in Christ Jesus" (Phil 3:14). Paul sees himself as a model of one who is in the process of being transformed by Christ into mature life in Christ.[79]

Peace traces the three essential elements of conversion (insight, turning and transformation) in the experience of Paul: *Paul saw, he turned and his life was changed.* First, Paul *saw* that Jesus was "the Son of God," as he preached a few days later (Acts 9:20) and that he had been persecuting Jesus in persecuting the church. He "discovered that he was not working for God, as he had assumed, but against God. This is the personal context within which Paul was converted."[80] Prior to the Damascus encounter, Paul was a model Jew, "there was no turmoil over the question of his righteousness"[81] (Acts 22:2-3; 23:6; 26:4-7; Gal 1:14; Phil 3:4-6), but then he discovered that he was persecuting God and he saw everything differently. This insight was essential to Paul's conversion.[82] Paul "discovers that the God who revealed his Son to him is the same God that he had served as a Pharisee. The coming of Jesus fulfills the old covenant and creates a new covenant. But it is still the same God at work. Paul has not joined a new religious movement or altered all his ideas about God,"[83] but he has certainly reached a new understanding of the identity of Jesus.

Paul came to see that the cross was not the curse spoken of in Deuteronomy but that it had redemptive value. When speaking to the Sanhedrin after his arrest in Jerusalem, Paul addresses them as "brothers" (Acts 23:1) and later says, "I worship the God of our ancestors, believing everything laid down according to the law or written in the prophets" (Acts 24:14). Paul did what he did because he was an orthodox Jew.[84] In the modern language of Jews for Jesus, he was a "completed" or "fulfilled" Jew, not a heretic.[85] But Paul's Jewish colleagues saw him as outside the camp and as a legitimate target for persecution. Given Paul's approval of the stoning of

---

[79]Everts, "Conversion and Call," p. 162.
[80]Peace, *Conversion*, p. 25.
[81]Ibid., p. 49.
[82]Ibid., p. 50.
[83]Ibid., p. 82.
[84]Ibid., p. 98.
[85]Ibid., p. 99.

Stephen (Acts 8:1) and his voting against Christians who were being condemned to death (Acts 26:10), Peace suggests that Paul may also have become aware of the immorality of his murderous acts as well as of his mistaken theology. Jesus connects Satan with the desire to murder (Jn 8:44), and Paul speaks of his commission as rescuing people from the "power of Satan" (Acts 26:18). "Perhaps Paul was chosen to call people away from Satan because he, as a Pharisee, had personally experienced a desire to kill induced by the power of Satan, and had been rescued by Jesus from it."[86]

Paul's new insight came in a moment. "Up to that point in time he had seen Jesus as a fake Messiah and himself as one faithfully doing God's work in accord with God's will. But in that instance on the Damascus road, all this has changed."[87] Paul did not only have an external encounter with Jesus; "there was an inner dimension to what happened."[88] Paul says Christ was revealed, literally, "in me" (Gal 1:16 NIV). "It was not merely a dialogue with spoken words. There was an inner knowing and an inner conviction. It was not just Paul's mind that was touched but his whole being at its depth."[89] Clearly, this encounter was initiated by God, not by Paul (Gal 1:16; Phil 3:12) and had an irresistible quality (1 Cor 9:16-17).[90] But for the power with which God confronted Paul, he could have seen all this and still turned his back on it. Many people do turn away from encounter with God's truth; they are given an insight for which they are accountable, but it does not bring about the essential turning.

Second, Paul *turned* from persecuting the church to joining it, from opposing Jesus to following him. He continued to be an orthodox Jew, but "now he saw the old facts in a new context. The Messiah had come. . . . Paul discovered that God was working in a new way in the world and that he had been blind to this fact. And now that he saw this new reality, he embraced it wholeheartedly."[91] And third, Paul's *life was changed* radically and he took a new direction. Paul then called for this same conversion experience in the lives of other people: they must "repent and turn to God and do deeds consistent with repentance" (Acts 26:20).

It is important, I think, to note that Peace's description of the second aspect of conversion in Paul's experience (his turning) is defined in terms of

---

[86]Ibid., p. 51.
[87]Ibid., p. 54.
[88]Ibid., p. 85.
[89]Ibid.
[90]Ibid., p. 87.
[91]Ibid., p. 26.

his conversion to Christianity. The various indications that Paul turned toward God in Christ and that he joined the Christian community illustrate both the difficulty we face when we try to identify the precise moment at which a person receives new life and the importance of not confusing that moment with the time of Christian affiliation. When Paul urges the Philippians to imitate him, it is in regard to his commitment to "press on toward the goal for the prize of the heavenly call of God in Christ Jesus" (Phil 3:14). Paul invites them to join him in the process in which he himself was involved—progress toward maturity in Christ.[92]

Jesus' twelve disciples. The twelve disciples of Jesus present a quite different situation from Paul's, and theirs is even more fuzzy. Their experience leads me to ask whether any of the disciples of Jesus were saved prior to their call to follow Jesus and, if not, at what point they were saved. We know that Judas was not saved before he began to follow Jesus—nor would he ever be, assuming the Calvinist understanding of the preservation of believers by God—yet he was a member of the community of disciples. Furthermore, there is little in the biblical narrative to indicate to us that his progress (or lack of it) in faith is different from the progress of the other eleven until near the end. The situation of the other disciples is much less clear, and they provide an important case study for the distinction between *believers*, that is, people who are saved by grace through faith, and *Christians*, followers of Jesus the Messiah.

Donald Bloesch writes,

> It is important to understand that the disciples were not believers until Pentecost. They were under the law but not yet under grace. They had been converted to the "way" of the cross, yet not to the gospel of the cross. They had accepted Jesus as Messiah in the Jewish sense, but they did not embrace him as Savior of the world. The Holy Spirit was *with* them, not yet *in* them (Jn 14:17). They were in the sphere of the kingdom but not yet sealed in the body of Christ. Jesus declared, "I tell you this now, before it takes place, that when it does take place you may believe that I am he" (Jn 13:19; cf. 14:29). Even at the time of the ascension the disciples still regarded Jesus only as Messiah of Israel rather than God in human flesh, as is evident in their words; "Lord, will you at this time restore the kingdom to Israel?" (Acts 1:6). We also read that after his resurrection Jesus upbraided his disciples for "their unbelief and hardness of heart, because they had not believed those who saw him after he had risen" (Mk 16:14). The disciples before Pentecost were seekers

---

[92]Everts, "Conversion and Call," p. 162.

rather than believers. They had an incipient faith but not the faith that is "the power unto salvation." They were faithful as servants but not as sons (cf. Heb 3:5-6). They received the gift of the Spirit when their hearts were purified by faith (Acts 15:8-9 JB).[93]

It is hard to discern Bloesch's intended meaning in this description of the disciples' growth toward full-blown Christian faith. If he means to say that the disciples did not become "Christians," sealed in the body of Christ by the promised Holy Spirit, until Pentecost, I doubt that anyone would disagree. From the perspective of "Christian faith" and the full experience of "Christian salvation" (in the degree to which it is experienced in this life, as opposed to the bodily glorification we all still anticipate at the resurrection), the disciples had an "incipient faith" and were only "seekers rather than believers." But if Bloesch intends to say that the disciples did not have "saving" (as opposed to "Christian") faith until Pentecost, I cannot agree. Such a statement would deny faith and salvation to anyone in the old covenant. But it is hard to believe that such is Bloesch's intention, so I read his words in the sense that I have suggested—identifying Pentecost as the moment at which the disciples became new covenant believers, Christians, united to Christ by his gift of the Holy Spirit.

Later, Bloesch expands on his point regarding the experience of the disciples. He observes that

> Jesus' declaration that his disciples were already clean by the word spoken to them (Jn 13:10; 15:3) has led some commentators to conclude that the disciples were regenerate before Pentecost. R. A. Torrey argues that the baptism of the Spirit was not given to the disciples for regeneration because they had already attained the regenerate state.[94]

But Bloesch finds Torrey's position to be lacking "exegetical grounding" because

> in John 13:1-20 Jesus washes his disciples' feet, an act that symbolizes their future cleansing by the blood (the cross) and the Spirit. They were now clean by virtue of being covered by the blood of Christ (1 Jn 1:7), but they were not actually clean. They did not yet have regeneration because they were not yet baptized into the death of Christ (Mk 10:34-35).[95]

---

[93]Donald Bloesch, *The Holy Spirit: Works and Gifts* (Downers Grove, Ill.: InterVarsity Press, 2000), pp. 298, 390 n. 78.
[94]Ibid., p. 306, quoting R. A. Torrey, *The Holy Spirit* (Old Tappan, N.J.: Revell, 1927), pp. 112-15.
[95]Bloesch, *Holy Spirit*, p. 306.

Once again, Bloesch appears to restrict the Holy Spirit's work of regeneration to the new covenant inaugurated in Christ's blood and made possible through Christ's sending of the Spirit. If "regeneration" is defined as a distinctively new covenant work by the Spirit of the resurrected Christ, then certainly the disciples were not "regenerated." But although we may find distinctive terminology helpful when designating the epochal differences in the work of the Holy Spirit, we must be careful not to draw too sharp a line between the Spirit's saving work in the old covenant and his saving work in the new. Certainly, we cannot restrict the Spirit's inner work in people's lives to the time following his being "sent" at Pentecost.

Sinclair Ferguson notes that the Spirit was at work in the old covenant in the moral ordering of the people, in "personal renewal of a moral and spiritual nature."[96] The moral and spiritual characteristics that the New Testament describes as produced by the Holy Spirit, such as the fruit of the Spirit (Gal 5:22-23), are already found in Old Testament believers who are set before New Testament believers as examples of justification by faith (e.g., Abraham, in Rom 4) but also as examples of the life of faith (e.g., Heb 11; Jas 2:14-26; 5:17-18). Ferguson rightly concludes, therefore, that "such exhibitions of the presence of the saving fruit of the Spirit argue for the presence of his soteriological ministry in the old covenant as well as in the new."[97]

Douglas Oss also calls attention to

> clear instances in which the inner-transforming work of the Spirit is implied. For example, God commands the Israelites to circumcise their hearts (Lev 26:41; Deut 10:16; cf. Rom 2:28-29); the Israelites are said to have grieved God's Holy Spirit in the desert through their rebellion (Isa 63:10-11); the Old Testament repeatedly asserts that God honors a humble and contrite spirit (e.g., 2 Sam 22:28; 2 Kings 22:19; 2 Chron 7:14; Ps 25:9; 51:17; Isa 57:15; 66:2); the Spirit gives both moral instruction and guidance (Neh 9:20; Ps 143:10).[98]

God also commands them "to rid themselves of immorality and acquire a new heart and a new spirit (Ezek 18:31)."[99] But Oss also notes that the Old Testament anticipates a future new age "in which the transformative work

---

[96]Sinclair B. Ferguson, *The Holy Spirit*, Contours of Christian Theology (Downers Grove, Ill.: InterVarsity Press, 1996), p. 25.
[97]Ibid.
[98]Douglas A. Oss, "A Pentecostal/Charismatic View," in *Are Miraculous Gifts for Today? Four Views*, ed. Wayne A. Grudem (Grand Rapids, Mich.: Zondervan, 1996), p. 246.
[99]Ibid.

of the Spirit will become a universal reality among God's people."[100]
Jesus' discussion with Nicodemus in John 3 indicates that

> Nicodemus should have been able to understand the need for a work of renewal, and the promise of a new covenant in which it would be effected, from his Hebrew Bible (John 3:7). He should not have been surprised. Already in the old covenant the Lord circumcised the hearts of the people (Deut 30:6).[101]

This is not to deny the epochal development from the old to the new covenant, which Paul describes in 2 Corinthians 3, specifically with reference to the ministry of the Spirit,[102] but it does make us very cautious toward any suggestion that "regeneration," the spiritual renewal of sinners by the Holy Spirit, is a brand-new work for the Spirit when he works in the establishment of the church after Pentecost.

Bloesch goes on to say that "the disciples were justified like the Old Testament patriarchs and prophets were justified—by the promise of the blood, not by actual immersion or participation in the blood."[103] This confirms my conclusion that Bloesch does not intend to assert that the disciples were not saved until they received the promised Spirit at Pentecost anymore than he would deny that the Old Testament patriarchs were saved, even though they were certainly not Christians. In regard to Christ, the patriarch's faith was "incipient" and the full experience of Christ's atoning work was still only anticipated. The critical point that is established in all of this is the importance of drawing a distinction between being "saved" and becoming a Christian. Bloesch puts "the disciples of Jesus prior to Pentecost, the God-fearers in Acts 10 and the Old Testament prophets," all into the category of "pre-Christian."[104] This is appropriate terminology, so long as we do not assume that *pre-Christian* is equivalent to *unsaved*, which hardly seems possible when the Old Testament prophets are included in the category.

Writing about the disciples, Richard Peace asks,

> Were they converted at the moment they responded to Jesus' invitation to become fishers of men (Mark 1:17-18)? Or did conversion take place when

---

[100]Ibid.
[101]Ferguson, *Holy Spirit*, p. 25.
[102]Ibid., p. 26.
[103]Bloesch, *Holy Spirit*, p. 307.
[104]Ibid., p. 327.

they were commissioned as apostles (3:13-15)? Perhaps it took place when they affirmed that Jesus was indeed the Messiah (8:29). Or did it occur at the moment of the miracle of the second touch? [n. 22: Which Mark portrays in a symbolic way in 10:46-52.][105]

Peace's own suggestion is that, "On the basis of the understanding derived from Paul's experience, none of these experiences would qualify as the moment of conversion. Instead, each played a vital part in the final experience of conversion."[106] Again, the meaning of Peace's terminology is critical but not entirely clear. Is *conversion* equivalent to *salvation* here, or does Peace distinguish these terms? I can make good sense of his language if he is referring to conversion to Christianity, but not if it is conversion in the salvific sense.

"When Jesus calls Simon, Andrew, James and John to follow him," Peace writes, "they would have understood him to be inviting them to become part of a band of disciples attached to a religious teacher."[107] They, along with the crowd, find Jesus to be an exceptional teacher with unusual authority (Mk 1:16-28). Their initial experience is summed up in their distress in the storm, when they address Jesus as "Teacher" (Mk 4:38; Matthew uses "Lord" in Mt 8:25 and Luke "Master" in Lk 8:24). When Jesus calms the storm, they learn that Jesus is more than a teacher and they ask, "Who then is this?" (Mk 4:41). Mark's narrative goes on to demonstrate Jesus' control over demons (Mk 5:1-20), illness (Mk 5:24-34) and even death (Mk 5:21-24, 35-43). Jesus then identifies himself as a prophet (Mk 6:4).

A further step in grasping Jesus' identity is reached with the confession that he is Messiah (Mk 8:29). Given the expectations of the first century, what Peter "has in mind is a conquering hero who will wage war on the Gentile nations and then establish the kingdom of God on earth."[108] In the narrative that follows, they learn what kind of Messiah Jesus is. As Peace notes, "It is one thing to assert that Jesus is the Messiah. It is another to understand what it means for Jesus to be Messiah. Peter still had a long way to go in his commitment even after he made his astonishing assertion."[109] Jesus taught them that he was not a conquering hero but a suffering servant who would die for the sins of others and rise again (Mk 8:31), which

---

[105]Peace, *Conversion*, pp. 12-13.
[106]Ibid., p. 13.
[107]Ibid., p. 165.
[108]Ibid., p. 187.
[109]Ibid., pp. 123-24.

shocked Peter into rebuking Jesus (Mk 8:32), on account of which Jesus then rebuked Peter for acting like Satan (Mk 8:33). To avoid the misconceptions in people's minds concerning the Messiah, Jesus identifies himself as the Son of Man, an ambiguous title because it could be simply reminiscent of God's address to Ezekiel (e.g., Ezek 2:1 NIV), but it also has messianic usage in Daniel 7:13 (NIV).[110] Nevertheless, it is as Davidic king that Jesus rides into Jerusalem (Mk 11:1-10) and cleanses the temple (Mk 11:15-19).

Jesus furthers his self-revelation by asking how the Messiah can be both Son of David and David's Lord (Mk 12:35-37) and goes on to demonstrate that he is the Son of God, an identification that comes from the mouth of the high priest (Mk 14:61) and from the centurion (Mk 15:39). This had been discerned and acknowledged by the demons (Mk 3:11; 5:7), but Jesus now admits his identity publicly (Mk 14:62), while qualifying it with reference to the future Son of Man who comes gloriously.[111]

Peace suggests that "New Testament conversion involves repentance and faith that is focused on the Jesus who died for one's sins and lives again as the Lord who brings new life. It is only after they [the disciples], like Paul, meet the resurrected Jesus that it all makes sense for them and the response of conversion is possible."[112] It seems very unnecessary to assume that all of those whom Jesus called to be his disciples were unbelieving Jews and that they only came to saving faith when they came to realize the identity of Jesus—that they became "children of Abraham by faith" only when they came to believe that Jesus was the Christ, the Son of God. Thus, people such as Cornelius, Nathanael, "probably" John's two disciples and others are included by Edwards in the four categories of people without explicit knowledge of Christ who might, nevertheless, be saved. They were "good men before [they met Christ], for they seemed to be found already in a disposition to follow [Christ] when [Christ] first appeared to them in his human nature and this seems to have been the case with Zacchaeus and with the woman of Canaan."[113] I am struck particularly by the words of Jesus concerning Nathanael, of whom he says, "Here is truly an Israelite in whom there is no deceit!" (Jn 1:47). And note how quickly Nathanael replies to Jesus: "Rabbi, you are the Son of God! You are the King of Israel!" (Jn 1:49). As McDermott notes, "The significance of

---

[110]Ibid., pp. 194-95.
[111]Ibid., p. 211.
[112]Ibid., p. 216.
[113]Jonathan Edwards, *Miscellanies* 847, quoted in McDermott, "Response," p. 78.

these New Testament saints is not that they eventually professed faith in Christ but that Edwards says they were regenerated before they made that explicit profession."[114]

Jesus makes it clear to Peter that he recognized Jesus as the Messiah only because of a special work of God, illumining his understanding. But this can hardly be taken as a declaration that Peter was unsaved and bound for hell prior to his belief in Jesus as Son of God. The disciples went through a process of growing understanding and increasing faith. At a number of points along the way, Jesus rebukes them for their lack of faith and understanding (Mk 4:40; 7:18; 8:17-21, 32-33; 9:19). Peace notes that "at no point in the Gospel are they commended for their faith,"[115] yet they do demonstrate some faith. "They go out on their mission with a minimum of provisions (6:8-11),"[116] and they actually engage in ministry, calling people to repentance (Mk 6:12), as John the Baptist had done. Both Jairus and the Canaanite woman had faith that Jesus could heal, so they came and asked for healing, but the disciples "need to understand that it is God working in and through Jesus; and then they themselves must put their trust in God through Jesus."[117]

Scot McKnight has taken note of the potential confusion created by failing to differentiate between the conversion of saving faith in Jesus and the conversion of affiliation with Jesus and his people, in his sociological study of conversion in the Gospels.[118] His own work, however, does not completely escape the confusion that I have identified in the study by Richard Peace and the language of Donald Bloesch. Most of the time, he speaks of conversion to Christianity or to a particular form of Christianity, but he occasionally speaks about conversion in language that indicates salvation. Nevertheless, he offers a helpful description of different kinds of conversion and of the various dimensions of conversion, not all of which are experienced by every convert in the same way or the same order.

In regard to salvation, Scripture indicates that there is a moment in the life of each person who is saved when they move from darkness to light. The experience of the first disciples of Jesus illustrates for us, however, just how difficult it is to identify that moment. McKnight proposes that Peace

[114]Ibid., p. 79.
[115]Peace, Conversion, p. 242.
[116]Ibid.
[117]Ibid., p. 243.
[118]Scot McKnight, Turning to Jesus: The Sociology of Conversion in the Gospels (Louisville, Ky.: Westminster John Knox, 2002).

may have oversimplified the evidence and stretched "the explanatory skin too tightly," by arguing that there is "just one conversion pattern that is experienced by Paul and the Twelve differently."[119] Contrary to the common evangelical tendency to make the crisis conversion of Paul normative, McKnight suggests that maybe "the Petrine experience of a growing conversion is more normative."[120] He writes:

> Those who understand conversion through the lens of Paul's experience move the conversion experience away from the norm to the dramatic. Paul's experience of conversion was profound; it finds Christian counterparts in some of the greats in Christian history—notable leaders like Augustine, Martin Luther, John Wesley, and Karl Barth. But Paul's experience is hardly typical. Instead, what we find is that a sociological approach to the Gospel evidence reveals that Peter's conversion illustrates most completely the normal pattern. Consequently, I am calling Christian thinking to consider Peter as the prototypical convert to Jesus.[121]

The apparent difference between Peace and McKnight arises, to a large degree, from the fact that they are focusing on different aspects or kinds of conversion. Peace primarily analyzes the process of salvation, conversion to faith in Christ as Savior and Lord, whereas McKnight's sociological study is more interested in the process by which people become formally or publicly affiliated with the church. Once again, the importance of not confusing the moment of salvation with the point of public identification with the church is evident. Both of these are "conversions to Jesus," but they differ in kind, and we need to be clear what sort of conversion we are talking about when we use the term. Only God can define accurately when a person is saved but a sociologist can identify a person's religious affiliation.

Many people who eventually express their willingness to follow Jesus as Lord and Savior, do reach that point through a process that looks more like the stages of developing understanding which we see in Peter's life than it is like Paul's dramatic turnabout after meeting Jesus on the road to Damascus. Even in regard to Paul, it is not easy to identify the moment of his salvation, but with regard to Peter and many others since then, we find it much easier to identify when they became Christians than when they were saved. Furthermore, the process of growth in knowledge of

---

[119]Ibid., p. 17.
[120]Ibid.
[121]Ibid., p. 176.

what it means to follow Jesus continues beyond the initial identification with him, so that conversion is an ongoing necessity until we are finally transformed into the image of Christ. So, some people are saved for a while before they become Christians, others are saved some time after they become Christians and, for others, the two forms of conversion occur together. But, none of us is well equipped to discern the timing of the critical event of salvation from sin and entrance into the kingdom of God by birth from above. What we should focus upon is the direction of people's lives. Are we and they oriented toward God in Christ or are we moving away from him?

Non-Jews whose faith Jesus commended. Jesus occasionally praised the faith of pagans and urged Jews to follow their examples. For example, in Nazareth, he spoke well of the widow at Zarephath in Sidon, to whom Elijah was sent, rather than to any of the many widows in Israel at the time (Lk 4:24-26). Zarephath was in the "heartland of the Baal cult (1 Kings 16:31)," but Jesus commends her for her faith in Elijah's order, which was the word of the Lord. "She had less evidence for faith than the residents of Nazareth had but believed that God was speaking and could be trusted."[122] Jesus also cited Naaman, the Syrian, who was healed through Elisha, even though there were many lepers in Israel at the time (Lk 4:27). The outcry of the Jewish people of Nazareth at that point indicates that they understood well the implied contrast that Jesus was making between these heathen and themselves (Lk 4:28-29). Further in Luke's narrative, Jesus showed amazement at the faith of a Gentile centurion who sought healing for his slave because the centurion's faith was greater than he had found "even in Israel" (Lk 7:9). Whether this was saving faith or only faith in Jesus as a miracle-worker we cannot discern, but it was a good example of trust, nevertheless. In much the same way, Matthew records Jesus' affirmation of the faith of the Canaanite woman in the district of Tyre and Sidon who sought help for her demonized daughter (Mt 15:21-28). When Jesus healed ten lepers, the only one who returned to "give praise to God" (Lk 17:18) was particularly noted by Jesus as "a foreigner." McDermott observes that in all these instances, Jesus encouraged those who were within the covenant community to learn from those who were outside.[123]

Along this line, we may notice also the way in which Jesus picked a Samaritan for the parable he used to teach a devout Jewish lawyer about the

---

[122]McDermott, *Can Evangelicals Learn,* p. 86.
[123]Ibid., p. 88.

neighbor whom the law requires us to love (Lk 10:25-37). The lawyer had asked what he must "do to inherit eternal life." (Lk 10:25) and when the lawyer identifies the Samaritan as the one who had acted properly as a neighbor to the man beaten by robbers, Jesus tells the lawyer, "Go and do likewise" (Lk 10:37).

Of course, it is one thing for us to note that Gentiles who encountered Jesus were commended for faith and quite another to draw conclusions from such instances about people who do *not* have such encounters. In the case of the Gentiles who demonstrated unusual faith, at the very least we have demonstrations of the Spirit's work of illumination to make the revelation effective even if the person's faith is not of the justifying kind. Granting that the story concerning the neighborly Samaritan is fictional, we cannot ignore Jesus' willingness to commend someone outside the covenant people as an example of the love required by the law—by contrast with the behavior of a priest and a Levite.

The twelve disciples of John the Baptist in Ephesus. The twelve disciples of John the Baptist, whom Paul met in Ephesus (Acts 19:1-7), provide another interesting case. Most of the attention given to this incident in recent years has been in the context of discussions regarding the baptism in the Spirit, in particular, whether this is something that is logically, if not necessarily chronologically, distinct from the reception of the Spirit in new covenant salvation. Our own interest is different, however, having to do with the disciples' relationship to God. Were they already "saved"? My own conclusion is that these were old covenant believers who had received the Johannine baptism of repentance but who had not been baptized in the name of Jesus, the one who would baptize them with the Spirit. They were even less knowledgeable concerning the Messiah than were the followers of Jesus who had gathered in the upper room in Jerusalem, awaiting the gift of the Spirit. They typify the old covenant believer after the epochal sending of the Holy Spirit, who has still not received the new covenant Spirit personally. When Paul taught them further, they were baptized in the name of Jesus, and as the Spirit came on them, they spoke in tongues and prophesied, just as the 120 had done on the day of Pentecost. This was, therefore, no experience of subsequent baptism with the Spirit by people who had already been united with Christ by the indwelling of the Spirit. Theirs was an old covenant experience of the Holy Spirit's saving work, like that which John the Baptist had known, and they now moved personally into the new covenant experience of the Spirit and were united with the body of Christ, being baptized in his name.

Applying inferences from these cases to Jews today. Can Jews in our own time, who have not heard of Jesus in a way that enables them to accept or reject him, be saved? I will deal with that question again when we consider other religions and God's saving program today, but the material here lays the groundwork for that discussion. The critical question is *when* or *whether* the quality of faith that saved people under the old covenant ceases to be saving. I believe that Anderson is right to draw an analogy between the situation of Old Testament believers and that of the unevangelized today. He posits that "their repentance and faith (themselves the result of God's work in their hearts) opened the gate, as it were, to the grace, mercy and forgiveness which he always longed to extend to them, and which was to be made for ever available at the cross." Anderson then asks, "Might it not be true of the follower of some other religion that the God of all mercy had worked in his heart by his Spirit, bringing him in some measure to realize his sin and need for forgiveness, and enabling him, in the twilight as it were, to throw himself on the mercy of God?"[124]

J. I. Packer responds to Anderson's question:

> The answer seems to be "yes." It might be true. Who are we to deny it? If ever it is true, such worshipers will learn in heaven that they were saved by Christ's death and that their hearts were renewed by the Holy Spirit. They will join the glorified Church in endless praise of the sovereign grace of God. Christians since the second century have hoped so, and perhaps Socrates and Plato are in this happy state even now. Who knows?[125]

At a later point, I will address the question of whether the other religions themselves have salvific value, but at this point, I am simply addressing the salvation of individuals within those religions, though not necessarily *through* those religions. This works if we recognize that the death of Christ is always the ground of salvation but that some people who are ignorant of it still live under the revelational terms of the old covenant, even though they are historically living in the new covenant. Edwards points us in a helpful direction with his emphasis on a person's disposition, which is "all that can be said to be absolutely necessary," because this is what God looks at. The Jews who were saved in the Old Testament "did not receive Christ in any conscious or explicit manner, but they had

---

[124] Anderson, *Christianity and World Religions*, pp. 101-2.
[125] J. I. Packer, "What Happens to People Who Die Without Hearing the Gospel?" *Decision*, January 2002, p. 11.

the proper disposition, which alone is necessary for salvation."[126]

Ecclesiocentrists face a particularly sticky problem in regard to Jews at the time of Jesus who had the faith of Abraham or in regard to Gentile God-fearers who did not know about Jesus. Did such people *lose* their salvation? And, if so, at what point—at the moment of Christ's resurrection, at the ascension or at Pentecost? As Sanders asks, "Are such people damned for failing to hear the *new* required content of belief?" Some theologians might cover such people under a "grandfather clause," but this is problematic within the principles of ecclesiocentrism. Thus, Sanders is right to ask, "If a 'grace period' is granted to people who are a dispensation behind (in terms of hearing), then why not a grace period for those unevangelized, who may be five or six dispensations behind?"[127] I doubt that a Dispensationalist would speak of "five or six dispensations" in this way but, nonetheless, we can speak of "generations" and still face the same "dispensational" problem that applies, whether or not one is formally a Dispensationalist.

To admit that Jews may be saved through old covenant repentance and faith is *not to argue that Christians ought not to evangelize Jews.* I am certainly not asserting a "two covenant theory" in which the Christian gospel is only for Gentiles. Jesus is the Messiah promised to Israel and, like the early apostles, who were themselves Jews, we must proclaim Jesus as Messiah to Jewish people today. What we cannot do, however, is assume that none of the Jews who are alive today and who have not believed in Jesus as Messiah and Lord are saved. We can say that any who have been enlightened by the Spirit concerning the identity of Jesus and who have rejected him are lost; they are not children of Abraham by faith, "circumcised of heart," and so they are not children of God. But Erickson is right: "Paul's preaching to the Jews need not mean that salvation without hearing this was impossible."[128] The same is true for us in our evangelism among Jewish people. I was initially a bit more reluctant to agree with Erickson that though

---

[126]Gerald R. McDermott, *Jonathan Edwards Confronts the Gods: Christian Theology, Enlightenment Religion and Non-Christian Faiths* (New York: Oxford University Press, 2000), p. 134.

[127]John Sanders, ed., *What About Those Who Have Never Heard? Three Views on the Destiny of the Unevangelized* (Downers Grove, Ill.: InterVarsity Press, 1995), 159 n. 18.

[128]Erickson, *How Shall They Be Saved?* p. 193. Consider, likewise, the conclusion of a Wesleyan theologian: "While it would be dreadfully anti-Wesleyan to minimize the role of the church in bringing persons to the fullness of salvation in Christ, it is perhaps equally anti-Wesleyan to suggest that the incarnation of God in Christ brought an end to God's saving activity in Judaism" (Thomas E. Phillips, "The Mission of the Church in Acts: Inclusive or Exclusive?" *Wesleyan Theological Journal* 38 [spring 2003]: 137).

it was not impossible that some unevangelized Jews were saved, "it was improbable."[129] On further reflection, however, Paul's own words about God's judicial hardening of the hearts of much of Israel (Rom 11:7-10), and the large numbers of Jewish people who did hear the gospel but still did not believe in Jesus, do lend support to Erickson's pessimism.

We must be aware, however, that Jews now are in a different position than were Jews in the apostolic period, given the centuries of anti-Semitism they have experienced at the hands of nominal Christians, expressed most vividly in the Holocaust. That factor looms very large in the minds of Jews today. Consequently, I am less ready to assume that even a Jew who rejects the proclamation of Jesus made by a Gentile Christian today has rejected Jesus himself, than I would be to say the same of a Jew in the apostle Paul's day. Erickson is right to suggest that "there is room for acknowledging that God alone may know in every case exactly whose faith is sufficient for salvation."[130] We need to leave this judgment with God while we make ourselves available to him as servants of his glorious gospel, which is powerful to salvation when the Spirit of God is at work too.

The story of Khaled AbdelRahman, from Iraq, has fascinating similarities to the Damascus experience of Saul of Tarsus, with the significant difference that AbdelRahman was a Muslim, not a Jew. It is definitely not my intention, however, to suggest that God's work in Islam is part of the special redemptive program that culminates in the incarnate Word, Jesus, the Christ. AbdelRahman "grew up in Iraq, believing that one day he would be an imam (leader) of a mosque."[131] He argued about religion with some young Christians, creating "many faith problems for them," but their priest gave him excellent answers to his questions.

> One night, as he slept, AbdelRahman saw a vision of a man with a beard. "Son," the man said, "why do you attack my sheep?" AbdelRahman replied, "Who are you, Sir?" [and the answer was:] "Jesus Christ." [AbdelRahman said:] "I'm not attacking your sheep, Sir, I'm trying to bring your lost sheep back to the straight path." [And, Christ replied:] "You are the one who is lost. I'm the straight path."[132]

Confused by this encounter, AbdelRahman gave up on religion and pur-

---

[129]Erickson, *How Shall They*, p. 93.
[130]Ibid., p. 195.
[131]Stan Guthrie, "Doors into Islam," *Christianity Today*, September 9, 2002, p. 40.
[132]Ibid.

sued a life of pleasure. His father was a high-ranking officer in the Iraqi army but was assassinated as a threat to the state, in what was made to look like an accidental car crash. Before AbdelRahman learned of the cause of his father's death, "he heard a commanding voice as he slept: 'Run away from your country now!' He knew it was the voice of Jesus,"[133] and he caught a flight to his mother's home country. When he called his mother and learned what had actually happened to his father and that he himself had been sought by the police, he passed out. When he woke up, hours later, he "began praying earnestly for God to show him the truth. Later, in a dream, Jesus told him, 'I love you. Why don't you love me likewise? Come to me, because I have a plan for you.'"[134] AbdelRahman responded to the call and has since been involved in Christian evangelistic ministry among Muslims.

God's gracious pursuit of AbdelRahman is unmistakable in his story; eventually, it led him to Christian faith, but it also took him through a process in which God's intention to save him and commission him for service was very clear. This did not come about apart from contact with Christian witnesses, but God went well beyond that witness to draw AbdelRahman to decisive faith in Jesus. We dare not establish a theoretical understanding of God's saving work from the fallible recollection of someone who reports specific revelation from God, without the Holy Spirit's special work of inspiration. Nevertheless, it is interesting to contemplate the sense in which Jesus would have addressed AbdelRahman as "son" at the point in his life when he was opposing Christians in his misguided efforts to lead them to the truth.

Summing Up

In answer to our question (who can be saved?), we have learned a good deal from the biblical narratives of the salvation experiences of the people we meet there. Many people in Israel were saved without faith in Jesus because they believed in the God of Abraham and looked forward to the fulfillment of God's promises, although the manner of that fulfillment became clear to them only very gradually. In fact, so indistinct was the knowledge of that fulfillment that it was easy for people not to see in Jesus the one whom for they were waiting. Consequently, earnest pursuers of the faith of Abraham, like Saul of Tarsus, thought it their duty to God to

---

[133]Ibid., p. 42.
[134]Ibid.

oppose Jesus and his followers. We have observed that God's work of salvation is often a gradual process in people's lives and that we are not able to identify the precise moment when an individual is saved. We have also seen that the moment of salvation does not necessarily coincide with the moment of conversion to Christianity, although it can, and it probably does for many of us who grew up in Christian homes.

I, for one, having grown up in a missionary home in India, cannot remember a time when I did not believe that Jesus had died for me. That does not mean that I was always saved, of course, but my becoming saved certainly happened early. It also means, however, that many people may now become Christians before they are saved, just as people in the New Testament were saved before they became Christians. What we must not do is confuse these two forms of conversion. Our primary purpose must always be to serve God in his work of salvation. It is a good and necessary thing to seek to bring people into the full knowledge of Jesus as the Son of God, but making people Christians is not our main goal.

Clearly, then, the biblical narrative gives us grounds for hope that God's saving program has been wider than his building of the covenant communities, both in the old and in the new covenant. Jesus had sheep who did not yet "belong to this fold." He felt a compulsion to "bring them also," and he knew they would listen to his voice so that there would be one fold with one shepherd (Jn 10:16). Although they were not yet in the fold, Jesus identified them as *his sheep*. I wonder—were some of those sheep in North America and Australia, as Jesus spoke? To Paul, in Corinth, God gave comfort in a vision after his weeks of fear and flight, on his second missionary journey. God assured Paul: "There are many in this city who are my people" (Acts 18:10). These people were not yet Christians; they were not gathered in Christian congregations or churches. Some of them were Jews, but most of them were Gentiles. God identified them as *his people*. Were some of them saved already and simply needing Paul's proclamation of Jesus as Son of God to be led on to fuller faith and the joy of new covenant life in Christ? Perhaps. We do not know. In any event, Paul was not the one who would make them God's people; he was there as God's instrument to lead them on to full faith in Jesus. I expect that most of them would have been saved simultaneously with their becoming Christians. The key thing is that *being saved and becoming a Christian are not the same thing*. Consequently, we need not assume that the unevangelized are not saved, simply because they are not (yet!) Christians.

In the next chapter we will look at another category of the unevangelized: those who never attain the intellectual and moral ability to hear and comprehend human proclamation of the gospel. Can they be saved? If so, how? We will also examine a proposal that all believers ultimately become "Christians," but that for some of them, this may not happen until the moment of death.

10

Can Infants Be Saved?

Thesis 12: The possibility and the process of salvation are no different for infants and the mentally incompetent than for competent adults. Those whom God elects to salvation are saved by grace through faith. Scripture is silent about how many of the infants who die in infancy are included among the elect, but we place our hope for their salvation in God's great mercy. The capabilities of infants and the mentally challenged to relate to God cannot be measured by their ability to communicate with us; we must not assume that the capabilities of their bodies and brains are indicative of the abilities of their souls and minds. Infant faith, like adult faith, would be a trusting response to God and his self-revelation by the means God chooses.

Thesis 13: All people meet Jesus Christ personally at the moment of death, and they respond to him in a manner consistent with the response they had been giving to God and his revelation during their lifetime. At that moment, those who had received forms of revelation less complete than the gospel, but who had responded in faith by a work of the Holy Spirit, will joyfully find in Christ the fulfillment of all their hopes and longings. Consequently, there is a sense in which we can say that only those who believe in Jesus will be (finally) saved, even though we affirm that some can be (initially) saved without knowing about Jesus.

IN MANY ASIAN AND AFRICAN CULTURES THE FATE OF ancestors comes up quickly in discussions of the salvation of the unevangelized. In North American and European cultures, the ancestors are not much of an issue, but infants and the mentally incompetent certainly are. Parents who have eagerly expected a child only to lose it through miscarriage or illness want to know where their baby is now. Certainly, the unborn and infants are unevangelized, but we concluded in chapter four that they, too, need to be saved. No one gets to enjoy God's fellowship in heaven except through the Son of God. So parents want to know, are their children automatically saved by Christ's atonement? If so, are they an exception to the principle that justification is by faith? And how then are we to understand the means by which salvation is applied to them? If we cannot say that they are included in the saving benefits of Christ's work, must we say that they are all certainly lost? Or do we have reason to believe that at least some of them (e.g., children of a believing parent) are saved? The issues are no less troubling for parents of mentally disabled children who may grow up without ever having the ability to understand their need of salvation or God's program for achieving it. What can we say about them? To these issues we turn our attention now.

THE IMPORTANCE OF THIS QUESTION

Innumerable human beings have died in infancy throughout human history, particularly if one assumes that human life begins with conception, as many Christians do. On this assumption, every egg that is fertilized but not implanted and every aborted human person (whether the abortion is spontaneous or induced) is someone about whose eternal destiny we may legitimately wonder. The numbers about which we are speaking here are immense. In fact, Gilbert Meilaender places the beginning of human life at some time *after* conception, in part because "research seems to indicate that as many as half of fertilized ova may fail to implant successfully." If this is true, and if life begins with fertilization, "we would be forced to conclude that half of the human race dies after a life of four to five days. Although it is logically possible," he suggests, "it is also rather counterintuitive."[1] When we add to these statistics concerning unimplanted but fertilized ova the number of spontaneous abortions, the tragically high number of medically induced abortions and all those people who grow physically but never attain mental capacity to grasp the gospel, we may well face a situation in which the *majority* of the human race does not reach a state in which they are able to hear and respond to any humanly communicated knowledge concerning God.

In light of the prevalence of abortion these days, we can appreciate Augustus H. Strong's suggestion that one reason for God's choosing not to give us clear revelation concerning the salvation of infants is that

---

[1]Gilbert Meilaender, *Bioethics: A Primer for Christians* (Grand Rapids, Mich.: Eerdmans, 1996), p. 30.

"knowledge of the fact that all children dying in infancy are saved might have seemed to make infanticide a virtue."[2] Millard Erickson also addresses the risk that some might conclude that mass infanticide is "the most efficient means of evangelism and the most compassionate treatment" of children, but he reminds us that we are not justified in promoting a good end by a "very evil means."[3] In a different vein, Norman Geisler proposes that "high infant-mortality rates in the overwhelmingly non-Christian third world have a salvific design: 'He takes his elect from those who are under the age of accountability in countries where if they had grown up they wouldn't have heard the gospel and they would have wanted to hear it.'"[4] This is an idea that John Ellenberger finds "abhorrent" and "inconsistent with the meaning of God's victorious 'gathering of the nations.'"[5] One can see how a proposal like Geisler's might reduce our desire to minimize the incidence of infant mortality around the world and thereby have the effect that Strong and Erickson fear could follow.

THE ANALOGY BETWEEN INFANTS AND UNEVANGELIZED ADULTS

The salvation of those who die as infants or those who are mentally incapable and the salvation of adults who are unevangelized are often treated quite separately, but the two cannot be so easily separated. We need a doctrine of salvation that accounts for all classes of the unevangelized—both those who *have not* heard and those who *cannot* hear. These two issues came together in the discussion at the Evangelical Affirmations conference at Trinity Evangelical Divinity School in May 1989. It was noticed that "the wording of the affirmations did not specifically rule out the possibility of salvation for the unevangelized" and a "stricter formulation" was called for, one stipulating that explicit knowledge of salvation is necessary for

---

[2]Augustus H. Strong, *Systematic Theology* (Westwood, N.J.: Revell, 1907), p. 663.
[3]Millard J. Erickson, *How Shall They Be Saved? The Destiny of Those Who Do Not Hear of Jesus* (Grand Rapids, Mich.: Baker, 1996), p. 253.
[4]Norman Geisler, "All You Wanted to Know About Hell and Were Afraid to Ask," Pippert Lectures, Alliance Theological Seminary, Nyack, N.Y., 1982, quoted in John D. Ellenberger, "Is Hell a Proper Motivation for Missions?" in *Through No Fault of Their Own? The Fate of Those Who Have Never Heard*, ed. William V. Crockett and James G. Sigountos (Grand Rapids, Mich.: Baker, 1991), p. 222. (Note Geisler's appeal to God's knowledge of counterfactuals to deal with the problem of the unevangelized.)
[5]Ellenberger, "Is Hell," p. 223.

salvation.[6] When it was pointed out that such a statement would "consign all infants who die to hell," the matter was not pursued. By contrast, Christian churches and organizations frequently write their statements regarding salvation in ecclesiocentric language, with competent unevangelized adults in mind, but without any mention of how these other groups of people who do not know of Christ can be saved.

Ronald Nash has noticed that accessibilists tend to treat infants and the mentally disabled in the same way as they treat unevangelized, but he sees these as different cases, precisely because condemnation is related to sins committed while in the body (2 Cor 5:10; cf. also Mt 16:27; Rom 2:6, 8; and esp. Ezek 18). In Nash's opinion, infants are a different case, because they "have no personal guilt of that type." They die physically because of their relationship to Adam, but they are incorporated into Christ without an act of their will just as they were into Adam.[7] On the other hand, the case of the unevangelized looks very different to Nash.

I agree with Nash that these two categories (infants and adults) are different in significant ways, but I suggest that Nash has ignored the significant point of analogy. He grants that infants can be regenerated in spite of their ignorance of Christ, but I am compelled to ask why the same could not be true of elect adults. Both are sinners who need salvation, and both are ignorant of Christ, though for different reasons. In previous chapters, I have offered reasons for believing that God can save sinners who do not know about Jesus and whose ignorance is inculpable; indeed we have seen scriptural instances of such people. I have insisted, however, that salvation of these people is by grace through faith, even though the content of that faith varies, depending on the means by which God has revealed himself to people. In any case, no adults—no matter when or where they lived—have ever lacked the revelation necessary to be saved. Nor has it ever been impossible for the Holy Spirit to graciously draw them to God by faith, if God so chooses.

John Sanders is correct, therefore, to criticize Nash's assumption that all infants are saved but that the unevangelized cannot be:

Nash's position means that all those throughout history who died in infancy

---

[6]John Sanders, *No Other Name: An Investigation into the Destiny of the Unevangelized* (Grand Rapids, Mich.: Eerdmans, 1992), p. 24.
[7]Ronald Nash, "Restrictivism," in *What About Those Who Have Never Heard? Three Views on the Destiny of the Unevangelized,* ed. John Sanders (Downers Grove, Ill.: InterVarsity Press, 1995), p. 119.

in unevangelized countries are saved, while those unfortunate enough to live into adulthood are damned. Apparently God loves these children and saves them through Christ but does not love the adults, for he does not make eternal salvation available to all of them.[8]

It is much better, I believe, for Reformed theologians to take the Westminster Confession's statement—that "elect infants dying in infancy are regenerated and saved by Christ through the Spirit" (10.3)—and then to extend this to unevangelized adults, as well. We might then say that "all elect *unevangelized adults* are regenerated and saved by Christ." In the case of both infants and adults, then, the prior issue is the same. It is the question, whom has God elected in Christ?

INFANT ELECTION

Unlike the earliest Arminians, John Wesley believed in original guilt, so that even a child born of two perfect Christians would be a sinner, but that original guilt is cancelled by the justification of all people in Christ.[9] Wesley deemed this to be one of the universal benefits of the atonement. Wesley would be able to assure any parent who has lost a child, whether or not the parents were Christians, that their child had originally been under condemnation for guilt in Adam but that Christ's salvation has accomplished their salvation. This position is certainly attractive from a pastoral perspective, as one ministers to the bereaved.

Regrettably, perhaps, this is not an avenue open to Calvinists, who believe in the perseverance of the saints. It would mean that some of the infants who live to moral and rational maturity forfeit their salvation through personal sin, which would be incoherent. Theologians who follow Augustine's understanding of election (or Martin Luther's) rather than John Calvin's do not face this problem. Augustine believed that election is to perseverance rather than to faith (as Calvin proposed). Consequently, it would be possible for some to be saved (justified) for a time in their lives but not saved in the final judgment. The elect will persevere, but the nonelect will fall away. This form of Augustinianism accords well with the doctrine of baptismal regeneration, but that is incompatible with

---

[8]John Sanders, "Response to Nash," in *What About Those Who Have Never Heard? Three Views on the Destiny of the Unevangelized* , ed. John Sanders (Downers Grove, Ill.: InterVarsity Press, 1995), p. 146.

[9]John Wesley, *A Plain Account of Christian Perfection* (1777; Minneapolis: Bethany Fellowship, 1966), p. 50.

the evangelical insistence on the necessity of personal faith.[10]

Concern about the eternal state of those who die as infants is a basic reason for Erickson's proposal that all humans are born corrupt in Adam but become guilty only by personal identification with Adam through individual choice.[11] "The infant who dies in infancy never comes to the age of accountability and thus never ratifies the Adamic sin," and "the same would be true for those who attain physical maturity, but never come to this point of moral responsibility. Consequently, there is no imputation of guilt. There need not be, in a sense, justification."[12] It is primarily here that I have a problem with Erickson's proposal. He undermines the universal saving work of Christ for guilty sinners. Given the statistics mentioned earlier, possibly well over half of the population of the new earth would be there—not because they are sinners who were saved by grace but because they never became sinners. More traditionally, Calvinists have posited that the reason that any infants are saved is *not* because they were excluded from implication in original guilt but because they are in solidarity with Christ. This is the move being taken by those who assert that all who die in infancy are known to be elect. It is superior to Erickson's proposal in that it makes the atoning work of Christ necessary for eternal life with God.

The Westminster Confession states that "elect infants dying in infancy are regenerated and saved by Christ through the Spirit who worketh when, where, and how he pleaseth. So also are all other elect persons, who are incapable of being outwardly called by the ministry of the Word of God" (10.3). So who are these "elect infants"? Strong tells us that "some of the framers" of the Westminster Confession taught that "in declaring that 'elect infants dying in infancy' are saved," the Confession "implies that non-elect infants dying in infancy are lost."[13] On that interpretation, the

---

[10] Among Augustinians who believe that baptism is regenerative, a complex of doctrinal proposals are appealed to concerning the state of infants. To start with, infants who are baptized are presumed to be saved. The tradition of "baptism of desire" might be further used to suggest that even some unbaptized infants may be saved. And, finally, some have held the belief that there is a *limbus infantum*, a place where unbaptized infants go; it is not the full blessedness of heaven but has none of the pain of hell. I understand the theological argument that lies behind the doctrine of baptismal regeneration, and I sympathize with the sensitivities that inform other provisions, but none of this is open to me. I am, by conviction, a Baptist, and even if I were Reformed in my ecclesiology as I am in my soteriology, that would not entail baptismal regeneration, since the Reformed see baptism as a sign of the covenant, not as a means of salvation.

[11] Erickson, *How Shall They,* pp. 249-51.

[12] Ibid., p. 251.

[13] Strong, *Systematic Theology,* p. 663.

parents of a deceased infant will surely want to know whether *their* baby
was an "elect infant" whose regeneration and salvation are sure. To avoid
any ambiguity, the American Presbyterian Church in the U.S.A. adopted a
statement in 1903 which said that the Confession "is not to be regarded as
teaching that any who die in infancy are lost. We believe," they said, "that
all dying in infancy are included in the election of grace, and are regenerated and saved by Christ through the Spirit, who works when and where
and how He pleases."[14]

Strong agrees that all who die in infancy are elect, and he cites Calvin[15]
and John Owen[16] as Reformed theologians who held this position before
him. Lyman Beecher and Charles Hodge are credited as the first to make
"current in this country [America] the doctrine of the salvation of all who
die in infancy."[17] While granting this to be the majority view among Calvinist theologians, however, Loraine Boettner judges that "the Scriptures
seem to teach plainly enough that the children of believers are saved; but
they are silent or practically so in regard to those of the heathens."[18] That
would at least provide comfort to Christian parents, as the *Canons of Dort*
asserted: "Godly parents ought not to doubt concerning the election and
salvation of those of their children whom God calls out of this life in infancy."[19] Interestingly, Charles Spurgeon extended this to all infants, since
the second commandment says that God shows mercy to the thousandth
generation of those who love him (Ex 20:6). From this, Spurgeon concludes

---

[14]Loraine Boettner, *The Reformed Doctrine of Predestination* (c. 1932; Philadelphia: Presbyterian
& Reformed, 1974), p. 146.

[15]John Calvin *Institutes of the Christian Religion* 4.16, Library of Christian Classics (Philadelphia: Westminster Press, 1965), 2:1327-31. Boettner also contends that "in none of Calvin's
writings does he say, either directly or by good and necessary inference, that any dying in
infancy are lost" (*Reformed Doctrine*, p. 146). But Sanders thinks it "best to interpret Calvin
as believing that God elects some but not all children who die for salvation" (*No Other Name*,
p. 295).

[16]John Owen, *Works*, 8:522 (These works are available in reprinted form from London: The
Banner of Truth Trust, 1965-1968). Charles Spurgeon said that all of the Calvinists he knew
in his day "hope and believe that all persons dying in infancy are elect" ("Infant Salvation
[Sermon 411]," *Metropolitan Tabernacle Pulpit, 1861* [Pasadena, Tex.: Pilgrim, 1975], 7:505-12.
This is also available at <http://www.spurgeon.org/sermons/0411.htm>).

[17]Strong, *Systematic Theology*, p. 664, quoting George L. Prentiss, *Presbyterian Review*, July 1883,
pp. 548-80.

[18]Boettner, *Reformed Doctrine*, p. 146.

[19]*Canons of Dort* 1.17, trans. Anthony Hoekema, *Created in God's Image* (Grand Rapids, Mich.:
Eerdmans, 1986), p. 165 n. 78. Hence, Hoekema himself posits that "the promise of the covenant of grace, that God will be the God not only of us who are believing adults but also of
our children, should give Christian parents assurance that their infants who die are not lost"
(ibid.).

that "infants who have had pious ancestors, no matter how remotely, dying as infants are saved," all of them being elect.[20] Even among Calvinist theologians there is not a clear consensus on this issue, so we must press on to examine it further in order to reach our own conclusions.[21]

Personally, I believe that Scripture leaves us ignorant as to how many of those who die in infancy are elect, though we may be hopeful of the greatness of God's mercy.[22] With this stance, I place myself alongside Reformed theologians such as Anthony Hoekema, who approves of Herman Bavinck's cautious claim that "we can on the basis of Scripture go no further than to refrain from uttering a determinative and decisive judgment either in a positive or negative sense."[23] Although it would certainly be nice to assume that all who die in infancy are saved, I concur with Erickson that many of the texts to which people allude "really do not seem to bear sufficiently upon the issue to be of help."[24]

Two texts are most frequently cited as evidence of the salvation of in-

---

[20]Spurgeon, "Infant Salvation," p. 2.

[21]I find it very interesting that Wesley "was prepared to accept that people such as the apostle Paul were 'unconditionally' elected to perform certain functions, that some nations were so elected to hear the gospel, and *even 'some persons' were 'unconditionally elected . . . to eternal glory.'* But he rejected that 'all those' not so 'elected to glory must perish everlastingly,' and 'That there is one soul on earth, who has not ever had a possibility of escaping eternal damnation'" (David Bennett, "How Arminian Was John Wesley?" *Evangelical Quarterly* 72, no. 3 [2000]: 239; emphasis mine). And Wesley could also "state that though grace does not generally 'act irresistibly, yet in some souls the grace of God is so far irresistible that they cannot but believe and be finally saved'" (ibid.). Consequently, if one were to follow Wesley's form of Arminianism, one might even hope that all those who die in infancy do believe because they are unconditionally elect and irresistibly graced with faith. So long as everyone receives the grace necessary to be saved, so that anyone can be saved who chooses to be, it poses no essential problem to a synergist position if some are efficaciously saved by God's working.

[22]Neal Punt approaches the question from his premise that all are elect in Christ except those who willfully reject God's self-revelation: "Among the redeemed in heaven there will be a countless number of infants who were taken from this earth without ever having willfully rejected God's revelation of himself. They will be eternally praising God for the electing love of the Father which gave them the right to eternal glory, for the cleansing blood of the Son which removed from them the stain of sin and gave them the gift of immortal life, and for the sanctifying work of the Holy Spirit which made them fit inhabitants of heaven" (*What's Good About the Good News? The Plan of Salvation in a New Light* [Chicago: Northland, 1988], p. 69). This is an encouraging picture, but what basis have we for assuming all these infants to be elect? Even if we start where Punt does, with the assumption of universal election in Christ until demonstrated otherwise, how can we know for sure that none of them will reject God's proffered grace?

[23]Hoekema, *Created in God's Image*, p. 165, quoting Herman Bavinck *Dogmatiek, 4: 810* in Hoekema's own translation.

[24]Erickson, *How Shall They*, p. 236.

fants. The first is David's statement that his dead child would not return to David but that David would "go to him" (2 Sam 12:23), which is interpreted as an indication that David expected to be together with his child in the afterlife (presumably in "Abraham's bosom"). The second text is Jesus' welcoming of the children because "it is to such as these that the kingdom of heaven belongs" (Mt 19:14; cf. Mk 10:14; Lk 18:16-17). I concur with Erickson that these texts "carry fairly significant problems."[25] David could have been saying no more than that he too would die, that nothing could be done to raise his son. Apart from the fact that the children to whom Jesus referred may well have been walking, we read too much into the text if we assume that Jesus was making a profound theological statement about the salvation of infants. Even if he were, at most he indicates that the kingdom of heaven belongs to "such as these," which scarcely amounts to a statement that every infant who dies before some "age of accountability" will be in heaven. In support of Boettner's confidence that at least the children of believers are elect, Reformed theologians sometimes cite Paul's statement that the children of one believing parent are "holy" (1 Cor 7:14). But whatever Paul's enigmatic statement meant, he can hardly have been asserting that those children are "saved." In the same verse, he says that "the unbelieving husband is made holy through his wife, and the unbelieving wife is made holy through her husband." Would any Reformed theologian want to say that unbelieving spouses of Christians are saved by that association?

Sanders is correct, I think, in judging that "those who affirm the salvation of all infants who die are clearly bringing extrabiblical beliefs with them to these texts."[26] In spite of my strong wish to be able to assert that all infants who die are saved, I have found no compelling "extrabiblical beliefs" to enable me to make that assertion. To David Clark's question, "Is the salvation of all infants who die held for sentimental reasons?"[27] Sanders answers yes, and I must agree. Perhaps Sanders is also correct that "the real reason is that current attitudes toward children in Western civilization make the prospect of infant damnation unbearable."[28]

Lest this conclusion seem rather pessimistic, I must stress that I am also not able to say for sure, on biblical or extrabiblical grounds, that any (or all)

---

[25]Ibid.

[26]Sanders, *No Other Name*, p. 290.

[27]David Clark, "Warfield, Infant Salvation and the Logic of Calvinism," *Journal of the Evangelical Theological Society* 27 (December 1984): 462, quoted in Sanders, *No Other Name*, p. 303.

[28]Sanders, *No Other Name*, p. 303.

of the infants who die are *not* elect. If any of them are graciously saved by God, however, I am certain that they were guilty sinners who will be saved only because Christ died for them; they were "in Christ," and they will be saved because they eventually trust in Christ, through God's gracious gift of faith. In short, Scripture is silent concerning the election of infants who die, and so we can express confidence in God's justice and hopefulness concerning God's grace, but we cannot be definite about the situation of any individual. We must leave this matter in the hands of the God whom we love and trust. Scripture witnesses to universal human solidarity with Adam in sin, but it consistently identifies our actions in this life as the ground of final condemnation.

INFANT FAITH

Princeton theologian B. B. Warfield posited that the destiny of those who die in infancy

> is determined irrespective of their choice, by an unconditional decree of God, suspended on no act of their own; and their salvation is wrought by an unconditional application of the grace of Christ to their souls, through the immediate and irresistible operation of the Holy Spirit prior to and apart from any action of their own proper wills.[29]

Although I agree with the unconditional nature of God's saving grace and the efficacious operation of the Holy Spirit, for reasons I have already stated, I believe that it is much better to conceive of infant salvation in terms of infant faith. We should consider infants and the incompetent no differently than we do competent adults, insisting on the necessity of God's gracious work of regeneration and on personal faith. Since faith is a gift of God, we can assert that it is a gift that he would give to any infants whom he may have chosen for salvation.

I come back, then, to the need for personal faith, and I see Jonathan Edwards headed in the direction that I commend to you. He posited that "infants who have a disposition in their hearts to accept Christ, if they were given the opportunity, will be 'looked upon and accepted as if [they] actually believed in Christ and so [are] entitled to Eternal Life through Christ.'"[30] I would nuance Edwards's proposal, however, in keeping with

---

[29]B. B. Warfield, *Two Studies in the History of Doctrine* (New York: Christian Literature Co., 1897), p. 230, quoted in Boettner, *Reformed Doctrine,* p. 144;

[30]Greg D. Gilbert, "The Nations Will Worship: Jonathan Edwards and the Salvation of the Heathen," *Trinity Journal,* n.s., 23 (spring 2002): 68.

the position I have already put forward concerning adults. Why say that God accepts infants with a disposition toward Christ "*as if* [they] actually believed"? It is much better to apply the point I have been making about how faith matures as more complete revelation is given. The disposition of which Edwards speaks must be evident to God through a response in the hearts of these infants toward the overtures that God makes to them. We may grant that this is something less than a fully developed presentation of the good news of God's saving program accomplished in Christ, but it has the character of what we have earlier seen called "implicit faith." It is explicitly faith, but it is implicitly faith *in Christ*. We might have said the same about Abraham or any other old covenant believers. They believed God explicitly and their trust in his promises was implicitly a faith in Christ. This may also be the case for some of the unevangelized, whether they are responding to God's revelation in creation or to some other faint trace of special revelation. It is faith that is exercised in a "disposition" of the heart. Faith is what God requires in order to reckon a person "righteous" on the ground of Christ's righteousness.

Two tenets of Reformed theology were deemed by Bavinck as putting Reformed theology in a good position regarding this question. First, the Reformed did not wish

> to determine the grade or extent of the knowledge that was considered indispensable for salvation. And, in the second place, they maintained that the means of grace were not absolutely necessary for salvation, but that God could also regenerate to eternal life outside of or without Word or sacraments.[31]

In short, God is able to save those who have no contact with the church, and the knowledge necessary for salvation is not something we can ascertain for certain. These are key aspects of an accessibilist approach within the framework of Reformed or Calvinistic theology.

In J. O. Buswell Jr., I find an idea that moves us even further in the right direction. He proposes "that the Holy Spirit of God prior to the moment of death, so enlarges the intelligence of one who dies in infancy (and I should make the same postulate to cover those who die in imbecility without having reached a state of accountability), that they are capable of accepting Jesus Christ."[32] I sympathize with Buswell's general intention in suggest-

---

[31]Herman Bavinck, *Dogmatiek* 4:810, as translated by Hoekema, *Created in God's Image*, p. 165.
[32]J. O. Buswell, *A Systematic Theology of the Christian Religion* (Grand Rapids, Mich.: Zondervan, 1963), p. 162.

ing this means by which infants and the mentally incapable are enabled to believe, but I suggest that it is too dependent on brain function. We should not assume that the capabilities of the human soul or mind are measurable by the ability to exercise these capabilities in bodily form, thereby making it possible for others to observe them. I propose, rather, that the same is true for those who die as infants as I believe to be true for those who live to adulthood. At some point in their lives, they are given a revelation of God that is sufficient for them to be saved if they respond to it properly, and they receive a spiritual enablement that makes them morally responsible for that response. (More will be said about the latter in the next chapter). The elect are graciously drawn to God in saving faith. Whether that revelational confrontation takes place at some point in the prenatal life of the infant or at the moment of death when the infant meets Christ, we do not know.

Strong posited that

> since there is no evidence that children dying in infancy are regenerated prior to death, either with or without the use of external means, it seems most probable that the work of regeneration may be performed by the Spirit in connection with the infant soul's first view of Christ in the other world. As the remains of natural depravity in the Christian are eradicated, not by death, but at death, through the sight of Christ and union with him, so the first movement of consciousness for the infant may be coincident with a view of Christ the Savior which accomplishes the entire sanctification of its nature (2 Cor 3:18; 1 Jn 3:2).[33]

I see significant merit in Strong's suggestion, but I consider it better to grant that God makes himself known in a saving way in *this* life even to people who lack the physical capacity to demonstrate this choice to others. One of the positive consequences of affirming a substance duality (body and soul) of human being, rather than a materialistic monism, is that it prevents us from evaluating people's personal ability by their physical ability. We must not reduce mind to brain. Thus, we cannot assume that people (infants or adults) are unable to communicate with God simply because they are unable to communicate with us.

When Erickson discusses the difference between two types of unevangelized people, he speaks of adults who are ignorant of the gospel but have general revelation and of infants who have no revelation whatsoever

---

[33]Strong, *Systematic Theology*, p. 663.

because of their "essential or necessary" inability, which is "not personal and responsible."[34] Strong apparently worked on the same assumption, so he posited that the infant receives the ability to know God at the moment of death. That might be the best approach for us to take, but I think that we should not rule out the possibility that God encounters the unborn in a Spirit-to-spirit communication that does not need the development of the brain that would later make it possible for us to see such communication at work. I wonder, for instance, what to make of the meeting between Elizabeth, the mother of John "the Baptizer," and Mary, the mother of Jesus. When Elizabeth's child "leaped in her womb," she tells Mary, "As soon as I heard the sound of your greeting, the child in my womb *leaped for joy*" (Lk 1:44, emphasis mine). Might there be other unborn infants leaping for joy when they encounter the now incarnate, crucified and resurrected Word?

I do think that Strong's proposal that the time when infants meet Christ and believe in him (if they do) is better taken to be the moment of death than some time after death, as Clark Pinnock suggests. Pinnock posits that the infants who die are "given time to grow up and mature, so then a decision could be made."[35] Between the two proposals, I prefer Strong's proposal regarding the *timing* of infant faith, but I think that Pinnock does better to insist on a *personal act* of faith. Hence, my own proposal that God reveals himself to infants (and the unborn) during their brief lives, and that their salvation can, therefore, take place before death, but that it does not occur without an act of personal faith. In any event, Strong's speculation regarding those who die as infants leads us on to the larger question of what happens when people die—not just infants but everyone.

ENCOUNTER WITH CHRIST AT THE MOMENT OF DEATH

Statement of my proposal. Will there be people who will be received by the Father but who have not known the Son? This seems highly implausible, given the insistence of Jesus that no one comes to the Father except through the Son and that no one knows the Father except the Son and "anyone to whom the Son chooses to reveal him" (Mt 11:27). One possible approach would be to stress the revelatory activity of the Son in all forms of divine self-revelation, so that whatever revelation of God one responds to is one that has been mediated by the Son. In fact, then, no one does come

---

[34]Erickson, *How Shall They*, p. 252.
[35]Clark Pinnock, *A Wideness in God's Mercy: The Finality of Jesus Christ in a World of Religions* (Grand Rapids, Mich.: Zondervan, 1992), p. 168.

(*nor ever has* come) to the Father except through the Son's mediatory and revelatory work.

Earlier, I mentioned Strong's proposal that those who die as infants are regenerated when they meet Christ. It is interesting that Erickson, who does not believe that these infants need justification, does consider their depravity to be "a continuing problem," but he cites 1 John 3:2 ("we will be like him, for we will see him as he is") as indication that the necessary transformation can occur for infants through the "appearance of Christ," without "any special action" on their part.[36] I submit that there is not a large difference between Strong's and Erickson's proposal on this point, since the glorification that occurs with the resurrection of the body at Christ's return happens only to those who were already saved by God prior to that time. Erickson asks: "But if sanctification and glorification are but the continuation and the completion of the renewing work begun in regeneration, may it not be that much the same thing, albeit on a more complete scale, is done for infants dying in infancy?"[37]

There is a logic about the economy of the Trinity, however, that makes the hypothesis of an at-death encounter with Jesus an attractive position to my mind. D. A. Carson comments on Pinnock's adoption of both inclusivism and postmortem evangelism (which is *not* what I am proposing), and he argues that it "leads to an uneasy synthesis."[38] He asks a good question: "If faith that is consciously focused on Jesus is not necessary for salvation, why should people be offered a further chance beyond death?"[39] That question allows me to clarify a couple of things about my own proposal: First, I am not positing "postmortem evangelism" if that is understood as teaching that people have a second chance beyond this life or that people who had no opportunity to respond to God's self-disclosure in saving faith during their lives will get such an opportunity beyond their lives. Second, I do think that even those whom God has graciously brought into saving relationship with himself during their lives, without giving them knowledge of the incarnation of the Son, need to know the Son in the process of coming to know the Father.

My proposal of universal at-death encounters with Christ allows one to confess that faith in Jesus Christ is necessary, while not overemphasizing

---

[36]Erickson, *How Shall They,* p. 252.
[37]Ibid.
[38]D. A. Carson, *The Gagging of God: Christianity Confronts Pluralism* (Grand Rapids, Mich.: Zondervan, 1996), p. 299.
[39]Ibid., p. 300.

the need-to-know information about Christ before death. It is a particularly useful hypothesis with regard to the salvation of those who die in infancy or who are mentally incompetent. It is interesting to recall that, for Irenaeus, in the second century, a major purpose of the millennium is so that Old Testament believers might meet Christ and thus be prepared for the vision of the Father. We might note the interesting prospects of this view also for the unevangelized who respond properly to general revelation.[40] Irenaeus did not make anything of this point because he assumed that the gospel had been taken throughout the world—he had no concept of unevangelized people.

As stated previously, whatever position we hold concerning the knowledge necessary for salvation must cover all the categories identified above. Admittedly, however, the proposal that we all meet Christ at death moves us beyond Scripture's explicit teaching into the speculative. Consequently, such a hypothesis can only be held tentatively, but it is consistent with everything that we do know from Scripture. Certainly, Paul expected to be with Christ at the point of his departure from the body, and I take this to be descriptive of the situation of all believers in Christ (2 Cor 5:6-8; Phil 1:23-24). There is nothing in Scripture which would exclude the possibility that a meeting with Christ is the experience of *all* people, not only believers, though it is obviously not a joy for those who have lived in disbelief and rebellion against God. The concept of at-death encounters with Christ is a view that has been found more commonly among Roman Catholic than among Protestant theologians, but there is nothing about it that is inconsistent with the tenets of Protestantism.

Distinction between my proposal and two different proposals. My own proposal of at-death encounters with Christ needs to be carefully distinguished from two other proposals for which it may be mistaken: The first such proposal is the *final fundamental option* theory, which holds "that the unevangelized will be given an opportunity to be saved at the moment of death."[41] A luminous presentation of this view is found, for instance, in the work of Ladislaus Boros, a Hungarian Jesuit now teaching in Austria.[42] I think this is the proposal that Jacques Dupuis has in mind when he makes his assessment that

---

[40]See Terrance Tiessen, *Irenaeus on the Salvation of the Unevangelized*, ATLA Monograph (Metuchen, N.J.: Scarecrow, 1993), 31:168-70.

[41]See Sanders, *No Other Name*, p. 164.

[42]Ladislaus Boros, *Pain and Providence*, trans. Edward Quinn (Mainz: Matthias-Grünewald-Verlag, 1965; London: Burns & Oates, 1966).

of all substitutes [for the ecclesiocentric approach] devised through the theological tradition, the theory of the "act of dying" is best capable of showing that salvation is possible not only for adults who, though not having heard the Gospel message, have made a moral decision during their earthly life but also for children and for the unborn who in this life have never reached the age of reason and of moral decision.[43]

Like the position I am proposing, this final-option theory affirms that every one encounters Jesus Christ at the moment of death rather than after death. But, *very different* from my position is this proposal's position that "prior choices we have made deeply influence but do not determine our final decision. We may choose to confirm the way we have lived or we may reject it,"[44] although "it would be an extreme case in the order of probability" that a person would reverse the direction of their lives in that final moment of decision.[45] The same concept is found in George Lindbeck's proposal

that dying itself be pictured as the point at which every human being is ultimately and expressly confronted by the gospel, by the crucified and risen Lord. It is only then that the final decision is made for or against Christ. . . . All previous decisions, whether for faith or against faith, are preliminary.[46]

By contrast with the above suggestion, my own contention is that the response one makes to Christ at that moment of death will be *consistent* with the response one has been making to God in whatever forms God has been revealing himself *prior* to death. I am not claiming that people who, before they die, have no opportunity to respond in faith to God and his revelation will get that opportunity for the first time at the moment of death.[47] All have the opportunity to respond to God in faith during their life. But not everyone meets Christ explicitly—face to face, as it were—rather than obliquely, as in the Word's involvement in less-complete forms of divine revelation. The response given to Christ at that personal meeting will be con-

---

[43]Jacques Dupuis, *Toward a Christian Theology of Religious Pluralism* (Maryknoll, N.Y.: Orbis, 1997), p. 118. Sanders cites others who endorsed this position, including John Cardinal Henry Newman and Joseph DiNoia (*No Other Name*, p. 164 n. 26).

[44]Sanders, *No Other Name*, p. 165.

[45]Ladislaus Boros, *The Mystery of Death*, trans. Gregory Bainbridge (New York: Herder & Herder, 1965), p. 97, quoted in Sanders, *No Other Name*, p. 167.

[46]George Lindbeck, *The Nature of Doctrine: Religion and Theology in a Postliberal Age* (Philadelphia: Westminster Press, 1984), p. 59.

[47]Sanders notes that some Roman Catholic scholars take this approach rather than the one that allows for a first-time turn to God at death; see *No Other Name*, p. 165 n. 27, quoting *The New Catholic Encyclopedia* (Washington, D.C.: Catholic University Press of America), 4:694.

sistent with one's responses to God prior to death; there will be no reversals. Even a death-bed conversion is a response to God that took place during life. For such people, however, the gap between their initial response and their encounter with Christ in all his glory will be very short.

Second, my proposal must be distinguished from the theory of *eschatological salvation,* the idea that the unevangelized get an opportunity to meet and accept Christ *after* death. Many who accept the basic proposal of a universal encounter with Christ expect it to come *after* death and base their view largely on 1 Peter 3:19-21; 4:6.[48] Early in the church's understanding of Peter's text, Origen and others had interpreted it as a reference to conversion and baptism beyond the tomb.[49] In our own day, Russell Aldwinckle has written, "We agree with Hick that physical death is not the end of our moral and spiritual development nor of significant decision making."[50] Gabriel Fackre also argues for this eschatological salvation but calls it "Divine perseverance."[51] Fackre identifies the "prisoners" in 1 Peter 3:19 read canonically (Gen 5:28—10:32), as "those outside of God's special saving history in Israel and Christ—human beings who, since Noah and right up to the present moment and into the future, are accountable to the patient God. They are accountable through what our forebears called the 'Noahic covenant.'"[52] Fackre cross-references Paul's teaching about Christ's descent into "the lower parts of the earth" (Eph 4:8-9), and he posits that "the same presence, freedom and regency of Christ in the place of death spoken of here are echoed in parallel passages elsewhere in the New Testament (Mt 12:40; Rom 10:7; Phil 2:10; Rev 1:18; 5:13; 21:25)."[53]

C. E. B. Cranfield sees in Peter's texts

> a hint . . . that those who in subsequent ages have died without ever having had a real chance to believe in Christ are not outside the scope of His mercy and will not perish eternally without being given in some way that is beyond our knowledge an opportunity to hear the gospel and accept Him as their Savior.[54]

---

[48]See the description of this position in Sanders, *No Other Name,* pp. 181-88.

[49]Dupuis, *Toward a Christian Theology,* p. 112.

[50]Russell F. Aldwinckle, *Jesus—A Savior or the Savior? Religious Pluralism in Christian Perspective* (Macon, Ga.: Mercer University Press, 1982), p. 182.

[51]Gabriel Fackre, "Divine Perseverance," in *What About Those Who Have Never Heard? Three Views on the Destiny of the Unevangelized,* ed. John Sanders (Downers Grove, Ill.: InterVarsity Press, 1995) , pp. 71-95.

[52]Ibid., p. 83.

[53]Ibid., p. 85.

[54]C. E. B. Cranfield, "The Interpretation of 1 Peter 3:19 and 4:6," *The Expository Times* 69 (September 1958): 372, quoted in Sanders, *No Other Name,* p. 188.

Sanders also cites Donald Bloesch as arguing the benefits of this proposal if one assumes that people can be "condemned to hell only for explicit rejection of Jesus as Lord."[55] Erickson suggests that John Peter Lange's commentary on 1 Peter 3:18-20 has been very influential in this direction. Lange wrote: "Holy Scripture nowhere teaches the eternal damnation of those who died as heathens or non-Christians; it rather intimates in many passages that forgiveness may be possible beyond the grave, and refers the final decision not to death, but to the day of Christ."[56]

It would be wonderful if people did, indeed, have opportunity after death to reverse decisions that they have made during their lives, but Nash's response to Fackre's proposal is correct: Scripture teaches that death is the "end of any human opportunity for salvation."[57] Hebrews 9:27-28 distinctly teaches that judgment follows death. Jesus' parable in Luke 13:23-30 makes a similar point: the owner of the house will close the door once and for all, and there will be no chance for people to change the decision they made when the opportunity was available during their lives. Now is the critical time. I also agree with Nash that a proper reading of 1 Peter 3—4 does not support a belief in salvation after death.[58] The text in 1 Peter 3 is notoriously difficult, and widely divergent readings of it have been proposed in the history of biblical interpretation. Without reviewing here the extensive literature on the subject, I am inclined to agree with Erickson that the text itself, when read in context, together with the witness of other clear texts regarding the finality of death, lends greatest support to the idea that Christ preached through Noah to the people of his day.[59] It is most significant, however, that even if 1 Peter 3 teaches that Christ preached to some who had died prior to his own death, we lack any biblical grounds for assuming that a similar postmortem opportunity is provided for others.[60]

Joseph Leckie considered the eternal destiny of those who die as infants to be a significant factor supporting the possibility of postmortem evangelism. He posits that infants "mature in the future life and then are given an

---

[55]Sanders, *No Other Name*, pp. 70-71.

[56]John Peter Lange, *The First Epistle General of Peter* (New York: Scribner, 1868), p. 75, quoted in Millard Erickson, "Is There Opportunity for Salvation After Death?" *Bibliotheca Sacra* 152 (April-June 1995): 132.

[57]Nash, "Restrictivism," p. 97.

[58]Ibid., p. 98.

[59]Erickson, *How Shall They*, pp. 165-73.

[60]Ibid., p. 173.

opportunity to hear the good news about Christ and accept him."[61] But this speculation is unnecessary if we grant that humans, in their soulish being, have capabilities that they are not able to manifest physically. We can, therefore, assume that God is able to relate to the unborn, even though we cannot do so, and that they may be responding to God's self-revelation in ways that will be decisive for their eternal condition. For them, too, an important moment in coming to know God more fully will be their meeting with Christ at death, but we need not assume that this is their *first* chance to respond to God.

Pinnock admits that "the scriptural evidence for postmortem encounter is not abundant," but he believes that "its scantiness is relativized by the strength of the theological argument for it."[62] But what Pinnock considers necessary theologically can be fulfilled just as well by an *at-death* encounter with Christ, so it does not require an encounter *after* death. Personally, I am definitely not proposing that the fundamental decision people make in relationship to God during their lives can be *reversed* at or after death, but neither is Pinnock.[63] Decisions made before death are not "preliminary": they are final and definitive. It is very important, therefore, that we not confuse this at-death encounter with a second chance.

This is *not* a chance for those who rejected Christ during their lifetime to accept him afterward, as is suggested by some proponents of eschatological salvation. In fairness, it should be noted that some of them would also want to avoid the idea of a *second* chance. Thus, Bloesch asserts that "what the descent doctrine affirms is the universality of a first chance, an opportunity for salvation for those who have never heard the gospel in its fullness."[64] Stephen Davis suggests that we are not in a position to know who has heard the gospel in this way: "Only God knows who will receive an opportunity after death to receive Christ."[65] It is peculiar, however, that Bloesch argues that God can even deliver people from hell, although we cannot know whether he does this in any actual cases.[66] This certainly

---

[61]Erickson, *How Shall They*, p. 165, quoting Joseph Leckie, *The World to Come and Final Destiny*, 2nd ed. (Edinburgh: T & T Clark, 1922), pp. 99-101.

[62]Pinnock, *Wideness in God's Mercy*, p. 169.

[63]Ibid., pp. 170-75.

[64]Donald Bloesch, "Descent into Hell," in *Evangelical Dictionary of Theology*, ed. Walter Elwell (Grand Rapids, Mich.: Baker, 1984), p. 314.

[65]Sanders, *No Other Name*, p. 194, quoting Stephen Davis, "Universalism, Hell and the Fate of the Ignorant," *Modern Theology* 6 (January 1990): 183-84.

[66]Donald Bloesch, *Life, Ministry, and Hope*, vol. 2 of *Essentials of Evangelical Theology* (San Francisco: Harper & Row, 1978), pp. 226-28.

seems to fall into the category of a "second chance," since at least the great day of judgment would have provided personal encounter with Christ and as much incentive as one can possibly imagine for repentance. From a monergistic perspective, of course, it is completely implausible that God would have chosen people in Christ, before he created the world, and then waited to effectually call them until after they had spent some time in hell. The final judgment day must certainly be the very end of opportunity, the point at which one's eternal destiny is fixed.

What I am proposing, then, is not a second chance for people who have rejected God's gracious initiatives right through their earthly lives. It is an opportunity, rather, for those who have had faith that God exists and that he rewards those who diligently seek him (Heb 11:6), who have honored God as God and given him thanks (Rom 1:21) or who "by patiently doing good" have sought "for glory and honor and immortality" (Rom 2:7) but who have never met Jesus. Having responded, by God's grace, to the form in which God revealed himself to them during their lives, they will then respond with faith and joy to the Son who had been at work in their lives, though they were ignorant of much about him. Jesus speaks of precisely this consistency of response to progressively clearer forms of divine revelation. He responded sternly to the religious authorities who criticized him when their own knowledge of Scripture should have produced a positive response to him. To those who rebuked Jesus for having healed on the sabbath, he said, "You do not have the love of God in you," and that is why they refused to come to Jesus so that they might have life (Jn 5:39-40, 42). If they had believed Moses, who wrote about Jesus, they would have believed Jesus (Jn 5:46). This is precisely the framework within which I am working. As the Spirit of God works in people's hearts, they believe the revelation that he gives them, and they have the love of God in them. Such people keep believing as God makes himself more clearly known to them. When encountering Jesus, those who have been graciously drawn to faith in less explicit ways recognize in Jesus the one for whom they have longed, and they come to him to have life.

Benefits of my proposal. The fruitfulness of this prospect for Japanese and Taiwanese believers, who are deeply concerned about their ancestors, is obvious. Given the proposal I am putting forward here, we are unable to say with certainty that all of those people who died without hearing the gospel are now eternally lost. God made himself known to all of them in some way; and those to whom he gave repentance and faith (however basic) during their lives will have met Jesus at the moment of death and rejoiced to know their Savior. The implications of this proposal are also worth contemplating from an ecclesiocentric viewpoint. Ecclesiocentrists sometimes argue that those who respond to the light they have received will eventually hear the gospel. For instance, Robertson McQuilkin asserts that "the repeated promise of additional light to those who obey the light they have is a basic and very important biblical truth concerning God's justice and judgment"[67] (citing Mt 13:10-16; Mk 4:21-25; Acts 10). Sanders cites others who believe in universally accessible revelation through universal sending of a messenger to those who are seeking God, including Thomas Aquinas and "most of the theologians from the twelfth through the fifteenth centuries," Buswell, Geisler, Wesley Gustafson, Earl Radmacher, Robert Lightner and David Dewitt.[68]

On the one hand, this concept seems best suited to synergistic theologies of salvation in which one's destiny is decided by one's own response to God's gracious enablement rather than by an efficacious work of the Spirit. But a Calvinist might appropriate the principle being enunciated here as part of a recognition that God often moves people along to their definitive act of justifying faith in Christ through a process of positive responses, in smaller steps. For instance, Strong, a Calvinistic Baptist theologian, wrote concerning the faith of the patriarchs and of "whoever among the heathen are saved" that their faith "is implicitly a faith in Christ, and would become explicit and conscious trust and submission, whenever Christ were made known to them (Matt. 8:11-12; John 10:16; Acts 4:12; 10:31, 34, 34, 35, 44; 16:31)."[69] I suggest to those who place large importance on the explicit knowledge of and faith in Jesus Christ that the final moment at which *fully formed faith in Christ* occurs may not take place for some people who have been ignorant of the gospel until the moment of death. My proposal asserts, however, that their response to Christ at that moment will be consistent with the responses they have been making to God's lesser forms of self-revelation prior to that decisive meeting with Christ.

My proposal would also serve well the Molinists who assert that unevangelized individuals can be saved if God knows that they *would have* be-

---

[67]Robertson McQuilkin, "Lost," in *Perspectives on the World Christian Movement: A Reader,* ed. Ralph Winter and Steven Hawthorne (Pasadena, Calif.: William Carey Library, 1999), p. 159, quoted in Miriam Adeney, "Rajah Sulayman Was No Water Buffalo: Gospel, Anthropology and Islam," in *No Other Gods Before Me? Evangelicals and the Challenge of World Religions,* ed. John G. Stackhouse Jr. (Grand Rapids, Mich.: Baker, 2001), p. 72.

[68]Sanders, *No Other Name,* pp. 156-63.

[69]Strong, *Systematic Theology,* p. 842.

lieved had they received the gospel. To the criticism that this would be salvation apart from any personal faith on the part of these individuals, Molinists may respond that such people *do believe* in Jesus but that this happens only at the moment of death when they meet Jesus in person.

Nash states that "people who teach post-mortem evangelism . . . are not really inclusivists. They are actually exclusivists [what I am calling ecclesiocentrists] who believe that a conscious act of faith in Jesus Christ really is necessary for salvation."[70] His observation would also apply to my own proposal of an at-death encounter. I, too, am arguing that no one comes to final, eschatological salvation without explicit faith in Christ. There is an important difference, however, that Nash's comment does not take into account: The critical distinction between ecclesiocentrism and the accessibilism that I am putting forward is that the former insists that none of those living after the first generation following Christ's resurrection can be saved without knowing about Christ and believing explicitly in him *while they are alive.* I, on the other hand, am suggesting that God does bring people into saving relationship with himself now even though they do not receive the gospel message, but that they meet Christ and place their faith in him at the moment of death. Thus, they do come to know the Father through the Son, but the moment of their explicit faith in Jesus is not the moment at which they move from the kingdom of darkness to the kingdom of light through God's grace.

A few reflections on the most appropriate terminology. During an earlier period of time in my life, I taught that the unevangelized are saved when the Holy Spirit does his work of illumination and elicits from them a faith response to some divine revelation of whatever sort they received. But I then began to wonder whether it might be better to speak of salvation as taking place only at the moment of encounter with Christ. Until then, perhaps, people who were responding positively to God's revelation would be in a position of readiness, but only when they met Christ would they actually come into the experience of God's salvation. This is the way in which V. Boublik spoke in his *Teologica delle religioni* (1974), a work that Dupuis describes as the first extensive study intending to be a synthetic treatment.[71] But it now seems to me that it is best to see this whole matter as another illustration of the fact that salvation is past, present and future for all of us who are at peace with God. We *were* saved when Christ died and rose again

---

[70]Ronald Nash, *Is Jesus the Only Savior?* (Grand Rapids, Mich.: Zondervan, 1994), p. 150.
[71]Dupuis, *Toward a Christian Theology*, p. 3.

from the dead, but we came into the existential experience of that salvation at the moment of saving faith; we are now *being* saved by the sanctifying work of the Holy Spirit; but the *final* declaration of our justification and our complete sanctification, or glorification, awaits the eschatological fulfillment of God's saving program. Thus, it is probably best not to withhold the designation "saved" from those who have been reconciled to God through a graciously enabled faith response to God's self-revelation, even though that revelation may have been less complete than the gospel concerning Jesus. In fact, it is likely important that we speak of such people as being "saved" so as to avoid giving the impression that those who die in a state of divine condemnation are moved from that state to salvation at the moment of death, as though this were a further chance for people who had been resisting God right up to the end of their earthly lives.

Precisely because we are speaking about "salvation outside the church," however, we do well to deny that the unevangelized who are saved in this age are incorporated into Christ with the Holy Spirit as recipients of the distinctively new covenant grace that forms the church. In this regard, the analogy between the unevangelized who are saved now and people who were saved before the incarnation is of further help. Bruce Demarest asks whether Old Testament believers were incorporated into Christ and concludes that they

> received a measure of atonement. They were justified by faith, they experienced the removal of the defilement of sins (albeit via repeated sacrifices), they enjoyed fellowship with God, and they possessed the hope of eternal life. But the fullness and perfecting of salvation as incorporation into Christ had to await the once-for-all sacrifice of the Messiah.[72]

Demarest reaches this conclusion on the grounds of four "lines of evidence":

- "Incorporation into Christ involves participation in our Lord's humanity (Jn 6:48-56)."

- "The basis of union with Christ is the Savior's atoning death and resurrection" (Jn 14:19; Rom 7:4; Gal 2:20), so that "union with Christ necessarily must await the Lord's death and resurrection from the grave."

- "The Holy Spirit is the bond by which believers are united to Christ.

---

[72]Bruce Demarest, *The Cross and Salvation: The Doctrine of Salvation,* Foundations of Evangelical Theology (Wheaton, Ill.: Crossway, 1997), p. 339.

The indwelling Christ and the indwelling Spirit are a coincident reality. But Jesus promised his disciples that he would return to them in a dynamic way through the Counselor after he was glorified (John 15:26; 16:7)."

- "The New Testament links union with Christ with distinctive *ministries* of the Spirit. The first such ministry is the Spirit's work of baptizing believers into Christ (Gal 3:27) and his body, the church (1 Cor 12:13). The second is the Spirit's work of sealing believers in this new relation (2 Cor 1:21-22; Eph 1:13; 4:30) unto the day of redemption."[73]

In regard to Demarest's last point, I would not want to speak of new covenant believers as being baptized *by* the Spirit since I am persuaded by exegetes who have argued that 1 Corinthians 12:13 should be understood as reference to baptism by Christ *with* or *in* the Spirit, as in all the other instances where baptism in or with the Spirit is spoken about in the New Testament.[74] In general, however, I think that Demarest's point is well demonstrated. In terms of the history of God's saving work, the new covenant has clearly been inaugurated, and the Spirit is now being given to all who believe in Jesus. I am arguing, however, that precisely because the unevangelized are, by definition, ignorant of Jesus, they live in a different "spiritual economy" and await the fuller revelation of God in Christ, as believers did prior to the Word's taking on flesh.

A narrative version of my proposal. For those who like their theology in narrative form, I recommend the story of Emeth's meeting Aslan in C. S. Lewis's delightful book *The Last Battle,* the final book in the Narnia series.[75] I cannot do the story justice by retelling it here for those who are unfamiliar with it. But, if you know it, you will remember what happens. You will recall how Emeth (Hebrew for *truth*) had served Tash (the evil "god" of the Calormenes) gladly all of his life. But on the other side of death, he meets the great lion Aslan (the Christ figure) coming toward him and feels wonderfully attracted to him even as he feels afraid. Aslan welcomes Emeth as a "son" and informs him that his earnest quest and the good that he had done in his life, though he had done them for Tash, had actually been received by Aslan.

---

[73]Ibid., pp. 338-39.
[74]Compare D. A. Carson, *Showing the Spirit: A Theological Exposition of 1 Corinthians 12-14* (Grand Rapids, Mich.: Baker, 1987), p. 47.
[75]C. S. Lewis, *The Last Battle: A Story for Children* (1956; Middlesex: Penguin, 1964), chap. 15, esp. pp. 148-50.

I read the Narnia series to each of our four children and, by the time I was reading it to our daughter, her three older brothers were usually on the bed too. One of the interesting things about the story of Emeth, as I contemplate my own theological pilgrimage, is that I thoroughly enjoyed the story each time I read it to our children, but the theology portrayed troubled me because I was then an ecclesiocentrist. Since my "conversion" to accessibilism, I have gained a new appreciation for Lewis's imagery. I hear the key point of the story as accessibilist in tone but, like all parables, it should not be exegeted too precisely. No doubt, one could probably draw from the tale conclusions that would trouble even an accessibilist.

Summing Up

In this chapter and the preceding two, we have been probing the question, what must a person know in order to be saved? We examined the situation of five groups of people:

- those within Israel (in the Old Testament) who had saving faith

- people who know only what God reveals about himself in the means of revelation accessible to everyone, that is, through "general revelation"

- people outside the covenants God made with Abraham and his descendants but who had saving relationships with God and who, therefore, are analogous to the unevangelized in our own day,

- Jews who met Christ

- infants and the mentally incompetent who die before reaching an age where they are mentally capable of learning about God or are making moral judgments

From the study of these five groups, I have concluded that God may save people by *any* of his means of self-revelation and that he does so by stirring within them a response of faith that is appropriate to the revelation they have received. One is judged only according to the revelation one has received, and no one lacks the external divine revelation necessary for salvation.

We have observed that God moves people along in a relationship where they grow in knowledge of him and in faith. Only God is able to say when a person is exercising the faith that saves, but we may be able to discern the direction in which people are moving. Our goal is to keep people moving toward God, but only God can save them. We "plant" and we "water," but only God can create spiritual growth (1 Cor 3:5-9). With regard to the unevangelized of all kinds, I have asserted that God is able to reveal himself to them and to give them the faith that pleases him. This is true, whether they are adults who are not given the gospel concerning Christ or people whose minds never develop to a level where they could understand the gospel, and whether they are infants who die very young or older people who are mentally incapacitated. If we were to map the situation, we would note that the boundary of those who are elect to salvation does not correspond to the boundary of clear gospel proclamation and mental or moral maturity. Many Reformed theologians have acknowledged this in regard to infants who die, but few of them have been prepared to treat all of the other "unevangelized" peoples under the same general theory of salvation. I take that to be a mistake, and I hope that my work will stimulate reconsideration.

I have postulated that people meet Jesus at the moment of death and that their response to him will be consistent with their previous response to God by whatever means God has made himself known to them. Thus, beyond death, all who come into fellowship with the Father will do so through knowledge of the Son. Conversely, those who live beyond death outside fellowship with God will not only have rejected God's various overtures during their lives but will have rejected Christ at the moment of that final personal meeting. Decisions made in this life are decisive. The elect of all nations will be brought to saving faith within their lifetimes. Some of us will have been graced with more knowledge of God than have others, but all of us will have much more to anticipate.

Frequently, when stating that everyone receives the revelation they need to be saved by grace through faith, I have observed that, because of the sinfulness of humankind after the Fall, no one *can* believe without the Spirit's enablement. Does everyone receive not only the revelation necessary for salvation but also the enablement to believe? To that question we proceed in the next chapter.

11

Who Is Able to Believe?

Thesis 14: God's saving grace is universally sufficient so that on at least one occasion in each person's life, one is enabled to respond to God's self-revelation with a faith response that is acceptable to God as a means of justification. Only those whom God effectively persuades (i.e., recipients of efficacious grace) will believe. Nevertheless, the universally sufficient grace vindicates God's judgment of unbelievers, and it removes from the doctrine of original sin a burden that it could not otherwise sustain, given the biblical witness concerning the grounds of final judgment.

WE HAVE SEEN THAT GOD MAKES HIMSELF KNOWN to everyone in a number of ways and that he only holds people accountable for the revelation that they receive from God. We have also seen that the sort of faith that pleases God varies according to the sort of revelation God has given to people. But this faith is itself God's gift to those whom God is drawing to himself. In the beginning of this part of the book, however, we saw that everyone comes into the world guilty before God and completely unable to please him. Is it possible, then, that some of the people who are condemned to God's eternal wrath for not responding to God's self-revelation by faith were *unable to believe* because of the spiritual inability that resulted from their solidarity with Adam? At this point in my proposal, I will put forward an idea that has not been characteristic of Reformed theology but that I believe deserves a careful hearing. I will argue that *God's saving grace is universally sufficient so that on at least one occasion in all people's lives, they are enabled to respond to God's self-revelation with a faith response that is acceptable to God as a means of justification.*

THE NECESSITY OF ILLUMINATION BY THE HOLY SPIRIT

Revelation is essential to sinners who need to be reconciled to God. But precisely because of our sinfulness, revelation does not have saving effects without illumination, that is, "a divine operation in the mind and heart of a recipient of grace that confirms to that recipient the reality of a supernatural truth or person."[1] This was what enabled Peter to recognize that Jesus was the Christ (Mt 16:17). It showed Paul the truth and reality of the gospel (Gal 1:12). Paul later told the Ephesians that he would ask God to give them "a spirit of wisdom and revelation as you come to know him, so that, with the eyes of your heart enlightened, you may know what is the hope to which he has called you, [and] what are the riches of his glorious inheritance among the saints" (Eph 1:17-18). Without this illumination, people do not understand and respond to the gospel (1 Cor 2:14; 2 Cor 4:4), but when it is present, it results in saving faith; it gives "the light of the knowledge of the glory of God in the face of Jesus Christ" (2 Cor 4:6). Without this divine inner work, the objective existence of divine revelation does not result in knowledge of God on the part of those who receive the revelation. I have taken care to demonstrate that everyone receives divine revelation that is sufficient for salvation if they respond to it in faith. But how significant is that fact if many of the people who receive the revelation lack the *ability* to give the required response?

THE TRADITIONAL REFORMED POSITION ON HUMAN INABILITY AND GOD'S ENABLING GRACE

Traditionally, Calvinistic theology has taught these two points: everyone is pervasively depraved, so that they are unable to do any spiritual good; but God remedies that spiritual disability and enables the elect to believe in such a way that all of them freely do so (this is dubbed *efficacious grace*). Calvinists have asserted that the Fall was totally spiritually debilitating. It left all of Adam's descendants guilty before God by virtue of their solidarity with Adam in his original disobedience (Rom 5:12-21). It also made them subject to death and placed them in bondage to sin and Satan. Their natures have been so seriously depraved that they can do nothing that pleases God. Being in a state of rebellion, their wills are bound. They sin willingly, but they are unable not to sin, and specifically they are not able to repent of their sin and trust in God for salvation. Unless the Spirit of

---

[1]Gerald R. McDermott, *Can Evangelicals Learn from World Religions? Jesus, Revelation and Religious Traditions* (Downers Grove, Ill.: InterVarsity Press, 2000), p. 66.

God intervenes and frees sinful human wills, people will not (and in a sense, cannot) believe.[2] They are, nevertheless, culpable for this unbelief because their inability is self-incurred in their union with Adam. As Louis Berkhof puts it, "We should not forget that the inability under consideration is self-imposed, has a moral origin, and is not due to any limitation which God has put upon man's being. Man is unable as a result of the perverted choice made in Adam."[3]

A Problem in the Traditional Reformed Understanding

The concept of "self-incurred inability in Adam" is a difficult one for individualistic Westerners to comprehend and even more difficult to accept. The legitimacy of such an arrangement should be more evident, however, if we consider that it is on a similarly constituted ground of union with Christ, the righteous one, that God is able to be just while justifying sinners (Rom 3:25). God graciously frees the wills of those whom he intends to save so that they entrust themselves to his mercy, willingly and joyfully, and are saved. This is generally identified as the *effectual calling* of God, which is made effectual by the Spirit's regenerating work, in the narrow sense in which regeneration precedes and enables the human response.

To many Christians who do not accept Calvinist theology, it seems patently unjust that those who are not given the ability to believe are condemned for not doing so. Even if we grant that people continue to pervert themselves by willful sin, the fact that this sinfulness derives from original sin makes many Christians feel that God is being unjust. Although I have found the Calvinist reading of Scripture very helpful and generally very plausible, I have not been completely satisfied with the classic Calvinistic responses to this charge of injustice. The particular concept that I commend to your consideration now is the fruit of my attempt to deal with my dissatisfaction with the classical answer.

I grant the propriety of a self-incurred inability in Adam through a divinely established solidarity of the race with Adam. It was God's prerogative to constitute humankind in that kind of relationship. Nevertheless, I find it striking that "Scripture universally relates man's ultimate judgment

---

[2]See, e.g., Louis Berkhof, *Systematic Theology* (London: Banner of Truth Trust, 1949), pp. 246-50.
[3]Ibid., p. 250.

to his own moral 'works,' which fall short of God's standards, and not in the first instance to his union with Adam (e.g., Mt 7:21-27; 13:41; 25:31-46; Lk 3:9; Rom 2:5-10; Rev 20:11-14)."[4] But here is a difficulty: if human responsibility is consistently attributed to actual or personal rather than to original sin, it is peculiar that the inability which made that sin unavoidable should remain located in the Adamic Fall. Likewise, the biblical expressions of God's hatred (Hos 9:15; Jer 12:8; Ps 5:5; 11:5) and anger (Ex 32:10-11; Judg 2:14; Jer 10:24; Ps 30:5; 106:40; Rom 2:5; 9:22) toward his people because of their sin are focused on the wicked and rebellious deeds that his people were doing at the time. The *strength* of this divine disapproval is difficult to understand if these people were absolutely incapable of repentance and faith.

I am not the first Calvinist to have been troubled on this point. "In 1977, the Christian Reformed Church received a formal complaint against its creedal teaching on reprobation" because the *Canons of Dort* were understood as teaching that some people are "consigned to everlasting damnation before they ever came into being."[5] The complaint was submitted to a three-year study to elucidate the teaching of the *Canons*. Neal Punt sums up what the official elucidation by the Synod in 1980 stated:

"God consigns someone to destruction [hell] only on the basis of what that person does; and whatever evil action that person performs." "God condemns to destruction [hell] only those who do, in fact, exhibit unbelief." All non-elect persons are "the agents of unbelief." [An agent is one who himself acts.] "The condition of the non-elect [headed for hell] results from their unbelief." "The basis for that condemnation [being sent to hell] is to be found solely in the persistent unbelief and sin of those so condemned."[6]

I came to my own proposal before learning of the CRC discussion, but I am encouraged by these conclusions. They have taken into account the critical point I made earlier about the criteria by which each of us is judged in the final divine tribunal. Punt has grasped that point too. Like me, he grants that everyone is worthy of eternal death due to the sin of Adam, but he notes that "nowhere in all of Scripture do we read—or is it implied, nor is it to be inferred—that anyone ever suffers eternal death by reason of

[4]Bruce Milne, *Know the Truth: A Handbook of Christian Belief* (Leicester, U.K.: Inter-Varsity Press, 1982), p. 106.
[5]Neal Punt, *What's Good About the Good News? The Plan of Salvation in a New Light* (Chicago: Northland, 1988), p. 21.
[6]Ibid., p. 22.

their sin in Adam, *apart from* individual, willful, final unbelief and sin on the part of the person so rejected."[7]

As a Calvinist, I do not question God's right to show grace and to have mercy on whomever he wishes and to judicially harden the hearts of whomever he wishes (Rom 9:18). On the other hand, I do feel the force of the common sense of injustice that those who are *unable* to believe should be condemned for not doing so.[8] Even though it was God's prerogative to establish humanity in solidarity with Adam, Scripture does not teach that the inability that all incurred in Adam is the cause or ground of their eternal condemnation for unbelief. Since salvation is of grace, it is, by definition, not deserved by anyone, and so God has a sovereign right to choose those whom he will save. But I am uncomfortable with the grounds for the condemnation of those who are left in their sin as these have been stated traditionally in Calvinist theologies. I have also found it rather difficult to understand some passages of Scripture that describe God's distress at the unbelief of those who reject him. A case in point is Jesus' pain at the rejection by most of the inhabitants of Jerusalem: "Jerusalem, Jerusalem, the city that kills the prophets and stones those who are sent to it! How often have I desired to gather your children together as a hen gathers her brood under her wings, and *you were not willing!*" (Mt 23:37, emphasis mine). Why, I have wondered, is Jesus so disturbed when he knows that only those whom the Father draws will come to him (Jn 6:44) and that all of them will do so (Jn 6:37)?

TWO ALTERNATIVE PROPOSALS THAT USE DIVINE/ HUMAN SYNERGISM

My own proposal may be most easily understood if I compare it with two other ways in which theologians have understood God's gracious enablement of sinners so that they might believe. As you hone your own position

---

[7] Ibid., pp. 22-23.

[8] Jonathan Edwards also granted that Arminians were right to be concerned about "the justice of damning men for those things that are necessary" ("A Careful and Strict Inquiry into the Modern Prevailing Notions of that Freedom of Will, Which Is Supposed to Be Essential to Moral Agency, Virtue and Vice, Reward and Punishment, Praise and Blame," in *The Works of Jonathan Edwards* [Carlisle, Penn.: Banner of Truth Trust], 1:65). To deal with this concern, Edwards proposed a distinction between natural and moral inability, or necessity. Although it is good to see Edwards's recognition of the problem, I do not think that he can evade the difficulty that Arminians have identified by describing the universal human inability as moral, so long as that moral inability is traced back to original sin, which makes the weight of final condemnation rest ultimately on sin in Adam.

on the question at hand—namely, who is able to believe?—this will also provide you with four options to ponder: the traditional Calvinist theory described above, the Lutheran approach, the Wesleyan approach and my modified Calvinist proposal, which appropriates aspects of the Lutheran and Wesleyan understandings.

The Lutheran proposal of enabling grace that accompanies the gospel. Lutheran theologians have generally been unwilling to affirm that God gives efficacious grace only to particular people and that these are the ones whom God elected to salvation unconditionally, that is, not based on anything the people do, such as believing in Jesus. Instead, they propose that the proclamation of the gospel is accompanied by an enabling grace that empowers *all* hearers not to resist the Word of God and hence to respond in faith. Paul Althaus indicates that in the theology of Martin Luther, God's word "is never merely an external word, spoken by human lips and heard with human ears. On the contrary, at the same time that this word is spoken, God speaks his truth in our hearts so that men receive it not only externally but also internally and believe it. This is the work of the Spirit."[9] As the *Formula of Concord* (1577) stated the situation, "With this Word is present the Holy Spirit, who opens the hearts of men, in order that, as Lydia did (Acts 16:14), they may diligently attend, and thus may be converted by the sole grace and power of the Holy Spirit, whose work, and whose work alone, the conversion of man is."[10]

Helmut Thielicke points out that in the Lutheran understanding, "the work of the Spirit is not an element that is added to God's words and deeds."[11] It is "a Word that contains the Spirit, i.e., a Word in which God himself is present. To refuse this Word is . . . hardening, *non* salvation."[12] It is in this way that the baptism of infants is understood to be justifying in its effect, although justification is by faith. Infants, given this enablement, are assumed not to resist the Word of God and hence to respond with infant faith and, thereby, to be justified.[13] Althaus notes that as late as 1521, Luther declared that "children are baptized on the basis of the faith and

---

[9] Paul Althaus, *The Theology of Martin Luther*, trans. Robert C. Schultz (Philadelphia: Fortress, 1966), p. 36.

[10] Formula of Concord 2.3, in Philip Schaff, *The Creeds of the Evangelical Protestant Churches* (London: Hodder & Stoughton, 1877), pp. 108-9.

[11] Helmut Thielicke, *The Evangelical Faith* (London: Hodder & Stoughton, 1877), 3:8.

[12] Ibid., 3:9.

[13] Luther's Larger Catechism 4, quoted in Adolf Harnack, *History of Dogma* (London: Williams & Norgate, 1899), 7:251 n 2. Compare Edmund Schlink, *Theology of the Lutheran Confessions* (Philadelphia: Fortress, 1961), pp. 151-54.

the confession of the sponsors."[14] In 1522, however, "in order to preserve the insight that we are saved not through someone else's faith but through our own," Luther began to teach infant faith.[15]

The Formula of Concord speaks of a universal mercy of God (Rom 11:32; Ezek 18:23; 33:11; 2 Pet 3:9; 1 Jn 2:2)[16] and states that Matthew 22:14

> is not to be so understood as if God were unwilling that all should be saved, but the cause of damnation of the ungodly is that they either do not hear the Word of God at all, but contumaciously contemn it, stop their ears, and harden their hearts, and in this way foreclose to the Spirit of God his ordinary way, so that he cannot accomplish his work in them, or at least when they have heard the Word, make it of no account, and cast it away. Neither God nor his election, but their own wickedness, is to blame if they perish [Lk 2:49, 52; Heb 12:25.; 2 Pet 2:1-2].[17]

The Saxon Visitation Articles (1592) taught that God "wills that all men should be saved" and that everyone is commanded "to hear Christ" and is promised "by his hearing, the virtue and operation of the Holy Ghost for conversion and salvation."[18]

The Wesleyan proposal of enabling grace that universally prevenes. The influence of Wesleyan theology reaches far wider than the Methodist Church and extends to many Christians (including many Baptists) who are quite unaware that the soteriology they affirm derives from the influence of John Wesley. Unlike the early Arminians, Wesley stressed that original sin is not merely a disease (corruption without guilt) but is really and truly sin and that it makes a person guilty before God. This guilt is imputed to all of Adam's descendants, so that even a child born of two perfect Christians would be a sinner.[19] Although the original guilt is canceled by the justification of all people in Christ (one of the universal benefits of the atonement), Wesley denied that humans, as they are by nature, have any ability whatever to cooperate with the grace of God. They are morally depraved and totally dependent on God's grace for salvation. In Wesley's view, however, no one actually exists in that state of in-

---

[14]Althaus, *Theology of Martin Luther,* p. 364.

[15]Ibid., pp. 364-65.

[16]Formula of Concord 11.9, in Schaff, *Creeds,* p. 168.

[17]Formula of Concord 11.11, in Schaff, *Creeds,* pp. 168-69.

[18]Saxon Visitation Articles 4, in Philip Schaff, *The Creeds of the Evangelical Protestant Churches* (London: Hodder & Stoughton, 1877), p. 185.

[19]John Wesley, *A Plain Account of Christian Perfection* (1777; Minneapolis: Bethany Fellowship, 1966), p. 50.

ability. In view of the universal character of redemption, God endows each person with sufficient enabling grace so that he or she can turn to God in faith and repentance.

The earliest Arminians held that it was only just that God should enable people to believe, since they could not be held accountable without spiritual ability. (This was also Charles Finney's position.) Wesleyans, however, believed that this was of the free grace of God, through preventing or prevenient grace. Everyone has grace in some measure, and one only sins because that grace is not used.[20] People are thus responsible free agents. In his 1773 essay "Predestination Calmly Considered," Wesley argued for a universal call that assumes an ability on the part of hearers to respond in faith. This is the only way that a person could be justly acquitted or condemned.[21] Wesley criticized Calvinist theology in strong words:

> And shall this man, for not doing what he never could do, and for doing what he never could avoid, be sentenced to depart into everlasting fire, prepared for the devil and his angels? [cf. Mt 25:41]. "Yes, because it is the sovereign will of God." Then you have either found a new God, or made one! This is not the God of the Christians. Our God is just in all his ways; he reapeth not where he hath not strewed. He requireth only according to what he hath given; and where he hath given little, little is required.[22]

Wesley's concern regarding the justice of God is clear. If people are unable to believe and yet are judged responsible to do so, then God is reaping where he has not sown. He is demanding more from people than he has made it possible for them to give. Consequently, the determining factor in an individual's salvation cannot be the grace of God; it must be the human's graciously enabled but libertarianly free decision. As Clark Pinnock puts it, "God's grace may be genuinely extended to people, but unless it meets the response of faith . . . it has no saving effect." God's grace is thus "non-manipulative and non-coercive."[23] Thomas Oden identifies this "synergy of grace and freedom" as "the consensual teaching of the believ-

---

[20]*The Works of John Wesley,* photographic reprint of the edition of 1872 (Grand Rapids, Mich.: Zondervan, 1958-1959), 6:512, quoted in Justo L. González, *From the Protestant Reformation to the Twentieth Century,* vol. 3 of *A History of Christian Thought* (New York: Abingdon, 1975), p. 313.

[21]William C. Placher, ed., *From the Reformation to the Present,* vol. 2 of *Readings in the History of Christian Theology* (Philadelphia: Westminster Press, 1988), p. 98.

[22]*Works of John Wesley,* 11:234, quoted in Placher, *From the Reformation,* p. 98.

[23]Clark Pinnock, introduction to *Grace Unlimited,* ed. Clark Pinnock (Minneapolis: Bethany Fellowship, 1975), p. 15.

WHO CAN BE SAVED?

ing church" in the early centuries, as demonstrated by the Third Ecumenical Council.[24] On this model, "those who cooperate with the prevenient grace that is always/already there will find that grace becomes effective. Grace cooperates with human freedom, and God elects those who respond to the evangelical call."[25]

A Brief Critique of Synergism in the Lutheran and Wesleyan Proposals

Both the Lutheran approach and the Wesleyan approach put sinners in the position of being graciously enabled to respond with faith to God's offer of salvation. In both cases, this faith is the fruit of grace, but whether or not this response occurs is ultimately decided not by God but by the person who believes. A similarly synergistic proposal had been put forward by Luis de Molina, a seventeenth-century Jesuit theologian who offered an alternative to the Augustinian theology of Thomas Aquinas. Recently, Thomas Flint has argued the benefits of a Molinist explanation of the interrelation of the human and divine agencies for our understanding of predestination.[26] In the Molinist scheme, "efficacious grace is not intrinsically different from sufficient grace: it is merely sufficient grace that 'works' "; the grace is "only contingently efficacious, and its being efficacious is determined by us, not by God."[27]

From the Calvinist perspective, the effect of the synergism in Luther's, Wesley's and Molina's approaches is seriously problematic precisely because it makes the decisive factor in a person's salvation that person's own decision. It seems to us that if salvation is realized through *cooperation* between God and the person saved, the absolute graciousness of salvation is compromised. Since the difference between those who are saved and those who are not lies within the action of the believer, it seems that these believers have cause for self-congratulation and that God's glory in salvation has been compromised (Eph 2:8-9). Thus, Ardel Caneday and Thomas Schreiner complain that "if we are ultimately responsible for our faith, then we can brag about our decision to believe."[28]

---

[24]Thomas C. Oden, *The Transforming Power of Grace* (Nashville: Abingdon, 1993), p. 89.
[25]Ibid.
[26]Thomas P. Flint, "Two Accounts of Providence," in *Divine and Human Action: Essays in the Metaphysics of Theism*, ed. Thomas V. Morris (Ithaca: Cornell University Press, 1988), p. 161.
[27]Ibid.
[28]Thomas R. Schreiner and Ardel B. Caneday, *The Race Set Before Us: A Biblical Theology of Perseverance and Assurance* (Downers Grove, Ill.: InterVarsity Press, 2001), p. 318.

From numerous conversations with Arminians and Wesleyans, I know that this perception is difficult for them to understand. It is argued that believers cannot boast because they simply accepted a free gift. I acknowledge the significance of grace in most synergistic theologies. But the fact remains that the critical difference between those who believe and those who do not is found in the believers rather than in God's gracious work. Since God enables all equally, the outcome is determined by the people who must respond to God's initiative. I fail to see why believers should not be commended for having responded to grace. However small their contribution has been, it was the decisive factor. With Kevin Vanhoozer, therefore, I seek a conception of the grace of salvation in God's effectual calling that does not reduce God "to a mere physical cause on the one hand, or to an ineffectual influence on the other."[29]

MY MODIFIED CALVINISTIC PROPOSAL OF UNIVERSALLY SUFFICIENT ENABLING GRACE

My quandary should now be obvious. I am not completely satisfied with the traditional Calvinist theory, but I cannot solve my problem by adopting either the Lutheran or the Wesleyan approach because of the synergism entailed. Consequently, I propose an approach to the issue that conforms to the Calvinist understanding of *efficacious* grace but to which I add a *sufficient* grace. Efficacious grace is given only to the elect and, by definition, it is what saves sinners who are spiritually disabled by the sinfulness of their hearts or natures. Sufficient grace, on the other hand, is universal. Since all are, in some sense, made able to believe, God is just in judging them for not doing so. I have found this approach helpful, and I hope others will as well.

I propose, then, that *it may be that God gives everyone sufficient grace to enable them to believe in him but that he only draws and persuades effectively the elect.* Not only does everyone receive revelation sufficient to lead to salvation if responded to with faith, but at least once in everyone's life that divine revelation is accompanied by a divine enabling that makes a faith response possible, *in the sense that people are justly condemned for failing to believe when God is made known to them on that occasion.*

With Lutherans, I affirm that this is an *accompanying* grace rather than the *prevenient* grace that Wesleyans propose. With Wesleyans, however, I

---

[29]Kevin J. Vanhoozer, *First Theology: God, Scriptures and Hermeneutics* (Downers Grove, Ill.: InterVarsity Press, 2002), p. 106.

assert that the enabling grace is *universal*. But I differ from the Lutherans by denying that this divine enabling grace *always* accompanies the proclamation of truth concerning God, particularly the truth of the gospel. As Vanhoozer notes, "Reformed theologians deny that the preached word works *ex opere operato*. To stipulate that God must always be salvifically at work wherever there is preaching is effectively to deny the freedom of God."[30] The Spirit of God blows wherever he pleases (Jn 3:8), in grace that is ineffectual to salvation as well as in the enabling or regenerative grace that effects salvation. The proclamation of God's Word accomplishes God's purposes, but those purposes are not the same for each individual or on every occasion. In the nice turn of phrase suggested by Vanhoozer, the proclamation of the gospel becomes effective because "the Spirit 'advenes' on truth to make it efficacious." The Spirit comes to the word that is being proclaimed and empowers it by his advent.[31]

With the Calvinist tradition, therefore, I affirm that salvation occurs only when and because God works effectively in the inner being (the heart and mind) of a person. The contingency thus lies with God, rather than with the human agent, preserving the sovereignty and pure graciousness of saving grace. The Word of God becomes an effective saving Word only when the Spirit of God empowers it, drawing to God those who are called by God's voice (Jn 6:44-45), which is being heard with the ears or seen with the eyes but also received with the heart that God opens—as happened with Lydia, in Philippi (Acts 16:14). As the Reformed tradition has regularly asserted, the call that effects salvation is a work of both Word and Spirit; in the terminology of contemporary philosophy of language, it is by both *illocution* and *perlocution*.[32] I believe, however, that a model incorporating universal *sufficient* accompanying grace while maintaining the particularity and divine sovereignty of *efficacious* grace addresses some of the problems I have identified in the usual Calvinist proposals, which lack the former component.

The general idea at work in my construct has a precedent of sorts in the tradition of Reformed orthodoxy. Seventeenth-century Reformed theologian Francis Turretin appealed to a distinction between sufficient and efficient grace, in order to demonstrate that Adam was properly held responsible for his first sin, even though the Fall had been decreed by God.

---

[30]Ibid., p. 112.
[31]Ibid., p. 122.
[32]Ibid.

Although man fell, still he had the ability to stand if he wished. Otherwise God would have placed him in an impossible condition. Hence a twofold help or assistance is commonly distinguished: help without which *(auxilium sine qua non)* or the power of not sinning (by which he had strength sufficient to stand if he wished); and the help by which *(auxilium quo)* or efficacious grace (which gave not only the ability if he wished, but to will what he could). The former was after the manner of a habit and faculty in man; the latter, however, after the manner of an action or efficacious motion to good. The former was necessary to his ability to persevere, but the latter to his actual perseverance. The former help was never absent from Adam, not even in the very moment in which he sinned; but the latter, God withheld from him freely as he was not bound to give it. Notwithstanding, neither can man be excused (because he sinned voluntarily and was impelled by no force) nor God be accused (because as a most free dispenser of his own goods, he was bound to the bestowal of that grace by no law, as will hereafter be more fully shown).[33]

Turretin expressed precisely what I am now recommending, but I propose that we apply it more broadly than to Adam's original situation, seeing it as descriptive of everyone's situation.

RESPONSE TO A POTENTIALLY SERIOUS OBJECTION TO MY PROPOSAL

I am aware that the concept I have put forward elicits a serious objection, so let me try to address that concern. Henri Blocher identifies the possible problem by way of commentary on Turrentin's proposal. Blocher notes that "the first help meant mere possibility for him, a possibility which never comes to fruition if the second help is not added!"[34] But Blocher is not impressed with the concept, and he cites Blaise Pascal's complaint against the Jesuits (in his *Lettres provinciales*) "that the chief characteristic of what they called 'sufficient grace' was that it was not sufficient."[35]

Much the same objection has been expressed by evangelical Arminians concerning my own proposal of universal sufficient grace. Of course, the reason why the enabling grace is "not sufficient" is different in my account than it was in the theory of the Jesuits whom Pascal criticized or in the Lutheran and Wesleyan models that I reviewed. In those synergist models, the grace

[33]Francis Turretin *Institutes of Elenctic Theology* 9.7.7, ed. James T. Dennison Jr., trans. George Musgrave Giger (Phillipsburg, N.J.: Presbyterian & Reformed, 1992), 1:607-8.
[34]Henri Blocher, *Original Sin: Illuminating the Riddle*, New Studies in Biblical Theology (Downers Grove, Ill.: InterVarsity Press, 1997), pp. 57-58.
[35]Ibid., p. 58.

does not suffice for salvation without the additional cooperative work of the *people* who receive it. In my monergist model, the grace suffices for salvation only when further *divine grace* is supplied, to make the enablement efficacious. Nevertheless, I too have been asked how I can call a grace *sufficient* when it is never, in any instance, sufficient to bring a person to salvation. I have wondered whether it might be better to call the universal grace of which I am speaking an *enabling grace,* in distinction from *efficacious grace.* At this point, however, I suggest that we maintain the term *sufficient* because there is an important sense in which this grace is, indeed, sufficient, even though it does not suffice for salvation. Its sufficiency lies particularly in its being enough to justify God's condemnation. Through this enablement by the Spirit, which all people experience at least once in their lifetime, they *could* respond to the revelation accompanied by the enabling grace if they *would* do so. I hope that my proposal and its merit will become even more clear as I explain some of the benefits that I believe to follow from this concept.

Calvinist theologians with a knowledge of the history of their tradition might be tempted to dismiss my proposal as a restatement of Amyraldianism. I grant that Amyraut, Richard Baxter and others were sensitive to some of the difficulties in Calvinism that I identified above. But my proposal for addressing those difficulties is different. Amyraut's "hypothetical universalism" treated the issue of God's intention in the atonement, which we examined in chapter five. My own interest here is not in the extent or intent of the atonement but in the grace that flows from it in the Spirit's work of enablement. This will probably not be an issue for most readers, but those who are interested can visit appendix two, "The Distinction Between My Proposal of Universal Sufficient Grace and Amyraldian 'Hypothetical Universalism.'"

THE BENEFITS OF MY PROPOSAL

God's justice. In a recent Wesleyan soteriology, Oden speaks well when he asserts that

> no human being has been condemned for Adam's sin alone, but in so far as anyone is subject to condemnation and judgment, it is due to one's own freely collusive cooperation with the conditions of sin resulting from the history of sin following Adam. The principle of free moral agency is preserved in and through the doctrine of sufficient grace.[36]

---

[36]Oden, *Transforming Power*, p. 45.

The justice of divine judgment is no longer an issue if all people receive a grace that remediates the effects of sin sufficiently to enable them to believe, if they will. There is thus no question about their not having been able to do so. People who do not believe *could* if they *would*. I argue that the problem is that, given the rebelliousness that characterizes us, we are still prone not to submit to God and receive his provision for our salvation. Without coercing us, however, God is able to draw us in a manner that effectively brings us to Jesus (Jn 6:44), to open our hearts (Acts 16:14) and to illumine our minds so that we will to come. As with the Lutheran accompanying grace and the Wesleyan prevenient grace, this work of God is sufficient but not efficacious. But along with traditional Calvinism, I posit that the explanation for the faith of those who do believe is not found in themselves but in the effective working of God. The Holy Spirit woos the elect to exercise an ability that all have graciously been given but that only these people *use* to respond to God's call. Contrary to Oden and other synergists, I contend that the act of saving faith is explained on the basis of efficacious grace, not on the basis of human choice, yet that choice is freely willed by the human agent (not coerced by God).

I hear a somewhat similar proposal in the work of J. O. Buswell Jr. when he suggests "that the convicting work of the Holy Spirit is to be understood as (1) sufficient and (2) universal."[37] By "the sufficiency of the convicting work of the Holy Spirit," he means "to point out that this work, as revealed to us in the Scripture and in Christian experience, is sufficient to justify for our finite minds the fact of the eternal wrath of God against those who reject His grace in Christ." By "universality," Buswell means that "the convicting work of the Holy Spirit is absolutely universal to the entire human race in all ages in all areas."[38]

The demand of justice does not require that people be continually enabled, with each experience of divine revelation. Scripture speaks of a hardening of the heart that occurs as one resists God's gracious drawing. Paul speaks of people storing up wrath for the day of God's righteous judgment by their "hard and impenitent" hearts (Rom 2:5). He tells the Thessalonians about "those who are perishing because they refused to love the truth and so be saved" (2 Thess 2:10). God sends such people a powerful delusion so that they believe the lie (2 Thess 2:11). Here we have

---

[37] J. O. Buswell Jr., *A Systematic Theology of the Christian Religion* (Grand Rapids, Mich.: Zondervan, 1963), p. 160.
[38] Ibid.

indication of the judicial hardening that results when people resist and refuse grace. They become "darkened in their understanding, alienated from the life of God because of their ignorance and hardness of heart," and consequently they lose all sensitivity (Eph 4:18-19).

Roger Forster and Paul Marston note that, in the case of Pharaoh, it was only after five warnings and penalties had been ineffective that God did the hardening. "Submission now would have meant prudence, not penitence; and it was against prudence, not penitence, that he was hardened" (Ex 9:12). For Pharaoh, "the last five plagues were not disciplinary, but wholly penal."[39] They further comment that

> it appears, then, that the Lord is never said to debauch Pharaoh's heart, but only to strengthen it against prudence and to make it dull; that the words used do not express the infusion of evil passion, but the animation of a resolute courage, and the overclouding of a natural discernment; and, above all, that every one of the three words, to make hard, to make strong, and to make heavy, is employed to express Pharaoh's own treatment of himself, before it is applied to any work of God, as actually taking place already.[40]

Paul describes this process of judicial abandonment in Romans 1:24-27. Furthermore, those who spurn God's grace may put themselves beyond the point where it will be offered again (Heb 6:4-6; 10:26-31). There comes a time when God no longer accompanies the objective revelations of himself with a gracious enabling. The personal responsibility for this self-incurred inability can surely be denied by no one. It is in this vein that we may understand the biblical truth concerning the slavery that grows as one continues to sin (Jn 8:34; Rom 6:17; 2 Pet 2:19). When people choose to believe the lies of Satan rather than the truth of God in spite of God's gracious enabling, Satan blinds them (2 Cor 4:4) and enslaves them (2 Tim 2:26). Having surrendered themselves into his power by these acts of their own will, they are responsible for this. The reality of death in sin becomes ever more obvious (Eph 2:1-2). It is in this light that I understand the warnings to the Hebrews that should they not harden their hearts when the Spirit gives a desire to repent (Heb 3:7-8; 12:17) because the opportunity will not last forever (Heb 3:15).

On the basis of Titus 2:11 ("For the grace of God has appeared, bringing

---

[39]Roger Forster and Paul Marston, *God's Strategy in Human History: God's Sovereignty and Man's Responsibility* (Minneapolis: Bethany, 1973; Crowborough, East Sussex: Highland, 1989), p. 172.
[40]Ibid., p. 175.

salvation to all"), Oden asserts that "to no one, not even the recalcitrant unfaithful, does God deny grace sufficient for salvation. Prevening grace precedes each discrete human act."[41] Oden doubts that God ever ceases to give sufficient grace, even to the obdurate.[42] Given the Scriptures I have cited, however, this is too optimistic a statement. Nevertheless, there is much cause for praise when we hear testimony of lives in which this hardening and blinding process had gone on for years in a descending spiral, yet God graciously moves in and frees them from the bondage that they have chosen and gloriously saves them. God owes no one grace, but his grace shines brightest where sin reigns most evidently (Rom 5:20-21).

As I indicated at the outset, I have not avoided the scandal of particularity, but I hope to have ameliorated the sense of injustice. I agree with Oden that "grace is effective as it elicits willing cooperation and sufficient in so far as it does what is necessary to lead the will to cooperate, even when the deficient will is resistant."[43] I differ from him, however, in my conviction that when the grace is effective, its efficacy lies in the peculiar working of the Spirit and not in *(though not apart from)* the response of the human will.

God's distress at human rejection. Through the prophet Ezekiel, the Lord pled with Israel to repent and turn from their transgressions so that they would not be ruined (Ezek 18:30). God states that he has "no pleasure in the death of anyone" and urges Israel, therefore, to "turn, then, and live" (Ezek 18:32; cf. 33:11). If God accompanies his appeal to the house of Israel to repent and turn to him with a gracious ability for them to do so—grace they spurn—we can discern one sense in which God may say that he has "no pleasure" in their death. Later in Ezekiel, God speaks of his efforts with the Israelites to cleanse them and turn them to himself and of his commitment to judge them according to their ways and doings (Ezek 24:14). Clearly this was not an efficacious working by God, but it does testify to a work of such sort that it justified the exercise of God's judgment against them for their deeds.

Through Amos, God repeatedly describes his disciplinary actions against Israel, and demonstrates distress that they "did not return" to him. This was in spite of the fact that he sent famine and drought, which ruined harvests and left the people frantically searching for water (Amos 4:6-8).

---

[41]Oden, *Transforming Power*, p. 48.
[42]Ibid., p. 81.
[43]Ibid.

God sent "blight and mildew" on their vineyards and locusts to devour their fig and olive trees, but they did not return (Amos 4:9). He sent plagues upon them as he had done the Egyptians and "killed [their] young men with the sword," but they "did not return" to him (Amos 4:10). He overthrew some of them as he had done Sodom and Gomorrah, but they still did not return (Amos 4:11). And so God's patience is wearing thin and he warns them to prepare to meet their God (Amos 4:12).

From a synergist perspective, this language of divine distress is easy to understand. They *could* return to God because of a prevening grace, but they did not. But if we work within the classic form of Reformed monergism, which concludes from Scripture that people cannot return without an efficacious work of God's grace and that they *will* return (gladly and willingly) whenever that grace works within them, the distress of God and his declarations of impending and just judgment are difficult to comprehend. We can make sense of them, however, if we postulate an enabling grace, which I am calling sufficient grace. On this postulate, it also becomes easier to understand passages that indicate there is a sense in which God does take delight in the death of the wicked. When Moses is warning Israel that God will judge them severely if they continue in their unrepentance, he says, "Just as the LORD took delight in making you prosperous and numerous, so the LORD will take delight in bringing you to ruin and destruction; you shall be plucked off the land that you are entering to possess" (Deut 28:63). "We are faced with the inescapable biblical fact that in some sense God does not delight in the death of the wicked (Ezek 18), and in some sense he does (Deut 28:63; 2 Sam 2:25)."[44] I find both cases equally difficult to understand unless there is also a sense in which it can be said that these people *could* have done righteous rather than wicked deeds. I locate that sense in the concept of *sufficient accompanying grace.*

The distress of Jesus as he looked down over Jerusalem now becomes more comprehensible. They *could* have come at his call. Nothing kept them from doing so except their own stubbornness. That resistance gave him great pain. We are still left, of course, with mysteries: Why did God not effectively woo them all? Why did the Father not reveal to all of them, as he had to Peter, that Jesus was the Christ (Mt 16:17)? Paul provides some insight into God's work of grace in hardening part of the nation in pursuit of

---

[44]John Piper, "Are There Two Wills in God?" in *Still Sovereign: Contemporary Perspectives on Election, Foreknowledge and Grace*, ed. Thomas R. Schreiner and Bruce A. Ware (Grand Rapids, Mich.: Baker, 2000), pp. 118-19.

his wider plan of grace for the Gentiles (Rom 11:25-32), and that only temporarily (Rom 11:25-26). Nevertheless, we echo Paul's sense that God's judgment is "unsearchable" and "his paths beyond tracing out" (Rom 11:33 NIV), and we give him glory (Rom 11:36).

God's "desire" for people to be saved. It may be that my proposal of God's universal grace offers us additional help in understanding some of the New Testament texts that speak in a language that has a universal ring to it. Roman Catholic theologians often speak of God's "universal salvific will."[45] This is a manner of speaking that is open to Wesleyans and Lutherans but problematic to Calvinists, if God's "will" is identified with his eternal purpose. On the understanding being proposed here, however, Calvinists could also speak of "universal salvific grace," indicating that God has, indeed, enabled all to believe, although he has not been uniformly persuasive in his gracious calling. There is universal grace that is salvific in its enabling though it does not achieve universal salvation because it is resisted by many. Thus, when Peter asserts that God is "not wanting anyone to perish" (2 Pet 3:9), God's "wanting" is easier to understand if he has given everyone grace sufficient to make salvation possible. One of the universal benefits of Christ's death is this grace.

With 1 Timothy 2:4 (cf. 2 Pet 3:9) in mind, Philip Edgcumbe Hughes has asked, "How can it be said that God desires all men to be saved, if by a fixed decree many are destined never to be saved and cannot therefore be helped by our prayers?"[46] Jaroslav Pelikan similarly observes that 1 Timothy 2:4 "had always been a conundrum to Augustinian doctrines of predestination and the will of God."[47] Traditionally, Calvinists have responded both by describing God's will in this instance as preceptive, that is, in the sense of God's command that everyone repent and believe; and by pointing out that, in the context (cf. 1 Tim 2:1-2), Paul is making reference to "all kinds" of people.[48] Arminian theologians frequently protest the "exceedingly paradoxical notion of two divine wills regarding salva-

[45]Compare Flint, "Two Accounts," p. 169 n. 44: "It is not quite *de fide* that God wills all to be saved. . . . Nevertheless, I am aware of no Thomist who would deny God's universal salvific will."

[46]Philip Edgcumbe Hughes, *The True Image: The Origin and Destiny of Man in Christ* (Grand Rapids, Mich.: Eerdmans, 1989), p. 173.

[47]Jaroslav Pelikan, *Reformation of Church and Dogma (1300-1700)*, vol. 4 of *The Christian Tradition* (Chicago: University of Chicago Press, 1984), p. 237.

[48]See Robert Letham, *The Work of Christ* (Downers Grove, Ill.: InterVarsity Press, 1993), pp. 242-43. Martin Bucer, John Calvin and Zacharias Ursinus all followed Augustine in understanding the text as a reference to "all classes" of people.

tion."[49] But Wayne Grudem has very aptly demonstrated that Arminians "*also* must say that God *wills* something more strongly than he wills the salvation of all people, *for in fact all are not saved.*"[50] Arminians argue that this is because God chooses to preserve human free will, whereas Reformed theologians attribute it to God's purpose to glorify himself. We may go further, in addressing this passage, however, if we posit that God actually enables everyone to repent and believe.

The free offer of the gospel. Among Calvinist theologians, there has been a controversy about the genuineness of the external call and the sincerity of making such an offer when not all have been included in God's intention in the atonement. Those who argue that it is legitimate to offer the blessings of salvation in our gospel preaching also point out that the call to repent and believe is for all people and that the promise of salvation can be freely offered on the basis of these conditions.[51] Some also contend that the Holy Spirit does a work of conviction that leaves people justly condemned for their unbelief (Jn 3:18). The blame for not accepting the gospel is clearly placed on sinful people who reject it: they perish "because they refused to love the truth and so be saved" (2 Thess 2:10). This makes best sense, however, if people have rejected the truth when they could have done otherwise, in the sense of God's having graciously enabled a positive response, which they stubbornly refuse to give.

In some cases, then, through this work of conviction, God prepares people for ultimate conversion. In others, it serves to increase their culpability. Oden correctly states that "even where the will is most recalcitrant, grace is still said to be 'sufficient,' for grace would have sufficed to guide the will had the will not resisted. It is not inconsistent to say that sufficiency from God's side may be met with resistance from the human side."[52]

John Bunyan rightly related the offer of the gospel to a universal sufficiency of the atonement, arguing that

if those that perish in the days of the gospel, shall have, at least, their damnation heightened, because they have neglected and refused to receive the gospel, it must needs be that the gospel was with all faithfulness to be ten-

[49]Pinnock, introduction to *Grace Unlimited*, p. 13.
[50]Wayne Grudem, *Systematic Theology: An Introduction to Biblical Doctrine* (Grand Rapids, Mich.: Zondervan, 1994), p. 684.
[51]See Letham, *Work of Christ*, p. 239. Anthony Hoekema demonstrates the consistency of the free offer of the gospel with both Scripture and the Reformed confessional standards (*Saved by Grace* [Grand Rapids, Mich.: Eerdmans, 1989], pp. 68-77).
[52]Oden, *Transforming Power*, p. 114.

dered unto them; the which it could not be, unless the death of Christ did extend itself unto them (Jn 3:16; Heb. 2:3); for the offer of the gospel cannot with God's allowance, be offered any further than the death of Jesus Christ doth go.[53]

It should be apparent, however, that a merely objective sufficiency of the atonement will still not serve Bunyan's purpose. Given the moral inability of fallen humankind, a gracious enabling must be part of the universal effect of the atonement, or neither the gospel call nor the just judgment of those who refuse can be assumed.

Anthony Hoekema warns against both the Arminian (synergist) proposal of sufficient grace and the hyper-Calvinist denial of God's desire for universal salvation. He urges readers to "maintain the Scriptural paradox" even though we cannot reconcile factors within its teaching.[54] My suggestion is that the biblical truths are maintained but the antinomy between God's universal salvific will and his particular election is lessened if we posit a universal sufficient grace, the efficacy of which lies in further gracious work on God's part.

John Calvin observes that God has said by the prophet Ezekiel, "As I live, says the LORD God, I have no pleasure in the death of the wicked, but that the wicked turn from their ways and live" (Ezek 33:11; cf. Ezek 18:23). But Calvin contends that "as the prophet is exhorting to penitence, it is no wonder that he pronounces God willing that all be saved. But the mutual relation between threats and promises shows such forms of speech to be conditional."[55] Here Calvin cites the Ninevites and the kings of Gerar and Egypt. He goes on:

> Since by repentance they averted the punishment promised to them, it is evident that it was not firmly decreed unless they remained obstinate. Yet the denunciation had been precise, as if it were an irrevocable decree. But after terrifying and humbling them with the sense of His wrath, though not to the point of despair, He cheers them with the hope of pardon, that they might feel there was room for remedy. So again with the promises which invite all men to sal-

---

[53]John Bunyan, "Reprobation Asserted," in *The Works of John Bunyan,* ed. G. Offor (London: Blackie and Son, 1855), 2:348, quoted in Alan C. Clifford, *Atonement and Justification: English Evangelical Theology 1640-1790: An Evaluation* (Oxford: Clarendon, 1990), p. 76.

[54]Hoekema, *Saved by Grace,* p. 73.

[55]John Calvin, *Concerning the Eternal Predestination of God,* trans. J. K. S. Reid (London: James Clarke, 1961), p. 105, quoted in Brian G. Armstrong, *Calvinism and the Amyraut Heresy: Protestant Scholasticism and Humanism in Seventeenth-Century France* (Madison: University of Wisconsin Press, 1969), p. 198.

vation. They do not simply and positively declare what God has decreed in His secret counsel but what He is prepared to do for all who are brought to faith and repentance. But, it is alleged, we thereby ascribe a double will to God, whereas He is not variable and not the least shadow of turning falls upon Him. ... God requires conversion from us; wherever He finds it, a man is not disappointed of the promised reward of life. Hence God is said to will life, as also repentance. But the latter He wills, because He invites all to it by His word. Now this is not contradictory of His secret counsel, by which He determined to convert none but His elect. He cannot rightly on this account be thought variable, because *as lawgiver He illuminates all with the external doctrine of life*, in this first sense calling all men to life. But in the other sense, He brings to life whom He will, as Father regenerating by the Spirit only His sons.

It is indeed certain that men are not converted to the Lord of their own accord; nor is the gift of conversion common to all. For this is one of the two heads of the covenant, which God promises to make with none but with His children and His elect people.[56]

It is apparent that Calvin considered the universal proclamation of the gospel and the summons to repentance and faith to be our legitimate responsibility. His own argument was that such proclamation is justified because God "illuminates all with the external doctrine of life." I, in turn, am proposing that this does not suffice for Calvin's own purpose unless there is an accompanying *inner* calling—at least on one occasion in an individual's life. Were this not so, then people would be finally condemned on the ground of their sin in Adam, for in the Fall we incurred the inability that makes all subsequent rejection of the gospel inevitable. This puts too much weight on original sin, and it fails to account for the consistent biblical witness that people are ultimately condemned for the deeds done in their lifetime.

The sovereign grace of sanctification. In his exposition of Open Theism, Pinnock identifies what seems to him to be a serious problem with monergistic views of sanctification:

According to theological determinism, . . . whatever state you are in now is the will of God since God's will covers everything that happens, including states of mind and heart. If one does not desire to grow in holiness, this lack of desire is God's will too. If God wants someone to desire holiness he will

---

[56]Calvin, *Concerning the Eternal Predestination*, pp. 105-6, quoted in Armstrong, *Calvinism*, pp. 198-99, emphasis mine. Commenting on this passage, Armstrong points out that Amyraut related God's role as lawgiver to the hypothetical covenant and his role as father to the absolute covenant (*Calvinism*, p. 199).

make them want it. . . . We, therefore, cannot be blamed for not wanting a higher level of holiness. If my desire is at a low level, it must be God's will that it is.[57]

Caneday and Schreiner tell of a man who used precisely such an appeal to divine monergism to excuse his personal sin. This person "kept having sexual relations outside marriage," but excused himself by saying: "God in his grace has not given me the desire to obey him. It would be legalistic of me to keep his commands without the desire."[58] I can understand Pinnock's sense that something is amiss in a monergistic understanding of sanctification if it necessarily leads to a situation in which God must be held accountable for the sins that Christians commit, since God deliberately withheld from them the sanctifying grace that would have kept them from sin. I find the treatment of sanctification by Reformed theologians to be somewhat ambiguous in regard to the respective roles of God and believers. Hoekema, for instance, states that "though sanctification is *primarily* God's work in us, it is not a process in which we remain passive but one in which we must be continually active"[59] (emphasis mine). To speak of sanctification as *primarily* God's work leaves the impression that it is *secondarily* ours; hence, we work together and God's work is not determinative, as it is in justification. Of course, we exercise repentance and faith in justification, so we are not passive there either, but a Reformed or monergist theologian would surely not say that justification is *primarily* God's work.

On the other hand, as Hoekema sums up his treatment of "God and his people in sanctification," he asks,

> Should we say, as some have done, that sanctification is a work of God in which believers cooperate? This way of stating the doctrine, however, wrongly implied that God and we each do part of the work of sanctification. . . . Summing up, we may say that sanctification is a supernatural work of God in which the believer is active. The more active we are in sanctification, the more sure we may be that the energizing power that enables us to be active is the power of God.[60]

[57]Clark H. Pinnock, *Most Moved Mover: A Theology of God's Openness* (Grand Rapids, Mich.: Baker, 2001), pp. 167-68.
[58]Schreiner and Caneday, *Race Set Before Us*, p. 316.
[59]Hoekema, *Saved by Grace*, p. 201.
[60]Ibid. When Hoekema writes "as some have done," he cites Louis Berkhof, *Systematic Theology* (London: Banner of Truth Trust, 1949), p. 534.

Yet a note of synergism might again be heard in Hoekema's quotation from J. C. Ryle:

> Sanctification . . . is a thing for which every believer is responsible. . . . Whose fault is it if they [believers] are not holy, but their own? On whom can they throw the blame if they are not sanctified, but themselves? God, who has given them grace and a new heart, and a new nature, has deprived them of all excuse if they do not live for his praise.[61]

In the citation from Ryle, it sounds as though we, not God, set the limits to our growth in holiness. God's grace has been sufficient for all of us to be perfect, but we do not appropriate it, and we are responsible for that failure. Such an idea has an obvious attraction, for it evades the position that Pinnock found so horrifying. Calvinists know that our *obedience* can only be attributed to God's grace so that we have no cause for boasting, but

---

[61]J. C. Ryle, *Holiness* (London: James Clarke, 1956), pp. 19-20, quoted in Hoekema, *Saved by Grace*, p. 201.

Similarly, Calvinistic Baptist Bruce Demarest writes: "Sanctification is a cooperative venture; the Spirit blesses believers with sanctifying grace, but the latter must faithfully *cooperate* therewith. Faith alone justifies but faith joined with our concerted efforts sanctifies" (*The Cross and Salvation: The Doctrine of Salvation,* Foundations of Evangelical Theology [Wheaton, Ill.: Crossway, 1997], p. 425). And Donald Bloesch speaks about the divine and human factors in sanctification as follows: "None of us can earn our salvation or make ourselves worthy of God's grace. But we can demonstrate and manifest God's grace in our daily lives, and if we do so we will be rewarded, not because we have been more open to the moving of the Spirit. Even then we can take no credit, since our openness is irrevocably tied to our election. We do good works because we have been separated by God for a life of service. If we cease to do good works we will be judged for having quenched and grieved the Spirit who lives within us and strives to perfect our union with Christ" (*The Holy Spirit: Works and Gifts* [Downers Grove, Ill.: InterVarsity Press, 2000], p. 206). On the other hand, Bloesch writes (later in the same book), more monergistically, that "salvation is *never a cooperative affair* between willing humans and the Spirit of God but always a surprising work of grace that does not merely negate our will but turns our will in a completely new direction so that we can act and believe—yet not to gain salvation but to give evidence that we are indeed recipients of saving grace" (p. 251).

R. C. Sproul does not hesitate to use the language of synergism in speaking of the process of sanctification: "As part of the process of sanctification, perseverance is a synergistic work. This means it is a cooperative effort between God and us. We persevere and he preserves" (*Grace Unknown: The Heart of Reformed Theology* [Grand Rapids, Mich.: Baker Books, 1997], p. 212). But it does not appear that he means to say more than that Christians are not passive in their growth in holiness. Later, using the analogy of a father and child holding one another's hands, Sproul says that "when the child loosens his grip on the father's hand, the father may let him stumble and scrape his knees. Though the child incurs the father's displeasure in the process, the father will not allow his grip on the child to be loosed entirely, preventing him from falling into an abyss. . . . We can fall from grace, but not absolutely" (p. 213). Here the monergistic action of God's preserving his children to the end is clearly described, but the action of the believer is not left out of the process.

there is an understandable reluctance to admit the converse—to attribute our *disobedience* to God. On the other hand, if we import synergism into our doctrine of sanctification to address this perceived problem, we commit theological suicide as monergists.[62] If we insist that salvation is all of grace, it will not do to argue that although our justification is accomplished by monergistic efficacious grace, our sanctification is achieved through a synergistic cooperation between God and ourselves. If the latter were the case, then final salvation would be brought about through a synergism, and all monergist complaints that synergism undermines the absoluteness of God's grace in salvation would come back to haunt the Calvinists, who describe sanctification synergistically.

Salvation, from beginning to end, is wrought by God. This includes both the initial faith that God graciously gives us and by means of which we are justified, on account of Christ's atoning work on our behalf, and the ongoing faith by means of which we grow in holiness and are conformed to the image of Christ. We have nothing that we did not receive from God (1 Cor 4:7), and we go forward in holiness by the work of the same Spirit who began that motion in us (Gal 3:1-5). If any part of the long process of salvation—which begins with our being regenerated by the Spirit and concludes when we are perfected in Christ in glorified bodies—is a matter of our cooperating with God, then our salvation is a cooperative work. It is thus incoherent to assert that regeneration and justification are God's sovereign work in us (monergism) but that sanctification is a work in which we cooperate (synergism). Arminians or Molinists, being consistently synergistic, posit a synergism from start to finish. At every stage, God's gracious initiative precedes human effort, but the human response to that grace determines the outcome. Calvinists and other monergists, who insist that God regenerates and justifies those whom *he* has eternally purposed to save, cannot introduce a *human* determinism into the measure of

---

[62]I am indebted to Schreiner and Caneday for fruitful dialogue growing out of their fine book on the doctrines of perseverance and assurance of salvation (*The Race Set Before Us*, cited above). I had been surprised by their analogy between justification and sanctification (including perseverance), both of which they portrayed as wrought sovereignly by God's grace, in a monergistic fashion. My conception of the situation in sanctification, at that time, was analogous to the Wesleyan understanding of justification: God provides believers with sufficient grace not to sin, but we choose whether or not we will appropriate it. I had arrived at my synergistic understanding of sanctification because, although I understood Scripture to teach that it is the eternal purpose of God which determined that some people will never believe and be justified, I found it hard to imagine that God eternally purposed that particular believers should be no more holy than they are.

progress in salvation without undermining entirely the sovereignty of God's saving work, which we are convinced is taught by Scripture. To consistently affirm that salvation is God's gracious work, from start to finish, giving us nothing of which to boast, we need to speak of the human activity in sanctification in completely the same way we speak of its role in justification. In both cases there is human activity, but it is an activity that occurs because of God's grace, which effects both faith and obedience in us.[63]

We must approach the inclusion of sins committed by believers within the will of God's eternal purpose, just as we do all the evil that occurs within the history of the world by the sovereign will of God. God hates the sin, and he does not will to bring it about in any way that would make him accountable for it. Nevertheless, he permits it to occur for reasons of his own, which are frequently hidden from us now. Just as God hardened the hearts of most of Paul's fellow Israelites as part of his saving purpose for all the nations of the world, so he wills that his work of grace among the Gentiles will one day serve to provoke Israel to jealousy and be instrumental in God's saving work among them (Rom 11:31-32). Likewise, his choosing not to effectively prevent a particular Christian from sinning, in some instance, has a purpose in the larger scheme of God both for that individual and for others, which will some day become apparent to us and will prompt us to glorify God's wisdom and grace.

So it is clear that sanctification cannot be the fruit of a synergistic cooperation between God and human beings, yet God cannot be held accountable for the sin that believers commit. The best way for us to understand this puzzle, I suggest, is my proposal regarding *sufficient* and *efficient* grace. In regard to justification, this proposal helped us to make some sense of God's justice in condemning sinners who do not believe. Simi-

---

[63]In an e-mail message of January 20, 2002 (which I obtained permission to cite), Caneday writes, "The issue is addressed by Paul again in Colossians 1:28-29 where he says, 'We proclaim him, admonishing and teaching everyone with all wisdom, so that we may present everyone perfect in Christ. To this end I labor, struggling with all his energy, which so powerfully works in me.' If Paul's labors as an apostle, on behalf of the sanctifying of others, are completely grounded in a non-synergistic way in God's grace, then surely his labors to the same end for himself are also non-synergistically grounded in God's grace alone. For all that he does he does by God's grace. Therefore, we have no problem at all in affirming that to whatever degree we are sanctified it is wholly accountable to God's grace working in us. For Paul makes it clear to us that we do not all receive the same measure of grace but that God who gives grace to us gives the effects of his grace, namely, varying measures of faith, to different individuals: 'For by the grace given me I say to every one of you: Do not think of yourself more highly than you ought, but rather think of yourself with sober judgment, in accordance with the measure of faith God has given you' (Romans 12:3)."

larly, concerning sanctification, we find in my proposal a construct within which believers are justly held accountable for their continuing acts of sin, even though God has deliberately not yet made them perfect. Helpfully, John Piper suggests that

> God has the capacity to look at the world through two lenses. He can look through a narrow lens or through a wide-angle lens. When God looks at a painful or wicked event through his narrow lens, he sees the tragedy or the sin for what it is in itself and he is angered and grieved. "I do not delight in the death of anyone, says the Lord God" (Ezek 18:32). But when God looks at a painful or wicked event through his wide-angle lens, he sees the tragedy or the sin in relation to everything leading up to it and everything flowing out from it. He sees it in all the connections and effects that form a pattern or mosaic stretching into eternity. This mosaic, with all its (good and evil) parts, he does delight in (Ps 115:3).[64]

I suggest that what makes the deeds of sin both tragic and sinful is that they are committed by individuals who are justly held accountable for their acts, an accountability possible only when we assume the gracious enablement that I have described as *sufficient accompanying grace.* Given these factors, we have some understanding of why "God can both grieve over the unholy speech of his people (Eph 4:29-30) and take pleasure in them daily (Psa 149:4)."[65]

Going back to the statements made by Hoekema and Ryle, it is evident that the synergistic note in their description of sanctification derives from a legitimate concern to hold believers responsible for their shortcomings. Ryle wants to make sure that we do not blame God for our not being more holy. (One is reminded of Paul's discussion of anticipated objections to electing grace in Romans 9.) For the holiness we do achieve, the glory must go to God; but for the ways in which we fall short of God's demands, we must take the blame. Our disobedience cannot be charged to God's failure to provide us with grace sufficient to enable us to obey.

Once again, then, I find it helpful to think in terms of God's *always* enabling believers to do the right thing. There is a sufficient enabling grace for sanctification that is universal within the community of faith, just as there is a sufficient enabling grace for justification that is universal within the human race. But God does not give the same measure of faith to all. We *could* all be perfect, in the sense that our imperfection cannot be charged to

---

[64]Piper, "Are There Two Wills," p. 126.
[65]Ibid., p. 127.

God but is blamed against us. We fail to respond to or "use" the grace that God gives us, which is not in any way deficient for our perfection. We are guilty of sinful disobedience precisely because there is an important sense in which we *could* have resisted sin, given God's grace to us in that instance. Nevertheless, our actual obedience is only secured when God effectively graces us to that end. It is in this sense that Scripture speaks of God's distributing different measures of faith. Whatever good we do, as followers of Jesus, is because God works in us, and so we have nothing of which to boast. Whatever evil we do, on the other hand (contra Pinnock's reading of the position of theological determinism), is sin for which we are responsible because we failed to appropriate the enablement of God, which was sufficient. None of us is ever tempted or tried beyond our strength; God provides a way out (1 Cor 10:13). I take this to be a statement concerning the sufficiency of his grace in the midst of our experiences of testing and temptation. If we fail to take that way out, we are to blame. Should we triumph over sin on that occasion, we will give praise to God for his deliverance, recognizing that we did not fall only because we were upheld by the effective grace of God.

Intriguingly, Donald Bloesch has suggested that "Lutherans are often better than Calvinists in affirming the paradox of divine agency in the procuring of salvation and human responsibility for the loss of salvation."[66] It is precisely this tightrope that I am trying to walk safely in this discussion. When contemplating sanctification, it is important that we recognize the limits of our perspective both on our own growth in holiness and on that of others.[67] We must measure ourselves against Christ, not against one another. If holiness is a measurable quantity, it is certainly not one that *we* can measure with any sort of accuracy. God is at work in each of his children in distinctive ways, both providentially and in saving grace, and no two lives can be compared. This prevents us from ever considering ourselves more holy than other people and forbids us to pass judgment on how holy or unholy another person is. We may, of course, recognize particular acts of sin in others, and we may need to help them respond properly. We may also see good works, the fruit of God's grace in the lives of other people in whom God's light shines, and this will cause us to glorify our Father in heaven (Mt 5:16). But to make an overall assessment of the relative sanctification of people, within any sort of comparative ranking, is completely

---

[66]Bloesch, *Holy Spirit*, p. 330.
[67]This point was well made by Caneday in an e-mail message to me on February 2, 2002.

beyond either our capability or our prerogative. Only God sees human hearts (1 Sam 16:7). We will need to keep this in mind not only when we contemplate the lives of other Christians, but also when we encounter people from other religious communities.

SUMMING UP

I hope that my proposal is now clear and that its benefits are evident. I believe that my suggestion is coherent with the overall Calvinist understanding of God's saving work in the world but that it improves significantly on that tradition in regard to God's justice in condemning unbelievers. Those who are not yet convinced that the concept is biblical (in spite of its eminent usefulness!) may wish to visit appendix three, "Scriptural Support for the Concept of Universally Sufficient Enabling Grace."

This chapter brings us to the end of our analysis of the process by which God gives eternal life to sinners. Everyone comes into the world guilty in Adam, and all are spiritually disabled as a consequence of this sinfulness. To redeem a people he had chosen for himself, even before creating them, God sent the Son, who lived a perfect and sinless life, which he gave for the restoration of the new race that was chosen in Christ. The saving effect of Christ's redemptive work only becomes effective in the life of a person, however, when it is appropriated by faith. The faith that unites people to Christ is itself a fruit of Christ's saving work, distributed to the elect by the Spirit of God. God gives everyone revelation of himself and, at some point in the life of each person, the Spirit of God does an inner work of enablement so that one could be saved if one responded to God's revelation with the faith appropriate to the revelation received. Thus, *although all human beings begin their lives as guilty sinners, if they fail to believe and remain in their condemnation, it will be because of their personal resistance to the Holy Spirit's enabling and their refusal to believe God's truth.* On the final day of judgment, each person will account for the deeds done during his or her lifetime. In the lives of those whom God has chosen in Christ, however, the Spirit of God does an effective work of drawing them to God, so that they do believe and are saved by Christ's righteousness. Because the entire saving work is accomplished by God—both objectively in Christ and subjectively through the Spirit—those who come to faith are aware that God has saved them, without any contribution of their own. All the glory is God's.

Suppose, once more, that you are sharing the gospel with an Asian friend, and she wants to know what you can say, from your Christian perspective, about the fate of her ancestors who died without any knowledge of this message that you insist will save her from eternal condemnation, if she trusts in the Jesus of whom you speak. Earlier, I suggested that you can tell her that her ancestors had sufficient revelation to believe and be saved. They may not have known about Jesus, but they were not without knowledge of God, and they will be held accountable for their response to God in the ways in which he revealed himself to them. If you are a monergist, and if you have had sufficient time to talk, your friend will know that you affirm that only those who are effectively enabled by the Spirit of God will believe in God and be saved. So *she may ask how God can hold her ancestors accountable for not believing,* even when they had sufficient revelation, *if they were spiritually unable* to believe in God through it. I suggest that you tell her that at least once (and perhaps many times) in each of her ancestors' lives, God will have accompanied his revelation with an enabling such that the ancestors *could* have believed if they *would* do so. The ancestors will only have believed and been saved if God efficaciously enabled them to do so. But, if not, the ancestors still had an ability to believe—an ability of such a kind that God was justly angry that they suppressed the truth in unrighteousness and refused to believe.

We can all be thankful that although people may suppress God's truth on numerous occasions, even under painful conviction by God's Spirit, God woos an immense number of sinful people until they finally submit, even though it may be at the end of a rebellious life. We may flee God "down the nights and down the days," and "down the arches of the years," and "down the labyrinthine ways" of our own minds until the "hound of heaven" from Francis Thompson's famous poem catches up with us and we discover that it was he whom we were seeking through our many fruitless and unsatisfying quests.[68]

If God gives everyone sufficient revelation to be saved if they respond appropriately, is it still important that we take the gospel to the world? I believe so, and I will make my case in the next chapter.

---

[68]Francis Thompson, "The Hound of Heaven," in *The College Survey of English Literature,* rev. ed., ed. Alexander M. Witherspoon (New York: Harcourt Brace, 1951), pp. 1162-64.

12

Why Should We Send Missionaries?

Thesis 15: Accessibilism is not detrimental to the church's missionary motivation. The point of accessibilism is not to undermine the uniqueness of the gospel or to diminish the necessity of its proclamation; it is to vindicate God's justice toward people who have not heard the gospel. God's ordinary means for saving people, since Pentecost, is through the proclamation of the gospel by the church, empowered by the Spirit. We engage zealously in evangelism out of obedience to the example and request of our Lord and out of our love for Christ and for our neighbor. Above all, we do Christian mission for the glory of God whose name will be magnified by those who come to know him as Father. Although God may be saving people beyond the reach of the church's gospel proclamation, he desires for them a fullness of life, here and now, that is impossible apart from full knowledge of Christ's bless-ings and life in a community of followers of Jesus.

Thesis 16: Scripture is silent about the final numbers of the saved relative to the unsaved, but we have reason to be very hopeful concerning the proportion of the human race that will enjoy life with God in the glorious new earth that he plans to bring about when his redemp-tive program is complete.

I HAVE LAID OUT AN ACCESSIBILIST UNDERSTANDING of God's saving program in the world, and I know from previous experience that this will raise concerns in some people's minds about the church's motivation for mission. In this chapter, I want to identify those fears and face them squarely, and I want to see whether there is an intrinsic incoherence be-tween the missionary mandate and the proposal that God may save some people without the efforts of the church. Then, I will lay out reasons for still pursuing global evangelism energetically.

CHRIST'S MANDATE TO THE CHURCH

In the first chapter, I gave you some background on my own involvement in and commitment to Christian mission, but I want to be very clear at the outset of this chapter that I believe evangelism to be an essential activity of Christian congregations, as mandated by our Lord (Mt 28:18-20; Mk 16:15; Lk 24:47; Jn 20:22-23; Acts 1:8). The church exists as the eschatological community in the world, and we point to the rule of God when we gather for worship, when we live as a community in the world and when we exercise a prophetic function through the reconciled human social relationships that God creates within the church.[1] But our mission is more than this powerful presence in the world; for it also involves proclamation of the good news concerning the kingdom of God.

The ministry of Jesus, who is the pattern for our own ministry, was strongly evangelistic; all three Synoptic Gospels summarize his ministry in terms of preaching the gospel (Mt 4:23; Mk 1:14-15; Lk 4:14-21).[2] Just before Jesus left the earth, the disciples asked him about his schedule for the kingdom. In response Jesus reconfirmed the commission he had given them previously; this was to be their (and our) major task in the interim before he returned to set up his kingdom in a more visible, tangible way. The disciples of Christ's church are those who bear witness to God's lawcase against the nations and their idols (cf. Is 41:21-22; 43:9-10).[3] Jesus was the faithful witness (Rev 3:14) who vindicated God's cause and bore truth to the Father's word and works. To the church, Christ gave the Spirit, who is both attorney and witness; he convicts the world of sin, righteousness and judgment, and he leads believers into all truth (Jn 16:8, 13). The church proclaims the apostolic witness found in the New Testament, and the Spirit continues to empower that witness (Acts 5:32). "The exalted Jesus continues to preach through the proclamation of the church (Eph 2:17)."[4]

THE FEAR THAT ACCESSIBILISM WILL UNDERMINE THE CHURCH'S MOTIVATION FOR SACRIFICIAL MISSION

Among mission leaders, in particular, I sense a fear that if we could not as-

---

[1]Stanley J. Grenz, *Theology for the Community of God* (Nashville: Broadman & Holman, 1994), p. 655.

[2]Everett Ferguson, *The Church of Christ: A Biblical Ecclesiology for Today* (Grand Rapids, Mich.: Eerdmans, 1996), p. 284.

[3]Edmund P. Clowney, *The Church,* Contours of Christian Theology, ed. Gerald Bray (Downers Grove, Ill.: InterVarsity Press, 1995), p. 47.

[4]Ferguson, *Church of Christ*, p. 286.

sure churches that everyone is lost who does not hear about Jesus from the lips of a human missionary, then the churches would be unprepared to make the sacrifices necessary to get the gospel to everyone in our generation and to those in every generation until the Lord returns. Such concern is noted, for instance, in the Manila Declaration of June 1992. Having stated that consensus was not achieved on the possibility of salvation for the unevangelized, the delegates said, "We agreed that our discussion of this issue must not in any way undercut the passion to proclaim, without wavering, faltering or tiring, the good news of salvation through trust in Jesus Christ."[5] To this, we can say a hearty "Amen!"

At the Iguassu Consultation in Brazil, in 1999, animated discussion followed Christopher Wright's expressed hope that the World Evangelical Fellowship (now the World Evangelical Alliance) would "have room for differences of opinion" on the issue of whether people must know about the sacrifice of Christ in order for it to be effective in their salvation. David Neff reported that consultation participants were asking, "Doesn't openness to some being saved outside of personal knowledge of Jesus cut the nerve of missions motivation?"[6] A pastor writes with considerable alarm:

> The modern church would do well to define clearly its position on the eternal destiny of those people who never hear the gospel. If they will be saved apart from the preaching of the gospel, then the very foundations of the traditional, conversionist missionary enterprise are stripped of legitimacy.[7]

Unquestionably, the ecclesiocentric conviction that people could not be saved apart from their hearing the gospel has been widely used by evangelical churches to motivate their members to missionary work since the great thrust that began in the nineteenth century, although it apparently did not have so large a role in missionary motivation prior to that time.[8] Harold Netland writes:

> Protestants maintained that those apart from the gospel of Jesus Christ were

[5]Harold Netland, *Encountering Religious Pluralism: The Challenge to Faith and Mission* (Downers Grove, Ill.: InterVarsity Press, 2001), p. 49.
[6]David Neff, "Much Ado About Footnotes." This article was previously available at <http://www.worldevangelical.org> but is no longer posted.
[7]Greg D. Gilbert, "The Nations Will Worship: Jonathan Edwards and the Salvation of the Heathen," *Trinity Journal*, n.s., 23 (spring 2002): 54.
[8]John Sanders told me (in an e-mail message on July 31, 2002) of a D.Min. dissertation in missiology that studied missionary motivation after the Reformation and found that ecclesiocentrism (which he dubbed "restrictivism") was not a prominent motivation until the late nineteenth century.

forever lost, and it was this assumption that drove early missionaries to
bring the gospel of Christ to the remote peoples of China, Africa, Latin
America and the islands of the Pacific. Hudson Taylor, the great missionary
to China, vividly expressed this perspective in his challenge to the Student
Volunteer Movement in Detroit in 1894: "There is a great Niagara of souls
passing into the dark in China. Every day, every week, every month they are
passing away! A million a month in China they are dying without God." One
simply cannot understand the remarkable Protestant missionary effort of the
nineteenth century, including the work of missionary pioneers such as William Carey, Adoniram Judson, David Livingstone and Hudson Taylor, without appreciating the premise underlying their efforts: salvation is to be
found only in the person and work of Jesus Christ, and those who die without the saving gospel of Christ face an eternity apart from God.[9]

EVANGELISM: GOD'S NORMAL OR ORDINARY MEANS OF SALVATION

The ordinary and the extraordinary means of salvation. Gordon Smith
suggests that it is helpful to distinguish between the main plot and the
subplot of the story. The main plot running through Scripture is surely that
God is at work through Christ and in his church. Even if there were pagan
saints, faithful outside of the covenant who are recognized by God, this
would at most be a subplot. The central theme is that we are to proclaim
the gospel and invite people into the kingdom that is embodied in the
community of God's people.[10]

As I have noted earlier, Calvinist theologians have frequently spoken in
decidedly ecclesiocentric language, but many of them stop short of absolutely denying the possibility that some of God's elect might be among the
unevangelized, even though this would be an *extraordinary* thing in God's
saving program. Loraine Boettner, for instance, a champion of five-point
Calvinism, states that "the Christian Church has been practically of one
mind in declaring that the heathens as a class are lost," and then he goes
on to cite numerous biblical texts to demonstrate that "such is the clear

---

[9]Netland, *Encountering*, p. 27. The Hudson Taylor quote is taken from Grant Wacker, "Second Thoughts on the Great Commission: Liberal Protestants and Foreign Mission, 1890-
1940," in *Earthen Vessels: American Evangelicals and Foreign Missions, 1880-1980*, ed. Joel A.
Carpenter and Wilbert R. Shenk (Grand Rapids, Mich.: Eerdmans, 1990), p. 285.

[10]Gordon T. Smith, "Religions and the Bible: An Agenda for Evangelicals," in *Christianity and
the Religions: A Biblical Theology of World Religions*, Evangelical Missiological Society Series,
ed. Edward Rommen and Harold Netland (Pasadena, Calif.: William Carey Library, 1995),
2:26.

teaching of the Bible."[11] But Boettner concludes his biblical demonstration with this statement: "The Scriptures, then, are plain in declaring that under *ordinary* conditions those who have not Christ and the Gospel are lost."[12] Furthermore, he says,

> We do not deny that God can save some even of the adult heathen people if He chooses to do so, for His Spirit works when and where and how He pleases, with means or without means. If any such are saved, however, it is by a miracle of pure grace. Certainly God's ordinary method is to gather His elect from the evangelized portion of mankind, although we must admit the possibility that by an *extraordinary* method some few of His elect may be gathered from the unevangelized portion.[13]

The Church of Scotland's Declaratory Act (1879) had used similar terminology: "While none are saved except through the mediation of Christ . . . it is not required to be held that . . . God may not extend his grace to any who are without the pale of ordinary means, as it may seem good in his sight."[14] Additionally, J. O. Buswell Jr. cited the 1581 Leiden Synopsis as follows:

> God does not always supply the two methods of calling possible to Himself (i.e., outward and inward calling), but calls some to Him only by the inner light and leading of the Holy Spirit without the ministry of His outward Word. This method of calling is of course *per se* sufficient for salvation, but very rare, extraordinary, and unknown to us.[15]

The issue of the possible salvation of the unevangelized is of great importance because of their great numbers. Neal Punt writes:

> It is conservatively estimated that throughout all of history 75 percent of those who have lived and died have never heard the gospel. Reasonable estimates range as high as 90 percent. . . . Whatever the estimated numbers are, we know that millions of people have lived and died without hearing the

---

[11]Loraine Boettner, *The Reformed Doctrine of Predestination* (1932; Philadelphia: Presbyterian & Reformed, 1974), p. 118.

[12]Ibid., p. 119, emphasis mine.

[13]Ibid., pp. 119-20.

[14]Church of Scotland's Declaratory Act para. 4, quoted in John Sanders, *No Other Name: An Investigation into the Destiny of the Unevangelized* (Grand Rapids, Mich.: Eerdmans, 1992), pp. 143-44.

[15]Leiden Synopsis (1581; sixth edition, 1652), quoted in Heinrich Heppe, *Reformed Dogmatics,* trans. by G. T. Thompson (London: Allen & Unwin, 1950), p. 514, quoted in J. O. Buswell Jr., *A Systematic Theology of the Christian Religion* (Grand Rapids, Mich.: Zondervan, 1963), p. 161.

gospel. In spite of our best efforts there will be millions more who, through no fault of their own, will live and die without being exposed to the gospel of Jesus Christ in a meaningful way.[16]

Since the incarnate Word is no longer visibly present on earth, the inspired Scriptures are the normal and normative means of God's self-disclosure. It is the preaching of this Word, accompanied by an inner witness of the Spirit (1 Cor 12:3; Tit 3:5), that God has designated as his normal means of bringing people to saving faith (Mt 24:14; 28:19-20; Rom 10:13-17). The church's proclamation of the gospel is, therefore, the major instrument that God is now using to bring people into union with Christ, thus adding them to the church as further witnesses to his grace (Acts 1:8; 2:40-47).

The church continues to proclaim the gospel with the confidence evidenced by Peter that all who repent and believe in Jesus (which they signify by baptism) will receive the promised Holy Spirit and the forgiveness of sins (Acts 2:38). This is a promise whose efficacy persists throughout all generations (Acts 2:39). In one of the most memorized verses of the Bible, Jesus himself had promised that "everyone who believes in him" will not perish but will have eternal life (Jn 3:16).

The sad corollary of that wonderful promise, however, is that those who reject Jesus continue in the state of condemnation as sinners before God (Jn 3:18-19). It is on this latter truth that Christians have often made a very significant mistake and have inferred from the passage something that the text does not teach. What Jesus tells us is that when people are confronted by him (as happens when he is intelligibly proclaimed) and respond in disbelief and rejection, that disbelief compounds their already condemned state. The text clearly assumes that people have a knowledge of Jesus. It says nothing at all, however, about those who are not rejecting Jesus or failing to believe in him because they have never heard of him. Two truths are affirmed: those who respond to Jesus in faith will be saved; and those who respond to Jesus in disbelief will continue in condemnation. Light has come to them and they have preferred darkness because their deeds are evil (Jn 3:19-20). In addition to these two truths, a third inference from the text has frequently been drawn: anyone who does not believe in Jesus is condemned. This is assumed to be the case even when people are ignorant of Jesus, but that assumption is an illegitimate extension of the intent of the passage. Jesus speaks very

---

[16]Neal Punt, *What's Good About the Good News? The Plan of Salvation in a New Light* (Chicago: Northland, 1988), p. 79.

specifically to this matter, on another occasion, when he says, "If I had not come and spoken to them, they would not have sin; but now they have no excuse for their sin" (Jn 15:22).

As D. A. Carson rightly asserts:

> The idea is not that if Jesus had not come the people would have continued in sinless perfection—as if the coming of Jesus introduced for the first time sin and its attendant guilt before God. . . . Rather, by coming and speaking to them Jesus incited the most central and controlling of sins: rejection of God's gracious revelation, rebellion against God, decisive preference for darkness rather than light.[17]

It is those who receive the light and prefer the darkness that are described in these words of Jesus, not those who have no knowledge of the light that came into the world in Jesus. Misunderstanding this critical difference has an unfortunate impact on the position one takes concerning the fate of the unevangelized.

The point of Romans 10. Romans 10 deserves very careful examination because it is a text that has been widely used within the evangelical tradition of missionary motivation to argue for the necessity of the preaching of the gospel for people to be saved. The conclusion has often been drawn that no one can be saved unless this gospel is heard from missionaries and is believed. I have preached this message myself in missionary conferences. Unfortunately, as I later came to realize, this use of the text distorts it from its context in Paul's letter. Briefly, let's examine Paul's point in his own situation and then see what we may and may not infer from his original teaching. In Romans 9:30—10:21, Paul is struggling with the tragedy that a large portion of his people Israel have not believed in Jesus as Messiah, whereas many Gentiles have. Frank Thielman sums up Paul's concern well:

> In 9:30—10:4 Paul has attempted to explain why believing Gentiles, once "no people" (9:25-26), now predominate among God's people, while Israel's representation has been reduced to a remnant. His explanation pictures two races, one in which Gentiles win the prize of "righteousness by faith" and one in which Israel fails to reach the goal of the law. Paul briefly describes the Gentiles' success in 9:30 and then discusses Israel's failure at length in 9:31—10:4. Israel's race involved the proper pursuit of the law, but Israel did not attain the "law" because it stumbled over the gospel and therefore over

---

[17]D. A. Carson, *The Gospel According to John* (Grand Rapids, Mich.: Eerdmans, 1991), p. 526.

the winning-post of the race, the prize toward which the law pointed. Instead of recognizing the end of the race as God had designed it, Israel continued to run along its own course, in its own works and by its own righteousness.[18]

Paul goes on to describe the "righteousness that is by faith" and argues that, on this matter, "there is no distinction between Jew and Greek . . . for, 'Everyone who calls on the name of the Lord shall be saved' " (Rom 10:12-13). Verse 13 concludes with a quotation from Joel 2:32 that Paul applies to the invocation of the exalted Christ, which, in its Old Testament context, was a promise that all who call upon the name of the Lord (Yahweh), in the Day of the Lord will be saved.[19] C. E. B. Cranfield aptly states the point that is being made in the much cited verses (Rom 10:14-15):

> At this point Paul is concerned to show that the Jews have really had full opportunity to call upon the name of the Lord in the sense of vv. 12 and 13, and are therefore without excuse. That all along the law which was constantly on their lips was pointing to Christ, that all along He had been its innermost meaning, did not by itself constitute this full opportunity. The fullness of opportunity was not present for them until the message that the promises have indeed now been fulfilled had actually been declared to them by messengers truly commissioned for the purpose by God Himself. Paul makes his point by asking the question whether this fullness of opportunity has really been present for the Jews by means of this chain of related questions, and then answering in the affirmative in v. 15b.[20]

Paul's argument is that in the case of the Jewish people, by and large, three of the necessary conditions for salvation had been met: God had commissioned messengers, the messengers had preached and their "report" (cf. Is 52:7) had been heard. But in spite of this, Israel had not believed, and so the final necessary condition had not been fulfilled. A possible explanation for Israel's unbelief in the Christ might have been that they had not heard, but Paul states strongly that this is not the case: "Have they not heard? Indeed they have" (Rom 10:18).

To describe the extent of the proclamation of the gospel concerning Jesus, which should have elicited faith and led to salvation, Paul cites from

---

[18]Frank Thielman, *Paul and the Law: A Contextual Approach* (Downers Grove, Ill.: InterVarsity Press, 1994), p. 208.

[19]C. E. B. Cranfield, *A Critical and Exegetical Commentary on the Epistle to the Romans,* International Critical Commentary (Edinburgh: T & T Clark, 1979), 2:532.

[20]Ibid., 2:533.

the Septuagint version of Psalm 19:4. These words, as used by the psalmist, referred to the universal self-revelation of God in his creative work. Paul does not quote it as a proof-text or as a fulfilled prophecy (note the absence of specific reference to Scripture), but he uses the words to refer to the Christian mission to the diaspora.

> This outreach had been going on for about 20 years, and since the Jerusalem agreement in a more systematic way (Gal 2:9—probably about 7 years earlier). And if his own tactics as apostle to the Gentiles were typical of the gentile mission as a whole (Jew first and also Gentile), the outreach to the diaspora must have been considerable (the implication of Rom 15:20-24 is that in Paul's view only the western regions of the Roman Empire remained so far untouched). Consequently there must have been few diaspora synagogues within the Roman Empire or Parthia which had not heard something of the claims made about Messiah Jesus. Allowing for an element of hyperbole in the psalmist's language, Paul's answer is clear and justified: it [the unbelief of Israel] cannot be explained or excused on the grounds that they have never had the opportunity to believe.[21]

John Calvin's commentary on Romans 10:14 is both interesting and significant. Calvin observes that it is "necessary to have the word, that we have a right knowledge of God."[22] But notice how Calvin continues:

> No other word has he [Paul] mentioned here but that which is preached, because it is the *ordinary* mode which the Lord has appointed for conveying his word. But were any on this account to contend that God cannot transfer to men the knowledge of himself, except by the instrumentality of preaching, we deny that to teach this was the apostle's intention; for he had only in view the *ordinary* dispensation of God, and did not intend to prescribe a law for the distribution of his grace.

J. N. D. Anderson notes that "Calvin does not specify in what ways (other than preaching the gospel) God may sometimes, in his grace, 'instil a knowledge of Himself,' " and Anderson does not want to suggest that Calvin would have approved of Anderson's own accessibilist proposal. Nevertheless, I agree with Anderson that "we cannot doubt, however, that God can— and sometimes does—communicate directly with individuals."[23]

---

[21]James D. G. Dunn, *Romans 9-16*, Word Biblical Commentary (Dallas: Word, 1988), p. 630.

[22]Quotations are taken from *Calvin's Commentaries* (Wilmington, Del.: Associated Publishers & Authors, n.d.), pp. 1469-70, emphasis mine.

[23]J. N. D. Anderson, *Christianity and World Religions: The Challenge of Pluralism* (Downers Grove, Ill.: InterVarsity Press, 1984), p. 150.

To insist that Romans 10:14-15 teaches an exclusive instrumentality of the preached gospel in God's saving program would require one to deny that saving faith is ever elicited by the many instances of God's direct encounter with individuals. Ecclesiocentrists would likely see those instances as pre-evangelistic, but I see no reason to insist that saving faith could not be elicited by the Holy Spirit in these cases, even if God may later bring knowledge of the gospel to these people. We know only of those to whom this has happened; others, who may never have gotten the gospel, are necessarily unknown to us.

In Romans 10:19-20, Paul then goes on to demonstrate that his people have "ignored so many of its own scriptures which are now being fulfilled in Israel's rejection and the nations' acceptance of the word of faith."[24] If the Gentiles, who are a "no-people," have believed, it can certainly not be argued that Israel has not heard. As Cranfield sadly notes, "The ignorance which is blameworthy has been characteristic of them; but the ignorance which would have constituted an excuse they cannot claim."[25] For as Cranfield says concerning Romans 10:18, "had the Jews not heard, they would have had an excuse for their not having believed"[26] (cf. Jn 15:22). Paul's point is that Israel is without excuse for their failure to experience the "righteousness that is by faith" in Jesus because the gospel was taken to them by divinely commissioned preachers and they refused to believe. Paul is not making a statement about whether they would have been guilty of unbelief if they had not heard the gospel. The point is that they *did* hear it and so they were guilty.

The basic principle of salvation by faith, which comes by hearing the "word," applies to *all forms* of revelation. As indicated above, however, there is no one who lives without receiving some form of divine self-revelation. To infer from Romans 10 that only through hearing the gospel concerning Jesus can people be saved is to beg the question at issue, namely, the salvific value of other forms of revelation. In the case of the Jewish people of whom Paul is thinking, that revelation had included the gospel concerning Jesus. Obviously, that was not true of people in the Old Testament who were, nevertheless, saved through calling on Yahweh. Could the Jews have been saved if Christ had died but they had not yet heard about him? And if they could have, what about the Gentiles who did not have the

---

[24]Dunn, *Romans 9-16*, p. 631.
[25]Cranfield, *Critical and Exegetical Commentary*, 2:538.
[26]Ibid., 2:537.

privileges of the law and covenants of promise that Israel had? Romans 10:14-15 ought not to be cited as clearly excluding all the unevangelized from salvation on the ground that the conditions of hearing the gospel have not been met. Paul was not addressing that issue at all. He was describing how it is that Israel is without excuse for not having attained the righteousness that comes by faith in Jesus, because they *have heard* the gospel but have not believed it.

Of course, we must be clear about what constitutes a "hearing" of the gospel. Bruce Nicholls points out that "to have heard the gospel does not mean to have heard it once, but rather to the point of understanding where the hearer recognizes that Jesus demands a decision for or against him."[27] Speaking from his many years of missionary work in north India, Nicholls observes that

> the goal of their search is to "see" God, not merely hear God. They are in search of experience and reality. Thus, unless those who have never heard the Gospel, can see the Gospel in the lives of those who tell it they are unable to hear it. A knowledge of the faith and evangelistic strategies are no substitute for the incarnational life of those who proclaim it.[28]

Consequently, we have to be very careful not to assume that those who have rejected messengers of the gospel, or who have rejected the *particular* message they actually heard, have rejected Jesus. We must also take into account that an illuminating work of the Holy Spirit is necessary for human understanding of Jesus to take place. Only God knows the hearts of those who hear the gospel message; only he knows who among them is resisting and rejecting the understanding of Christ that the Spirit of God is making clear to their minds.

THE CHURCH'S MOTIVATION FOR EVANGELISTIC MISSION

In spite of my conclusion that God has not restricted his saving work to the church's obedience to its missionary mandate, I believe that the church still has very strong motivation for evangelism and mission. We should not fear that churches will lose the heart for mission work if they believe that God can save some people without their evangelistic help.

Incorrect motivation. Millard Erickson makes the helpful observation

---

[27]Bruce Nicholls, "The Exclusiveness and Inclusiveness of the Gospel of Jesus Christ," in *Salvation: Some Asian Perspectives*, ed. Ken Gnanakan (Bangalore: Asia Theological Association, 1992), p. 34.
[28]Ibid.

that "the missionary endeavor is a means to an end, not an end in itself, although those personally involved in missions sometimes express themselves as if the latter were the case."[29] He goes on to warn that we should not fall into a pragmatic view of truth, affirming an ecclesiocentric theory of salvation simply because it is an effective means to the desired end of motivating people to missionary effort.[30] Ecclesiocentrists who argue for the necessity of evangelization to salvation on the grounds that it provides the greatest motivation to missionary activity ought to logically appropriate also the "church dominion model" of providence and prayer. In that model, God has chosen to do only what members of the church ask him to do, as a means of training us to regain the dominion that was lost in the Fall in Eden. It is hard to imagine a model of divine providence that offers greater motivation to prayer.[31] But if effectiveness in motivation is our only criterion for truth, we are in a dangerous position, as Erickson properly warns.

Although arguing for ecclesiocentrism, John Barrett rejects the proposal "that Christians must not accept any theology that would tend to lessen their zeal to convert people to Christ." He contends, rather, that

> Christians are required to accept a particular theology (if it is biblically sound) irrespective of its perceived consequences. . . . The point is, if after investigation, it eventuates that a fully developed inclusivism [i.e., accessibilism or religious instrumentalism] is a sounder biblical response than (say) restrictivism [i.e., ecclesiocentrism], then Christians will be required to accept that conclusion irrespective of how they might feel it undermines evangelism.[32]

In short, the questions, who can be saved? and, how are people saved? must be answered through careful study of Scripture, unfettered by fears of what consequences might result for Christian mission from any particular conclusion.

Neff has expressed concern about the use of ecclesiocentrism as a primary means of motivating people for missions because it is anthropocentric, focusing on human lostness. Correctly, he asserts that our primary

---

[29]Millard J. Erickson, *How Shall They Be Saved? The Destiny of Those Who Do Not Hear of Jesus* (Grand Rapids, Mich.: Baker, 1996), p. 255.

[30]Ibid., pp. 255-56, 269.

[31]See Terrance Tiessen, *Providence and Prayer: How Does God Work in the World?* (Downers Grove, Ill.: InterVarsity Press, 2000). In chapter 6, I describe this model as it is espoused by Paul Bilheimer, Watchman Nee and Brother Andrew.

[32]John K. Barrett, "Does Inclusivist Theology Undermine Evangelism?" *Evangelical Quarterly* 70, no. 3 (1998): 243-44.

motivation must be the glory of God. He believes that it is ultimately "God who gives the gifts of repentance and faith." Consequently, he desires to "exalt the sovereign grace of God in salvation and then get on with the job he has commanded us to do," preaching the gospel to everyone.[33] Lesslie Newbigin observes how Wesley Ariarajah cites the story of Cornelius as evidence that "there is no need to channel God to people; God has direct access."[34] However, Newbigin says,

> Now it is certainly true that this story shows how God's mission is not simply an enterprise of the Church. It is a work of the Spirit who goes ahead of the Church, touches the Roman soldier and his household, prepares them for the message, and teaches the Church a new lesson about the scope of God's grace. But it is a complete misreading of the story to conclude from it that the going of the missionary is unnecessary. On the contrary, if Peter had not gone to Cornelius's house there would have been no conversion and no story. God prepared the heart of Cornelius before Peter came. But God also sent Peter, and Peter had to go and tell the story of Jesus. It was the telling of the story that provided the occasion for the radically new experience which made Cornelius a Christian, and which radically changed the Church's own understanding of its gospel. To use this story to suggest that the missionary journey is unnecessary or even improper is to distort it beyond recognition. It is indeed true, gloriously true, that God goes ahead of his Church. But it is also true that he calls the Church to follow. The Holy Spirit is not domesticated within the Church, but it is through the Church, the company of those (often unworthy like Jonah) who confess Jesus as Lord, that the Spirit brings others to that confession.[35]

David Bosch correctly states that mission is "a divine activity—God manifesting his glory in the sight of the nations by saving his people." But, he continues,

> it is a perversion to suggest if God is the primary "agent" of mission, people are inactive, or vice versa. That would be to argue that God's activity is the enemy of human freedom, that the more one emphasizes God's actions the less one can emphasize ours. Rather, the opposite is true: the more we recognize mission as God's work, the more we ourselves become involved in it. This is what Paul means when he says, "I worked harder than any of [the

---

[33]Neff, "Much Ado," p. 2.

[34]Wesley Ariarajah, *The Bible and People of Other Faiths* (Geneva: World Council of Churches, 1985), p. 17, quoted in Lesslie Newbigin, *The Gospel in a Pluralist Society* (Grand Rapids, Mich.: Eerdmans, 1989), p. 167.

[35]Newbigin, *Gospel,* p. 168.

other apostles]—though it was not I, but the grace of God that is with me" (1 Cor 15:10).[36]

We should not act as though the success of mission is completely dependent on us and our work. This sometimes happens through what Bosch describes as the

> tendency—particularly in Protestant circles—to interpret the Matthean version of the Great Commission (Matt. 28:18-20) primarily as a *command* and, with that, to overemphasize the auxiliary verb "go." . . . This is based on a faulty exegesis. . . . It is also, however, the product of a deficient theology: in semi-Pelagian manner, we tend to prioritize human intervention and relegate the power of God to secondary status.

We must not forget that "the commission proper *follows upon* the promise, in verse 20b, of the abiding presence of him who is the real missionary."[37]

The relative motivational effect of various positions. Erickson grants that "the strongest motivation for evangelism is attached logically to the exclusivist [i.e., ecclesiocentric] view, since without hearing the gospel explicitly, people are eternally lost."[38] But he also insists that "at the same time, it simply is not true that no other view supplies a motive for evangelism and missions." Similarly, John Ellenberger posits that far from cutting the "nerve cord" of missions, "admitting that God is working above and beyond the work of missionaries and pastors enhances our motivation to evangelize the lost."[39]

In chapter eight, I discussed Molinism and pointed out that some have used Luis de Molina's theory that God knows counterfactuals (i.e., things that never actually happen but which would have happened if the circumstances had been different) to support an accessibilist conclusion. They have suggested that God will save the unevangelized whom he knows *would have* believed if they *had been* evangelized. Objections have been raised that this theory diminishes motivation for evangelism, just as other forms of accessibilism do. It might seem that the second Molinist strategy,

[36]David J. Bosch, "Reflections on Biblical Models of Mission," in *Toward the Twenty-First Century in Christian Mission: Essays in Honor of Gerald H. Anderson,* ed. James M. Phillips and Robert T. Coote (Grand Rapids, Mich.: Eerdmans, 1993), p. 184.

[37]Ibid., p. 185.

[38]Erickson, *How Shall They?*, p. 268.

[39]John D. Ellenberger, "Is Hell a Proper Motivation for Missions?" in *Through No Fault of Their Own? The Fate of Those Who Have Never Heard,* ed. William V. Crockett and James G. Sigountos (Grand Rapids, Mich.: Baker, 1991), p. 225.

the one put forward by William Lane Craig, would be less demotivating to mission: Craig posited that no one is unsaved because of a failure to receive the gospel, but ecclesiocentrists have also objected against that view. They have asked, "Why, then, should we engage in the enterprise of world mission, if all the people who are unreached would not believe the gospel even if they heard it?"[40] Craig aptly observes that the question "forgets that we are talking about people who *never* hear the gospel." In the view that he puts forward, "anyone who wants or even would want to be saved will be saved." Thus, those who do not hear the gospel are people who *would* not have believed even if we preached it to them. We can still be strongly motivated, then, says Craig, to be the ones who get the gospel to people whom God knew *would* believe it if they received it.

Nevertheless, I note that while Craig's use of Molinism may not risk cutting the nerve of mission as seriously as opponents fear accessibilism will, it does invalidate the use of the particular message of which ecclesiocentrists are so fond. At missions conferences, these speakers often tell their audience that some people will be lost if we do not get the gospel to them—those who would not have been lost if we had evangelized them. Yet Craig denies that this is true. A ground for motivation certainly remains, he protests, even if it is not the particular one to which appeal is so fervently made by many ecclesiocentric mission speakers.

Perhaps the agnostic approaches the matter of motivation to evangelistic mission from a slightly stronger position than does the accessibilist. J. I. Packer, for instance, has affirmed that "it might be true" that the Spirit of God will bring some people to realize their sin and need for forgiveness and enable them to throw themselves on the mercy of God. He posits, however, that

> we have no warrant to affirm categorically that this is true in the sense of having actually happened to people to whom God's promises never came; nor are we entitled to expect that God will act thus in any single case where the Gospel is not known or understood. Therefore our missionary obligation is not one whit diminished by our entertaining this possibility.
>
> Our job, after all, is to spread the Gospel, not to guess what might happen to those whom it never reaches. Dealing with them is God's business. He is just and also merciful. When we learn, as one day we shall, how He has

---

[40]William Lane Craig, "Politically Incorrect Salvation," in *Christian Apologetics in the Post-Modern World*, ed. Timothy R. Phillips and Dennis L. Okholm (Downers Grove, Ill.: Inter-Varsity Press, 1995), p. 95.

treated them, we shall have no cause to complain. In the meantime, let us keep before our minds humanity's universal need of forgiveness and the new birth, and the graciousness of the "whomsoever will" invitations of the Gospel. And let us redouble our efforts to make known Jesus Christ, who saves all who come to God through Him.[41]

In summing up this comparison of the relative motivational power of the first three theories in my scheme, I want to repeat Craig's observation. It is true that accessibilists cannot use the warning that some people—those who would not be lost if we had preached—will be lost without our preaching. It is further true that agnostics may be able to use that message, at least tentatively. They are not sure that it would happen, but they are also not sure it would not occur. If that one message were the sum and substance of missionary motivation, then ecclesiocentrists are clearly the best suited to stirring up the church for involvement in global evangelism. What I suggest, however, is that we have ample motivation to mission without that ecclesiocentric message and that use of the message might actually have negative consequences for missionary zeal.

The New Testament pattern of motivating for evangelistic work. I find it particularly interesting that the New Testament never used ecclesiocentrism as a motivation for mission, nor does it "make a direct link between missionary motivation and the fear of eternal damnation."[42] Jesus commanded his followers to disciple the nations, and they did so, without any record of his warning them that apart from their gospel preaching no one could be saved. "The apostles did not take it upon themselves to decide that those who did not hear the gospel were lost. Rather, they were simply following Jesus' marching orders."[43] They had also learned from Jesus' own motivation: "They saw their master weeping for the lost and they were driven by the same compassion for those who needed to hear. To them, the task was urgent. The disciples were eager to participate with God in world evangelism—the last great chapter before the coming of Christ (2 Pet 3:11-12)."[44]

No one showed more missionary drive than Paul, but he never speaks

---

[41]J. I. Packer, "What Happens to People Who Die Without Hearing the Gospel?" *Decision,* January 2002, p. 11.

[42]Amos Yong makes this point from his own reading of the New Testament (*Beyond the Impasse: Toward a Pneumatological Theology of Religions* [Grand Rapids, Mich.: Baker, 2003], pp. 51-52).

[43]Erickson, *How Shall They,* p. 260.

[44]Ellenberger, "Is Hell," p. 227.

with any sense of urgency about how people in Spain are dying and going to hell because he has not yet arrived there with the gospel, nor does he urge the Romans to send someone immediately, since he is still unable to go himself. Newbigin notes a difference between the goal of missionary action as generally defined today ("conversion of the greatest possible number of individuals and their incorporation into the Church" or "the humanization of society") and Paul's criterion. He told the Christians in Rome that he had completed his work in the vast region from Jerusalem to the Adriatic and that there was "no further place for me in these regions" (Rom 15:23). Paul had not converted everyone in those regions, but he had "left behind communities of men and women who believe the gospel and live by it. So his work as a missionary is done."[45]

Newbigin finds it "striking, for a modern reader, that [Paul] does not agonize about all the multitudes in those regions who have not yet heard the gospel or who have not accepted it," although Paul did "agonize over the fact that the Jews, to whom the gospel primarily belongs, have rejected it." Yet Paul "is certain that in the end 'the fullness of the Gentiles will be gathered in' and 'all Israel will be saved' (Rom 11:25-26)."[46] In the meantime, Paul considered his missionary task complete because believing communities had been established in the regions that he had visited. In much the same response to Paul's comment in Romans 15:19, Eckhard Schnabel asserts that the early Christians "would not have thought in terms of presenting the Good News to every individual in all the regions of the earth."[47]

Newbigin further addresses the concern about motivation that follows if Scripture does not permit an ecclesiocentric stance.

> But it may be asked: if it is true that those who die without faith in Christ are not necessarily lost, and if it is also true that those who are baptized Christians are not necessarily saved, what is the point of missions? Why not leave events to take their course? In answer to that question, I would refer again to the word of Paul which I quoted earlier, "I do it all for the sake of the gospel, that I may share in its blessings" (1 Cor 9:23). Jesus said as he was on his way to the cross, "Where I am, there shall my servant be" (John 12:26). The one who has been called and loved by the Lord, the one who wishes to love and

---

[45]Newbigin, *Gospel*, p. 121.
[46]Ibid.
[47]Eckhard J. Schnabel, "Mission, Early Non-Pauline," in *Dictionary of the Later New Testament and Its Developments*, ed. Ralph P. Martin and Peter H. Davids (Downers Grove, Ill.: InterVarsity Press, 1997), p. 755.

serve the Lord, will want to be where he is. And he is on that frontier which runs between the kingdom of God and the usurped power of the evil one. When Jesus sent out his disciples on his mission, he showed them his hands and his side. They will share in his mission as they share in his passion, as they follow him in challenging and unmasking the powers of evil. There is no other way to be with him. At the heart of mission is simply the desire to be with him and to give him the service of our lives. At the heart of mission is thanksgiving and praise. We distort matters when we make mission an enterprise of our own in which we can justify ourselves by our works. . . . Mission is an acted out doxology. That is its deepest secret. Its purpose is that God may be glorified.[48]

Ellenberger neatly sums up the factors that "stirred Paul to invest his life in world evangelism":[49]

1. A sense of obligation to God
    a. A trust committed to him (1 Cor 9:16-17)
    b. Obedience to the divine commission (Rom 1:1, 5)
    c. Fear of disappointing his beloved master (2 Cor 5:11)
    d. Speaking in God's stead (2 Cor 5:20)
    e. Reward for labor (1 Cor 3:8-9)

2. A desire to increase God's glory (2 Cor 4:13-15)

3. The rule of God's love in his life (2 Cor 5:14-20)

4. A sense of obligation to people (Rom 1:14-15)

5. A sense of urgency because of the shortness of time (1 Cor 7:29-30)

Of these Pauline motivations, Ellenberger discerns the third, "the rule of God's love," to be primary, because the first two "are an expression of gratitude for Christ's love" and the last two express love "in dedicated service."[50] Whereas the focus of Ellenberger's study was Paul's explicit statements regarding his reasons for evangelistic activity, others have noted the importance of the gospel to Paul and have argued that "the dynamic nature of the gospel is key to understanding what motivated the church to engage in mission."[51]

---

[48]Newbigin, *The Gospel*, p. 127.
[49]Ellenberger, "Is Hell," p. 221.
[50]Ibid.
[51]Robert L. Plummer, "A Theological Basis for the Church's Mission in Paul," *Westminster Theological Journal* 64 (fall 2002): 255. Plummer also lists other studies which have taken note of this theme (p. 255 n. 11).

What is noticeably missing from this carefully constructed list is any hint of ecclesiocentrism, any sense that Paul was stirred to evangelism by a conviction that the unevangelized would certainly all be eternally lost. Paul felt compelled by the love of Christ to proclaim the good news wherever he could because he knew that the gospel "is the power of God for salvation" to both Jew and Gentile and that God had "decided, through the foolishness of our proclamation, to save those who believe" (Rom 1:16-17; 1 Cor 1:21). Commenting on this role of believers within the Pauline mission, Andreas Köstenberger and Peter O'Brien note the way in which Paul stresses "the dynamic, almost personal character of the gospel."[52] The gospel is the means by which God works powerfully in people's lives (cf. Col 1:6, 10; 1 Thess 1:5; 2:13; 2 Thess 3:1-2).

From the words of the Lord to Paul when he told Paul of the task to which he was sending him, Ronald Nash concludes "that *God* does not speak or act like an inclusivist." In Acts 26:17-18, Jesus said to Paul: "I am sending you to open [the Gentiles'] eyes so that they may receive forgiveness of sins and a place among those who are sanctified by faith in me."[53] But it is surely over-reading this text to hear an ecclesiocentric message in the Lord's commission to Paul. No accessibilist questions that God's normative redemptive work in this age is through the gospel proclamation of the church. In conjunction with the preaching of Jesus, the Spirit of God opens sinners' eyes, giving them the repentance that leads to forgiveness of sin, and Christ gives them his Spirit, who unites them to the communion of believers, the church. It is precisely because God has chosen to use the preaching of the gospel to lead sinners from darkness to light, and to build the church, that we must give ourselves unstintingly to that task. That God may be able to save people apart from such human effort should in no way deter us from zealously serving him in the work to which he has called us.

Paul knew that the preaching of the gospel was the means that God planned to use to draw people to himself. But in the writings inspired by the Holy Spirit, Paul never speculated about what would happen to those to whom that gospel was not preached. It was enough that he did what he could and that other believers followed suit (which they did). Along this line, it is interesting to note Newbigin's reasons for finding it difficult to

---

[52]Andreas J. Köstenberger and Peter T. O'Brien, *Salvation to the Ends of the Earth: A Biblical Theology of Mission*, New Studies in Biblical Theology, ed. D. A. Carson (Downers Grove, Ill.: InterVarsity Press, 2001), 11:192.

[53]Ronald Nash, *Is Jesus the Only Savior?* (Grand Rapids, Mich.: Zondervan, 1994), p. 174.

believe that "all who do not accept Jesus as Lord and Savior are eternally lost."[54] If that were true, "then it would be not only permissible but obligatory to use any means available, all the modern techniques of brainwashing included, to rescue others from this appalling fate."[55] But the fallacy in Newbigin's suggestion is rightly pointed out by Carson, since no ecclesiocentrist would actually approve of brainwashing: "The Arminians among them would insist on the importance of free will; the Calvinists, that it is God who saves by the preaching of the Word, so that brainwashing is not only counterproductive but usurps the place of God."[56]

The urgency of mission in accessibilist perspective. If nothing else, we have the necessity of obedience to Christ's command, as Daniel Clendenin points out: "Although our theoretical knowledge of salvific exceptions will always remain ambiguous, our practical obedience to the Great Commission should be decidedly unambiguous."[57] Kenneth Kantzer posited that "Scripture has not given us enough information to resolve" the problem of the fate of the unevangelized. But, he urged,

> While God does not want us to waste time speculating about the fate of those about whom we can do nothing, there is something we can do. And he will hold us responsible for doing it. We can and must, with all our ability and strength, faithfully bear witness by word and life to our next-door neighbor, and to all those whoever and wherever they may be whom we can reach with the gospel. *That* he has revealed, and to that command we must be obedient.[58]

Obedience to Christ should be enough for us, but it is not where we should place our emphasis. Paul pointed to a higher motivation than mere obedience—the love of Christ that compelled him. And we must surely not lose sight of our ultimate goal in life to glorify God. John Stott speaks well to this point:

> Our supreme motivation in world evangelisation will not primarily be obedience to the great commission, nor even loving concern for those who do not yet know Jesus, important as these two incentives are, but first and

---

[54]Newbigin, *Gospel*, p. 173.

[55]Ibid.

[56]D. A. Carson, *The Gagging of God: Christianity Confronts Pluralism* (Grand Rapids, Mich.: Zondervan, 1996), p. 287.

[57]Daniel Clendenin, *Many Gods, Many Lords* (Grand Rapids, Mich.: Baker, 1995), p. 119.

[58]Kenneth S. Kantzer, preface to *Through No Fault of Their Own? The Fate of Those Who Have Never Heard*, ed. William V. Crockett and James G. Sigountos (Grand Rapids, Mich.: Baker, 1991), p. 15.

foremost a burning zeal (even "jealousy") for the glory of Jesus Christ. For God has exalted him to the highest place, and desires everybody to honour him too.[59]

When we stop to consider the matter carefully, there is plenty of motivation for missionary service, even if we abandon an ecclesiocentric understanding of the means God uses for salvation. For starters, we are probably best off viewing all alternate means as unusual (and possibly rare, in the case of adults) evidences that God's grace is not limited to the church, though the church is his primary means of bringing people into the kingdom. Erickson takes this approach, arguing that a wider hope need not undercut missionary work: "Very few, if any, actually come to such a saving knowledge of God on the basis of the natural revelation alone."[60] As John Sanders paraphrases Clark Pinnock on this matter, "All people need the gospel of Jesus. Those who are not seeking God need to be challenged and need to experience messianic salvation in the dimension of Pentecost, to experience the power of Christ and assurance of salvation."[61] Peter Cotterell has also stated this well:

> Christian mission is valid not only because it is commanded, and not only as a rescue from God's judgment. It is valid because only in Christ, in an overt knowledge of the good news, can we hope to live a truly human, meaningful life. . . . All peoples *deserve* to have the good news preached to them because it is good news, not only for the life beyond this one, but for the life we live now.[62]

It is a truly wonderful thing to know ourselves to be God's adopted children (Eph 1:5) and to understand all of the blessings that are ours because of this relationship through Jesus Christ. The abundant life that Christ came to give us starts here; it does not wait for our glorification. Thus, Anderson observes that everyone "needs teaching, heart assurance, and a message he can communicate to others." Anderson asks: "Can we deny others the present experience of joy, peace and power which a conscious knowledge of Christ, and communion with him, alone can bring?"[63]

---

[59]John Stott, *Evangelical Essentials: A Liberal-Evangelical Dialogue* (Downers Grove, Ill.: InterVarsity Press, 1988), pp. 328-29.

[60]Millard J. Erickson, "Hope for Those Who Haven't Heard? Yes, But . . . ," *Evangelical Missions Quarterly* 11 (April 1975): 126.

[61]Sanders, *No Other Name*, p. 263.

[62]Peter Cotterell, "The Unevangelized: An Olive Branch from the Opposition," *International Review of Mission* 77 (January 1988): 134, quoted in Sanders, *No Other Name*, pp. 284-85.

[63]Anderson, *Christianity and World Religions*, p. 155.

By contrast, Nash seems to assume that if people can be saved through general revelation, there is no need for Christian mission; but John Sanders rightly points out that although God does reach people through his witness in creation, "he wants much more for their lives. He desires that we all receive the blessing that can come only through a personal relationship with Jesus."[64] Thus, William Larkin is wrong to say that the whole episode in the house of Cornelius is "superfluous if Cornelius already has salvation."[65] It would, perhaps, be superfluous if eschatological salvation were God's only goal for people, but God not only wanted Cornelius to be "acceptable" in old covenant terms: he wanted him to receive the new covenant gift of the Spirit and to become part of the new covenant people of God in which the wall between Jew and Gentile is broken down.

Paul's passion to "win" as many as possible (1 Cor 9:19-23) is instructive.

> Although the verb to "win" has been taken to refer to Paul's goal of *converting* "as many as possible" (v. 19), including Jews and Gentiles (vv. 20-21), it cannot refer only to their conversion, since in verse 22 he speaks of his aim of winning "the weak," a designation which should be understood of Christians (rather than non-Christians; cf. Rom 5:6) whose consciences trouble them about matters which are not in themselves wrong (cf. 1 Cor. 8). Paul's goal of winning Jews, Gentiles and weak Christians has to do with their full maturity in Christ and thus signifies *winning them completely*. To win Gentiles has to do with his ultimate purpose for them, namely, their being brought to perfection in Christ on the final day. Nothing short of this will fulfill Paul's ambitions for them. Similarly, his goal of winning "weak" Christians has to do with their full maturity and blamelessness at the second coming.[66]

Paul's vision to see Christians brought to full maturity in Christ can obviously be extended to indicate the importance of bringing into the church those whom God has graciously reconciled to himself outside the church, so that they can come to understand the glorious work of God's grace and grow to the full maturity in Christ. It is, after all, one of the tasks of congregations of believers in Christ to nurture one another, through the gifts

---

[64]John Sanders, "Responses," in *What About Those Who Have Never Heard? Three Views on the Destiny of the Unevangelized*, ed. John Sanders (Downers Grove, Ill.: InterVarsity Press, 1995), p. 145.

[65]William J. Larkin Jr., "The Contribution of the Gospels and Acts to a Biblical Theology of Religions," in *Christianity and the Religions: A Biblical Theology of World Religions*, Evangelical Missiological Society Series, ed. Edward Rommen and Harold Netland (Pasadena, Calif.: William Carey Library, 1995), 2:81.

[66]Köstenberger and O'Brien, *Salvation*, 11:181.

given to us by the Spirit, until we all grow up into the fullness of Christ.

Carson cites Peter's words at Pentecost, "Repent, and be baptized every one of you in the name of Jesus Christ so that your sins may be forgiven" (Acts 2:38), and then he asks, "Would an inclusivist assume that all of his hearers *need* to repent and be baptized and have their sins forgiven?"[67] His question is rhetorical and assumes that the answer is "no," but that indicates a faulty understanding of the accessibilist (which he terms "inclusivist") position. On the one hand, we know that God has chosen to use the gospel to lead people to the repentance and faith that are necessary to receive forgiveness of sin. We *should* indeed call on everyone to repent of their sin and to believe in Jesus so that they might be saved in the last day. Even those among Peter's hearers who might have experienced God's old covenant grace needed to move on in new covenant trust in Jesus. To resist the Spirit's conviction and illumination and to spurn Jesus as their promised Messiah would be fatal.

The problem is that Carson stopped too soon in his citation of Peter's words. Not only did Peter promise forgiveness of sins to those who repent and are baptized in the name of Jesus; he also assured them that they would "receive the gift of the Holy Spirit" (Acts 2:38). This is the new covenant blessing that 120 old covenant believers had just received earlier that morning, and Peter urged his Jewish audience to move forward into the experience of that covenant. Peter had no need to know who of his hearers may have been a child of Abraham by faith, saved under the old covenant. He knew that God's redemptive program had moved on and that the way into the full experience of the blessings of the new covenant was through incorporation into the church through the new covenant repentance and faith that were signaled in baptism in the name of Jesus the Messiah. Only those who die in a state of repentance and faith will hear God declare their sins forgiven in the Day of Judgment.

Having asserted that "the church should be seen not so much as the ark of salvation but as the locus of witness to and experience of the fullness of the work of Christ, which is made manifest in Jesus of Nazareth,"[68] William Abraham is quick to assure readers that "it does not follow from this that Christians should in any way or to any degree slacken in their efforts to take the gospel to everyone. Paul sets the pace in this matter," Abraham suggests, because Paul argues

---

[67]Carson, *Gagging of God*, p. 306.
[68]William J. Abraham, *The Logic of Evangelism* (Grand Rapids, Mich.: Eerdmans, 1989), p. 220.

for Abraham as a model of the justified believer, yet he is so keen to see Abraham's descendants become followers of Jesus Christ that he is prepared to be accursed and cut off from Christ for their sake (Rom 9:1-3). His untiring efforts in evangelism and missionary zeal confirm this commitment to take the gospel everywhere.[69]

It is because "God has summed up and concentrated the vastness of his grace in creation and Israel in his action in Jesus of Nazareth" that "the whole world has a right of access to such grace. So generosity and love compel Christians to share the unsearchable riches of Christ."[70] Abraham therefore considers it to be "only right that those who have already responded to the light of God that they have received outside the gospel should know of the true source of that light." Such people "should also have access to the full measure of God's grace and power, which is made available in Jesus Christ"[71] and, I might add, through the distinctive new covenant gift of the Holy Spirit, which we receive as we are incorporated into the body of the risen Christ, the church.

Abraham further proposes that "it is entirely appropriate that those who have rejected God be given the opportunity to respond to him afresh. If God has come to us uniquely in Jesus Christ, then the fullness of God's grace in Jesus may awaken them from sin and bring them to eternal life."[72] From a Reformed perspective, this is not to be construed as indicating that the revelation of God in the gospel has a persuasiveness lacking in other forms of divine revelation, as though the Spirit's inner work were limited to particular means of external self-disclosure. But it conforms with my own argument that God in these days has chosen as his normal means of grace to effectively draw to himself in repentance and faith those whom he chose in Christ before the creation of the world through the church's proclamation of the good news concerning Jesus.[73]

We must also not underestimate the importance of the formation of the church as a community of those who are consciously endeavoring to be obedient to Christ in every avenue of life. Donald Macleod notes that those who are freed from sin by Christ's atoning work

---

[69]Ibid., pp. 220-21.
[70]Ibid., p. 221.
[71]Ibid.
[72]Ibid.
[73]Compare also Ellenberger, "Is Hell," p. 226: "Believing faith, sparked by the preaching of the sent ones, is the normal pattern (Rom 10:14-15)."

become themselves an irresistible force for social change. They can never themselves become oppressors of others; or be cowed into silence by the blusterings of earthly potentates. The saving grace which produces free individuals also produces free communities. . . . The Christian is free: free because Christ has died. It is the life lived out of this freedom (including our prophetic witness, our cross-bearing and our willingness to be nothing) which changes the sinful structures.[74]

This should bring home to us a dimension of God's purpose in the church's evangelistic mission, which is missed if we focus only on the salvation of individuals and assume that our mission work is less important if God can save individuals without it. Wonderful things happen to communities that are transformed by the gospel as they follow Christ together and seek to do his will socially as well as personally. God does not only want to save individuals; he wants to build churches as communities that give the world a small foretaste of the shalom of God that is produced when the kingdom of God breaks into our history. The manifestation of God's gracious work in the life of these communities of the redeemed is itself a powerful witness to the world, which longs for God's shalom, even when they are unable to name it.

Miriam Adeney's discussion of whether Islam nurtures disciples of Jesus is helpful on this point. She posits that

> as long as evangelicals remain fixated on the question of whether someone can be "saved" through another religion, our theology of religions will remain superficial. After all, who knows what God's Spirit does or does not do in human hearts? But if we enlarge the question to whether someone can grow up to maturity in Christ in another religious context, whether someone can become a full-fledged disciple of Christ while worshiping in another faith, then the limitation of other religions and the value of missionary work become clearer.[75]

She goes on to demonstrate that "Islam impeded discipleship in doctrinal, communal and sacramental areas."[76]

We must realize that *the point of accessibilism is not to undermine the*

---

[74]Donald Macleod, *The Person of Christ*, Contours of Christian Theology (Downers Grove, Ill.: InterVarsity Press, 1998), p. 259.

[75]Miriam Adeney, "Rajah Sulayman Was No Water Buffalo: Gospel, Anthropology and Islam," in *No Other Gods Before Me? Evangelicals and the Challenge of World Religions,* ed. John G. Stackhouse Jr. (Grand Rapids, Mich.: Baker, 2001), p. 79.

[76]Ibid.

uniqueness of the gospel or to diminish the necessity of its proclamation; it is to
vindicate God's justice toward people who have not heard the gospel. That distinction may be difficult to maintain, but it is essential if a position such as
I have set forward here is to be affirmed without dulling the church's sense
of urgency for mission. It is to this end that W. G. T. Shedd wrote that the
"extraordinary work of the Holy Spirit" in the salvation of the elect among
the unevangelized is mentioned

> to illustrate the sovereignty of God in the exercise of mercy, not to guide his
> church in their evangelistic labor. His command is, to "preach the gospel to
> every creature." The extraordinary work of God is not a thing for man to ex-
> pect and rely upon, either in the kingdom of nature or of grace. It is his ordi-
> nary and established method which is to direct him. The law of missionary
> effort is, that "faith cometh by hearing, and hearing by the word of God,"
> Rom. 11:17.[77]

Anderson thus draws our attention to God's statement to Paul in Corinth
to not be afraid but to speak "for there are many in this city who are my
people" (Acts 18:10). Concerning this verse, G. Campbell Morgan comments that the words were not spoken of those who were already Christians, but of "those whom his Lord numbered among His own."[78]

Charles Kraft has noted that

> people are lost because they lack the willingness to respond properly to God's
> revelation, not because they lack essential information. The principal prob-
> lem is not ignorance. Consequently, the true purpose for missions is "stimu-
> lating the hearers to action," not just imparting new information. Evangelism
> is important because it challenges people to respond to the gospel.[79]

Calvinists, of course, will assume not that the challenge is itself efficacious
but that God has committed himself to accompany the proclamation of the
Word with a working of his Spirit so that it has a power to pierce the heart
and mind, to bring conviction and elicit faith. God has decided to save
people through faith, in response to "the foolishness [from the perspective
of secular wisdom] of our proclamation" (1 Cor 1:21). But this is not necessarily because they cannot be saved otherwise. When it comes to the ef-

---

[77]W. G. T. Shedd, *Dogmatic Theology* (1888; Grand Rapids, Mich.: Zondervan, 1969), 2:710-11.
[78]G. Campbell Morgan, *The Acts of the Apostles*, 13th ed. (New York: Revell, 1924), p. 334,
quoted in Anderson, *Christianity and World Religions*, p. 155.
[79]Charles Kraft, *Christianity in Culture* (Maryknoll, N.Y.: Orbis, 1979), p. 255, as paraphrased
by Sanders, *No Other Name*, p. 267.

ficacy of God's saving work in people's lives, *more* revelation is not necessarily the answer. This point is also made by the patriarch Abraham, in the story of the rich man and Lazarus. Out of his desire to prevent his brothers from joining him in his torment in Hades, the rich man asked that Lazarus be raised from the dead and sent to warn the rich man's brothers of the destiny toward which they were heading. Abraham replied that the rich man's brothers had Moses and the prophets and that "they should listen to them" (Lk 16:29). The rich man was sure that a messenger who had been raised from the dead would succeed where the Scriptures had failed. Abraham replies that this is not so: "If they do not listen to Moses and the prophets, neither will they be convinced if someone rises from the dead" (Lk 16:31). Neither the persuasiveness of the messenger nor the content of his revelation determines the effectiveness of gospel proclamation. Although the story Jesus told did not make this point, we know from the general witness of Scripture that people are saved because God saves them. He has used various forms of revelation to bring this about, but there is clearly no mathematical progression through which fuller revelation guarantees that a larger percentage of those who receive such revelation will respond in faith.

We can reasonably assume that most of those who live to an age of moral discretion and are saved by God will come into that experience of eternal life through a knowledge of Jesus Christ that is brought to them by human preachers of the gospel. The joy of being God's instruments, of being co-workers with him, in this eternally important task is wonderfully motivating. We plant and we water, but only God can make things grow (1 Cor 3:6-9). Yet, how exciting it is for us when God does produce that growth. It is God's plan, however, to make things grow precisely through our planting and our watering. Although we are rarely given the specific encouragement given to Paul in Corinth—when God assured him that he had many people in that city (Acts 18:10)—we labor in faith that God will indeed use our witness to draw his people to himself.

J. H. Bavinck neatly describes the missionary task in the context of God's gracious work in people's lives:

> When a missionary or some other person comes into contact with a non-Christian and speaks to him about the gospel, he can be sure that God has concerned Himself with this person long before. That person had dealings more than once with God before God touched him, and he himself experienced the two fatal reactions—suppression and substitution. Now he hears the gospel for the first time. As [I have] said elsewhere, "We do not open the

discussion, but we need only make it clear that the God who has revealed
His eternal power and Godhead to them, now addresses them in a new way,
through our words." The encounter between God and that man enters a new
period. It becomes more dangerous but also more hopeful. Christ now appears in a new form to him. He was, of course, already present in this man's
seeking; and, because He did not leave Himself without a witness, Christ
was wrestling to gain him, although he did not know it. John describes this
in a most delicate way: the *Logos* "lighteth every man" and "the light shineth
in the darkness; and the darkness comprehended it not" (John 1:9, 5). In the
preaching of the gospel Christ once again appears to man, but much more
concretely and in audible form. He awakes man from his long, disastrous
dream. At last suppression and substitution cease—but this is possible only
in a faithful surrender.[80]

In the final analysis, of course, what is important is that we grasp the biblical truth about God's ways and means of saving sinners and live accordingly. There is no question that a powerful message of motivation to mission has been found in the statement that no people can be saved unless
human missionaries take the gospel to them. If this statement is not true,
however, it would be wrong for us to use it as a motivator, regardless of its
effectiveness. We need not fear that motivation will be lacking in the ways
that Scripture does genuinely offer it. The fact remains that, in this epoch,
God desires to save people through the proclamation of the gospel and
that he has graciously chosen us to be his co-workers in this wonderful
plan of grace. The timing of his return is related to the completion of the
church's task of evangelism (Mt 24:14; Acts 3:19-21). All those who long for
the Lord's coming in glory will be involved in the task of world evangelism so that the "times of refreshing may come from the presence of the
Lord, and that he may send the Messiah" whom he has appointed (Acts
3:19-20). "Amen. Come Lord Jesus!" (Rev 22:20).

   The danger of attempting to motivate people to mission by insisting
that the unevangelized cannot be saved. I have tried to address the fear
that if the absolute necessity of human gospel messengers is denied,
church members will lose their motivation to be involved in global mission. Another factor needs to be considered, however. It is apparent from
surveys done in churches that large numbers of evangelicals have *not* ac-

---

[80]J. H. Bavinck, *The Church Between Temple and Mosque: A Study of the Relationship Between the*
Christian Faith and Other Religions (Grand Rapids, Mich.: Eerdmans, n.d.), p. 127. Bavinck
takes the quote ("We do not open . . .") from one of his earlier works: *The Impact of Christian-*
ity on the Non-Christian World (Grand Rapids, Mich.: Eerdmans, 1948), p. 109.

cepted the ecclesiocentric message, in spite of the fact that it has been forcefully presented to them by missionaries in their churches. Nash (an ecclesiocentrist himself) estimated, back in 1982, that more than 50 percent of "evangelical leaders in places of denominational or missions leadership along with professors at mainstream evangelical colleges and seminaries" were inclusivist (what I have been calling "accessibilist"), as were "a third or more of nonprofessionals in evangelical churches."[81] If the ecclesiocentric message is true, we must preach it whether or not it is believed. On the other hand, if we have been overzealous in our attempts to motivate people, their refusal to believe the message may actually backfire. If we focus too strongly on a message that they do not accept, we may be in danger of failing to motivate them with a message that conforms better to their intuitions about God's justice and grace and that will therefore be more powerful. Regardless of a particular message's effectiveness in motivating people to mission, we will certainly not want to use it in a manner that misleads people. If my proposal is biblical, we must not speak one truth loudly (namely, that all who believe in Jesus are saved) while denying or ignoring another truth (that God is savingly at work apart from human gospel proclamation), even if partial truth seems to provide better motivation to mission than does the whole truth. We need not fear the truth. The same Spirit whose gracious work is absolutely essential to the salvation of sinners is the Spirit who stirs up God's people to willing service in God's work of reconciling sinners to himself through the good news concerning Jesus. Just as we trust him to empower our proclamation of the gospel, we must trust him to empower our call to involvement in the church's missionary outreach.

We need also to consider the impact of the ecclesiocentric message on two other groups of people: first, people who accept the message as true but who do so with deep-seated doubts about the sort of God who is being presented to them and, second, unbelievers to whom we are presenting the gospel. In the latter group, I mention again the people in many cultures who have very high regard for their ancestors and for whom the thought of being separated from their ancestors if they were to believe in Jesus is a large stumbling block. As I have noted earlier, we cannot say how any individual among their ancestors was related to God, but at least we can assure them that God's means of reaching those ancestors were not limited to the missionary work of churches or the vagaries of governments or

---

[81]Nash, *Is Jesus*, p. 107.

world affairs. I make these last points simply to remind us that the situation with regard to motivation is more complex than has sometimes been assumed by ecclesiocentrists who are concerned that accessibilism will undermine the church's passion for evangelization of the world.

HOW MANY OF THE UNEVANGELIZED MIGHT BE SAVED?

Even if we grant the probability that God saves some of the unevangelized, it is impossible to know the extent to which this may occur. As Erickson observes, it is "possible to be an inclusivist and yet believe that very few if any will actually be saved through these alternate channels," so that "relatively few, overall, will be saved," but it is also "possible to be an exclusivist and to believe in most persons who will ever have lived being saved, if one holds that the exclusive gospel will be preached efficaciously."[82] So the issue between ecclesiocentrists and accessibilists is *not* a difference concerning the relative proportion of the saved and the lost in the final day.

Whether or not one is optimistic about the proportion of the human race that is finally saved is also not determined by whether one is a monergist (e.g., Calvinist) or a synergist (e.g., Arminian). Calvinists can disagree about whether God has elected many or few of the race to salvation, and Arminians can differ about how many will libertarianly freely choose to repent and believe. Nevertheless, if one does conclude from Scripture, as I have done, that God's saving work is not restricted to the church's proclamation of the gospel, the question of how many of the unevangelized might be graciously saved naturally arises.

Despite his speaking in strongly ecclesiocentric words regarding the salvation of adults, Calvinist theologian Boettner includes in his "summary of the Reformed doctrine of election" the optimistic statement that "much the larger portion of the human race has been elected to life." This hopefulness probably rests, however, in his next point, namely, that "all of those dying in infancy are among the elect."[83] With similar hopefulness, Pinnock, an Arminian accessibilist, claims that "salvation is going to be ex-

---

[82]Erickson, *How Shall They,* p. 197.

[83]Boettner, *Reformed Doctrine,* p. 149. One of Charles Spurgeon's arguments for the salvation of those who die in infancy is that Scripture portrays the number of the saved at the end as being so great. He wrote: "I do not see how it is possible that so vast a number should enter heaven, unless it be on the supposition that infant souls constitute the great majority" ("Infant Salvation [Sermon 411]," *Metropolitan Tabernacle Pulpit, 1861* [Pasadena, Tex.: Pilgrim, 1975], 7:505-12; also available at <http://www.spurgeon.org/sermons/0411.htm>).

tensive in number and comprehensive in scope."[84] Although claiming agnosticism as to the method by which God may save the unevangelized, Stott asserts:

> I am imbued with hope. I have never been able to conjure up (as some great Evangelical missionaries have) the appalling vision of the millions who are not only perishing but will inevitably perish. . . . . I cherish the hope that the majority of the human race will be saved. And I have a solid biblical basis for this belief.[85]

On the other hand, as an accessibilist, Clendenin proposes that, "Except for any pious hope we might have about those who have not heard or cannot hear the gospel, we should remain silent as to the particulars of this matter."[86] My own inclination is to be fairly limited in my hopefulness regarding the salvation of unevangelized *adults* prior to the return of Christ, partly because belief in Christ is unusual, even among the evangelized. It would seem surprising if God actually had a larger proportion of elect among the unevangelized than among the evangelized. Nevertheless, Scripture has prepared us to be surprised and delighted on judgment day. As Jesus put it: "Then people will come from east and west, from north and south, and will eat in the kingdom of God. Indeed, some are last who will be first, and some are first who will be last" (Lk 13:29-30).

Three texts—Matthew 7:14; Luke 13:23-24; Matthew 22:14—have classically served to support what B. B. Warfield calls the "dogma of the fewness of the saved."[87] But Warfield is correct, I believe, in contending that

> a scrutiny of these passages will make it sufficiently apparent that they do not form an adequate basis for the tremendous conclusion which has been founded on them. In all of them alike our Lord's purpose is rather ethical impression than prophetic disclosure. . . . What He says is directed to inciting His hearers to strenuous effort to make their calling and election sure, rather than to revealing to them the final issue of His saving work in the world. . . . We can always learn from these passages that salvation is difficult and that it is our duty to address ourselves to obtaining it with diligence and earnest effort. We can never learn from them how many are saved.[88]

---

[84]Clark Pinnock, *A Wideness in God's Mercy: The Finality of Jesus Christ in a World of Religions* (Grand Rapids, Mich.: Zondervan, 1992), p. 135.

[85]Stott, *Evangelical Essentials*, p. 327.

[86]Clendenin, *Many Gods*, pp. 118-19.

[87]Benjamin Breckinridge Warfield, "Are They Few That Be Saved?" in *Biblical and Theological Studies*, ed. Samuel G. Craig (Philadelphia: Presbyterian & Reformed, 1968), p. 337.

[88]Ibid., p. 338.

Jesus' statement concerning the "narrow way" that is found by few has often been cited as indication of the relative "fewness" of the number of those who will finally be saved (Lk 13:23-24). But, as Darrell Bock observes, Jesus "does not describe the number of saved as few, but he shows that people come into blessing from everywhere (13:29), and he suggests that many who thought they were inside will find themselves outside."[89] It is highly doubtful that Jesus intended to make a statement regarding the final numbers of the saved. On the other hand, we must take seriously the clear warning of Jesus that "many, I tell you, will try to enter and will not be able" (Lk 13:24). But note that this is spoken to people who profess to have known Jesus—to have eaten and drunk with him when he taught in their streets (Lk 13:26)—and, hence, it has more to tell us about the importance of a genuine work of grace in true repentance among those who are *within* the visible membership of the Christian church than about those who are ignorant of him. It provides a stronger warning about presuming that Christians are saved than it does a statement about the status of the unevangelized.

Carson observes that Matthew 7:14 establishes proportions and asks, "Are there any texts where the question of *relative* proportions is directly addressed and the proportions go the other way?" He suggests that "the proportionality envisaged by Jesus in this passage is entirely in line with the entire history of the people of God across the Bible's story-line."[90] This is a sobering point, for it is true that the old covenant people were a small proportion of the world population in their day, and the faithful remnant within that people was often perilously small—not as small as Elijah once feared (namely, only himself; see 1 Kings 19:10), but still very small (seven thousand; see 1 Kings 19:18). But, once again, I take Warfield to be right in his conclusion that the point Jesus makes is "that the way of life is hard, and it is our first duty to address ourselves with vigor to walking firmly in it" and that the proportional statement was not an assertion "that in the ultimate distribution of the awards of human life, few are to be found among the saved, many among the lost."[91]

Again, in Matthew 22:14, it is not the Lord's intention to make a statement of the final result of the entire redemptive program. Spoken at the close of Jesus' parable regarding the feast, the phrase is

---

[89]Darrell L. Bock, *Luke* (Grand Rapids, Mich.: Baker, 1996), 2:1234.
[90]Carson, *Gagging of God*, p. 300.
[91]Warfield, "Are They Few," p. 343.

from the standpoint of the moment rather than that of the distant Judgment Day. The bit of history which the parable portrays, however, relates only the contemptuous and ultimately violent rejection of the Kingdom of God by the Jews and the consequent turning to the Gentiles with the result of attracting to it a mixed multitude.[92]

Nevertheless, given the usual minority response to the gospel where it is faithfully proclaimed, I find no biblical warrant for asserting that the proportion of the faithful is now larger among those who do not hear the gospel than among those who hear it. What I am not able to assert, on the basis of Scripture, is that *none* of the elect are to be found among the unevangelized. As to the proportion of the entire human race that will be saved when the final judgment is revealed, I agree with Warfield that the "established dogma" that only few are saved is not biblically supported, despite its widespread acceptance.[93]

Warfield's own optimism was based particularly on his postmillennial expectation that the return of Christ would be preceded by an extended period of time when most of the people on earth would be brought into the kingdom of God through the preaching of the gospel. I do not share Warfield's postmillennial eschatology, but I have previously expressed my doubt about the legitimacy of Iain Murray's suggestion that premillennialism necessarily takes away hopefulness about the success of the church's missionary work.[94] There have been wonderfully fruitful responses to the gospel, at particular times and places, in the history of the church's mission. Given the fact that the Lord has not returned two millennia after promising that he would, we have no way of knowing how long he may yet delay his coming, in order to give time for repentance (2 Pet 3:9).

The majority of the members of the Christian church are now found outside the Western world, which was God's primary instrument for more than a century of evangelistic effort. Who can say what lies ahead as churches in Africa, Asia and South America get even more involved in mission work, both within and outside their continents? We need not assume that the currently discouraging secularization of the West and the relative ineffectiveness of the church within it is indicative of the future.

---

[92]Ibid., p. 345.

[93]Ibid., pp. 334-50.

[94]Iain H. Murray's suggestion is found in *The Puritan Hope: Revival and the Interpretation of Prophecy* (Carlisle, Penn.: Banner of Truth Trust, 1971), p. 198. My doubt concerning his suggestions is expressed in Terrance Tiessen, "The Optimistic Activism of Postmillennial Eschatology," *Didaskalia* 3 (October 1991): 15-20.

The Spirit of God, like the wind, "blows where [and when] it chooses" (Jn 3:8), and we can labor in hope that God will yet breathe his gracious Spirit on the world, in our own day and in the years still to come before the Lord's return, making our planting and watering more fruitful than it has ever been. Given Jesus' statements about how difficult it is to enter into the kingdom of God, about the dangers of presumption and even about the relatively small number who were choosing to follow Christ at the time of his earthly ministry, we need not assume that there will never be a time when large numbers of people will come to faith. As I have said elsewhere, "It is not necessary for us to believe that the millennial reign of Christ is a spiritual reign brought in by the Spirit-empowered preaching of the gospel, prior to Christ's return, in order for us to be optimistic about what the gospel can accomplish in our time."[95]

On the other hand, when considering the final numbers, premillennialists also have reason for the sort of optimism that Warfield finds in postmillennialism. In the long period of time that Christ rules on earth, with ideal physical and spiritual conditions, even though not all will have regenerate hearts, we can look forward to an immense spiritual harvest. Into the picture of the blessed population of the new earth, we must factor the elect from among those who die in infancy. Charles Hodge, a postmillennialist, like Warfield, concludes his three-volume systematic theology with this hopeful judgment: "We have reason to believe as urged in the first volume of this work, and as often urged elsewhere, that the number of the finally lost in comparison with the whole number of the saved will be very inconsiderable."[96] Hodge was convinced that "all who die in infancy are saved,"[97] for he argued that

> the Scriptures nowhere exclude any class of infants, baptized or unbaptized, born in Christian or in heathen lands, of believing or unbelieving parents, from the benefits of the redemption of Christ. All the descendants of Adam, except Christ, are under condemnation; all the descendants of Adam, except those of whom it is expressly revealed that they cannot inherit the kingdom of God, are saved.

It is on this basis, opines Hodge, that the apostle Paul "does not hesitate to say that where sin abounded, grace had much more abounded, that the benefits of redemption far exceed the evils of the fall; that the number of

---

[95]Tiessen, "Optimistic," p. 16.
[96]Charles Hodge, *Systematic Theology* (Grand Rapids, Mich.: Eerdmans, 1946), 3:879-80.
[97]Ibid., 1:26.

the saved far exceeds the number of the lost" (Rom 5:18-19).[98] Hodge takes Matthew 7:14 to be referring only to adults.[99] Similarly, the statement in John 3:3 ("whoever believes in the Son has eternal life; whoever disobeys the Son will not see life, but must endure God's wrath") does not speak of infants. "No one understands this to preclude the possibility of the salvation of infants."[100]

In the opinion of Warfield, however, Hodge threw the "weight of his doctrine too heavily on the salvation of those that die in infancy."[101] Be that as it may, each of us must consider the state of those who die in infancy when considering the proportion of the race who will finally be saved. Even though I have not found clear biblical grounds to assert the salvation of all such people, I have reason to be hopeful of the greatness of God's grace in their case. Putting together the large number of adults who profess faith in Christ in the time before Christ's return, the ideal conditions that will exist during Christ's interim reign, the fact that Scripture does not limit the elect to the evangelized and the vast numbers of those whose relationship to God is hidden from us because of their physical incapabilities (including the aborted, those who die as infants and the cognitively disabled), I am very hopeful concerning the proportion of the human race that will enjoy life with God in the glorious new earth, which God plans to bring about when his redemptive program is complete—when "the kingdom of the world has become the kingdom of our Lord and of his Messiah" (Rev 11:15).

SUMMING UP

God's grace is amazing, and it is a particular wonder that he should have chosen to use us as his normal means of getting the good news concerning Jesus to the ends of the world in these last days. Having sent his Spirit to the church to empower it, Christ now sends us out to be his witnesses. *Nowhere* has Scripture stated that God will not save anyone whom we do not reach with the gospel. But this is insignificant to us, in our obedience to Christ, as we vigorously carry the gospel wherever we can, in hope that God will call out a people for his Name in the places to which we go. Like the apostle Paul, we are not driven by a fear that God cannot save people

---

[98]Ibid.
[99]Ibid., 1:26, 2:648.
[100]Ibid., 1:26.
[101]Warfield, "Are They Few," p. 350 n. 37.

whom the church does not evangelize, but we are compelled by love for God and our neighbor. We have experienced the great blessings in this life that come to us, both individually and in the community of God's people, through the knowledge of Christ and the gift of God's Spirit. Although we anticipate that God has already brought some people into saving relationship with himself before we reach them with the gospel, we long to see them mature in Christ and to see whole societies transformed by the power of the gospel. Indeed, we may hope that God *has* been savingly at work before we arrive with his fuller message, because we know that those who have believed in God's more limited forms of revelation will gladly welcome news of what God has done for them in Christ.

We are given no indication in Scripture as to how large a proportion of the total human population will live in eternal fellowship with God, but we are hopeful that God, who is rich in mercy, will be expansive in his grace. Eagerly, we look forward to the time when we will stand with the redeemed from "every tribe and language and people and nation" (Rev 5:9) and worship the Lamb who was slaughtered because he is worthy "to receive power and wealth and wisdom and might and honor and glory and blessing" (Rev 5:12). We are concerned less with how they get there than with the truth that God wonderfully saves them. Yet I cannot doubt that we will take particular joy in seeing among that great company of God's people those to whom we witnessed, for whom we prayed and to whom we sent missionaries.

PART 2

HOW DO
THE RELIGIONS
FIT INTO
GOD'S PURPOSES
IN THE WORLD?

13

How Do Religions Come into Being?

Thesis 17: Religions develop as inherently religious people respond to God's revelation in the forms that are accessible to them. Consequently, religions are ambiguous constructions, incorporating both the appropriation of divine truth and its suppression, due to human fallenness and demonic deception. The value of religions is therefore measured both by the completeness of the revelation to which they have responded and by the extent to which they have believed and obeyed, rather than suppressed, the truth that God has revealed.

Thesis 18: Among the religions of the world, Christianity has the great advantage of being constructed in response to God's revelation in Jesus Christ and the scriptures of the New and Old Testaments. But, even so, there is no particular communion or congregation of the Christian church that is a pure appropriation of God's revealed truth. As we construct the Christianity that we teach and practice, we must beware of syncretism. Nevertheless, the Christian religion we formulate should be at home in its cultural context to the fullest extent possible while faithfully living out God's revealed truth.

IN SPITE OF THE SECULARIZATION THAT CONTINUES in Western societies, an interest in spirituality is on the increase, and the religions of the world have become more rather than less prominent in our awareness. Agencies of the Christian church carry on vigorous missionary activity, yet large segments of the world remain dominantly non-Christian. What should we make of this? Christian attitudes toward mission and opinions about the status of the adherents of other religions are far from unified. In this second part of the book, I will propose a theology of religions or, as Amos Yong puts it, "an attempt to understand the human ultimate concern within a theistic framework."[1] I am seeking to answer the question, how do the religions fit into God's purposes in the world? Naturally, my perspective is a Christian one, grounded in my reading of biblical teaching, as I will lay out briefly in the next chapter. Consequently, this is a specifically Christian theology of religions, an "attempt to reflect on the relationship between God and the phenomenon of the religions from the standpoint of Christian faith."[2]

Since the definition of religion has itself been a matter of some controversy, it is tempting to leave each reader of this book to consider the subject with his or her own definition in mind. But that may create more problems than it solves, so I will offer a brief description of what I have in mind when I speak of religions. Then, I will review some of the attitudes toward other religions that are commonly found among Christians. Finally, I will unpack the perspective that I find most plausible and coherent with the accessibilism that I have put forward thus far. It is my proposal that *religions come into being as ambiguous responses to divine revelation.* The ambiguity derives particularly from the fact that when people formulate their religious convictions and gather together in religious institutions, demonic deception and sinful human construction are at work, as are God's revelation and grace. I want to propose a framework for understanding the religious situation in the world from the perspective of God's purposes in the world and for relating to the adherents of other religions as unapologetically evangelical Christians.

WHAT I MEAN BY *RELIGION*

Theology focuses on beliefs about God and his relationships to the world, so we can examine the theologies that are operative in particular religions, but we must not reduce religion to theology. Religions encompass more of a person's life and worldview. Millard Erickson suggests that an adequate perspective on religion will include the three aspects that were the exclusive focus of different periods or individuals.[3] In the Middle Ages, Christians thought of religion as *dogma or belief.* Friedrich Schleiermacher, reacting to the threat which Enlightenment rationalism posed to scholastic Christian thought, defined religion as *feeling,* particularly the feeling of ab-

---

[1] Amos Yong, *Beyond the Impasse: Toward a Pneumatological Theology of Religions* (Grand Rapids, Mich.: Baker Academic, 2003), p. 17.
[2] Ibid., p. 14.
[3] Millard Erickson, *Christian Theology* (Grand Rapids, Mich.: Baker, 1984), pp. 18-19.

solute dependence. Immanuel Kant, on the other hand, saw religion as an object of practical reason (because a transcendent object cannot be known theoretically), so that religion becomes *ethics*, a direction largely followed by Albrecht Ritschl. We may note that different religions place a different emphasis on the three factors identified by Erickson but, generally, they all include some beliefs, some feelings or attitudes, and some practices that are considered to be good or moral.

Because humans are creatures in the image of God, we are invincibly religious, a point aptly noted by Paul in his lecture to the "extremely religious" Athenians (Acts 17:22, 26-28). Consequently, it is often difficult to distinguish a people's religion from their culture, especially in situations where secularism has little or no impact. This being the case, anthropologists can be helpful in our task of defining religion. Paul Hiebert, Daniel Shaw and Tite Tiénou claim that "anthropologists now define 'religion' as beliefs about the ultimate nature of things, as deep feelings and motivations, and as fundamental values and allegiances."[4]

Missionary theologian Lesslie Newbigin uses the term *religion* to refer to "all those commitments that, in the intention of their adherents, have an overriding authority over all other commitments and provide the framework within which all experience is grasped and all ideas are judged."[5] This does not differ significantly from the theological and anthropological proposals I have cited, but it captures particularly well what I will have in mind as I speak of *religion*. From this perspective, no one is without a religion, whether or not one identifies oneself with any of the established religious institutions. Most (if not all) of the time, however, in our discussion of religions, I will have in mind those that have a recognizable institutional form and to which people identify themselves as belonging. In most of those situations, the commitments that have an "overriding authority" are derived from the supernatural and are con-

---

[4]Paul G. R. Hiebert, Daniel Shaw and Tite Tiénou, *Understanding Folk Religion: A Christian Response to Popular Beliefs and Practices* (Grand Rapids, Mich.: Baker, 1999), p. 35. They also cite a more complex definition of religion that has been offered by Clifford Geertz: "religion is (1) a system of symbols which acts to (2) establish powerful, pervasive and long-lasting moods and motivations in men by (3) formulating concepts of a general order of existence and (4) clothing these conceptions with such an aura of factualness that (5) the moods and motivations seem uniquely realistic" ("Religion as a Cultural System," in *Reader in Comparative Religion*, 4th ed., ed. William A. Lessa and Evon Z. Vogt (New York: Harper & Row, 1989], pp. 79-80, quoted in Hiebert, Shaw and Tiénou, *Understanding Folk Religion*, p. 35).

[5]Lesslie Newbigin, *The Open Secret: An Introduction to the Theology of Mission*, rev. ed. (Grand Rapids, Mich.: Eerdmans, 1995), p. 160.

nected with "gods." It is this factor that serves as my primary criterion for distinguishing the religious from the other factors in a particular cultural context.

THE DIVERSITY OF CHRISTIAN ATTITUDES TO OTHER RELIGIONS

On the question of the value of other religions, Filipino David Lim, an evangelical theologian, has helpfully identified four approaches, and I will add a fifth, which has arisen since Lim described the situation.[6] It is not possible to relate these five approaches to the alternatives that I described in the second chapter in an exact one-to-one correspondence.

The no-agreement approach. Providing the most negative assessments of other religions is a view that Lim describes as the *no-agreement approach.* This perspective is most likely to be found among ecclesiocentrics, although an agnostic might have this attitude as well. It views other religions "at best as nonredemptive, and at worst as partaking of the domain of darkness (e.g., Ex 20:3-6; 1 Chron 13:9; Is 37:18-19; 40; Jer 2:11; 5:7; 16:20; Acts 26:17-18; Col 1:13). As for those Gentiles who remain apart from Jesus Christ, God's wrath abides on them (1 Thess 2:16)."[7] Non-Christian religions are considered to be the result either of Satanic deception or of human aspirations toward God, and Christianity is deemed incompatible with, and completely different in essence from, other religions. "Those rays of truth which they indubitably contain are explained in terms of the fact that even Satan himself can and does sometimes appear as an angel of light (2 Cor 11:14)."[8] This is part of a stream of very negative assessments of the religions that goes back to the earliest days of the post-apostolic church, identified with the likes of Tatian and Tertullian.[9] Within the past century, this negative perspective toward non-Christian religions has sometimes been taken up in a way that opposed all religions, including Christianity, to revelation, following the lead of Karl Barth's earlier ap-

---

[6]For David Lim's four approaches, see his "Biblical Christianity in the Context of Buddhism," in *Sharing Jesus in the Two Thirds World: Evangelical Christologies from the Contexts of Poverty, Powerlessness and Religious Pluralism,* ed. Vinay Samuel and Chris Sugden (Bangalore: Partnership in Mission-Asia, 1983), pp. 282-87.

[7]Douglas R. Geivett and Gary W. Phillips, "A Particularist View: An Evidentialist Approach," in *More Than One Way? Four Views on Salvation in a Pluralistic World,* ed. Dennis L. Okholm and Timothy R. Phillips (Grand Rapids, Mich.: Zondervan, 1995), p. 237.

[8]J. N. D. Anderson, *Christianity and World Religions: The Challenge of Pluralism* (Downers Grove, Ill.: InterVarsity Press, 1984), p. 171.

[9]Daniel Clendenin, *Many Gods, Many Lords* (Grand Rapids, Mich.: Baker, 1995), pp. 55-56.

proach in his dialectical theology.[10] It is commonly identified with Hendrik Kraemer (1888-1965) through *The Christian Message in a Non-Christian World,* which he prepared for the World Missionary Conference to be held at Tambaram, Madras, in 1938.[11] The attitude has also been described as the general approach of Western Protestant missions in India from 1600 to 1900, evident in the concern of Christian theologians to point out the errors and supposed irrationality of Hindu religions.[12]

The common-faith approach. At the other end of the spectrum, representing a highly positive attitude toward all religions, is the *common-faith* perspective taken by proponents of relativism. Their general inclination is to assert that no one religion is exclusively true and that behind the diverse expressions of the sacred there is a shared core, a universal essence, that is expressed in all of them. Christianity is therefore deemed compatible and complementary with other religions; it is one of many paths all headed toward the same ultimate end. This idea has had a natural attraction to Asian theologians who live in the midst of religions such as Hinduism and Buddhism, which are often prepared to accept the validity of other religions. Hence the situation of Sri Ramakrishna, founder of the Ramakrishna Mission, who meditated on Christ, recognized Christ's divinity as an avatar (incarnation) of the Supreme, like Krishna and Buddha, and encouraged his disciples to worship Christ.[13] Indian Christian leaders who had also been shaped by the liberal tradition in Western Christianity, which had located God solely in the individual's inner experience, searched for parallels in Hindu religious experience.[14] In the Western world, this perspective has frequently been identified with Protestant philosopher John Hick and Roman Catholic theologians Paul Knitter and Hans Küng.

The different-ends approach. A third approach—the one I mentioned as not included in Lim's survey—was first ventured by Joseph DiNoia.[15] It

---

[10]Ibid., p. 55.

[11]Hendrik Kraemer, *The Christian Message in a Non-Christian World* (New York: Harper & Brothers, 1938).

[12]C. M. N. Sugden and Vinay K. Samuel, "Indian Christian Theology," in *New Dictionary of Theology,* ed. Sinclair B. Ferguson and David F. Wright (Downers Grove, Ill.: InterVarsity Press, 1988), p. 335.

[13]Bong Rin Ro, "Asian Theology," in *New Dictionary of Theology,* ed. Sinclair B. Ferguson and David F. Wright (Downers Grove, Ill.: InterVarsity Press, 1988), p. 50.

[14]Samuel and Sugden ("Indian Christian Theology," p. 335) cite as proponents of this method people such as Ram Mohan Roy (1772-1833), Brahmabandhab Upadhyaya (1861-1907) and P. Chenchiah (1886-1959).

[15]Joseph DiNoia, "The Universality of Salvation and the Diversity of Religious Aims," *World Mission* (winter 1981-1982): 4-15.

has been expanded by S. Mark Heim, who puts the *different-ends* idea forward in an attempt to resolve the issue between relativism and all the other positions that believe salvation is exclusively accomplished in Christ.[16] That so-called exclusivism would include the ecclesiocentrists, agnostics and accessibilists of my own scheme. Heim proposes that, in fact, there is not just one end that can only be reached by one religious path (exclusivism) or that can be reached by many different paths (pluralism). The reality is, rather, that there are many ends and that there are distinctive paths appropriate to reaching those ends. The question is not, is there one way or many ways? but rather, to what does this way lead?[17] Each religion has its own religious aim, and we can respect its own claim to be the means to attain that aim. "If different religious practices and beliefs aim at and constitute distinct conditions of human fulfillment, then a very high proportion of what each tradition affirms may be true and valid in very much the terms that the tradition claims." In fact, "two religious ends may represent two human states that no one person can inhabit at the same time."[18] So "each road will get you to a real destination—but not the same destination."[19] On the other hand, Heim suggests that

> there is no logical reason why a universe with a single religious ultimate might not also encompass a variety of religious ends. The variety could arise because some people establish a primary religious relationship to something other than the religious ultimate, or because there are distinctly different ways to relate to that ultimate, or for both reasons.[20]

Heim's interest in this proposal is "that it validates particularistic Christianity," whose distinctive end is salvation, but it also "supports those in other religious traditions committed to the distinctive truth in their confession."[21]

The common-ground or fulfillment approach. This approach corresponds very closely to what I have identified as religious instrumentalism. It considers other religions to be preparations for the Christian message, as the Old Testament was for the Jews. "God has left traces of himself and of his salvific plan in the other religious traditions. They have

---

[16]S. Mark Heim, *The Depth of the Riches: A Trinitarian Theology of Religious Ends* (Grand Rapids, Mich.: Eerdmans, 2001).
[17]S. Mark Heim, "Dreams Fulfilled: The Pluralism of Religious Ends," *Christian Century*, January 17, 2001, p. 14.
[18]Ibid.
[19]Ibid., p. 17.
[20]Ibid., p. 16.
[21]Ibid., pp. 15, 19.

some insight into God, truth, [and] spiritual riches but only partly rather than wholly. Hence Christ fulfils them and brings them to perfection."[22] Like the common-faith approach, this view may also be found among other religions. For instance,

> several Muslim theologians (Ghazâli, taken up again by Md. 'Abduh and R. Ridâ) declare that whoever follows what one believes to be the truth in matters of religion and is unintentionally ignorant of the coming of Muhammed will be saved. Many cultured Muslims think that what is essential is for each one to follow one's conscience.[23]

This perspective was common among early liberal theologians and early neo-orthodox theologians, who considered God to be savingly at work through the other religions but still "retained a sense of the absoluteness or superiority of Christianity." Among these, have been listed people such as Schleiermacher, Ritschl, Rudolf Bultmann, Emil Brunner, Reinhold and H. Richard Niebuhr, Paul Tillich and the early Ernst Troeltsch.[24] The idea of Christianity as the fulfillment of other religions is well captured in this summary of Friedrich Schelling's view:

> Christ "was present in every age to every race," but he was not known as such. Heathenism is related to Christianity as law to gospel, reason to faith, nature to grace. The heathen is like a blind man, feeling the sun's warmth but not seeing the sun itself. Christ was within heathenism as natural potency but not yet as a personal principle.[25]

Perhaps the best-known twentieth-century proponent of this perspective is Karl Rahner, whose concept of "anonymous Christianity" is so well known.[26]

The point-of-contact approach. In this brief review, the last way of approaching the other religions has been described as the *point-of-contact approach*, and it is probably the best counterpart to the accessibilism that

---

[22]Mariasusai Dhavamony, *Christian Theology of Religions: A Systematic Reflection on the Christian Understanding of World Religions*, Studies in the Intercultural History of Christianity (New York: Peter Lang, 1998), 108:63.

[23]Roman Catholic Study Group in Tunisia, "A Muslim Question to Christians: Why Do You Come to Live Among Us?" in *Faith Meets Faith,* ed. Gerald H. Anderson and Thomas F. Stransky, Mission Trends (Grand Rapids, Mich.: Eerdmans, 1981), 5:231.

[24]Clendenin, *Many Gods*, p. 62.

[25]E. L. Allen, *Christianity Among the Religions* (London: G. Allen & Unwin, 1960), p. 70, quoted in Anderson, *Christianity and World Religions*, p. 170.

[26]I have briefly expounded Rahner's view in *Irenaeus on the Salvation of the Unevangelized*, ATLA Monograph (Metuchen, N.J.: Scarecrow, 1993), 31:11-28.

I have presented in the first part of this book. This perspective grants that there is no fundamental agreement between the religions, but it emphasizes common points from which dialogue and evangelism can be started because the grace of God is at work in the lives of many devout people even in the other religions, although that does not assure a saving response in all those cases. Alister McGrath uses the phrase to describe his own perspective and says: "We are talking about 'points of contact' and occasional convergences, not identity nor even fundamentally consistent agreement."[27] Since my own proposal in this second part of the book falls generally in this category, I will not say more about it at this point.

A BRIEF CRITIQUE OF PROBLEMS IN THREE OF THESE ALTERNATIVES

Books have been written in criticism of these various positions, with particular concern expressed by evangelicals about the common-faith or relativist approach to the religions. Since others have contributed very helpful critique, I will not do much of it here, but I will focus on the presentation of a positive evangelical and Reformed proposal. Nevertheless, a few comments are in order regarding what I discern to be the key deficiencies of three of the approaches described above.

The common-faith approach. The primary fallacy of the common-faith approach is its refusal to acknowledge incommensurable differences between the various religions of the world. Gavin D'Costa is correct when he proposes that "no non-tradition-specific approach can exist, and such an apparently neutral disembodied location is in fact the tradition-specific starting point of liberal modernity, what [Alasdair] MacIntyre calls the Encyclopedic tradition."[28] D'Costa posits that,

> logically, pluralists simply present themselves as honest brokers to disputing parties, while concealing the fact that they represent yet another party which invites the disputants actually to leave their parties and join the pluralist one: then, of course, interreligious harmony will be attained. Ironically, there would be no religions left when such harmony was attained.[29]

---

[27] Alister McGrath, in *More Than One Way? Four Views on Salvation in a Pluralistic World*, ed. Dennis L. Okholm and Timothy R. Phillips (Grand Rapids, Mich.: Zondervan, 1995), p. 165.

[28] Gavin D'Costa, *The Meeting of Religions and the Trinity*, Faith Meets Faith (Maryknoll, N.Y.: Orbis, 2000), p. 19.

[29] Ibid., p. 20.

This is because all would have left their religions and joined a new one, "liberal modernity."

There is no place for the trinitarian God in these schemes, which are unitarian, deistic or agnostic. Thus, self-professed relativists are really being exclusivistic despite their constant criticism of that position. Tim Perry aptly notes the palpable irony of this position, "for it claims at bottom that the only way to preserve religious diversity in practice is to deny it in theory."[30] Knitter's appeal to a liberative justice, for instance, is in clear conflict with the concept of justice that derives from a traditional understanding of karma, and so Knitter's position is not ultimately pluralistic but

> is exclusive in that its consciously embedded conception of justice reserves for itself the ability to evaluate accurately all other culturally embedded conceptions. It is inclusive in so far as it argues that only those religions sharing its commitment to *soteria* are ultimately saving.[31]

Lest religious relativism seem to be an innovation of modern times, however, Vinoth Ramachandra aptly points out the considerable similarity between this ideology and the assumptions of second-century Gnosticism.[32]

In spite of its principle motivation, relativism turns out not to be a form of tolerance to other religions. Real tolerance is believing "that my neighbour is wrong in her beliefs and that as long as she clings to her beliefs she will suffer eternal ruin, and yet at the same time to defend and protect her

---

[30]Tim S. Perry, *Radical Difference: A Defence of Hendrik Kraemer's Theology of Religions,* Editions SR, ed. H. Martin Rumscheidt and Theodore S. de Bruyn (Waterloo, Ontario: Wilfrid Laurier University Press, 2001), 27:2.

[31]Ibid., 27:22.

[32]Vinoth Ramachandra, *The Recovery of Mission: Beyond the Pluralist Paradigm* (Carlisle, U.K.: Paternoster, 1996), pp. 249-50. These similarities include "a denigration (in practice, if not always explicitly in theory) of the personal Creator of biblical revelation in favour of an unknowable Absolute/Mystery"; an understanding of salvation "that is essentially individual and 'spiritual' in some vague sense (e.g., Hick's 'transformation of self-centredness to reality-centredness,' Samartha's and Panikkar's diffuse *advaitic* framework)"; a portrayal of "Jesus as essentially a teacher of divine truths, never as one whose death and resurrection have decisively altered the condition of humankind in any way"; an emphasis on " 'religious experience' over and above belief, doctrine and scripture in all the world's faiths"; a diminishment of "the historical and literal elements in the scriptures of all faiths in favour of mythological reinterpretations"; the postulation of "a universal, unifying spiritual principle (e.g., Panikkar's 'cosmotheandrism,' Pieris' 'salvific principle'), coming to expression in many saviour-figures who all stand in varying distance from the source"; and "an incipient elitism which distinguishes between the devout but misguided faithful in all religions and the select few (the pluralists, drawn from within all) who alone grasp the true meaning of all religion and are the vanguard of the future."

freedom to hold to those beliefs."[33] Furthermore, to stave off the risk of un-justified guilt feelings among Christians, we should note that *all religions are exclusivistic*. The religions "offer unique and competing truth claims about the basic makeup of the world"; they "offer us radically divergent pictures of God, the world, life, death, history, and humanity" because of "their historical particularity and specificity." As we would expect, "ad-herents of any given religion . . . believe that their own world-view offers the truest and best interpretation of the world."[34]

Even Raimundo Panikkar, though he himself is very partial to relativis-tic pluralism, says,

> A believing member of a religion in one way or another considers his reli-gion to be true. Now, the claim to truth has a certain built-in exclusivity. If a given statement is true, its contradictory cannot also be true. And if a certain human tradition claims to offer a universal context for truth, anything con-trary to that "universal truth" will have to be declared false.[35]

Even the religions that have classically been considered the most tolerant and pluralist, like Hinduism and Buddhism, believe that their own reli-gion is the most true and the best. As Daniel Clendenin points out, "the Bhagavad Gita reads that God accepts people whatever path they may choose to approach him (4.11), but it also insists that those who worship other gods in reality worship Krishna alone, albeit 'improperly' (9.23) or 'unknowingly' (9.24)."[36] These religions are also exclusive in an explicit way, in that they make truth-claims that are logically incompatible with the truth-claims of other religions: for instance, one must choose between monotheism and polytheism; one believes human life either has a tempo-ral end or is eternally recurring; Jesus either is or is not fully divine. This is even true, sometimes, *within* different strands of the same religion.[37] For example, take Theravada Buddhism, which "teaches salvation by self-ef-fort, whereas Pure Land Buddhism of the Mahayana tradition teaches the opposite, a salvation based upon faith in the power and merit of the Amida Buddha."[38]

---

[33]Ibid., p. 271.

[34]Clendenin, *Many Gods*, p. 64.

[35]Raimundo Panikkar, *The Intrareligious Dialogue* (New York: Paulist, 1978), p. xiv, quoted in Harold Netland, *Encountering Religious Pluralism: The Challenge to Faith and Mission* (Down-ers Grove, Ill.: InterVarsity Press, 2001), p. 296.

[36]Clendenin, *Many Gods*, p. 65.

[37]Ibid., pp. 65-66.

[38]Ibid., p. 66.

Traditionally, Judaism, Christianity and Islam have each claimed to be the exclusive medium of salvation, but Hinduism and Buddhism did not. Nevertheless, Harold Netland's careful discussion of "religions and truth" expertly demonstrates that the religions are diverse, even in the way they define what the key issues are.[39] But where they provide answers to common questions, they clearly make "mutually incompatible claims about the nature of reality." As a result, "so long as the meanings of the doctrines within the respective religious communities are preserved, they cannot be jointly accepted without absurdity."[40] As Russell Aldwinckle notes, "a religious pluralism, which relativizes all religions, is as much a threat to Judaism as to Christianity. Exodus-Sinai is not more normative than is Jesus Christ for such a pluralism."[41]

Examples of this point could be multiplied, but these should be sufficient to establish the commonality of exclusivism amongst the religions. From this fact, John Taylor argues that "one of the most significant things we have in common on which to build our mutual understanding is the experience of having a conviction that by definition precludes the other's belief, and being unable to accommodate it with integrity."[42]

The common-ground approach. The common-ground approach, which is generally taken up by those whom I have labeled religious instrumentalists, is definitely better than relativism because it seeks to preserve the uniqueness and centrality of Christ as God's means of salvation. Its affirmation of the possibility of salvation apart from the church's proclamation is also better than ecclesiocentrism's, for reasons explained in the last section. But in its assessment of the intentions of God for and in the religions of the world, it goes too far. It is more likely to be demotivating of evangelism than accessibilism is, and it may minimize the newness of the gospel.[43] Religious instrumentalists, in affirming common ground between the religions, don't deny that there is error in other religions, but they tend to minimize it.

As D'Costa points out, it is problematic to assert that other religions

---

[39]Chapter 6 of Netland's *Encountering* is titled "Religions and Truth."

[40]Ibid., p. 186.

[41]Russell F. Aldwinckle, *Jesus—A Savior or the Savior? Religious Pluralism in Christian Perspective* (Macon, Ga.: Mercer University Press, 1982), p. 50.

[42]John V. Taylor, "The Theological Basis of Interfaith Dialogue," in *Faith Meets Faith,* Mission Trends, ed. Gerald H. Anderson and Thomas F. Stransky (Grand Rapids, Mich.: Eerdmans, 1981), 5:105.

[43]Calvin E. Shenk, *Who Do You Say that I Am? Christians Encounter Other Religions* (Scottdale, Penn.: Herald, 1997), p. 50.

may be means to salvation because "religious traditions are properly to be considered in their unity of practice and theory, and in their organic interrelatedness," so they "cannot simply be dismembered into parts (be they doctrines, practices, images, or music) which are then taken up and 'affirmed' by inclusivists, for the parts will always relate to the whole and will only take their meaning in this organic context."[44] Calvin Shenk observes that "many elements of religion are common only if separated from their specific contexts or if parallels are based on selective data. Resemblances in form must not be allowed to obscure great differences in content."[45] It is not the religion, as such, but a reinterpretation of it that is deemed to be fulfilled in Christ, because what is taken from it is included in a different paradigm, where it can only "bear some analogical resemblance to its meaning and utilization within its original paradigm."[46]

An example of this fulfillment approach is Sikhism, which took what it deemed best in Hinduism and Islam and produced a new religious tradition. We might also recall Christianity's "inclusion" of Judaism as well as Islam's "inclusion" of Christianity and Judaism. Shenk is right to warn that points of contact should not be assumed to be common ground.[47] "The gospel can fulfill the religious aspiration of people or reinterpret certain practices of religion, but the gospel does not fulfill the whole religious system."[48] Other religions are not tutors or midwives preparing the way for Christ as the Torah was.[49]

The different-ends approach. Heim does well to recognize the genuine differences between religions and to avoid the relativism that "colonizes" them all under Christianity. His proposal of three possible human destinies—"lostness, penultimate religious fulfillments, and communion with the triune God"—is very intriguing.[50] It might be viewed as another form of the common-ground theory, but it has quite a distinctive approach, and so I have not subsumed it under that theory. My primary hesitation concerning his proposal comes from my view of the Bible as unique, sufficient

---

[44]D'Costa, *Meeting of Religions*, pp. 22-23.
[45]Shenk, *Who Do You Say*, p. 152.
[46]D'Costa, *Meeting of Religions*, p. 23.
[47]Shenk, *Who Do You Say*, p. 152.
[48]Ibid., p. 154.
[49]Ibid., p. 155.
[50]S. Mark Heim, *Salvations: Truth and Difference in Religion* (Maryknoll, N.Y.: Orbis, 1995), p. 163, quoted in Perry, *Radical Difference*, 27:129.

and universally normative divine revelation. In Scripture, I find no evidence that there are other ends to which God is taking some people. Heim's fascinating proposal forces us to face the questions that religious instrumentalism inevitably puts on the table: Is it possible that the special revelations God gave to Israel and to the church were specifically for them but not universally normative? Might it be that God has revealed to Jews and Christians ends that he wanted them to pursue but revealed to other peoples different ends? Is this, ultimately, a form of relativism that does not reduce all of the religious ends to one but affirms their distinctness and authenticity? I think not, because, as just indicated in Heim's three possible destinies that face human beings, communion with the triune God is set apart.

There appears to be a hierarchy of ends, in Heim's proposal, so that other religions are penultimate and moving toward fulfillment in Christ. That would head us in the direction of the fulfillment approach commonly taken by religious instrumentalists. So, then, is Scripture only the account of the supreme end of "salvation," allowing us to assert that those who reject "salvation" may, nevertheless, not go to hell, provided that they are responding positively to another dimension of God's revelation? For the proposal to work, there would have to be movement up the hierarchy of ends in the afterlife. That vision (as put forward by Dante, whom Heim exegetes in *The Depth of the Riches: A Trinitarian Theology of Religious Ends*) is certainly attractive, but it does not conform to my sense of the finality of spiritual decisions in this life, as I indicated in chapter ten. So I will not be taking Heim's path, but he certainly stimulates productive thinking.[51] I am open to the possibility that God may be working savingly in the hearts of individuals within the various religious communities of the world; and I see Jesus Christ as the final word from God (Heb 1:1-3) and, hence, as the end toward which God is drawing all the people of the world through every mode of his self-revelation. But I have proposed that decisions made in this life are critical and that the final movement along a trajectory toward (or away from Christ) will

---

[51]Perry criticizes Heim for not giving "sufficient weight to those biblical passages—central to the regulation of Christian eschatological grammar—that speak not of three possible human destinies, but of the final reconciliation of all things." He argues that passages such as Phil 2:5-11; 3:10-11; Eph 1:15-23; Col 1:15-20; and Rev 21:22-27 "seem to preclude an indefinitely long period of penultimate religious fulfilment and, therefore, place limits on Heim's proposal—limits that he does not address" (*Radical Difference*, 27:130). Perry puts his finger on my own concern.

occur at the moment of death, not afterward. I would also put less emphasis on the continuity between people's experience in other religions and their entrance into communion with Christ than Heim does.[52] As I will indicate in a later chapter, there are people who come to Christ out of other religions with a sense of having been moving steadily along a trajectory toward Christ, but there are many others who have a very strong sense of needing to make an about-face to find life with God in Christ. I think that our understanding of God's saving work in the world of many religions needs to allow for both of these experiences, and it must insist that, either way, the process concludes at the moment of death when one gives a decisive response to Jesus, in person.

THE AMBIGUITY IN ALL RELIGIONS

The phenomena of the religions as they arise from this essentially religious character of humanity are ambiguous responses to divine revelation. This is the framework for our evaluation of their possible role in God's providential program. Religions are fundamentally the consequence of the fact that God has not left himself without witness in the world. As J. H. Bavinck observes, "Buddha would never have meditated on the way of salvation if God had not touched him. Mohammed would never have uttered his prophetic witness if God had not concerned Himself with him. Every religion contains, somehow, the silent work of God."[53] But,

> from a biblical perspective, religions are multidimensional. . . . They reflect God's activity in the world, the human search for God, and the human attempt to flee from God. They seek to reverence the God or gods they know, and they try to manipulate God or gods. They are cries for help and efforts at self-justification.[54]

We must "distinguish between profound spiritual impulses which are the moving of God and the local clothing in which such impulses ap-

---

[52]Se, e.g., Heim, *Depth of the Riches,* p. 282: "Those who take their way through Buddhist or Hindu or Muslim tradition to the final and distinctive religious ends of those faiths will see their whole journey, rightly, as directed at the goal achieved. For those who follow their way through a Buddhist or Hindu or Muslim tradition and finally follow the ridge that leads them into communion through Christ, their entire journey will seem a providentially ordered way to conversion. Knowledge of God through this religious tradition served as the basis for accepting the fulfillment the gospel offers."

[53]J. H. Bavinck, *The Church Between Temple and Mosque: A Study of the Relationship Between the Christian Faith and Other Religions* (Grand Rapids, Mich.: Eerdmans, n.d.), p. 200.

[54]Shenk, *Who Do You Say,* p. 75.

pear. The light is reflected with varying degrees of brightness as the moon is reflected differently in a mud puddle, the sea, or a clear mountain lake."[55]

"Cosmic religions are founded on the revelation of God in creatures; ethical religions attest that an absolute will makes itself felt in the conscience of men; salvific religions are founded on the fact of fall and salvation."[56] The consciousness of God, which is an aspect of God's universal revelation that is imprinted on the being of humans created in his image, makes people naturally religious, but sin tends their religious expressions toward idolatry.

The account of Cain's and Abel's attempts to worship God concludes with this statement: "At that time [the birth of Adam and Eve's grandson Enosh, the son of Seth] people began to invoke the name of the LORD" (Gen 4:26). People have been doing so ever since, but this took a form of idolatry at Babel, and it has taken many idolatrous forms in a great diversity of languages and cultures through the centuries.[57] As John Goldingay and Christopher Wright have observed,

> Genesis 1—11 suggests that the religions, like all human activity, belong in the context of a world that needs restoration to the destiny and the relationship with God which were intended for them, which God purposed to bring about through the covenant with Israel which culminated in the mission and accomplishment of Jesus.[58]

We observe that religion can be an expression of our rebellion as well as of our response to God. Of course, this was "as true for Israelite religion (as the prophets pointed out) and for Christianity as 'religious observance' as for any other faith."[59]

There are certainly good and positive things that have resulted from the religions, but we must also recall the evils of temple prostitution, human sacrifice, caste systems, satanic worship, cannibalism and other such departures from God's norms—including the Christian justification of sla-

---

[55]Ibid., p. 99.
[56]Dhavamony, *Christian Theology*, 108:31.
[57]Clendenin, *Many Gods*, p. 126.
[58]John E. Goldingay and Christopher J. H. Wright. " 'Yahweh Our God Yahweh One': The Oneness of God in the Old Testament," in *One God, One Lord: Christianity in a World of Religious Pluralism*, 2nd ed., ed. Andrew D. Clarke and Bruce Winter (Grand Rapids, Mich.: Baker, 1992), p. 46.
[59]Ibid.

very and racism at times in history.[60] All of this has been done in the name
of religion, as have been the hateful speeches of Louis Farrakhan, the
mind-control of the cults and the corrupt practices of some Christian television preachers.[61] In assessing religions, therefore, we must begin with an
awareness of the profound ambiguity in all religious experience. Just because something is religious is no guarantee that it is good for humans or
that it aids them in relationship to God. Christian realism recognizes that
human religiosity "sometimes contains elements of truth, goodness, and
beauty, but also elements of error, evil, and ugliness."[62]

Properly recognizing the ambiguity of all religions helps us to avoid
"both the undue negativism of atheism and the romantic optimism of pluralism about human religiosity."[63] As Bavinck suggests,

> If we could acquire a complete oversight of the history of religion among all
> peoples, [we would] see the process of continuous degeneration and decay
> caused by man's rebellion against God, by his flight from God, and his anx-
> iety in God's presence. We would also see clear proof that God had not aban-
> doned man, has not left himself without a witness, but is unceasingly con-
> cerned and active with man.[64]

Taylor observes how both the response of disobedience and the response
of obedience "gets built into the tradition and passed on to later generations. And they, in their turn, may respond more readily to the unceasing
calls and disclosures of the Spirit, and so be moved to reform some part of
the tradition."[65] Thus, Gordon Smith warns us not to be too quick to condemn as rebellion the religious activity of "the honest seeker after God
whose only avenue of expression is the religious environment in which he
lives. . . . It may be rebellion, but it could also be viewed positively as an

---

[60]I am grateful to Kenneth Stewart for his comments on a paper I wrote. At that time, I had
mentioned the Inquisition and the Crusades as examples of evils done in the name of Christianity. He noted that Christians are still debating the merits and demerits of these two items
and that I might do better to mention something "now universally looked upon as hid-
eous," such as the justification of slavery. I follow his astute historian's judgment, but I remain convinced, personally, that both the Inquisition and the Crusades are a blot on the
church's record.

[61]Clendenin, *Many Gods*, p. 54.

[62]Ibid., p. 51.

[63]Ibid.

[64]J. H. Bavinck, *An Introduction to the Science of Missions*, trans. David Hugh Freeman (Kampen: J. H. Kok, 1954; Philadelphia: Presbyterian & Reformed, 1960), p. 236.

[65]Taylor, "Theological Basis," 5:97-98.

authentic and sincere quest that is distorted by human fallenness."[66]

It is serious folly to assume that all religions are leading people toward God, by their own paths, as universalists propose. Scripture condemns all other religions *as such* as darkness (Eph 4:18), ignorance (Acts 17:30; Rom 1:18-21; 1 Pet 1:14) and foolishness (1 Cor 1:18-23). The heathen gods are not gods (Is 41:29; 42:17; Jer 2:28; Acts 14:15; 19:26; Gal 4:8), and heathen religions even demonstrate demoniacal power (Deut 32:17; 1 Cor 10:20-21; Rev 9:20). Although idols are not real gods, they are perceived as such by those who worship them, and behind such worship is the activity of demons.

Thus, Don Howell, a former missionary in Japan, writes:

> The elaborate systems of idol worship centered in temple activities are not neutral social events the believer may freely dabble in. There are dark spiritual forces ultimately at work behind the most frivolous of ceremonies, capturing the allegiance of people and leading to spiritual ruin. This explains Paul's consistent insistence, in his letters, that the worship of the true God and the worship of idols are mutually exclusive (1 Co 10:14-22; 2 Co 6:15-18; 1 Th 1:9).[67]

The religions are one instrument that Satan, the "father of lies," uses to keep people from the only Savior.[68] Sadly, the demons can also be at work within biblical covenantal religion, as is evident in Christ's warnings to the churches in Smyrna, Pergamum and Thyatira (Rev 2:8-25).

Magic and the occult are condemned, as in Paul's strong words to Bar-Jesus (Elymas), a magician and a false prophet whom Paul denounced as "son of the devil . . . enemy of all righteousness, full of all deceit and villainy" who was "making crooked the straight paths of the Lord" (Acts 13:10). The confrontation with magic led to the destruction of magic paraphernalia in Ephesus (Acts 19:11-20). Accordingly, Lesslie Newbigin notes that

> the sphere of the religions is the battlefield *par excellence* of the demonic. New converts often surprise missionaries by the horror and fear with which they

---

[66]Gordon T. Smith, "Religions and the Bible: An Agenda for Evangelicals," in *Christianity and the Religions: A Biblical Theology of World Religions,* Evangelical Missiological Society Series, ed. Edward Rommen and Harold Netland (Pasadena, Calif.: William Carey Library, 1995), 2:18.

[67]Don N. Howell Jr., "The Apostle Paul and First-Century Religious Pluralism," in *Christianity and the Religions: A Biblical Theology of World Religions,* Evangelical Missiological Society Series, ed. Edward Rommen and Harold Netland (Pasadena, Calif.: William Carey Library, 1995), 2:104.

[68]J. N. D. Anderson, *Christianity and World Religions,* p. 172.

reject the forms of their old religion—forms that to the secularized Westerner are interesting pieces of folklore and that to the third-generation successors of the first converts may come to be prized as part of national culture.[69]

Any religion, including Christianity, may become "the sphere in which evil exhibits a power against which human reason and conscience are powerless."[70] Newbigin notes soberingly that "it was the guardians of God's revelation who crucified the Son of God. It is the noblest among the Hindus who most emphatically reject the gospel. It is those who say, 'We see,' who seek to blot out the light (John 9:41)."[71]

Given the Bible's frequent depictions of the evilness of human hearts, we have to ask to what extent religions are a manifestation of sinful flight from and rebellion against God. Ecclesiocentrists who propound the no-agreement approach see all non-Christian religions as expressions of evil. On the other hand, accessibilists, who posit a work of the Spirit of God in the other religions, are hopeful that God may be at work even in the midst of the religious devotional practices of non-Christians. J. N. D. Anderson, for instance, says that his study of Islam convinces him "that one cannot deny that some of the great Muslim mystics have sought the face of God with a whole-heartedness that cannot be questioned." And he does not doubt that "in some cases it was God himself whom they were seeking, not self-justification or a mystical experience *per se*. Like everyone else, they could be 'saved' by grace alone." But, Anderson asks, "may they not have been responding to some initiative of that grace which was *uniquely* operative in the cross and resurrection of One whose story they had never really heard?"[72]

Similarly, Newbigin, after nearly forty years of missionary work in India, writes: "Anyone who has had intimate friendship with a devout Hindu or Muslim would find it impossible to believe that the experience of God of which his friend speaks is simply illusion or fraud."[73] Newbigin notes that

the contemporary debate about Christianity and the world's religions is generally conducted with the unspoken assumption that "religion" is the pri-

---

[69]Newbigin, *Open Secret*, p. 170.
[70]Ibid.
[71]Ibid.
[72]Anderson, *Christianity and World Religions*, pp. 152-53.
[73]Lesslie Newbigin, *The Gospel in a Pluralist Society* (Grand Rapids, Mich.: Eerdmans, 1989), p. 174.

mary medium of human contact with the divine. But this assumption has to be questioned. When the New Testament affirms that God has nowhere left himself without witness, there is no suggestion that this witness is necessarily to be found in the sphere of what we call religion. The parables of Jesus are notable for the fact that they speak of secular experiences. When the Fourth Gospel affirms that the light of the Logos who came into the world in Jesus shines on every human being, there is no suggestion that this light is identified with human religion. The text goes on to say that this light shines in the darkness, and the ensuing story constantly suggests that it is religion which is the primary area of darkness, while the common people, unlearned in religious matters, are the ones who respond to the light. And it is significant that Justin Martyr, one of the earliest apologists to use this Johannine teaching in making contact with the unbelieving world, affirms that the true light did indeed shine on the great philosophers like Socrates, but that the contemporary religion was the work of devils. Our thought must therefore be directed not just to the religions so called; we must ask about the relation of the gospel to all who live by other commitments, whether they are called religious or secular.[74]

CHRISTIANITY AS ONE INSTANCE OF THE AMBIGUITY OF RELIGIONS

Arthur Glasser reminds us that "the empirical church is no less than, and no more than humankind's response to God's self-disclosure in Jesus Christ. Being human, it is a historically shaped religious movement, a product of culture, and thus limited, as is any human institution."[75] Thus, Christianity is no exception to what I have said about the ambiguity of religions. It is included in our general assessment that religion "often results merely in self-righteousness instead of an encounter with God in his holiness and majesty."[76] When we speak of "Christianity," we are not talking about the ways of thinking, feeling and living that are exactly what God prescribed. We are talking about the phenomenon we observe as the global Christian church and as individual churches; we are talking about institutions, theologies and ways of life that have developed as people have tried to follow Jesus.

[74]Ibid., pp. 172-73.
[75]Arthur F. Glasser, "Response to Stanley J. Samartha's 'The Lordship of Jesus Christ and Religious Pluralism,' " in *Christ's Lordship and Religious Pluralism*, ed. Gerald Anderson and Thomas F. Stransky (Maryknoll, N.Y.: Orbis, 1981), p. 38.
[76]R. W. F. Wootton, *Christianity and Other Faiths: An Evangelical Contribution to Our Multi-Faith Society* (Exeter: Paternoster, 1983), p. 23.

The Old Testament clearly attests that some institutionalized and well-intentioned religious practices—in spite of the fact that they had been specifically commanded by God—not only were self-serving, but were an outright abomination to God (1 Sam 15:22-23; Is 1:10-15; Amos 5:21-27; Mic 6:6-8).[77] There was a Jewish zeal for the Mosaic law that sometimes represented a human attempt to earn salvation (Mt 23:1-37; Lk 11:37-52), and the same is true of many of the ascetic practices, pilgrimages, prayer and meditation that different religions, including Christianity, enjoin on their followers.

So institutional Christianity is no different from any other religion in its character as a humanly constructed institution. Christianity is a response to the supreme revelation of God in Christ and should, therefore, most closely approximate what God wants in a religion. Some of its expressions are a response to the divine initiative in revelation and illumination that is elicited by, and is pleasing to, the Spirit of God. But in other expressions it represses God's truth and evidences deception that is both self-incurred and influenced by the demonic adversary. Like other religions, it is both a movement toward and a flight from God. Some of Satan's most subtle and most dangerous work in the world may well be taking place within, rather than against, the Christian church as a visible religious phenomenon.

Nevertheless, Christianity is intrinsically superior because of its being the institutional response to the *ultimate* revelation of God in Christ (God's final word; Heb 1:1-3), even though it is also ambiguous, as a sinful human response to that revelation. It is not superior by virtue of being the fulfillment of the other religions, as though it were the best genus of a species called *religion*.[78] Tragically, thousands of people are being kept from Christ by Christian churches. Wonderfully, even in those churches where the official teaching or practice of the faith is significantly erroneous, God still draws people to himself through the special revelation that is never totally suppressed in the religious forms that have been constructed.

CONTEXTUALIZATION AND SYNCRETISM IN THE CONTEXT OF OTHER RELIGIONS

Since Christianity is a human construct, we must be careful how we build it. Our goal, of course, is to produce a religion that approximates as closely

---

[77]Clendenin, *Many Gods*, p. 55.

[78]Compare Hendrik Kraemer's critique of that fulfillment perspective—which was proposed by J. N. Farquhar (1971), Friedrich Schleiermacher and Karl Rahner (1966)—as this is reviewed by Perry, *Radical Difference*, 27:88.

as possible the religion that God prescribes. We want to think, feel, worship and live in the ways that God instructs us to—both as individuals and as organized communities. Because Christians live in the context of other (sometimes dominant) religions, our expressions of faith must beware of *syncretism,* of constructing a religious system that puts error from other religions together with biblical truth in a manner that ultimately distorts that truth. I am using the term *syncretism* here with a negative sense, as a way of describing the introduction of error into the formulation of Christian truth. I speak of taking beliefs (or practices) that do not really cohere and putting them together, of drawing them from various religious systems, as though each of these has equal validity, with the result that Christian truth is compromised. The term is not always used this way, so one has to read it within each user's context. Andrew Walls, for instance, says, "Christianity is in principle perhaps the most syncretistic of the great religions."[79]

Gerald McDermott understands Walls to mean "that the Christian God has chosen to unfold his truth gradually through time rather than in one blinding and all-encompassing flash of revelation and that he has used other religious and philosophical systems to help unfold and interpret his reality."[80] As McDermott puts it, "Christianity has always borrowed from other faith traditions and baptized these borrowings into Christ by relating them to, and reconfiguring them in, the larger vision of God's revelation in Christ."[81] This is a good and necessary thing for God's people to do as they move out into the world, but I would prefer to call it *contextualization* and to reserve *syncretism* for the improper distortion of Christian truth that results when this process is not done properly.

Churches that were planted by Western missionaries have complained that those missionaries used the label *syncretism* to stifle all attempts by believers to express their Christian faith in ways more appropriate to their own culture than rather than adopting the practices that Western missionaries brought with them from their own culture. Since the contextualization of theology and of church practice is always necessary in every time and place, we must not allow fear of syncretism to inhibit it. On the other

---

[79]Andrew F. Walls, *The Missionary Movement in Christian History: Studies in the Transmission of Faith* (Maryknoll, N.Y.: Orbis, 1996), p. 173.

[80]Gerald R. McDermott, "What If Paul Had Been from China? Reflections on the Possibility of Revelation in Non-Christian Religions," in *No Other Gods Before Me? Evangelicals and the Challenge of World Religions,* ed. John G. Stackhouse Jr. (Grand Rapids, Mich.: Baker, 2001), p. 21.

[81]Ibid., p. 22.

hand, we must be sure that the theology and worship constructed in each context are authentically Christian. Clearly, then, we must identify a way of measuring whether a given response to God's revelation in Christ is, in fact, Christian—whether it is the God who revealed himself in Jesus Christ who is being accurately represented in the theological, liturgical or practical formulation. Because of the ambiguity of the religions and cultures among which Christians must live and worship Christ, we need a way of discerning truth, as well as error, when we encounter it in the cultures of the world (including our own) and in the religions that are so intricately interwoven with many of those cultures.

I suggest that we should apply six criteria to the beliefs and practices that make up the Christianity we teach and live.[82] First, our own theological formulation or practice should be *oriented in the same direction as other successful or approved formulations.* Tradition is not normative, as Scripture is, but we must be very careful when departing from long-lasting and broad consensus in the church's understanding of truth. Contextualization has to do with formulating the truth in ways appropriate to the context, not with formulating new truth relevant only to that context. Consistency with the faith handed down within the church through the centuries is to be highly valued. This was the main emphasis of James Orr in his classic work *The Progress of Dogma.*[83] Drawing on the work of John Henry Newman, Orr attempted to show that there is an organic unity of doctrine in the history of the Christian church and that we need to judge new proposals to see whether or how well they carry on that organic unity. An abrupt change of direction, such as Orr discerned in nineteenth-century Liberalism, evidenced that an illegitimate move had been made. This was not "progress" but diversion.

Of course, we face serious difficulties when we try to assess accurately whether a particular way of speaking about God in a culture other than our own is in continuity with the church's understanding. We need to recall, for instance, the significant difficulties that the church encountered in

---

[82]In this proposal, I have drawn on the three criteria suggested by J. de Mesa and L. Wostyn and the five that Robert Schreiter suggests. See J. de Mesa and L. Wostyn, *Doing Theology: Basic Realities and Processes* (Manila: Maryknoll School of Theology, 1982); and Robert Schreiter, *Constructing Local Theologies* (Maryknoll, N.Y.: Orbis, 1985). Both of these are cited by Stephen B. Bevans, S.V.D., *Models of Contextual Theology,* Faith and Culture (Maryknoll, N.Y.: Orbis, 1992), pp. 18-19.

[83]James Orr, *The Progress of Dogma, Being the Elliot Lectures, Delivered at the Western Theological Seminary, Allegheny, Pennsylvania, U.S.A.* (London: James Clarke, 1901).

formulating a common understanding of the Trinity because some of its theologians were working in Greek and some in Latin. On a smaller but still important plane, many North American churches are experiencing significant tension these days over the so-called worship wars, which are largely the result of cultural differences between different age groups within congregations. We must not be precipitous in pronouncing a theological construct or a church practice "syncretistic" when we have limited knowledge of the thought forms in the context where these developed.

A second criterion, therefore, is that theology and practice developed by a particular Christian community must be *accepted by the people of God*, since theology and Christian worship and morality are the work of the whole church. Consequently, Robert Schreiter suggests that a particular church's theology should be open to criticism from other churches. We can be greatly enriched in our understanding of Scripture when we hear it through the ears of others who approach it with different experiences than we have, particularly when their experience is more like the context of the biblical writers than is our own culture.

Third, the formulation must *lead to Christian orthopraxis*. "A theology that justifies an oppressive status quo would be as wrong as a theology of liberation that calls for violent action against oppressors."[84] As William Dyrness emphasizes, the truth of Scripture must be worked out in the "fabric of our lived worlds."[85] In short, when a purportedly Christian theology is lived out, it must lead to genuinely Christian behavior.

Fourth, there should be *inner consistency* in the system; for lack of this, the church rejected Arius's proposal concerning Jesus (which denied his eternal deity), because it undermined the doctrine of salvation. Fifth, the theology formulated must be *able to be translated into worship*. Once again, Arianism fell short on this account. Because Christians pray to Christ as to God, the Arian formula was unacceptable. Sixth, each church's formulation should *make a positive contribution to a dialogue among various contextual theologies*. Stephen Bevans suggests, for instance, that

> one of the signs of the truth of the theology of liberation is how radically it has challenged not only other Latin American theologies, but also theologies from various parts of the world. Similarly, one of the signs of the authenticity of feminist and Black liberation theology is that they speak significantly to

[84]Bevans, *Models*, p. 19.
[85]William Dyrness, *Learning About Theology from the Third World* (Grand Rapids, Mich.: Zondervan, 1990), p. 32.

other theologies and uncover hitherto unthought-of areas for theological re-flection.[86]

The polemic against Baal in the Former Prophets (Joshua—Kings) is an excellent illustration of contextualization that does not fall into syncretism. Robert Chisholm sums up the main features of Yahweh's anti-Baal strategy:

> Yahweh contextualized his self-revelation, usurping Baal's position as king and his role as the sovereign dispenser of human and agricultural fertility. Rather than philosophically denying Baal's existence, Yahweh took a much more practical approach which accommodated the cultural situation of ancient Israel. Through word and deed he demonstrated that he alone could meet the very real needs which Baalism claimed to satisfy. In this way he destroyed any basis or motivation for Baal worship. It was irrelevant whether or not Baal really existed; the important point for Israel was that Baal could not deliver what he promised, while Yahweh could. In short, Yahweh contextualized his self-revelation for maximum effect without compromising to any degree his claim for exclusive allegiance. To put it another way, contextualization compelled one to exclusivism; it did not blur the distinction between Yahweh and Baal and foster syncretism.[87]

D. A. Carson observes that

> when the people of God avoid syncretistic entanglements, it is a sign that the Lord is with them (Josh. 22:31). By contrast, when they oppress one another and follow other gods, it is because truth has perished (Jer. 7:28) and the people have rejected the word of the Lord (Jer. 8:9). Again and again Deuteronomy warns the people to be careful to follow all that the Lord has commanded, to avoid entanglements, including marriage, with the surrounding peoples, for fear of learning and following their ways (e.g., Deut. 4; 6:13-19; 7:21-26; 13:6-8). In part, the preservation of the covenant community depends on each generation carefully passing on to the next the exclusive greatness and covenant fidelity of Yahweh.[88]

Syncretism was a danger in New Testament times, as it continues to be to-

---

[86]Bevans, *Models*, p. 19.
[87]Robert B. Chisholm Jr., " 'To Whom Shall You Compare Me?' Yahweh's Polemic Against Baal and the Babylonian Idol-Gods in Prophetic Literature," in *Christianity and the Religions: A Biblical Theology of World Religions*, Evangelical Missiological Society Series, ed. Edward Rommen and Harold Netland (Pasadena, Calif.: William Carey Library, 1995), 2:63-64.
[88]D. A. Carson, *The Gagging of God: Christianity Confronts Pluralism* (Grand Rapids, Mich.: Zondervan, 1996), p. 252.

day, threatening the purity of our response to God's special revelation. This is particularly apparent in Paul's letter to the Colossians, who tried to put together Jewish ritual practices, angel worship and speculative ideas, which seem to reflect an incipient Gnosticism, and to then add Christ to a spiritual hierarchy. They "advocated specific kinds of behavior (ceremonialism and asceticism) consistent with that worldview."[89] It was a subtle heresy that "both compromised and denied the gospel—it posed God as remote and inaccessible except through a long chain of intermediaries, one of whom was Jesus," and these "intermediaries (spirits or angels) needed to be worshiped or placated because cosmic reconciliation was a model for personal reconciliation. Followers of this religion sought mystical illumination and higher knowledge of things heavenly; redemption was understood as the ascent of the soul to the higher world."[90] Against this, Paul urged the complete adequacy of Christ, which left no need for "elemental spirits" because Jesus fully embodied deity. The Colossians had been delivered from the kingdom of darkness to the kingdom of the Son and should not regress (Col 1:13).

SUMMING UP

God has left no one without witness, and because humans are intrinsically religious beings, they have constructed religions in the ambiguous expression of their response to God's revelation. In some ways, they have incorporated truth made known to them by God, but at other points they have suppressed God's truth and substituted for it either ideas of their own imagination or the lies of the Adversary. The usefulness of religions is therefore measured by both the completeness of the revelation to which they have responded and the extent to which they have believed, rather than suppressed, the truth that God has revealed. Among the religions of the world, Christianity has the great advantage of being constructed in response to God's revelation in Jesus Christ and the scriptures of both Testaments. But even so, there is no particular communion or congregation of the Christian church that is a pure appropriation of God's revealed truth. In all of them, human imagination and the lies of the Evil One have triumphed over truth at some point of belief, attitude or practice at different periods of their history. Constant self-criticism, a continual listening to the Word of God under the direction of the Spirit of God and an openness to

---

[89]Shenk, *Who Do You Say*, p. 113.
[90]Ibid.

correction from the rest of the body of Christ—these are essential for Christian churches. Humility is always in order.

Christian churches must strive to incarnate God's truth in the worlds in which they live, both in their ways of speaking about God and his relationships with creation, and in their practices of worship. Faithfulness to God's revelation and effective inculturation are both essential to churches' effectiveness in serving God's purposes for them in their part of his creation. Syncretism, as a putting together of truth and error, is always a danger; and that error may be appropriated from various aspects of the churches' context, from the neighboring religions, the culture, and the intellectual or political contexts. It is a testimony to the great grace of God in preserving his church that it persists and continues to serve God, despite the many dangers it faces.

An aspect of the humility that comes from recognizing the ambiguity of our own expressions of Christian faith is that we are also open to the ambiguity in other religions. We are never completely right and they are never completely wrong, and we can be grateful for the truth and the manifestations of common grace that we encounter in our meetings with members of other religions. More will be said in succeeding chapters about how we should live this out in our relationship with others.

14

How Did the Covenant People Relate to Other Religions?

Thesis 19: The biblical writers consistently bear witness to the uniqueness of the God who created all that exists and who established a covenant relationship with the people of Israel, which was later extended to the Gentiles, in the church. The gods worshiped by the other nations are not real and are unable to save; in fact, the worship of these gods might be stirred up by demonic forces as a means to hold people in spiritual bondage. To his covenant people, God gave special revelation of himself and prescribed the way in which he was to be worshiped. Sadly, despite this great privilege, idolatry was always a grave threat among the covenant people. The people of Israel were called to bear witness to the true God primarily by the purity of their own lives and worship, but God also acted on their behalf and in the lives of neighboring nations to exalt his own name. As is true in the areas of theological and moral truth, the practice of religion for which God holds people accountable is assessed by the revelation of God's will that they have received.

Thesis 20: God appropriated divine names and religious forms from contemporary culture without endorsing the religion of Israel's neighbors. Thus, God modeled accommodation and assimilation without syncretism, and this should be our own goal as we establish Christian communities in the contexts of the religions of our own day.

THE EXISTENCE OF OTHER RELIGIONS IS NOTHING NEW for God's people, so a Christian theology of religions needs to observe with particular care the attitudes of biblical writers to the religious worlds of their times. That is our task in this chapter. In the midst of the plurality of religions they encountered, biblical writers in both Testaments consistently announced the uniqueness of Yahweh, the Lord God, and condemned idolatry. Yet they also testify to the gracious work of God in the lives of individuals among the nations. Furthermore, the covenant people drew on language and concepts in the religions of their neighbors to formulate their own faith in the only true God.

OLD TESTAMENT PERSPECTIVES

Israel's awareness of other religions. Israel's monotheism developed within
the context of Egyptian polytheism and the Canaanite worship of Baal and
Asherah,[1] the god and goddess of fertility.[2] In that context, "the prophets
were intolerant of all other religions,"[3] but their condemnations were elicited not so much by a mandate to instruct the other nations directly as by a
need to keep Israel faithful to the one true God of all the earth. The Israelites
were, obviously, not fully aware of the extent of the development of other
religions. For example, when Jeremiah and Ezekiel judged Israel,

> Confucius (551-479 B.C.) and Lao-tzu, the founder of Taoism (c. 604-531 B.C.),
> were active in China, Zoroaster (c. 628-551 B.C.) expounded his version of re-
> ligious dualism in the Persian Empire, Socrates (c. 470-399 B.C.) searched for
> wisdom in Greece, while Guatama [sic] the Buddha of India (563-483 B.C.)
> forsook a life of leisure for religious asceticism, enlightenment and solitude,
> and Mahavira (c. 599-527 B.C.) founded Jainism.[4]

Furthermore, "a millennium earlier, while the Assyrians of Nineveh worshiped Ashur, the cruel god of war, far away in India Brahmin priests offered sacrifices to the fire god Agni."[5]

J. H. Verkuyl observed that

> the whole Old Testament (and the New Testament as well) is filled with de-
> scriptions of how Yahweh-Adonai, the covenant God of Israel, is waging war
> against those forces which try to thwart and subvert his plans for his cre-
> ation. He battles against those false gods which human beings have fash-
> ioned from the created world, idolized, and used for their own purpose . . .
> the Baals, and the Ashteroth, whose worshippers elevated nature, the tribe,
> the state and the nation to a divine status. God fights against magic and idol-
> atry which, according to Deuteronomy, bend the line between God and his
> creation. He contends against every form of social injustice and pulls off
> every cloak under which it seeks to hide.[6]

---

[1]Daniel Clendenin, *Many Gods, Many Lords* (Grand Rapids, Mich.: Baker, 1995), p. 14.
[2]Richard S. Hess, "Yahweh and His Asherah? Religious Pluralism in the Old Testament
World," in *One God, One Lord: Christianity in a World of Religious Pluralism*, 2nd ed., ed. Andrew D. Clarke and Bruce Winter (Grand Rapids, Mich.: Baker, 1992), p. 15.
[3]Ibid.
[4]Clendenin, *Many Gods*, p. 14.
[5]Ibid.
[6]J. H. Verkuyl, *Contemporary Missiology: An Introduction* (Grand Rapids, Mich.: Eerdmans,
1978), p. 95, quoted in Vinoth Ramachandra, *The Recovery of Mission: Beyond the Pluralist Paradigm* (Carlisle, U.K.: Paternoster, 1996), p. 232.

Because of Israel's distinctive calling by the true God, "for Israel to have accepted Canaanite and other religions as equally valid and acceptable alternatives to their own faith would have been no act of tolerance, kindness or maturity. It would have been an utter betrayal of the rest of mankind, for the sake of whose salvation they had been chosen and redeemed."[7]

The worship of the one true God of all the earth. The Old Testament steadfastly maintains that the religion of Israel is fundamentally different from other religions because of who Israel's God is. The biblical narrative indicates, however, that the people of Israel were frequently more tolerant of other religions than they should have been, to the point of adopting the religious practices of their neighbors. If Israel failed in single-hearted devotion to Yahweh, the God who created the world and formed them into a people for himself, then God's ultimate purposes for the good of all the nations would not be realized. The number who remained faithful to Yahweh was sometimes perilously small, but God always kept a faithful remnant until he finally brought into the world the visible image of the invisible God, the Word incarnate, who was welcomed by the faithful in whose hearts God was working.

When the nation of Israel came under severe oppression, after having flourished in Egypt for many generations, God moved to deliver them with his mighty hand as a testimony to the nations. Yahweh sent plagues on Pharaoh and his people so that they might "know that there is no one like [him] in all the earth" (Ex 9:14). And as Moses blessed the Israelites before his death, he reminded them that "there is none like God, O Jeshurun, who rides through the heavens to your help, majestic through the skies," and that the Lord who had come to them at Sinai "subdues the ancient gods, shatters the forces of old" (Deut 33:26-27). "From the very beginning, Israel linked the uniqueness of Yahweh with her salvation from Egypt (Ex 20:2)."[8] This was a creedal confession that expressed Israel's experience of God's deliverance, which was certainly not a concept borrowed from their pagan neighbors.[9]

We recall Elijah's encounter on Mt. Carmel with Jezebel's 850 proph-

---

[7]Christopher J. H. Wright, *The Uniqueness of Jesus,* Thinking Clearly Series (Grand Rapids, Mich.: Monarch, 1977), p. 117.

[8]Ed Mathews, "Yahweh and the Gods: A Theology of World Religions from the Pentateuch," in *Christianity and the Religions: A Biblical Theology of World Religions,* Evangelical Missiological Society Series, ed. Edward Rommen and Harold Netland (Pasadena, Calif.: William Carey Library, 1995), 2:35.

[9]Ibid.

ets to determine the one true God (1 Kings 18:17-40), which ended in Elijah's putting to death the priests of the other deities. Indeed, Yahweh had ordered Israel to "annihilate" (Deut 20:17) the pagan peoples as they entered the land God gave them "so that they may not teach you to do all the abhorrent things that they do for their gods, and you thus sin against the LORD your God" (Deut 20:18). They were called upon to "put away the foreign gods that are among you" through "merciless campaigns of extermination" (Josh 24:23; see also Josh 6:21, 24; 8:8, 19, 26; 11:20).[10]

It was in such a context that the Hebrews proclaimed "the LORD is our God, the LORD alone" (Deut 6:4) and obeyed his command that anyone who sacrificed to another god should be "devoted to destruction" (Ex 22:20).[11] That there is no God beside Yahweh is a theme repeated constantly throughout the Exodus narrative (Ex 7:5, 17; 8:10, 22; 9:14; 10:2; 12:12; 14:4, 18; 16:12; Deut 4:35, 39; 32:39; etc.). In fact, one of God's primary purposes in liberating Israel from Egypt was to proclaim his name through all the earth (Ex 9:14-16) and to execute judgments "on all the gods of Egypt" (Ex 12:12). This demonstration to "all the peoples of the earth . . . that the hand of the LORD is mighty" continued in the acts of Yahweh as they crossed the Jordan under Joshua (Josh 4:24).[12]

Although there is a strong thematic and literary relationship between ancient Near Eastern and Hebrew Wisdom literature,

> one fundamental difference remains. Unlike the other ancients who paid homage to assorted pantheons of deities, the Israelite wisdom of the Old Testament acknowledged only one God, Yahweh (Pr 22:17-19). Thus, the Hebrews denied materialism (since matter was created by God), pantheism (because Yahweh as Creator was above all creation), and dualism (since creation was originally made "good" by God). Ideologically, this meant that the Hebrews owed allegiance to Yahweh alone and had neither room nor time for these false deities and competing religious systems.[13]

Unfaithfulness to the true God among his covenant people. Sadly, God's demand that his covenant people give him their complete alle-

---

[10]Clendenin, *Many Gods*, p. 15.
[11]Ibid.
[12]Ibid., p. 127.
[13]Michael Pocock, "Selected Perspectives on World Religions from Wisdom Literature," in *Christianity and the Religions: A Biblical Theology of World Religions,* Evangelical Missiological Society Series, ed. Edward Rommen and Harold Netland (Pasadena, Calif.: William Carey Library, 1995), 2:53.

giance, though clearly and often expressed, was not always obeyed in the actual history of that people. In fact,

> most of the kings and queens who ruled in ancient Israel saw no difficulty in tolerating and at times participating in cults in which rulers of neighbouring states worshipped other deities. For them Yahweh, God of Israel, was not the only deity, but the one who ruled over their own state, whether the Northern or Southern kingdom.[14]

The prophets firmly condemned this, but "many of the rulers of ancient Israel accepted the state deities of other nations and acknowledged their worship through political and marital alliances with the rulers of these foreign states."[15]

As Richard Hess observes, among "many or most of the citizens,"[16] Yahweh was the state deity,

> the official god whom they recognized as supreme above all others in Israel. However, most people lived away from state politics for most of their daily existence. At these times the official god held little importance. Instead, the people sought family and local deities whom they felt could help them in their work life. They sought local deities, local manifestations of Baal and Asherah, for example, to aid them in providing rain so that their crops would grow and they and their families would have enough to eat during the coming year.[17]

The vision given in Ezekiel 8 is a chilling description of the way in which the temple of Jerusalem had become the home of many idols. And 2 Kings 21 gives a similarly shocking view of the idol worship fostered during the reigns of Manasseh and Amon, which the writer describes as "the abominable practices of the nations that the LORD drove out before the people of Israel" (2 Kings 21:2). An important part of the prophets' work was to combat all such idolatrous tendencies (see, e.g., Isaiah, Jeremiah, Ezekiel, Hosea and Amos), which included this sort of disparagement of the alleged gods of other nations. They stressed the nothingness of idols (Jer 2:26-28; 3:6-13; 10:1-16; Hos 8:4-7; Amos 5:26).

> Among the Prophets, adultery and fornication routinely constitute the analogies for any relationship between Israel and the worship of foreign gods. Isaiah scorns those who commit adultery: "Among the oaks and under every spread-

---

[14]Hess, "Yahweh," p. 15.
[15]Ibid.
[16]Ibid.
[17]Ibid., pp. 15-16.

WHO CAN BE SAVED?

ing tree: you sacrifice your children in the ravines. . . . You made your bed on a
high and lofty hill; there you went to offer your sacrifices" ([Is] 57:3-8).[18]

Consequently, "the tragedies of the Assyrian and Babylonian captivities
are specifically attributed to Israel's idolatrous perversions (2 Kings 17;
2 Chron 28:22-23; 36:11-21)."[19]

On occasion, "a foreign cult was imported and made the national cult," an
example being Ahab's establishment of the worship of Baal in his capital after his marriage to Jezebel, daughter of the king of Tyre.[20] This was strongly
opposed by Elijah (1 Kings 18); yet Jezebel's daughter, Athaliah, later ruled in
the south for a few years and tried to introduce foreign worship as the state
cult (2 Kings 11). Thankfully, this was universally rejected, and she was over-
thrown and executed through a coup by the military and priestly leaders.[21]

Israel's witness among the nations. Jacques Dupuis states that Israel's
monotheistic faith "imposes upon it a missionary vocation: Israel must
preach Yahweh's exclusive dominion, the nonexistence of other gods" (Is
40—55),[22] but this was not something that the nation was commissioned
by God to do in an active proclamation of the message of Yahweh's
uniqueness to the people of other nations. Israel believed that Yahweh
alone is God and that they were called on to live out a single-minded obedience to Yahweh before the surrounding nations. Thus, Eckhard Schnabel
(along with numerous others) observes that "the prophetic announcement, the historical reality, and the legal stipulations surrounding the exodus indicate that Israel's role as a witness among the nations and to the
nations was a passive one at best."[23] In neither the Torah nor the Prophets

---

[18]Pocock, "Selected Perspectives," 2:51. See also Jer 3:8; 23:13-14; Hos 2:2.

[19]Clendenin, *Many Gods*, p. 130.

[20]Hess, "Yahweh," p. 16.

[21]Ibid.

[22]Jacques Dupuis, *Toward a Christian Theology of Religious Pluralism* (Maryknoll, N.Y.: Orbis,
1997), p. 39.

[23]Eckhard J. Schnabel, "Israel, the People of God and the Nations," *Journal of the Evangelical
Theological Society* 45 (March 2002): 37. See also Andreas J. Köstenberger and Peter T.
O'Brien, *Salvation to the Ends of the Earth: A Biblical Theology of Mission*, New Studies in Biblical Theology, ed. D. A. Carson (Downers Grove, Ill.: InterVarsity Press, 2001), 11:35, quoting G. Goldsworthy, "The Great Indicative: An Aspect of a Biblical Theology of Mission,"
Reformed Theological Review 55 (1996): 7. Robert L. Plummer claims that "most scholars are
in agreement that the missionary witness of God's people in the Old Testament is overwhelmingly passive" ("A Theological Basis for the Church's Mission in Paul," *Westminster
Theological Journal* 64 [fall 2002]: 270), and he cites other biblical scholars who have reached
this conclusion. I find very plausible Plummer's proposal that the key to the difference between the Old Testament and the New Testament in this regard is the nature of God's Word
(the gospel) and the presence of the Holy Spirit (p. 270).

do we find "any hint that Israel has a historical mission to bring members of other nations to a saving knowledge of Yahweh."[24] After Israel had failed disastrously in its God-given role, and had done so with such speed in the sin of the golden calf (Ex 32—34), it became increasingly obvious that "the extension of the covenant blessings to the nations would come through 'an Israel within Israel.' The concept of a remnant within the nation had already begun."[25] Israel had been given "a unique historical experience of Yahweh's character and purpose for his creation," which was what "enabled them to bear witness to *his* uniqueness as the living God (e.g., Is 43:8-13). Israel existed as a nation at all only because of Yahweh's intention to redeem people from every nation."[26]

Isaiah 41:21-23 challenges the other gods to prove their existence, and Isaiah 44:9-20 is a scathing satire on idolatry. Similarly, Psalm 115:3-8 compares dead idols with the living God (cf. Deut 4:28); gods made by human hands are nothing. For this reason, when Solomon prayed at the dedication of the temple, he asked that "all the peoples of the earth" might know the only true God (1 Kings 8:23, 41-43, 60); and Hezekiah "makes an almost identical confession" (2 Kings 19:15).[27] Yet, John Goldingay and Christopher Wright make the intriguing observation that "condemnation of religious deficiency is reserved for the people of God (cf. Amos 2). The gods of the nations are regarded as simply impotent. Worship of them is not so much culpable as futile. They cannot save."[28] This message is seen in the narrative of Jonah, where it is clear that Yahweh saved the sailors who cried out in fear, whether they "prayed to Yahweh consciously or to whatever they recognised as God."[29] Likewise, in Elijah's confrontation with the prophets of Baal and in the prophecies of Isaiah 40—55, the impotence of the other so-called gods is emphasized. In fact, they are represented as

> an encumbrance to their worshippers. It is Yahweh alone who saved. The question, therefore, of whether there is salvation in other religions, is in Old

---

[24]Schnabel, "Israel," p. 38.
[25]Köstenberger and O'Brien, *Salvation*, p. 37.
[26]Ramachandra, *Recovery of Mission*, p. 231.
[27]Clendenin, *Many Gods*, p. 61.
[28]John E. Goldingay and Christopher J. H. Wright, " 'Yahweh Our God Yahweh One': The Oneness of God in the Old Testament," in *One God, One Lord: Christianity in a World of Religious Pluralism*, 2nd ed., ed. Andrew D. Clarke and Bruce Winter (Grand Rapids, Mich.: Baker, 1992), p. 52.
[29]Ibid.

Testament terms a non-question. There is salvation in *no* religion because religions don't save. Not even Israel's *religion* saved them.[30]

The Old Testament's denunciation of idol worship was primarily announced when it occurred among the Israelites, whom the prophets denounced for behaving like an unfaithful wife. But Moses left the people in
no uncertainty that many of the religious practices of their neighbors were
"abhorrent" to God (Deut 18:9). This included the sacrifice of children,
divination, soothsaying, sorcery and the casting of spells (Deut 18:10-11).
It was for such "abhorrent practices" that God drove the nations out before
Israel. This indicates clearly that such religious practices were intolerable,
regardless of whether they were committed by God's special covenant
people or by other nations.[31]

On the other hand, the practice of such abominations among Israel's
neighboring nations did not lead to God's complete rejection of them. As
J. H. Bavinck points out, in the Old Testament "the future of the nations is
a point of the greatest concern. It is in itself striking how often the Old Testament discusses the future of these peoples and interests itself in the salvation that will one day be their lot."[32] Israel rejected "the notion of entire
God-fearing nations"[33] but knew that not all people among the nations
were idolatrous. Some had recognized the living God who manifested
himself through the cosmic covenant, but these were "presented frequently as individuals who stand against the tide of their own people."[34]
For instance, Abraham tried to prevent the destruction of Sodom by appealing for protection of righteous individual Gentiles who may have
been there (Gen 18:16-33). And Ezekiel speaks of God's unwillingness to
save all of a rebellious nation, even if three individuals as righteous as
Noah, Dan'el and Job were in it (Ezek 14:14, 20), a probable reference to
"the names of venerable righteous Gentiles (Noah, Dan'el and Job) to indicate the universal truth of his point."[35] It is commonly believed that the
Dan'el of Ezekiel 14:14, 20 is the figure referred to in the Ugaritic epic of

---

[30]Ibid.

[31]R. W. F. Wootton, *Christianity and Other Faiths: An Evangelical Contribution to Our Multi-Faith
Society* (Exeter: Paternoster, 1983), p. 16.

[32]J. H. Bavinck, *An Introduction to the Science of Missions*, trans. David Hugh Freeman (Kampen: J. H. Kok, 1954; Philadelphia: Presbyterian & Reformed, 1960), p. 11.

[33]R. Bryan Widbin, "Salvation for People Outside Israel's Covenant?" in *Through No Fault of
Their Own? The Fate of Those Who Have Never Heard*, ed. William V. Crockett and James G.
Sigountos (Grand Rapids, Mich.: Baker, 1991), p. 82.

[34]Ibid.

[35]Ibid., p. 82 n. 20.

Aqht, rather than the biblical Daniel, given the appeal made in Ezekiel 28:3 "to the standard set by Dan'el before the ruler of Tyre, a Phoenician (Canaanite) city,"[36] and the likelihood that "the Biblical Daniel's righteousness probably had not become proverbial so soon."[37]

Dupuis cites the conversion of the inhabitants of Nineveh, who worshiped the God of Israel under the common name of Elohim (Jon 3:1-10) as "a striking witness to the universality of God's love and pardon extending to other peoples."[38] The story reports how hard it was for Jonah to learn that God is graciously at work outside the covenant community.[39] Yet Jonah "is not presented as a missionary whose preaching to Nineveh (even if for tragic reasons) is intended to serve as a paradigm for Israel's outreach to the nations,"[40] and Jonah's reaction to God's sending him "indicates that the thought that a prophet of Israel should go and preach to a pagan audience with the goal of saving them from God's judgment was quite foreign to him."[41]

I think that Solomon's dedicatory prayer for the temple is also significant for its indication of an expectation within Israel that people would come to Jerusalem to worship Yahweh. Writes Dupuis,

> The Old Testament does not tell us how many among the nations have recognized the living God. What it says is that all are called to it. Israel's vocation is to announce the living God to all the nations. The 'Psalms of the Reign' (47; 93; 97; 98; 99) praise God in his universal royalty and invite the nations to share in his praise.[42]

In Isaiah 42:10-12, all the nations from the ends of the earth are invited to sing a new song to the Lord. "The history of the nations is seen as part of the universal dominion of the Creator. All peoples are called upon to acknowledge that the God of Israel is the only God and there is no other (Is 45:14, 21-24). The perspective is that of the universality of salvation. All the

---

[36]Ibid., p. 82. The NRSV offers "Daniel" as an alternative reading but, in editorial comment on my manuscript, Daniel Reid affirmed that Widbin's opinion here is "common and widely accepted."

[37]Note on Ezek 14:14, 20 in *The NIV Study Bible,* gen. ed. Kenneth Barker (Grand Rapids, Mich.: Zondervan, 1985).

[38]Dupuis, *Toward a Christian Theology,* p. 39.

[39]In the New Testament, James and John had to learn the same lesson about the Samaritans (Lk 9:51-56) as did Peter with regard to the so-called unclean Gentiles (Acts 10—11). See Clendenin, *Many Gods,* p. 132.

[40]Köstenberger and O'Brien, *Salvation,* p. 45.

[41]Schnabel, "Israel," p. 39.

[42]Dupuis, *Toward a Christian Theology,* pp. 39-40.

nations will walk in the light of God's glory" (cf. Is 60:3; 66:18-19; Jer 1:5; 3:17).[43] It is very clear that God wants the nations to know that he is Lord (Ezek 20:9, 14, 22, 41; 21:5); and it was through God's chastisement of Israel that the following peoples were to discover that he alone is God: the Ammonites, the Moabites, the Philistines, the residents of Tyre and Sidon, and the Egyptians (Ezek 25:5, 11, 17; 26:6; 28:22-24; 29:6, 9, 16; 30:19, 26; 32:15).[44]

Within the Old Testament, we frequently meet people who ask God to deliver them so that his power could be seen by the other nations, causing them to glorify Israel's God who was, indeed, the God of all the world. As Bavinck writes:

> Israel knew that it lived under the constant surveillance of the then contemporary world. This note is heard in the lament of Moses after Israel had worshiped the golden calf and God had expressed his sentence upon the people. "Wherefore should the Egyptians speak, and say, for mischief did he bring them out, to slay them in the mountains; and to consume them from the face of the earth" (Exodus 32:12)? Later after God had inflicted severe punishment Moses said, "Then the nations which have heard the fame of thee shall speak, saying, because Jehovah was not able to bring his people into the land which he sware unto them, therefore he hath slain them in the wilderness" (Numbers 14:16).[45]

Along this line, as David prays to the Lord, following Nathan's prediction of the establishment of David's throne, he acknowledges the uniqueness of the Lord: "There is no one like you, O LORD, and there is no God besides you" (1 Chron 17:20). Thus, God's making of Israel to be his people and his act of redemption on their behalf are recognized as having been for God's purpose of making for himself "a name for great and terrible things" (1 Chron 17:21). Israel was established so that the name of the Lord would be "established and magnified forever" (1 Chron 17:24).

This point was made very explicitly in the Ten Commandments, which prohibited idolatry and the misuse of God's name. God is not to be confused with any other gods, such as those of Egypt or Canaan, in a manner that would permit Israelites to worship those gods. It is true that God had placed Israel in a situation where they became more aware of other religions, but his purpose was to make the adherents of those religions aware

---

[43]Ibid., p. 40.

[44]Gerald R. McDermott, *Can Evangelicals Learn from World Religions? Jesus, Revelation and Religious Traditions* (Downers Grove, Ill.: InterVarsity Press, 2000), p. 75.

[45]Bavinck, *Introduction,* pp. 14-15. See also Deut 9:28; Josh 7:9; Ps 67:2; Is 37:20.

of himself. This inevitably generated spiritual and social conflict between Yahweh and every other claimant to deity. The temptation to which Israel repeatedly succumbed "was to think of Yahweh too as simply another tribal deity and to worship him in terms derived from an alien religious framework, thus betraying the revelation entrusted to her for the sake of the nations."[46]

The Servant of Yahweh, whose coming Isaiah predicts (Is 42:1-4; 49:1-6; 50:4-9; 52:13—53:12), will do a work that affects the whole world. He will be "a covenant to the people" (Is 42:6), and he will restore the people of God (Is 49:6)

> by replacing the first servant, Israel (49:3), because he is deaf and blind (42:18-20). He serves at the same time as "a light to the nations" (42:6), as he will "bring forth justice to the nations" (42:1) as the "coastlands wait for his teaching" (42:4; cf. 49:1). He is "a light to the nations that my salvation may reach to the end of the earth" (49:6b).[47]

After Israel has been redeemed, she

> will call other nations to her, and they will come running (55:3-5). In response to Yahweh's invitation to turn to him and be saved (45:14, 22), the nations will bow down before the Lord's people (45:14; cf. 49:23), acknowledging that there is no other God than Yahweh and that he is certainly with them. Even kings and queens will be in attendance on Israel (49:23).[48]

But more soberingly, those who oppose him will be destroyed (Is 49:26).

In the texts that describe the eschatological gathering of the nations around the Lord (Is 2:2-5; 60:1-20), the doctrine of Israel's election often prevails over the call to the nations. "The call to the nations keeps an ethnocentric perspective: gentiles could become Jews and thus share in Israel's privileged status." In the future, however, the nations would—with Israel—form one elect people acclaiming God.[49] But elsewhere there is a decentralization of Israel, as in the oracle on Egypt in Isaiah 19:19-22: Egypt becomes the "people of God," but Israel remains the Lord's "heritage": "On that day Israel will be the third with Egypt and Assyria, a blessing in the midst of the earth, whom the LORD of Hosts has blessed,

---

[46]Goldingay and Wright, "Yahweh," p. 53.
[47]Schnabel, "Israel," p. 41.
[48]Köstenberger and O'Brien, *Salvation,* p. 48.
[49]Dupuis, *Toward a Christian Theology,* p. 40.

saying, 'Blessed be Egypt my people, and Assyria the work of my hands, and Israel my heritage'" (Is 19:24-25).[50]

It is not a people's ethnic descent but their contrite spirits and righteous responses to God's command that will determine their participation in the future restoration, when God's kingdom is established (Is 58:8-14).[51] Isaiah provides the only prophetic text that indicates a centrifugal movement from Israel to the nations, involving human messengers (Is 66:18-21). "The 'survivors' of Isaiah 66:19 are Jews who have survived God's judgment on his people: they are sent to the nations, to the remote regions of the earth, in order to proclaim Yahweh and the salvation that he has made possible."[52]

God's direct providential work as witness to the nations. The God of biblical revelation is the God of universal history, "but he brings that history to its goal ('salvation') through the particular history of a particular people."[53] The Old Testament teaches us that Yahweh was not simply Israel's tribal deity but "the sovereign God of the whole earth, actively involved in nations other than Israel."[54] We recall, for instance, God's work in pre-Israelite Canaan, giving Ar as a possession to the descendants of Lot, who became the nations of Moab and Ammon (Deut 2:9-12, 19-21), and Seir to the descendants of Esau (Deut 2:21-23). In these instances, God displaced other peoples to make room for these groups. Yahweh cared about the destinies of other nations. He not only brought Israel out of Egypt, but he also brought the Philistines from Caphtor and the Arameans from Kir (Amos 9:7), and he judges Israel's neighbors (Amos 1:3—2:5) as well as Israel (Amos 2:6-16). The prophets anticipated a day when the knowledge of the Lord will cover the earth as the waters cover the sea (Is 11:9; Hab 2:14).

Even Israel's unfaithfulness to God served as an opportunity for God to declare himself among the nations. God told Gog, "the chief prince of Meshech and Tubal," for instance, that he would use him to invade Israel "so that the nations may know me, when through you, O Gog, I display my holiness before their eyes" (Ezek 38:2, 16). But God says that he will then destroy Gog and, thereby, "will display my greatness and my holi-

---

[50]Ibid., p. 41. See also Mariasusai Dhavamony, *Christian Theology of Religions: A Systematic Reflection on the Christian Understanding of World Religions,* Studies in the Intercultural History of Christianity (New York: Peter Lang, 1998), 108:82.

[51]Schnabel, "Israel," p. 41.

[52]Ibid., p. 42.

[53]Ramachandra, *Recovery of Mission,* p. 230.

[54]Ibid.

ness and make myself known in the eyes of many nations. Then they shall know that I am the LORD" (Ezek 38:23).

Indeed, God complained through Malachi that "from the rising of the sun to its setting [God's] name is great among the nations, and in every place incense is offered to [his] name, and a pure offering," but that Israel has profaned it (Mal 1:11-12). Mariasusai Dhavamony suggests that this text was in Jesus' mind when he pointed to the faith of the Roman Centurion and said, "Many will come from east and west and will eat with Abraham and Isaac and Jacob in the kingdom of heaven, while the heirs of the kingdom will be thrown into the outer darkness" (Mt 8:11-12).[55]

An excursus on the use of force to spread the faith. Violence in the name of religion has become very prominent in the news of our day, particularly because of public attestation by Muslim radicals that they are engaged in *jihad,* or a holy war against infidels, in the name of Allah, and the pronouncement of *fatwahs,* or judicial sentences of death against individuals such as novelist Salman Rushdie. This increased focus on the use of force to propagate orthodox belief in God, or to suppress heresy, has generated new attention to Israel's conquest of Canaan by God's command. Particularly troubling to modern sensitivities is the *herem,* or ban, in which God ordered Israel to utterly destroy all the people, including women and children, and the animals in a city that was attacked (1 Sam 15:3), because they are all dedicated to God. When John Collins addressed the matter in his presidential address at the annual meeting of the Society of Biblical Literature in 2002, he noted that one "does not have to work very hard to find biblical precedents for the legitimation of violence."[56] He cites instances in which Christians have appealed to the biblical example to justify their own use of force. These include the English Puritan revolution, Oliver Cromwell's treatment of Catholics in Ireland, the New England Puritans' analogy between Native American tribes and the Canaanites and Amalekites, Boers' resistance to British rule in South Africa and later black African liberationists fighting the Boers, and the Zionist movement in Israel.[57]

Collins reviews strategies that have been used to minimize the offensiveness of these texts and concludes that the best way to "relativize the more problematic ones" is to "note the diversity of viewpoints within the

---

[55]Dhavamony, *Christian Theology,* 108:83.
[56]John J. Collins, "The Zeal of Phinehas: The Bible and the Legitimation of Violence," *Journal of Biblical Literature* 122 (spring 2003): 3.
[57]Ibid., pp. 13-14.

Bible"[58] and to recognize that the Bible, "for all the wisdom it contains, is no infallible guide on ethical matters."[59] Most helpful of all, suggests Collins, is to learn the lesson that "certitude leads to violence" and to lessen the contribution of the Bible to violence in the world by showing "that certitude is an illusion."[60] None of these strategies hold much promise for evangelicals. I, for one, prefer to suggest that a degree of certitude on some clearly revealed truths (e.g., God the Father, Son and Holy Spirit is the only true God) is not an illusion, but that certitude need not lead to violence.[61] One can believe that something is certainly and universally true without also believing that force should be used to convince others of this fact. I am also convinced that the Bible is, indeed, an infallible guide on ethical matters, although our interpretations of it are not infallible. I believe that it is possible to interpret Israel's conquest of Canaan and the application of the ban in a manner that will *not* justify the use of violence against unbelievers by Christians today. It is significant that a similar interpretive controversy is going on among Muslim scholars concerning the use of the Qur'an to support violence.[62]

The ban was not a concept unique to Israel. It was also used by its neighbors,[63] and it did not operate, in Israel, only in the context of war against outsiders: Exodus 22:20, for instance, commanded that a member of the covenant people who "sacrifices to any god, other than the LORD alone, shall be devoted to destruction." And if a town should be led astray by a "scoundrel" from within Israel into the worship of other gods, that town should be destroyed under the ban (Deut 13:12-16). Those who carried out the destruction were instructed not to keep anything that was devoted to

---

[58]Ibid., p. 19.

[59]Ibid., p. 21.

[60]Ibid.

[61]This response to the postmodernist complaint that a Christian conviction about truth leads to violence is well handled by Brian J. Walsh and J. Richard Middleton in *Truth Is Stranger Than It Used to Be: Biblical Faith in a Postmodern Age* (Downers Grove, Ill.: InterVarsity Press, 1995).

[62]See, for instance, the description offered by John Kelsay, "Suicide Bombers: The 'Just War' Debate, Islamic Style," *Christian Century*, August 14-27, 2002, pp. 22-28.

[63]Collins, "Zeal of Phinehas," p.5; Walter C. Kaiser Jr., *Toward Old Testament Ethics* (Grand Rapids, Mich.: Zondervan, 1983), p. 75. William Sanford Lasor, David Allan Hubbard and Frederic William Bush observe that this action's being customary did not make it right, but "it does help to explain why the Israelites did not think it wrong." They also appeal to progressive revelation, to account for the unreadiness of the Israelites to receive teachings such as the Sermon on the Mount (*Old Testament Survey: The Message, Form and Background of the Old Testament* [Grand Rapids, Mich.: Eerdmans, 1982], p. 208).

destruction so that the Lord might "turn from his fierce anger" and show them compassion (Deut 13:17). The rationale for this shocking destruction was provided in Deuteronomy 7:2-6: the destruction of everyone in the land into which God was bringing Israel was for the protection of Israel as "a people holy to the LORD" their God, a nation chosen "out of all the peoples on earth to be his people."[64] It was for this reason that intermarriage was forbidden and the items involved in pagan worship (altars, pillars and idols) were to be completely destroyed (Deut 7:5).

Deuteronomy records instructions given by Moses to the covenant people as they were about to enter into the land across the Jordan and to dispossess the nations there. He reminds them that they were not being used of God to occupy the land because of their righteousness or the uprightness of their hearts, "but because of the wickedness of these nations" (Deut 9:5). In regard to some other nations, Israel was ordered to offer them conditions of peace rather than to exterminate them (Deut 20:10-15), but the sin of the Canaanites had been patiently tolerated by God for many years and "the iniquity of the Amorites" was now "complete" (Gen 15:16). Thus, they were to be destroyed "so that they may not teach [the Israelites] to do all the abhorrent things that they do for their gods, and [Israel] thus sin against the LORD [their] God" (Deut 20:18). The peoples in Canaan were aware of God's mighty deliverance of Israel from Egypt, as we see in Rahab's confession to the Hebrew spies in Jericho that the Lord their God "is indeed God in heaven above and on earth below" (Josh 2:11). Nevertheless, most of the people had apparently hardened their hearts and refused to believe the signs God had given in the mighty deeds that brought about Israel's exodus so that nations would know that he was the Lord (Ex 9:16; Rom 9:17); therefore, God's long-delayed judgment was now to fall on them.[65] But the killing stopped "when faith in Yahweh was sufficiently established to meet challenges of Baalism."[66]

Rather than being shocked at the severity of God's judgment on people whose religious practices were abhorrent to him (Lev 18:21-24; 20:3)—so that the land itself was defiled and "vomited out its inhabitants" (Lev 18:25)—we should take care concerning our own responses to God's revelation and be grateful for the grace that restrains God's outpouring of

---

[64]Kaiser, *Toward Old Testament Ethics*, p. 75.

[65]Ibid., p. 268.

[66]Paul Ferguson, "Devote, Devoted," in *Evangelical Dictionary of Biblical Theology*, ed. Walter A. Elwell (Grand Rapids, Mich.: Baker, 1996), p. 175.

wrath on evil-doers today. It is also worthwhile to note that this expression
of God's judgment against wickedness was not restricted to nations other
than Israel, nor was Israel its exclusive instrument. "If the whole nation incurred God's displeasure, as they often did, then the agents of retribution
could be the very pagans whom God had previously repudiated (Is 10:5-
6; Hab 1:5-11)."[67] This occurred, for instance, when God fought against Israel and on the side of the Babylonians (Jer 21:5-7).

We should also observe that God condemned and punished Jehu's
"brutal and politically inspired purges of Baal worship" (2 Kings 9:10) in
Hosea 1:4-5.[68] "Opposing Baal worship and other religious expressions did
not give one a license to kill or to use brutality."[69] In fact, it may be that the
shortness of the time for which Baal worship was eradicated in Israel by
Jehu was "because it was a revolution of force and not a reformation of
heart."[70] Indeed, the worship or recognition of other gods was usually
countered, even in the Old Testament, by preaching rather than force.
Most critical of all, therefore, is the fact that Israel's conquest of Canaan,
with the attendant direction to exterminate the inhabitants, was not aimed
at converting the Canaanites to monotheism. Its purpose was divine judgment on evil and the creation of a context within which a pure testimony
to God could be established and within which a covenant community
would reach the full realization of its divinely intended purpose in the
coming of its Messiah, the Savior of the world.

Although Christians have not always considered the sword an inappropriate way to advance the program of God in the world, including propagation of the gospel, it is generally agreed within the church today that
physical force is not an appropriate instrument for the church to use in the
world.[71] My ancestors were Mennonites, and I have great respect for the
price they paid to obey what they understood to be Christ's call to complete nonviolence. I do not hear the New Testament message in that way,
personally, so I affirm the just-war or just-peace tradition of Christian eth-

---

[67]R. P. Gordon, "War," in *New Bible Dictionary*, ed. N. Hillyer (Wheaton, Ill.: Tyndale House,
1982), p. 1241.
[68]Hess, "Yahweh," p. 17.
[69]Ibid. Christopher Wright observes that "Jehu's *methods,* as a response to religio-political oppression, receive no commendation in the Old Testament" (*An Eye for an Eye: The Place of Old
Testament Ethics Today* [Downers Grove, Ill.: InterVarsity Press, 1983], p. 129).
[70]Wright, *Eye for an Eye,* p. 129.
[71]This reflects a remarkable success on the part of the Radical Reformation, which innovated
by insisting on the separation of church and state and the liberty of conscience, which entailed freedom of religion within a society.

ics. Thus, I consider Christians to have responsibilities both in the sphere of the civil society in which they live and in the church where they regularly worship.

For the restraint of sin and the well-being of society, God has established the institution of civil government and given to it the power to use the "sword" to defend its citizens against evil-doers both within and outside the state (Rom 13:1-7). To the church, however, Christ has only given the instrument of his written Word, which is to be proclaimed in the power of the Spirit of God for the advancement of God's redemptive purposes in the world. The church is forbidden to use coercive or forceful means to further the purposes of saving grace. However we may interpret the situation in Israel's occupation of Canaan, nothing in the instructions to God's new covenant people authorizes us to use physical force to bring about someone's acceptance of the lordship of Christ, whether that person is inside or outside the covenant community. We should warn people of the terrible judgment of God that awaits those who persistently rebel against him, but he will not use us to bring that judgment down on sinners through physical force or the taking of life.

Where the church has failed to act according to this principle in the history of Christianity, we need to be ready to confess its sin. We should be the first to decry vigilante efforts taken by individuals or groups, in the name of Christ and morality—whether it be the murder of an abortionist by a misguided Christian zealot or acts of violence by groups bearing the name of Christ in places like Ireland, Bosnia, Nigeria and Indonesia. In the current world tensions, it is particularly important that well-known Christian leaders regularly disassociate the Christian church from government use of force in places like Afghanistan and Iraq. Even Christians who believe that actions by political entities were justified in those situations, and who may have participated in a military capacity as citizens of the state, should be very clear that Christianity is not at war with anyone and especially not with other religions. In recent years, many Christian mission organizations have wisely resolved to be very cautious about using the language of spiritual warfare to describe their activities and have stopped using the word *crusade* to refer to evangelistic meetings. As followers of the Prince of Peace, we seek to be agents of peace wherever we are, first focusing on the reconciliation of people with God but also being interested in working for reconciliation in situations of human enmity.

The way God wanted to be worshiped. Through his prophets God made it very clear to Israel that they could not construct just any means they chose to worship the one true and living God. This was true within Israel and, by extension, is true for everyone. As Daniel Clendenin points out,

> The Israelites wore liturgical tassels on their garments for the express purpose of reminding them not to follow God according to their own hearts and minds (Num 15:37-41). In seeking the only true God, it is disastrous to do what is right in our own eyes (Deut 12:8; Judges 17:6; 21:25), for the way which seems right to us may well be a way of death (Prov 14:12; 21:2).[72]

That was a key criterion of false prophets: they prophesy "out of their own imagination" rather than from the direction of Yahweh (Ezek 13:17). Clendenin writes that

> Jeroboam's comprehensive alternative cultus became synonymous with Israel's self-destruction (1 Kings 12:25-33). Sacrifices were to be offered in designated places, not wherever one might choose (Deut 12:13-14; 16:5-6). They were to be performed by designated people, not by just anyone, so that even King Uzziah was rebuked and punished for his insolence and presumption in offering priestly incense (2 Chron 26:16-21).[73]

Divine judgment on Aaron's golden calf (Ex 32) and on the "strange fire" of Aaron's sons Nadab and Abihu (Lev 10), "however well-intentioned their actions may have been, reenforces this point."[74]

Elijah challenged the people to choose between Yahweh and Baal (1 Kings 18:21); "both could not mediate salvation."[75] God will bless the whole world, "but it is wrong to imagine that all the world can worship the Lord any way it chooses, still less that the many religions of the world are equally valid phenomenal manifestations of the one noumenal Reality."[76] Since I have reasoned that faith in God which is elicited by revelation less complete than the revelation given in Jesus can still be saving faith, it is very important to note, as Millard Erickson does, that

> while knowledge of this God may not include all the details about him (which, to some extent, is true even of those who know him from special revelation), the conception of God should not be contradictory to the nature of the true God. Thus, one could not have been an "implicit Jehovist" while

---

[72]Clendenin, *Many Gods*, p. 128.

[73]Ibid., p. 129.

[74]Ibid., p. 130.

[75]Calvin Shenk, *Who Do You Say That I Am? Christians Encounter Other Religions* (Scottdale, Penn.: Herald, 1997), p. 83.

[76]Clendenin, *Many Gods*, p. 131.

worshiping Baal, for instance. This would be true of the worship of many of those in other world religions. . . . It must always be an abandonment of reliance on anything other than the grace of God himself.[77]

NEW TESTAMENT PERSPECTIVES

The attitude of Jesus toward the faith of Gentiles. The historical mission of Jesus was principally, if not exclusively, to Israel (cf. Mt 10:5-6; 15:24), but he admired the faith of the centurion—a pagan whose faith was greater than he had found in Israel (Mt 8:10)—which led him to announce that many, coming from east and west, will be admitted to the kingdom of heaven (Mt 8:11-12). The entry of others into the kingdom is not purely eschatological; it comes about first in history, as the parable of the banquet testifies (Mt 22:1-14; Lk 14:15-24).[78] In the Syro-Phoenician region, Jesus is again astonished at the faith of these "pagans," and he performs miracles for them, including healing the possessed daughter of the Canaanite woman in Tyre and Sidon, at whose faith Jesus marvels (Mt 15:21-28). These miracles have the same meaning as always: they signify that the reign of God is present and at work already (Mt 11:4-6; 12:25-28; Lk 4:16-22). It extends to all who enter it by means of faith and conversion (Mk 1:15). At the well near Sychar, Jesus is impressed with the Samaritan woman's thirst for living water (Jn 4:7-15). He does not reject the worship on Mt. Gerizim, but he announces a future time when true worship will be in Spirit and truth and need not be at either Jerusalem or Gerizim.[79]

Jesus commends the actions of the "good Samaritan" in contrast with those of a priest and a Levite (Lk 10:29-37). It is the Samaritan who models for the Jews God's ideal of the neighbor (Lk 10:36-37). The faithful leper cleansed by Jesus was also a Samaritan (Lk 17:11-16) and was the only one—though a "foreigner"—out of the ten who were healed who returned to give thanks and whom Jesus commended for his faith (Lk 17:18-19). Toward the end of Jesus' ministry, some Greeks asked to see him:

> This inquiry reminds Jesus of the great lifting up of the Son of man (John 12:23). The coming of the nations is always regarded as one of the plain signs of the Messiah. It is thus evident throughout the entire gospel that Jesus always viewed his own life within the greater context of the Old Testament

---

[77]Millard J. Erickson, *How Shall They Be Saved? The Destiny of Those Who Do Not Hear of Jesus* (Grand Rapids, Mich.: Baker, 1996), p. 195.
[78]Dupuis, *Toward a Christian Theology*, p. 46.
[79]Ibid.

prophecies of salvation, and one element in this prophecy of salvation was always the approach of men from other lands and nations.[80]

In the context of Jesus' ministry and teaching, saving faith is clearly not just remotely accessible to pagans and foreigners; it is operative among them. They too may belong to the kingdom of God, "the call to which extends beyond the limits of Israel's chosen people."[81] Initially, this seems to contrast with Jesus' attitude in Matthew 15:24 ("I was sent only to the lost sheep of the house of Israel"). But the eschatological banquet with the patriarchs (Mt 8:10-12), which Jesus announced in response to the centurion's faith, is not just for the end of time: "it is established in Jesus' death and resurrection (Lk 22:16) and is to be announced by the Church (Mk 16:15; Acts 28:30-31) until it grows into its fullness (Mt 6:10; 25:31-32; Lk 11:2)."[82] As Dupuis says, "the Kingdom of God to which the nations have access is at one and the same time historical and eschatological."[83]

The New Testament presents both the particularity of Jesus and the universality of his mission.[84] Jesus told Nicodemus that God loves "the world" and gave "his only Son" (Jn 3:16-17). As John puts it, God "sent his only Son into the world so that we might live through him" (1 Jn 4:9). And Paul says that "in Christ God was reconciling the world to himself" (2 Cor 5:19). Although God desires all kinds of people to be saved and come to the knowledge of the truth, there is only one mediator between God and humankind (1 Tim 2:3-6).

The attitude of New Testament writings toward other religions. The New Testament writers were keenly aware of calls to worship other gods—the "many gods and many lords" (1 Cor 8:5) of Greek and Roman polytheism—but they confessed that Christ was the uniquely normative revelation of God.[85] In fact, a riot broke out in Ephesus when Paul declared that "gods made with hands are not gods" at all (Acts 19:26), thereby threatening the trade of the silversmiths who made the images of Artemis. As Georges Khodr says, the apostles' openness to the pagan world (cf. Acts 10:35; 14:16-17; 17:28) "confers no theological status on it."[86]

---

[80]Bavinck, *Introduction*, p. 33.
[81]Dupuis, *Toward a Christian Theology*, p. 47.
[82]Ibid.
[83]Ibid., p. 48.
[84]Shenk, *Who Do You Say*, p. 96.
[85]Dhavamony, *Christian Theology*, p. 15.
[86]Georges Khodr, "The Economy of the Holy Spirit," in *Faith Meets Faith*, Mission Trends, ed. Gerald H. Anderson and Thomas F. Stransky (Grand Rapids, Mich.: Eerdmans, 1981), 5:38.

In Athens, Paul preached to Stoics and Epicureans, whose schools had "adopted the principle of accommodation of their beliefs with popular religion for their followers." In the imperial period, they "had to endorse religious pluralism if they were to maintain their following, given the growing cult of the veneration of the deceased emperor as one of the ways of affirming loyalty to the Principate."[87] Yet, in Acts 17:27-28, "Paul explicitly sets out his theology of God over against the divine plurality espoused by both Stoics and Epicureans in the Athenean audience. He did so, whatever the consequences for the imperial policy."[88]

In Corinth, Christians discussed whether they should dine in the pagan temples and eat meat sacrificed to idols (1 Cor 8—10; cf. Rev 2:20). "Paul is quite categorical: 'a false god has no existence in the real world' (1 Cor 8:4)."[89] Here "Paul sides with the strong in their contention that idols have no real, objective, ontological existence" (cf. 1 Cor 10:19-20), making an appraisal of idolatry that Paul inherits from Old Testament poets and prophets (cf. Ps 115:4-7; 135:15-17; Is 44:9-20; 46:1-7; Rev 9:20; see also 1 Cor 12:2, "idols that could not speak").[90] The so-called gods to whom the non-Christians attributed deity were not so; "they had no existence in the form their worshippers believed them to have."[91] Indeed, Paul later described them as demons (1 Cor 10:20), and his statement "yet for us, there is one God, the Father" (1 Cor 8:6) "indicates that there was a clear dividing line for the Christian community on the issue of religious pluralism"[92] in the sense of accepting other religions as equally valid with Christian faith. Paul says of the people of Thessalonica that they "turned to God from idols, to serve a living and true God" (1 Thess 1:9). Paul reminds the believers in Ephesus that in their pre-Christian days, they were living without hope and "without God in the world" (Eph 2:12). As Bavinck observes, "In spite of their religiosity, their beautiful temples, and their appearance of piety, they journeyed without God through this bewildering world."[93] They had followed

---

[87]Bruce Winter, "In Public and in Private: Early Christians and Religious Pluralism," in *One God, One Lord: Christianity in a World of Religious Pluralism,* 2nd ed., ed. Andrew D. Clarke and Bruce Winter (Grand Rapids, Mich.: Baker, 1992), p. 140.

[88]Ibid., p. 142.

[89]Khodr, "Economy of the Holy Spirit," 5:38.

[90]Don N. Howell Jr., "The Apostle Paul and First-Century Religious Pluralism," in *Christianity and the Religions: A Biblical Theology of World Religions,* Evangelical Missiological Society Series, ed. Edward Rommen and Harold Netland (Pasadena, Calif.: William Carey Library, 1995), 2:101.

[91]Winter, "In Public," p. 144.

[92]Ibid., p. 145.

[93]Bavinck, *Introduction*, p. 53.

"the ruler of the power of the air, the spirit that is now at work among those who are disobedient" (Eph 2:2).

The church's missionary role in the world. From the missionary work assigned to the church, it is clear that God wishes the nations to know the good news of what Christ has accomplished. It is only after Christ's resurrection that missionary outreach gets under way as the norm for God's new covenant people—when Jesus sends out his disciples to carry on the work that began when the Father sent the Son (Jn 20:21). Jesus had called the disciples so they could be with him and be sent out to preach the gospel (Mk 3:14). In the Great Commission, therefore, "the prophetic vision of nations coming to Jerusalem (Is 2:2-5; Mic 4:1-5; Zech 8:20-23) is replaced by the reality of Jewish missionaries going to the nations."[94]

The church does not completely replace Israel, but it is the continuing covenant community of the people of God united in Jesus, the one in whom the promises to Israel are fulfilled. As Vinoth Ramachandra aptly puts it, "the church is a particular community among other particular communities in the world. But it has a universal mission. To be elect in Christ Jesus means to be incorporated into his mission to the world, to be the bearer of God's saving purpose for his whole world."[95] So "the gospel creates new human community, and that new human community is itself part of the gospel to be proclaimed."[96]

In fact, we can put the missionary thrust of the church in the larger context of the Noahic covenant. Thus, Roman Catholic bishop from Malawi, Patrick Kalilombe, sees in Acts 17:26-28

> a validation of the insights found in the first chapters of Genesis: there is a cosmic Covenant of love between God and mankind by the very fact of creation. Mankind may break this Covenant through sin and infidelity. But again and again God renews it and reaffirms his salvific intention. His special choices (that of Israel and that of the church) are not an abolition of the cosmic Covenant. If anything, they are a hopeful sign or proof of what in less evident ways he is doing all along with the whole of mankind, and they are meant to serve this wider Covenant.[97]

---

[94]Schnabel, "Israel," p. 47.
[95]Ramachandra, *Recovery of Mission,* p. 235.
[96]Ibid., p. 266.
[97]Patrick Kalilombe, "The Salvific Value of African Religions," in *Faith Meets Faith,* Mission Trends, ed. Gerald H. Anderson and Thomas F. Stransky (Grand Rapids, Mich.: Eerdmans, 1981), 5:62-63.

Walter Kaiser proposes, quite plausibly, that Isaiah's prediction that Yahweh's Servant will be the instrument of salvation to the Gentiles should not be restricted to a time still future for us. When Jesus promised the Holy Spirit and announced his plan that the early Christian believers were to be his witnesses in Jerusalem, Judea and Samaria and to the ends of the earth (Acts 1:8), "he authoritatively gave the meaning of what he had intended for the listeners of Isaiah's day to understand from Isaiah 49:6."[98]

> There are three repeated allusions to this text from the prophet in the New Testament. (1) The expression "to the ends of the earth" is verbally identical to the Greek rendering of the same phrase in Isaiah 49:6. The extent and scope of the witness are the same in both Testaments.
>
> (2) The coming of the Holy Spirit in Acts 1:8 is closest to the wording in Isaiah 32:15, where the destruction of Jerusalem is predicted "till the Spirit is poured upon us from on high, and the desert becomes a fertile field." This is reminiscent of the Spirit's coming in Isaiah 44:3-4 as rain on a dry and thirsty land. In this context, the clause, "I will pour out my Spirit on your offspring, and my blessing on your descendants" (Isa. 44:3b) does not refer to abundant rain, but is used metaphorically of the conferring of spiritual blessings. Thus, as numerous progeny was taken as a sign of God's blessing, so spiritual progeny are likewise a sign of God's blessing. The work of the Holy Spirit would elicit bold testimony from his people Israel, just as it will from early Christian believers.[99]

The apostle Paul cites the promise that the Servant will be "a light to the nations" (Is 49:6) and announces this as a command for himself, explaining why he, too, went to the Gentiles (Acts 13:47). So the command was not limited to the Messiah as Servant, but it also "embraced the remnant of Israel."[100] Paul "understood his missionary activity to Gentiles within the context of an Old Testament expectation in which the Gentile nations would on the final day partake of God's ultimate blessings to Israel."[101] James had likewise identified Peter's Gentile mission as fulfillment of the prediction of Amos 9:11-12 that God would restore David's fallen tent with the possession of all the nations that bear the Lord's name.[102]

---

[98]Walter C. Kaiser Jr., *Mission in the Old Testament: Israel as a Light to the Nations* (Grand Rapids, Mich.: Baker, 2000), p. 61.

[99]Ibid., pp. 61-62.

[100]Ibid., p. 63.

[101]Köstenberger and O'Brien, *Salvation*, p. 164.

[102]Kaiser, *Mission*, p. 76.

GOD'S USE OF ASPECTS OF THE RELIGIOUS CONTEXT IN FORMING HIS UNIQUE COVENANT COMMUNITIES

In establishing his special covenant relationships with Israel and the church, God appropriated divine names and religious forms from contemporary culture and transformed them into something new, without falling into syncretism. Because we regularly face both the need to contextualize and the danger of syncretism, we do well to watch carefully how God did this. Ramachandra asks, for instance, what we should make of "the fact that God addressed the patriarchs of Israel and entered into covenant with them in terms of divine names and religious forms that they derived from their contemporary culture."[103] His response is excellent: "The covenant between God and Abraham was grounded in God's saving initiative ('grace') and self-disclosure, and not on the sincerity or validity of Abraham's previous worship."[104]

We cannot abstract Abraham from the context of developments in Mesopotamian religion at the time. In the polytheistic systems of the ancient world,

> the great cosmic deities, while respected and worshiped in national and royal contexts, "had little contact with the common people." In Mesopotamia in the first part of the second millennium B.C. people began to relate to minor deities who were thought of as "personal gods" that took interest in a family or individual. . . . "Abraham may have viewed Yahweh as a personal god that was willing to become his 'divine sponsor.'"[105]

As Gerald McDermott says, "the point is not that Yahweh took on all the characteristics of these personal gods but that Abraham may have used this religious framework to understand Yahweh and that Yahweh in turn may have used and then adapted this framework to teach Abraham truths about Himself."[106] The smoking fire pot and blazing torch in Genesis 15 and the practice of circumcision are further examples of features existent in Mesopotamian religious rituals that God may have used "to teach new religious concepts about Himself and His ways with His people."[107]

---

[103]Ramachandra, *Recovery of Mission,* p. 232.

[104]Ibid., pp. 232-33.

[105]McDermott, *Can Evangelicals Learn,* p. 81, quoting John H. Walton and Victor H. Matthews, *The IVP Bible Background Commentary: Genesis-Deuteronomy* (Downers Grove, Ill.: InterVarsity Press, 1997), pp. 36-37.

[106]McDermott, *Can Evangelicals Learn,* pp. 81-82.

[107]Ibid., p. 82, quoting Walton and Matthews, *IVP Bible Background Commentary,* pp. 42, 44.

God accommodated his self-revelation to a social-religious framework of concepts, myths, rites and divine titles, but he broke "through that framework with new and richer promises and acts."[108] God's purpose in electing Abraham in his Mesopotamian context "was not to endorse the religion of El and the Mesopotamian pantheon," but to move Abraham and his descendants beyond that beginning point through a personal relationship with God that would prepare them "for the full experience of redemption and thereby for full knowledge of his true name and character."[109] Wright thus sees the Pentateuchal tradition as illustrative of "accommodation or assimilation" rather than of syncretism.[110]

Calvin Shenk finds in these biblical incidents the suggestion

> that God relates to people in terms of their existing concept of deity . . . but such initiative prepares for fuller revelation and redemption. It would be wrong to conclude that the worship of other gods is always an unconscious worship of the triune God. El, understood as the creator God, was acceptable, but lesser deities and idols were not.[111]

There was some similarity among ancient Semitic religions, but the Old Testament rejected idolatry, immorality and occult practices, consistently illustrating the opposition to syncretism, even as aspects of the cultural and religious context were used in the new formulation of covenantal religious life. "When legal, societal, or religious structures were taken from the surrounding cultures, they were cleansed of their polytheistic elements."[112] For instance, no deity list was included in the treaty or covenant, idols were excluded from the place of worship, priests and prophets were forbidden to engage in sorcery, there was no magic in the sacrifices, and the king was not a deity.[113]

Even when other religions believed in a creator God and had elements of truth, it was understood that sin had distorted the truth, so that followers of other religions were invited to learn from Yahweh. "The salvation

---

[108]Ramachandra, *Recovery of Mission*, p. 233.

[109]Ibid.

[110]Christopher J. H. Wright, "The Christian and Other Religions: The Biblical Evidence," *Themelios* 9 (January 1984): 6.

[111]Shenk, *Who Do You Say*, p. 80.

[112]G. Herbert Livingston, "The Relation of the Old Testament to Ancient Cultures," in *Introductory Articles*, vol. 1 of *The Expositor's Bible Commentary*, ed. Frank E. Gaebelein and J. D. Douglas (Grand Rapids, Mich.: Zondervan, 1979), p. 356.

[113]Ibid.

disclosed in Israel was for all nations."[114] Consequently, "The worship of El was acknowledged but the worship of Baal was repudiated because it implied the worship of other gods. . . . Israel had no need to choose between Yahweh and El but was obliged to choose between Yahweh and the gods of their neighbors."[115] At Mount Carmel, Elijah made very clear the necessity that Israel choose between Yahweh and Baal; both of them could not be God (1 Kings 18:21; cf. Josh 24:14-15).[116] By contrast, "Ezra, Nehemiah, and Daniel identify Yahweh as the 'God of heaven,' a local title used in the Persian empire. Daniel identified Yahweh as the Lord of Heaven, the Syrian high God. Similarly, Ezra and Nehemiah express their theology using the terms of the surrounding culture."[117]

An analysis of Genesis 1—11 turns up considerable similarity between biblical and nonbiblical thinking, but the differences are even more noticeable. In fact, "many of the individual episodes in Gen 1—11 may be seen to have a distinctly polemical thrust in their own right, particularly against the religious ideas associated most closely with Mesopotamia."[118] The account of the tower of Babel is a good case in point. Whereas Babylon claimed to be the center of civilization, with its temple tower being the gate of heaven, "Babel does not mean gate of God, but 'confusion' and 'folly.' Far from its temple's top reaching up to heaven, it is so low that God has to descend from heaven just to see it!" (Gen 11:4-9).[119] The flood account in Genesis is remarkably parallel to the Mesopotamian accounts, but the relationship between the divine and the human worlds are portrayed in a very different manner. "Whereas the Mesopotamian gods destroyed mankind out of caprice and their 'Noah' just happened to be lucky enough to worship the right deity, Genesis declares that man's wickedness provoked the flood and that Noah was saved because he was righteous."[120]

These marked differences between the religion of Israel and its neighbors notwithstanding, the Hebrews appropriated the Semitic name *El* for God, and the New Testament writers used the Greek *theos*.

---

[114]Shenk, *Who Do You Say*, p. 80.

[115]Ibid., p. 83.

[116]Goldingay and Wright, "Yahweh," p. 56.

[117]Shenk, *Who Do You Say*, p. 85. See Ezra 1:2; 5:11-12; 6:9-10; 7:12, 21, 23; Neh 1:4-5; 2:4, 20; Dan 2:18-19, 37, 44; 5:23.

[118]Gordon J. Wenham, *Genesis 1-15*, vol. 1 of *Word Biblical Commentary* (Waco, Tex.: Word, 1987), p. xlviii.

[119]Ibid., p. xlix.

[120]Ibid.

The *El* of the sixth-century B.C. history of Phoenicia by Sanchuniathon was a fierce warrior god—in most respects unlike Yahweh, but like Yahweh a god of battles. The Hellenistic *theos* was often understood to be a single godhead behind many names and mythologies or an impersonal One behind all that is.[121]

Theos, as it describes the God of the New Testament, is highly personal, unlike the Hellenistic counterpart; but it is "the ground and force behind everything that exists," which may indicate that there was some continuity as well as discontinuity in the appropriation of a term already in use.

McDermott takes note of remarkable parallels between Psalm 104 and an Egyptian hymn of Amenhotep IV (Akhenaten, early fourteenth century B.C.). The latter is "a hymn of praise to the deity that is manifested by Aten, the sun disk. It is a remarkable example of monotheism, made all the more remarkable by its presence in a long history of ancient Egyptian polytheisms. Perhaps for this reason it vanished as soon as its progenitor died."[122] Both of these texts

> speak of God sending rain to water the earth and satisfy the beasts of the field and the birds of the air, of the earth returning to darkness and lions emerging when the sun retires, of God's manifold works fulfilling the divine will, of ships and fish sporting in the oceans before God, of humans getting their food from God, and of all creaturely life depending on the divine spirit.[123]

Although the possible connection between these two texts is a matter of scholarly debate, McDermott considers it likely that

> either these ideas were common to the ancient Near East and the psalmist used them, under the inspiration of the Holy Spirit, to describe Yahweh's providence, or there was a direct borrowing from the Egyptian hymn. In either case non-Hebrew sources influenced the Hebrew writer in ways that eloquently depicted God's loving care for His creatures.[124]

---

[121]McDermott, *Can Evangelicals Learn,* p. 82, quoting Patrick D. Miller Jr., *The Divine Warrior in Early Israel* (Cambridge: Harvard University Press, 1973), and J. Schneider, "Theos," in *New International Dictionary of New Testament Theology,* ed. Colin Brown (Grand Rapids, Mich.: Zondervan, 1976), 2:66-67.

[122]McDermott, *Can Evangelicals Learn,* p. 83.

[123]Ibid., pp. 83-84, quoting "The Hymn to the Aton," from *An Anthology of Texts and Pictures,* vol. 1 of *The Ancient Near East,* ed. James B. Pritchard (Princeton: Princeton University Press, 1958), pp. 226-30.

[124]McDermott, *Can Evangelicals Learn,* p. 84.

This seems a plausible assessment.

C. S. Lewis refers to the fact that Moses "was instructed in all the wisdom of the Egyptians" (Acts 7:22) and suggests

> it is conceivable that ideas derived from Akhenaten's system formed part of that Egyptian "wisdom" in which Moses was bred. Whatever was true in Akhenaten's creed came to him, in some mode or other, as all truth comes to all men, from God. There is no reason why traditions descending from Akhenaten should not have been among the instruments which God used in making himself known to Moses.[125]

On the other hand, there were marked differences between the God worshiped by the Hebrews and the high god of the Egyptians. The Egyptians concentrated the attributes of many deities into a mighty sun-god, but theirs was "a naturalistic monism." In contrast, "Israel was dedicated to a purely spiritual sovereign creator not identified with any aspect of nature or with any essence of nature."[126]

Scholars frequently assert that Proverbs 22:17—24:22 is drawn from an earlier Egyptian wisdom tradition known as the *Teaching of Amenemope* because both the structure and the subject matter are so similar.[127] In both, we find thirty precepts or exhortations, many of which use the same images. R. B. Y. Scott notes that there is no way to prove literary dependence, but

> he thinks that the profession of scribe in that era was international and that scribes probably were trained in a wide range of wisdom writings. If the Hebrew scribe did not have the Egyptian text before him or was not recalling it from memory, he probably was calling upon a tradition that was international rather than merely Hebrew.[128]

It is interesting to note also that the floor plan for the tabernacle, about which God instructed Moses (Ex 26:30), "was similar to that of the Egyptian temples, which possessed an inner sanctuary having no source of light, a larger room, and an outer court," features that were also "common to some Semitic temples."[129]

---

[125]C. S. Lewis, *Reflections on the Psalms* (Glasgow: Fontana, 1958), p. 74, quoted in McDermott, *Can Evangelicals Learn*, p. 85.

[126]Livingston, "Relation of the Old Testament," p. 346.

[127]McDermott, *Can Evangelicals Learn*, p. 85, quoting James D. G. Dunn, "Biblical Concepts of Revelation," in *Divine Revelation*, ed. Paul Avis (Grand Rapids, Mich.: Eerdmans, 1997), p. 7.

[128]McDermott, *Can Evangelicals Learn*, pp. 85-86, quoting R. B. Y. Scott, *The Anchor Bible: Proverbs and Ecclesiastes* (Garden City, N.Y.: Doubleday, 1965), pp. 20-21.

[129]Livingston, "Relation of the Old Testament," p. 346.

In their use of the word *logos,* John (in his Gospel) and Paul (in Colossians) resist the tendency to syncretism "by deliberate *assimilation* of current vocabulary into a thoroughly Christian (Old Testament based and Jesus centered) theology." In doing this, they differed greatly from the second-century apologists who found Christ in the faiths and philosophies of humankind.[130] So we find in the Scriptural practice

> no basis for concluding that the other nations in the Old Testament were in reality worshiping Yahweh under a variety of names and should be left to worship their own gods. Instead, Israel's relationship with Yahweh was to be a witness to others; other people were invited to join in the worship of Yahweh.[131]

But we also find that the concepts and practices of Israel's neighbors and their religions were not so thoroughly depraved that God was unable to use some of them in communicating to his covenant people who he was and how he wanted to be worshiped and served.

CONTEMPORARY ATTEMPTS TO FOLLOW THE APPROACH MODELED IN SCRIPTURE

Deciding whether names for gods used in another religion are appropriate for us to use when we speak about God or translate his written Word is a very complex task. The practice in Scripture itself indicates that we cannot rule it out in principle, but it also provides some guidelines. Christian use of a name already used has advantages in terms of affirming another religion's truth, but because religions are systems, we must observe carefully all that is entailed in the understanding of the name within its original religious context. There will always be new content, or *discontinuity,* when we speak of the triune God by appropriating the name being used by a people to whom we bring the gospel. So thorough education will be necessary. Accordingly, Michael Pocock's study of the Wisdom literature of the Old Testament leads him to the conclusion that "the lesson for relationships between the people of God and other cults and cultures will be that the use of communicational *forms* common to both is acceptable and advisable, while the biblical distinctives of worldview and theology must be maintained."[132]

---

[130]Wright, "Christian and Other Religions," p. 13.
[131]Shenk, *Who Do You Say,* p. 83.
[132]Pocock, "Selected Perspectives," 2:46.

There is no reason to doubt that a significant factor in Protestant missionaries' success in Korea was their conclusion that the Korean name for the High God, Hananim, was the only appropriate term for them to use in reference to Yahweh. They told Koreans about how Hananim had revealed himself supremely in the sending of his Son, Jesus, whose death and resurrection provided atonement for the sins of repentant believers.[133] Similarly, Shenk contends that "to the question . . . 'Is Allah of the Muslims the same God as the Christian God?' we can respond confidently, 'Allah is the same God but understood differently.'"[134] This was Muhammad's own perception of the situation. He "understood his calling as a prophet to be in full continuity with the God of Abraham."[135]

Timothy George has asked, "Is the God of Muhammad the Father of Jesus?" and he concludes that the answer is both yes and no. It is yes because "the Father of Jesus is the only God there is" and because "Christians and Muslims can together affirm many important truths about this great God—his oneness, eternity, power, majesty." But the answer is also no because "no devout Muslim can call the God of Muhammad 'Father,'" which would compromise divine transcendence, or assert that God is a Trinity. And yet no one who knows God as he has revealed himself to us in Christ can refuse to call God "Father" or deny that God is Father, Son and Holy Spirit.[136] Shenk's clear yes and George's ambiguous yes and no are not so much different responses to the religious phenomenon of Islam as they are answers to slightly different questions. Both affirm that there is only one God, and both grant that this God is understood differently by Christians and Muslims.

Timothy Tennent helpfully proposes a distinction between three levels at which a name is used: the linguistic, the revelational and the positional. At the linguistic level, Allah and God are "semantically identical" and "completely interchangeable," since "Allah is the Arabic translation of the English word God," and its use "as a divine designation in Arabic precedes the rise of the Islamic faith in the seventh century."[137] At the revelational

---

[133]Compare Don Richardson, *Eternity in Their Hearts*, rev. ed. (Ventura, Calif.: Regal, 1984), pp. 66-69.

[134]Shenk, *Who Do You Say*, p. 190.

[135]Patrick Gaffney, quoted in Agnieszka Tennant, "The Prophet's Pulpit: An Interview with Patrick Gaffney," *Books and Culture*, January-February 2002, p. 21.

[136]Timothy George, "Is the God of Muhammad the Father of Jesus?" *Christianity Today*, February 4, 2002, p. 34.

[137]Timothy C. Tennent, *Christianity at the Religious Roundtable: Evangelicalism in Conversation with Hinduism, Buddhism and Islam* (Grand Rapids, Mich.: Baker, 2002), p. 205.

level, however, although attributes of the Allah of the Qur'an and the God of the Bible overlap considerably, they are also incompatible at points. But it is at the positional level that the greatest difference appears, that is, in regard to the position of worshipers relative to God whom they endeavour to worship. Tennent argues that the Muslim "does not know the Father" and hence "stands in a position of profound discontinuity," being "in need of reconciliation."[138]

I concur with Tennent's proposal regarding the first two levels (linguistic and revelational), but I would urge caution regarding our ability to judge the situation at the third level (positional). His ecclesiocentric position dictates his conclusion. If it is possible, however, that God can draw people into saving relationship with himself prior to their knowledge of Jesus as Christ and hence of God as triune, we find ourselves unable to say with certainty what a particular individual's positional relationship is with God, even though that individual lacks full revelation. The cogency of this point may be easier to see if we consider two Christians who worship God by the same name and essentially the same theology, that is, they are identical on the first two levels. Because only God knows the heart, we are unable to assert with certainty that both of them are properly related to God in the critical "positional" dimension. As the Old Testament prophets warn us, it is possible to say the right things and do the right liturgical actions but have hearts that are far from God.

Considering the proper Christian attitude toward Islamic worship of Allah brings to mind a similar need to assess the situation of Jews, many of whom (being neither atheistic nor messianic) also worship a God who is not trinitarian. N. T. Wright has pointed out very helpfully, however, that the monotheism of the period from the Maccabean revolt (second century B.C.) to the Bar-Kochba revolt (second century A.D.) was not a "unitarianism."[139] Those who prayed the Shema held a monotheism that appears not to have had "anything to do with the numerical analysis of the inner being of Israel's god himself."[140] Israel's concept of God as developed in the Old Testament scriptures was a creational, providential and covenantal monotheism that was aimed at establishing a clear distinction between the true God and the conceptions of God found in paganism and dual-

---

[138]Ibid., p. 206.
[139]N. T. Wright, *The New Testament and the People of God*, Christian Origins and the Question of God (Minneapolis: Fortress, 1992), 1:259.
[140]Ibid.

ism.[141] But there were Jewish groups and individuals who speculated "on the meaning of some difficult passages in scripture (Daniel 7, for example, or Genesis 1)" and "suggested that the divine being might encompass a plurality." Among these was Philo, who wondered whether the Logos might, effectively, be a second divine being and whether the *Similitudes of Enoch* may "portray the Son of Man/Messiah as an eternal divine being."[142] Wright argues that it was the rise of Christianity and, possibly, the influence of both "polemical constraint and Hellenizing philosophy" that led Jews during and after the second century to reinterpret "monotheism" as "the numerical oneness of divine being."[143]

Wright's analysis is a good reminder that religions develop and that there is diversity within them. As a result, we must listen very closely to individuals within other religions as they speak about God and their relationship to him. We dare not assume to know what a particular individual believes because he or she is a Muslim, a Jew, a Hindu or a Buddhist. Wright's description of Judaism indicates the effect of interaction with Christianity and other religious ideas. The same has gone on in other religions as they encounter one another. We must, of course, keep our own eyes open to the ways Christian concepts of God have been influenced and shaped by the environment in which its members lived—the cultural, religious, philosophical, political and other factors of the worlds within which Christians have formulated their own faith. To remind ourselves of this, we need go no further than the recent complaints of Open Theists that classical theism has been badly affected by Greek philosophical concepts of God and needs to be purified!

Let me emphasize again that the fact that some people may be rightly related to God, in spite of the incompleteness of the revelation made available to them, is no reason to withhold the full revelation of God in Christ that is brought to us through the New Testament scriptures. For those from whom God has elicited a faith response to lesser revelation, the further revelation will lead them on to fuller knowledge of God and draw them into the community of those who are God's witnesses in the world. In this regard, the experience of first-century Jews who had the faith of Abraham but who learned to worship Jesus and the Spirit as God, together with the Father, is paradigmatic.

---

[141]Ibid., 1:248-52.
[142]Ibid., 1:259.
[143]Ibid.

In choosing how to name God, in new contexts, we will obviously have to be very sensitive to the ways in which the divine names already present in the context are conceptualized. And if we decide that there is sufficient truth in the theological content of a particular name for God to make it possible for us to refer to the God who revealed himself in Jesus by that particular name, we must be prepared for a careful process of instruction. This is, of course, true in every context, including those that are predominantly Christian. All of us must continually be clarifying and purifying the thought that comes to our minds when we say "God," because the temptation to suppress the truth will always be with us and the risk of substituting an image of our own creation for the true and living God is one against which we must be perpetually vigilant.

SUMMING UP

In pursuing an understanding of the way the world's many religions fit into God's program, we have found a consistent voice among the writers of Scripture; they insist that there is only one true and living God and that only he must be worshiped and only in the ways he has prescribed. Sadly, we have noticed that idolatry is not restricted to those who are ignorant of God's covenantal revelation; it is a persistent threat within the community of those who know about God's gracious covenantal work and who identify themselves as God's covenant people. Of course, *as with salvation, the practice of religion for which people are held accountable is determined by the extent to which they have had access to revelation of God's will on the matter.*

Ecclesiocentrists posit that only people who receive God's universally normative revelation can be saved. Since Pentecost, this revelation is the gospel concerning Jesus; as to the old covenant, ecclesiocentrists generally assume that revelation concerning the coming redeemer was the basic knowledge necessary for people to be saved. I suggest that an ecclesiocentric position faces a very serious challenge when we consider the missionary role of the covenant people that was identified above. It is extraordinary that Israel's role as a witness to the nations was a passive one, if in fact God could not save people without such human missionary activity. Such an idea poses an insurmountable problem for synergists, who emphasize the freedom of the human will. From a monergist perspective, the proposal is not incoherent, but it is certainly peculiar. It requires us to believe that God's redemptive program was extremely limited in extent under the old covenant and that God chose for salvation no one outside the relatively small covenant community, except for a few others who came into contact with them. This is not impossible but it is seems implausible, as I have observed in the first part of the book.

It is evident in God's covenant with Abraham that God had gracious purposes for all the nations of the world, who would be blessed through Abraham's progeny. But that program of universal blessing was pursued very slowly, from our limited perspective. Many centuries passed before God the Word finally came in the flesh to fulfill the covenant promise and move forward the program of universal blessing. Even with the establishment of the new covenant, the missionary thrust of the church was necessarily limited, given their small numbers and their inability to travel to the ends of the earth. Once again, it is not impossible that God's program of salvation was so limited geographically, but it does not accord well with the expansive comments concerning God's grace and mercy that we have examined more closely in the first part of the book.

Christian missionary work entails the conversion of people from other religions and the establishment of Christian churches in the context of the religions from which those new believers in Jesus have come. This calls for great wisdom, as noted in the previous chapter. We must contextualize the faith so that converts and potential converts are able to follow Christ in all areas of their lives but without disrupting their cultural background in ways not necessitated by their new Christian faith. Achieving this without syncretism, which distorts Christianity, and without unnecessary dislocation of Christians from their surrounding culture is one of the great challenges of Christian mission work. Indeed, it is an ongoing challenge for Christians and their churches, long after they have been thoroughly established. Much of the weakness of Christian churches in the Western world may be attributable to uncritical conformity to our surrounding (materialistic and hedonistic) culture. On the other hand, our mission in the world is enhanced when we are at home in our society in all the ways that God allows. God's appropriation of certain aspects of the religious context that surrounded Israel provides us with a good model. Our goal is a personal and communal expression of Christian faith that is completely faithful to Jesus but that has the winsome attractiveness to sinners which Jesus himself had while living in Galilee and Judah.

The nuanced approach to religions that we find in an accessibilist proposal should make us both self-critical as Christians and gracious toward others, in whatever state of relative theological ignorance we find them.

We seek to be useful servants of the God who has called us to be his witnesses in the world, where he leaves no one without witness (Acts 14:17). In the next two chapters, then, we will examine the nature of God's work of grace in the context of other religions, both in regard to God's general providence and with reference to eternal salvation.

15

Is There Revelation in Other Religions?

Thesis 21: Formalized religions are ambiguous responses to divine revelation, and so are the religious commitments of individual members of those religions. Both the institutional religions and the persons within them are responding to general revelation, but they may also be responding to universally normative special revelation that they have encountered or to remnants of such revelation that may exist in the traditions that have been passed down. Additionally, there may have been instances of particular, but not universally normative, revelation that contributed to the formation of an established religion or to the personal religious commitment of an individual within one of those religions.

Thesis 22: The scriptures of other religions are not themselves instances of divine revelation. Because these scriptures lack the Holy Spirit's inspiration, they are a mixture of truth and error, depending on the relative extent to which they have appropriated and suppressed revealed truth, whether through human rebellion or error, or through demonic deception.

Thesis 23: After the supreme self-revelation of God in Jesus, the incarnate Word, there have been no divinely appointed prophets on the order of those in the old covenant, such as Moses and Isaiah. In the church, the Spirit of God gifts individuals for prophecy, and this may include the reception of messages from God that are beneficial to the building up of the congregation in their lives of faith. Such new covenant prophecies are fallible reports of messages believed by the reporter to have been received from God, and these must be judged within the congregation by others who have spiritual discernment. God may reveal to individuals outside the church messages containing truth that would further God's purposes in the world if it were appropriated. Only in a very limited sense could the communication of such messages be dubbed "prophecy," and the communicators could not be called "prophets" of God by any but the most restricted definition. They lack the charism of the Spirit that operates in the Christian church. Obviously, the communication of such messages from God is fallible and liable to an admixture of error that greatly exceeds the communication of messages from God by individuals who are indwelt by the Spirit of God. Such messages, particularly when regarded by members of the religious community as having come from God, will contribute significantly to the formation and development of the religion.

Thesis 24: In God's gracious providence, he may have caused or allowed ideas to emerge within a religious context that provide a bridge or stepping stone toward the gospel, thereby facilitating communication of the gospel to those people and becoming an instrument of the Spirit of God in eliciting faith in Christ.

IN THE FIRST PART OF THE BOOK, WE NOTED THAT GOD has revealed himself more specifically to some individuals than to others and that these instances of revelation were not exclusively the revelatory acts by which God established his covenant people. We have seen that a knowledge of God that has not arisen out of the response of God's covenant people to his covenantal revelation may be found within religions. If this is true, we need to assess the implications with reference to two radically opposite approaches. On the one hand, representatives of a no-agreement approach (found only in ecclesiocentrism) find no truth at all in other religions and certainly no response to gracious divine revelation. On the other hand, some more relativistic theologians have suggested that there is a fundamental similarity between God's self-revelation to Israel and the church and his revelation to other people. Consequently, they accept the religious scriptures of other religions as "inspired" works. They might even call these writings the "Old Testament" of particular peoples and may consider them permanently normative and adequate revelation for the particular people to whom the revelatory scriptures were given.

Critically important questions now confront us. What should be our attitude toward the claims of other religions that God has revealed himself to them and that they worship him according to his dictates? How should we regard their scriptures when these are considered divinely authoritative? Did God speak specifically to people outside his covenant relationships with Israel and the church? If so, were these people prophets of the true and living God, even if they were fallible in their reports of God's message? To such questions, we now attend.

THE REVELATION TO WHICH OTHER RELIGIONS CONSTITUTE A RESPONSE

Unquestionably, what we have identified as "general" revelation is a major factor in the religious practice of many people in the world. Everyone has a conscience and contemplates the nature and origin of the physical world in which we live. Everyone is made in the image of God and is seeking ways of dealing with the awareness of and hunger for God that is intrinsic to our human being. Some of the major philosophical religions and even of the more popular "folk" religions have also had exposure to special revelation in the covenantal form, which is now fixed in the Christian Scripture. Particularly important at this point, however, is the evidence that the divine revelation to which other religions are responding *may* include a form of revelation that is neither "general," because it is not uni-

versally available, nor "special," in the sense of being universally normative revelation given to reveal the way of salvation from sin and death. It
is not in the line of revelation that God gave as he established a people
with whom he formed a special covenantal relationship for the blessing of
the world. This is important to our assessment of the value of other religions and particularly of their scriptures.

In chapter six, I cited a few reports of quite remarkable personal revelation by God apart from the inspired Scriptures, but those were in situations where people had contact with the Christian church and its message.
In the first part of the book, our primary interest was in the question of
what forms of revelation God might use to save *individuals*. In this second
part of the book, however, we are focusing on the *religions* that come into
being, within which people accept a common set of beliefs, attitudes and
practices that are ultimate for them, in and through which they deal with
the God consciousness that is built into humans as creatures made in
God's image. So I now want to mention a few reports of special revelation
made to individuals who live in completely non-Christian contexts. Of
course, these are accounts that have been passed on to us through many
hands and the development of which, within the contexts of their occurrence, would be difficult to study, given time and distance. Nevertheless,
they are reported by credible Christian witnesses, and particular significance has been attributed to them by groups of people who eventually
came to faith in Christ. With these factors in mind, I now cite a few of these
reports for your pondering.

REPORTS OF PARTICULAR DIVINE REVELATION TO INDIVIDUALS OR GROUPS

A Pakistani woman named Gulshan Esther

reports having been healed after an apparition of Jesus at a time in her life
when she was a devout Muslim and her only knowledge of Christianity
was the little information found in the Quran. She was crippled by typhoid
when only six months of age. She claims that Jesus and his apostles all appeared to her, and that she was taught the Lord's Prayer during this encounter nineteen years later. It was her knowledge of this prayer that convinced
a Christian missionary in Pakistan to risk his right to stay in the country by
catechizing her.[1]

---

[1]Phillip H. Wiebe, *Visions of Jesus: Direct Encounters from the New Testament to Today* (New York: Oxford University Press, 1997), p. 84.

When Phillip Wiebe wrote of this incident, Esther was living in Oxford, England, and conducting missions to Pakistan. Wiebe considers this case unusual because "the knowledge apparently exhibited about Christian beliefs by the percipient seems to have been very minimal."[2]

Such experiences are frequently cited by missionaries among Muslim peoples, but they are not restricted to Muslims; indeed, my father, who was a missionary in India, frequently met Hindus whose first encounter with Jesus was in a dream or vision. J. Oswald Sanders tells of a couple who visited the home of a missionary in Thailand, saying to them, "There is a matter which is troubling me, and I think you are the one who can help me. . . . I had a dream about a man called Jesus. Could you tell me who he is?" The woman "knew nothing of Jesus except that she and her husband had been seeking peace, and together they had tried to live a holy life after the precepts of Buddha, but peace had not come." The missionary taught them from the Scriptures for three hours, "and the Holy Spirit guided and gave understanding. It was a thrill beyond telling to see this simple couple perceive the deep things of the Word of God," said the missionaries. The following week, the couple said, "We have found peace and joy now as we never had before."[3]

From the history of cross-cultural missionary work, we have numerous stories of God's sending to individuals messages that were significant in their later conversion to Christianity. Among these are intriguing stories about a "lost book" from God for which people have been waiting expectantly, as among the people of Myanmar, for instance.[4] Along this line, we can include also messages about the coming of messengers to whom the people should give attention. For example, H. Townsend, a pioneer missionary among the Abeokuta in southwestern Nigeria, wrote of how their *Ifa* oracle had predicted the coming of the missionaries and said that they should be permitted to teach. Indeed, Townsend reported, "The great oracle, that is to them as a Bible, has been consulted again and again about us, and has, I am told, never been induced to utter a word against us."[5] This

---

[2]Ibid.

[3]J. Oswald Sanders, *How Lost Are the Heathen?* (Chicago: Moody Press, 1972), pp. 67-70, quoted in Ajith Fernando, *The Christian's Attitude Toward World Religions* (Wheaton, Ill.: Tyndale House, 1987), p. 135.

[4]See Don Richardson, *Eternity in Their Hearts*, rev. ed. (Ventura, Calif.: Regal, 1984), chapter 2.

[5]The Rev. H. Townsend, letter, August 27, 1850, in "Proceedings of Church Missionary Society," 1851, pp. 100-101, quoted in Tokunboh Adeyemo, "Unapproachable God: The High God of African Traditional Religion," in *The Global God: Multicultural Evangelical Views of God*, ed. Aída Besançon Spencer and William David Spencer (Grand Rapids, Mich.: Baker, 1998), p. 143.

raises fascinating questions about which only tentative answers can be given, with so little knowledge of the situation. I do not assume that the *Ifa* oracle was a means of special revelation from God but think it more likely to have been part of the demonic activity among the Abeokuta people. Nevertheless, God can use even evil spirits to achieve his revelational purposes (see, e.g., God's use of a lying spirit to deceive Ahab in 1 Kings 22:13-28), and God can prevent false prophets from speaking things he does not wish (as Balaam testified in Num 22:38).

My interest now lies with a different issue. Given that these revelations about the "lost book" or coming messengers are preparatory to the arrival of the gospel in the instances of which we are aware, we have to wonder about the status of those who die before the gospel reaches them but who waited expectantly for the message that had been promised to them through a "revelation." For reasons I have given in part one, I am ready to grant the possibility that if the Spirit of God generated in an individual's heart an eager longing for the message that was believed to have been promised by God, this anticipation might itself be an evidence of the saving work of God in that individual's life.

Don Richardson recounts the experience of the Santal people in northeast India, who had an ancient oral tradition concerning Thakur Jiu, the "Genuine God," whom nineteenth-century Scandinavian missionaries later identified as the God who made reconciliation with himself possible through Jesus Christ. The result of their ministry and that of other missionaries who followed was a large people movement to Christ.[6] Richardson reflects that

> one of the amazing characteristics of this benign, omnipotent "sky-god" of mankind's many folk religions is His propensity to identify Himself with the God of Christianity! For "sky-god," though regarded in most folk religions as remote and more or less unreachable, tends to draw near and speak to folk religionists whenever—unknown to themselves—they are about to meet emissaries of the Christian God![7]

God graciously witnesses to many of these people, preparing them for the coming of those who bring the good news concerning Jesus. At the very least, God is at work preparing people for the reception of the gospel message. What we do not know is the extent to which God's saving

[6]Richardson, *Eternity in Their Hearts,* pp. 41-47.
[7]Ibid., p. 50.

work may already be under way in the hearts of those who look forward hopefully to the realization of a promised blessing that is not realized within their lifetimes.

Among the Gedeo people of Ethiopia, amazing response resulted when the gospel was preached by Albert Brant and Glen Cain in December 1948. Thirty years later, there were more than two hundred churches among the Gedeo people, averaging more than two hundred members each.[8] The Gedeo believed in a benevolent and omnipotent Creator, called Magano, but few prayed to Magano, and they sacrificed to Sheit'an. When asked by Brant why this was so, they replied, "We sacrifice to Sheit'an, not because we love him, but because we simply do not enjoy close enough ties with Magano to allow us to be done with Sheit'an!"[9] But one of the Gedeo, a man named Warrasa Wange, did approach Magano and asked him to reveal himself to the Gedeo people. He was given vivid visions of white men who came and built "flimsy shelters for themselves under the shade of a large sycamore tree near Dilla, Warrasa's hometown" and later built "more permanent shiny-roofed structures" that eventually "dotted an entire hillside." Then a voice told Wange: "These men will bring you a message from Magano, the God you seek. Wait for them." Eight years passed, during which time "several other soothsayers among the Gedeo people prophesied that strangers would soon arrive with a message from Magano." Finally, Brant and Cain arrived and parked their truck under precisely the sycamore tree that had been featured in Wange's vision.[10]

I am particularly fascinated by the story of the Mbaka people in the Central African Republic because the content of the revelation given to them went beyond the simple announcement that a messenger would come to tell them about God. There was amazing response to the preaching of Ferdinand Rosenau and other Baptist missionary colleagues when they contacted the Mbaka in the early 1920s. Mbaka tribesmen explained the reason for their responsiveness to Eugene Rosenau, son of one of the pioneers:

> Koro, the Creator, sent word to our forefathers long ages ago that He has already sent His Son into the world to accomplish something wonderful for all mankind. Later, however, our forefathers turned away from the truth about Koro's Son. In time they even forgot what it was that He accomplished for mankind. Since the time of "the forgetting," successive generations of our

---

[8]Ibid., p. 56.
[9]Ibid., p. 54.
[10]Ibid., p. 56.

people have longed to discover the truth about Koro's Son. But all we could learn was that messengers would eventually come to restore that forgotten knowledge to us. . . . In any case, we resolved that whenever Koro's messengers arrived we would all welcome them and believe their message![11]

Many Christians are inclined to interpret these exciting incidents as divine preparation for the gospel and to assume that no one was actually saved until the gospel arrived. But I suggest that we need to be cautious about making such assumptions, on two accounts: first, precisely because we are, by definition, ignorant of what God is doing among the peoples about whom we know nothing; and second, because we are not in a position to judge at what point God accepts, as justifying, a faith that is wrought in the heart of a sinner by the gracious act of the Spirit of God (as noted earlier). On the other hand, we would be foolish to put our hope in experiences about which we are necessarily ignorant or about which we have knowledge in relatively rare instances. In short, there is a means of divine revelation that we cannot deny but the value of which we must not overstate. Concerning the divine intent and effectiveness of it, we must be tentative in our statements. We should not ignore, however, the significance of God's using supernatural revelations in the process of people's salvation, even if these are only preparatory to the hearing of the gospel from a human messenger. It certainly gives evidence that God's initiatives of grace toward people are not evenly distributed, which poses a problem for synergists who usually consider this to be "unfair."

Stephen Neill tells, for instance, about Mariamma, a childless widow who feared that she had lost her husband because of sin she had committed in another existence. In her quest for peace, she went to numerous holy sites, but all of them failed to give her peace.

It was about this time that the catechists had first come to her village, but she had resisted them. When they bade her "join 'the Way,' " she had replied, "I have taken hold of this, how can I then take hold of that?" (This was illustrated by catching hold with one hand of one twig of the tree under which we were standing, and another twig with the other hand.) . . . [But] the matter had been decided for her by a dream. She had seen one of the catechists coming to her and saying, "Why do you resist? What we tell you is true." After that she had yielded and believed and been baptized. "Do you not feel tempted sometimes," we had asked her, "to go back to Hinduism as others have done?" "Never," she replied with determination. "See, I have clung to

---

[11]Ibid., p. 57.

Him as this creeper clings to this tree. I will never leave Him; even if He should leave me, I would never leave Him."[12]

HAS SPECIAL DIVINE REVELATION BEEN INVOLVED IN THE DEVELOPMENT OF NON-CHRISTIAN RELIGIONS?

I am encouraged by the above accounts of what God has been doing to make himself known to people who have had no contact with the Christian church. Many more such instances could be recounted, and we have no way of knowing how many similar encounters with God may have taken place in the lives of individuals who never met a Christian within their lifetime. A different kind of situation needs to be considered, however: we must ask whether there have been particular instances of divine revelation in the lives of individuals who were later influential in the establishment of religions that now compete with Christianity for people's allegiance. Might Muhammad and Siddhartha Gautama (known to most as Buddha) and others have had particular disclosures from God that were beyond general revelation but apart from the universally normative special revelation given in connection with the covenant program of God with Israel and the church? Here a proposal made by Dutch Calvinist and theologian of mission J. H. Bavinck bears close attention. Bavinck believed that God did reveal himself to these leaders of other religions:

> In the night of the *bodhi* when Buddha received his great, new insight concerning the world and life, God was touching him and struggling with him. God revealed Himself in that moment. Buddha responded to this revelation, and his answer to this day reveals God's hand and the result of human repression. In the "night of power" of which the ninety-seventh sura of the Koran speaks, the night when "the angels descended" and the Koran descended from Allah's throne, God dealt with Mohammed and touched him. God wrestled with him in that night, and God's hand is still noticeable in the answer of the prophet, but it is also the result of human repression. The great moments in the history of religion are the moments when God wrestled with man in a very particular way.[13]

Tragically, because of the characteristic repression of divine revelation (of which Paul wrote in Romans 1), these devout people who sought God

---

[12]Stephen Neill, *Out of Bondage: Christ and the Indian Villager* (London: Edinburgh House Press, 1930), pp. 53-54.

[13]J. H. Bavinck, *The Church Between Temple and Mosque: A Study of the Relationship Between the Christian Faith and Other Religions* (Grand Rapids, Mich.: Eerdmans, n.d.), p. 125.

formed a concept of him that is different from what has been revealed in Jesus. Consequently, the religions that follow from their encounters with God—Buddhism and Islam—while bearing the marks of divine revelation, represent primarily the human rejection of God. Yet the work of the Spirit is evident at times when God, "as it were, stop[s] the noiseless engines of repression and exchange and overwhelm[s] man to such an extent that he is powerless for the moment."[14]

Bavinck cites Cyrus as such a case: God anointed him with his Spirit and empowered him for the task to which God called him, even though Cyrus did not know God. Thus, says Bavinck,

> we meet figures in the history of the non-Christian religions of whom we feel that God wrestled with them in a very particular way. We still notice traces of that process of suppression and substitution in the way they responded, but occasionally we observe a far greater influence of God there than in many other human religions. The history of religion is not always and everywhere the same; it does not present a monotonous picture of only folly and degeneration. There are culminating points in it, not because certain human beings are much better than others, but because every now and then divine compassion interferes, compassion which keeps man from suppressing and substituting the truth completely.[15]

I have argued that religions are ambiguous responses to God's revelation, and I think that we must take very seriously the possibility presented by Bavinck's statements. I see no reason why we should not grant the possibility that there have been genuine personal encounters with God by key individuals in the formation of religious systems. These encounters may go beyond general revelation and beyond the illumination by which God might open one's eyes to worship of the Creator or make one aware of one's sinfulness before the supreme Judge of all people, before whom we cry for mercy and grace.

If, as I have claimed, there are some aspects of various religions that result from an appropriation of truth revealed by God, then we can expect to find some positive and commendable features within the beliefs, attitudes and practices of other religions and of their adherents. Gerald McDermott has asked whether evangelicals can learn from other religions, and I think he has demonstrated well that "the Bible contains hints and suggestions that God has given knowledge of Himself to people and traditions outside

---

[14]Ibid.
[15]Ibid., p. 126.

the Hebrew and Christian traditions."[16] This has the character not of doctrine or historical event but of "inner experience or new awareness."[17] In McDermott's judgment, "the evidence is neither overwhelming nor crystal clear, but it is sufficient to make a claim for revelation in the religions biblically *plausible*."[18]

Within Scripture, Abram's encounter with Melchizedek, priest of El Elyon, is a very interesting incident. Melchizedek blessed Abram by El Elyon ("the high god of the Canaanite pantheon"[19]) and said that El Elyon is maker of heaven and earth (Gen 14:19). Then Melchizedek blessed El Elyon and declared that he had delivered Abram's enemies into his hand (Gen 14:20). Abram then tells the king of Sodom that he cannot take any of the spoils because he had "sworn to the LORD [Yahweh], God most high [El Elyon], maker of heaven and earth, that [he] would not take a thread or a sandal-thong" or anything that belonged to Melchizedek, so that he "might not say, 'I have made Abram rich' " (Gen 14:22-23). McDermott comments:

> Notice what Abram has done in these words: he has identified Yahweh with El Elyon in two ways. He has conjoined the two names in a gesture that suggests they point to the same God, and—as if it were not completely clear—he has given Melchizedek's description of El Elyon to Yahweh: maker of heaven and earth. Claus Westermann argues that both Abram's acceptance of Melchizedek's blessing and his tithe to the Canaanite priest indicate that Abram acknowledged the legitimacy of Melchizedek's priesthood and sanctuary.[20]

So "Melchizedek is represented as worshipping the true God under the name of a Canaanite deity."

> [He] had knowledge of the true God despite all appearances of *not* having received revelation from the Hebrews. This is not to suggest that Melchizedek's beliefs about God were the same as Abram's, and it certainly does not imply that all Canaanite beliefs about El Elyon were accurate. But the text *does* seem to imply that Melchizedek had some sort of knowledge of the God who manifested Himself as the Holy One of Israel. It means that true

---

[16]Gerald R. McDermott, *Can Evangelicals Learn from World Religions? Jesus, Revelation and Religious Traditions* (Downers Grove, Ill.: InterVarsity Press, 2000), p. 73.

[17]Ibid., p. 72.

[18]Ibid., p. 74.

[19]Walter Brueggemann, *Genesis,* Interpretation: A Bible Commentary for Teaching and Preaching (Atlanta: John Knox, 1982).

[20]McDermott, *Can Evangelicals Learn,* pp. 77-78, quoting Claus Westermann, *Genesis: A Practical Commentary* (Grand Rapids, Mich.: Eerdmans, 1987), p. 115.

knowledge of God came to Melchizedek apart from revelation given through the Abrahamic lineage.[21]

With a very similar reading of the incident, John Goldingay and Christopher Wright opine that

> the implication seems to be that Abram and Genesis itself recognize that Malkisedeq (and presumably other people in Canaan who worship El under one manifestation or another) does serve the true God but does not know all there is to know about that God. It is in keeping with this that Israel in due course takes over Malkisedeq's city of Shalem and locates Yahweh's own chief shrine there. "Yahweh roars from Sion" (Amos 1:2); indeed, "El, God, Yahweh" shines forth from Sion (Ps 50:1).[22]

A similar thing takes place, in Genesis 18:33, when Abraham calls on God as Yahweh El Olam. "El Olam appears only here as a designation of Yahweh, but comparable phrases come elsewhere to designate Canaanite deities. Such Canaanite texts also more broadly refer to El as one who blesses, promises offspring, heals, and guides in war."[23] There are correspondences between Yahweh and El as the Canaanites know him, "but these correspondences do not constitute identity."[24]

Discussing a later incident, Goldingay and Wright propose that Joseph and the Pharaoh

> seem to work on the basis that the God they serve is the same God (see Gen. 41:16, 39; and cf. the Pharaoh's giving and Joseph's accepting an Egyptian theophoric name and a wife who was a priest's daughter, 41:45). However, this common understanding changes dramatically in Exodus when a later Pharaoh refuses point-blank to recognize Yahweh as God. It is a major subplot of the ensuing narrative to show the stages by which he was forced to do so (notice the train of thought running through Exod. 5:2, 7:5, 17, 8:10, 22, 9:15, 29, 14:18, 25). No matter how positively we view the openness to other people's experience and worship in God, there are circumstances where the conflictual stance is unavoidable. In this case it was because of rival claims to deity, resistance to God's redemptive work in history, and manifest, unrepentant oppression and injustice.[25]

---

[21]McDermott, *Can Evangelicals Learn*, p. 78.
[22]John E. Goldingay and Christopher J. H. Wright, " 'Yahweh Our God Yahweh One': The Oneness of God in the Old Testament," in *One God, One Lord: Christianity in a World of Religious Pluralism*, 2nd ed., ed. Andrew D. Clarke and Bruce Winter (Grand Rapids, Mich.: Baker, 1992), p. 48.
[23]Ibid.
[24]Ibid.
[25]Ibid.

It is significant that John indicates that the Word of God is "the life" who was "the light of all people" (Jn 1:3-4). Whatever knowledge humans possess of God has been given by Christ, and this knowledge has been given to the pagans as well, since John says that the true light who was coming into the world "enlightens everyone" (Jn 1:9). As Christian philosophers have been prone to assert in recent decades, "all truth is God's truth." Thus, when Paul acknowledges that Epimenides and Aratus—the sixth- and third-century B.C. Greek poets whom he quoted at Athens—have spoken truth about God (Acts 17:28), this knowledge must have been mediated to Epimenides and Aratus by Christ, suggests McDermott.[26]

Carl Braaten wisely warns us, however, against "making any sweeping judgments about what can be known of God in the world religions apart from his self-revelation in Israel, Jesus and the church."[27] To this I add that where revelation is encountered apart from the supreme self-giving in the incarnate Christ—as in God's more general self-disclosure or in particular moments of his personal encounter with individuals—that the God who is revealing himself to these people is always the triune God who made covenant with Israel and the church and who revealed himself in Jesus, even though the people receiving the revelation live outside the bounds of the covenant community of God's people. Braaten is correct to object to Raimundo Panikkar's proposal that the universal Christ goes by many names—Rama, Krishna, Purusha, Tagatha and the like. Like John Hick, who speaks of a "universal God," Panikkar makes a jump "directly from phenomenological facts to theological judgments without benefit of the kind of christological critique that a trinitarian theology of the cross would require."[28] Although the Word mediates all God's self-revelation, his personal manifestation in the flesh is distinctive and complete and must be distinguished from all other purportedly personal appearances of God. As Gabriel Fackre so clearly observes, because Jesus, the Word, is the Way, the Truth and the Life (Jn 14:6), "*wherever* the truth is spoken . . . the Son of the Father, the Word of the Father, Jesus Christ speaks it. Truth is the gift of the Logos at work in the narrative of revelation . . . by the power of the Holy Spirit."[29]

---

[26]Ibid.

[27]Carl E. Braaten, *No Other Gospel! Christianity Among the World's Religions* (Minneapolis: Fortress, 1992), p. 72.

[28]Ibid., p. 78.

[29]Gabriel Fackre, *The Doctrine of Revelation: A Narrative Interpretation,* Edinburgh Studies in Constructive Theology (Grand Rapids, Mich.: Eerdmans, 1997), p. 30.

THE NATURE AND STATUS OF THE SCRIPTURES OF OTHER RELIGIONS

Christianity is a religion of the book, and it learned to be so from its Lord and "founder," whose own life was consciously lived in fulfillment of the scriptures that we now designate the Old Testament. Jesus himself regarded the Old Testament as God's Word, absolutely reliable (cf. Mk 12:24-37; Lk 20:15-18), and he promised that the Holy Spirit would continue to lead his followers into truth, so that the New Testament would eventually also become part of the Word of God. The authority in Jesus' own life was the Word of God. He repeatedly insisted that it must all be fulfilled (Mt 5:17-19), and he appealed to it continually in disputes (e.g., Mk 12:24-27). The Holy Spirit of God leads us to faith in the resurrected Jesus, and we follow his directive to obey the Word of God. As Gerald Bray wisely states, "the person of Jesus Christ cannot be divorced from the written Word of God, and if the latter goes there are few grounds for maintaining the divinity of the former."[30] It is because of the completeness of the revelation in Christ that objective special revelation, of the universally normative kind, ceases with the apostolic, inspired interpretation of his work and words. God spoke his last word in Jesus (Heb 1:1-3), and Scripture now brings Christ to us as the Spirit enlightens our minds and empowers his Word.

The sufficiency and finality of the scriptures of the Old and New Testament have prevented the church from acknowledging any further revelation, verbal or written, as universally normative for the people of God. Only those writings that the Spirit of God inspired in the process of leading his covenant people into fellowship with himself warrant human obedience. This exclusive claim on the part of Christian orthodoxy is not popular in a relativistically pluralist environment, such as the one that characterizes the postmodern Western world, but it is the inescapable consequence of commitment to Jesus as Lord and of belief that Jesus is the ultimate in God's program of self-revelation.

The scriptures of other religions, therefore, are definitely *not* parallel to the Old Testament as God's revelation for them, preparing them for Christ, nor are they additional revelation that supplements or even supplants the New Testament as religious authority. I am made decidedly uneasy, for instance, by the kind of proposal put forward by Steve Charleston when he suggests that "instead of speaking about Native American spirituality" we

---

[30]Gerald Bray, *The Doctrine of God*, Contours of Christian Theology (Downers Grove, Ill.: InterVarsity Press, 1993), p. 237.

should begin to speak of "an Old Testament of Native America."[31] By contrast, I agree once more with J. N. D. Anderson:

> I have heard of more than one Muslim whose study of the Qur'an made him seek after Christ; but I think we must ascribe this to the Spirit of God meeting him in his need, rather than attribute it to the Qur'an as such. Yet there are certainly elements in non-Christian religions—and, indeed, in the heart of man—that testify in some measure to the righteousness and judgment of God, to the sin and guilt of man, and to the need of men and women everywhere for expiation and forgiveness, through all of which God can speak.[32]

Jacques Dupuis has proposed that the Qur'an in its entirety is not the authentic word of God for it contains error but that it is an imperfect transmission of genuine revelation given to Muhammad.[33] But Charleston states that the "old testament" of Native America "is full of mistakes, false starts, guesses, hopes, dreams, wishes, just like any other Old Testament."[34] To the contrary, I insist, it is precisely here that the scriptures of other religious traditions differ from the Scriptures of God's covenant revelation. Although the former may well have been written in response to a number of forms of genuine divine revelation, and although they contain truth as a consequence of this fact, they are human writings without the benefit of the Spirit's inspiration, which protected the writers of the covenant Scriptures from error. Therefore, other religions' scriptures (or, indeed, any noncanonical scriptures to which Christians might make appeal) are fallible writings. They record a response to divine revelation that includes the characteristic ambiguity of openness to and repression of truth. We cannot emphasize too strongly the distinctive operation of the Holy Spirit in the production of the covenant Scriptures—the Old and New Testaments—which makes them infallible and therefore unique.[35]

Charleston's suggestion that groups other than the Jews might have

---

[31]Steve Charleston, "The Old Testament of Native America," in *Lift Every Voice: Constructing Christian Theologies from the Underside*, rev. and exp. ed., ed. Susan Brooks Thistlethwaite and Mary Potter Engel (Maryknoll, N.Y.: Orbis, 1998), p. 72.

[32]J. N. D. Anderson, *Christianity and World Religions: The Challenge of Pluralism* (Downers Grove, Ill.: InterVarsity Press, 1984), p. 173.

[33]Jacques Dupuis, *Toward a Christian Theology of Religious Pluralism* (Maryknoll, N.Y.: Orbis, 1997), p. 245.

[34]Charleston, "Old Testament," p. 74.

[35]In commenting on an earlier draft of this manuscript, Harold Netland made the helpful observation that "not all scriptures in non-Christian traditions claim the same kind of divine inspiration that is associated with the Bible or the Qur'an. Sacred texts of Hinduism, Buddhism, Jainism and Daoism typically do not fit this model."

been given an "old testament" is intended to provide a positive appraisal of other religious traditions as possibly the work of God, in the same way that Israel's scriptures were produced by God. This brings to mind Paul's concerns in Galatians 4:1-11,[36] because we find there a negative assessment of both the Galatian Gentiles' pagan religious experience and of the position taken by Judaizers who refused to move on to Christ, which was God's intention in the giving of the law (Gal 3:24). Interpreters disagree about Paul's meaning when he writes to the Galatians about the *stoicheia*[37] but, whatever its sense, Paul parallels the experiences of Jews under the law and the experiences of idolatrous Gentiles. In regard to the theme of our present analysis, the feature that I find most striking in Paul's analysis is the contrast (rather than the analogy) which he draws between the pre-Christian situation of Jewish Christians and Gentile Christians. Paul does not denigrate the old covenant or its scriptures. It was God's instrument to lead people toward Christ, who breaks down the ethnic distinction between Jews and Greeks and fulfils the promise which the law had not replaced. In its time and for its disciplinary, pedagogical purpose, the law was good and Jews who had the faith of Abraham knew God as they anticipated fulfilment of the covenant promises and were taught about their sinfulness by the law. By contrast, the Gentiles, who had worshipped idols, had not known God but had been "enslaved to beings that by nature are not gods" (Gal 4:8).

Reading the *stoicheia* as "basic principles of religion," R. N. Longenecker sees a parallel between "the Mosaic Law in its condemnatory and supervisory functions" and the pagan "veneration of nature and cultic rituals."[38] On the other hand, if the *stoicheia* are spiritual powers, as many interpreters conclude, then N. T. Wright's proposal that Paul refers to "local presiding deities" with territorial jurisdiction may be a good way to understand the analogy in Paul's mind.[39] "Paul, faced with Judaizers at

---

[36]I am indebted to Daniel Reid for drawing my attention to this text.

[37]Daniel Reid summarizes the three primary options: "(1) basic principles of religious teaching such as the Law; (2) essential, rudimentary substances of the universe such as earth, water, air and fire; or (3) personal spiritual beings of the cosmos such as demons, angels, or star deities" ("Elements/Elemental Spirits of the World," in *Dictionary of Paul and His Letters*, ed. Gerald F. Hawthorne, Ralph P. Martin and Daniel G. Reid [Downers Grove, Ill.: InterVarsity Press, 1993], p. 229).

[38]R. N. Longenecker, *Galatians*, Word Biblical Commentary (Dallas: Word, 1990), 41:166, quoted in Reid, "Elements," p. 232.

[39]N. T. Wright, *Colossians and Philemon*, Tyndale New Testament Commentaries (Grand Rapids, Mich.: Eerdmans, 1986), pp. 101-2, 115-16), quoted in Reid, "Elements," p. 232.

Galatia, would then be likening Jewish religion governed by the Law to paganism; both were characterized by bondage to religious forces that were but local, national, tribal deities."[40] To require Gentile Christians to submit to "works of the Law" would be, in effect, to regard "the triumph of Christ as the victory of one national deity over all others."[41] Whichever of these readings may represent most accurately the ideas Paul wished to convey, the effect of the parallelism is the same. Pagan religions are not pedagogical preparations for Christ; they are a refusal to follow through with the implications of Christ's fulfillment of both the law and the promises of the old covenant, stifling the freedom into which Christ wants to bring both Jews and Gentiles. For it is "for freedom" that "Christ has set us free" (Gal 5:1), and those who know the truth about Christ but refuse to let him set them free are enslaved, just as are those who worship idols that are not really gods.

Like Bavinck, I am willing to grant the possibility that Muhammad may have had God speak to him in particular ways.[42] I have argued that even if God had spoken to Muhammad in a particular nonuniversally normative manner, Muhammad's writing (the Qur'an) was not inspired scripture. Nevertheless, the Qur'an provides a peculiar opportunity for God to work in the hearts of Muslims, using the testimony concerning Jesus that is contained there, albeit inaccurately. I am reminded of the remarkable experience of Mallam Ibrahim, a Qur'anic teacher in Nigeria, in the mid nineteenth century.[43] Through his reading of the Qur'an, he became convinced that Isa (Jesus) must have been greater than Muhammad because he healed the sick, raised the dead and ascended to heaven. Ibrahim gathered many followers but was eventually summoned before the Muslim clerics in Kano, who demanded that he recant. He refused to do so and was martyred. Before he died, he told his followers (who were called the Isawa) to flee to the boundaries of the emirates of Kano, Bauchi and Zaria and remain there until a man came who would lead them into all of the truth about Isa. Decades later, Walter Miller arrived in northern Nigeria, and in 1913 he was heard preaching in the marketplace by one of the Isawa who concluded that this was the man of whom Ibrahim had

---

[40]Reid, "Elements," p. 232.

[41]Ibid.

[42]Bavinck, *Church Between,* p. 125.

[43]I am indebted to Ian Ritchie for first drawing this incident to my attention in an e-mail message posted to the Canadian Evangelical Theological Association Discussion List on March 23, 1999.

prophesied. Many of the Isawa came to mature faith in Christ under the ministry of Miller in Zaria.

Harvie Conn writes about this incident:

> To the small coteries of Muslims in northern Nigeria, still loyal after perse-cution to their leader, Ibrahim, and to his prophecies that God would one day reveal the true faith to them concerning Isa, the Word of God, the Breath from God, the message in 1913 from a missionary concerning Jesus as Ful-filler turned them to Christ.[44]

A number of things stand out in this historical incident. God spoke through Ibrahim to prepare people for the proclamation of the gospel by a Christian missionary, and God kept that expectation alive in their hearts until Miller arrived many years later. But God had used the Qur'an— which is not divinely inspired as is the Bible but which contains elements of the truth—to give Ibrahim some knowledge of Jesus. The Spirit of God then created in Ibrahim's heart a faith that I assume to be saving, despite the fact that he could hardly be considered "evangelized." The Isawa re-joiced to learn the fuller truth concerning Jesus years after Ibrahim's death, but I expect that Ibrahim would already have had the joy of meeting Christ personally, at the moment of his death, and of worshiping the one infi-nitely greater than Muhammad.

ARE THERE "PROPHETS" OUTSIDE THE COVENANT COMMUNITY?

So much for the scriptures of Islam. But what are we to say about Muham-mad himself, who is so highly revered within Islam as the final and great-est prophet from God? Should we identify Muhammad as a prophet if he received revelation from God and if the message he then preached accom-plished some relative good, in that it opposed polytheism and idolatry? It is hard to conceive that such a message was intended by God for Muham-mad alone, without God's desiring that it be communicated more widely. But is everyone who proclaims a message that has beneficial effects on oth-ers because it contains some truth, albeit truth mixed with error, to be con-sidered a prophet? We need to make a few distinctions. First, we should

---

[44]Harvie M. Conn, "The Muslim Convert and His Culture," in *Faith Meets Faith*, Mission Trends, ed. Gerald H. Anderson and Thomas F. Stransky (Grand Rapids, Mich.: Eerd-mans, 1981), 5:224, quoting Martin Jarrett-Kerr, *Patterns of Christian Acceptance: Individual Response to the Missionary Impact, 1550-1950* (New York: Oxford University Press, 1972), pp. 319-20.

distinguish between messages derived from general revelation and those derived from special revelation.[45]

In the category of messages derived from general revelation, I would include the scientific or moral truth that even a non-Christian might apprehend and propound. We give credit to scientists who "discover" truths concerning the physical world, but we do not dub them "prophets," even if we assert that "all truth is God's truth" and grant that their discovery of this truth involved illumination by the Spirit of God. I am prepared to affirm both of these provisos and to see the Spirit of God at work in the scientific efforts of unbelieving scientists, whose discoveries have the potential to do good in the world and to contribute to greater wholeness or *shalom* within the creation that groans under the effects of sin. (Sadly, of course, we are not always wise in our use of this knowledge, and so discoveries with great potential for good are often used for evil.) In short, scientists may apprehend truth through general revelation and may even use it to further God's purposes for the good of humanity; but they may suppress the call to worship God, which their examination of God's creation should have elicited. They may even deny that God exists. In some informal sense, we might then dub them "false prophets."

It is special revelation that requires our closer examination. In chapter six, I indicated that special revelation is of two kinds: some of it is universally normative—truth revealed by God for all people everywhere—and some of it is given for particular people for a limited time and place. The divinely commissioned prophets of Israel were instruments of God's universally normative revelation. When they spoke for God, they were to be believed and obeyed, and the test of their authenticity was that they were never wrong in what they declared as God's word (Deut 18:22). But that prophetic role did not continue; it became obsolete when the prophet greater than Moses arrived, the Word in the flesh. God had spoken to Israel's ancestors "by the prophets, but in these last days he has spoken to us by a Son, whom he appointed heir of all things, through whom he also created the worlds. He is the reflection of God's glory and the exact imprint of God's very being" (Heb 1:1-3). In Jesus, God spoke the last word, and there was nothing further to be said. The apostles whom Jesus chose to be with him and whom he trained to preach the gospel of the kingdom

---

[45]I am grateful to the anonymous external reader of the first draft of my manuscript, who raised a question about the coherence of my original denial that prophecy has occurred in non-Christian religions. I wrote this section in response to that question.

were not prophets like Moses and Isaiah. Under the inspiration of the Holy Spirit, they wrote letters that were received within the new covenant community as "other scriptures" (2 Pet 3:16), but they added nothing to revelation in Christ. They simply unpacked it, so to speak. After the time of the original apostles, there have been no further divinely authoritative writings.[46] It is for this reason that the orthodox consensus of the Christian church precludes new prophets with universally normative messages from God, despite the claim by Muhammad or, more recently, by Joseph Smith.

That being said, we must be quick to mention that at the Feast of Pentecost after Christ's resurrection, Christ sent the Spirit, as he had promised he would. Galilean followers of Jesus spoke about "God's deeds of power" in many different languages that day, when the Spirit of God filled them (Acts 2:4-11). In explanation of the strange occurrence, Peter announced that the prophecy of Joel had been fulfilled (Joel 2:28). The last days had arrived, and God had poured out his Spirit on both men and women so that they would prophesy (Acts 2:17-18). Since then, prophecy has been among the grace gifts that the Holy Spirit bestows on members of the church for the building up of other members in the body (Rom 12:6; 1 Cor 12:8-10). Prophecy was exercised in the church in Corinth, and Paul gave the Corinthians instructions for its use. Clearly, this form of prophecy does not have the divine authority and infallibility of Israel's divinely appointed prophets.

This issue has become controversial, particularly because of the rise of the "charismatic movement" in the Christian church, but that discussion may illuminate our analysis of prophecy in the non-Christian religions, too. Within that context, I have appreciated C. Samuel Storms's definition of prophecy, in the context of the church today, as "the human *report* of a divine *revelation*." It is based on a spontaneous revelation,[47] and here I am speaking of the second kind of special revelation—particular messages

---

[46]I am aware of the claim within the Roman Catholic Church that the pope might speak *ex cathedra* (from his throne) infallibly, or with divine authority. But since Vatican II, there has been a general consensus in the Catholic Church concerning the sufficiency of Scripture. Although the Catholic Church has a different opinion from Protestants concerning the list of books that should be regarded as Scripture, that difference occurs only in regard to the Old Testament. For the New Testament, the canon is the same in all branches of the church. Furthermore, the pope's pronouncements are not considered to be new revelation additional to Scripture; they are infallible interpretations of Scripture.

[47]C. Samuel Storms, "A Third Wave View," in *Are Miraculous Gifts for Today? Four Views*, ed. Wayne Grudem (Grand Rapids, Mich.: Zondervan, 1996), p. 207.

communicated to individuals, which are not universally normative. Prophecy, even within a New Testament congregation, may occasionally be fallible because there are always these four elements: the revelation, the perception or reception of the revelation, the interpretation of what has been disclosed, and the application of that interpretation. The revelation is infallible, but the report of it is not, because of misperception, misinterpretation and misapplication. Storms illustrates from the case of Agabus in Acts 21. God had given to Agabus the special revelation that Paul was going to be arrested and bound in Jerusalem, but Agabus drew his own conclusions from that revelation and passed them along to Paul, together with the message God had given to him. Paul knew what awaited him in Jerusalem because God had revealed this to others, as well. But Paul felt constrained in his spirit to proceed to Jerusalem with the gift from the Gentiles, and so he rejected the counsel that Agabus gave to him (Acts 21:13). Because error can occur in the passing along of particular messages that God gives to individuals in the new covenant age of the Spirit, extrabiblical prophecy has to be carefully judged (1 Cor 14:29; 1 Thess 5:19-22). As Storms rightly observes, the gift of prophecy does not guarantee the infallible transmission of the revelation.[48]

Agabus and the daughters of Philip were prophets, just as there were other prophets in the church in Antioch, through whom God communicated to the believers there his desire that Barnabas and Saul should be commissioned as missionaries to the Gentiles (Acts 13:2). So far, so good, you may be thinking. But Muhammad was not a Christian believer, he did not have the gift of the Spirit, and he was not operating within the framework of a Christian congregation. Consequently, even if we grant that Agabus was not a prophet of the type of Moses or Isaiah, we can hardly lump Muhammad and Agabus in the same group. But can we apply the definition offered by Storms to the experience of Muhammad? If Bavinck is correct about the operation of divine special revelation outside the covenant people, and if Muhammad is an instance of someone to whom God spoke, then might we say that Muhammad's preaching was a form of "prophecy"? It would then have been a "human *report* of a divine *revelation*." This brings me to a conclusion that will certainly not satisfy a Muslim, but it may not close off conversation as quickly as might otherwise happen. If my line of reasoning is valid, we can say that Muhammad *may* have prophesied, in the sense that he received a mes-

---

[48]Ibid., p. 209.

sage from God and passed it along, though it was mixed with ideas of his own and possibly even with the fruit of demonic deception along the way. So we cannot say that Muhammad was a prophet, as was Moses, in the sense that faithful Muslims must affirm. But we need not deny that God *may* have spoken to him and that he may even have done some good, within God's *providential* purpose in the world. (More on that subject will come up in the next chapter.)

At first thought, it might even appear that some salvation-related good should be attributed to Muhammad's preaching and to the Qur'an, which grew out of it. On a hierarchy of errors, a monotheism that acknowledges Jesus as a prophet may seem superior to a polytheism, even a polytheism that grants some value to Jesus as a holy man or teacher. Those who see other religions as preparatory to Christianity (like the Old Testament revelation is seen as preparatory) might suppose that God could be leading people from polytheism to trinitarian monotheism by means of unitarian monotheism, just as he led the Israel of faith through nontrinitarian monotheism to trinitarianism. In addition to having theological reasons for not accepting an analogy between Judaism and other religions as schoolmasters that lead people to Christ, I am given serious pause by history. Christian evangelism among Muslims has not met with great positive response, despite what one might expect if it were a divine work of preparation.

If I were convinced of the fulfillment approach, I might, perhaps, appeal to Romans 11 and suggest that the movement from Judaism to Christianity has also not been large because of temporary divine hardening. While I find the parallel intriguing, it is highly speculative and would only be attractive if one had some other biblical reason for believing that Israel's role as a covenant people was not unique; such reason is lacking. The testimony of Scripture is clear: Israel had a unique place in God's saving program in the world. As the apostle Paul put it, they are the ones to whom "belong the adoption, the glory, the covenants, the giving of the law, the worship, and the promises; to them belong the patriarchs, and from them, according to the flesh, comes the Messiah, who is over all, God blessed forever. Amen" (Rom 9:4-6). It was Israel's unique role to be the people from whom Messiah would come, the one through whom God's promise to Abraham of blessing for the whole world would be fulfilled. There is only one such Savior of the world and, therefore, no other people share an analogous position or have either prophets or scriptures that are preparatory to the Lord Christ.

DID GOD PLACE STEPPINGSTONES OF PREPARATION FOR THE GOSPEL IN THE RELIGIONS?

I have rejected the proposal that the scriptures of other religions are divine revelation like the divinely inspired Bible. I have also denied that the founders or leading spiritual teachers of other religions should be called "prophets" in the line of divinely authoritative messengers within Israel that went back to Moses. They cannot even be likened to new covenant prophets like Agabus and the daughters of Philip, nor can their utterances be deemed Spirit-gifted prophecy, such as the charism in Christian congregations, because they lack the indwelling presence of the Spirit of the resurrected Christ. One further suggestion is worth examining, however, because it makes less lofty claims: it has been proposed that God has worked to plant within religious contexts steppingstones that assist people toward Christ, preparing them for the gospel message. This is an idea that might be acceptable to ecclesiocentrists, who would want to insist that no salvation occurred until the gospel arrived but that God had prepared people for that time. Accessibilists, on the other hand, might want to leave open the possibility that a trusting acceptance of the "seed" planted by God might be an act of faith within one's movement toward Christ, even if that movement had to continue, not fully satisfied, until the personal encounter with Christ at the moment of death.

McDermott notes that Christian thinkers have "argued that foreign systems of thought—both philosophical and religious—can be steppingstones or schoolmasters to lead the heathen to Christ."

> Perhaps the religions will serve this function: as providential preparations for future peoples to receive the full revelation of God in Christ. This does not mean that there is direct continuity from the religions to Christ, but it does mean that the religions may be used by Jesus to prepare their devotees to understand and receive himself—just as the practice of animal sacrifice instituted by the Triune God (and copied by nearly every world religion thereafter) prepared the Jews to be able to understand and receive Christ as the Lamb of God who takes away their sins.[49]

According to Harold Netland, Anglican theologian F. D. Maurice

---

[49]Gerald R. McDermott, "What If Paul Had Been from China? Reflections on the Possibility of Revelation in Non-Christian Religions," in *No Other Gods Before Me? Evangelicals and the Challenge of World Religions,* ed. John G. Stackhouse Jr. (Grand Rapids, Mich.: Baker, 2001), p. 32.

adopted a remarkably positive view of non-Christian religions, admitting God's presence and revelation within them. Thus Islam, Hinduism and Buddhism should not be rejected outright but should be affirmed as *serving God's purposes*, and missionaries in their encounters with other religions should build upon the "precious fragments of truth" contained within them.[50]

Given my previous demonstration that God's revelation and grace may, indeed, have been factors in the development of the religions and that not every non-Christian religion's beliefs and practices are completely false, Maurice's perspective on the Christian evangelistic approach to adherents of other religions has some merit. We can, indeed, affirm God's ability to use these fallible human constructions to serve his purposes, but we should not give the impression that their development as religious institutions was something that God intentionally brought about, as Maurice's words may imply.

In speaking about "providential preparation" for the gospel, I would want to make it clear that God was not intentionally developing these religious systems, as a whole, in preparation for the gospel, as a parallel to his work with Israel. Since McDermott alluded to the animal sacrifices that were "instituted" by Yahweh in Israel's worship, I want to distinguish from that special covenantal revelation the other religious concepts that may, in some sense, have been "instituted" by God in noncovenantal communities. Those could, at least, be part of God's general providential work, which includes everything in history, both good and evil.

In this vein, Jonathan Edwards

> believed that God has planted types [in the sense of Old Testament types, pointing forward to Christ] of true religion even in religious systems that were finally false. God outwitted the devil, he suggested, by using diabolically deceptive religion to teach what is true. For example, the practice of human sacrifice was the result of the devil's mimickry of the animal sacrifice that God had instituted after the Fall.[51]

Animal sacrifice was the main type of Christ in the Old Testament, but it was also revealed to all the Gentiles. Satan distorted this and led the

---

[50]Harold Netland, *Encountering Religious Pluralism: The Challenge to Faith and Mission* (Downers Grove, Ill.: InterVarsity Press, 2001), p. 33.

[51]McDermott, *Can Evangelicals Learn*, p. 106. McDermott provides a detailed examination of this concept in Jonathan Edwards's works in chapter 6, "Parables in All Nations: Typology and the Religions," of *Jonathan Edwards Confronts the Gods: Christian Theology, Enlightenment Religion and Non-Christian Faiths* (New York: Oxford University Press, 2000).

Gentiles to sacrifice human beings, even their own sons, and Satan then

> believed he had "promote[d] his own interests," outsmarting God; but God outflanked the devil. He permitted this diabolical deception because through it "the devil prepared the Gentile world for receiving . . . this human sacrifice, Jesus Christ." Similarly, the devil induced human beings to worship idols and think that the Gentile deities were united to their images. But God used this deception as well for his own purposes, to prepare the Gentile mind for the concept of incarnation, perfectly realized in Christ: "And so indeed was [the] heathenish doctrines of deities' being united to images and the heathenish fables of heroes being begotten [by] gods, a preparation for their receiving the doctrine of the incarnation, of the Deity's dwelling in a human [body], and the Son of God's being conceived in the womb of a virgin by the power of the Spirit of [God]."[52]

These "pagan practices thus pictured divine realities in distorted (and sometimes horrific) fashion"; they were "not merely human insights but developments (albeit twisted and broken) of original perceptions granted by God himself."[53]

This is the sort of divine providential work that I want to affirm. Edwards's proposal puts an interesting twist on the no-agreement contention that the religions are the product of demonic deception. He grants that Satan is at work in the religions, but he then puts Satan's work under subjection to God, who is able to use it for his own good purposes. Thus, we do not have to conceive of entire religious constructions as designed or intended by God, but we can still see his providential work *within* them, bringing good and gracious effects out of what has become intrinsically evil, although it originated, at least in part, in response to God's revelation that occurred prior to the inception of this particular religious institution or community.

As further examples of "revealed types" such as Edwards found in other religions, McDermott adds "the idea that human beings are accepted by the divine on the basis of divine love rather than human effort" as taught by Mahayana Buddhists and Hindu *bhaktas*.[54] This is not the product of "general revelation," but it is also not "special revelation" of the universally normative, covenantal type, because it does not reveal salvation through Jesus Christ. McDermott is quick to observe that

---

[52]McDermott, *Can Evangelicals Learn*, p. 107, quoting Jonathan Edwards, *Miscellanies* 307.
[53]McDermott, *Can Evangelicals Learn*, p. 114.
[54]Ibid., p. 113.

the grace taught by these communities is not the same as the grace shown by
the God of Jesus Christ. Humans are sometimes expected to do something to
merit this grace, and the Hindu and Buddhist deities do not manifest the holiness of the God of Israel. Hence the grace is not as costly as for the Christian
Trinity. Nevertheless, the basic idea of divine love overruling legal demands
is present.[55]

Richardson's account of the concept of the peace child found among the
fierce, cannibalistic Asmat people of New Guinea appears to be an instance of this typology present in other religious structures, what Richardson calls "redemptive analogies."[56] Missionaries often find in the religious
concepts of a new audience something that provides a strikingly apt
bridge or jumping-off point for the presentation of gospel truth. Again,
McDermott is careful to note, as I have done, that

> this is not to equate the Christian Scriptures, which contain types, with other
> scriptures that may contain types. The Bible is in a different category of rev-
> elation from that of the religions since it alone mediates the reality of the tri-
> une God as incarnate in Jesus of Nazareth.[57]

But, "among the religions are scattered promises of God in Christ," and
"these promises are revealed types planted there by the triune God."[58]
Once more, provided we do not read the word *planted* too strongly, imply-
ing thereby that the religions per se are an intentional divine development,
I concur with McDermott.

SUMMING UP

Since we have defined religions as ambiguous responses to divine revelation, it has been necessary to examine closely the particular forms of revelation to which religious communities are responding. Obviously, general
revelation will be one contributing factor, but I have proposed that there
may also have been encounters with special revelation. This encounter
may have been with special revelation given to the covenant community
(and hence universally normative) that is passed on when the people of
another religious group have had contact with members of Israel or the
church. As indicated in an earlier chapter, special universally normative
revelation may also have been passed down within the life of a community

---

[55]Ibid., p. 113 n. 38.
[56]Don Richardson, *Peace Child* (Glendale, Calif.: Regal, 1974).
[57]McDermott, *Can Evangelicals Learn*, p. 114.
[58]Ibid.

from a member's encounter at a much earlier time. Distortion is bound to occur in that process of transmission and tradition, but some truth may also remain. In addition to contact with this universally normative revelation, however, their may be instances in which God has given particular revelation of himself to individuals—revelation that is not universally normative and that might be quite limited in its content, but that contributes to the formation of a religion because it is deemed to have divine authority. Religions develop through a mixture of appropriation and suppression of these various forms of divine revelation, the latter coming about because of human error and rebellion as well as through demonic deception.

Scriptures are not as important in many religious groups as they are in Judaism, Christianity and Islam, which are often described as "religions of the Book." Where writings are deemed authoritative, however, even if they include appropriation of revealed truth to a significant degree, they are not in themselves divine revelation because they lack the inspiration of the Holy Spirit, such as constitutes the Old and New Testaments, the written word of God. To the extent that these writings convey truth, however, they can be beneficial in a community's life and may be providentially used of God. We should not consider the spiritual leaders within other religions to be prophets, even if we grant that some of them may have received particular nonuniversally normative messages from God. No one since Jesus Christ, God's complete and final revelation, has had the sort of divine appointment and function that old covenant prophets like Moses had. Prophecy, as a gift of the Spirit for ministry in the church, is also different from old covenant prophecy; but even that is not a good comparison to the special communication with which God may privilege some people outside the church. Such experiences heighten the demand for a faith response from the individuals who receive that revelation. There is certainly no counterpart to the Old Testament scriptures as revelation preparatory for Christ, but God might providentially bring about, or permit, within communities the development of ideas that serve as bridges or stepping-stones for the later communication and reception of the gospel.

Now we need to move beyond examining the revelation from God that contributes to the development of religions and ask whether or how God may be at work within the context of other religions in bringing about his program of salvation. We will also ask how the religions might fit into God's general (nonsalvific) providence in the world over which he is sovereign, whether or not he is acknowledged as Lord.

16

Is There Salvation in Other Religions?

Thesis 25: No religion saves people—only God does. But because religions are ambiguous responses to divine revelation and because they pass along to their devotees aspects of God's truth that have been appropriated by the religious tradition, God may graciously give faith to individuals while they live in the context of a non-Christian religion. In such instances, God may use the revealed truth that people encounter as a part of their religious tradition to elicit that saving faith. The religions that have not arisen primarily from God's universally normative special revelation cannot be viewed as having been raised up by God with the intent that they should serve as vehicles of special (saving) grace.

Thesis 26: We can observe signs of the work of God's common grace in the world through religions, and we should give thanks to God for this when we discern it in religions we encounter. Religions, like governments, may be used (and perhaps even intended) by God to restrain sin and evil and to create an environment where good may flourish. In religions, as in cultures, God may work graciously for the well-being of his creatures. Christians can engage in worthwhile ministry activities that serve only the purposes of God's common grace, but our greatest desire is to be useful to God in his purposes of special, saving grace. On the other hand, the line between God's works of common and special grace is not something that we are well able to discern.

I HAVE PROPOSED THAT GOD, IN HIS EXTRAORDINARY WORK, may save people apart from the church and its gospel witness. As is true in God's ordinary work, this salvation takes place by grace through faith. The content of that faith will vary, depending on the type of revelation that God makes available to people. Some of that revelation takes place within people's individual context, so should we say that some people might be saved *through* religions other than Christianity? Ecclesiocentrism denies that anyone can be saved without being a Christian. On the other hand, what I have dubbed "religious instrumentalism" posits that God has raised up the various religions of the world as specific *means* for the communication of his saving grace to the people among whom these religions have developed. The accessibilism that I am laying out and defending in this book finds its path in between those two positions. I am hopeful that God is saving some who are outside the Christian church, but I do not think that God has raised up other religions, as such, to be instrumental in his saving work. Nevertheless, it seems impossible to deny that people's religious education and context has a significant part in the way they relate to God, moving either toward or away from him. How are we to understand and speak about this?

When Christians contemplate the place of religions in the world, we tend to think in terms of salvation. This is not surprising, particularly for evangelicals, because we view our own Christian religious experience predominantly in terms of the wonderful grace by which God has saved us from sin and condemnation and has given us new life. On the other hand, that new life is not simply eternity in heaven; it is life now, in this world, where God has given us a purpose to live and has transformed our relationships. God has placed us within communities where his grace is both experienced and lived out in service that extends beyond the boundaries of the community, bringing blessing to the world. Naturally, we view other religions by comparison with our own, and we ask whether those religions are, similarly, communities formed by saving grace. Are those religious communities instruments of God's grace in the world, as our religious community is called to be? Once we have addressed that pressing question, however, I want to get to another one that has been given much less attention: Is it possible that God may have nonsalvific purposes for the religions of the world? Might there be ways in which he is at work in, and even through, religions to achieve purposes that are not about eternal salvation but that still have genuine value—purposes for which we can give him thanks? In short, do the religions have a positive role within God's general providential working in the world? I will propose that the religions do have a role and that, at least in part, they function as media of God's common (universal and nonsaving) grace.

THE SAVING WORK OF GOD WITHIN THE CONTEXT OF THE RELIGIONS

Salvation through religion. For reasons spelled out in part one, I believe that God does save people who do not receive the special revelation with which the covenant people have been blessed. Some of these people are involved in the life of other religions. I emphasize, however, that although God's saving work is going on within the context of the religions, it is not being done *through* them. Indeed, given what I have said about the ambiguity of Christianity as a religion, I would have to say that even Christianity is not a means by which God accomplishes salvation. When speaking of salvation, I am a bit reluctant to speak so negatively of Christianity, because it is difficult to draw so sharp a line between the organic Christian church that Christ is building (Mt 16:18) and the organizational church that is constructed by humans (not all of whom are in union with Christ) in response to God's revelation. Nevertheless, assuming the points I made earlier about the distinct advantages of Christianity over other religions as a humanly constructed institution, I think my point will be understood. Christianity is an ambiguous phenomenon, with purely human and even demonic influence in its construction, expressing both appropriation and suppression of God's truth in its beliefs, attitudes and practices.

As Carl Braaten put it, "all religions fall short as ways of salvation, including all their mystical and moralistic attempts at self-elevation to the level of God."[1] But even Braaten goes too far when he proposes a model that "pictures Jesus Christ as the revelation of the eschatological fulfillment of the religions" and suggests that "the gospel of Jesus Christ does not destroy but fulfills the religions."[2] D. A. Carson wisely objects, arguing that

> in the Bible, the fulfillment of the old covenant in Jesus Christ (e.g., Matt. 5:17-20) is the fulfillment of what systematicians have called special revelation, and "fulfillment" itself means not the satisfaction of religious and personal aspirations, but the arrival of the eschatological event to which the old covenant Scriptures pointed in promise and type. Although the Bible as a whole can sometimes speak of the gospel and of Jesus as bringing to fruition the *aspirations* of pagans who surround the covenant community, it does not speak of the gospel or of Christ as fulfilling their *religion*. Nor would the adherents of such religions see themselves in such light; indeed, they would be insulted at the suggestion.[3]

Carson's last concern is the least important, of course, since we must eval-

---

[1]Carl E. Braaten, *No Other Gospel! Christianity Among the World's Religions* (Minneapolis: Fortress, 1992), p. 75.
[2]Ibid., p. 78.
[3]D. A. Carson, *The Gagging of God: Christianity Confronts Pluralism* (Grand Rapids, Mich.: Zondervan, 1996), p. 31.

uate the religions from a biblical perspective regardless of the self-perception of other religions' adherents. The unique thing about Christianity as a religion is that it tells the story of what God has done to save people from sin and its consequences, and God uses that proclamation as a means of salvation.[4]

The role that religions may play in God's saving work in an individual's life. It is one thing to say that God can be known savingly by those who are outside Christianity; it is quite another to say that people can know God savingly *through* other religions. Patrick Kalilombe, a Roman Catholic bishop in Malawi, speaks too positively:

> The African Bible reader will thus not fear to state that the religious systems of his ancestors were not just tolerated by God. They were the results of the efforts of our cultures wherein the Spirit of God was an active agent. And therefore, there would be no fear in me to assert that, as long as these religions were the serious searchings of our cultures for the deity, they are to be respected as the normal divinely given means for salvation, put by God in his will for the salvation of all the peoples.[5]

I believe that we can respect that these African ancestors searched for God, but we should not view their religious constructs as the "normal divinely given means for salvation."

Clark Pinnock's forthrightness on this matter is thoroughly appropriate: "The idea that world religions ordinarily function as paths to salvation

---

[4]Christopher Wright, "What Difference Does Jesus Make?" in *Practicing Truth: Confident Witness in Our Pluralistic World,* ed. David W. Shenk and Linford Stutzman (Scottdale, Penn.: Herald, 1999), p. 247. I take this to be the point of the denial stated in article 5 of the 1999 declaration of "The Gospel of Jesus Christ": "We deny that anyone is saved in any other way than by Jesus Christ and his Gospel. The Bible offers no hope that sincere worshipers of other religions will be saved without personal faith in Jesus Christ" ("The Gospel of Jesus Christ: An Evangelical Celebration," *Christianity Today,* June 14, 1999, p. 54). Since the denial follows the affirmation "that Jesus Christ is the only way of salvation, the only mediator between God and humanity" (citing Jn 14:6 and 1 Tim 2:5), I take article 5 to be a reference to the uniqueness of Jesus Christ as Savior. Consequently, I do not assume the statement necessarily asserts that knowledge of the gospel is necessary to salvation by Christ, for reasons presented earlier in the book. As to the religions, I understand the point to be that the religions are not God's saving instruments, as though sincere fulfillment of the requirement of those religions would itself serve as a means of salvation. I repeat that salvation only comes through a Spirit-illumined faith response to the self-revelation of God and that all who are finally saved will have joyfully received Christ at some point in their life, even if it is not until the moment when they left this world and met Jesus, at their death.

[5]Patrick Kalilombe, "The Salvific Value of African Religions," in *Faith Meets Faith,* Mission Trends, ed. Gerald H. Anderson and Thomas F. Stransky (Grand Rapids, Mich.: Eerdmans, 1981), 5:67.

is dangerous nonsense and wishful thinking."[6] As Pinnock says, "There are so many evil sides to religion that a fulfillment paradigm (the idea that religions point people to Christ) is out of the question. Religions are not ordinarily stepping stones to Christ. More often, they are paths to hell."[7] But here I see a distinction in regard to the relative value of Christianity. As a human institution, Christianity does not save. But because of its orientation around the supreme revelation of God in Christ, when a religious body strives to be the church of Christ—to be a worshiping Christian community—it has a distinctive place among the religions. Nevertheless, membership within it or participation in its practices is not of itself a *means* of salvation.

Having stated that we should not assume God is working through other religions as such, Pinnock grants that some people in those religions do worship the true God. Buddhism and Islam are not reliable vehicles of salvation, but God can call people to himself from within these religious systems. Pinnock believes that "there is enough truth in most religions for people to take hold of and put their trust in God's mercy."[8] He also suggests that God may be at work changing religions to make them more helpful to people seeking him. Religions are among the powers "that Jesus Christ is challenging in the coming of the kingdom of God."[9] If people are saved in other religions, it is not *because of* those religions as such. It could only be because God, in his great grace, has drawn them to faith through those aspects of their experience and knowledge that are true to God's self-revelation and that have come to them as a part of that self-revelation, either directly or through a transmission of special revelation made in the past. In this regard, I find animistic religions, which practice animal sacrifice for the appeasement of the gods, very intriguing. But we might say the same thing about Christianity as a religion constructed by people responding to God's special revelation in Christ. Its salvific value is also very ambiguous, when viewed in the institutional forms and expressions that it has taken through the centuries.

It is important that we not leap from the recognition that there is truth in other religions, even truth that owes its origin to divine revelation, to the assumption that the religions themselves are God's intended instruments

---

[6]Clark Pinnock, *A Wideness in God's Mercy: The Finality of Jesus Christ in a World of Religions* (Grand Rapids, Mich.: Zondervan, 1992), p. 90.
[7]Ibid., p. 91.
[8]Ibid., p. 111.
[9]Ibid., p. 120.

for leading people to salvation. The official statement of the International Missionary Council's second missionary conference (held in Jerusalem in 1928) welcomed "every noble quality in non-Christian persons or systems as further proof that the Father, who sent His Son into the world, has nowhere left himself without witness."[10]

But Carson notes that the statement does not address the critical question of whether the revelation that has come to non-Christian persons or systems is a *saving* knowledge, and he rightly observes that "a truth set in the wrong context, valuable as it may be intrinsically, can be damning."[11]

The basic reason that the religions themselves, as structures of thought and practice, cannot be divinely instituted means of salvation is that

> there is no direct continuity from the religions to Christ. They are not beginnings or foundations of which Christ is the completion or superstructure. There may be lines of continuity between a non-Christian religion whose method of advancement is human effort and a particular construal of Christianity in which salvation is earned by human striving, but this is a version of Christianity that Christ repudiated.[12]

Other religions "face in different directions, ask different questions and look for different kinds of religious fulfillments."[13] That is precisely the truth that S. Mark Heim has grasped in his proposed alternative to relativistic pluralism.

When Christians speak about the condition of faithful adherents of other religions, they seem to appreciate most those who are sincere or devout in their religious practice. But precisely because religions institutionalize some forms of the suppression of the truth of God's revelation, this sort of appreciation for religiousness as such is dangerous. As Gerald McDermott has observed, "the religious person is not . . . necessarily closer to God than is the nonreligious."[14] In fact, John Barrett has noticed "that the most committed practitioners in other religions are often those least open

---

[10]"The Christian Life and Message in Relation to Non-Christian Systems of Thought and Life," in *The Jerusalem Meeting of the International Missionary Council: March 24-April 8, 1928*, 8 vols. (New York: International Missionary Council, 1928), 1:410-11, quoted in Carson, *Gagging of God*, p. 180.

[11]Carson, *Gagging of God*, pp. 180-81.

[12]Gerald R. McDermott, *Can Evangelicals Learn from World Religions? Jesus, Revelation and Religious Traditions* (Downers Grove, Ill.: InterVarsity Press, 2000), p. 91.

[13]Ibid.

[14]Ibid.

to the message of the gospel."[15] This was often the case, even in the response to Jesus' ministry. Barrett suggests that "those most dedicated to
the traditions of their forefathers were the very ones most vehemently opposed to Christ,"[16] but he speaks much too categorically. What he says was
possibly more true of the scribes than of the Pharisees, for instance.
Among the latter group, we find attraction to Jesus, rather than repulsion
from him, in a number of instances.

Consider Nicodemus, for example, who sought Jesus out because he
had concluded that Jesus was "a teacher who has come from God" (Jn 3:2),
or the Pharisee who invited Jesus to dine with him in his house (Lk 7:36).
When the temple police returned to the Sanhedrin without having arrested Jesus, they explained that this was because no one had ever spoken
like him before (Jn 7:46). To intimidate the police, some Pharisees asked
whether they had been deceived by Jesus since none of "the authorities or
of the Pharisees believed in him" (Jn 7:48). But they, too, may have been
speaking too hastily, as is evident from Nicodemus's challenge that no one
should be judged "without first giving them a hearing to find out what
they are doing" (Jn 7:51). After the Spirit had been sent, Luke tells us that
"a great many of the priests became obedient to the faith" (Acts 6:7), and
we know that there were Pharisees other than Paul in the congregation in
Jerusalem (Acts 15:5). So it is good to be warned that sincerity and religious devotion are not necessarily evidences of God's gracious work, but
they should not be categorically criticized either. Jesus was most severe
with the religious leaders because they had the greatest knowledge of
God's revelation and had responsibility for the spiritual well-being of the
people. Self-righteousness and hypocrisy especially elicited condemnation from the Lord.

"There may be revelations *from* God in other religions, but only in the
religion of the Christ is there the revelation *of* God as incarnate in Jesus
of Nazareth," says McDermott.[17] I would probably say it this way: "Only
in the religion that is a proper response to the revelation of God in Christ
do we find direct continuity from Christ to the religion," but his point is
a good one. And yet Lesslie Newbigin writes of an "element of continuity" that

---

[15]John K. Barrett, "Does Inclusivist Theology Undermine Evangelism?" *Evangelical Quarterly*
70, no. 3 (1998): 237.
[16]Ibid., p. 238.
[17]McDermott, *Can Evangelicals Learn*, p. 92.

is confirmed in the experience of many who have become converts to Christianity from other religions. Even though this conversion involves a radical discontinuity, yet there is often the strong conviction afterwards that it was the living and true God who was dealing with them in the days of their pre-Christian wrestlings.[18]

That God has made himself known to peoples of the world apart from the distinctive revelation of his covenant relationships may explain, for instance, the experience of Steve Charleston. He sat in an introductory Old Testament class during his first year of seminary and heard the professor describe "what was unique about the religious worldview of ancient Israel."[19] Charleston then came up with a list of fifteen items mentioned by his professor as unique, all of which Charleston found in Native American tradition:

> 1. God is one. 2. God created all that exists. 3. God is a God of human history. 4. God is a God of all time and space. 5. God is a God of all People. 6. God establishes a covenant relationship with the People. 7. God gives the People a "promised land." 8. The People are stewards of this land for God. 9. God gives the People a Law or way of life. 10. The People worship God in sacred spaces. 11. God raises up prophets and charismatic leaders. 12. God speaks through dreams and visions. 13. The People maintain a seasonal cycle of worship. 14. The People believe God will deliver them from suffering. 15. God can become incarnate on earth.[20]

It would be difficult to get a reliable answer, but it might be worth asking, nonetheless, to what extent these beliefs, which Charleston learned within the native community, were influenced by contact with Christians in the process of the formation and transmission of this religious tradition.

Speaking out of personal conversations with Muslim-background believers and the missionaries among them, Miriam Adeney writes: "Muslim-background believers usually do not speak of coming to a new God when they meet God in Jesus. Rather, they feel that the One whom they worshiped in ignorance, inaccurately and incompletely, now has become

---

[18]Lesslie Newbigin, *The Finality of Christ* (London: SCM Press, 1969), p. 59, quoted in J. N. D. Anderson, *Christianity and World Religions: The Challenge of Pluralism* (Downers Grove, Ill.: InterVarsity Press, 1984), pp. 173-74.

[19]Steve Charleston, "The Old Testament of Native America," in *Lift Every Voice: Constructing Christian Theologies from the Underside,* rev. and exp. ed., ed. Susan Brooks Thistlethwaite and Mary Potter Engel (Maryknoll, N.Y.: Orbis, 1998), p. 76.

[20]Ibid., p. 77.

their personal Father. They feel completed."[21] If not specifically *through*, it is not completely *apart from* the religious experience of these God-seekers that God drew them to himself through the years. Thus, there is both continuity and discontinuity between the believers' pre-Christian and Christian experiences. As Gordon Smith puts it,

> There is no wasted time with God. With a change of allegiance, there is a gradual redemption of the whole of one's life including one's past. All that we are and all that we have been is brought into perspective by our change in allegiance. There is discontinuity; there must be. But the point of discontinuity is at the point of fundamental allegiance. This is the issue.[22]

Consider, for instance, the case of Hinduism's bhakti movement and of Mahayana Buddhism, where the emphasis on divine gift approximates the Christian doctrine of grace.[23] Furthermore, Joseph D'Souza, director of Operation Mobilization of India, observes that "there are other systems [within Hinduism] that allow for a personalized, incarnated God . . . which allows for *bhakti* (worship). This has become a great bridge builder to millions of people who are favorable and responsive to the gospel."[24]

It is significant to mark, however, the possibility that this doctrine of grace in bhakti Hinduism may be a result of its contact with Christianity. Alister McGrath points out that the distinction between "kitten salvation" (the tigress carries her cubs) and "monkey salvation" (the babies have to hang on to their mothers)

> is not found in any of the foundational documents of Hinduism, dating from the Vedic period (2000-600 B.C.), in which a synthesis between the polytheistic sacrificial religion of the Aryans and the pantheistic monism of the Upanishads took place, nor during the pantheistic period (600 B.C.-A.D. 300). It emerged during the Puranic period (A.D. 300-1200), during which time Syrian forms of Christianity became established in the southern regions of In-

---

[21]Miriam Adeney, "Rajah Sulayman Was No Water Buffalo: Gospel, Anthropology and Islam," in *No Other Gods Before Me? Evangelicals and the Challenge of World Religions*, ed. John G. Stackhouse Jr. (Grand Rapids, Mich.: Baker, 2001), p. 73.

[22]Gordon T. Smith, "Religions and the Bible: An Agenda for Evangelicals," in *Christianity and the Religions: A Biblical Theology of World Religions*, Evangelical Missiological Society Series, ed. Edward Rommen and Harold Netland (Pasadena, Calif.: William Carey Library, 1995), 2:22.

[23]McDermott, *Can Evangelicals Learn*, p. 92.

[24]Adeney, "Rajah Sulayman," p. 78, takes this quote from Stan Guthrie, "Sticks and Stones: Christians Examine Role of Rhetoric in India Violence," *World Pulse* (January 21, 2000): 2.

dia; it is especially associated with the medieval writer Sri Ramanuja (ca. 1050-1137).[25]

Dependence is always hard to demonstrate, but McGrath plausibly suggests that "perhaps it is a specifically Christian understanding of grace that has found its way into some strands of the movement."[26]

Concluding thoughts on salvation in the context of the religions. I am aware of a certain amount of ambiguity in the discussion we have just concluded. Since I have granted that God saves people outside Christianity, it is obvious that some of the people whom he might save may be living within the context of another established religion. People are saved because God graciously elicits from them a faith response to the revelation that he has given them. But religions are ambiguous responses to divine revelation. Even if one were to insist that the only revelation to which other religions are responding is general revelation, it would have to be granted that some of the truth of God's revelation is transmitted to people through their religious tradition. If people's religious community teaches that the world is created by one supreme being, whom they call God, those people have received a religious truth from their religion. If they honor him as God and give him thanks, it will be because the Spirit of God used the truth that they received through their religious instruction. Furthermore, if we grant that there may even have been moments of nonuniversally normative special revelation at work in the formation of particular religious communities, the situation becomes even more complex. To say that people whom God saves within the context of these religious communities are not saved *through* their religion would be peculiar. It would be like saying that even though you were saved through hearing the good news concerning Christ from Christian messengers who were undeniably members of the Christian religion, you were not saved *through* Christianity.

I am, in fact, *admitting* that God's grace may be at work in the formation or development of religions and that the manifestations or outworkings of that grace in the teaching and practices of a religion may be used by the Holy Spirit to draw people to God in faith. It happens within the context of Christianity, despite the human failures and demonic deception that are obvious at times and places in its history; and it happens within the con-

---

[25]Alister McGrath, "A Particularist View: A Post-Enlightenment Approach," in *More Than One Way? Four Views on Salvation in a Pluralistic World,* ed. Dennis L. Okholm and Timothy R. Phillips (Grand Rapids, Mich.: Zondervan, 1995), p. 171.
[26]Ibid., p. 172.

text of other religions, too, as I have indicated in a few of the personal stories recounted earlier in the book. What I am *denying*, however, is what I
identify as the key point of difference between accessibilism and religious
instrumentalism: *I am denying that God raised up other religions with the same
intentionality that he raised up Israel and for the same purpose, namely, to be recipients of special divine revelation designed to prepare people for and lead people
toward Christ.* It is the intentional instrumentality that I reject, and I think
that the difference is significant. Its implications should have been clear in
my discussions of the uniqueness of the Christian Scriptures and of the divinely appointed prophets of Israel. Jesus is the "prophet greater than
Moses," but he is not the "prophet greater than Siddhartha Gautama" because there is no analogy between Moses and Gautama in the covenantal
development of God's program of salvation.

Might there be, however, some other sense in which we can speak more
positively of a divine intention in the life and development of religions?
That is a question not often asked by evangelicals, but I think it needs to
be considered.

The Role of the Religions in the General Providence of God

A Reformed doctrine of divine providence affirms God's complete control of all things in his creation, so everything that occurs is part of the
outworking of God's eternal purpose (sometimes spoken of as God's
"decree"). Within this framework, an important distinction is made between the things that God wills to *effect*, or to bring about by his own initiative, and the things that God wills to *permit*, incorporating them into
the larger program whereby he achieves his purposes and brings good,
even out of evil, while not being morally accountable for the evil that
creatures freely do. On the assumption that everything in human history is ordered by God's providential governing of his creation, the
question here is, then, which kind of divine purpose is at work in regard
to the religions? I have posited that God is not actively at work bringing
the religions into being because he has redemptive purposes for them,
as fulfillment theories would suggest. But I now want to suggest that
God may nevertheless have good intentions, of a nonsalvific sort, for the
world's religions.

I have asserted that God's Spirit is working to illuminate, at significant moments, the religious experience of individuals and that these experiences occasionally contribute to developments in the life and

thought of religions. Consequently, the work of God within the development of religions should not be ignored, even though we are unable to affirm positively the final result, because of the additional negative contribution of human suppression of the truth and of demonic deception. This point is nicely made by Amos Yong, who suggests that we "see religious traditions as serving divine purposes in greater or lesser degrees at each stage of their evolution" and that we include Christianity in this assessment.[27]

Few Christians (whether monergist or synergist) would deny that God's providential work in the world has had some effect on the development of the world's religions and that they factor, somehow, within God's purposes. Christopher Wright and John Goldingay posit that "Deuteronomy suggests that worship of other deities offered by non-Israelites is ordained by God (see Deut. 4:19; cf. 32:8-9 RSV, NIV mg following the Qumran ms and LXX)."[28] However, they take note of the ambiguity in regard to God's providence, which I have identified above, and suggest that

> this may be an example of the way the Hebrew Bible attributes to Yahweh as sole cause phenomena which we tend to attribute to secondary human volition—as it does, for example, in some cases of human lying, or disobedience, or hardening of the heart. If Israelites observed that other nations worshipped their own deities, and if Yahweh was sovereign high God over all, then he must in some way be responsible for the fact.[29]

Goldingay and Wright see this, however, as only an "interim acceptance," given that such religion is shown to be inadequate by the later fuller awareness.[30] Carson puts it well:

> Even if one decides that what is meant is that God apportions the worship of the heavenly array to the pagan nations, this may mean, within the context of the story-line (not least in Deuteronomy), no more than that God's sovereign sway extends even over the pagan nations and their false gods, but that is no reason for the covenant community who truly know God to follow in their path. In other words, the verse provides no optimism for the view that

[27] Amos Yong, *Discerning the Spirit(s): A Pentecostal-Charismatic Contribution to Christian Theology of Religions* (Sheffield: Sheffield Academic Press, 2000), p. 50. See also pp. 48-49.
[28] John E. Goldingay and Christopher J. H. Wright, " 'Yahweh Our God Yahweh One': The Oneness of God in the Old Testament," in *One God, One Lord: Christianity in a World of Religious Pluralism*, 2nd ed., ed. Andrew D. Clarke and Bruce Winter (Grand Rapids, Mich.: Baker, 1992), p. 51.
[29] Ibid.
[30] Ibid.

the worship of idols is an acceptable alternative approach to the one living and true God.[31]

Common grace. In chapter five, I proposed that God's general kindness to undeserving and unthankful sinners is one of the universal benefits of Christ's work of atonement. This kindness is referred to by Reformed theologians as "common grace." It is grace because it is undeserved. It is common because God gives this kind of undeserved blessing to everyone, in some measure, because the media of its communication are of a very general nature and because it is not aimed specifically at individuals' salvation. I have suggested that the religions play a very limited role in God's specifically salvific intentions, but let's consider whether or how they might serve his more general purposes of undeserved kindness—ways in which they might be permitted by God so that certain relative but authentic benefits might come to their members. As Creator and Lord of all the earth, God has an interest in the well-being of all of his creatures (including the sparrows who could be bought so cheaply in the market in Jesus' day). In particular, he is concerned about the creatures whom he created in his image. Even when they live in rebellion against him and live under his just condemnation, God is merciful to them and gives them much that is good. Might some of that good be communicated through the religious environments in which these people live, however mixed the blessing of these ambiguous entities might be? After all, God is able to use even evil to bring about some of his good purposes.

Religions as analogous to governments. Stanley Grenz has suggested a parallel between religions and human government, the latter being "God's agent in promoting good and punishing evil" (Rom 13:1-6).[32] Like many other Christians, I understand human government to be an institution set up by God to function as an instrument of common grace in the world, providing order and justice in a society where sin inevitably works toward disorder and injustice. To parallel religions to government would be to recognize a divine intention in the existence of religions as institutions while not suggesting that every religion serves God completely as he wishes it to do. Grenz himself is quick to note that "religion readily becomes an expression of human fallenness, even falling prey to the de-

---

[31]Carson, *Gagging of God,* p. 296 n. 76.

[32]Stanley J. Grenz, "The Universality of the 'Jesus-Story' and the 'Incredulity Toward Metanarratives,'" in *No Other Gods Before Me? Evangelicals and the Challenge of World Religions,* ed. John G. Stackhouse Jr. (Grand Rapids, Mich.: Baker, 2001), p. 106 n. 54.

monic" and, thus, a parallel to government is further demonstrated. Governments, too, though ordained by God to do good, can be perverted and can work against the moral purposes of God for humanity instead of promoting them.

Grenz identifies one particular way in which the religions may have a providential role in the work of God in history:

> The biblical visionaries anticipate the establishment of the eternal community of a reconciled humankind dwelling within the renewed creation and enjoying the presence of the redeeming God. Although the fullness of community comes only as God's gift at the culmination of history, the biblical writers also assert that foretastes of the future reality can be found in the present. The providential place of human religious traditions, therefore, may lie in their role of fostering community. . . .
>
> Whatever their ultimate vision of reality may be, all religious traditions contribute to identity formation and social cohesion. Their immediate goal is to assist their adherents in the task of gaining a sense of identity as persons standing in relationship to something "larger" than the individual, however that encompassing reality may be understood. In this sense, religions fulfill a divinely sanctioned function. Because God's ultimate purpose is the establishment of community, evangelicals ought to affirm each religious tradition in its intent to promote social cohesion among human beings, for in this manner each contributes to the present experience of community.[33]

In the phenomenon observed by Grenz, I see evidence of God's work of common grace, one of those aspects of a religious construct that we can affirm as good, and for which we can give praise to God. But I do not suggest that God has intentionally raised up particular religions to accomplish this purpose. Like government, which is an institution in the abstract, religions, in general, can have a helpful role in society. This is one of those cases where the ambiguity of all religions is evident. Some religious groups have, indeed, fostered a strong sense of communal identity and loyalty but have then misused these good things and led members to suicide or acts of terror. Nevertheless, where the effects are good we see a sign of the grace of God, and we can welcome that sign without, thereby, endorsing the whole religious construct.

Religions as analogous to cultures. Points of similarity can be found between governments and religions as human institutions that can serve a providential purpose within God's common-grace work in the world, but

---

[33]Ibid., pp. 104-6.

I prefer to parallel religion and culture, as Harold Netland does.[34] Of course, this comparison gets complicated in many parts of the world; in nonsecular cultures, it is often difficult to distinguish the culture from the religion because religion is such a large part of the culture. In these cultures, where there may have been only one religion, which is shared by every member of the group, religious conversion can be extremely difficult.

Yet even granting the difficulty of separating the elements of a culture according to those that are religious from those that are not, I think we can benefit from drawing an analogy between culture and religion. They are often closely intertwined but must be distinguished as long as we live in a fallen world. Like governments, every particular culture should not be viewed as having been developed by specific divine providential intention. Cultures have come about through a mixture of God's good creative activity and of human activity which is both good and evil. Much can be gained by applying the insights offered by Richard Mouw on culture and common grace to the aspect of religion.[35] In both religions and cultures, we can see the grace of God at work: some of the fruit borne gives God pleasure, and we too can delight in it—without affirming the entire system. Where religions serve to restrain the expression of sin (as biblically defined) within their community and to foster works of civic good, we can be thankful, and we should attribute these relative goods to the grace of God. The values of cultures are frequently moral in nature, and morality is intrinsically religious.

The values we appreciate in a particular culture, such as the respect for parents or care for the environment, may be specifically derived from a religious framework, or they may have become part of the society's way of life without conscious religious grounding. Whether these function as merely cultural values or as specifically religious values, we Christians recognize in them an external obedience to God's law. Unless it proceeds from faith in God, it is sin, because it is not done for the right motive, to glorify God (Rom 14:23), for "without faith it is impossible to please God" (Heb 11:6). But these texts are speaking of the pleasure God takes in deeds that are righteous because they are the fruit of Christ's righteousness lived out within our daily lives. The unregenerate are unable to please God in that sense.

---

[34]Harold Netland, *Encountering Religious Pluralism: The Challenge to Faith and Mission* (Downers Grove, Ill.: InterVarsity Press, 2001), p. 328.

[35]Richard J. Mouw, *He Shines in All That's Fair: Culture and Common Grace* (Grand Rapids, Mich.: Eerdmans, 2001).

On the other hand, there is surely a sense in which God is more pleased with unregenerate children who honor their parents (Deut 5:16) than with unregenerate children who dishonor their parents, or even better pleased than with regenerate children who dishonor their parents. Even when an act that conforms to the letter of God's law is not done in the spirit of the law (faith and love), it has a relative goodness by virtue of its conformity to God's moral standard. Such an act is not the righteousness that proceeds from and evidences God's saving work, but it is an evidence of nonsalvific grace. It is an evidence that sin has been restrained in this one respect—in the lives of these particular people from whom even external conformity to God's law does not come naturally, given their fallenness. Common grace accounts for these relative goods, and when such moral and social goods are encouraged by a culture or by a religion, we can be thankful that these structures are serving God's gracious purposes in this sinful world.

Implications and applications of seeing the religions as instruments of common grace. By keeping clearly in view the differences between God's common and his special (saving) grace, we can see in the religious systems we encounter cause for gratitude to God and his grace, as well as opportunity to proclaim and to model the much greater blessings that God communicates through union with Christ. Ironically, evangelism seems easiest where God's common grace has least been experienced, because the restraint of sin and its consequences that comes about through God's gracious working in a community makes it more difficult to convince people of their need of saving grace. As Jesus himself observed, it is to sinners who are aware of their own sinfulness and the desperateness of their situation that the liberating message of the gospel is most evident as good news. Nevertheless, as Mouw helpfully demonstrates, Christians should seek to be agents of common grace, doing "common grace ministries."[36] These have an intrinsic legitimacy and value, even though we must not be satisfied to stop with them, knowing that we are also called to be agents of special grace.

As agents of special grace, the religions not based on the revelation of God in Christ fail disastrously, but as agents of common grace, they may at times exceed some Christian communities. Recognizing this sobering reality should keep us from triumphalism in our relationship with the other religions of the world and enable us to be positively appreciative of ways in which God is at work in and through them. That the grace of God we observe in those religions is not saving grace should not prevent us

---

[36]Ibid., pp. 80-82.

from valuing the evidences of common grace that we recognize. Indeed, we may need to be humble about our ability to define the line between common and special grace, as Mouw warns us with his observation that for all he or "any of us can know—much of what we now think of as common grace may in the end time be revealed to be saving grace."[37]

Addressing the Lystrans (Acts 14:15-17) and the Athenians (Acts 17:24-28), the apostle Paul appealed to God's general revelation and common grace to lead them on to the higher knowledge of God as he had revealed himself in Christ. In the same way, we may start by affirming the good features that we observe in the lives of other religious communities and by seeking to open their eyes to the Giver of all these goods in human experience. We can show them how their own life experiences are illumined by the biblical narrative and how the longings of their souls, unsatisfied by even the best features of their religious system, can be satisfied by Christ.

As we think about similarities and differences in an analogy between religions and cultures or societies, we might reflect on Jeremiah's instructions to the exiles in Babylon living between the first deportation and the destruction of Jerusalem. He urged them to "build houses and live in them; plant gardens and eat what they produce. . . . But seek the welfare of the city where I have sent you into exile, and pray to the LORD on its behalf, for in its welfare you will find your welfare" (Jer 29:5, 7). "The very practice of prayers for the foreign city and its rulers acknowledges the reign of God,"[38] but it is inconceivable that God's people could be instructed to pray for the flourishing of other religions that predominated where they lived in the same way that they were urged to pray for the wellbeing of the civil state within which they lived. Here the inseparability of religion from culture, in some social contexts, becomes critical. Christians in such an environment should seek and pray for the welfare of their village, city or nation, but they can hardly do the same for the religion. Becoming Christians does not change one's political status, except to put the authority of the government in subjection to God, which might necessitate disobedience at some time if the two authorities come into conflict. But with regard to the religion from which Christians have converted, their new commitment to serve God's purposes of bringing everyone into his kingdom through the spread of Christ's Lordship immediately puts them

---

[37]Ibid., p. 100.
[38]Allen Verhey, *Christian Community, Scripture and the Moral Life* (Grand Rapids, Mich.: Eerdmans, 2002), p. 378.

in conflict with their former religion. They cannot pray for its welfare, except in a very limited sense, namely, that it might at least serve God's purposes of common grace. In those areas, they may even work together with adherents of other religions. But the survival of the religion as such is clearly threatened by the Christian mandate to evangelism, which Christ uses to build his church.

It is precisely this distinction between the respective roles of governments and religions within the providence of God that puts Christians in such a difficult situation when they live or minister in nonsecular societies. Where a religion makes no distinction between itself and the state, it is inevitable that the leaders of such a religion will view Christians as a political threat. In such a context, it is extremely difficult for Christians to convince their neighbors that they are loyal citizens of their nation and society while remaining, effectively, opponents of the religion with which the state is inextricably allied. This includes a wide range of contexts, including states in which the head is considered to be divine, those in which religious law (such as Islamic sharia) constitutes the law of the state, or even traditional African contexts in which the Christian aversion to ancestor veneration (when viewed as "worship") imperils the status of the chief whose power and authority derives from his relationship to those ancestors. This also puts most forms of Christianity in the Catch-22 of being perceived as a dangerous proponent of secularism precisely because they insist that the government should not be preferentially related to any religious institution but should foster religious freedom.

Divine providence at work in the diversities within religions. It is sometimes difficult to know how finely to draw the line between or within religions. One thinks of the great variety of formulations commonly grouped together as Hinduism, and even the diversity within Christianity raises a question for us. Are Eastern Orthodoxy, Roman Catholicism and Protestantism, for instance, different religions, branches or denominations? Obviously, there is a sense in which they are versions of Christianity; they share a trinitarian confession of faith, such as is found in the Apostles' Creed. On the other hand, the differences between them can be quite significant, and Protestant apologists have sometimes spoken of Roman Catholicism as a "false cult," which is to say that it is a different religion than Protestantism. I recall the distress of one of my Roman Catholic students who attended an evangelical Protestant seminary when she told me of her fellow students who differentiated between Roman Catholics and Christians, with the unstated assumption that *Christians* identified the group who are saved, among whom they did not include Roman Catholics. Of course, this drawing of the line between authentic Christianity and non-Christianity is certainly not unique to the Protestant wing!

When we think about God's providential action with regard to the religions, we can appropriately include in that consideration the various manifestations of those religions, including Christianity and even the denominations or schools of theology within Protestantism. My mind was led in this direction by reading Valentine Hepp's 1930 Stone Lectures at Princeton. In these he argued that "only the Calvinistic world-view can create any order in the chaotic condition of science, because Calvinism is the most consistent and harmonious Christendom. . . . . Only in Calvinism do you find the correct appreciation of nature."[39] This contention leads him to propose that Calvinism "is appointed to serve the world by furnishing a believing philosophy of nature."[40] Here, we see a concept of divine providential intentionality at work not just in the development of Christian religion generally, but in the rise of a particular theological movement within it. What is not clear is whether Hepp viewed Calvinism alone as a divinely intended theological instrument or whether Lutheranism and Thomism might have different contributions to make, in different areas of thought, within the divine program.

More recently, Mouw has suggested that "one legitimate way to think positively about the fact of multiple Christian denominations may be to see different denominational groups as having different vocations—different assignments from the Lord to work out different virtues and to cultivate different spiritual sensitivities."[41] I am definitely not extending the language of denominations within Christianity to the various religions of the world, which would give the impression that the divine assignments given to Lutheranism and Presbyterianism are analogous to different assignments given to Christianity and Buddhism. That would be the road of thoroughgoing relativism, down which a biblically informed theology cannot walk. But granting the more general analogy between culture and religion, without suggesting that the religions *as such* are divinely ordered, we can see how the common-grace purposes of God for a fallen world may be providentially served by the religions; and we can also see how God

---

[39]Valentine Hepp, *Calvinism and the Philosophy of Nature: The Stone Lectures Delivered at Princeton in 1930* (Grand Rapids, Mich.: Eerdmans, 1930), pp. 51-52.

[40]Ibid., p. 52.

[41]Mouw, *He Shines*, pp. 79-80.

might bless particular communities through the ways in which sin is restrained, the needy are cared for, those who do good to others are encouraged and assisted, and human well-being in general is fostered. The generous hospitality shown in the meals served at a Sikh temple is not the same thing as feeding the hungry in Christ's name, but that does not negate the commendableness of Sikh hospitality. It originates in the grace of God that accounts for all deeds that conform externally to God's moral will, even when they fail to be worthy of eternal reward because they are not consciously done from the motive of faith in God through Christ.

Christianity is unique among religions as a response to the most complete self-revelation of God who lived among us as one of us (Jn 1:14). No particular institutional response to the revelation in Christ adequately represents him; Christian denominations and Christian congregations are all the product of ambiguous responses to God's revelation. So, as Hepp points out, we can identify ways in which one of these institutional responses to God manifests particularly well the grace of God, but we can also see ways in which Christian bodies have institutionalized the suppression of some truth of God's revelation. This makes it difficult for us to know when a particular Christian body has been specifically raised up by God for a specific divine purpose and when it is simply a faithful response to the revelation that others have not appropriated so well. Clearly, God's grace is at work in all the good that we find in Christian churches, but the degree of divine intentionality, of permission or effectuation, is hidden from us.

I underline again the important difference we have noted between Christianity and other religions: although no religion saves, Christianity has come out of Christ's building of his church, and that church is directly intended to be an instrument of God's redemptive program in the world. Having said that, however, Hepp's comments and Mouw's discussion of common grace force me to grant that particular religions may well have a particular role to play within the *common grace* purposes of God in the world, restraining the expression of sin and stirring up actions that conform, at least externally, to the moral will of God. It is in this regard that an analogy between religions and governments has a measure of validity.

SUMMING UP

In the following chapters we will contemplate the implications of the conviction that the religions (and the ways in which they teach people relate to God and to other people) are ambiguous responses to God's revelation and to other expressions of God's grace. Accepting the position I have put forward to this point will provide a framework and guidelines for these interreligious relationships. In this chapter, I have reasserted my conviction that members of other religions who have not rejected Christ himself may already be living in saving relationship with God, despite their not having the knowledge of the gospel, which God wants us to communicate to them. Recognizing that they may be saved, however, does not lead us to affirm the religious system within which they are endeavoring to worship God. In no way are we led to diminish the exclusive claims of Jesus Christ to being uniquely the Way, the Truth and the Life. There is an inescapable exclusivism in this Christian insistence that the one and only true God has revealed himself fully only in Jesus and that all other purported revelation must be tested by its consistency with Jesus. This is offensive to the relativistic mood that characterizes postmodernity, but that offense is unavoidable for all who allow Jesus and the written Word of God to define reality. Nevertheless, because accessibilism refuses to reject everything about all other religions as worthless and because accessibilism is hopefully open to signs of God's common grace in the lives and institutions of people of other religions, it fosters a gracious spirit in our relationships with others.

17

How Do We Discern God's Grace in Other Religions?

Thesis 27: We can discern the work of God's grace in the teaching and life of other religions and in the lives of individuals who adhere to other religions by using three criteria. Most important for our process of discernment is the extent to which the truth revealed in Scripture is attested and practiced, that is, the degree to which the religion or the individual is orthodox. A second criterion is the morality taught and practiced by religions and their members (i.e., orthopraxy). By the fruit, we know the nature of the tree. God's grace is evident where human well-being is fostered—where personal morality and social justice are valued, encouraged and practiced. Although human theory is often better than its practice, the grace of God may be discernible particularly in situations where we are led to commend good behavior that seems unlikely to have been derived from the erroneous religious theory being propounded. The third criterion is most important from God's perspective but is most difficult for us to use, namely, the orientation of an individual's heart or even a community's heart. Only God knows the motives from which people do good, but his moral assessment is largely determined by that attitude of heart. Religions can teach ideas and foster forms of behavior, but only God can turn hearts toward himself.

I HAVE PROPOSED THAT GOD IS GRACIOUSLY AT WORK in the context of other religions but that the religions themselves are not God's means of communicating *saving* grace. This being so, we need to discern what we encounter as we relate to other religious people, *even when they identify themselves as Christian.* Because God has revealed his truth to us in Jesus and in inspired Scriptures, we have a means by which to identify God's work in our lives or the lives of others. But our judgments are always fallible because none of us has an infallible interpretation of God's revealed truth and because we have no guarantee that we have rightly discerned the motives of other people.

In our current context, which is frequently identified as postmodern, skepticism about our ability to know things that are absolutely true, that is, true for everyone, leads to widespread relativism. Even many who acknowledge that objective truth exists are hesitant to evaluate the beliefs and practices of others, religious or otherwise, because they have a strong sense of the situational limits of their own beliefs and perceptions; but as Harold Netland rightly observes, "If we reject a thorough relativism holding that all judgments about the truth or falsity of alternative worldviews are merely the products of particular contexts, then there emerges at least the possibility of making responsible judgments on the basis of criteria that transcend particular contexts."[1] Colin Gunton aptly puts his finger on the key problem in any denial of objective truth such as is common in contemporary relativism.

> The concept of God is intrinsically universal. . . . We cannot . . . evade the fundamental implications of the concept of God as the one who is the source of all being, meaning, and truth. That is why I believe that the denial of the concept of objective truth—however that objectivity be understood—is tantamount to a denial of belief in God, as some postmodernists have realized. To invert Dostoyevsky's famous saying, if everything is permitted, then there is no God. The obverse is that the notion that God exists generates a concept of objective truth, and therefore believers must face up to the questions of the conflict of claims and the criteria for choosing one alleged truth rather than another. If my story differs from yours at a fundamental level, then at least one of us has got things wrong.[2]

Our Christian evaluation of religions (including our evaluation of manifestations of Christianity itself) and of the state of their adherents, however, will be made on the basis of God's self-revelation as contained supremely in Scripture, even though we will need to grant that our own grasp of revealed truth is partial and fallible. The consensus of the Christian community will be important in assessing which things we believe to be true are essential or fundamental and which are to be held more lightly. An implication of this approach is, of course, that we cannot rely significantly on "foundational" truths, which we deem to be obvious to all reasonable peo-

---

[1]Harold Netland, *Encountering Religious Pluralism: The Challenge to Faith and Mission* (Downers Grove, Ill.: InterVarsity Press, 2001), p. 290.

[2]Colin Gunton, "The Trinity, Natural Theology and a Theology of Nature," in *The Trinity in a Pluralistic Age: Theological Essays on Culture and Religion*, ed. Kevin J. Vanhoozer (Grand Rapids, Mich.: Eerdmans, 1997), p. 92.

ple; we are dependent on the Spirit of God to convince people of the truth of his own revelation. Our single foundation will be the one laid by Jesus Christ, "our Lord, the one in whom the creation holds together."[3]

Nevertheless, despite the exclusiveness of this epistemological starting point, we can proceed with a measure of hopefulness because of our convictions that God does not leave himself without witness and that his Spirit is at work in the lives of people, particularly those whom he chooses to draw to himself. We can plant and we can water, but only God can produce a harvest. God has established a moral order, thereby creating universal moral truth, but only God's Spirit can bring people to acceptance of this truth. Thus, Netland notes:

> It is no accident that most people respond favorably to morally respectable figures such as Confucius, Jesus, the Buddha, Gandhi, the Dalai Lama and Mother Teresa, and that the plausibility of their religious claims is enhanced by the moral integrity of their lives. By contrast, the religious claims of Jim Jones, David Koresh and Shoko Asahara were widely dismissed, in part because they were rightly perceived to be lacking in moral virtue. Implicitly, then, people *do* use a moral criterion in assessing claims from various religious traditions, and surely this is as it should be.[4]

At this point in our study, however, my interest is not in apologetics, that is, in the demonstration of the truthfulness of Christianity or in the superiority of Christianity over all other religions. Our challenge, as members of the community of people who have come to know God in Christ by the Spirit, is to discern where *else* God is graciously at work, whether savingly or in common-grace ways.

As an anthropologist, Paul Hiebert "is aware that the discoveries in the history of religions no longer allow proclamation of the superiority of the Christian message based on miracles, religious experiences, spiritualities, religious-moral codes, or even resurrections." Hiebert posits that there are "no simple phenomenological criteria by which we can test the presence of the Holy Spirit."[5] I admit that it is difficult to discern such things, but it must be done. A helpful place to start is given in Daniel Clendenin's sug-

---

[3]Gunton, "Trinity," p. 103.

[4]Netland, *Encountering*, pp. 297-98.

[5]Paul G. R. Hiebert, "Discerning the Work of God," in *Charismatic Experiences in History*, ed. Cecil M. Robeck Jr. (Peabody, Mass.: Hendrickson, 1985), p. 151, quoted in Amos Yong, *Discerning the Spirit(s): A Pentecostal-Charismatic Contribution to Christian Theology of Religions* (Sheffield: Sheffield Academic Press, 2000), p. 139.

gestion that there are "three characteristic traits of the person who truly knows God: orthodoxy, orthopraxis, and orthokardia."[6] Perhaps a measure of all three of these can be found in Peter's assessment of Cornelius (Acts 10:35): both the orthodox and the orthokardic (right-heartedness) aspects are seen in his fear of God and the orthopraxic dimension was identified in his doing of "what is right."

When conversing with people who identify themselves with a particular religion, we must, of course, be aware of the great diversity within religions, as I have noted earlier. Consequently, we cannot assume that we know what people believe or experience about God simply because we have a religious label for them. Their own religious situation will have to be discovered and discerned through our careful listening and observation. In his missionary work among Hindus in South India, for instance, Hiebert

> found that most villagers knew little more than the rudiments of Hindu theology. He found himself teaching them their theology in order to present Christ as the better way. He also found that much of village religion has little to do with Hinduism. Hinduism stresses *ahimsa*, not taking life, but many of the village ceremonies involved blood ceremonies.[7]

ORTHODOXY

The key factor we are looking for in another person's life is saving faith, the trust in the grace and mercy of a holy and trustworthy God, which was demonstrated paradigmatically by Abraham (Rom 4:16-18; Gal 3:28-29) and by the diverse group of people cataloged in Hebrews 11. People's beliefs should be harmonious with the whole context of the biblical message, particularly with those truths on which the church has reached a consensus of interpretation.

God forbade the Israelites to worship any deity alongside the true God (Ex 20:3); their God Yahweh was the only real god (Deut 6:4) and had to be the sole object of their allegiance. They could borrow names (El) and ritual forms from their neighbors, provided these did not conflict with Yahweh's fundamental character, but other gods and religious practices, like Molech and child sacrifice, were clearly incompatible with worship of Yahweh. Here we find a clear doctrinal criterion for acceptable worship; the true God has particular qualities or attributes that are essential. In Romans 1,

---

[6]Daniel Clendenin, *Many Gods, Many Lords* (Grand Rapids, Mich.: Baker, 1995), p. 137.
[7]Paul G. R. Hiebert, Daniel Shaw and Tite Tiénou, *Understanding Folk Religion: A Christian Response to Popular Beliefs and Practices* (Grand Rapids, Mich.: Baker, 1999), p. 9.

for instance, I hear a critical bottom line: people must acknowledge the Creator as God and give him thanks.

John Goldingay and Christopher Wright posit that

> the Hebrew Bible is not explicit on the basis for [the] contrast in attitudes to the religion of El and that of Baal, though one can guess aspects of the reasons for it. The high god El could more easily become the sole God Yahweh than would be the case with the subordinate Baal; worship of Baal implied worship of other gods than Yahweh rather than worship of Yahweh as Baal. Israel's history recalled the way Baal worship led the wilderness generation into sexual immorality (Num. 25:1-3), and Hosea attacks the way Israel let itself be influenced by this aspect of Canaanite religion—even if the nature of Yahweh also gained in definition under the influence of Baalism as Yahweh was more explicitly declared to be lord of the crops and was portrayed as Israel's own lover. In coming to describe the relationship between Yahweh and Israel in marriage terms Hosea thus adopts language and imagery from Canaan even while he is in the course of attacking the theology which the Canaanites expressed by means of it.[8]

In this biblical criterion, Goldingay and Wright see a possible "implication for the inter-faith issue," namely, "that we regard adherence to (e.g.) an African traditional religion as a God-given starting point for people on their way to recognizing that the definitive act and revelation of God are found in the story of Israel which comes to a climax in Jesus." They further suggest that "it might be possible to take the same stance in relation to a religion such as Islam or to British folk-religion, though here the question is complicated by the fact that these are at least in a formal sense post-Christian religions which explicitly or implicitly presuppose a conscious rejection of the gospel."[9]

An example of this kind of assessment is provided by Clark Pinnock, who notes a significant difference between the confession of people in Ghana—that the transcendent God is "the shining one, as unchangeable as a rock," one who is "all-wise and all-loving"—and the situation of the "Zen master who intends to place the void over against a theistic belief."[10]

---

[8]John E. Goldingay and Christopher J. H. Wright, " 'Yahweh Our God Yahweh One': The Oneness of God in the Old Testament," in *One God, One Lord: Christianity in a World of Religious Pluralism,* 2nd ed., ed. Andrew D. Clarke and Bruce Winter (Grand Rapids, Mich.: Baker, 1992), pp. 56-57.

[9]Ibid., pp. 52-53.

[10]Clark Pinnock, *A Wideness in God's Mercy: The Finality of Jesus Christ in a World of Religions* (Grand Rapids, Mich.: Zondervan, 1992), p. 97.

I suggest, however, that we need to distinguish between the evaluation we make of religions as systems and our assessment of the situation of the individuals within those religions. What many people know about Jesus, if they know anything at all, has usually come to them through the religion that has incorporated (and possibly distorted) some aspect of universally normative special revelation. The religious system may, therefore, be "post-Christian," as Goldingay and Wright observe. But the individual, who is moving either toward or away from God while living in the context of that religion, is not necessarily "post-Christian," personally. He or she may not have had any direct personal meeting with Christ.

Jesus Christ will be our primary criterion for discerning the Spirit's work beyond the church. What the Spirit says can never oppose the revelation we have of Christ because it is the Spirit's role to glorify Christ and what Christ shows us of God. Pinnock rightly proposes, therefore, that

> the question to ask is christological (1 Jn 4:2-3). Spirit is in agreement with the Son and agrees with what he said and did. . . . What the Spirit says and does cannot be opposed to revelation in Christ, because Spirit is bound to Word of God. . . . To identify prevenience, we look for the fruit of the Spirit and for the way of Jesus Christ.[11]

From the narrative of the gospel we learn the pattern of God's ways, so that "wherever we see traces of Jesus in the world and people opening up to his ideals, we know we are in the presence of Spirit."[12] Because the immanent Trinity is the economic Trinity, "we cannot discover anything new about God *in se* that is unrelated or contradictory to the second person of the economic Trinity—the only Trinity we know."[13] We know, for instance, that we will never find a fourth or fifth person in the Godhead. Allah and Brahman

> must be understood within the context of the triune God. They may give us hints of hidden riches within the Trinity that we had not previously seen, but such insight will be the unveiling of what is already lying within the revelation we possess, not a new revelation coming from outside of what God disclosed of Himself through Israel and Jesus.[14]

---

[11]Clark Pinnock, *Flame of Love: A Theology of the Holy Spirit* (Downers Grove, Ill.: InterVarsity Press, 1996), p. 209.

[12]Ibid.

[13]Gavin D'Costa, "Revelation and Revelations: Discerning God in Other Religions: Beyond a Static Valuation," *Modern Theology* 10 (April 1994): 168-69, quoted in Gerald R. McDermott, *Can Evangelicals Learn from World Religions? Jesus, Revelation and Religious Traditions* (Downers Grove, Ill.: InterVarsity Press, 2000), p. 71.

[14]McDermott, *Can Evangelicals Learn*, pp. 71-72.

I agree with Netland that "the most important question is not what a given religion does for society at large or for any of its members, but rather whether what it affirms, explicitly and implicitly, about reality is in fact true. The most significant question we can ask of any religion is whether its fundamental claims are true."[15] Not all beliefs are equally essential to the religious worldview of which they are a part. "Acceptance or rejection of belief in baptism by immersion as opposed to say, sprinkling, does not alter substantially the nature of the Christian worldview. On the other hand, acceptance of belief in the existence of an eternal creator God is clearly essential to Christian faith."[16] Each religion has a set of defining beliefs, although there may be debate about what this set comprises and, if any of the defining beliefs of a religion are false, about whether the religion is false.[17]

It is one of the faults of relativists that they ignore the doctrinal incompatibilities between religions. In assessing the value of other religions, Christians will appeal to the normative divine revelation in Christ and Scripture, which brings Christ to us. Relativists tend to emphasize experience and subjective response, but we must not ignore the fact that people's subjective activity, worship or prayer, assumes a particular objective reality. But "if people's thoughts about an object are sufficiently mistaken, they will just not be able to connect their thoughts with that object at all."[18]

Stanley Samartha says that "the question of truth is indeed important, but God's love is even more important. . . . . Love takes precedence over truth."[19] This proposal is confusing because of the way it disjoins love and truth.[20] To love God, one must believe that certain facts about God, such as his existence and certain traits of his character, are true. Consequently, truth is a more important factor in our assessment of religions and of the experience of religious people than love is, because whom or what they

[15]Harold Netland, *Dissonant Voices: Religious Pluralism and the Question of Truth* (Grand Rapids, Mich.: Eerdmans, 1991), p. 165. By "truth," Netland intends to speak of "a property of propositions such that a proposition is true if and only if the state of affairs to which it refers is as the proposition asserts it to be. Otherwise it is false" (p. 181).
[16]Ibid.
[17]Ibid., p. 182.
[18]Peter Byrne, "John Hick's Philosophy of World Religions," *Scottish Journal of Theology* 35 (1982): 293, quoted in Clendenin, *Many Gods*, p. 106.
[19]Stanley J. Samartha, "The Lordship of Jesus Christ and Religious Pluralism," in *Christ's Lordship and Religious Pluralism*, ed. Gerald Anderson and Thomas F. Stransky (Maryknoll, N.Y.: Orbis, 1981), pp. 54-55.
[20]Netland, *Dissonant Voices*, p. 166.

love is critical. It is not just love that counts; it is the love of God and of one's neighbor for God's sake.

Lesslie Newbigin speaks wisely about those who want to relativize religious claims and evaluate them by values such as justice, compassion, love and mercy:

> Why should these abstract nouns have a more ultimate status than a concrete life lived out on the actual plane of history? The gospel is not the assertion that in Jesus certain qualities such as love and justice were present in an exemplary manner. If this were so, we could of course dispense with the example once we had learned the lesson which the example teaches. The gospel is not just the illustration (even the best illustration) of an idea. It is the story of actions by which the human situation is irreversibly changed. The concreteness, the specificity, the "happenedness" of this can in no way be replaced by a series of abstract nouns. The difficulty of words like justice and love is that their content has to be given them in particular situations where action has to be taken. Both "justice" and "love" can be used and are frequently used as masks for special interests. One has always to ask, "Whose justice? What kind of love?" Where there is no Judge, each of us is judge in our own cause. On the other hand, when we point to Jesus, and to the story which has its center in the cross, we are invoking a criterion by which all our claims to justice are humbled and relativized. To affirm the unique decisiveness of God's action in Jesus Christ is not arrogance; it is the enduring bulwark against the arrogance of every culture to be itself the criterion by which others are judged. The charge of arrogance which is leveled against those who speak of Jesus as unique Lord and Savior must be thrown back at those who assume that "modern historical consciousness" has disposed of that faith.[21]

Doctrine does matter, and the teaching of other religions must be scrutinized for compatibilities and incompatibilities with Christian Scripture. As Goldingay and Wright properly observe,

> however much theological and spiritual insight other religions may have, then, by definition they cannot encompass the gospel, because they do not tell the gospel story. So, while one can honour them as starting points for people, one cannot in love view them as finishing points. There is no salvation in them, not because they are somehow inferior as religions to the religion of Christianity, but because they are not witnesses to the deeds of the God who saves.[22]

---

[21]Lesslie Newbigin, *The Gospel in a Pluralist Society* (Grand Rapids, Mich.: Eerdmans, 1989), p. 166.
[22]Goldingay and Wright, "Yahweh," p. 54.

When it comes to identifying the specific doctrinal content of the faith that saves, we need to be cautious not to raise the bar too high, particularly when we consider the situation of those whose knowledge of God in Christ is in the context of Christian traditions other than our own Protestant evangelicalism. Article 7 of "The Gospel of Jesus Christ: An Evangelical Celebration," a statement drawn up by some evangelical leaders in June 1999, denies "that anyone who rejects the humanity of Christ, his incarnation, or his sinlessness, or who maintains that these truths are not essential to the Gospel, will be saved (1 John 4:2-3)."[23] Donald Bloesch is appropriately "uncomfortable" with the statement, and he comments that "we must not confuse faith in the gospel with assent to particular doctrines in the church, even assent to the doctrine of justification. . . . We are saved not by our theological sophistication or maturity but only by faith in the crucified and risen Christ."[24]

Bloesch's comment reminded me of an evangelistic Bible study I was leading in the home of a nominally Roman Catholic family in the Philippines. We were studying Romans together, and I was drawing the family's attention to Paul's emphasis on faith as the instrument of justification when the mother in the home said, "But *everyone* in the Philippines believes in Jesus." She spoke from her context, growing up in a nation largely "Christianized" by the Spanish conquerors, four centuries before, where some 92 percent of the population deemed themselves to be Christians and members of the Roman Catholic Church. A Jesuit historian once commented, in a course I was taking on the history of the Catholic Church in the Philippines, that the church there is "full of baptized pagans." He recognized that in a church where the ratio of priest to parishioner was about one priest for every 100,000 members, the level of Christian instruction was very poor. So theology was not the forte of most of the members of that part of the Christian church. But how God assesses the faith of each of those poorly catechized Christians is not something we are in a good position to say for certain. Reflecting on my experience in that Bible study, I recall discussing with my wife a question that somewhat took me by surprise, even as I raised it: must a person know that "justification is by faith and not by works" to be justified by faith? Bloesch thinks not, and I am in-

---

[23]"The Gospel of Jesus Christ: An Evangelical Celebration," *Christianity Today*, June 14, 1999, p. 54.
[24]Donald G. Bloesch, *The Church: Sacraments, Worship, Ministry and Mission*, Christian Foundations (Downers Grove, Ill.: InterVarsity Press, 2002), p. 285.

clined to agree with him.[25] I take the apostle John's concern to be the perverse denial of truth by people who are believed to know better but who refuse to submit themselves to the truth, twisting it, instead, to their own destruction, as Peter said (2 Pet 3:16).

I recall reading an e-mail message on a theology list, in which an evangelical Arminian theologian asked whether Calvinists and Arminians worship the same God. It strikes me that the answer would have to be yes and no, just as it was when we asked about Muslims and Christians, though the yes is much more significant—in this case, both worship the God who is Father, Son and Holy Spirit. On the other hand, they define that God rather differently. Many Arminians consider the Calvinist doctrine of unconditional election to be abhorrent, whereas Calvinists express similar horror at the depiction of God offered by Bible believing Open Theists, who deny that God knows the future comprehensively.

I have had students protest that we cannot draw an analogy between Calvinists and Arminians, on the one hand, and Christians and Muslims, on the other. Yet when I ask them whether Jews and Christians today worship the "same God," they are much less ready to answer. Abraham was not a trinitarian, but he had justifying faith. In short, we can identify some definitions of God that put the one who believes in such a "god" outside the community of those who worship the true God, just as we can distinguish between Baal and Yahweh. But I doubt that we are able to define exactly the theological boundaries outside which God is definitely not doing a saving work in the life of the person who is theologically ignorant, rather than theologically perverse.

ORTHOPRAXIS

When warning his disciples that many who thought themselves to be included in the citizenship of his kingdom would be excluded, Jesus uses deeds as a criterion. Such people will remind Jesus of their association with him, "We ate and drank with you, and you taught in our streets" (Lk 13:26), but Jesus will dismiss them as "evildoers" (Lk 13:27). Scripture identifies care for the poor, the afflicted and oppressed, widows and or-

---

[25]As N. T. Wright puts it, "One is not justified by faith by believing in justification by faith. One is justified by faith by believing in Jesus. It follows quite clearly that a great many people are justified by faith who don't know they are justified by faith" (*What St. Paul Really Said: Was Paul of Tarsus the Real Founder of Christianity?* [Cincinnati, Ohio: Forward Movement Publications, 1997]). My thanks to Daniel Reid for drawing my attention to this quotation.

phans as a sign of knowledge of God and of genuine faith (Jer 22:13-17; Jas 1:27; cf. Is 1:10-17; 58:1-14) and stipulates that it is the standard by which we shall be judged in the last day (Mt 25:31-46).[26] John emphasizes the importance of believing in the name of God's Son Jesus Christ (1 Jn 3:23), but he warns that orthodoxy without obedience is of no account. In particular, God's gracious presence in a person's life will be evident in love, "because love is from God; everyone who loves is born of God and knows God" (1 Jn 4:7). As John tells us elsewhere, when those who have been doing "what is true come to the light," it is "clearly seen that their deeds have been done in God" (Jn 3:21).

Abraham and Rahab are exemplars of faith for the writer of Hebrews but of good works for James (Jas 2:20-26), that is, of the good works that give evidence of living faith. This was also Jeremiah's message to people coming to the temple to worship (Jer 7:1-7). The prophets taught that all the nations stood under God's judgment. As Allen Verhey comments, Amos "announced God's judgment on the nations around Israel (greeted, no doubt, by the cries of his hearers, 'Amen, brother! Preach it, Amos') before he announced God's judgment on Israel (greeted, [Verhey suspects], with the guilty silence that can make no reply without invoking a double standard)" (Amos 1:3—2:8).[27] "The judgment of God was announced 'in the midst of the gods' (Ps 82:1), and while it was familiar to Israel, it was a vocation for the politics of the nations, too" (cf. Ps 82:2-4, 8).[28] Such oracles of judgment against the nations, on moral grounds, were frequently pronounced by the prophets (e.g., Is 13—23; Jer 46—51; Ezek 25—32).[29]

We can assume that God judges religions, as he does nations, for the extent to which they do his moral will, as he has made this known to them both in conscience and in the various forms of special revelation that have been their privilege. Job was characterized as righteous because he cared for the poor, the widow, the lame, the orphan, the blind and the needy (Job 29:12-16; 31:16-23).[30] God requires us "to do justice, and to love kindness, and to walk humbly with your God" (Mic 6:8), and Paul tells us that God will "give eternal life" to "those who by patiently doing good seek for glory and honor and immortality" (Rom 2:7).

---

[26]Clendenin, *Many Gods*, p. 112.
[27]Allen Verhey, *Christian Community, Scripture and the Moral Life* (Grand Rapids, Mich.: Eerdmans, 2002), p. 379.
[28]Ibid.
[29]Ibid.
[30]Clendenin, *Many Gods*, p. 138.

E. Luther Copeland is thus wise to question the common practice of tracing the signs of the life-giving Logos among the sages, as Justin and Clement had done. "While I would not rule out the quest for the revealing work of the Logos among the sages and prophets," Copeland says,

> from Jesus' own evaluation of character it seems much more appropriate to seek those who have been enlightened—and redeemed—by him as eternal Logos among the lowly: the poor, the mourners, the meek, those who long for righteousness, the merciful, the pure in heart, the peacemakers, those persecuted for righteousness's sake (Matthew 5:3-10; Luke 6:20-22), and those who serve the needy (Matthew 25:31-46).[31]

Similarly, Pinnock observes that "as in Jesus' day, it is often the noblest representatives of religion who reject God's action emphatically, while ordinary people welcome it."[32]

It is important to remember, at this juncture, what has been said earlier about the common grace of God. Not all evidences of the grace of God at work in the lives of individuals and communities are indications that salvation has occurred. But all of this nonsaving grace is fruit of the atoning work of Christ, and thus here, as in the work of salvation, the activity of the Spirit is intricately related to the work of Christ. In his study of culture and common grace, Richard Mouw finds "intriguing" Alasdair MacIntyre's "suggestion that a 'moral philosophy . . . characteristically presupposes a sociology,' such that 'we have not yet fully understood the claims of any moral philosophy until we have spelled out what its social embodiment would be like.' "[33] Mouw suggests that, in the same way, "every theological system has an associated sociology, such that we can fully understand the claims of a theological perspective only if we attempt to see what it would look like if those claims were fleshed out in the life of a community" and that we might use this link "to test cautiously the adequacy of the theological position in question."[34]

Extending Mouw's point, we can use this criterion to assess not only Christian theological constructions but also the religious constructs of other religions. Of course, the sociological implications of the truth we

---

[31]E. Luther Copeland, *A New Meeting of the Religions: Interreligious Relationships and Theological Questioning* (Waco, Tex.: Baylor University Press, 1999), p. 56.

[32]Pinnock, *Wideness in God's Mercy*, p. 91.

[33]Richard J. Mouw, *He Shines in All That's Fair: Culture and Common Grace* (Grand Rapids, Mich.: Eerdmans, 2001), p. 73, quoting Alasdair MacIntyre, *After Virtue: A Study in Moral Theory* (Notre Dame, Ind.: University of Notre Dame Press, 1981), p. 22.

[34]Mouw, *He Shines*, p. 74.

have drawn from Scripture will serve as our criteria for recognizing positive signs of God's grace in the sociological outworking of the convictions of other religious systems; we will also use these criteria for identifying points at which the errors in a belief system are made evident in the harmful sociological outworkings of those beliefs.

Given Stanley Grenz's focus on God's purposes to foster human community, he naturally suggests that we assess a religion "according to both the personal identity/social structures it fosters and the underlying belief system that sanctions the social order."[35] Here the interrelationship of belief and practice are evident. As Grenz notes, "just as in the Old Testament setting, to choose the true God is to opt for the truly human as well, whereas the worship of false gods leads to injustice."[36] Nevertheless, however much we may appreciate the positive result of community formation that another religion produces, "other religious visions cannot provide community in its ultimate sense, because they are *theologically* insufficient. They do not embody the fullest possible understanding of who God actually is."[37]

Once again, the priority of beliefs becomes apparent. Practices are important, and they may be aspects of particular religions that we can affirm, but they are never enough, because the underlying theological inadequacy of non-Christian religions, which do not begin from the understanding of God as triune, will keep them from leading people into all that God wants for them. Having said this, we need to remind ourselves that no Christian religious community now attains to the full expression of what God will bring about in the new heaven and earth; and, meanwhile, there may be times at which a particular non-Christian community better approximates God's ideal than does a particular Christian community. Recognition of that fact should foster our humility. We should call others to participate in the life with God in Christ that God has graciously drawn us into, but we dare not pretend that we have arrived at the fullness of what he is bringing about. We can paint the biblical picture of what we eagerly hope for and call others to join us in that hope through faith in Jesus, without pretending to have arrived at the state of the world that we eagerly wait for God to bring into being.

---

[35]Stanley J. Grenz, "The Universality of the 'Jesus-Story' and the 'Incredulity Toward Metanarratives,' " in *No Other Gods Before Me? Evangelicals and the Challenge of World Religions,* ed. John G. Stackhouse Jr. (Grand Rapids, Mich.: Baker, 2001), p. 107.

[36]Ibid. Christopher J. H. Wright has made a very similar point ("The Christian and Other Religions: The Biblical Evidence," *Themelios* 9 [January 1984]: 8).

[37]Grenz, "Universality," p. 109.

Although we may observe and admire behavior in non-Christians that looks like fruit of the Spirit, it is essential that we remember that salvation is not by works. We are saved not *by* but *for* good works (Eph 2:8-10).[38] Yet Paul asserts that God will judge impartially according to what each person has *done* (Rom 2:5-11; cf. Ps 62:12; Rev 20:12-13). At this point, I think that the classic Reformed distinction between common and special grace is especially helpful. Within the history of Christianity, there have certainly been times of cruelty and behavior that are contradictory to the Christian gospel, whereas there are instances of self-sacrificial love in the lives of the devout members of other religions. And there are teachings within other religions that foster attitudes and behavior that conform to God's moral requirements as revealed in the Scriptures of the Old Testament and New Testament.

Because of the universal revelatory work of Christ, of which John 1:9 speaks, the line is not always easy to discern. As Newbigin says,

There is light and there is darkness. But light shines on the darkness to the uttermost; there is no point at which light stops and darkness begins, unless the light has been put under a bushel. When the light shines freely one cannot draw a line and say, "Here light stops and darkness begins." But one can and must say, "*There* is where the light shines; go towards it and your path will be clear; turn your back on it and you will go into deeper darkness."[39]

On the other hand, it does raise the question of whether these works are evidence of a saving-faith relationship with God, such as Ulrich Zwingli described in the case of the elect who do not hear the gospel. But because of common grace, we must also realize that not every manifestation of objective goodness is the fruit of faith; it could be the fruit of self-righteousness. It is not just *what* people do but *why* they do it that is important to God who looks on the *heart*.

Vinoth Ramachandra clearly reaffirms the uniqueness of Jesus as divine, but he argues that this does not cancel out all other stories of the divine-human encounter. Rather, "it enables us to discern signs of God's new order, inaugurated in Jesus, in all human struggles against fear, greed, violence, sickness, oppression and injustice."[40] All grace—common grace as well as

[38]Clendenin, *Many Gods*, p. 138.
[39]Lesslie Newbigin, *The Open Secret: An Introduction to the Theology of Mission*, rev. ed. (Grand Rapids, Mich.: Eerdmans, 1995), pp. 174-75.
[40]Vinoth Ramachandra, *Faiths in Conflict? Christian Integrity in a Multicultural World* (Leicester, U.K.: Inter-Varsity Press, 1999), p. 117.

the forms of God's gracious encounters with people that are not specifically oriented toward making them aware of Christ's solution for sin—are the fruit of the saving work of Christ. Pinnock suggests that wherever

> we find self-sacrificing love, care about community, longings for justice, wherever people love one another, care for the sick, make peace not war, wherever there is beauty and concord, generosity and forgiveness, the cup of cold water, we know the Spirit of Jesus is present. Other spirits do not promote broken and contrite hearts.[41]

So also, says Verhey, " 'Whatever is true, whatever is honorable, whatever is just, whatever is pure, whatever is pleasing, whatever is commendable' (Phil 4:8) is not to be denied but credited to God and counted as God's gifts to humanity."[42] I take this to apply not only to individuals but to the religions that people construct in their ambiguous responses to God's revelation.

Given that religions are structures or systems that tend toward justice, mercy and humility (Mic 6:8) or toward injustice, oppression and pride, we can evaluate the effect of a religious system on the lives of the people who live according to its regulations. The concept of structural evil, which Liberation theologians have helpfully drawn to our attention, comes to the fore here. Paul Knitter's emphasis on the liberating effect of true religion, for both humans and the earth we inhabit, is not without merit. It bears mention again that the Old Testament 's condemnations of the nations did not focus on belief in the wrong gods. "Condemnation of the nations, where reasons are given, is usually based on their moral and social behaviour (see the oracles against the nations, e.g., Amos 1—2; Is 13—23)."[43]

> The presenting cause of Yahweh's hostility to Pharaoh (god himself and representative of the gods of Egypt) is his oppression of the Hebrews. There is no such conflict and hostility in the narratives of Genesis when first Joseph and then his brothers have their long interaction with Egypt. On the contrary, there is a recognition of the God of Joseph by the Pharaoh, in a way echoed later in the book of Daniel (e.g., Gen. 41). But the Exodus Pharaoh having initiated a state policy of oppression which has political, economic, social and spiritual aspects, refuses to acknowledge the God of Moses (Ex 5:2). It is that which arouses Yahweh to action—action for justice in the biblical sense of judging the oppressor and rescuing the oppressed. The destruc-

---

[41]Pinnock, *Flame of Love,* pp. 209-10.
[42]Verhey, *Christian Community,* p. 459.
[43]Goldingay and Wright, "Yahweh," p. 52.

tion of Pharaoh is thus a declaration of Yahweh's opposition to a religion that sanctions a social order that in turn sanctions inhumanity and oppression.[44]

The longer struggle carried on within Israel against Baalism is a similar situation. There seems to have been a moral deterioration in the life of the inhabitants of Canaan from the time when the patriarchs first settled there to the time when God moved against them in judgment. "The less conflict-ual attitude to Canaanite religion in Genesis goes along with the statement that 'the iniquity of the Amorites is not yet full' (Gen. 15:16), whereas the evil of the inhabitants of the land in the later centuries is enough to make the land itself vomit them out (Lev. 18:24-28)."[45] Thus, we see a different "response to other religions related to the kind of social and moral charac-teristics they foster among their adherents."[46] Yahweh not only opposed worship of the wrong God or "no-god," as on Mt. Carmel,

> but the hijacking of the whole social, economic and legal ethos of Israel by the religious vandalism of Jezebel's Phoenician Baalism, as focused in the Naboth incident (1 Kgs. 21). The struggle was not simply over what was the right religion, but what was a right and just society for Naboth to live in. Baal religion undergirded—or at least imposed no restraint on—the way Ahab and Jezebel treated Naboth.[47]

Goldingay and Wright argue, therefore, that "the moral, social and cul-tural effects of a major religious tradition do give us some grounds for a discriminating response to it—fully aware that this can be as uncomfort-able for Christianity as a cultural religion as for any other."[48] This is a very important point, which we dare not ignore, if we wish to be the sort of peo-ple through whom God's glory can be magnified among the nations—and among the religions.

Frank Macchia appeals to both christological and pneumatological cri-teria when discerning the spirits at work in the world.

> If God created humanity in the divine image and laid claim to humanity in the birth, death, and resurrection of Christ, then any attempt to dehumanize anyone for any reason contradicts God's love for humanity and serves the forces of darkness. If the Spirit anointed Christ to preach the good news to the poor, the blind, and the imprisoned (Luke 4:18), then those structures

---

[44]Ibid., p. 57.
[45]Ibid., pp. 57-58.
[46]Ibid., p. 58.
[47]Ibid.
[48]Ibid.

and forces that encourage poverty, sickness, and crime serve the forces of darkness. If Satan blinds the minds of the ungodly to the gospel (2 Cor 4:4), then those things that discourage our gospel witness, both word and deed, to the needy also serve the forces of darkness.[49]

One further potentially productive approach to evaluating other religious systems is suggested by Netland in his own application of the moral criterion of internal coherence to Zen Buddhism. "The issue," Netland suggests,

> is not whether Buddhism manifests moral awareness, nor even whether individual Buddhists can be persons of outstanding moral character (undoubtedly many are); the issue is whether the metaphysical commitments of Buddhism, and Zen in particular, *allow* for the moral insights and imperatives we find within Buddhist traditions.[50]

Netland identifies two points where Buddhist ontology and moral awareness are in tension. First, Zen is "unable to account for, or explain adequately, the phenomena of moral obligation." Second, "Zen's ontology clashes sharply with a widely shared aspect of human experience, namely the awareness of a real and irreducible distinction between good and evil, right and wrong."[51] This sort of analysis may be more useful in apologetics than in our work of personal discernment in our relationships with others whose eternal good we seek, but we cannot ignore the strengths and weaknesses of the religious systems within which people live when we assess their own personal situations.

ORTHOKARDIA OR ORTHOPATHY

Moses posed a question like Jeremiah's: "Now, O Israel, what does the LORD your God require of you?" (Deut 10:12), and Clendenin notices that Moses answered "rather comprehensively": love and fear God, walk in his ways, serve him with all your heart and soul. But then Moses sums up his exhortation: "Circumcise, then, the foreskin of your heart" (Deut 10:16).[52] The "circumcised" heart was also identified by Joel and Jeremiah (Jer 4:4; Joel 2:12-13) as an essential characteristic of true religion. Here, then, the

---

[49]Frank Macchia, "Created Spirit Beings: Satan and Demons," in *Systematic Theology*, rev. ed., ed. Stanley M. Horton (Springfield, Mo.: Logion, 1995), pp. 211-12, quoted in Yong, *Discerning*, p. 244.

[50]Netland, *Encountering*, p. 304.

[51]Ibid., p. 307.

[52]Clendenin, *Many Gods*, p. 139.

critical distinction between outward religious ritual and inward attitudes and intentions comes to the forefront.

What Jesus identified as the "greatest and first commandment" (Mt 22:38; citing Deut 6:4-5) calls for a particular attitude of the heart, for complete love for God. And Moses promises Israel that God will do such a work in them: "The LORD your God will circumcise your heart and the heart of your descendants so that you will love the LORD your God with all your heart and with all your soul, in order that you may live" (Deut 30:6). Clendenin further observes that "the sacrifices that please God do so because of the attitude of the one who offers them, namely, righteousness (Ps 4:5), a broken spirit and a contrite heart (Ps 51:16-17), gratitude (Ps 50:7-15), loyalty and the knowledge of God (Hos 6:6), and obedience (1 Sam 15:22)."[53] Only a person who has a "pure heart" may approach the Lord (Ps 24:3-4), and Jesus reaffirms that it is the "pure in heart" who will "see God" (Mt 5:8). When it comes to this criterion, of course, only God can judge. He is the only one who knows our hearts, and "he has promised not to forsake anyone who truly seeks him (Ps 9:10; 2 Chron 16:9; 1 Cor 4:3-5)."[54]

SUMMING UP

We need to exercise discernment on two levels: in assessing religious systems or institutions and in evaluating the situation of individuals within them. We dare not assume that an assessment of the institution to which one belongs gives us an adequate means of assessing the person's own spiritual situation.

Of the three criteria that we have discussed—right belief, right action and right attitude—unquestionably the first is the most important in regard to *our* assessment of systems. It is on this point that all religions other than Christianity fall drastically short; they do not believe in and worship the triune God: Father, Son and Holy Spirit. On the other hand, not all theological deficiencies are equally serious, and an individual can be seriously wrong about points of theology and still be properly related to God. At the individual level, it is clear that God's primary interest is a person's attitude, and it is here that the Spirit of God is especially at work in people's lives. Churches can teach the faith in its creedal form, and that has value, but only the Spirit of God can produce the faith or trust that pleases God.

God is always graciously at work in the lives of individuals and com-

[53]Ibid.
[54]Ibid.

munities, sending rain on their fields, giving them joy and producing in them the characteristics that no sinner could produce apart from the Holy Spirit's goodness. This common-grace work can also be manifested and structured into the life of religious communities and the fruit they bear, both individually and socially. At this level, we may be most likely to find aspects of other religions, and features in the lives of their adherents, that we admire and for which we can be grateful to God for his grace. We must not belittle the importance of this gracious work of God, as though only saving grace is of any value. So we need to glorify God for all of his work in the world. We have to be very careful, however, not to emphasize the second criterion (right behavior or practice) so exclusively that we allow moralistic judgments to determine our sense of what sort of ministry people or institutions need. Just because people are "good," it does not mean that they are "saved"; but if they are radically (at the root) "bad," we can be sure that they are not saved.

We must be particularly tentative in judging people's hearts, which only God can see (1 Sam 16:7). Good trees will bear good fruit, but we are simply unable to definitively judge where people are in their relationship to God when the signs of grace in their lives are ambiguous and when their motives are hidden from us. As Newbigin says, we should be particularly interested in the direction in which people are moving. Only God can move people from darkness to light, but he may do so over long periods of time. We can be his servants in that process, if we are sensitive to the Spirit of God to give us discernment and to minister the word or deed that God will use next to move people closer to God. Of course, the more clearly God's light shines in our own lives, the more likely he is to attract others to the light through us. And so we move on now to consider ways in which we should relate to people of other religions in our religiously plural society and in a world where many societies are very uninterested in religious plurality.

18

Should We Participate
in Interreligious Dialogue?

Thesis 28: Dialogue with members of other religions is valuable. It is not a substitute for evangelism, but it is also not simply a means of evangelism. Nevertheless, Christians engaged in dialogue will be hopeful that God might use their conversations to lead dialogue partners to faith in Christ or to further other good purposes that God may have for the lives of those with whom we are in dialogue. Christians can also benefit personally from dialogue in various ways, learning as well as teaching.

IN RECENT DECADES, *DIALOGUE* HAS BECOME A COMMON TERM in relationships between religious groups—relationships between different religions as well as relationships within particular religions, such as between denominations or branches of Christianity. Attitudes to the interreligious form of such dialogues have been quite diverse. The no-agreement approach rules it out, since there is really no point to it. All that is needed, from that Christian standpoint, is evangelism. On the pluralist or common-faith end of the spectrum, however, dialogue has been viewed as highly fruitful and frequently replaces evangelism as an alternative way of relating. The subject raises many questions. Why would we, or should we, dialogue with representatives of other religions? What would we hope to gain from or to give through such discussion? If we do dialogue, how should we go about it? It is the answer to such questions that I want to consider in this chapter.

A DEFINITION OF *DIALOGUE*

By *interreligious dialogue*, I mean "a sustained conversation between parties who are not saying the same thing and who recognize and respect the contradictions and mutual exclusions between their various ways of thinking."[1] As a "sustained conversation," this is intentional and extended,[2] and our primary goal is not to achieve agreement but to achieve understanding. This is not a quest for a lowest common denominator that we can all agree on, although it will probably identify points of agreement as well as points of difference and may even lead to common action on matters of shared concern, such as secularism or social justice. This sort of dialogue is not a substitute for evangelism, but evangelism need not be its only goal, either. Yet, as the Lausanne Covenant stated, the "kind of dialogue whose purpose is to listen sensitively, in order to understand" is "indispensable to evangelism," and John Stott supports this notion by reference to Proverbs 18:13: "If one gives answer before hearing, it is folly and shame."[3]

Objections to interreligious dialogue within the Christian community have generally been based on the doctrine of separation (2 Cor 6:14-17) and the conviction that to collaborate in seeking mutual understanding is to be complicit with evil and error.[4] Christianity is at its heart a missionary religion, and any approach to dialogue that sees itself as an *alternative* to evangelism destroys the heart of the Christian's love for neighbors whose greatest need is to be at peace with God and to be part of the community of God's people. Dialogue and evangelism are not the same thing, but they are also not completely different—"no absolute line can be drawn" between them.[5] In dialogue, we give testimony to our relationship with God through Christ, and we seek the good of the one with whom we speak and to whom we listen. Paul appears to have expected that Christians would be in dialogue with non-Christians (Col 4:5-6): that they would be receiving questions from them and that their responses would be gracious and "seasoned with salt."

---

[1]John V. Taylor, "The Theological Basis of Interfaith Dialogue," in *Faith Meets Faith*, Mission Trends, ed. Gerald H. Anderson and Thomas F. Stransky (Grand Rapids, Mich.: Eerdmans, 1981), 5:94.

[2]Terry C. Muck, "A New Testament Case for Interreligious Dialogue?" (paper presented at the Evangelical Theological Society meeting, Washington, D.C., November 18-20, 1993), p. 3.

[3]John R. Stott, "Dialogue, Encounter, Even Confrontation," in *Faith Meets Faith*, Mission Trends, ed. Gerald H. Anderson and Thomas F. Stransky (Grand Rapids, Mich.: Eerdmans, 1981), 5:172, quoting paragraph 4 of the Lausanne Covenant.

[4]Muck, "New Testament Case," p. 5.

[5]Thomas Finger, "Confessing Truth in a Pluralistic World," in *Practicing Truth: Confident Witness in Our Pluralistic World*, ed. David W. Shenk and Linford Stutzman (Scottdale, Penn.: Herald, 1999), p. 216.

A critical question we must answer is whether we are in dialogue because God has not revealed himself to our neighbor or because he has done so.[6] In my accessibilist construction, the answer is the latter. We believe that God has already made himself known to the person with whom we speak and that they already experience God's grace in their lives. Therefore, we seek to be useful to God in the *furthering* of his purposes in the life of this neighbor, which we hope are purposes of grace. I believe that accessibilists are in an excellent position to engage in sincere dialogue with devotees of other religions and that it helps if we approach the conversation as critical realists, transparent about our own fallibility and limitations in knowing and doing truth.

THE SUPERIORITY OF DIALOGUE OVER DEBATE

Dialogue is a very different form of engagement with others than is debate, and it has distinct advantages. J. N. D. Anderson has found this to be particularly true in regard to Muslims who would want to draw him into an argument about the relative excellencies of Jesus *(Isa)* or Muhammad but with whom, in such settings, "any spirit of rivalry or competition, inevitably militates against spiritual understanding."[7] As Harold Netland puts it, "one can win the debate but lose the person."[8] He warns that we must be "especially careful about apologetics encounters with religious communities, such as Jewish and Muslim communities, that have suffered greatly in the past at the hands of Christendom." In such contexts we "must learn first to listen humbly in silence, cultivating relationships of trust before proceeding into encounters over truth."[9]

Because of Anderson's missionary experience, he generally tries to avoid controversies and makes a more peaceful proposal to Muslims with whom he converses:

> "Don't you think it might be more helpful for us to put argument on one side," I would say, "at least for the present? May I ask you instead to tell me, as fully and frankly as you can, what your knowledge of God, as this is ministered to you through the Qur'an, really means to you? I can prom-

---

[6]S. Wesley Ariarajah, *Not Without My Neighbour: Issues in Interfaith Relations* (Geneva: World Council of Churches Publications, 1999), p. 107.

[7]J. N. D. Anderson, *Christianity and World Religions: The Challenge of Pluralism* (Downers Grove, Ill.: InterVarsity Press, 1984), p. 187.

[8]Harold Netland, *Encountering Religious Pluralism: The Challenge to Faith and Mission* (Downers Grove, Ill.: InterVarsity Press, 2001), p. 282.

[9]Ibid., p. 283.

ise you that I will listen to what you say with both interest and respect, and that I will make a genuine attempt to understand the nature of that knowledge and its practical implications—trying to stand, as it were in your shoes. And then, perhaps, you will permit me to tell you, to the best of my ability, what God has come to mean to me as he is revealed in Jesus Christ my Lord."[10]

This kind of dialogue can change both parties, as was the case in the encounter between Peter and Cornelius, who both learned things through the experience. Wesley S. Ariarajah was involved in interfaith dialogue for years, on behalf of the World Council of Churches. He notes a very important contribution of dialogue in terms of the prevention or avoidance of conflict. When Christians acted violently against people of other religions, Ariarajah was often asked what the WCC dialogue program was doing about it. His answer is excellent: "Dialogue is not an ambulance service; it is a public health program."[11] It is extremely difficult to work for reconciliation between religious groups once violence has occurred. Building relations of mutual respect, a "community of conversation," is much better. "It seeks to make people 'at home' with plurality, to develop an appreciation of diversity, and to make those links that may just help them to hold together when the whole community is threatened by forces of separation and anarchy."[12]

J. H. Bavinck indicates one particular danger we face when we rely on successful rational argument to lead people to a relationship with God through Christ.

At any moment someone will come who will upset our fine arguments and thereby push this man back into his former faith. This world is so complicated, so full of contradictions, so confused, that it is frequently difficult for those of us who have been blessed by God's word in Christ to see everything in the light of God's omnipotent wisdom and greatness. How much more difficult it must be for someone who has always bowed down to numerous gods and powers but who now, on the basis of philosophical reasoning, has come to the idea that there can only be a single God. As long as he has not really met God in Christ, as long as he has not bowed down before him and recognized him as Father, everything in him is still extremely weak and vulnerable. The deepest cause of this is, as Paul expressed it so strikingly, that

---

[10]Anderson, *Christianity and World Religions*, p. 187.
[11]Ariarajah, *Not Without*, p. 12.
[12]Ibid., p. 14.

his faith rests too much upon "the wisdom of men," and too little upon "the power of God" (1 Cor 2:5).[13]

RESPECT FOR THE OTHER PERSON'S INTEGRITY AND RELIGIOUS FREEDOM

As we enter into dialogue with people committed to a different religion, we must respect and defend their right to believe and practice according to their own convictions, and we must refrain from coercion. Jesus called on us to love our neighbors (Mk 12:29-31) and even our enemies (Mt 5), and this includes respecting them as fellow creatures who bear the image of God. Loving our neighbors who have religious convictions different from our own, according to 1 Corinthians 13, will mean being patient, kind and tolerant toward them, not easily provoked by them, not thinking evil thoughts of them, being humble and aware that our own knowledge is only partial at this time. It means "taking them seriously, being open to them and interested in them, trying to understand them better, learning from them something about their life."[14] As Kevin Vanhoozer reminds us, "True dialogue demands the practice, and not simply the discourse, of Christian love. Indeed, might we not venture, in light of our trinitarian re-flections, to suggest that it is *only* by opening ourselves up to the Other and to difference that we are true to our Christian distinctives?"[15]

This respect for the right of others to believe differently from we do does *not* mean that we accept what they believe as equally true, only that we grant them the right to hold their own convictions, right or wrong, just as we want them to grant us the same right. This will be easier for us if we can cultivate "the gracious acceptance of the reality of religious plurality and the end of Christendom."[16] We must not resent the presence of other faiths or the views of their adherents. The radical Christian commitment to defend every one's religious freedom is itself very attractive to people

---

[13]J. H. Bavinck, *An Introduction to the Science of Missions*, trans. David Hugh Freeman (Kampen: J. H. Kok, 1954; Philadelphia: Presbyterian & Reformed, 1960), p. 231.

[14]Charles W. Forman, "Christian Dialogues with Other Faiths," in *Toward the Twenty-First Century in Christian Mission: Essays in Honor of Gerald H. Anderson*, ed. James M. Phillips and Robert T. Coote (Grand Rapids, Mich.: Eerdmans, 1993), p. 341.

[15]Kevin J. Vanhoozer, "Does the Trinity Belong in a Theology of Religions? On Angling in the Rubicon and the 'Identity' of God," in *The Trinity in a Pluralistic Age: Theological Essays on Culture and Religion* (Grand Rapids, Mich.: Eerdmans, 1997), p. 69.

[16]Gordon T. Smith, "Religions and the Bible: An Agenda for Evangelicals," in *Christianity and the Religions: A Biblical Theology of World Religions*, Evangelical Missiological Society Series, ed. Edward Rommen and Harold Netland (Pasadena, Calif.: William Carey Library, 1995), 2:19.

of other religions, as is evident in immigration patterns, even when their own religion does not ground a similar respect for others when it is allowed to dictate a nation's policy.

In current discussions of conflict between religions, the term *proselytism* often arises, and it frequently carries a negative connotation, particularly in media reports. On the other hand, it may simply refer to the propagation of one's faith in an effort to convert others, which evangelicals will insist is a right both for themselves and for the members of other religions in the genuine pluralism that Christianity should foster. The WCC used the term negatively when it stated that "proselytism embraces whatever violates the right of the human person, Christian or non-Christian, to be free from external coercion in religious matters."[17] When defined in that way, proselytism is inconsistent with the Christian spirit that must inform our relations and our efforts at dialogue with other religious or nonreligious people. Because of the term's ambiguous meanings, we will need to define its sense carefully when we defend the right of people to proselytize others.

Expression of Friendship

In establishing relationships with people of other religions, we should not make our friendship with them contingent on their agreement with us. From his work in Britain, Christopher Lamb notes that the "need in many contemporary situations is for a Christian *ministry of welcome*, which makes it clear that people of other faiths are regarded by Christians as human beings with the same feelings and needs as everyone else, and as people who have every right to be where they are."[18] He sees this welcome and the giving of practical help to immigrants as "pre-supposed by the way that Jesus treated disadvantaged people of all kinds, and by the particular dialectical ministry which . . . [Jesus had] with religious leaders," and he finds it "alarming to listen to Christian views about mission and evangelism to those of other faiths and to realize that the speakers have little or no interest in Muslims or Hindus or Sikhs as people, or indeed as religious believers, except in so far as their beliefs can be made to yield angles of approach for Christian propaganda."[19]

---

[17]"Christian Witness, Proselytism and the Jews," in Gerald H. Anderson and Thomas F. Stransky, eds., *Faith Meets Faith*, Mission Trends (Grand Rapids, Mich.: Eerdmans, 1981), 5:190.

[18]Christopher Lamb, "Dialectical Ministry: Christian Life and Mission in the Multi-Faith Situation," *Themelios* 9, no. 2 (1984): 23.

[19]Ibid.

Lamb uses that harsh word intentionally "because of the essentially in-human attitude which such views betray."[20]

RECOGNITION OF GENUINE DIFFERENCE

We recognize the existence of genuine and important differences between religious traditions. This makes dialogue possible in a way that is impossible when differences are assumed to be transcended or resolved in an overarching unity, but it also underlines the great difficulty of genuine dialogue. This is ironic, because one of pluralists' key goals has been to enable dialogue between religions! Yale theologian Kathryn Tanner has spoken well to this point:

> Pluralist generalizations about what all religions have in common conflict with genuine dialogue, in that they prejudge its results. Commonalities, which should be established in and through a process of dialogue, are constructed ahead of time by pluralists to serve as presuppositions of dialogue. Pluralists therefore close themselves to what people of other religions might have to say about their account of these commonalities. Moreover, . . . a pluralist focus on commonalities slights differences among the religions of the world. The pluralists' insistence on commonalities as a condition of dialogue shows an unwillingness to recognize the depth and degree of diversity among religions, or the positive importance of them.[21]

Rather than fostering harmony in the relationships between religions, this "can all too easily lead to the deliberate suppression of differences in the interests of harmony."[22]

Interreligious dialogue is fraught with difficulty because the differences between us are often subtle. "We shall frequently find that the same word carries an entirely different cluster of meanings in the different traditions; we may also discover with surprise that quite different words are used to mean the same thing."[23] John Taylor recalls, for instance,

> a very well-known and respected participant in the dialogue between Christians and Hindus exclaiming in the course of a conversation—"What makes

---

[20]Ibid.

[21]Kathryn Tanner, "Respect for Other Religions: A Christian Antidote to Colonialist Discourse," *Modern Theology* 9 (January 1993): 2, quoted in Alister McGrath, "A Particularist View: A Post-Enlightenment Approach," in *More Than One Way? Four Views on Salvation in a Pluralistic World*, ed. Dennis L. Okholm and Timothy R. Phillips. (Grand Rapids, Mich.: Zondervan, 1995), p. 160.

[22]McGrath, "Particularist View," p. 162.

[23]Taylor, "Theological Basis," 5:98.

this so painful is that again and again, when my Hindu brother and I seem to be drawing closer than ever before, and at a deeper level, at that very moment the immense gulf between us opens up again."[24]

Thus, at the very least, interreligious dialogue can further "mutual comprehension of conflicting truth claims," which is essential to "real communication of the Christian faith."[25]

Yves Raguin, a Jesuit professor at the Ricci Institute for Chinese Studies in Taipei, Taiwan, notes that "there is no dialogue possible unless we realize the magnitude of the differences, and try from this to find a common ground" because we need a place to start.[26] Consequently, we cannot start with what is specific of a religion, such as the Christian claim to the exclusiveness of Christ. Raguin proposes that our common ground is "that all people are bound to God by a destiny which is inscribed at the depth of their being. It is what we mean when we say that man is made in the image of God."[27] But rather than starting anthropologically, Christians in dialogue do better to start theologically, from the trinitarian nature of God, which is the distinctive of Christian understanding. As Vanhoozer argues, the Trinity, "far from hindering conversation, is the transcendental condition of interfaith dialogue with the Other. Without the Trinity, theological dialogue lacks the necessary specificity (i.e., Logos, Christ) and the necessary spirit (i.e., love, Spirit) to prosper."[28] Vanhoozer proposes that "one may seek in charity to be, as far as is conceptually and confessionally possible, at peace with all positions, but one must then seek, in clarity, to enumerate the differences that remain."[29]

LEARNING FROM ADHERENTS OF OTHER RELIGIONS

Since religions are ambiguous responses to God's revelation, we can grant that aspects of other people's belief may be true and that we can learn from them in this discussion. As Thomas Finger puts it, "If universal truth is not only something that I already possess in part, but also something that is not

---

[24]Ibid.

[25]David J. Hesselgrave, "Evangelicals and Interreligious Dialogue," in *Faith Meets Faith*, ed. Gerald H. Anderson and Thomas F. Stransky (Grand Rapids, Mich.: Eerdmans, 1981), 5:125-26.

[26]Yves Raguin, S.J., "Differences and Common Ground," in *Faith Meets Faith*, ed. Gerald H. Anderson and Thomas F. Stransky (Grand Rapids, Mich.: Eerdmans, 1981), p. 175.

[27]Ibid.

[28]Vanhoozer, "Does the Trinity," p. 68.

[29]Ibid.

yet fully known to me and toward which I strive, dialogue with sincere partners can help me better understand my own faith as well as theirs."[30] Lesslie Newbigin also rejects the proposal that "other religions and ideologies are wholly false and the Christian has nothing to learn from them" for three reasons. First, "the sensitive Christian mind, enlightened by Christ, cannot fail to recognize and to rejoice in the abundant spiritual fruits to be seen in the lives of men and women of other faiths."[31] Later, Newbigin writes,

> The Christian confession of Jesus as Lord does not involve any attempt to deny the reality of the work of God in the lives and thoughts and prayers of men and women outside the Christian church. On the contrary, it ought to involve an eager expectation of, a looking for, and a rejoicing in the evidence of that work. There is something deeply wrong when Christians imagine that loyalty to Jesus requires them to belittle the manifest presence of the light in the lives of men and women who do not acknowledge him, to seek out points of weakness, to ferret out hidden sins and deceptions as a means of commending the gospel. If we love the light and walk in the light we will also rejoice in the light wherever we find it—even the smallest gleams of it in the surrounding darkness.[32]

Newbigin's second reason for being open to learning from others is that

> in almost all cases where the Bible has been translated into the languages of the non-Christian peoples of the world, the New Testament word *Theos* has been rendered by the name given by the non-Christian peoples to the one whom they worship as the Supreme Being. It is under this name, therefore, that the Christians who now use these languages worship the God and Father of Jesus Christ. The very few exceptions, where translators have sought to evade the issue by simply transliterating the Greek or Hebrew word, only serve to prove the point; for the converts have simply explained the foreign word in the text of their Bibles by using the indigenous name for God.[33]

It is, therefore, "impossible to claim that there is a total discontinuity between" the other religion and Christianity. Third, Newbigin points out that "John tells us that Jesus is the light that enlightens every man. This text does not say anything about other *religions*, but makes it impossible for the Christian to say that those outside the church are totally devoid of the truth."[34]

---

[30]Finger, "Confessing Truth," p. 216.

[31]Lesslie Newbigin, *The Open Secret: An Introduction to the Theology of Mission*, rev. ed. (Grand Rapids, Mich.: Eerdmans, 1995), p. 169.

[32]Ibid., p. 175.

[33]Ibid., p. 169.

[34]Ibid., p. 170.

Gerald McDermott makes the point nicely: "Commitment to Jesus precludes commitment to the finality of other faith," but "it does not rule out acceptance of the truth that other faiths may contain."[35]

> [For] if Saint Augustine learned from Neo-Platonism to better understand the gospel, if Thomas Aquinas learned from Aristotle to better understand the Scriptures, and if John Calvin learned from Renaissance humanism, perhaps evangelicals may be able to learn from the Buddha—and other great religious thinkers and traditions—things that can help them more clearly understand God's revelation in Christ.[36]

That we are speaking about learning from members of other *religions*, whereas theologians of earlier centuries spoke of learning from *philosophies* is insignificant, as Stephen Williams rightly observes. On the other hand, conceptual borrowing "does not entail that Advaitic Hindus or Yogacarin scholars are having an experience of God, still less a saving one."[37] In regard to Aquinas, for instance, it is particularly interesting to note that Aquinas's access to Aristotle was "by way of the Muslim philosopher Ibn Rushd (Averroes) and the Jewish philosopher Moses ben Maimon (Maimonides)."[38]

Anderson remarks that it is "a common experience for a Christian to learn much from men of other faiths—in devotion, humility, courage and a host of other virtues; and it is perfectly possible for him to learn from the teaching of some other religion a lesson he has failed to learn from his own."[39] Note that when Jesus wanted to teach his disciples a lesson about love for one's neighbor, which is central to the piety of both Testaments, he cited a good Samaritan—a representative of another religious tradition— as an example (Lk 10:25-37).[40]

Our cultural conditioning may prevent us from "learning some of the things clearly taught in the Scriptures," suggests Ajith Fernando. "Other

---

[35]Gerald R. McDermott, *Can Evangelicals Learn from World Religions? Jesus, Revelation and Religious Traditions* (Downers Grove, Ill.: InterVarsity Press, 2000), p. 20.

[36]Ibid., p. 12.

[37]Stephen Williams, "The Trinity and 'Other Religions,' " in *The Trinity in a Pluralistic Age: Theological Essays on Culture and Religion* (Grand Rapids, Mich.: Eerdmans, 1997), p. 29.

[38]Michael S. Jones, "Evangelical Christianity and the Philosophy of Interreligious Dialogue," *Journal of Ecumenical Studies* 36 (summer-fall 1999): 383.

[39]J. N. D. Anderson, *Christianity and Comparative Religion* (Leicester, U.K.: Inter-Varsity Press, 1970), p. 93, quoted in R. W. F. Wootton, *Christianity and Other Faiths: An Evangelical Contribution to Our Multi-Faith Society* (Exeter: Paternoster, 1983), p. 22.

[40]Duane Friesen, "The Discernment of Wisdom in the Encounter Between the Christian Faith and People of Other Religious Faiths," *Mission Focus: Annual Review* 8 (2000): 129.

cultures may not have these cultural hindrances. So, even without the light of the gospel, people of other cultures may achieve heights in these areas simply by availing themselves of general revelation."[41] He cites meditation, devotion and reverence in prayer, as things about which he could learn much from a friend converted from Hinduism. "We know," he argues, "that the fullest revelation about reverence is found in the Scriptures, but we had been blinded from seeing it because of the defective Christianity we inherited."[42] Fernando posits, further, that Christianity's deficiency in the meditative or contemplative aspect of life

> is one reason why Christianity has made minimal inroads into the societies of Asia, where the religions with a high emphasis on the contemplative are practiced. Many Buddhists and Hindus, for example, have been unimpressed by Christianity. They view Christians as irreligious people because of our lack of emphasis on the meditative and contemplative aspects of life.[43]

From Buddhists, Miriam Adeney has learned "sensitivity to suffering, paradox, and ambiguity." From Confucianists, she has written,

> [I have] learned the importance of courtesy and the glory of the extended family. Primal religionists remind me that the transcendent supernatural breathes mystery immanently in every part of life, calling forth our awe and our ceremony. Jews encourage me to wrestle with God's world, and even with God himself. Mystics of various traditions inspire me to cultivate spiritual passion. Religious social activists, including Muslims, spur me to sacrifice for justice and righteousness.[44]

Back in 1928, the International Missionary Council had made similar observations at its meeting in Jerusalem. It cited, as positive elements within other religious systems,

> the sense of the Majesty of God and the consequent reverence in worship which are conspicuous in Islam; the deep sympathy for the world's sorrow and unselfish search for the way of escape, which are at the heart of Buddhism; the desire for contact with Ultimate Reality conceived as spiritual, which is prominent in Hinduism; the belief in a moral order of the universe

---

[41]Ajith Fernando, *The Christian's Attitude Toward World Religions* (Wheaton, Ill.: Tyndale House, 1987), p. 111.

[42]Ibid., p. 112.

[43]Ibid., p. 113.

[44]Miriam Adeney, "Rajah Sulayman Was No Water Buffalo: Gospel, Anthropology and Islam," in *No Other Gods Before Me? Evangelicals and the Challenge of World Religions*, ed. John G. Stackhouse Jr. (Grand Rapids, Mich.: Baker, 2001), p. 68.

and consequent insistence on moral conduct, which are inculcated by Confucianism; the disinterested pursuit of truth and human welfare which are often found in those who stand for secular civilizations but do not accept Christ as their Lord and Saviour.[45]

Duane Friesen recalls "hearing several persons who spent time in Africa refer to how their encounter with African culture and spirituality sensitized them to the issue of spiritual powers and healing in the New Testament—aspects they had overlooked in their one-dimensional 'scientific' Western culture."[46] As many of these illustrations have indicated, dialogue does not necessarily mean learning entirely new things but seeing old things in new ways, gaining new understanding of familiar concepts.[47]

We see "new development in the history of revelation as Christ makes himself more fully known by the progressive illumination of the Holy Spirit."[48] For example, "justification by grace through faith was not foreign to the Christian tradition before Luther, but when Luther placed paramount emphasis on the idea and situated it at the center of Christian faith, all the rest of what had been revealed looked new and different."[49] Similarly, "Islam's emphasis on submission to God can help evangelicals correct a misplaced emphasis on self-determination."[50] Buddhism's resistance to materialism can be beneficial to Western evangelicals.[51] It is in this vein that Philip Yancey speaks of the things he learned from Mahatma Gandhi, who was himself trying to live according to principles that he believed had been taught by Jesus, though not followed by Christians in the way that Gandhi understood them.[52]

Of course, we will "change the shape of the ideas" that we appropriate

---

[45]"The Christian Life and Message in Relation to Non-Christian Systems of Thought and Life," in *The Jerusalem Meeting of the International Missionary Council: March 24-April 8, 1928,* 8 vols. (New York: International Missionary Council, 1928), 1:410-11, quoted in D. A. Carson, *The Gagging of God: Christianity Confronts Pluralism* (Grand Rapids, Mich.: Zondervan, 1996), p. 180.

[46]Friesen, "Discernment," p. 135.

[47]McDermott, *Can Evangelicals Learn,* p. 14.

[48]Gerald R. McDermott, "What If Paul Had Been from China? Reflections on the Possibility of Revelation in Non-Christian Religions," in *No Other Gods Before Me? Evangelicals and the Challenge of World Religions,* ed. John G. Stackhouse Jr. (Grand Rapids, Mich.: Baker, 2001), p. 25.

[49]McDermott, *Can Evangelicals Learn,* p. 15.

[50]Ibid.

[51]Jones, "Evangelical Christianity," p. 383.

[52]Philip Yancey, *Soul Survivor: How My Faith Survived the Church* (New York: Doubleday, 2001), pp. 147-77.

from other traditions to help us better understand God in Christ, because we fit them into a Christian framework rather than adopt the framework in which those ideas appear in other religious traditions. But this does not negate that we have learned from another tradition.[53] Further examples of how this learning may be pursued can be found in McDermott's very interesting book *Can Evangelicals Learn from World Religions?* He devotes four chapters to a detailed examination of contributions that he believes can be made to a Christian understanding of God in Christ when we give our attention to features in Buddhism, Daoism, Confucianism and Islam.[54]

D. A. Carson has expressed concern about the statement made by John Goldingay and Christopher Wright that Yahwism was "able to reach its own mature expression" with the aid of things observed in the religious expression of Israel's neighbors.[55] Carson dubs this "remarkable rhetoric"[56] and suggests that "one might as well say that Jesus reached his own mature expression with the aid of the Pharisees. At one level, that is not entirely incorrect, but it so misrepresents the relationship that it is misleading."[57] Carson asks, "God's gracious self-disclosure is given to specific people in concrete historical situations: why should the historical connections be taken as a sign of necessary syncretism?"[58] I have noted the serious danger of syncretism, and I have insisted that the clear revelation of God in the Scriptures must always be our criterion as we assess concepts, no matter where they originate—whether from philosophers, scientists or religious teachers. But to deny that we might gain any benefit from learning of the religious experience of others who are responding to divine revelation that is less clear and complete would be unnecessarily triumphalistic.

Greek Orthodox bishop Georges Khodr writes:

> If obedience to the Master means following Him wherever we find traces of His presence, we have an obligation to investigate the authentic spiritual life of non-Christians. This raises the question of Christ's presence outside

---

[53]McDermott, *Can Evangelicals Learn*, p. 18.

[54]Ibid., chapters 6-9.

[55]John E. Goldingay and Christopher J. H. Wright, " 'Yahweh Our God Yahweh One': The Oneness of God in the Old Testament," in *One God, One Lord: Christianity in a World of Religious Pluralism*, 2nd ed., ed. Andrew D. Clarke and Bruce Winter (Grand Rapids, Mich.: Baker, 1992), p. 41.

[56]Carson, *Gagging of God*, p. 251.

[57]Ibid.

[58]Ibid.

Christian history. The strikingly evangelical quality of many non-Christians obliges us, moreover, to develop an ecclesiology and a missiology in which the Holy Spirit necessarily occupies a supreme place.[59]

I appreciate the tone of Khodr's approach, but I would want to be careful not to eclipse the work of the Son by that of the Holy Spirit, whose role it is to glorify the Son. In our ecclesiology and missiology, a thoroughly trinitarian theology will prevent us from giving any of the persons a "supreme place," although we can distinguish the economic "specialties" within the Godhead without endangering God's ontological unity.

When we approach conversation with adherents of other religions in the spirit of learning, we need not (indeed must not) deny the firmness of our own theological convictions. We start from our commitment to Jesus Christ as Lord, as the Way, the Truth and the Life. But as Newbigin reminds us, "There is no dichotomy between 'confession' and 'truth-seeking.' "[60] We approach our conversation partners with the hope of gaining an even better understanding of the truth we believe that we have apprehended already, but we will inevitably "seek to grasp the new truth by means of those ways of thinking and judging and valuing" that we have "already learned and tested."[61] Our presuppositions are drawn from the gospel, and we can be both explicit and unapologetic about this. "Jesus is for the believer the source from whom his or her understanding of the totality of experience is drawn and therefore the criterion by which other ways of understanding are judged."[62]

Of course, the situation is the same for the other partners in the dialogue, whether they be Hindu, Muslim, Buddhist or a member of some less-established religious community. The final authority to which they appeal will be different from ours. Unless the Spirit of God convinces them of the truth of Scripture and of its witness to Jesus, we have few commonalities which can serve as starting points for dialogue. Being up front about this, however, should foster honesty and transparency in the conversation.

Obviously, these efforts to listen sincerely to what others have to say, with an openness to learning even religious truth or its better application, need to be undertaken by Christians who are very well grounded in their own faith.

---

[59]Georges Khodr, "The Economy of the Holy Spirit," in *Faith Meets Faith*, Mission Trends, ed. Gerald H. Anderson and Thomas F. Stransky (Grand Rapids, Mich.: Eerdmans, 1981), 5:38.
[60]Newbigin, *Open Secret*, p. 168.
[61]Ibid.
[62]Ibid.

Such dialogue would be dangerous for poorly trained Christians, who are incapable of discerning error and may be drawn into syncretism or even converted out of the Christian faith. We have to be continuously aware of the deceptive power of the evil one and dare not overestimate our own invulnerability to his power. I am certainly not suggesting that dialogue with members of other religions is one of our most effective ways to learn truth. Of course, we are most likely to get that benefit from Scripture itself and from those whose minds and lives are immersed in the study of the Bible and devotion to its Author. I do believe, however, that it is appropriate to approach conversation with people convinced of the truth of other religions with a Holy Spirit-led willingness to see what God may have been doing in their lives. If our conversation partners will come with a reciprocal openness, it is wonderful to contemplate what the Spirit of God might do for them. God has promised that those who truly seek him will find him.

TEACHING PEOPLE OF OTHER FAITHS, EVEN WHEN IT DOES NOT RESULT IN CONVERSION

Precisely because we know that we do not fully comprehend the truth and its implications, we are able to ask for our partners in dialogue to admit the same. We may be able to gain insight into other faiths that their own devotees do not share, so that in the dialogical process we can teach as well as learn.[63] McDermott is perceptive when he suggests that "revelation can remain within a religion as a partly or even totally concealed revelation. Christians might see that revelation in a way that transforms the religion out of all recognition to an adherent but that nonetheless is faithful to the intent of the author of the revelation, God's Spirit."[64] He cites, as an example, the early church's interpretation of passages in Torah that pointed to Jesus Christ, although most Jewish readers saw them as prophecies pointing to someone else or referring to Israel as a whole.

Carl Braaten suggests that "as we can only read road signs at night when headlights shine on them, so when the light of Christ shines on other religions, we see meaning there which we would not understand without Christ."[65] In the process of dialogue, we may hope that God will enable us to shine the light of Christ on the experience of others in such a way that

---

[63]McDermott, *Can Evangelicals Learn*, p. 19.

[64]Ibid., p. 71.

[65]Carl E. Braaten, *No Other Gospel! Christianity Among the World's Religions* (Minneapolis: Fortress, 1992), p. 61.

they will be drawn to the Source of the light, which has been suppressed as well as reflected in the ambiguous construction of their own religious construct. Of course, what we wish for them we also wish for ourselves, recognizing that the form of Christianity within which we endeavor to follow Jesus is also an ambiguous response to God's self-revelation, one in which the Truth has been both reflected and suppressed.

Developing Mutual Awareness of Unconscious Presuppositions

None of us is completely aware of all the beliefs that inform our behavior or on which our explicitly enunciated convictions may rest. Dialogue with others who do not share our faith can help us to become aware of our unconscious presuppositions.[66] It can help us to be self-critical as we see ourselves through others' eyes. But we can also help others to recognize their own unconscious presuppositions, some of which they may reject once they are aware of them, leading to larger changes.

Learning About Worship

There may be factors in the *form* of worship practiced by members of other religions from which we can learn, but we may also gain a better understanding of the important distinctives of Christian worship by observing its alternatives. Ariarajah illustrates this from his experience with a Hindu friend.[67] When Ariarajah attended a Hindu temple to observe the *puja*, he was struck with the extent to which the senses were engaged—sight, smell, sound and taste (through the sharing of the *prasad*, a mixture of milk, water and fruit)—and the whole process happened very quickly. When his Hindu friend came to one of their Christian services, Ariarajah expected him to be bored by the lack of sensory stimulation and the length of the service. Instead, the man was deeply moved and appreciated the teaching, the intercession for member's needs and the intentional participation of three hundred people in worship together. Similarly, we may recall Fernando's comments about Hinduism and his observation that Christians have things to learn about the meditative or contemplative aspects of life, particularly when they minister in Asian societies.[68]

In speaking of the danger of syncretism, Carson notes that the Israelites

---

[66]Jones, "Evangelical Christianity," p. 383.
[67]Ariarajah, *Not Without*, pp. 46-48.
[68]Fernando, *Christian's Attitude*, p. 113.

were "not even to inquire about how the surrounding pagans worship, lest they be tempted to follow them ([Deut] 12:30). 'You must not worship the Lord your God in their way, because in worshiping their gods, they do all kinds of detestable things the Lord hates' ([Deut] 12:31)."[69] This is an important caution, but we need to recall the the degradation of religious practice and general morality in the societies from which God wished to protect Israel as they settled in Canaan, after the exodus from Egypt. Obviously, terrible things are still done in the name of religion in many parts of the world. We need to apply the discernment of which I spoke in the last chapter. Not all religions and not all members of a particular religion make equally beneficial partners in dialogue. The potential for good needs to be carefully assessed before much time is devoted to the sort of extended conversation that genuine dialogue requires. Furthermore, I am definitely not calling for syncretistic worship practices. We will learn how to worship God from the normative revelation given to us in inspired Scripture, and nothing needs to be added to that instruction from the scriptures or traditions of other religions. My point is that, in observing faithful members of other religions, we may find instances of that to which Scripture enjoins us but which has not been adequately emphasized or implemented in our own Christian tradition. Thus, while we may be stimulated, through observing non-Christians at worship, to greater reverence in prayer and encouraged to use all our senses in the worship of God, as Fernando and Ariarajah have suggested, we are almost certain to be more impressed by the difference between Christian worship and that of other religions.

Sunand Sumithra nicely sums up these differences between the prayer and spirituality of Christians and that of Hindus—particularly the lack of personal relationship between the worshiper and the one being worshiped as well as the lack of thanksgiving, confession and repentance, which are basic elements of Christian prayer.[70] Masao Uenuma does a similar comparison with Buddhism and Michael Nazir-Ali with Islam.[71] Having an

---

[69]Carson, *Gagging of God*, p. 252.

[70]Sunand Sumithra, "A Christian View of Prayer and Spirituality in Hindu Thought," in *Teach Us to Pray: Prayer in the Bible and the World*, ed. D. A. Carson (Grand Rapids, Mich.: Baker, 1990), pp. 187-89.

[71]Masao Uenuma, "A Christian View of Prayer and Spirituality in Buddhist Thought" (pp. 192-204), and Michael Nazir-Ali, "A Christian View of Prayer and Spirituality in Muslim Thought" (pp. 205-10), in *Teach Us to Pray: Prayer in the Bible and the World*, ed. D. A. Carson (Grand Rapids, Mich.: Baker, 1990).

awareness of the dominant religious context in which Christians follow Jesus may help us to be alert to areas in which we must emphasize Christian distinctiveness. Sumithra notes, for instance, that it is generally "hard for Indian Christians to take the holiness of God seriously in their everyday life," perhaps because the great "gap between God and man is not to be found in any Hindu Scriptures or experience."[72] Commenting on the Buddhist context, Uenuma sees the "ontological differences between God and man" as "perhaps the fundamental element that distinguishes Christian spirituality from any 'Eastern' spirituality."[73]

HOPE THAT OUR CONVERSATION PARTNERS MIGHT ALREADY BE SAVED

Given the perspective that I have put forward, I grant that the member of another religion *may* be personally in saving relationship to God, in spite of the fact that their religion, as such, is erroneous and, as a system, is counterproductive for people seeking God. I agree with Hendrik Kraemer's position (as summed up by Tim Perry) that "the biblically realistic world of revelation in Christ is systematically incommensurate with the similarly holistic worlds of non-Christians religions," so that there is no common ground between religions, but that at the level of personal encounter between Christians and members of other religions, there are points of contact because of God's revelatory work in individual lives.[74] Again, I find Newbigin helpful, as he describes his own position in this regard:

> It is almost impossible for me to enter into simple, honest, open, and friendly communication with another person as long as I have at the back of my mind the feeling that I am one of the saved and he is one of the lost. Such a gulf is too vast to be bridged by any ordinary human communication. But the problem is not really solved if I decide from my side of the abyss that he also is saved. In either case the assumption is that I have access to the secret of his ultimate destiny. . . . All such pronouncements go beyond our authority and destroy the possibility of a real meeting. The truth is that my meeting with a person of another religion is on a much humbler basis. I do not claim to know in advance his or her ultimate destiny. I meet the person simply as a witness,

---

[72]Sumithra, "Christian View," p. 190.
[73]Uenuma, "Christian View," p. 204.
[74]Tim S. Perry, *Radical Difference: A Defence of Hendrik Kraemer's Theology of Religions*, Editions SR, ed. H. Martin Rumscheidt and Theodore S. de Bruyn (Waterloo, Ontario: Wilfrid Laurier University Press, 2001), 27:61.

as one who has been laid hold of by Another and placed in a position where I can only point to Jesus as the one who can make sense of the whole human situation that my partner and I share as fellow human beings.[75]

Newbigin suggests that in relating to people of other faiths,

> we shall expect, look for, and welcome all the signs of the grace of God at work in the lives of those who do not know Jesus as Lord. In this, of course, we shall be following the example of Jesus, who was so eager to welcome the evidences of faith in those outside the household of Israel. . . . In our contact with people who do not acknowledge Jesus as Lord, our first business, our first privilege, is to seek out and to welcome all the reflections of that one true light in the lives of those we meet. There is something deeply repulsive in the attitude, sometimes found among Christians, which makes only grudging acknowledgment of the faith, the godliness, and the nobility to be found in the lives on non-Christians.[76]

Richard Peace's discussion of the gradual process through which the eleven disciples came to faith in Jesus—who died and rose again from the dead for their sins—prepares us to be sensitive to the particular experience of each individual with whom we converse about God. As Peace says,

> If, however, you understand conversion to be a process that unfolds over time, as it did for the Twelve, then your question to others is apt to be "Where are you in your spiritual pilgrimage and with what issue are you wrestling when it comes to God?" You assume that different people are at different places in their spiritual pilgrimages and that they need to be assisted in conscious reflection on that pilgrimage (even as you too are engaged in a spiritual pilgrimage and need the help of others to walk in the way of Jesus).[77]

Evangelism then "becomes the process of assisting others to move beyond their assumptions about Jesus to a new and radical understanding of who he actually is."[78] Unable to discern people's hearts or to know for certain what their relationship is to God, we try to move them steadily further toward the Light.[79]

---

[75]Newbigin, *Open Secret*, p. 174.

[76]Lesslie Newbigin, *The Gospel in a Pluralist Society* (Grand Rapids, Mich.: Eerdmans, 1989), p. 180.

[77]Richard V. Peace, *Conversion in the New Testament: Paul and the Twelve* (Grand Rapids, Mich.: Eerdmans, 1999), p. 286.

[78]Ibid., p. 309.

[79]A very similar approach is recommended by John Stackhouse in his excellent work on apologetics, *Humble Apologetics: Defending the Faith Today* (New York: Oxford University Press, 2002). The chapter on conversion is particularly appropriate and was condensed in "What Conversion Is and Is Not," *Christianity Today*, February 2003, pp. 71-75.

FOSTERING THE WAYS IN WHICH RELIGIONS ARE GOOD FOR THEIR MEMBERS AND FOR THE WORLD

Unquestionably, our primary desire for others is that they be reconciled to God. In that regard, as I have been careful to note, non-Christian religions (and, sadly, some forms of Christianity) are not helpful. Nevertheless, we can grant that some factors in the religions are beneficial to people, even when they are not in saving relationship to God. I treated this matter at length in the previous chapter, but I want to underline one point I made very briefly there. Having observed that God is working in common-grace ways within the religions, I suggested that we should value Christian ministry that encourages or participates in the operation of God's common grace. When we see aspects that we admire in the lives of non-Christians, including the sort of things from which Christians cited earlier have learned from other religions, we can affirm and encourage those relative goods. For example, we know God wants us to care for widows and orphans and to exercise responsible dominion over creation. When we see these things being done in and by other religions, we should affirm them and encourage continuance of these good works. Such good cannot be done apart from the grace of God, and we can express to our dialogue partners our gratitude to the true and living God for what he has accomplished in their lives.

This is an excellent illustration of the difference between *dialogue* and *debate*. In debate, one's objective is to score points against the opponent. To concede that a point has been well made or to grant to a debating opponent her superiority in some way would be counterproductive. This is not so in dialogue. Here, we are not trying to make points. We are trying to serve God in furthering whatever gracious intentions he has for the people with whom we converse. We may recall Jesus' point that "those who do what is true come to the light, so that it may be clearly seen that their deeds have been done in God" (Jn 3:21). Seeing members of another religion "do what is true" should encourage us to pray that God might indeed draw them to the light, since he is already at work in their lives in some measure. When we find teaching and practice within the context of the cultures and religions of the world that we recognize as true wisdom, given its agreement with the teachings of the inspired Scriptures, we can be grateful for it and for the good that will come to those who live according to this truth even though that good may fall short of reconciliation with God.

In recent months, we have become particularly aware of the hatred toward America that exists in some people's hearts and of the evil they are prepared to do in expression of that hate. What has been most striking has been the religious rhetoric used by some of the leaders of terrorist organizations, among whom Muslims have been most prominent in recent news. What is encouraging to all people of goodwill is that other Muslims have repudiated these acts and denied that they are genuinely demonstrative of the will of Allah. People whose hearts are turned toward God (though they may not yet be fully reconciled to him) and who desire shalom in God's creation should encourage one another. A few words from an essay by Miroslav Volf make the point well:

> If we were more self-critical about our violent proclivities and more suspicious about violence in media, we might note, on the religious landscape, the steady flow of work that religious people do to make the world a more peaceful place. Our imagination would not be captured, for instance, with religion as motivating force for a dozen or so not particularly religious terrorists who destroyed the Twin Towers. Instead, we would be impressed with the degree to which religion serves as a source of solace and orientation for a majority of Americans in a time of crisis. We'd note the motivation it gave to many to help the victims, protect Muslims from stereotyping, and build bridges between religious cultures. We should promote religion—this kind of religion—and not be indifferent toward it.[80]

UNAPOLOGETIC EVANGELISM

When engaging in dialogue (or serious conversation) with members of other religions, we can readily admit that we seek their conversion. We need not apologize for this fact, nor be ashamed of the scandal of the gospel, of the cross and resurrection, although we must listen very carefully before speaking. Dialogue is not an alternative to Christian mission, in which we seek to be agents of God's saving work in people's lives through Christ and by the life-giving work of the Spirit. Regrettably, the two have often been seen as alternative activities between which we must choose. This has been true both on the part of relativists, who object to Christian efforts to convert others, and on the part of ecclesiocentrists, who see dialogue as a failure to proclaim clearly the truth concerning God in Christ and to call people to repentance and faith.

A poll conducted in 2002 by the television program *Religion and Ethics News Weekly* and *U.S. News & World Report* magazine found that only 22

---

[80]Miroslav Volf, "Guns and Crosses," *Christian Century*, May 17, 2003, p. 39.

percent of Americans approved of conversion goals, and 71 percent said that Christians should leave people of other faiths alone.[81] In this poll, "78 percent said that a statement declaring 'all religions have elements of truth' is closer to their views, compared to 17 percent who identified with a statement saying that their religion is 'the only true religion.' " With similar findings, "a Pew poll released in March [2002] found only 18 percent said their own religion is 'the one true faith.' "[82]

It is unfortunate that the concept of "mission"—which aims at converting others from the religious faith they now hold to the faith in God which we, as Christians, believe to be saving—has been tarnished by association with colonialism and coercion. As a consequence, John Howard Yoder suggests that we speak of " 'heralding' or *kerygma.*"[83] Heralds announce an event as true and as "very important for their hearers, especially for those who have not heard it before. . . . Yet, no one is forced to believe." What keeps heralds from using coercion "is not doubt or being unsettled by the tug of older views. The herald believes in accepting weakness, because the message is about a Suffering Servant whose meekness it is that brings justice to the nations."[84] It is for this reason that there is no contradiction or tension between the kerygmatic truth claim and the posture of dialogue. The distinction is, rather, from "colonial or Crusader truth."[85] From Yoder's perspective,

> the error in the age of triumphalism was not that it was tied to Jesus but that it denied him, precisely in its power and its disrespect for the neighbour. . . Its error was not that it propagated Christianity around the world but that what it propagated was not Christian enough. Then the adjustment to Christianity's loss of élan and credibility is not to talk less about Jesus and more about religion but the contrary.[86]

What makes our faith in Jesus a source of fruitful dialogue with people of other faiths is precisely the content of the message of Jesus, which includes, as Yoder notes, "the love of the adversary, the dignity of the lowly, repentance, servanthood, the renunciation of coercion."[87]

---

[81]"Poll: Americans Shun Conversion Goals," *Christian Century,* May 8-15, 2002, p. 16.
[82]Ibid.
[83]John Howard Yoder, *The Royal Priesthood: Essays Ecclesiological and Ecumenical,* ed. Michael G. Cartwright (Grand Rapids, Mich.: Eerdmans, 1994), p. 256.
[84]Ibid.
[85]Ibid.
[86]Ibid., p. 257.
[87]Ibid., p. 258.

Newbigin notes that C. S. Song "wishes to play down the role of truth because, as he says, truth judges, polarizes, divides. Truth, he says, cannot unite the ununitable; only love can. So the Christian mission must be an affair of love, not an affair of truth."[88] But surely it is not love that encourages people to believe a lie. Newbigin sees the human race as being

> on a journey and we need to know the road. It is not true that all roads lead to the top of the same mountain. There are roads which lead over the precipice. In Christ we have been shown the road. We cannot treat that knowledge as a private matter for ourselves. It concerns the whole human family. We do not presume to limit the might and the mercy of God for the ultimate salvation of all people, but the same costly act of revelation and reconciliation which gives us that assurance also requires us to share with our fellow pilgrims the vision that God has given us the route we must follow and the goal to which we must press forward.[89]

Stephen Neill gives us this insight:

> If I take my partner in dialogue seriously, I cannot wish for him anything less than I wish for myself. What I desire for myself is that Christ should be all in all to me, that he should reign unconditionally supreme over every thought and word and deed, that my going out and my coming in should be ordered by his Spirit, and that he should be glorified in my body whether it be by life or death. This is the surrender to which I desire that my interlocutor should also come.[90]

The critical realistic perspective from which I have been approaching truth, our knowledge of it and our apology for it is well described by Trevor Hart. It fosters an attitude that

> is not one of arrogance or dismissive intolerance, but precisely one of humility and openness. Since such truth-claims are non-demonstrable in the sense usually intended by that term, and since the knower knows only on the basis of a personal commitment to certain fundamental assumptions, she has no universally recognized or intellectually superior case with which to bludgeon those who do not stand where she does, or on the basis of which to call into question their intelligence or common sense. She, as one who believes that truth is indeed to be known in one way rather than another, but who must submit in her knowing to reality itself in its willingness

---

[88]Newbigin, *Gospel*, p. 183, quoting C. S. Song, *Tell Us Our Names* (Maryknoll, N.Y.: Orbis, 1984), p. 114.

[89]Newbigin, *Gospel*, p. 183.

[90]Stephen Neill, *Salvation Tomorrow* (Nashville: Abingdon, 1976), p. 38.

to be known, can only enjoin those who see things radically differently to "come and stand where I am standing, view the world from this place and using these tools, and see whether what you find here doesn't make more sense." Thus if the mode of certainty is that of faith, then the mode of proclamation is that of witness.[91]

We want to discern the areas in which God is at work in the lives of others, and we want to participate in the work that God is doing as he draws them to himself. We definitely do not want to coerce or manipulate them into agreeing with us and our Christian tradition. In dialogue, we gain a clearer understanding of what a particular individual believes and where he is in regard to the quest for God. The risk in proclaiming the gospel is that we may fail to communicate the gospel of Christ effectively because we do not understand the hearer's own thought and religious position adequately, and we may fail to grasp the areas from which resistance to the gospel arises in his life.

Timothy Tennent describes this need to listen carefully, drawing from his own experience:

> I thought that Hindus were mostly polytheists until I talked to Hindus and discovered that the majority are not. I thought that Islam had advanced into sub-Saharan Africa mainly through the sword until I studied the history of the Islamic spread into Africa. I never understood the significance of translating the Buddhist doctrine of *śunyatā* emptiness instead of nothingness until a Buddhist explained it to me. True witness to someone of another faith means that we must understand his or her actual position, not a caricature of it.[92]

First Peter 3:15-16 urges us to be ready to give reasons for the hope that is within us, but in order for these reasons to be comprehensible and persuasive, we must understand the perspective from which our dialogue partners will hear them. Likewise, if we are to join Paul in becoming all things to all people in order to win some of them to allegiance to Christ (1 Cor 9:22), we must have a good understanding of where these people are spiritually and be able to discern in which areas we can identify with them and in which areas we must distance ourselves; then we can main-

---

[91]Trevor Hart, "Karl Barth, the Trinity and Pluralism," in *The Trinity in a Pluralistic Age: Theological Essays on Culture and Religion*, ed. Kevin J. Vanhoozer (Grand Rapids, Mich.: Eerdmans, 1997), p. 128.

[92]Timothy C. Tennent, *Christianity at the Religious Roundtable: Evangelicalism in Conversation with Hinduism, Buddhism and Islam* (Grand Rapids, Mich.: Baker, 2002), p. 241.

tain our authentic Christian position but present it winsomely and at-
tractively.[93]

We are obligated to help others in their quest for truth,[94] and dialogue
is sometimes necessary to enable others to come to a full understanding of
Christian faith, particularly when they have many misconceptions. Accordingly, Kenneth Cragg writes that

> a Christian theology has first to listen to the questions explicit for it in other
> religions. It has then to undertake them in the common denominator of hu-
> man experience as the place from whence they all emerge and to which an-
> swers must return. Shared humanity, interpret it how we may, best con-
> duces to realism in our response. It is the best hope of relevance translated
> and received.[95]

Cragg speaks of the way in which Islam "encloses Jesus strictly within the
dimension of prophethood," disallowing the significance he has for Christians.[96] He then posits: "Only in a careful attention to the Muslim partnership with us *and* the Muslim consensus against us can a Christian theologian clarify and pursue the one and interpret the other."[97] Cragg warns us,
however, not to abandon the exclusiveness of Christ's saviorhood. We
must beware that, from the perspective of Islam, Judaism, Hinduism and
Buddhism, Christology

> must be de-monopolized to admit of numerous saviourhoods, multiplying
> or diversifying the paradigm (as we esteem it) of the cross on Calvary. The
> endlessly varied psyches of mankind, their myth-making fertility, their pri-
> mordial image-ing must be allowed free reign. The distinctiveness of the
> Christian gospel and the resultant will to a missionary inclusiveness of hu-
> man range must be abandoned. We must surrender the will to recruit the
> world. At best, pluralism suggests to us, there can only be a sort of common
> market of "salvations," each by its own lights and means. We have too
> readily said that around the cross of Jesus all the ground is level and "who-
> soever will may come." Asia caps these warnings by assuring us that our
> Christian sense of personality conspires, in fact, to its own deception by af-
> firming its loved and cherished creaturehood, a loved and redeemed iden-
> tity, heir to eternal life.[98]

---

[93]Muck, "New Testament Case," p. 11.
[94]Jones, "Evangelical Christianity," p. 384.
[95]Kenneth Cragg, *The Christ and the Faiths* (London: SPCK, 1986; Philadelphia: Westminster
Press, 1987), p. 11.
[96]Ibid., p. 14.
[97]Ibid.

Paul's sermon in Athens is a very interesting example of both affirmation and negation of the religious ideas of his hearers that ended in a call for repentance, not just for enlightenment.[99] Paul began with the unknown god but did not commend all of the Athenians' religious conclusions. He criticized their shrines and those who served in them. He granted that the Athenians were religious, but he pronounced them ignorant and confused. "By calling God the Creator of heaven and earth, Paul was refuting the Stoic doctrine of eternal matter. By affirming God's intimate concern for people, he corrected the Epicurean idea of distant and uncaring gods."[100] Yet Paul acknowledged common beliefs with the Stoics in their teaching that God preserves and guides all of life and is immanent in the world in his providential work. Human beings were created to seek and find God who is not far away, as even their own poets affirmed (Acts 17:27-28). Indeed, John Sanders argues that "most of Paul's message would find agreement in both the Old Testament and Stoic teaching. True, Paul quotes from only one Stoic poet, but the bulk of his ideas and the very wording of them can be found in Stoicism."[101] But having affirmed and negated some of their ideas, Paul invites them to repentance (Acts 17:30) and warns them of coming judgment (Acts 17:31). Despite some truths in their beliefs, they would remain under the judgment of God if they were now to reject Christ as Paul proclaimed him to them.

Braaten wisely warns us of the dangers in talking about salvation in the non-Christian religions, because

> the resurrection gospel is the criterion of the meaning of salvation in the New Testament sense. When Christians enter into dialogue with persons of other religions, they must do their utmost to communicate what they mean by the assertion that Jesus lives and explain how this gospel intersects the hopes and fears of every person whose fate is to anticipate death as the final eschaton. . . . The gospel falls upon the human situation and illuminates the universal existential problem. This is the hypothesis that Christians bring into an interreligious dialogue. A Christology that is silent about the resurrection of Jesus from the dead is not worthy of the Christian name and should not be called Christology at all.[102]

---

[98]Ibid., p. 20.

[99]Calvin E. Shenk, *Who Do You Say that I Am? Christians Encounter Other Religions* (Scottdale, Penn.: Herald, 1997), pp. 105-6.

[100]Ibid., p. 105.

[101]John Sanders, "Response to Nash," in *What About Those Who Have Never Heard? Three Views on the Destiny of the Unevangelized,* ed. John Sanders (Downers Grove, Ill.: InterVarsity Press, 1995), p. 145.

[102]Braaten, *No Other Gospel!* pp. 84-85.

As Newbigin says, our obligation is to tell the story of Jesus, the story of the Bible, which is the power of God for salvation. It is not our responsibility to convert others, though we long for that to happen so that others may share our joy. "But it is only the Holy Spirit of God who can so touch the hearts and consciences of others that they are brought to accept the story as true and to put their trust in Jesus." So the Christian "will not imagine that it is her responsibility to insure that the other is persuaded. That is in God's hands."[103]

MUTUAL HUMILITY

There are skeletons in the closet of every religion, and it is tempting to compare the best manifestations of Christianity with the worst manifestations of other religions. If we want genuine and fruitful dialogue, this temptation will have to be resisted. We will need to distinguish between the essence of our Christian faith and the empirical manifestations of it, and we may need to admit Christian guilt and even ask forgiveness for some of these manifestations. But we must also be willing to allow our dialogue partner from another religion to do the same. As Adeney notes, "other religions' idols often appear obvious, our own are more elusive. Yet the ideologies we cherish are riddled with sin."[104] So we "should not be too hasty" when we are "faced with *other* people's idols."[105]

Bernard Lewis has made a very helpful observation given the current public tensions between Christianity and Islam in the wake of September 11. He observes that Christianity and Islam are the only two religions in the world that define civilizations.[106] In the Christian world, in English (and in most of the other languages of the Christian world), we have two words, *Christianity* and *Christendom*. We use the first term to describe our religion, "a system of belief and worship with certain ecclesiastical institutions." But we use *Christendom* to speak of "a civilization that incorporates elements that are non-Christian or even anti-Christian. Hitler and the Nazis, it may be recalled, are products of Christendom, but hardly of Christianity," suggests Lewis.[107] The problem is that we have no similar terms for distinguishing between Islam the religion and Islam the civilization, and this leads to misunderstanding. Thus we speak of "Islamic art" or "Is-

---

[103]Newbigin, *Gospel*, p. 182.
[104]Adeney, "Rajah Sulayman," p. 68.
[105]Ibid., p. 69.
[106]Bernard Lewis, "I'm Right, You're Wrong, Go to Hell," *Atlantic Monthly*, May, 2003, p. 37.
[107]Ibid.

lamic science" to describe art and science done in Muslim countries, whether or not these have a particularly religious character. As we enter into dialogue with Muslims especially (and this may be the most needed direction of dialogue these days, for the peace of the world), we need to grant them the same distinction we make for our own religion, even if words to describe the distinction are harder to come by.

Monika Hellwig (a Roman Catholic professor of theology at Georgetown University) notes that the church has not always served well its role as agent of the Reign of God.

> Therefore, although it may puzzle and antagonize the outsider to the Christian tradition, Christian partners in the dialogue may say without any sense of hypocrisy or inconsistency that "the church does not condone" actions and situations which the outsider sees being done by Christians and perhaps even by those who appear as church representatives.[108]

Hellwig posits that "the strong and fairly monolithic alignments of interest in the case of both Jews and Muslims on a worldwide basis render it urgent, but also difficult, for Christians to represent their own total allegiance to the gospel as taking priority over their qualified allegiance to any particular group."[109] In the wake of September 11, this strikes me as even more urgent than when Hellwig first penned the words (in 1981). It is unhealthy that public statements by Muslim leaders so often speak as though there is a war going on between Islam and Christianity, partly because the United States is predominantly Christian and because its political leaders are often outspoken about their own Christian faith. Polls have even found that not all evangelical Christians perceive conflicts between Palestinians and Israel in the same way, yet Christians are frequently portrayed as "pro-Israel," which to the ears of many in the Middle East sounds like "anti-Palestinian, anti-Arab and anti-Muslim." Would that the voice of practicing Christians were heard as an earnest quest for justice and peace for all, committed to these things because God wants them, and willing to carefully analyze the complex circumstances of each conflict situation in pursuit of what is morally right, not what is politically partisan.

Historically, the Christian religion has "often proved itself incapable of

---

[108]Monika Konrad Hellwig, "Christian-Jewish-Muslim Relations," in *Faith Meets Faith*, Mission Trends, ed. Gerald H. Anderson and Thomas F. Stransky (Grand Rapids, Mich.: Eerdmans, 1981), 5:205-6.

[109]Ibid., p. 207.

encompassing the gospel or reflecting it, so that the response of someone who belongs to another religion can understandably be that even if Christianity has rightly diagnosed the human problem, it has still not identified the solution."[110] Those sobering words, written by Goldingay and Wright, are well illustrated by an experience recounted by Yoder. He tells of a friend in Algiers who "was once told by a neighbor, 'Jesus is French, and we are Arabs' " because "the only 'Jesus' he had any reason to know about was the tribal deity of the French colonists." But Yoder observes that if the Algerian had been more knowledgeable of his own Algerian history in the sixteenth century, "Jesus would have been Spanish, for it was then that a Spanish fleet, whose admiral was a cardinal, had taken over the Algerian coast, including the massacre of ten thousand in the port city of Oran." Yoder asks the sobering question: "What does it do for the usability of the name of Jesus . . . when for a whole culture that name is defined not by the apostles but by the crusaders?"[111]

Recognizing Christians' failure to live up to God's covenantal expectations of us and to serve God's rule in the world will help us to understand why some people in other religions have such a difficult time seeing Jesus as the Christ. I think, for example, of Jewish people in whose memories the Holocaust remains strong and who think of it as a horror perpetrated by Christians. Is it any wonder that when they hear Christians present Jesus to them as the Jewish Messiah, the association of Jesus with Christianity makes it extremely difficult for them to hear the message? It would be folly for us to assume that when they reject our message concerning Jesus, they have rejected Jesus himself, their promised Messiah. On the one hand, we will want to assert that what was done then by the Nazis was terribly contrary to the moral will of God and that we too repudiate it as evil. On the other hand, we must be careful not to exonerate the Christian church too quickly for the failure of Christians to protest soon enough or loudly enough what was being done to the Jews in Germany and elsewhere in Europe. Indeed, we must admit that aspects of Christian thought did contribute to and condone that evil.

In his review of a number of books dealing with the role and response of the church to Nazi persecution of Jews, David Gushee notes that the Institute for the Study and Eradication of Jewish Influence on German Religious Life, which was opened in 1929, was "led by a New Testament

---

[110]Goldingay and Wright, "Yahweh," p. 55.
[111]Yoder, *Royal Priesthood*, p. 259.

scholar, Walter Grundmann."[112] "Along with some other learned biblical scholars," Grundmann

> made the argument that Jesus was not Jewish, but instead an "Aryan" who was Judaism's greatest critic and in fact sought its destruction. The Institute also published a New Testament (the Old Testament, illegitimate by defini-tion, was simply abandoned), a catechism, and a hymnbook, all scrubbed clean of any "Jewish elements."[113]

As Gushee reports, citing the work of David Kertzer, Catholic documents of the late nineteenth to early twentieth centuries demonstrate "that nearly every anti-Semitic theme the Nazis used in the 1920s and 1930s could be found in the Catholic press (including journals and papers very close to the Vatican) either during the same period or just before"[114] and that racial anti-Semitism appeared in the Catholic press. Gushee is convinced that "there can be no doubt that Catholics—like their Protestant counterparts— contributed to the toxic brew of hatred that reached its logical conclusion in the Holocaust."[115]

Commenting on Gandhi's experience in South Africa, "E. Stanley Jones concludes, 'Racialism has many sins to bear, but perhaps its worst sin was the obscuring of Christ in an hour when one of the greatest souls born of a woman was making his decision.' "[116] Jones reminds us of how the church's failure to be what it should be can result in our alienating people from Christ rather than drawing them to him. Thankfully, because of the sover-eign work of God's grace, we are unable to keep people from being saved if God chooses to save them. But this must not diminish our eagerness to be the sort of community that God can easily use to draw people to himself. At the very least, it would appear that we may be guilty of keeping people from enjoying the blessings of membership in the church. On the other hand, I would not be too quick to suggest that Gandhi would have become a Christian but for the failure of Christianity to live up to the full demands of the gospel. His protests are reminiscent of the complaints one sometimes hears from non-Christians that the church is full of hypocrites and hence

---

[112]David P. Gushee, " 'Rescue Those Being Led Away to Death': The Church, the Nazis and the Holocaust," *Books and Culture* 8 (March-April 2002), p. 23.
[113]Ibid.
[114]Ibid., p. 40, quoting David I. Kertzer, *The Popes Against the Jews: The Vatican's Role in the Rise of Modern Anti-Semitism* (New York: Alfred A. Knopf, 2002).
[115]Gushee, "Rescue," p. 40.
[116]Quoted in Yancey, *Soul Survivor*, p. 175.

they have no interest in becoming part of the church. Self-justification and scapegoating are ancient strategies used by sinners who are unwilling to be honest about their own sinfulness and to submit to God as he has revealed himself in Christ.[117] Complaints about the failures of the church are too frequently an excuse for people's stubborn resistance to the Spirit of God, who makes them aware of their own sinfulness and of the changes that Christ will demand if they follow him. The church should be willing to admit its failures, but it is as a community of self-confessed but pardoned sinners that we invite other sinners to accept God's grace and join the company of those who live in eager anticipation of the day when God's grace will perfect us in the likeness of Christ, after whose image we were created.

According to Bavinck,

> The more you learn to know heathendom in its deepest motives (which lie hidden behind its foolish and childish reasonings), the more you recognize yourself therein; you see that you yourself are repeatedly busy, in the same way, trying to flee from God and to push him aside, although you do so in a much more refined and sophisticated manner. Your own life, in which God's grace has performed and patiently continues to perform a wonderful work against the unruliness of your own heart, itself constitutes a basis for your elenctic efforts.[118]

That is, a basis for our work of rebuking and calling for repentance.

From a meeting that Taylor had with the staff of the Islamic Research Institute in Rawalpindi in 1968, he reports that an open discussion

> was dramatically upset by the intervention of a young historian from North Africa who protested that the contemporary Church was as relentlessly hostile to Islam as it had ever been, and he instanced missionary sympathy with the Southern Sudanese revolt, widespread Christian rejoicing over Israel's capture of the Old City of Jerusalem, and the churches' support of Biafra. . . .
>
> Dialogue, as I understand it, means overcoming the immediate urge to dismiss these suspicions as untrue, accepting the fact that, true or not, the suspicions are part of the data of our relationships, and facing the possibility that perhaps the other person has more reason to be suspicious of me than I have hitherto admitted. If we all made that effort of imagination it might make us humbler and gentler.[119]

---

[117]Compare Ted Peters, *Sin: Radical Evil in Soul and Society* (Grand Rapids, Mich.: Eerdmans, 1994), pp. 169-83.

[118]Bavinck, *Introduction,* p. 230.

[119]Taylor, "Theological Basis," 5:96.

Fernando tells of an outbreak of violence in Sri Lanka in 1983 "in which many from the Buddhist majority had a hand. Some Christians were quick to use this as evidence for the bankruptcy of Buddhism. But as we began to get a clearer picture of what had happened," Fernando says, "news began to emerge that Christians too had been involved in the violence."[120] Fernando observes that "Buddhists believe that the moral restraint of Buddhism is the answer to the immorality found in the West. The Hindus believe the devotion of Hinduism is the answer to the materialism found in the West. The Muslims believe that the brotherhood of Islam is the answer to the racial prejudice found in the West."[121] All of these people probably assume, in the process of this critique, that the culture of Western societies is the product of Christianity, which, to a significant extent, is undeniable.

Calling for humility in dialogue, Stott notes that

> we have to recognize humbly that some of [our dialogue partner's] misconceptions may be our fault, or at least that his continuing rejection of Christ may be in reality a rejection of the caricature of Christ which he has seen in us or in our fellow Christians. As we listen to him, we may have many such uncomfortable lessons to learn. Our attitude toward him changes. There may after all have been some lingering sense of superiority of which we were previously unconscious. But now no longer have we any desire to score points or win a victory. We love him too much to boost our ego at his expense. Humility in evangelism is a beautiful grace.[122]

For dialogue to go forward, repentance and forgiveness are necessary, so that we can make a new beginning. In the words of Yoder: "There is no alternative but painstakingly, feebly, repentantly, patiently, locally, to disentangle . . . Jesus from the Christ of Byzantium and of Torquemada."[123]

OPENNESS TO BEING CONVERTED OURSELVES?

Raimundo Panikkar writes this concerning dialogue: "The religious person enters this arena without prejudices and preconceived solutions, knowing full well he may in fact have to lose a particular belief or particular religion altogether. He trusts in truth. He enters unarmed and ready to be converted himself. He may lose his life—he may also be born

---

[120]Fernando, *Christian's Attitude*, p. 92.
[121]Ibid., p. 93.
[122]Stott, "Dialogue," 5:171.
[123]Yoder, *Royal Priesthood*, p. 261.

again."[124] This is a shocking thought, but critical realism challenges us to acknowledge that we do not apprehend the truth completely. Still, I find the prospect of conversion from faith in Christ frankly inconceivable. Could I possibly be so wrong as to have built my faith on the wrong foundation? I can certainly not approach dialogue with serious doubt. I have a firm confidence in the resurrected Jesus as revealer of God because he was himself the Son of God. I believe the Christian Scriptures to be the revelation of God, inspired by the Holy Spirit. I cannot dialogue as though I am uncertain about these things. Thus, I agree with Stott that "we should not cultivate a total 'openness' in which we suspend even our own convictions concerning the truth of the gospel and our personal commitment to Jesus Christ. To attempt to do this would be to destroy our own integrity as Christians."[125] On the other hand, surely I must expect this confidence to be found in my dialogue partner as well. In spite of this mutual confidence in radically opposite understandings of the truth, our dialogue with members of other religions should be characterized by humility, including the willingness to confess sins that have been committed and to renounce whatever we come to believe was erroneous.

As Newbigin says, "A dialogue which is safe from all possible risks is no true dialogue. The Christian will go into dialogue believing that the sovereign power of the Spirit can use the occasion for the radical conversion of the partner as well as of the Christian."[126] To some extent, we put our Christianity at risk, remembering that in his encounter with Cornelius, Peter was also profoundly changed.[127] "But," says Newbigin,

> to put *my* Christianity at risk is precisely the way by which I can confess Jesus Christ as Lord—Lord over all the world and Lord over my faith. It is only as the church accepts the risk that the promise is fulfilled that the Holy Spirit will take all the treasures of Christ, scattered by the Father's bounty over all the people and cultures of mankind, and declare them to the church as the possession of Jesus.[128]

Inevitably, when we face seriously the firm confidence of people whose religious sincerity and the relative goodness of whose lives we cannot eas-

---

[124]Raimundo Panikkar, "The Rules of the Game," in *Faith Meets Faith*, Mission Trends, ed. Gerald H. Anderson and Thomas F. Stransky (Grand Rapids, Mich.: Eerdmans, 1981), 5:113.
[125]Stott, "Dialogue," 5:159.
[126]Newbigin, *Open Secret*, p. 187.
[127]Ibid., p. 186.
[128]Ibid., p. 188.

ily dismiss, our own conviction that we alone know the truth may be shaken. Cragg cites John Bunyan's disquiet in this regard:

> The tempter also would much assault me with this: "How can you tell but that the Turks has as good scriptures to prove their Mahomet the Saviour, as we have to prove our Jesus is? And, could I think so many ten thousands, in so many countries and kingdoms should be without knowledge of the right way to heaven . . . and that we only, who live in a corner of the earth, should alone be blessed therewith? Every one doth think his own religion rightest, both Jews and Moors and Pagans: and how if all our faith, and Christ, and scriptures, should be but a think so too?"[129]

Cragg notes how John Henry Newman found his own confidence and security by submission to "what 'mother Church' had infallibly authenticated for him."[130] But Cragg rightly observes that this stance, if "duly reciprocated by all, would foreclose everything. To adopt it would simply be to refuse all cognizance of pluralism and so to opt out of this world. It would be to enthrone one authority unilaterally or to imprison one and all incommunicado."[131]

Stephen Neill offers a better approach:

> The Christian is committed to the view that all truth, in whatsoever guise it may manifest itself, is from God. He is free to recognize truth which is not evidently and clearly related to the revelation of God in Jesus Christ; but he is not likely to give up his conviction that every truth (in ways that we can see or in ways that we cannot see) is related to that supreme manifestation of the truth. In this sense, but in no other, the truths to be found in other religions may be seen as roads which lead, albeit circuitously and indirectly, to the one God.[132]

SUMMING UP

From an accessibilist perspective, dialogue with people of other religions is highly worthwhile. It is not a substitute for evangelism, nor is it just one more means of doing evangelism. It is legitimate to desire, above else, the conversion of one's partners in dialogue, but that is not our sole purpose. We dialogue to better understand one another, to learn from one another, to teach one another. We do it because—even though people on each side

---

[129]John Bunyan, *Grace Abounding,* para. 97, quoted in Cragg, *Christ and the Faiths,* p. 314.
[130]Cragg, *Christ and the Faiths,* p. 316.
[131]Ibid.
[132]Neill, *Salvation Tomorrow,* p. 43.

WHO CAN BE SAVED?

of the dialogue are convinced of the general correctness and superiority of their religious beliefs, attitudes and practices—Christians believe that God is also at work in the life of the neighbor who does not yet acknowledge that Jesus is Lord. We want to discover what God has been doing in other people's lives, and we want to put ourselves into situations where God can use us to further his gracious purposes in other people's lives. We dialogue because we love our neighbor and because we want to work to remove all possible hindrances to our neighbor's love for God. But dialogue is simply extended conversation—can we go further and actually cooperate formally with people of other religions? The final aspect of this constructive proposal will address that question.

19

Should We Cooperate
in Interreligious Activities?

Thesis 29: Some concerns are common to various religions, such as the dangers of secularism, the protection of innocent human life, the protection of the ecosystem and the quest for social justice. Peace through justice in the world is the desire of all people of goodwill but, regrettably, religious differences frequently contribute to both injustice and violence. In the face of these issues of global importance, whatever the members of different religions can do together for the common good, for the shalom of God's world, without compromising their distinctive faith allegiances, is to be pursued. Religious communities need to work together against common threats in ways that do not compromise or syncretize their different belief systems.

Thesis 30: It is impossible for Christians to join in worship with members of other religions. To do so would be to deny the uniqueness of the triune God whom Christians worship through Christ by the impulse of God's Spirit. Words and acts of worship to God, even when offered in the name of Jesus, are not acceptable to him when the heart of the worshiper is not right. On the other hand, we do not know to what extent God may receive the prayers and worship of people whose theology is inadequate but whose hearts are rightly oriented toward God. Nevertheless, we are not authorized to worship together, as though the differences in our understanding of the God whom we worship were not significant. In civic events where there is a common desire to acknowledge our human finitude and to seek the help and blessing of the Supreme Being, Christians may pray, as long as they are free to do so in the name of Jesus their Lord, as participants in a series of prayers offered by members of different religions. This is not an act of common worship, provided each participant prays according to his or her own faith and so long as no effort is made to formulate a generic prayer to be prayed by all participants, regardless of religious differences.

I HOPE MY REFLECTIONS ON DIALOGUE HAVE DEMONSTRATED that there are good reasons for Christians to converse intentionally and at length about religious commitments with members of other religions. Should we do more than talk? Given the state of the world, with the deadly influences of secularism and the many religious conflicts that are creating terrible living conditions for millions of people, are there ways in which people of faith (albeit of diverse faiths) can work together for the good of humanity and of the earth? Numerous religious groups share concerns about the ill effects of secularism, the need to protect the lives of the unborn and the deterioration of the family unit, which is fundamental to a healthy society. Would interreligious cooperative action on such issues of common concern necessitate a relativistic suspension of our faith differences to make it work? This is the sort of question we face as we contemplate the opportunities for Christians to pursue our goals in the world in cooperation with members of other religions.

THE CHALLENGE OF PEACEFUL COEXISTENCE

I have made it clear that I believe there is only one true and living God who has revealed himself definitively in the person of Jesus Christ, who was God the Word in the flesh. Although granting that none of us has grasped that truth (or Truth) completely or expressed it perfectly, I believe that we can make many theological statements with a strong conviction that they are true. Relativists have frequently asserted that we must abandon this exclusivism because it inevitably leads to imperialism, oppression and violence. It is impossible to deny that these have occurred in the history of relationships between peoples in the world. But as Daniel Clendenin notes,

> pluralist historiography is at best inconsistent and at times blatantly selective and reductionistic. Typically, religion has been only one of several important factors in historical tragedies; cultural, social, economic, linguistic, and political matters were and are just as important (consider, e.g., the war between Christian Armenians and historically Muslim Azerbaijanis over Nagorno-Karabakh, or the war in the former Yugoslavia among Catholics, Orthodox, and Muslims).[1]

The extent to which Christianity is the guilty party throughout history has been very seriously distorted by relativists like Rosemary Radford Ruether, who has stated that "it probably would not be difficult to prove that more violence, chauvinism, and hostility between groups have been fomented by Christianity than by most other religions, partly because it has

---

[1]Daniel Clendenin, *Many Gods, Many Lords* (Grand Rapids, Mich.: Baker, 1995), p. 94.

had more global power than any other religion."[2] Clendenin draws attention, for instance, to the relative silence about violence perpetrated in other religious contexts, "Afro-tribal (Rwanda, Uganda), Asian (Indian and Pakistani warfare over Kashmir, the Cambodian killing fields), Islamic (Armenian genocide, modern jihad), Jewish (extermination of Canaanite peoples), or Soviet (50 million deaths)."[3]

This is not to deny serious aberrations in Christian history. As was indicated in the previous chapter, we need to be ready to admit these and to express our sorrow about them, but this has not been a problem unique to Christianity. Vinoth Ramachandra, for example, observes that whereas Islam is frequently viewed by the West as involving unavoidable conflict, Hinduism is assumed to be tolerant and pluralistic. He presents a quite different picture in *Faiths in Conflict? Christian Integrity in a Multicultural World.*[4] Recent events in India, with the rise of militant Hindu fundamentalism supported by Hindu nationalistic political fervor, give further support to Ramachandra's case. Ramachandra's own proposal for the resolution of violence resulting from clashes between the religions is what he calls "constitutional secularism," as distinguished from social or cultural secularism.[5] He uses the term in a strictly political sense to describe the state's efforts to deal impartially with all the religious communities within it, while not assuming either official atheism or relativism in regard to the truth claims of religions.

The freedom of religion that is now so widely affirmed through the United Nations Charter of Human Rights, at least in principle, is fundamentally a fruit of the convictions of the radical Reformers who innovated this freedom, even within Christianity. That gain needs to be continually reaffirmed, and Christians need to be peacemakers in the world by continually working for religious freedom. Particularly important to evangelicals is the right to propagate our faith—not only the right to practice it personally. It is here that Christians are currently experiencing great pressure around the world. In areas where Islamic law is being enforced, converts from Islam are being beaten and killed, and evangelism is forcefully pro-

---

[2] Rosemary Radford Ruether, "Feminism and Jewish-Christian Dialogue," in *The Myth of Christian Uniqueness,* ed. John Hick and Paul Knitter, p. 141, quoted in Clendenin, *Many Gods,* p. 94.

[3] Clendenin, *Many Gods,* p. 94.

[4] Vinoth Ramachandra, *Faiths in Conflict? Christian Integrity in a Multicultural World* (Downers Grove, Ill.: InterVarsity Press, 1999).

[5] Ibid., p. 147.

hibited. In some dominantly Hindu situations, similar prohibitions of conversionist efforts are being sought. But closer to home, religiously speaking, there have been efforts in Israel to prohibit proselytism, and within the boundaries of Christianity itself, some Orthodox churches are engaged in very serious political efforts to establish a religious monopoly in their regions. In the irony of God's gracious work in the world, however, we hear frequent reports from Christian ministries who reach out to Muslims that there is a greater responsiveness now to the gospel than ever before, in the wake of Islamic militantism. Thanks to the work of God's grace in people's lives, many are repulsed by the hatred and violence that is being perpetrated in the name of God. We need the wisdom of serpents and the harmlessness of doves if we are to serve the Prince of Peace effectively in a world where Christians themselves are frequently and violently opposed. We need to guard our own hearts, lest the enemy get a foothold through hatred and the thirst for vengeance, when we suffer as the Lord assured us we would. But we also discern an ongoing struggle for the soul of some of the world's great religions, perhaps especially Islam. Not all within those religious communities are pleased with the militant actions taken by their coreligionists. We can certainly pray that God will work in those contexts, so that lasting good will come out of the current situation both for God's covenant people and for other people. But this is also an important time for people across the religious spectrum who want to see the world at peace and the earth properly cared for to work together to that end. Religion need not be the problem; it can be part of the solution, in the grace of God.

THE PROSPECTS AND LIMITS OF CHRISTIAN COOPERATION WITH OTHER RELIGIOUS GROUPS

The "Guidelines on Dialogue" prepared by the World Council of Churches Central Committee in 1979 suggested that

> common activities and experiences are the most fruitful setting for dialogue on issues of faith, ideology and action. It is in the search for a just community of humankind that Christians and their neighbours will be able to help each other break out of cultural, educational, political and social isolation in order to realize a more participatory society.[6]

---

[6]"Guidelines on Dialogue: World Council of Churches," in *Faith Meets Faith,* Mission Trends, ed. Gerald H. Anderson and Thomas F. Stransky (Grand Rapids, Mich.: Eerdmans, 1981), 5:152.

Lesslie Newbigin suggests that a consequence of recognizing the goal of missions to be the glory of God is "that the Christian will be eager to cooperate with people of all faiths and ideologies in all projects which are in line with the Christian's understanding of God's purpose in history." He observes that he has

> repeatedly made the point that the heart of the faith of a Christian is the belief that the true meaning of the story of which our lives are a part is that which is made known in the biblical narrative. The human story is one which we share with all other human beings—past, present, and to come. We cannot opt out of the story. We cannot take control of the story. It is under the control of the infinitely patient God and Father of our Lord Jesus Christ. Every day of our lives we have to make decisions about the part we will play in the story, decisions which we cannot take without regard to the others who share the story.[7]

Newbigin's list of those who share the story includes "Christians, Muslims, Hindus, secular humanists, Marxists, or of some other persuasion." He knows that these people "will have different understandings of the meaning and end of the story," but he hopes that "along the way there will be many issues in which we can agree about what should be done." He proposes, in particular, that "there are struggles for justice and for freedom in which we can and should join hands with those of other faiths and ideologies to achieve specific goals, even though we know that the ultimate goal is Christ and his coming in glory and not what our collaborators imagine."[8]

On the other hand, David Hesselgrave encourages "interreligious dialogue concerned with meeting human need" but suggests that "it may be necessary that this dialogue stop short of complete cooperative action because it is incumbent upon the Christian that all he does in word and deed be done in the name of his Lord Christ (Col 3:16)." So he is prepared to go only as far as "discussion of ways and means," although he thinks that even this "may be invaluable in view of overwhelming and increasing human need."[9] Hesselgrave's warning is apt but perhaps overly restraining. A cooperative venture involving members of different religious communities would have to be done as a purely humanitarian effort, not as an in-

---

[7]Lesslie Newbigin, *The Gospel in a Pluralist Society* (Grand Rapids, Mich.: Eerdmans, 1989), p. 181.

[8]Ibid.

[9]David J. Hesselgrave, "Evangelicals and Interreligious Dialogue," in *Faith Meets Faith*, ed. Gerald H. Anderson and Thomas F. Stransky (Grand Rapids, Mich.: Eerdmans, 1981), 5:125.

terreligious one, because the latter might give the impression that the religions represented can somehow be merged. A syncretism would be communicated, even if that was not the intention.

On the other hand, if the humanitarian effort can be organized most effectively by a single administrative structure, perhaps it would be wise to promote such a structure, though not one with a religious identification, while allowing the various workers on the project to be forthright about their own reasons for serving. Thus, a Christian could give "a cup of cold water in Jesus' name" because she serves the needy person as an act of Christian love, even though the project itself is not done for Christ. In such a case, it would be service with a "nongovernment organization," like similar efforts in an explicitly nonreligious government organization, except that there might be less pressure to stifle one's religious motivation. Hendrik Kraemer encouraged cooperation "on a pragmatic basis and with a pragmatic goal in mind, out of a common feeling of responsibility and concern for man and his needs," provided that "one does not seek first for a common religious basis which transcends or presumably unites the religions."[10] This is an excellent limitation that leads along the same route I am affirming.

Newbigin suggests that Christians should "not be eager to have their particular contributions to the common human task separately labeled as 'Christian.' They will be happy only if what they do can serve the reign and righteousness of the Father of Jesus who loves all, gives life to all, and purposes the blessing of all."[11] The Evangelical Alliance in Britain took a similar approach. It spoke of the work done by "the secular agencies, such as community relations councils, whose members include Christians together with people of other faiths and men and women of good will without any religious commitment." And it proposed that "Christians should not stand aside as mere observers or critics but be actively involved. It is not easy work," they admitted, "as clashes and misunderstandings often arise; the Christian will need to listen patiently to the appeals and complaints of the various groups concerned, to assess the situation carefully and to serve *along with* the leaders of the other-

---

[10]Hendrik Kraemer, "The Role and Responsibility of the Christian Mission," in *Philosophy and the Coming World Civilization: Essays in Honor of William Ernest Hocking,* ed. Leroy S. Rouner (The Hague: Martinus Nijhoff), p. 249, quoted in Tim S. Perry, *Radical Difference: A Defence of Hendrik Kraemer's Theology of Religions,* Editions SR, ed. H. Martin Rumscheidt and Theodore S. de Bruyn (Waterloo, Ontario: Wilfrid Laurier University Press, 2001), 27:81.

[11]Lesslie Newbigin, *The Open Secret: An Introduction to the Theology of Mission*, rev. ed. (Grand Rapids, Mich.: Eerdmans,) p. 176.

faith communities, rather than as one coming from outside to do things *for* them."[12] The Alliance identifies racism as something against which Christians must particularly be opposed.[13] Since the people of other faiths in a British community would frequently also be of other ethnicities (British Christians being a predominantly white Christian community), this is an important area in which cooperation can be achieved toward a firmly biblical goal.

Given that many who create tension in our world operate under the guise of religion, to the detriment of much true religious faith, such cooperative ventures could be a valuable means to the reducing of such tension, whereas separate humanitarian efforts by religious communities could actually exacerbate the sense of conflict. Such cooperation would be aimed at something that Hesselgrave does affirm as a positive goal in interreligious dialogue, the breaking down of "barriers of distrust and hatred in the religious world."[14]

The Vatican Commission for Religious Relations with the Jews issued "Guidelines and Suggestions for Implementing the Conciliar Declaration *Nostra Aetate* (N.4)" on December 1, 1974.[15] It suggests that "in the spirit of the prophets, Jews and Christians will work willingly together, seeking social justice and peace at every level—local, national and international."[16] Given the terrible impression of Christians that followed the Holocaust, efforts by Christians to seek justice and peace for Israel can be particularly significant. Of course, this cannot mean countenancing injustice by Israelis to Palestinians! After all, we are also seeking to present Christ to Palestinians, and numbers of them are already our brothers and sisters in Christ.

Similarly, Terry Muck argues for cooperation for two reasons. First, we are to love our neighbor. Second, we need to take advantage of

> the role religion plays in the world today. Put simply, religion is perhaps our last hope for civilized, humane cooperation among the peoples of the world. If part of the gospel is to support and even to create just social systems, then

---

[12]R. W. F. Wootton, *Christianity and Other Faiths: An Evangelical Contribution to Our Multi-Faith Society* (Exeter: Paternoster, 1983), p. 28.

[13]Ibid.

[14]Hesselgrave, "Evangelicals," 5:125.

[15]"Guidelines and Suggestions for Catholic-Jewish Relation, by Vatican Commission for Religious Relations with the Jews," in Gerald H. Anderson and Thomas F. Stransky, eds., *Faith Meets Faith*, Mission Trends (Grand Rapids, Mich.: Eerdmans, 1981), 5:181.

[16]Ibid., 5:187.

cooperation with other religions to the extent that they contribute to those systems is a gospel requirement.[17]

John Jefferson Davis wisely counsels us to ensure that any group formed for cooperative effort has a clear written statement that does not conflict with Scripture.[18] This does not mean, however, that the group must be explicitly Christian.

THE QUESTION OF INTERRELIGIOUS PRAYER AND WORSHIP

In the wake of September 11, there was a strong desire in many quarters in the United States to minimize alienation among members of different religions, particularly between Muslims and Christians. This frequently put Christian clergy in the difficult position of deciding when and how they should cooperate in interreligious events. Illustrative of this was the controversy that followed the participation of David Benke, a Lutheran minister, in the nationally televised memorial service called "A Prayer for America," which was held at Yankee Stadium on September 23, 2001.[19] On the other hand, Franklin Graham has been criticized for excluding millions of Americans from other faiths by invoking the name of Jesus in his prayer at the inauguration of President George Bush Jr.

Prior to the rise of these real life dilemmas, Gavin D'Costa had contemplated the issue of whether we should pray with members of other religions or whether that would be "like marital infidelity."[20] In the wake of the post-September 11 controversies, Gilbert Meilaender has expanded on the set of questions that we face in developing guidelines for prayer with people of other faiths. He frames the issue for us quite helpfully.

> Suppose a group of Catholics, Lutherans, Jews, Muslims, Episcopalians, Greek Orthodox, Sikhs, Buddhists, Presbyterians and Hindus come together to pray about some shared concern. Thinking now from within the Christian faith, what should we say about questions such as the following: What are they doing? (Before we decide whether doing it is a good idea, it might be nice if we could say what they are doing.) Are they praying together? Are they praying alongside each other but not with each other? Are they address-

---

[17]Terry C. Muck, "Missiological Issues in the Encounter with Emerging Buddhism," *Missiology* 28 (January 2000): 43.

[18]Ajith Fernando, *The Christian's Attitude Toward World Religions* (Wheaton, Ill.: Tyndale House, 1987), p. 115, quoting Randy Frame, *Eternity* (January 1985): 21.

[19]"The Interfaith Public Square: An Editorial," *Christianity Today*, March 11, 2002, pp. 34-35.

[20]Gavin D'Costa, *The Meeting of Religions and the Trinity*, Faith Meets Faith (Maryknoll, N.Y.: Orbis, 2000), p. 143.

ing the same god? If they are addressing the same god—and it is that One whom Christians confess as the true God—does that mean their praying with each other is unproblematic?[21]

D'Costa's own conclusion is that "a refusal to even consider encountering the mystery of God within the other in shared prayer runs the risk of idolatry; worshiping only the god of our own construction." He posits, therefore, that

> there is a case to be made that the prayers of others might be reconfigured in the act of shared prayer, such that the Christian might discover the mystery of the triune God more fully, and also share with the other the "gift" that prayer always is: an invitation to communion with the triune God.[22]

The same Spirit who helps us may be at work in other religions, so the prayers of non-Christians may tell us more than we can predict. "When interreligious prayer is done with a reverence and devotion to God in real love of God, with the consequent thirst for greater love between people, which stems from and is nourished by a greater love of God," proposes D'Costa, "then in love's celebration of love by the lovers, we glimpse the reality of the trinity in human community—even if not by common accord in name, but by one accord in the heart of love."[23]

Wesley Ariarajah makes a significant distinction between *prayer* and *worship*, defining the latter as "an ordered response to a realized experience of the Sacred within a specific religious community."[24] It is in the sense of "worship" that the greatest difficulty arises for Christians, and that is where I would not be able to participate, as a Christian, either in a joint worship gathering or in the worship of another religious community, even if they invited me to do so. I share Kraemer's assessment that common worship is wrong "for the simple reason that it is spiritual quackery to maintain that one is praying to the same God named alternatively God, Ram, Allah. . . . It is not allowable to experiment with God. This softheartedness leads to a corruption of truth and loss of identity and spiritual character unintentional though this may be." Kraemer claimed that "Christians should be the first to point out and keep to the

---

[21]Gilbert Meilaender, "Interfaith 'Prayer': What Is It and Should We Do It?" *Christian Century*, October 23-November 5, 2002, p. 33.

[22]D'Costa, *Meeting of Religions*, p. 144.

[23]Ibid., p. 165.

[24]S. Wesley Ariarajah, *Not Without My Neighbour: Issues in Interfaith Relations* (Geneva: World Council of Churches Publications, 1999), p. 38.

rules of sound inter-religious cooperation." To participate in common worship is "overstepping the boundaries and creating . . . newly constructed gods, unwittingly used as toys."[25]

On a similar note, as Meilaender ponders the questions he raised, he observes that Muslims worship "the god of Abraham and Ishmael—not of Abraham, Isaac and Jacob," and he suggests that "it is hard to think of Jesus as having prayed to that god and, therefore, hard to suppose that Christians address that god when they pray in and with Jesus."[26] On the other hand, Meilaender considers Amos 9:7, which speaks of God's bringing up the Philistines from Caphtor and the Syrians from Kir, as he had brought Israel from Egypt; and he concludes that "other peoples have their own history of dealing not with a generic god but with Yahweh, the God of Israel, whom we can identify rightly only through the story of his dealings with Israel, even though those are not his only dealings."[27] I note that Meilaender is not asking whether these people are saved, only "whether, when the peoples of the world cry out to god in their need, there are Christian grounds for supposing that, at least sometimes, it may be the true God whom they address."[28] And he concludes that sometimes this is the case. "Although they do not fully know that God, he still is present to them and may receive their prayer as directed to himself."[29] Consequently, there is a sense "in which a Christian and a Hindu, praying alongside each other, might also be said to be praying 'to the same God—both directing their prayer to the objectively present God who is the Father of the Lord Jesus Christ, though that God is incompletely known to one of those who prays."[30] But this does not lead us to an unproblematic inference that they are praying *together*.

Reflecting on the issue of eating meat offered to idols, which Paul addresses in 1 Corinthians 8—10, Meilaender suggests that "Paul could, with some theological justification, have told the Corinthians that in those sacrificial rituals the pagans were actually reaching out unwittingly to the true God."[31] After all, Paul told the Athenians that their altar "to an un-

---

[25]Hendrik Kraemer, *Religion and the Christian Faith* (London: Lutterworth, 1956), p. 370, quoted in Perry, *Radical Difference*, 27:81.
[26]Meilaender, "Interfaith 'Prayer,' " p. 34.
[27]Ibid., p. 35.
[28]Ibid.
[29]Ibid., p. 36.
[30]Ibid.
[31]Ibid.

known God" was "though unknown to them, built for the worship of the God whom he preached." But

> it would have been another matter entirely for him to have joined in their worship of that unknown God—as if he were not able to identify the One to whom all worship must be directed. So it would be possible for Christians to acknowledge that they and their pagan neighbors pray, in the complicated sense [Meilaender has] specified, "to" the same God. And there might be a sense in which they could pray "alongside" each other, with the Christians knowing that, in the sense specified, all were praying to the same God. But it would be harder to specify a sense in which, even granting all this, they could avoid seeming to deny the Lord Jesus if they were to present themselves as praying "with" their pagan neighbors.[32]

As to praying together, I share Meilaender's discomfort about participating in joint prayer *if* the assumption is that we are all praying to the same God. On the other hand, if there is a mutual recognition that we each love God according to the knowledge we now have of him, there may be reason for a Christian and a non-Christian to pray when they are together, in an attitude of respect for the other's sincere quest for God, provided they both acknowledge that they are each praying about the same concern but they are not praying *together*. In a public gathering, this would be facilitated in the form of a succession of prayers within the context, perhaps, of a community event in which members of different religions share a common goal and do not want their participation to be completely secular. That is quite different from a coordinated act of worship, which is inappropriate for Christians.

In retrospect of Graham's prayer at the presidential inauguration, Roberta Albert, an associate professor of religion at Temple University said, "I think when praying in public, there is an obligation to speak to everyone. Otherwise you are treating non-Christians as if they are not American. That is very wrong and counter to Christian beliefs."[33] But this confuses issues, from a Christian perspective. In prayer, one speaks to God, and Christians speak to God the Father in the name of Jesus. No one could possibly pray a public prayer that represented all Americans. Public officials who want the different religious perspectives of their citizens represented in prayer at a public occasion should therefore request several adherents

---

[32]Ibid.
[33]Roberta Albert, quoted in Marion Callahan, "With Franklin Graham, Prayer Leads to Argument," *The Philadelphia Inquirer,* August 18, 2002.

of various faiths to pray, but it should be assumed that they will all pray to their own god (or gods) in the manner appropriate within their religious tradition. Religious faith is, in principle, exclusive, and the assumption that anyone could pray a generic prayer on behalf of every citizen of a nation is ridiculous. To ask a Christian to invoke God's blessing on a civic event but to then forbid her to pray in the name of Jesus is to make it impossible for the Christian to pray at all.

Also writing in the wake of the tragedy of September 11, James Lewis said, "In this new and dangerous epoch of world history, which threatens to embroil us in religious wars and civilizational clashes, we may do well to seek Muslim prayer partners and together beseech the true, one and only God to have mercy on us."[34] This is surely not meant to imply that every understanding of God is acceptable, for Lewis denies that Muslims and Christians worship the same God.[35] But I hear his recognition of the value of religious people commonly seeking the good of the world, without relativizing the differences in our religious understandings. Living in a religiously plural society, we who are religious should not behave together secularly, as though we were all atheists. We want to reduce interreligious tension without blurring the significance of the religious differences between us. Being faithful to God and his revealed truth will keep us from becoming relativistic pluralists, but it will also prevent us from privatizing faith.

R. W. F. Wootton, writing up the conclusions of an Evangelical Alliance study group, recalls the March 1981 "Observance for Commonwealth Day" in Westminster Abbey, which included "hymns, readings from the scriptures of different faiths, affirmations about humanity, justice, love and service, and nine prayers and blessings by various religious leaders; so it was clearly an act of inter-faith worship."[36] He asserts that "evangelical Christians will have little hesitation in rejecting worship of this kind" for four reasons. First, "it is shot through with contradictions, because of the radically different conceptions of God and fundamental beliefs among the different faiths. Thus in the Westminster service, for example, God is called 'Father' (something quite unacceptable to the Muslims present), while reference is made to 'gods' and to the transmigration of souls."[37] Sec-

---

[34]James Lewis, "Does God Hear Muslims' Prayers?" *Christianity Today,* February 4, 2002, p. 31.

[35]Ibid., p. 30.

[36]Wootton, *Christianity and Other Faiths,* p. 35.

[37]Ibid.

ond, it gives the impression "that the Christian participant accepts the other faiths as equally valid with his own." Third, it conflicts with the task of evangelism, and fourth, it would "cause great perplexity in the minds of Christians converted from other religions and any who are weak in the faith."[38]

As I have done, Wootton suggests that

> it does not necessarily follow that circumstances can *never* arise where it would be right for Christians to engage in prayer with people of other faiths. Thus at Asian funerals Christian ministers have sometimes felt that no principle was sacrificed by accepting a request to pray aloud with leaders of other faiths; and at week-end dialogue conferences between Christians and Muslims times of intercessory prayer have been arranged in which both faiths participated.[39]

What must be kept very clear is the distinctiveness of each person's prayer in such circumstances. Recognizing that worship is at the heart of a religion and that dialogue seeks to get inside another religion as much as possible, Wootton suggests religious people visit other faiths' centers of worship to observe the people at worship—visiting as observers, not as participants.[40]

Barbara Brown Taylor takes students in her class on world religions to visit the Hindu temple in Atlanta, but she has learned to prepare them for the field trip so that they can plan their action ahead of the time when they will be invited to participate, not just observe. On one such visit, Taylor and her students were taken by surprise as the priest turned toward them and started to offer each of them the *prasad*—food that had been blessed in the presence of Lakshmi, Vishnu's wife.[41] From the Hindu priest's perspective, the Christian observers "can be perfectly good Christians and still eat Vishnu's almonds."[42] The question of whether this is true arises from the Christian side, and at the time of writing about the experience, Taylor was still struggling to formulate her own answer.

Paul's instructions to the Corinthians who wondered about whether Christians could eat meat that had been offered to idols are certainly helpful on this issue. Don Howell sums it up, reflecting on his own con-

---

[38]Ibid., p. 36.
[39]Ibid.
[40]Ibid.
[41]Barbara Brown Taylor, "Vishnu's Almonds," *Christian Century*, March 22-29, 2000, p. 352.
[42]Ibid.

text when he was a missionary in Japan:

> The new union of the believer with Christ and solidarity with other believers
> in the worship of Christ, celebrated in the Lord's Supper, rules out participa-
> tion *(koinonia)* in temple feasts which binds the person to the other partici-
> pants in the worship of demons (1 Cor 10:14-22). Behind the festive social oc-
> casion, Paul says, are evil spiritual beings beckoning the time and attention
> of the celebrants.[43]

To enter the temple of an idol and eat with people who are, themselves, intentionally fellowshipping with "this non-god, this hand-made pseudo
god," would be "to invite created powers to have an authority over one
which they do not possess, a power which belongs only to the creator-God
revealed in and through Jesus the Messiah."[44] Taking note of Paul's concern that younger or "weaker" Christians might be misled by those who
are more firmly grounded in their Christian faith, we need to be sensitive
to the way in which any act of cooperation with members of other religions
will be understood by fellow Christians.

I do believe that God may hear the prayers of non-Christians who are
ignorantly reaching out to the transcendent in acknowledgment of their
need. But when he does so, it is an act of grace like his sending rain on the
fields of the unrighteous. When the sailors on the ship Jonah took to Nineveh fasted and cried out to Elohim, they met with a "response from the
one whom Jonah can call both *'elohim*, Yahweh, and El."[45] But, non-Christians do not have the *assurance* that Christians have, knowing God is attentive to their prayers; for Christians come to God in the name of Jesus, as
led by the Holy Spirit. Nevertheless, we should encourage prayer as a
means of seeking after God. Jesus promised us that those who seek God
will find him!

In *The Book of Lights,* Chaim Potok tells the story of two American rabbis
who were army chaplains in Japan during the Korean War. They passed a

---

[43]Don N. Howell Jr., "The Apostle Paul and First-Century Religious Pluralism," in *Christianity and the Religions: A Biblical Theology of World Religions,* Evangelical Missiological Society
Series, ed. Edward Rommen and Harold Netland (Pasadena, Calif.: William Carey Library,
1995), 2:104.

[44]N. T. Wright, *The Climax of the Covenant: Christ and the Law in Pauline Theology* (Minneapolis:
Fortress, 1991), p. 134.

[45]John E. Goldingay and Christopher J. H. Wright, " 'Yahweh Our God Yahweh One': The
Oneness of God in the Old Testament," in *One God, One Lord: Christianity in a World of Reli-
gious Pluralism,* 2nd ed., ed. Andrew D. Clarke and Bruce Winter (Grand Rapids, Mich.:
Baker, 1992), p. 50.

Japanese man who was praying devoutly at a roadside shrine, and one of the rabbis said: "Do you think our God is listening to that man?" He went on to ruminate, "If our God is *not* listening, what do we mean when we say 'God'? And if he *is* listening, what do we mean when we say 'our'?"[46] Apt questions, indeed, but I discern a certain ambiguity arising from the term *listen.* Certainly, God "hears" everything that everyone says, including prayers, in the sense of being aware of these utterances. But when we speak of God's "hearing" prayer, we often mean that God is attentive to our prayers with an intention of answering requests that accord with God's will. In the former sense, certainly God "listened" to the prayer of the man praying at a roadside shrine, but in the latter sense, we have no grounds for asserting that God attended positively to the prayer. After all, Scripture makes it clear that even the prayers of God's covenant people are unwelcome when our behavior and the orientation of our hearts are not in keeping with the tenor of our words.

In this regard, I find the perspective of Pope John Paul II intriguing. Regarding the prayer of non-Christians, he says,

> What seems to bring together and unite, in a particular way, Christians and believers of other religions is an acknowledgment of the need for prayer as an expression of human spirituality directed towards the Absolute. Even when, for some, he is the great Unknown, he nevertheless remains always in reality the same living God. We trust that wherever the human spirit opens itself in prayer to this Unknown God, an echo will be heard of the same Spirit who, knowing the limits and weakness of the human person, himself prays in us and on our behalf, "expressing our plea in a way that could never be put into words" (Rom 8:26). The intercession of the Spirit of God who prays in us and for us is the fruit of the mystery of the redemption of Christ, in which the all-embracing love of the Father has been shown to the world.[47]

On December 22, 1986, reflecting on the World Day of Prayer for Peace (which had been held at Assisi in October), the pope said,

> Every authentic prayer is under the influence of the Spirit "who intercedes insistently for us . . . because we do not even know how to pray as we ought." He prays in us "with unutterable groanings" and "the One who searches the hearts knows what are the desires of the Spirit" (cf. Rom 8:26-27). We can in-

---

[46]Bob Abernethy, "Faithful and Respectful: Paradox of Pluralism," *Christian Century* March 15, 2000, p. 294, quoting Chaim Potok, *The Book of Lights* (New York: Alfred A. Knopf, 1981).

[47]Quoted in Jacques Dupuis, *Toward a Christian Theology of Religious Pluralism* (Maryknoll, N.Y.: Orbis, 1997), pp. 174-75.

deed maintain that every authentic prayer is called forth by the Holy Spirit, who is mysteriously present in the heart of every person.[48]

The final statement sounds a bit strong to me. I would not deny the presence of God, by his Spirit, *with* all people, but I believe that the statement "the Holy Spirit . . . is present *in the heart*" applies only to true believers. On the other hand, I see no reason to deny that the Holy Spirit calls forth prayer from sincere seekers who are not yet believing.

When Lewis asks, "does God hear Muslim prayers?" he concludes that "while nearly all would deny the Trinity if it were explained to them, their prayers might compare favorably with the experience of Cornelius in Acts 10 and so could be regarded as 'God-fearing.' "[49] In this regard, Lewis suggests, the prayers of devout Muslims are like those of "children who pray to God generally and in nondescript ways in their pre-Christian state." He believes that these children "address God and that God hears them."[50] This is not to suggest that all Muslims who are reaching out to God are finding him, but Lewis is encouraged by the experience of Begum Bilquis Sheikh (as told in the book *I Dared to Call Him Father*). Through "extraordinarily mystical circumstances," she came to a "new conception of God as 'Father,' " and then "over time she spoke to God as she understood him until, under the guidance of Christian friends, she entered a personal relationship with God as Father" that transformed her life.[51] It is precisely this process—in which God gradually draws people toward himself—that gives us reason to encourage others to pray, even when we doubt that their knowledge of God is adequate to fully formed faith.

Paul Helm has suggested a particularly helpful approach to understanding the usefulness of prayer by people who lack full biblical revelation of God.[52] He suggests that God has essential properties that he alone possesses or could possess. These include properties such as being underivedly just, supremely good and infinitely wise. He asks us to

suppose that a person, ignorant of God's special revelation in Scripture, were to pray using words which mean any of God's individual essential proper-

---

[48]Quoted in Dupuis, *Toward a Christian Theology*, p. 174.

[49]Lewis, "Does God Hear," p. 30.

[50]Ibid., p. 31.

[51]Ibid., quoting Begum Bilquis Sheikh, *I Dared to Call Him Father* (Old Tappan, N.J.: Chosen Books, 1978).

[52]Paul Helm, "Are They Few That Be Saved?" in *Universalism and the Doctrine of Hell: Papers Presented at the Fourth Edinburgh Conference on Christian Dogmatics, 1991*, ed. Nigel M. de S. Cameron (Grand Rapids, Mich.: Baker, 1993), pp. 276-79.

ties. Suppose he were to say, "O most merciful one, have mercy upon me." If the description "most merciful one" is necessarily true of God and is true of God only, then it would appear to follow that in using such an expression the speaker successfully refers to God. For God is essentially most merciful, and only God can be.

If the speaker refers successfully to God, he does so whether or not he believes that in using the expression he is referring to the God and Father of our Lord Jesus Christ. Moreover, he succeeds in making such a reference no matter from what source the terms he uses have come, whether from special revelation, or from some tradition of piety whose pedigree is not clear. In other words successful reference of this sort does not require an intact causal link from God's special revelation in Scripture to what the person believes. The answer to the question, "From where has such a person gained his belief?" need not necessarily be "From Scripture."

Suppose, then, a person with little or no acquaintance with special revelation, but in deep personal need and despair, who cries out "O most merciful one, have mercy on me." I suggest that this is a prayer that is sincerely addressed to God and sincerely addressed to the only true God, even though the one who is speaking may not realise the fact.[53]

Helm finds it "hard to imagine that such a prayer could not or would not be answered," and I concur, recognizing, of course, that God does not grant every request he receives, even if the one praying were the most knowledgeable and devout believer. Since God is the Creator of the universe, anyone who addresses "the Creator" is addressing the only true God. "And anyone who, in addressing the Creator pleads for his mercy, is in fact casting himself on the mercy of Christ."[54] Consequently, I agree that even the prayer of self-professed atheists would be received by God, when they cry out in sincere desperation that God, "if there is a God," would deliver them.[55] Concerning such moments, we can be thankful that professing atheists, like confessing believers, are not always completely self-consistent. I am reminded of the young man who fled China for Hong Kong in its days as British colony. Although he had been educated as an atheist, he kneeled down at the base of a tree and prayed that the one who had made the tree would assist him in his escape. He did escape and eventually met Christians who taught him about the one who had made that tree as well as the good news of what the Creator had done in the sending of the Son as the world's Savior.

---

[53]Ibid., pp. 276-77.
[54]Ibid., p. 278.
[55]Ibid.

SUMMING UP

The writer to the Hebrews has exhorted us to "pursue peace with everyone" (Heb 12:14), and this is certainly as important a time as ever to follow that injunction. The cause of religion, as opposed to secularism, is not being helped by the fact that so many of the contemporary conflicts raging around the world are identified as religious in nature. We cannot deny that religion is a very large factor in many of them but, sadly, many of the most active agitators on both sides are not good representatives of the official religious ideals of their faith communities. This conflict results in suffering on all sides and the sort of chaos that is far from the shalom God wants for his world. It is God's desire that his people should be a blessing in the world, and this should not be restricted to the spiritual blessing that comes through the proclamation of the gospel. The God who sends rain on the fields of the unrighteous is well served when his followers likewise care for the needy and do so in the name of Christ.

Precisely because we do all that we do for the glory of God and act explicitly in the name of Christ our Lord, it is impossible for us to cooperate in interreligious ventures (however good their goal) in any way that would suggest that there are not real religious differences between the worshipers of God through Christ and others who worship God as they deem best. We can certainly not participate in common worship. We can, however, work together for the good of the communities in which we live—we simply cannot do so as an explicitly joint religious venture. We can and should pray about the same concerns, but we cannot pray *together,* as though we address the same God by different names. This is not to say that the true and living God may not hear a prayer unless it is addressed to him by the proper name. But it does mean that he gives no promise to do so. Having providentially withheld rain from a farmer's field, God may well provide help to the desperate farmer who calls out for it, though he be ignorant of God's real identity. When that help arrives, however, a sense of gratitude to God for his having answered one's prayer is critical. By the grace of God and the work of the Spirit, God may reveal himself more fully to the one in whose heart he has first stirred prayer, however ill informed the one praying may be.

May God see fit to glorify himself in the world through the grace expressed in and through the lives of his people, as we seek to do good to all people (especially to the household of faith) and to foster relationships with people of other faiths that will demonstrate the winsomeness of Christ and be used of God for his purposes of grace, both common and saving.

20

Concluding Reflections

WE LIVE IN A TIME OF GREAT OPPORTUNITY AND OF GREAT DANGER for the Christian church as a missionary people. As adherents of many different religions migrate to countries where the Christian church is present and where religious freedom is protected, we are given great missionary opportunities. On the other hand, there is a growing public awareness of religious differences and a widespread sense that these contribute to conflict rather than to the peaceful progress of the world. In this context, evangelism is often viewed negatively, and Christians may become embarrassed to commend Jesus Christ to members of other religions, even when there is freedom to do so. As Christians get to know people with different religious convictions and discover much about them that is admirable—particularly by comparison with the secularism of many people in Western societies—the sense of evangelistic urgency may be challenged in Christians' minds. Achieving a healthy, biblically informed perspective on the world's religions and the people within them is crucial to the effectiveness of Christians and their churches in serving God's purposes in the world, in our time. I have offered a view from my own study of Scripture, and I trust that God will use it for his glory and the good of his church, through which God wants to bless the world.

We have looked at two main questions: How does God save people? And how do the religions fit into God's purposes in the world? Each of these raises a host of other subordinate questions, and I hope the answers that I have offered will be deemed helpful, even by those who disagree with me but who may find greater clarity in the formulation of their own ideas through interaction with mine.

I hear Scripture saying that God constituted the whole human race in solidarity with Adam in his moral probation, so that we all became guilty "in him" when he disobeyed God; and as a result of that guilt, we are alienated from the life of God and unable to do anything pleasing to him, unless he graciously intervenes for our justification and sanctification. Consequently, all human beings are in need of a savior. Thankfully, God has provided a Savior, but only one, the Son of God himself, who took on human nature, lived a perfect life and offered that life to the Father as a perfect substitute for those whom the Father had chosen "in him" before anything was created. All who have ever been saved (that is, restored to fellowship with God), who are now being saved, or who ever will be saved, are saved because Jesus Christ died and rose again for them.

In addition to the objective salvation that God accomplished by himself, God has determined that only those who believe in him will be saved by Christ's work. To that end, he has made himself known to everyone, leaving no one without a witness. God requires that people respond to that witness in faith, but he does not require a faith that would be impossible for anyone by virtue of their ignorance. In the day of judgment, God will hold all people accountable for their response to the revelation that was made available to them, and only for that revelation. They will not be able to offer the excuse that they were ignorant, and no one will have been kept from salvation by ignorance. Contrary to John Wesley's perception of Calvinist teaching, as cited earlier in the book, I do not believe that God reaps where he has not sown. I argue, therefore, that not only does God provide salvific revelation to all human beings, but he also gives each of us, at least once in our lives, a gracious enablement to respond in faith, such that we are justly held accountable if we fail to do so. Yet Scripture indicates that those who do respond to God in faith do so because of an effectual calling by God—a work that goes beyond enablement and secures response. God actually gives the required repentance and faith to those whom he has chosen, so that salvation is all of God and the saved make no contribution about which they could boast.

I am well aware that the accessibilist position, which I have set forward in this book, is viewed by some as threatening to the church's global mission. I believe that such is not the case, and I have endeavored to put forward a strong biblical rationale for making sacrifices to get the good news of what God has done in Christ to everyone in the world, in each generation, even though we are aware that God may give eternal life to some whom we do not reach with the gospel. I have no way of knowing how many of these people there may be, and I have expressed doubt that the percentage of the elect among the unevangelized will be significantly greater than it is among the evangelized, in the case of those whom we perceive to be mentally and morally capable. We know, however, that the fullness of the joy of salvation, in *this* life, is experienced only by those who know that God has accepted them in Christ and who have been given God's new covenant Spirit, testifying to them that they are children of God, and who are part of a vibrant community of God's Spirit-gifted people. Maximizing the number of God's elect who have this full experience of salvation is one of the primary goals of Christian missionary work. It is eminently worth all our effort, even if God may bring some people into a less satisfying experience of salvation apart from the church's proclamation.

In regard to infants or others who die without attaining the mental capacity to hear and understand any of the usual forms of God's self-revelation, I have not found biblical reason to assert that these are all definitely among the elect whom God saves. I posit, however, that those whom God does save from among this group (and I am hopeful that their numbers are very large) are saved by grace through faith, despite our inability to explain how that might come about. In any event, I argue that no one will come to the Father without having known the Son, even if the first moment at which one attains informed knowledge of Jesus is at the moment of death. In hypothesizing that everyone meets Christ at death, I still argue that this will not provide people with an opportunity to reverse decisions made during their lifetime, but that we will all respond to Jesus, in person, in the same manner that we have been responding to God just prior to that at-death encounter.

Because human beings are creatures in the image of God, we are inherently religious beings. We were made for fellowship with God, and we are hungry for that fellowship and will never be fully satisfied until it is fully realized. We may experience a foretaste of this joy through knowledge of Christ in this life, but it is only fully attained when we are finally with him. Because humans are intrinsically religious beings and because God has revealed himself to us, formal ways of responding and relating to God have arisen through the ages in what we identify as "religions." These come about through a combination of factors. There is human response to divine revelation, both by way of appropriation and by way of suppression. There is the subtle but terribly dangerous work of the adversary, who works ceaselessly against God's purposes, and who, given his penchant to pervert what is inherently good, often uses the human hunger for God in ways that are harmful to those who yield to his deception. Then too, there is the natural creativity of humans hungry for God, who strive to satisfy their longings by means of their own devising.

Many religions—with widely different beliefs about God, practices of worship and moral instruction—were already flourishing when God called Abram to leave Ur and to go where God would send him as the beginning of a program through which God would establish a peculiar covenant relationship with one people in the world for the sake of bringing blessing to the whole world. As God revealed more and more about himself to this covenant people, a body of knowledge about God grew and was recorded in written Scriptures under the inspiration of the Spirit of God. Israel knew that there is only one God and that he is the God of the whole world. They recognized that some of their neighbors had knowledge of God, though theirs was less well informed than was Israel's; they recognized also that still others had developed a concept of God that terribly distorted the truth and that had to be avoided and condemned. Meanwhile, Israel had its own ups and downs, periods of faithfulness and periods of rebellion against God, but through it all God preserved a remnant who were faithful. This remnant included a young woman named Mary, and through her the Son of God came into the world to bring to fulfillment all the promises made to the covenant people. Through Jesus—the prophet greater than Moses, the priest greater than Aaron and the king greater than David—salvation came to the world. In turn, Jesus established a new covenant community, one in which there is no distinction between Jews and Gentiles, that we call the assembly of God, the church.

Neither Israel nor the church was established in special covenant relationship with God as an end in itself; each was instituted as part of God's plan to bless the world. In the case of the new covenant church, this has been done not only through the visible witness of the community, living in a godly way within the world, just as Israel had been called to do, but also through active propagation of the good news concerning Jesus. The church is a missionary people. In reaching out to people who worship God in the context of other religions, however, Christians are aware that these people are not completely ignorant of God. In each person's life there is the same pattern of appropriation and suppression of God's truth as it has been revealed to them, and the nature of each person's relationship to God can only be ascertained on an individual basis, through a process of careful listening. We know, however, that God has revealed himself most fully in Jesus, to whom reliable testimony has only been given in the inspired

Scriptures of the New Testament. And we know that the hunger for God that is in the hearts of all people (however strangely it may be manifested) can be fully satisfied only through knowledge of God in Christ and by the Holy Spirit. We hope, therefore, that God has brought us into the lives of all the people we encounter to move them steadily closer to God himself. Only God's Spirit can actually achieve this, but he has chosen to involve us in the process as agents of his powerful word.

Even though we know that no religion that is not founded on the worship of God through Jesus by the power of the Holy Spirit is true, as a religious system, we cannot regard everything about the religions of the world as useless and evil. The grace of God is manifested in the liberality with which he gives good gifts to those who are largely ignorant of him. And even to those who are vigorously suppressing God's truth in unrighteousness, this grace is also evident in the cultural and religious institutions that humans develop. When we encounter aspects of religious belief and practice that conform to God's truth as we understand it from Scripture, we are grateful to God and can affirm all those things that contribute to the restoration of shalom in God's world—even as we recognize that these are goods that fall short of the salvation that we want everyone to enjoy. It is essential that we not fall into a moral dualism, regarding the material goods of life in this world as worthless, if not evil, and assuming that only the things that are spiritual and eternal have any value. This world, which God has created, matters. Our stewardship of the physical world and our contribution to justice and the general well-being of the peoples of the world are a service to the God whose world this is. Other religions, as systems, are counterproductive in enhancing the eternal well-being of their adherents. But because remnants of truth have been appropriated in their systems, these religions can serve God's common-grace purposes in the world. We can affirm these contributions and can work together with non-Christians as citizens of the world to seek the temporal well-being of all God's human creatures, without dulling our witness to the uniqueness of Christ as the world's Savior and Lord.

As we seek to live peacefully in this fallen world with people of all religions and to further the temporal good of the world, we must strive to foster mutual understanding. It is to that end that conversation, formal and informal, is valuable. Such conversation can also help remove stumbling blocks that keep people from seeing God's grace and goodness in the church, as a people gathered around the worship of God through Christ. In a world torn by strife that is caused by sin, but which often masquerades as religion, we in the church are called to be God's witnesses and servants. More than anything we long to see people at peace with God, but we dare not minimize the value of peace between the peoples of the world. Where cooperation for the good of the community is possible, across religious lines, we should be ready participants, while being careful not to blur the important religious differences among our communities in a way that would compromise our commitment to Jesus as Lord.

God is at work in the world. Christ is in the process of bringing all things under his lordship. May God give us spirits of discernment and sensitivity so that we can be useful to him in the realization of his purposes as we eagerly look forward to the day when the kingdoms of the world will be the kingdoms of our God and when he will reign forever. To God alone be the glory.

Glossary

accessibilism: Accessibilism asserts that Jesus Christ is exclusively God's means of salvation but that there is biblical reason to be hopeful about the possibility of salvation for those who do not hear the gospel. It grants that non-Christians can be saved but does not regard the religions as God's designed instruments in their salvation. (See the chart in chapter two.)

agnosticism: Within the typology of this study, agnosticism asserts that we do not know for sure whether God saves anyone who does not hear the gospel. Consequently, it affirms neither ecclesiocentrism nor accessibilism. (See the chart in chapter two. See also ACCESSIBILISM and ECCLESIOCENTRISM.)

Amyraldianism: Amyraldianism derives its name from the thought of Moise Amyraut (or Amyraldus), who posited a twofold covenant or will of God, whereby God wills the salvation of all humankind on condition of faith but wills the salvation of the elect specifically and unconditionally. In this view, Christ dies in a hypothetical sense for all humanity but in a particularist sense for the elect alone. (See also LIMITED ATONEMENT and UNIVERSAL ATONEMENT.)

compatibilism: Compatibilism asserts that a person can act freely even though that action is determined by God. To the compatibilist, actions are free if the actors do them voluntarily, spontaneously or willingly, without coercion by anything outside of themselves, even though their action may be predictable as an expression of their own desires. It is often affirmed by monergists as their alternative to libertarianism, which is asserted by synergists. (See also LIBERTARIAN FREEDOM, MONERGISM and SYNERGISM.)

contextualization: Contextualization is formulating Christian truth and practicing Christian faith in ways that are faithful to biblical revelation and appropriate to the audience's context. (See also SYNCRETISM.)

counterfactuals: Counterfactuals are events that do not in fact occur but that *would* occur if the circumstances were different. They are hypothetical but true as hypotheses about what would pertain in a given situation if it were realized, although this particular situation never actually occurs. (See also MOLINISM.)

critical realism: Critical realism asserts that truth exists and that it can be known, but it concedes that what knowers perceive or understand is significantly affected by their situation and their presuppositions. Consequently, no one has completely objective knowledge, but one's subjectivity does not make significant apprehension of the truth impossible.

determinism: In the *scientific* sense, determinism is the theory that each event is necessarily as it is because of the factors or events that precede it. *Theological* determinism believes that events are as they are because God has determined they should be so. There is an ongoing controversy between compatibilists and incompatibilists/libertarians over whether a human act can be both free on the part of the human actor and determined by God. (See also COMPATIBILISM, HARD DETERMINISM, LIBERTARIAN FREEDOM AND SOFT DETERMINISM.)

ecclesiocentrism: Ecclesiocentrism asserts that since Christ ascended and sent the Holy Spirit, only those who hear the gospel can be saved. Thus, the possibility of salvation is coextensive with the presence of the church. (See the chart in chapter two.)

efficient (or efficacious) grace: God's gracious enabling of sinners is deemed to have been efficient when a person acts rightly, relative to the sort of enablement provided. Monergists believe that its efficiency (or effectiveness) is due to the work of God, whereas synergists believe that its efficiency derives from the person's appropriation of the enabling given to them. (See also MONERGISM, SUFFICIENT GRACE and SYNERGISM.)

evangelical: In this study, I use the term *evangelical* to describe a person or theology that regards the Bible as the truthful and uniquely authoritative means of God's self-revelation in our time, and that believes salvation comes about only by God's grace through human faith.

hard determinism: Hard determinism is mechanistic in its assumption that an event is completely the product of the preceding state, so that the idea that the event was brought about by some one's will is completely illusory. (See also SOFT DETERMINISM.)

incompatibilism: Incompatibilism posits that people do not act freely if their action is determined by God even if they act willingly. It proposes that genuine freedom must be libertarian and indeterminate.

libertarian freedom: Libertarian freedom is the state of freedom in which there is a real possibility that one could make at least two different choices in exactly the same circumstances, both external and internal. It is frequently referred to as the *power of contrary choice*. It is the type of freedom affirmed by incompatibilists, as the usual alternative to compatibilism. (See also COMPATIBILISM.)

limited atonement: The doctrine of limited atonement (or particular redemption) by Christ teaches that Christ died and rose again with the intent of saving those whom the Father had elected for salvation. This does not mean that the death of Christ was insufficient for the salvation of everyone. In fact, one could believe in both limited atonement and universalism. (See also AMYRALDIANISM, UNIVERSAL ATONEMENT and UNIVERSALISM.)

middle knowledge: The term *middle knowledge* is often associated with Luis de Molina, who asserted that God has three kinds of knowledge: In addition to God's natural knowledge (by which he knows all truth that is entailed in things as they are) and his free knowledge (which is what God knows by virtue of his decision that it should be so), God knows what creatures would do in every possible circumstance. This last form of knowledge is designated middle knowledge because it is believed that God chose what would actually occur from all the possibilities that he knew could occur. God's middle knowledge includes knowledge of counterfactuals. Although the concept of middle knowledge has often been appropriated by synergists, who (as Molinists) believe that creatures have libertarian freedom, it is also appropriated by monergists, who believe that creatures have compatibilist freedom. (See also COMPATIBILISM, COUNTERFACTUALS, LIBERTARIAN FREEDOM, MOLINISM, MONERGISM and SYNERGISM.)

Molinism: Molinism designates the view put forward by Luis de Molina that creatures have libertarian freedom but that God knows what they would do in any situation, even if those situations are never realized, as part of his middle knowledge. Thus, God knows counterfactuals of libertarian freedom. (See also COUNTERFACTUALS, LIBERTARIAN FREEDOM and MIDDLE KNOWLEDGE.)

monergism: Monergism asserts that everything comes about because God has determined that it occur, even though creatures may have authentic agency in bringing about some of those occurrences. (See also SYNERGISM.)

original corruption: Original corruption is the natural inclination toward sin that humans incur through their solidarity with Adam in the Fall.

original guilt: Original guilt is the state of being regarded as sinners, under the condemnation of God, because of solidarity with Adam in the Fall.

particular atonement or redemption: See LIMITED ATONEMENT.

Reformed theology: Reformed theology is frequently used as a synonym for *Calvinism,* being the theology that derived from the thought of the sixteenth-century Reformers in Switzerland. It should not be confused with Reformation theology, which would include Lutheran, Anabaptist and other streams of Protestant thought.

relativism: Within the typology of this study, relativism designates the position which asserts that all the major religions have true revelation in part and are more or less equally true and valid as paths to salvation. (See the chart in chapter two.)

religious instrumentalism: Religious instrumentalism asserts that Jesus is, in some sense, unique, normative and definitive but that God reveals himself and provides salvation through other religions and their structures. (See the chart in chapter two.)

soft determinism: Soft determinism is essentially the same thing as compatibilism. It affirms that everything is determined by God, but it denies that this can be understood in regard to moral creatures in a mechanistic (or hard deterministic) fashion analogous to the form of determinism that may occur in the physical world. (See also COMPATIBILISM and HARD DETERMINISM.)

sufficient grace: God's gracious enabling of sinners is deemed sufficient when it is adequate to their needs to an extent whereby they may be justly held accountable for a failure to act rightly, relative to the sort of enablement provided. (See also EFFICIENT GRACE.)

syncretism: In the context of this study, syncretism refers to the construction of a religious system that puts error from other religions together with biblical truth in a manner that ultimately distorts that truth. (See also CONTEXTUALIZATION.)

synergism: Synergism asserts that events occur through the cooperation of God and his creatures, such that God does not always have his way and creatures determine the outcome in some (or many or all) events of human history. (See also MONERGISM.)

unevangelized: The unevangelized are people who do not hear the gospel. Usually this is understood to include hearing the gospel from a human witness, hence it entails being in contact with the church.

universal atonement: The doctrine of universal atonement asserts that Christ died and rose again with the intention of saving the entire human race. It does not entail a belief that everyone is, therefore, saved, which would be universalism. It is an alternative view to limited atonement, or particular redemption. (See also AMYRALDIANISM, LIMITED ATONEMENT and UNIVERSALISM.)

universalism: Universalism asserts that every human being will finally be saved.

Appendix 1

A "Particular Atonement" Reading of the Apparently Universal References Concerning Salvation

In chapter five, I stated reasons for believing that God did not intend to save everyone and that he is not trying to do so. Some biblical texts, however, give the distinct impression that God does want to save everyone and that Christ died for everyone. Since the Bible teaches that God actually achieved salvation by Christ's incarnate work and that not everyone is saved, the universal references need to be reconsidered. If these texts do *not* mean that Christ died with the intention to save the world, what *do* they mean? Here is a brief look at those biblical statements and texts as they might be understood within a monergistic perspective, which believes that God always accomplishes his purposes and further entails that He saves everyone he wills to save.

Christ died for the world (Jn 1:29; 3:16; Rom 11:12, 15; 2 Cor 5:19; 1 Jn 2:2). A study of the references to *world* in Scripture indicates that the term rarely refers to each and every individual person in the world (see, e.g., Lk 2:1; Jn 1:10; Acts 11:28; 19:27; 24:5; Rom 1:8; Col 1:6). Robert Letham notes, regarding John 3:16, for instance, that the world for whom God sent the Son is the world that stands under judgment, the world qualitatively in enmity against God, rather than each and every individual. Note the purpose clause in John 3:17; the reason for sending the Son is to save those who believe![1] Often, the term *world* indicates that salvation is for non-Jews as well as Jews (Mt 24:14; Mk 16:15; Rom 10:18; probably also Jn 1:29; 6:33, 51; 2 Cor 5:19; 1 Jn 2:2), or it may mean "all nations." In a few cases it could

---

[1] Robert Letham, *The Work of Christ* (Downers Grove, Ill.: InterVarsity Press, 1993), p. 240.

mean the world of believers, that is, the church (possibly in, e.g., Jn 6:33, 51; Rom 4:13; 11:12, 15). In reference to a text such as John 1:29 ("the Lamb of God who takes away the sin of the world"), I reiterate the possibility (mentioned in chapter five) that Christ bore the penalty of all the *unconsciously* committed sins of all sinners.

First John 2:2 is a text that quickly comes to mind as an apparent affirmation of universal atonement: Jesus Christ "is the atoning sacrifice for our sins, and not for ours only but also for the sins of the whole world." But the text can also be well understood within the framework of a particular saving intent in Christ's work. On the one hand, we might naturally hear a note of ethnic universalism; Christ is the Savior of both Jews and Gentiles. This is particularly significant in the context of current proposals of religious pluralism. John's thought could be applied, for instance, in denial that Christ is the atoning sacrifice for Gentiles in the West but that God has other means of salvation for other peoples of the world. Christ is not only the Savior of Westerners who have grown up in the "Christian world"; he is also the Savior of Jews, Arabs, Africans, South Americans and of everyone in the world. There is no other objective way of salvation. All who have ever been saved, or are ever going to be saved, are saved because Jesus made an atoning sacrifice or propitiation *(hilasmos)* for his sin. That is good news to be proclaimed to the ends of the world by those of us who have been graced with the knowledge of this truth. In other words, this is a statement of the *exclusiveness* of Jesus' propitation; he is the only propitiation available in the world.[2] Furthermore, John also testifies to the *perpetuity* of Jesus' propitation, as John Murray puts it; Christ continues to be the world's Savior.[3]

Christ died for all people (*Rom 5:18; 1 Cor 15:22; 2 Cor 5:14; 1 Tim 2:4-6; Tit 2:11; Heb 2:9; 2 Pet 3:9*). The context of each of these passages is important. In Romans 5:18 and 1 Corinthians 15:22, Paul says that "all" die in Adam but that "all" are made alive in Christ. If the *all* in both cases refers to each and every human being, then Paul is teaching thoroughgoing universalism. Just as everyone became a sinner in Adam, so everyone will be saved in Christ. Likewise, in 2 Corinthians 5:14, Paul says that "one has died for all; therefore all have died." Clearly, however, Paul does not believe that all people will live again with God; the context of Paul's state-

---

[2]Ibid., p. 242.
[3]John Murray, *Redemption Accomplished and Applied* (Grand Rapids, Mich.: Eerdmans, 1955), pp. 73-74.

ment is Christ's union with his people. Similarly, in Hebrews 2:9-10, where Christ is spoken of as having tasted "death for everyone," it is explicitly stated that God's intention is "bringing many children to glory," which is why "the pioneer of *their* salvation" (emphasis mine) is made "perfect through sufferings."

Titus 2:11 ("the grace of God has appeared, bringing salvation to all") is best read as referring to "all without distinction" rather than "all without exception," that is, all classes of people. As D. A. Carson points out,

> if we take "all men" to mean all without exception the statement is demonstrably false. In terms of the foundational "appearance" of the grace of God in the incarnation, the recipients were relatively few people, almost all of them citizens of one small vassal state at the eastern end of the Mediterranean; in terms of the existential "appearance" of the grace of God in the salvation of men and women, the recipients were a rising number of people in the Roman Empire, plus a few outsiders like the emissary from Candace's court (Acts 8), but the vast majority of human beings then living, to say nothing of those who lived before and after that time, had seen nothing of this "appearance" of the grace of God.[4]

Paul's point is that the grace of God has appeared not only to Jews "but to Jews and Gentiles alike, without distinction, to slave and free alike, without distinction."[5]

First Timothy 2:4-6, Hebrews 2:9 and 2 Peter 3:9 refer to the revealed will of God that both Jews and Gentiles be saved. In 1 Timothy 2:1-2, for instance, this focus is clear. It is not individuals but all kinds of people, including "kings and all who are in high positions," who are to be the subject of our prayers, and this is because of God's desire for the proclamation of the gospel to all (cf., 2 Pet 3:8-9). Once again, therefore, the emphasis is on the uniqueness of Christ's ransom. God wants everyone "to come to the knowledge of the truth because Christ is the only mediator between God and humans."[6] In the same way, we note in Romans 8:32 that God gave up his Son "for all of us," but the context is Christ's intercession for the elect, whom God justifies.

***The possibility that people might be eternally condemned, even though Christ died for them** (Rom 14:15 [possibly not regarding salvation]; 1 Cor 8:11*

---

[4]D. A. Carson, *The Gagging of God: Christianity Confronts Pluralism* (Grand Rapids, Mich.: Zondervan, 1996), p. 288.
[5]Ibid.
[6]Letham, *The Work of Christ*, p. 243.

[likewise]; 2 Pet 2:1; Heb 10:26-30). Frequently, the warning in Hebrews 10:26-30 is viewed as hypothetical.[7] That is, if the action against which warning is being made were continued, it would lead to death. By means of these warnings the Spirit keeps us from that end. Thus, no one for whom Christ died will actually go to hell, but God preserves his people by warning them of the need to persevere in faith. As to the false prophets who bring "swift destruction" on themselves by denying "the Master who bought them" (2 Pet 2:1), it seems most plausible that these people had claimed to be saved ("bought by Christ") but that their heresies actually constitute a denial of Christ. Thus, they deny the Christ by whom they claimed to have been redeemed.[8]

In the case of Romans 14:15, on the other hand, the "ruin" about which Paul is concerned may not be loss of salvation; and the "destruction" of those whose consciences are weak and who are led to sin against them (1 Cor 8:11) may also be something less than eternal punishment. Nevertheless, even if these texts are to carry the strongest sense, it is helpful to understand these texts as warnings designed to keep the elect from irrevocable apostasy.

---

[7]For example, A. A. Hodge, *Outlines of Theology,* enl. ed. (1879; London: Banner of Truth Trust, 1972), p. 421.

[8]Simon Kistemaker, *New Testament Commentary: Exposition of the Epistles of Peter and of the Epistle of Jude* (Grand Rapids, Mich.: Baker, 1987), pp. 282-83.

Appendix 2

THE DISTINCTION BETWEEN MY PROPOSAL OF UNIVERSAL SUFFICIENT
GRACE AND AMYRALDIAN "HYPOTHETICAL UNIVERSALISM"

IN 1996, I OFFERED A VERSION OF MY PROPOSAL CONCERNING universal
sufficient grace in a paper read at an Evangelical Theological Society meeting.[1] A Calvinist theologian who later read the paper suggested to me that
I was reiterating Amyraldianism. I had made a number of references to
Moise Amyraut, who addressed some of the concerns to which I am trying
to speak, but our proposals are distinct in a very fundamental way.

Amyraut (1596-1664) agreed with the Synod of Dort's position concerning God's unconditional election, but he contended that election was the
secret counsel of God and should not be made the basis for the church's
doctrine. He argued that God's stated purpose was to save all humankind.
This was made possible by the universal sufficiency of Christ's death and
by the external call that moved the elect to respond in faith. God's purpose
was declared in a series of covenants: God the Father made the first covenant with humans in their innocence and perfect obedience, and this was
also in effect in the period of law, when salvation was offered on the basis
of obedience to the law given to Moses. God the Son, however, established
a covenant of grace. This was a *hypothetical* covenant, based on universal
atonement, which is why Amyraut's view is sometimes called "hypothetical universalism."[2] Forgiveness was offered to sinners without personal
merit, and salvation was available to those who responded in faith. But

---

[1]Terrance Tiessen, "The Universal Salvific Work of the Holy Spirit: Reducing the Scandal of
Calvinism" (paper presented at the Evangelical Theological Society meeting, Jackson, Mis-
sissippi, November 22, 1996).
[2]Andrew T. B. McGowan, "Amyraldianism," in *The Dictionary of Historical Theology*, ed.
Trevor A. Hart (Grand Rapids, Mich.: Eerdmans, 2000), p. 12.

faith was a gift through the persuasion of the Holy Spirit, in keeping with the mysterious and secret absolute will of God.

In Amyraut's construct, there is thus a twofold will of God, "whereby he wills the salvation of all humankind on condition of faith but wills the salvation of the elect specifically and unconditionally."[3] Therefore, Christ dies in a hypothetical sense for all humanity but in a particularist sense for the elect alone.

My proposal in chapter five should have made it clear that I do not affirm a hypothetical universalism. I believe that Christ died to accomplish the Father's intent to save the elect and that the Spirit applies Christ's work in efficacious enabling of those elect, so that they believe the revelation God gives them. The *universal sufficient enabling grace* of which I speak is one of the universal benefits of Christ's death, but this does not necessitate an affirmation of a hypothetical intent, on Christ's part, to save everyone.

Fairly recently, Alan Clifford has argued that John Owen's concept of a single intent for the atonement (namely, the salvation of the elect) is problematic because it "cannot make sense of the sin of unbelief. If unbelievers are guilty of rejecting Christ, whence their guilt, if Christ was not given for them?"[4] Clifford's own answer to the problem is to affirm the hypothetical or conditional universalism of Amyraut and of the Puritan theologian Richard Baxter. For reasons I gave in chapter eleven, I sympathize with Clifford, but I suggest the problem that Clifford locates in a limited intent of the atonement (for the elect alone) is much more clearly a problem at the *subjective* level of human ability, as Jonathan Edwards rightly discerned.

Against Owen, Baxter asserted that Christ's sacrifice for sin was "satisfactory and meritorious for all" people and that no one "shall be damned for want of a Saviour to die for him, and fulfil all righteousness, but only for abusing or refusing his mercy."[5] Two things are necessary if Baxter's concern is to be properly addressed: first, the death of Christ must be sufficient for all sin, as the Synod of Dort (and I) affirmed; and second, sinners must be in a position to accept or reject that salvation. To accept the first condition, we need not assert a hypothetical universalism, but I am arguing that the second truth does require a universal enabling grace.

---

[3]Ibid.
[4]Alan C. Clifford, *Atonement and Justification: English Evangelical Theology 1640-1790: An Evaluation* (Oxford: Clarendon, 1990), p. 100.
[5]*Richard Baxter's Catholick Theologie* (1675), 1.2.51, quoted in Clifford, *Atonement*, p. 101.

Appendix 3

SCRIPTURAL SUPPORT FOR THE CONCEPT OF UNIVERSALLY
SUFFICIENT ENABLING GRACE

IN CHAPTER ELEVEN, I INDICATED MY REASONS for coming to the conviction that God enables everyone to respond to his self-revelation in faith, on at least one occasion in their lives, in a way that leaves them accountable for their response. The critical issue is, of course, whether Scripture teaches universal sufficient grace of the sort that I have proposed. The Wesleyan appeal has generally been made to John 1:4, 9, "the true light, which enlightens everyone," who came into the world in incarnate form, in Jesus. The proposal that John is referring to a universal illumination of human intellectual and moral faculties by the Logos has also been affirmed by theologians with Calvinist inclinations.[1] The major problem with the Wesleyan model of a universal prevenient grace, which enables everyone to repent and believe through a remedial work in their nature, is that it does not accord well with biblical descriptions of the state of the unregenerate prior to the efficacious work of saving grace. Paul describes sinners in their "natural" state as unable to submit to the law or to please God (Rom 8:7-8). Without the Spirit of God, people are unable to understand or accept the things that come from God (1 Cor 2:14). These are descriptions of the way people are without God's enabling grace, and it does not seem reasonable to read them as descriptive of the human condition only prior to a work of grace that all people experience at a very early point in life. If there is an enabling of those who receive revelation, it would seem more likely that it *accompanies* the revelation than that it precedes it indiscriminately. It is improbable

---

[1]For example, Bruce Demarest and Gordon Lewis, *Integrative Theology* (Grand Rapids, Mich.: Zondervan, 1987), pp. 1, 71. They also cite R. V. G. Tasker and William Plummer to this effect.

WHO CAN BE SAVED?

that God does a permanent work of grace in the life of all people, which ameliorates the ill effects of sin in human nature. That would be tantamount to arguing for a universal but nonefficacious regeneration (in its narrow sense). It is more likely that the inner enablement that accompanies the divine revelation, at some points in the life of everyone, is limited to the time of reception of that revelation and does not constitute a change in the nature of the sinner. That deep and permanent change is only wrought by the Spirit in those who are effectively drawn to faith in Christ.

By way of specific explicit biblical teaching, one is hard put to cite texts specifically indicating a universal distribution of grace to all people that enables them to respond to divine revelation in a responsible way. This gives us pause but it does not invalidate the proposal if, first, there are biblical passages that provide an implicit ground for this deduction and, second, there are no biblical passages that negate it. I am convinced that both of these criteria are satisfied.

Thomas Oden makes this helpful observation concerning our experience:

> As one moves in a progression from those justified by grace through faith to incorrigible sinners, the boundaries of sufficient grace are tested. The first of these is easy to establish; the argument for sufficiency becomes progressively harder as one proceeds along the spectrum.[2]

IMPLICIT IN OTHER BIBLICAL TEACHING

The first criterion (that an implicit ground for this deduction is provided by biblical passages) is met through the analysis of the factors discussed above as benefits of this proposal:

- In God's righteous judgment of sinners, personal acts of unrighteousness are the ground on which God's wrath falls on the unrepentant.

- God is genuinely distressed when humans reject his overtures of love and his calls for repentance.

- In some significant sense, God desires that all people be saved.

- Scripture commands us to proclaim the good news that Christ died for sinners and to call people to repent and believe.

- And, finally, salvation is completely God's gracious work, including our growth in holiness.

---

[2]Thomas C. Oden, *The Transforming Power of Grace* (Nashville: Abingdon, 1993), p. 78.

In all of these areas, I have attempted to demonstrate that a coherent position is best supported if God enables people to repent and believe when he addresses them in his self-revelation.

NOT NEGATED BY OTHER BIBLICAL PASSAGES

Is the second criterion met? Or are there biblical passages that would invalidate the proposal? At first sight, it might seem that the passages to which Calvinists have traditionally appealed to demonstrate the spiritual inability of sinners would have this negative effect. These passages include particularly John 3:3-5; 6:44; Romans 8:7; 1 Corinthians 2:14; Ephesians 2:1-2, 4-5.[3] A closer analysis, however, indicates that this is not so. What these passages teach us is that, in our fallen condition, *apart from the gracious intervention of God,* none of us comes to God. None of us can say that Jesus is Lord without the working of the Holy Spirit in our minds and wills. Calvinist theologians have frequently distinguished between an external call and an internal call. The former is the summons that comes through God's self-revelation but that is sometimes rejected (Mt 10:15; 11:21-24; Jn 5:40; 16:8-9; Acts 13:46; 2 Thess 1:8; 1 Jn 5:10). The internal call, however, is the work of the Spirit, within the hearts and minds of recipients of revelation, that enables their positive response and therefore effects salvation.

John Murray, for instance, admits that the Bible does not use these terms, but he argues for their validity because, in most cases, the Bible uses terms for calling in regard to salvation to indicate not the universal call but "the call that ushers men into a state of salvation and is therefore effectual."[4] This work, which is done by the Spirit to make the call effective, is described as revelation (Mt 16:17; Gal 1:16), as an opening of the heart (Acts 16:14), as an opening (Lk 24:45) or illumination of the mind (1 Cor 2:6-16), and as God's causing of growth in the Word that is sown by preachers (1 Cor 3:5-9). I am proposing that another distinction needs to be made *within the "inner call"* between an enablement that makes people duly responsible for their failure to respond to the call of divine revelation and an enablement that makes the call efficacious. It is to the latter that Murray refers when he writes of the internal call, which is simply designated as *calling* in the New Testament passages cited above.

---

[3]Compare Anthony Hoekema, *Created in God's Image* (Grand Rapids, Mich.: Eerdmans, 1986), p. 150; and *Saved by Grace* (Grand Rapids, Mich.: Eerdmans, 1989), pp. 81-82.
[4]John Murray, *Redemption Accomplished and Applied* (Grand Rapids, Mich.: Eerdmans, 1955), p. 88; see also Hoekema, *Saved by Grace,* pp. 82-86. (Compare Lk 14:23; Rom 1:6-7; 8:30; 9:23-24; 11:29; 1 Cor 1:9, 26-27; Gal 1:15; Eph 1:18; 4:1, 4; Phil 3:14; 1 Thess 2:12; 2 Thess 1:11-12; 2 Thess 2:14; 2 Tim 1:8-9; Heb 3:1; 1 Pet 2:9; 2 Pet 1:10; Jude 1; Rev 17:14.)

Anthony Hoekema has suggested that we speak of an efficacious call rather than an inner call because he notes that in a passage like Matthew 13:19, Scripture speaks of something happening "in the heart" of some who are not saved, through the preaching of the Word. He is on the right path, but I wish to go further. In Acts 7:51, for instance, Stephen complains that the people *resist the Holy Spirit*. This could be simply the Spirit's work of conviction of sin, but it could well be more than that, including an illumination or enablement. Consequently, it seems wise to continue to speak of an inner calling but to distinguish between a work of grace that is merely enabling and one that is effective.

Oden speaks of three aspects of calling: external, internal ("addressed to the heart through the Spirit") and efficacious ("wherein God's intent is fulfilled through grace awakening a fitting human response").[5] What distinguishes his position as Wesleyan is the belief that the reason for the efficacy is found in the human response rather than in the power of the divine drawing. Louis Berkhof identifies, and biblically supports, three factors in the external call: a presentation of the gospel facts, an invitation to accept Christ in repentance and faith, and a promise of forgiveness and salvation. He then comments:

> From the fact that these elements are included in external calling, it may readily be inferred that they who reject the gospel not merely refuse to believe certain facts and ideas, but resist *the general operation of the Holy Spirit which is connected with this calling,* and are guilty of the sin of obstinate disobedience. By their refusal to accept the gospel, they increase their responsibility, and treasure up wrath for themselves in the day of judgment, Rom 2:4, 5.[6]

Berkhof argues that the external calling is a bona fide calling in spite of one's spiritual inability, since a person's "inability in spiritual things is rooted in his unwillingness to serve God. The actual condition of things is not such that many would like to repent and believe in Christ, if they only could."[7] While speaking of common grace, Berkhof states that "it does not effect the salvation of the sinner, though in some of its forms (external calling and *moral illumination*) it may be closely connected with the economy of redemption and have a soteriological aspect" (emphasis in the original).[8] Like-

---

[5]Oden, *Transforming Power*, p. 202.
[6]Louis Berkhof, *Systematic Theology* (London: Banner of Truth Trust, 1949), p. 460, emphasis in the original.
[7]Ibid., pp. 462-63.
[8]Ibid., p. 436.

wise, John Owen stated that "even *common* illumination and conviction of sin have, in their own nature, a tendency unto sincere conversion." Alan Clifford notes that clearly "there is a procurement of grace which is broader than the thesis of [Owen's] *Death of Death* will allow."[9] John Gill, on the other hand, denied a ministry of the Spirit in conviction of sin to those not chosen to salvation,[10] and it was precisely on this ground that Gill and other hyper-Calvinists denied the validity of universal offers of grace.[11]

The critical question is, what is the effect of this "general operation of the Holy Spirit which is connected with this calling" of which Berkhof speaks? The seeds of my proposal can be found here. It is human unwillingness that must ultimately be overcome by the persuasion of God's drawing power, but a person's inability to be willing need not always be assumed, given God's gracious work in those to whom his revelation (itself an act of grace) is addressed. Berkhof teaches that the internal call that is efficacious works "by moral suasion plus the powerful operation of the Holy Spirit."[12] "The Spirit of God operates through the preaching of the Word only in a morally persuasive way, making its persuasions effective, so that man listens to the voice of his God." This is only effective, suggests Berkhof, when there is an additional "powerful operation of the Holy Spirit, applying the Word to the heart."[13]

We are obviously unable to observe the working of the Spirit within a human mind or heart. We see only its effects. When people come to faith, we know that the Spirit has done this work of persuasion and application. I propose that the justice of God's judgment of unbelievers suggests to us a work of the Spirit, persuading and enabling, even in those who do not believe—a work that leaves them responsible for their unbelief, but not one that is effective in leading them on to belief. Using the image of the parable of the sower (Mt 13:19-23), perhaps the seed that falls on rocky ground and among thorns is illustrative of a measure of positive response to the gospel on the part of those who have sufficient but not efficacious grace. God does a distinctive work of preparing the ground for the seed that falls on the good soil.

---

[9]John Owen, "A Discourse Concerning the Holy Spirit" (1674), in *The Works of John Owen* (London: Banner of Truth Trust, 1965-1968), 3:236, quoted in Alan C. Clifford, *Atonement and Justification: English Evangelical Theology 1640-1790: An Evaluation* (Oxford: Clarendon, 1990), p. 102.
[10]John Gill, *A Collection of Sermons and Tracts* (London: printed for G. Keith, 1773), p. 123, quoted in Clifford, *Atonement,* p. 104.
[11]Clifford, *Atonement,* p. 113.
[12]Berkhof, *Systematic Theology,* p. 469.
[13]Ibid., p. 470.

Author Index

Subject Index

504

Scripture Index

2:4-8, *87*
2:9, *495*
3, *221*
3—4, *221*
3:18-20, *221*
3:19, *220*
3:19-21, *220*
3:20, *170*
4:1-2, *90*
4:6, *220*

2 Peter
1:1, *86*
1:10, *495*
1:11, *86*
1:19, *113*
1:21, *113*

2:1, *490*
2:1-2, *236*
2:5, *170*
2:12, *129*
2:19, *244*
2:20, *86*
3:2, *86*
3:8-9, *489*
3:9, *236, 247, 291,*
488, 489
3:11-12, *274*
3:15-16, *113*
3:16, *376, 414*
3:18, *86*

1 John
1:1-3, *105*

1:7, *189*
1:7-9, *102*
2:2, *89, 236, 487*
3:2, *53, 215,*
217
3:23, *415*
4:2-3, *410, 413*
4:7, *415*
4:9, *342*
4:10, *89*
5:10, *495*

Jude
1, *495*

Revelation
1:18, *220*

2:8-25, *313*
2:20, *343*
3:14, *260*
5:9, *93, 294*
5:12, *294*
5:13, *220*
9:20, *313, 343*
11:15, *293*
17:14, *495*
20:11-14, *82,*
233
20:12-13, *148,*
418
21:9, *78*
21:22-27, *309*
21:25, *220*
22:20, *286*